HUMAN MEMORY

A READER

Edited by
David R. Shanks
Reader in Experimental Psychology
University College London, UK

A member of the Hodder Headline Group
LONDON • NEW YORK • SYDNEY • AUCKLAND

First published in Great Britain in 1997 by
Arnold, a member of the Hodder Headline Group
338 Euston Road, London NW1 3BH
175 Fifth Avenue, New York, NY 10010
http://www.arnoldpublishers.com

Distributed exclusively in the USA by
St Martin's Press, Inc.
175 Fifth Avenue, New York, NY 10010

British Library Cataloguing in Publication Data
A catalogue entry for this book is available from the British Library

Library of Congress Cataloging-in-Publication Data
Human memory: a reader/edited by David Shanks.
    p.   cm.
   Includes bibliographical references and index.
   ISBN 0–340–69194–8. — ISBN 0–340–69195–6 (pbk.)
   1. Memory.   I. Shanks, David R.
  BF371.H755 1997
  153.1'2—dc21

                                                 97–8638
                                                      CIP

ISBN 0 340 69195 6 (pb)
ISBN 0 340 69194 8 (hb)

Production Editor Julie Delf
Production Controller Rose James
Cover designer Andy McColm

Composition by J&L Composition Ltd, Filey, North Yorkshire
Printed and bound in Great Britain by JW Arrowsmith Ltd, Bristol

CONTENTS

ACKNOWLEDGEMENTS

The editor and publishers would like to thank the following for permission to use copyright material in this book.

Academic Press Inc. for 'The effect of context on the structure of categories' by E. M. Roth and E. J. Shoben, *Cognitive Psychology*, vol. 15 (1983); the American Psychological Association for 'A critical evaluation of the semantic–episodic distinction' by G. McKoon, R. Ratcliff and G. S. Dell, *Journal of Experimental Psychology: Learning, Memory, and Cognition*, vol. 12, copyright © 1986 by the American Psychological Association, reprinted with permission; 'Concepts and conceptual structure' by D. L. Medin, *American Psychologist*, vol. 44, copyright © 1989 by the American Psychological Association, reprinted with permission; 'Distributed memory and the representation of general and specific information' by J. L. McClelland and D. E. Rumelhart, *Journal of Experimental Psychology: General*, vol. 114, copyright © 1985 by the American Psychological Association, reprinted with permission; 'Implicit memory: history and current status' by D. L. Schacter, *Journal of Experimental Psychology: Learning, Memory, and Cognition*, vol. 13, copyright © 1987 by the American Psychological Association, reprinted with permission; 'Investigating dissociations among memory measures: support for a transfer-appropriate processing framework' by T. A. Blaxton, *Journal of Experimental Psychology: Learning, Memory, and Cognition*, vol. 15, copyright © 1989 by the American Psychological Association, reprinted with permission; 'Misleading postevent information and memory for events: arguments and evidence against memory impairment hypotheses' by M. McCloskey and M. Zaragoza, *Journal of Experimental Psychology: General*, vol. 114, copyright © 1985 by the American Psychological Association, reprinted with permission; and 'Semantic integration of verbal information into a visual memory' by E. F. Loftus, D. G. Miller and H. J. Burns, *Journal of Experimental Psychology: Human Learning and Memory*, vol. 4, copyright © 1978 by the American Psychological Association, reprinted with permission; Annual Reviews Inc. for 'The structure and organization of memory' by L. R. Squire, B. Knowlton and G. Musen, reproduced, with permission, *Annual Review of Psychology*, vol. 44, © 1993, by Annual Reviews Inc.; the Canadian Psychological Association for 'Memory skill' by K. A. Ericsson, *Canadian Journal of Psychology*, vol. 39, © 1985, Canadian Psychological Association, reprinted with permission; Erlbaum (UK), Taylor & Francis and the author for 'Is working memory working? The fifteenth Bartlett lecture' by

A. D. Baddeley, *Quarterly Journal of Experimental Psychology*, vol. 44A (1992), reprinted by permission of the Experimental Psychology Society; Lawrence Erlbaum Associates, Inc. for 'Relation between encoding specificity and levels of processing' by E. Tulving, *Levels of Processing in Human Memory*, eds L. S. Cermak and F. I. M. Craik (1979); and Thieme New York for 'Lasting consequences of bilateral medial temporal lobectomy: clinical course and experimental findings in H.M.' by S. Corkin, *Seminars in Neurology*, vol. 4 (1984).

PREFACE

The purpose of this book is to make available a collection of some of the most important articles on human memory from the past two decades. Like many others who teach courses on this topic, I have found that students are often reluctant to consult the primary literature when there are so many excellent textbooks available which summarize the major issues and debates for them. Unsurprisingly, students wonder what purpose is served by reading the original journal articles or book chapters. But there is a purpose: a much clearer understanding of the methods and strengths and weaknesses of psychological research can be gained from studying the primary literature than from reading the somewhat glossed-over views that textbooks necessarily convey. I hope that by reading some of the most significant articles collected in one place, students will be better enabled to form a true picture of what experimental memory research is all about.

The articles have been chosen to provide a broad and up-to-date reflection of the main issues currently occupying memory researchers, with an emphasis on theoretical problems. The articles are divided into eight sections and each section is preceded by a short introduction in which I have tried to provide some context. In addition, these introductions briefly describe issues of current debate and suggestions for further reading.

I am very grateful to a number of colleagues who discussed with me the selection of articles for this book. I also thank Naomi Meredith at Arnold for her help with many aspects of the production process.

D. R. S.

SECTION ONE
CONCEPTS AND KNOWLEDGE

Editor's introduction

Probably the main foundational question about memory is this: what are the basic building blocks from which memories are formed? Philosophers usually refer to these building blocks as concepts, and psychologists attempt to find out about the nature of concepts via laboratory or natural experiments. Douglas **Medin**'s article 'Concepts and conceptual structure' (Chapter 1) provides, as its title suggests, a discussion of current understanding of the various ways in which concepts might be represented in memory, starting with the classical view that concepts are characterized by necessary and sufficient features and ending with what has come to be called the 'Theory' theory of conceptual representation. Medin also considers a second key question, namely how are our concepts linked together? This question is the focus of Emilie **Roth** and Edward **Shoben**'s article (Chapter 2). Roth and Shoben consider the possibility that concepts are linked via some sort of fixed structure or network, and go on to challenge this view on the basis that changes in context have dramatic effects on the properties of this structure or network. The context effects demonstrated by Roth and Shoben have proved to be deeply problematic for many traditional models of conceptual representation.

The study of concepts and concept learning is currently one of the most active areas in cognitive psychology. Important topics for further reading include the instability of concept structure (Barsalou, 1987), the possibility that categories are defined by 'essences' (Braisby *et al.*, 1996; Malt, 1994), the current status of prototype theory (Hampton, 1995), the question of whether mental representations are compositional (Fodor and Pylyshyn, 1988; van Gelder, 1990), and the nature of representations in connectionist networks (van Gelder, 1991). Finally, Chang (1986) reviews current formal models of conceptual representation and relates them to the empirical evidence.

References

Barsalou, L. W. (1987). The instability of graded structure: implications for the nature of concepts. In *Concepts and conceptual development* (ed. U. Neisser) pp. 101–140. Cambridge University Press.

Braisby, N., Franks, B. and Hampton, J. (1996). Essentialism, word use, and concepts. *Cognition*, 59, 247–274.

Chang, T. M. (1986). Semantic memory: facts and models. *Psychological Bulletin*, 99, 199–220.

Fodor, J. A. and Pylyshyn, Z. W. (1988). Connectionism and cognitive architecture: a critical analysis. *Cognition*, 28, 3–71.

Hampton, J. A. (1995). Testing the prototype theory of concepts. *Journal of Memory and Language*, 34, 686–708.

Malt, B. C. (1994). Water is not H_2O. *Cognitive Psychology*, 27, 41–70.

van Gelder, T. (1990). Compositionality: a connectionist variation on a classical theme. *Cognitive Science*, 14, 355–384.

van Gelder, T. (1991). What is the 'D' in 'PDP'? A survey of the concept of distribution. In *Philosophy and connectionist theory* (ed. W. Ramsey, S. P. Stich and D. E. Rumelhart) pp. 33–59. Erlbaum, Hillsdale, NJ.

1 Douglas L. Medin
'Concepts and Conceptual Structure'

Reprinted in full from: *American Psychologist* **44**, 1469–1481 (1989)

What good are categories? Categorization involves treating two or more distinct entities as in some way equivalent in the service of accessing knowledge and making predictions. Take psychodiagnostic categories as an example. The need to access relevant knowledge explains why clinical psychologists do not (or could not) treat each individual as unique. Although one would expect treatment plans to be tailored to the needs of individuals, absolute uniqueness imposes the prohibitive cost of ignorance. Clinicians need some way to bring their knowledge and experience to bear on the problem under consideration, and that requires the appreciation of some similarity or relationship between the current situation and what has gone before. Although clinical psychologists may or may not use a specific categorization system, they must find points of contact between previous situations and the current context; that is, they must categorize. Diagnostic categories allow clinicians to predict the efficacy of alternative treatments and to share their experiences with other therapists. Yet another reason to categorize is to learn about etiology. People who show a common manifestation of some problem may share common precipitating conditions or causes. Ironically, the only case in which categorization would not be useful is where all individuals are treated alike; thus, categorization allows diversity.

More generally speaking, concepts and categories serve as building blocks for human thought and behavior. Roughly, a *concept* is an idea that includes all that is characteristically associated with it. A *category* is a partitioning or class to which some assertion or set of assertions might apply. It is tempting to think of categories as existing in the world and of concepts as corresponding to mental representations of them, but this analysis is misleading. It is misleading because concepts need not have real-world counterparts (e.g., unicorns) and because people may impose rather than discover structure in the world. I believe that questions about the nature of categories may be psychological questions as much as metaphysical questions. Indeed, for at least the last decade my colleagues and I have been trying to address the question of why we have the categories we have and not others. The world could be partitioned in a limitless variety of ways, yet people find only a minuscule subset of possible classifications to be meaningful. Part of the answer to the categorization question likely does depend on the nature of the world, but part also surely depends on the nature of the organism and its goals. Dolphins have no use for psychodiagnostic categories.

Given the fundamental character of concepts and categories, one might think that people who study concepts would have converged on a stable consensus with respect to conceptual structure. After all, Plato and Aristotle had quite a bit to say about concepts, medieval philosophers were obsessed with questions about universals and the essence of concepts, and concept representation remains as a cornerstone issue in all aspects of cognitive science. However, we have neither consensus nor stability. The relatively recent past has experienced at least one and probably two major shifts in thought about conceptual structure, and stability is the least salient attribute of the current situation. In the remainder of this article, I will briefly describe these shifts and then outline some ways of integrating the strong points of the various views.

The first shift: classical versus probabilistic views

It is difficult to discuss concepts without bringing in the notion of similarity at some point. For example, a common idea is that our classification system tends to maximize within-category similarity relative to between-category similarity. That is, we group things into categories because they are similar. It will be suggested that alternative views of conceptual structure are associated with distinct (though sometimes implicit) theories of the nature of similarity.

The classical view

The idea that all instances or examples of a category have some fundamental characteristics in common that determine their membership is very compelling. The classical view of concepts is organized around this notion. The classical view assumes that mental representations of categories consist of summary lists of features or properties that individually are necessary for category membership and collectively are sufficient to determine category membership. The category *triangle* meets these criteria. All triangles are closed geometric forms with three sides and interior angles that sum to 180 degrees. To see if something is a triangle one has only to check for these three properties, and if any one is missing one does not have a triangle.

What about other concepts? The classical view suggests that all categories have defining features. A particular person may not know what these defining features are but an expert certainly should. In our 1981 book, *Categories and Concepts*, Ed Smith and I reviewed the status of the classical view as a theory of conceptual structure. We concluded that the classical view was in grave trouble for a variety of reasons. Many of the arguments and counterarguments are quite detailed, but the most serious problems can be easily summarized.

1. Failure to specify defining features. One glaring problem is that even experts cannot come up with defining features for most lexical concepts (i.e., those reflected in our language). People may believe that concepts have necessary or sufficient features (McNamara and Sternberg, 1983), but the features given as candidates do not hold up to closer scrutiny. For example, a person may list 'made of wood' as a necessary property for violins, but not all violins are made of wood. Linguists, philosophers, biologists, and clinical psychologists alike have been unable to supply a core set of features that all examples of a concept (in their area of expertise) necessarily must share.

2. *Goodness of example effects.* According to the classical view, all examples of a concept are equally good because they all possess the requisite defining features. Experience and (by now) a considerable body of research undermines this claim. For example, people judge a robin to be a better example of bird than an ostrich is and can answer category membership questions more quickly for good examples than for poor examples (Smith *et al.*, 1974). Typicality effects are nearly ubiquitous (for reviews, see Medin and Smith, 1984; Mervis and Rosch, 1981; Oden, 1987); they hold for artistic style (Hartley and Homa, 1981), chess (Goldin, 1978), emotion terms (Fehr, 1988; Fehr and Russell, 1984), medical diagnosis (Arkes and Harkness, 1980), and person perception (e.g., Cantor and Mischel, 1977).

Typicality effects are not, in principle, fatal for the classical view. One might imagine that some signs or features help to determine the presence of other (defining) features. Some examples may have more signs or clearer signs pointing the way to the defining properties, and this might account for the difference in goodness of example judgments or response times. This distinction between identification procedures (how one identifies an instance of a concept) and a conceptual core (how the concept relates to other concepts) may prove useful if it can be shown that the core is used in some other aspect of thinking. It seems, however, that this distinction serves more to insulate the classical view from empirical findings, and Smith *et al.* (1984) argued that there are no sharp boundaries between core properties and those used for purposes of identification.

3. *Unclear cases.* The classical view implies a procedure for unambiguously determining category membership; that is, check for defining features. Yet there are numerous cases in which it is not clear whether an example belongs to a category. Should a rug be considered furniture? What about a clock or radio? People not only disagree with each other concerning category membership but also contradict themselves when asked about membership on separate occasions (Barsalou, 1989; Bellezza, 1984; McCloskey and Glucksberg, 1978).

These and other problems have led to disenchantment with the classical view of concepts. The scholarly consensus has shifted its allegiance to an alternative, the probabilistic view.

The probabilistic view

The rejection of the classical view of categories has been associated with the ascendance of the probabilistic view of category structure (Wittgenstein, 1953). This view holds that categories are 'fuzzy' or ill-defined and that categories are organized around a set of properties or clusters of correlated attributes (Rosch, 1975) that are only characteristic or typical of category membership. Thus, the probabilistic view rejects the notion of defining features.

The most recent edition of the *Diagnostic and Statistical Manual of Mental*

Disorders (*DSM-IIIR*, American Psychiatric Association, 1987) uses criteria based on lists of characteristic symptoms or features to describe diagnostic categories and thereby endorses the probabilistic view. For example, a diagnosis of depression can be made if a dysphoric mood and any five of a set of nine symptoms are present nearly every day for a period of at least two weeks. Thus, two people may both be categorized as depressed and share only a single one of the nine characteristic symptoms!

The probabilistic view is perfectly at home with the typicality effects that were so awkward for the classical view. Membership in probabilistic categories is naturally graded, rather than all or none, and the better or more typical members have more characteristic properties than the poorer ones. It is also easy to see that the probabilistic view may lead to unclear cases. Any one example may have several typical properties of a category but not so many that it clearly qualifies for category membership.

In some pioneering work aimed at clarifying the structural basis of fuzzy categories, Rosch and Mervis (1975) had subjects list properties of exemplars for a variety of concepts such as *bird, fruit,* and *tool*. They found that the listed properties for some exemplars occurred frequently in other category members, whereas others had properties that occurred less frequently. Most important, the more frequently an exemplar's properties appeared within a category, the higher was its rated typicality for that category. The correlation between number of characteristic properties possessed and typicality rating was very high and positive. For example, robins have characteristic bird properties of flying, singing, eating worms, and building nests in trees, and they are rated to be very typical birds. Penguins have none of these properties, and they are rated as very atypical birds. In short, the Rosch and Mervis work relating typicality to number of characteristic properties put the probabilistic view on fairly firm footing.

1. Mental representations of probabilistic view categories. If categories are not respresented in terms of definitions, what form do our mental representations take? The term 'probabilistic view' seems to imply that people organize categories via statistical reasoning. Actually, however, there is a more natural interpretation of fuzzy categories. Intuitively, probabilistic view categories are organized according to a *family resemblance* principle. A simple form of summary representation would be an example or ideal that possessed all of the characteristic features of a category. This summary representation is referred to as the *prototype*, and the prototype can be used to decide category membership. If some candidate example is similar enough to the prototype for a category, then it will be classified as a member of that category. The general notion is that, on the basis of experience with examples of a category, people abstract out the central tendency or prototype that becomes the summary mental representation for the category.

A more radical principle of mental representation, which is also consistent with fuzzy categories, is the exemplar view (Smith and Medin, 1981). The exemplar view denies that there is a single summary representation and instead claims that categories are represented by means of examples. In this view, clients may be diagnosed as suicidal, not because they are similar to some prototype of a suicidal person, but because they remind the clinician of a previous client who was suicidal.

A considerable amount of research effort has been aimed at contrasting exemplar and prototype representations (see Allen *et al.*, 1988; Estes, 1986a, 1986b; Medin, 1986; Medin and Smith, 1984; Nosofsky, 1987, 1988a; and Oden, 1987). Genero and Cantor (1987) suggested that prototypes serve untrained diagnosticians well but that trained diagnosticians may find exemplars to be more helpful. For my present purposes, however, I will blur over this distinction to note that both prototype and exemplar theories rely on roughly the same similarity principle. That is, category membership is determined by whether some candidate is sufficiently similar either to the prototype or to a set of encoded examples, where similarity is based on matches and mismatches of independent, equally abstract, features.

2. Probabilistic view and similarity. To give meaning to the claim that categorization is based on similarity, it is important to be specific about what one means by similarity. Although the consensus is not uniform, I believe that the modal model of similarity with respect to conceptual structure can be summarized in terms of four assumptions as follows. (a) Similarity between two things increases as a function of the number of features or properties they share and decreases as a function of mismatching or distinctive features. (b) These features can be treated as independent and additive. (c) The features determining similarity are all at roughly the same level of abstractness (as a special case they may be irreducible primitives). (d) These similarity principles are sufficient to describe conceptual structure, and therefore, a concept is more or less equivalent to a list of its features. This theory of similarity is very compatible with the notion that categories are organized around prototypes. Nonetheless, I will later argue that each of these assumptions is wrong or misleading and that to understand conceptual structure theories of similarity are needed that reject each of these assumptions. Before outlining an alternative set of similarity assumptions, however, I will first describe a set of observations that motivate the second, still more recent, shift in thinking concerning conceptual structure.

Problems for probabilistic view theories

Problems for prototypes

Although the general idea that concepts are organized around prototypes remains popular, at a more specific, empirical level, prototype theories have not fared very well. First of all, prototype theories treat concepts as context-independent. Roth and Shoben (1983), however, have shown that typicality judgments vary as a function of particular contexts. For example, tea is judged to be a more typical beverage than milk in the context of secretaries taking a break, but this ordering reverses for the context of truck drivers taking a break. Similarly, Shoben and I (Medin and Shoben, 1988) noted that the typicality of combined concepts cannot be predicted from the typicality of the constituents. As an illustrative example, consider the concept of *spoon*.

People rate small spoons as more typical spoons than large spoons, and metal spoons as more typical spoons than wooden spoons. If the concept *spoon* is represented by a prototypic spoon, then a small metal spoon should be the most typical spoon, followed by small wooden and large metal spoons, and large wooden spoons should be the least typical. Instead, people find large wooden spoons to be more typical spoons than either small wooden spoons or large metal spoons (see also Malt and Smith, 1983). The only way for a prototype model to handle these results is to posit multiple prototypes. But this strategy creates new problems. Obviously one cannot have a separate prototype for every adjective-noun combination because there are simply too many possible combinations. One might suggest that there are distinct sub-types for concepts like *spoon*, but one would need a theory describing how and when subtypes are created. Current prototype models do not provide such a theory. A third problem for prototype theories grows out of Barsalou's work (1985, 1987) on goal-derived categories such as 'things to take on a camping trip' and 'foods to eat while on a diet.' Barsalou has found that goal-derived categories show the same typicality effects as other categories. The basis for these effects, however, is not similarity to an average or prototype but rather similarity to an ideal. For example, for the category of things to eat while on a diet, typicality ratings are determined by how closely an example conforms to the ideal of zero calories.

Laboratory studies of categorization using artificially constructed categories also raise problems for prototypes. Normally many variables relevant to human classification are correlated and therefore confounded with one another. The general rationale for laboratory studies with artificially created categories is that one can isolate some variable or set of variables of interest and unconfound some natural correlations. Salient phenomena associated with fuzzy categories are observed with artificially constructed categories, and several of these are consistent with prototype theories. For example, one observes typicality effects in learning and on transfer tests using both correct-ness and reaction time as the dependent variable (e.g., Rosch and Mervis, 1975). A striking phenomenon, readily obtained, is that the prototype for a category may be classified more accurately during transfer tests than are the previously seen examples that were used during original category learning (e.g., Homa and Vosburgh, 1976; Medin and Schaffer, 1978; Peterson *et al.*, 1973).

Typicality effects and excellent classification of prototypes are consistent with the idea that people are learning these ill-defined categories by forming prototypes. More detailed analyses, however, are more problematic. Prototype theory implies that the only information abstracted from categories is the central tendency. A prototype representation discards information concerning category size, the variability of the examples, and information concerning correlations of attributes. The evidence suggests that people are sensitive to all three of these types of information (Estes, 1986b; Flannagan *et al.*, 1986; Fried and Holyoak, 1984; Medin *et al.*, 1982; Medin and Schaffer, 1978). An example involving correlated attributes pinpoints part of the problem. Most people have the intuition that small birds are much more likely to sing than large birds. This intuition cannot be obtained from a single summary prototype for birds. The fact that one can generate large numbers of such correlations is a problem for the idea that people reason using prototypes. More generally, prototype representations seem to discard too much information that can be shown to be relevant to human categorizations.

Yet another problem for prototypes is that they make the wrong predictions about which category structures should be easy or difficult to learn. One way to conceptualize the process of classifying examples on the basis of similarity to prototypes is that it involves a summing of evidence against a criterion. For example, if an instance shows a criterial sum of features (appropriately weighted), then it will be classified as a bird, and the more typical a member is of the category, the more quickly the criterion will be exceeded. The key aspect of this prediction is that there must exist some additive combination of properties and their weights that can be used to correctly assign instances as members or nonmembers. The technical term for this constraint is that categories must be linearly separable (Sebestyn, 1962). For a prototype process to work in the sense of accepting all members and rejecting all nonmembers, the categories must be linearly separable.

If linear separability acts as a constraint on human categorization, then with other factors equal, people should find it easier to learn categories that are linearly separable than categories that are not linearly separable. To make a long story short, however, studies employing a variety of stimulus materials, category sizes, subject populations, and instructions have failed to find any evidence that linear separability acts as a constraint on human classification learning (Kemler-Nelson, 1984; Medin and Schwanenflugel, 1981; see also Shepard *et al.*, 1961).

The cumulative effect of these various chunks of evidence has been to raise serious questions concerning the viability of prototype theories. Prototype theories imply constraints that are not observed in human categorization, predict insensitivity to information that people readily use, and fail to reflect the context sensitivity that is evident in human categorization. Rather than getting at the character of human conceptual representation, prototypes appear to be more of a caricature of it. Exemplar models handle some of these phenomena, but they fail to address some of the most fundamental questions concerning conceptual structure.

Exemplar-based theories

The problems just described hold not only for prototype theories in particular but also for any similarity-based categorization model that assumes that the constituent features are independent and additive. To give but one example, one could have an exemplar model of categorization that assumes that, during learning, people store examples but that new examples are classified by 'computing' prototypes and determining the similarity of the novel example to the newly constructed prototypes. In short, the central tendency would be abstracted (and other information discarded) at the time of retrieval rather than at the time of storage or initial encoding. Such a model would inherit all the shortcomings of standard prototype theories.

Some exemplar storage theories do not endorse the notion of feature independence (Hintzman, 1986; Medin and Schaffer, 1978), or they assume that classification is based on retrieving only a subset of the stored examples (presumably the most similar ones or, as a special case, the most similar one). The idea that retrieval is limited, similarity-based, and context-sensitive is in accord with much of the memory literature (e.g., Tulving, 1983). In addition, these exemplar models predict sensitivity to category size, instance variability, context, and correlated attributes. It is my impression that in head-to-head competition, exemplar models have been substantially more successful than prototype models (Barsalou and Medin, 1986; Estes, 1986b; Medin and Ross, 1989; Nosofsky, 1988a, 1988b; but see Homa, 1984, for a different opinion).

Why should exemplar models fare better than prototype models? One of the main functions of classification is that it allows one to make inferences and predictions on the basis of partial information (see Anderson, 1988). Here I am using classification loosely to refer to any means by which prior (relevant) knowledge is brought to bear, ranging from a formal classification scheme to an idiosyncratic reminding of a previous case (which, of course, is in the spirit of exemplar models; see also Kolodner, 1984). In psychotherapy, clinicians are constantly making predictions about the likelihood of future behaviors or the efficacy of a particular treatment based on classification. Relative to prototype models, exemplar models tend to be conservative about discarding information that facilitates predictions. For instance, sensitivity to correlations of properties within a category enables finer predictions: from noting that a bird is large, one can predict that it cannot sing. It may seem that exemplar models do not discard any information at all, but they are incomplete without assumptions concerning retrieval or access. In general, however, the pairs of storage and retrieval assumptions associated with exemplar models preserve much more information than prototype models. In a general review of research on categorization and problem-solving, Brian Ross and I concluded that abstraction is both conservative and tied to the details of specific examples in a manner more in the spirit of exemplar models than prototype models (Medin and Ross, 1989).

Unfortunately, context-sensitive, conservative categorization is not enough. The debate between prototype and exemplar models has taken place on a platform constructed in terms of similarity-based categorization. The second shift is that this platform has started to crumble, and the viability of probabilistic view theories of categorization is being seriously questioned. There are two central problems. One is that probabilistic view theories do not say anything about why we have the categories we have. This problem is most glaringly obvious for exemplar models that appear to allow any set of examples to form a category. The second central problem is with the notion of similarity. Do things belong in the same category because they are similar, or do they seem similar because they are in the same category?

Does similarity explain categorization?

1. Flexibility. Similarity is a very intuitive notion. Unfortunately, it is even more elusive than it is intuitive. One problem with using similarity to define categories is that similarity is too flexible. Consider, for example, Tversky's (1977) influential contrast model, which defines similarity as a function of common and distinctive features weighted for salience or importance. According to this model, similarity relationships will depend heavily on the particular weights given to individual properties or features. For example, a *zebra* and a *barber pole* would be more similar than a *zebra* and a *horse* if the feature 'striped' had sufficient weight. This would not necessarily be a problem if the weights were stable. However, Tversky and others have convincingly shown that the relative weighting of a feature (as well as the relative importance of matching and mismatching features) varies with the stimulus context, experimental task (Gati and Tversky, 1984; Tversky, 1977), and probably even the concept under consideration (Ortony *et al.*, 1985). For example, common properties shared by a pair of entities may become salient only in the context of some third entity that does not share these properties.

Once one concedes that similarity is dynamic and depends on some (not well-understood) processing principles, earlier work on the structural under-pinnings of fuzzy categories can be seen in a somewhat different light. Recall that the Rosch and Mervis (1975) studies asked subjects to list attributes or properties of examples and categories. It would be a mistake to assume that people had the ability to read and report their mental representations on concepts in a veridical manner. Indeed Keil (1979, 1981) pointed out that examples like *robin* and *squirrel* shared many important properties that almost never show up in attribute listings (e.g., has a heart, breathes, sleeps, is an organism, is an object with boundaries, is a physical object, is a thing, can be thought about, and so on). In fact, Keil argued that knowledge about just these sorts of predicates, referred to as ontological knowledge (Sommers, 1971), serves to organize children's conceptual and semantic development. For present purposes, the point is that attribute listings provide a biased sample of people's conceptual knowledge. To take things a step further, one could argue that without constraints on what is to count as a feature, any two things may be arbitrarily similar or dissimilar. Thus, as Murphy and I (Murphy and Medin, 1985) suggested, the number of proper-ties that plums and lawn mowers have in common could be infinite: both weigh less than 1000 kg, both are found on earth, both are found in our solar system, both cannot hear well, both have an odor, both are not worn by elephants, both are used by people, both can be dropped, and so on (see also Goodman, 1972; Watanabe, 1969). Now consider again the status of attribute listings. They represent a biased subset of stored or readily inferred knowledge. The correlation of attribute listings with typicality judgments is a product of such knowledge and a variety of processes that operate on it. Without a theory of that knowledge and those processes, it simply is not clear what these correlations indicate about mental representations.

The general point is that attempts to describe category structure in terms of similarity will prove useful only to the extent that one specifies which principles determine what is to count as a relevant property and which principles determine the importance of particular properties. It is important to realize that the explanatory work is being done by the principles which specify these constraints rather than the general notion of similarity. In that sense similarity is more like a dependent variable than an independent variable.

2. Attribute matching and categorization. The modal model of similarity summarized in Table 1.1 invites one to view categorization as attribute matching. Although that may be part of the story, there are several ways in which the focus on attribute matching may be misleading. First of all, as Armstrong *et al.* (1983) emphasized, most concepts are not a simple sum of independent features. The features that are characteristically associated with the concept *bird* are just a pile of bird features unless they are held together in a 'bird structure.' Structure requires both attributes and *relations* binding the attributes together. Typical bird features (laying eggs, flying, having wings and feathers, building nests in trees, and singing) have both an internal structure and an external structure based on interproperty relationships. Building nests is linked to laying eggs, and building nests in trees poses logistical problems whose solution involves other properties such as having wings, flying, and singing. Thus, it makes sense to ask why birds have certain features (e.g., wings and feathers). Although people may not have thought about various interproperty relationships, they can readily reason with them. Thus, one can answer the question of why birds have wings and feathers (i.e., to fly).

In a number of contexts, categorization may be more like problem solving than attribute matching. Inferences and causal attributions may drive the categorization process. Borrowing again from work by Murphy and me (1985), 'jumping into a swimming pool with one's clothes on' in all probability is not associated directly with the concept *intoxicated*. However, observing this behavior might lead one to classify the person as drunk. In general, real world knowledge is used to reason about or explain properties, not simply to match them. For example, a teenage boy might show many of the behaviors associated with an eating disorder, but the further knowledge that the teenager is on the wrestling team and trying to make a lower weight class may undermine any diagnosis of a disorder.

3. Summary. It does not appear that similarity, at least in the form it takes in current theories, is going to be at all adequate to explain categorization. Similarity may be a byproduct of conceptual coherence rather than a cause. To use a rough analogy, winning basketball teams have in common scoring more points than their opponents, but one must turn to more basic principles to explain why they score more points. One candidate for a set of deeper principles is the idea that concepts are organized around theories, and theories provide conceptual coherence. In the next section, I will briefly summarize some of the current work on the role of knowledge structures and theories in categorization and then turn to a form of rapprochement between similarity- and knowledge-based categorization principles.

Table 1.1 Comparison of two approaches to concepts

Aspect of conceptual theory	Similarity-based approach	Theory-based approach
Concept representation	Similarity structure, attribute lists, correlated attributes	Correlated attributes plus underlying principles that determine which correlations are noticed
Category definition	Various similarity metrics, summation of attributes	An explanatory principle common to category members
Units of analysis	Attributes	Attributes plus explicitly represented relations of attributes and concepts
Categorization basis	Attribute matching	Matching plus inferential processes supplied by underlying principles
Weighting of attributes	Cue validity, salience	Determined in part by importance in the underlyng principles
Interconceptual structure	Hierarchy based on shared attributes	Network formed by causal and explanatory links, as well as sharing of properties picked out as relevant
Conceptual development	Feature accretion	Changing organization and explanations of concepts as a result of world knowledge

The second shift: concepts as organized by theories

Knowledge-based categorization

It is perhaps only a modest exaggeration to say that similarity gets at the shadow rather than the substance of concepts. Something is needed to give concepts life, coherence, and meaning. Although many philosophers of science have argued that observations are necessarily theory-labeled, only recently have researchers begun to stress that the organization of concepts is knowledge-based and driven by theories about the world (e.g., Carey, 1985; S. Gelman, 1988; S. Gelman and Markman, 1986a, 1986b; Keil, 1986, 1987; Keil and Kelly, 1987; Lakoff, 1987; Markman, 1987; Massey and R. Gelman, 1988; Murphy and Medin, 1985; Oden, 1987; Rips, 1989; Schank *et al.*, 1986; and others).

The primary differences between the similarity-based and theory-based approaches to categorization are summarized in Table 1.1, taken from Murphy and Medin (1985). Murphy and Medin suggested that the relation between a concept and an example is analogous to the relation between theory and data. That is, classification is not simply based on a direct matching of properties of the concept with those in the example, but rather requires that the example have the right 'explanatory relationship' to the theory organizing the concept. In the case of a person diving into a swimming pool with his or her clothes on, one might try to reason back to either causes or predisposing conditions. One might believe that having too much to drink impairs judgment and that going into the pool shows poor judgment. Of course, the presence of other information, such as the fact that another person who cannot swim has fallen into the pool, would radically change the inferences drawn and, as a consequence, the categorization judgment.

One of the more promising aspects of the theory-based approach is that it begins to address the question of why we have the categories we have or why categories are sensible. In fact, coherence may be achieved in the absence of any obvious source of similarity among examples. Consider the category comprised of children, money, photo albums, and pets. Out of context the category seems odd. If one's knowledge base is enriched to include the fact that the category represents 'things to take out of one's house in case of a fire,' the category becomes sensible (Barsalou, 1983). In addition, one could readily make judgments about whether new examples (e.g., personal papers) belonged to the category, judgments that would not be similarity-based.

Similarity effects can be overridden by theory-related strategies even in the judgments of young children. That fact was very nicely demonstrated by Gelman and Markman (1986a) in their studies of induction. Specifically, they pitted category membership against perceptual similarity in an inductive inference task. Young children were taught that different novel properties were true of two examples and then were asked which property was also true of a new example that was similar to one alternative but belonged to a different category, and one that was perceptually different from the other example but belonged to the same category. For example, children might be taught that a (pictured) flamingo feeds its baby mashed-up food and that a (pictured) bat feeds its baby milk, and then they might be asked how a (pictured) owl feeds its baby. The owl was more perceptually similar to the bat than to the flamingo, but even four-year-olds made inferences on the basis of category membership rather than similarity.

Related work by Susan Carey and Frank Keil shows that children's biological theories guide their conceptual development. For example, Keil has used the ingenious technique of describing transformations or changes such as painting a horse to look like a zebra to examine the extent to which category membership judgments are controlled by superficial perceptual properties. Biological theories determine membership judgments quite early on (Keil, 1987; Keil and Kelly, 1987). Rips (1989) has used the same technique to show that similarity is neither necessary nor sufficient to determine category membership. It even appears to be the case that theories can affect judgments of similarity. For example, Medin and Shoben (1988) found that the terms *white hair* and *grey hair* were judged to be more similar than *grey hair* and *black hair*, but that the terms *white clouds* and *grey clouds* were judged as less similar than *grey clouds* and *black clouds*. Our interpretation is that white and grey hair are linked by a theory (of aging) in a way that white and grey clouds are not.

The above observations are challenging for defenders of the idea that similarity drives conceptual organization. In fact, one might wonder if the notion of similarity is so loose and unconstrained that we might be better off without it. Goodman (1972) epitomized this attitude by calling similarity 'a pretender, an imposter, a quack' (p. 437). After reviewing some reasons to continue to take similarity seriously, I outline one possible route for integrating similarity-based and theory-based categorization.

The need for similarity

So far I have suggested that similarity relations do not provide conceptual coherence but that theories do. Because a major problem with similarity is that it is so unconstrained, one might ask what constrains theories. If we cannot identify constraints on theories, that is, say something about why we have the theories we have and not others, then we have not solved the problem of coherence: it simply has been shifted to another level. Although I believe we can specify some general properties of theories and develop a psychology of explanation (e.g., Abelson and Lalljee, 1988; Einhorn and Hogarth, 1986; Hilton and Slugoski, 1986; Leddo *et al.*, 1984), I equally believe that a constrained form of similarity will play an important role in our understanding of human concepts. This role is not to provide structure so much as it is to guide learners toward structure.

The impact of more direct perceptual similarity on the development of causal explanations is evident in the structure of people's naive theories. Frazer's (1959) cross-cultural analysis of belief systems pointed to the ubiquity of two principles, homeopathy and contagion. The principle of homeopathy is that causes and effects tend to be similar. One manifestation of this principle is homeopathic medicine, in which the cure (and the cause) are seen to resemble the symptoms. In the Azande culture, for example, the cure for ringworm is to apply fowl's excrement because the excrement looks like the ringworm. Schweder (1977) adduced strong support for the claim that resemblance is a fundamental conceptual tool of everyday thinking in all cultures, not just so-called primitive cultures.

Contagion is the principle that a cause must have some form of contact to transmit its effect. In general, the more contiguous (temporally and spatially similar) events are in time and space, the more likely they are to be perceived as causally related (e.g., Dickinson *et al.*, 1984; Michotte, 1963). People also tend to assume that causes and effects should be of similar magnitude. Einhorn and Hogarth (1986) pointed out that the germ theory of disease initially met with great resistance because people could not imagine how such tiny organisms could have such devastating effects.

It is important to recognize that homeopathy and contagion often point us in the right direction. Immunization can be seen as a form of homeopathic medicine that has an underlying theoretical principle to support it. My reading of these observations, however, is not that specific theoretical (causal) principles are constraining similarity but rather that similarity (homeopathy and contagion) acts as a constraint on the search for causal explanations. Even in classical conditioning studies, the similarity of the conditioned stimulus and the unconditioned stimulus can have a major influence on the rate of conditioning (Testa, 1974). Of course, similarity must itself be constrained for terms like homeopathy to have a meaning. Shortly, I will suggest some constraints on similarity as part of an effort to define a role for similarity in conceptual development.

Similarity is likely to have a significant effect on explanations in another way. Given the importance of similarity in retrieval, it is likely that explanations that are applied to a novel event are constrained by similar events and their associated explanations. For example, Read (1983) found that people may rely on single, similar instances in making causal attributions about behaviors. Furthermore, Ross (1984) and Gentner and Landers (1985) have found that superficial similarities and not just similarity with respect to deeper principles or relations play a major role in determining the remindings associated with problem solving and the use of analogy.

In brief, it seems that similarity cannot be banished from the world of theories and conceptual structures. But it seems to me that a theory of similarity is needed that is quite different in character from the one summarized in Table 1.1. I will suggest an alternative view of similarity and then attempt to show its value in integrating and explanation with respect to concepts.

Similarity and theory in conceptual structure

A contrasting similarity model

The following are key tenets of the type of similarity theory needed to link similarity with knowledge-based categorization. (a) Similarity needs to include attributes, relations, and higher-order relations. (b) Properties in general are not independent but rather are linked by a variety of interproperty relations. (c) Properties exist at multiple levels of abstraction. (d) Concepts are more than lists. Properties and relations create depth or structure. Each of the four main ideas directly conflicts with the corresponding assumption of the theory of similarity outlined earlier. In one way or another all of these assumptions are tied to structure. The general idea I am proposing is far from new. In the psychology of visual perception, the need for structural approaches to similarity has been a continuing, if not major, theme (e.g. Biederman, 1985, 1987; Palmer, 1975, 1978; Pomerantz *et al.*, 1977). Oden and Lopes (1982) have argued that this view can inform our understanding of concepts: 'Although similarity must function at some level in the induction of concepts, the induced categories are not 'held together' subjectively by the undifferentiated 'force' of similarity, but rather by structural principles' (p. 78). Nonindependence of properties and simple and higher-order relations add a dimension of depth to categorization. Depth has clear implications for many of the observations that seem so problematic for probabilistic view theories. I turn now to the question of how these modified similarity notions may link up with theory-based categorization.

Psychological essentialism

Despite the overwhelming evidence against the classical view, there is something about it that is intuitively compelling. Recently I and my colleagues have begun to take this observation seriously, not for its metaphysical implications but as a piece of psychological data (Medin and Ortony, 1989; Medin and Wattenmaker, 1987; Wattenmaker *et al.*, 1988). One might call this framework 'psychological essentialism.' The main ideas are as follows. People act as if things (e.g., objects) have essences or underlying natures that make them the thing that they are. Furthermore, the essence constrains or generates properties that may vary in their centrality. One of the things that theories do is to embody or provide causal linkages from deeper properties to more superficial or surface properties. For example, people in our culture believe that the categories *male* and *female* are genetically determined, but to pick someone out as male or female we rely on characteristics such as hair length, height, facial hair, and clothing that represent a mixture of secondary sexual characteristics and cultural conventions. Although these characteristics are more unreliable than genetic evidence, they are far from arbitrary. Not only do they have some validity in a statistical sense, but also they are tied to our biological and cultural conceptions of *male* and *female*.

It is important to note that psychological essentialism refers not to how the world is but rather to how people approach the world. Wastebaskets probably have no true essence, although we may act as if they do. Both social and psychodiagnostic categories are at least partially culture specific and may have weak if any metaphysical underpinnings (see also Morey and McNamara, 1987).

If psychological essentialism is bad metaphysics, why should people act as if things had essences? The reason is that it may prove to be good epistemology. One could say that people adopt an *essentialist heuristic*, namely, the hypothesis that things that look alike tend to share deeper properties (similarities). Our perceptual and conceptual systems appear to have evolved such that the essentialist heuristic is very often correct (Medin and Wattenmaker, 1987; Shepard, 1984). This is true even for human artifacts such as cars, computers, and camping stoves because structure and function tend to be correlated. Surface characteristics that are perceptually obvious or are readily produced on feature listing tasks may not so much constitute the core of a concept as point toward it. This observation suggests that classifying on the basis of similarity will be relatively effective much of the time, but that similarity will yield to knowledge of deeper principles. Thus, in the work of Gelman and Markman (1986a) discussed earlier, category membership was more important than perceptual similarity in determining inductive inferences.

Related evidence

The contrasting similarity principles presented earlier coupled with psychological essentialism provide a framework for integrating knowledge-based and similarity-based categorization. Although it is far short of a formal theory, the framework provides a useful perspective on many of the issues under discussion in this article.

   1. Nonindependence of features. Earlier I mentioned that classifying on the basis of similarity to a prototype was functionally equivalent to adding up the evidence favoring a classification and applying some criterion (at least X out of Y features). Recall also that the data ran strongly against this idea. From the perspective currently under consideration, however, there ought to be two ways to produce data consistent with prototype theory. One would be to provide a theory that suggests the prototype as an ideal or that makes summing of evidence more natural. For example, suppose that the characteristic properties for one category were as follows: it is made of metal, has a regular surface, is of medium size, and is easy to grasp. For a contrasting category the characteristic properties were: it is made of rubber, has an irregular surface, is of small size, and is hard to grasp. The categories may not seem sensible or coherent but suppose one adds the information that the objects in one category could serve as substitutes for a hammer. Given this new information, it becomes easy to add up the properties of examples in terms of their utility in supporting hammering. In a series of studies using the above descriptions and related examples, Wattenmaker *et al.* (1986) found data consistent with prototype theory when the additional information was supplied, and data inconsistent with prototype theory when only characteristic properties were supplied. Specifically, they found that linearly separable categories were easier to learn than nonlinearly separable categories only when an organizing theme was provided (see also Nakamura, 1985).

   One might think that prototypes become important whenever the categories are meaningful. That is not the case. When themes are provided that are not compatible with a summing of evidence, the data are inconsistent with prototype theories. For instance, suppose that the examples consisted of descriptions of animals and that the organizing theme was that one category consisted of prey and the other of predators. It is a good adaptation for prey to be armored and to live in trees, but an animal that is both armored and lives in trees may not be better adapted than an animal with either characteristic alone. Being armored and living in trees may be somewhat incompatible. Other studies by Wattenmaker *et al.* using directly analogous materials failed to find any evidence that linear separability (and, presumably, summing of evidence) was important or natural. Only some kinds of interproperty relations are compatible with a summing of evidence, and evidence favoring prototypes may be confined to these cases.

The above studies show that the ease or naturalness of classification tasks cannot be predicted in terms of abstract category structures based on distribution of features, but rather requires an understanding of the knowledge brought to bear on them, for this knowledge determines interproperty relationships. So far only a few types of interproperty relationships have been explored in categorization, and much is to be gained from the careful study of further types of relations (e.g., see Barr and Caplan, 1987; Chaffin and Herrmann, 1987; Rips and Conrad, 1989; Winston *et al.*, 1987).

2. Levels of features. Although experimenters can often contrive to have the features or properties comprising stimulus materials at roughly the same level of abstractness, in more typical circumstances levels may vary substantially. This fact has critical implications for descriptions of category structure (see Barsalou and Billman, 1988). This point may be best represented by an example from some ongoing research I am conducting with Glenn Nakamura and Ed Wisniewski. Our stimulus materials consist of children's drawings of people, a sample of which is shown in Figure 1.1 There are two sets of five drawings, one on the left and one on the right. The task of the participants in this experiment is to come up with a rule that could be used to correctly classify both these drawings and new examples that might be presented later.

One of our primary aims in this study was to examine the effects of different types of knowledge structures on rule induction. Consequently, some participants were told that one set was done by farm children and the other by city children; some were told that one set was done by creative children and the other by noncreative children; and still others were told that one set was done by emotionally disturbed children and the other by mentally healthy children. The exact assignment of drawings was counterbalanced with respect to the categories such that half the time the drawings on the left of Figure 1.1 were labeled as done by farm children and half the time the drawings on the right were labeled as having been done by farm children.

Although we were obviously expecting differences in the various conditions, in some respects the most striking result is one that held across conditions. Almost without exception the rules that people gave had properties at two or three different levels of abstractness. For example, one person who was told the drawings on the left were done by city children gave the following rule: 'The city drawings use more profiles, and are more elaborate.

Figure 1.1 Children's drawings of people used in the rule induction studies by Nakamura, Wisniewski and Medin.

The clothes are more detailed, showing both pockets and buttons, and the hair is drawn in. The drawings put less emphasis on proportion and the legs and torso are off.' Another person who was told the same drawings were done by farm children wrote: 'The children draw what they see in their normal life. The people have overalls on and some drawings show body muscles as a result of labor. The drawings are also more detailed. One can see more facial details and one drawing has colored the clothes and another one shows the body under the clothes.' As one can see, the rules typically consist of a general assertion or assertions coupled with either an operational definition or examples to illustrate and clarify the assertion. In some cases these definitions or examples extend across several levels of abstractness.

One might think that our participants used different levels of description because there was nothing else for them to do. That is, there may have been no low-level perceptual features that would separate the groups. In a followup study we presented examples one at a time and asked people to give their rule after each example. If people are being forced to use multiple levels of description because simple rules will not work, then we should observe a systematic increase in the use of multiple levels across examples. In fact, however, we observed multiple levels of description as the predominant strategy from the first example on. We believe that multiple levels arise when people try to find a link between abstract explanatory principles or ideas (drawings reflect one's experience) and specific details of drawings.

There are several important consequences of multilevel descriptions. First of all, the relation across levels is not necessarily a subset, superset, or a part–whole relation. Most of the time one would say that the lower level property 'supports' the higher level property; for example, 'jumping into a swimming pool with one's clothes on' supports poor judgment. This underlines the point that categorization often involves more than a simple matching of properties. A related point is that features are ambiguous in the sense that they may support more than one higher level property. When the drawings on the right were associated with the label *mentally healthy*, a common description was 'all the faces are smiling.' When the label for the same drawing was *noncreative*, a common description was 'the faces show little variability in expression.' Finally, it should be obvious that whether a category description is disjunctive (e.g., pig's nose or cow's mouth or catlike ears) or conjunctive or defining (e.g., all have animal parts) depends on the level with respect to which the rule is evaluated.

3. Centrality. If properties are at different levels of abstraction and linked by a variety of relations, then one might imagine that some properties are more central than others because of the role they play in conceptual structure. An indication that properties differ in their centrality comes from a provocative study by Asch and Zukier (1984). They presented people with trait terms that appeared to be contradictory (e.g., kind and vindictive) and asked participants if these descriptions could be resolved (e.g., how could a person be both kind and vindictive?). Participants had no difficulty integrating the pairs of terms, and Asch and Zukier identified seven major resolution strategies. For present purposes, what is notable is that many of the resolution strategies involve making one trait term more central than the other one. For example, one way of integrating *kind* and *vindictive* was to say that the person was fundamentally evil and was kind only in the service of vindictive ends.

In related work, Shoben and I (Medin and Shoben, 1988) showed that centrality of a property depends on the concept of which it is a part. We asked participants to judge the typicality of adjective–noun pairs when the adjective was a property that other participants judged was not true of the noun representing the concept. For example, our participants judged that all bananas and all boomerangs are curved. Based on this observation, other participants were asked to judge the typicality of a straight banana as a banana or a straight boomerang as a boomerang. Other instances of the 20 pairs used include *soft knife* versus *soft diamond* and *polka dot fire hydrant* versus *polka dot yield sign*. For 19 of the 20 pairs, participants rated one item of a pair as more typical than the other. Straight banana, soft knife, and polka dot fire hydrant were rated as more typical than straight boomerang, soft diamond, and polka dot yield sign. In the case of boomerangs (and probably yield signs), centrality may be driven by structure–function correlations. Soft diamonds are probably rated as very atypical because hardness is linked to many other properties and finding out that diamonds were soft would call a great deal of other knowledge into question.

Most recently, Woo Kyoung Ahn, Joshua Rubenstein, and I have been interviewing clinical psychologists and psychiatrists concerning their understanding of psychodiagnostic categories. Although our project is not far enough along to report any detailed results, it is clear that the *DSM-IIIR* guidebook (American Psychiatric Association, 1987) provides only a skeletal outline that is brought to life by theories and causal scenarios underlying and intertwined with the symptoms that comprise the diagnostic criteria. Symptoms differ in the level of abstractness and the types and number of inter-symptom relations in which they participate, and as a consequence, they differ in their centrality.

Conclusions

The shift to a focus on knowledge-based categorization does not mean that the notion of similarity must be left behind. But we do need an updated approach to, and interpretation of, similarity. The mounting evidence on the role of theories and explanations in organizing categories is much more compatible with features at varying levels linked by a variety of interproperty relations than it is with independent features at a single level. In addition, similarity may not so much constitute structure as point toward it. There is a dimension of depth to categorization. The conjectures about psychological essentialism may be one way of reconciling classification in terms of perceptual similarity of surface properties with the deeper substance of knowledge-rich, theory-based categorization.

References

Abelson, R. P., and Lalljee, M. G. (1988). Knowledge-structures and causal explanation. In D. J. Hilton (Ed.), *Contemporary science and natural explanation: Commonsense conceptions of causality* (pp. 175–202). Brighton, England: Harvester Press.

Allen, S. W., Brooks, L. R., Norman, G. R., and Rosenthal, D. (1988, November).

Effect of prior examples on rule-based diagnostic performance. Paper presented at the meeting of the Psychonomic Society, Chicago.

American Psychiatric Association. (1987). *Diagnostic and statistical manual of mental disorders* (rev. ed.). Washington, DC: Author.

Anderson, J. R. (1988). The place of cognitive architectures in a rational analysis. In *The Tenth Annual Conference of the Cognitive Science Society* (pp. 1–10). Montreal, Canada: University of Montreal.

Arkes, H. R., and Harkness, A. R. (1980). Effect of making a diagnosis on subsequent recognition of symptoms. *Journal of Experimental Psychology: Human Learning and Memory, 6,* 568–575.

Armstrong, S. L., Gleitman, L. R., and Gleitman, H. (1983). What some concepts might not be. *Cognition, 13,* 263–308.

Asch, S. E., and Zukier, H. (1984). Thinking about persons. *Journal of Personality and Social Psychology, 46,* 1230–1240.

Barr, R. A., and Caplan, L. J. (1987). Category representations and their implications for category structure. *Memory and Cognition, 15,* 397–418.

Barsalou, L. W. (1983). Ad hoc categories. *Memory and Cognition, 11,* 211–227.

Barsalou, L. W. (1985). Ideals, central tendency, and frequency of instantiation as determinants of graded structure in categories. *Journal of Experimental Psychology: Learning, Memory and Cognition, 11,* 629–654.

Barsalou, L. W. (1987). The instability of graded structure: Implications for the nature of concepts. In U. Neisser (Ed.), *Concepts and conceptual development: Ecological and intellectual factors in categorization* (pp. 101–40). Cambridge, England: Cambridge University Press.

Barsalou, L. W. (1989). Intra-concept similarity and its implications for inter-concept similarity. In S. Vosniadou and A. Ortony (Eds.), *Similarity and analogical reasoning* (pp. 76–121). Cambridge, England: Cambridge University Press.

Barsalou, L. W., and Billman, D. (1988, April). *Systematicity and semantic ambiguity.* Paper presented at a workshop on semantic ambiguity, Adelphi University.

Barsalou, L. W., and Medin, D. L. (1986). Concepts: Fixed definitions or dynamic context-dependent representations? *Cahiers de Psychologie Cognitive, 6,* 187–202.

Bellezza, F. S. (1984). Reliability of retrieval from semantic memory: Noun meanings. *Bulletin of the Psychonomic Society, 22,* 377–380.

Biederman, I. (1985). Human image understanding: Recent research and a theory. *Computer Vision, Graphics, and Image Processing, 32,* 29–83.

Biederman, I. (1987). Recognition-by-components: A theory of human image understanding. *Psychological Review, 94,* 115–147.

Cantor, N., and Mischel, W. (1977). Traits as prototypes: Effects on recognition memory. *Journal of Personality and Social Psychology, 35,* 38–48.

Carey, S. (1985). *Conceptual change in childhood.* Cambridge, MA: Massachusetts Institute of Technology Press.

Chaffin, R., and Herrmann, D. J. (1987). Relation element theory: A new account of the representation and processing of semantic relations. In D. Gorfein and R. Hoffman (Eds.), *Learning and memory: The Ebbinghaus centennial conference* (pp. 221–245). Hillsdale, NJ: Erlbaum.

Dickinson, A., Shanks, D., and Evenden, J. (1984). Judgment of act-outcome contingency: The role of selective attribution. *Quarterly Journal of Experimental Psychology, 36A,* 29–50.

Einhorn, J. H., and Hogarth, R. M. (1986). Judging probable cause. *Psychological Bulletin, 99,* 3–19.

Estes, W. K. (1986a). Memory storage and retrieval processes in category learning. *Journal of Experimental Psychology: General, 115*, 155–175.

Estes, W. K. (1986b). Array models for category learning. *Cognitive Psychology, 18*, 500–549.

Fehr, B. (1988). Prototype analysis of the concepts of love and commitment. *Journal of Personality and Social Psychology, 55*, 557–579.

Fehr, B., and Russell, J. A. (1984). Concept of emotion viewed from a prototype perspective. *Journal of Experimental Psychology: General, 113*, 464–486.

Flannagan, M. J., Fried, L. S., and Holyoak, K. J. (1986). Distributional expectations and the induction of category structure. *Journal of Experimental Psychology: Learning, Memory and Cognition, 12*, 241–256.

Frazer, J. G. (1959). *The new golden bough.* New York: Criterion Books.

Fried, L. S., and Holyoak, K. J. (1984). Induction of category distribution: A framework for classification learning. *Journal of Experimental Psychology: Learning, Memory and Cognition, 10*, 234–257.

Gati, I., and Tversky, A. (1984). Weighting common and distinctive features in perceptual and conceptual judgments. *Cognitive Psychology, 16*, 341–370.

Gelman, S. A. (1988). The development of induction within natural kind and artifact categories. *Cognitive Psychology, 20*, 65–95.

Gelman, S. A., and Markman, E. M. (1986a). Categories and induction in young children. *Cognition, 23*, 183–209.

Gelman, S. A., and Markman, E. M. (1986b). Young children's inductions from natural kinds: The role of categories and appearances. *Child Development, 58*, 1532–1541.

Genero, N., and Cantor, N. (1987). Exemplar prototypes and clinical diagnosis: Toward a cognitive economy. *Journal of Social and Clinical Psychology, 5*, 59–78.

Gentner, D., and Landers, R. (1985). *Analogical reminding: A good match is hard to find.* Paper presented at the International Conference of Systems, Man and Cybernetics, Tucson, AZ.

Goldin, S. E. (1978). Memory for the ordinary: Typicality effects in chess memory. *Journal of Experimental Psychology: Human Learning and Memory, 4*, 605–616.

Goodman, N. (1972). Seven strictures on similarity. In N. Goodman (Ed.), *Problems and projects.* New York: Bobbs-Merrill.

Hartley, J., and Homa, D. (1981). Abstraction of stylistic concepts. *Journal of Experimental Psychology: Human Learning and Memory, 7*, 33–46.

Hilton, D. J., and Slugoski, B. R. (1986). Knowledge-based causal attribution: The abnormal conditions focus model. *Psychological Review, 93*, 75–88.

Hintzman, D. L. (1986). "Schema abstraction" in a multiple-trace memory model. *Psychological Review, 93*, 411–428.

Homa, D. (1984). On the nature of categories. In G. Bower (Ed.), *The psychology of learning and motivation* (Vol. 18, pp. 49–94). New York: Academic Press.

Homa, D., and Vosburgh, R. (1976). Category breadth and the abstraction of prototypical information. *Journal of Experimental Psychology: Human Learning and Memory, 2*, 322–330.

Keil, F. C. (1979). *Semantic and conceptual development: An ontological perspective.* Cambridge, MA: Harvard University Press.

Keil, F. C. (1981). Constraints on knowledge and cognitive development. *Psychological Review, 88*, 197–227.

Keil, F. C. (1986). The acquisition of natural kind and artifact terms. In W. Demopoulos and A. Marras (Eds.), *Language learning and concept acquisition* (pp. 133–53). Norwood, NJ: Ablex.

Keil, F. C. (1987). Conceptual development and category structure. In U. Neisser

(Ed.), *Concepts and conceptual development: Ecological and intellectual factors in categorization* (pp. 175–200). Cambridge, England: Cambridge University Press.

Keil, F. C. and Kelly, M. H. (1987). Developmental changes in category structure. In S. Harnad (Ed.), *Categorical perception: The groundwork of cognition* (pp. 491–510). Cambridge, England: Cambridge University Press.

Kemler-Nelson, D. G. (1984). The effect of intention on what concepts are acquired. *Journal of Verbal Learning and Verbal Behavior, 23,* 734–759.

Kolodner, J. L. (1984). *Retrieval and organizational structures in conceptual memory: A computer model.* Hillsdale, NJ: Erlbaum.

Lakoff, G. (1987). *Women, fire, and dangerous things: What categories tell us about the nature of thought.* Chicago: University of Chicago Press.

Leddo, J., Abelson, R. P., and Gross, P. H. (1984). Conjunctive explanation: When two explanations are better than one. *Journal of Personality and Social Psychology, 47,* 933–943.

Malt, B. C. and Smith, E. E. (1983). Correlated properties in natural categories. *Journal of Verbal Learning and Verbal Behavior, 23,* 250–269.

Markman, E. M. (1987). How children constrain the possible meanings of words. In U. Neisser (Ed.), *Concepts and conceptual development: Ecological and intellectual factors in categorization* (pp. 256–287). Cambridge, England: Cambridge University Press.

Massey, C. M., and Gelman, R. (1988). Preschoolers' ability to decide whether a photographed unfamiliar object can move itself. *Developmental Psychology, 24,* 307–317.

McCloskey, M., and Glucksberg, S. (1978). Natural categories: Well-defined or fuzzy sets? *Memory and Cognition, 6,* 462–472.

McNamara, T P., and Sternberg, R. J. (1983). Mental models of word meaning. *Journal of Verbal Learning and Verbal Behavior, 22,* 449–474.

Medin, D. L. (1986). Commentary on 'Memory storage and retrieval processes in category learning.' *Journal of Experimental Psychology: General, 115*(4), 373–381.

Medin, D. L., Altom, M. W., Edelson, S. M., and Freko, D. (1982). Correlated symptoms and simulated medical classification. *Journal of Experimental Psychology: Learning, Memory and Cognition, 8,* 37–50.

Medin, D. L., and Ortony, A. (1989). *Psychological essentialism.* In S. Vosniadou and A. Ortony (Eds.), *Similarity and analogical reasoning* (pp. 179–195). New York: Cambridge University Press.

Medin, D. L., and Ross, B. H. (1989). The specific character of abstract thought: Categorization, problem-solving, and induction. In R. J. Sternberg (Ed.), *Advances in the psychology of human intelligence* (Vol. 5, pp. 189–223). Hillsdale, NJ: Erlbaum.

Medin, D. L., and Schaffer, M. M. (1978). A context theory of classification learning. *Psychological Review, 85,* 207–238.

Medin, D. L., and Schwanenflugel, P. J. (1981). Linear separability in classification learning. *Journal of Experimental Psychology: Human Learning and Memory, 7,* 355–368.

Medin, D. L., and Shoben, E. J. (1988). Context and structure in conceptual combination. *Cognitive Psychology, 20,* 158–190.

Medin, D. L., and Smith, E. E. (1984). Concepts and concept formation. In M. R. Rosenzweig and L. W. Porter (Eds.), *Annual Review of Psychology, 35,* 113–118.

Medin, D. L., and Wattenmaker, W. D. (1987). Category cohesiveness, theories, and cognitive archeology. In U. Neisser (Ed.), *Concepts and conceptual development:*

Ecological and intellectual factors in categories (pp. 25–62). Cambridge, England: Cambridge University Press.

Mervis, C. B., and Rosch, E. (1981). Categorization of natural objects. In M. R. Rosenzweig and L. W. Porter (Eds.), *Annual Review of Psychology, 32,* 89–115.

Michotte, A. (1963). *Perception of causality.* London: Methuen.

Morey, L. C., and McNamara, T. P. (1987). On definitions, diagnosis, and DSM-III. *Journal of Abnormal Psychology, 96,* 283–285.

Murphy, G. L., and Medin, D. L. (1985). The role of theories in conceptual coherence. *Psychological Review, 92,* 289–316.

Nakamura, G. V. (1985). Knowledge-based classification of ill-defined categories. *Memory and Cognition, 13,* 377–384.

Nosofsky, R. M. (1987). Attention and learning processes in the identification and categorization of integral stimuli. *Journal of Experimental Psychology: Learning, Memory, and Cognition, 13,* 87–108.

Nosofsky, R. M. (1988a). Exemplar-based accounts of relations between classification, recognition, and typicality. *Journal of Experimental Psychology: Learning, Memory, and Cognition, 14,* 700–708.

Nosofsky, R. M. (1988b). Similarity, frequency, and category representations. *Journal of Experimental Psychology: Learning, Memory, and Cognition, 14,* 54–65.

Oden, G. C. (1987). Concept, knowledge, and thought. In M. R. Rosenzweig and L. W. Porter (Eds.), *Annual Review of Psychology, 38,* 203–227.

Oden, G. C., and Lopes, L. (1982). On the internal structure of fuzzy subjective categories. In R. R. Yager (Ed.), *Recent developments in fuzzy set and possibility theory* (pp. 75–89). Elmsford, NY: Pergamon Press.

Ortony, A., Vondruska, R. J., Foss, M. A., and Jones, L. E. (1985). Salience, similes and the asymmetry of similarity. *Journal of Memory and Language, 24,* 569–594.

Palmer, S. E. (1975). Visual perception and world knowledge. In D. A. Norman and D. E. Rumelhart (Eds.), *Explorations in cognition* (pp. 279–307). San Francisco: W. H. Freeman.

Palmer, S. E. (1978). Structural aspects of visual similarity. *Memory and Cognition, 6,* 91–97.

Peterson, M. J., Meagher, R. B., Jr., Chait, H., and Gillie, S. (1973). The abstraction and generalization of dot patterns. *Cognitive Psychology, 4,* 378–398.

Pomerantz, J. R., Sager, L. C., and Stoever, R. G. (1977). Perception of wholes and their component parts: Some configural superiority effects. *Journal of Experimental Psychology: Human Perception and Performance, 3,* 422–435.

Read, S. J. (1983). Once is enough: Causal reasoning from a single instance. *Journal of Personality and Social Psychology, 45,* 323–334.

Rips, L. (1989). Similarity, typicality, and categorization. In S. Vosniadou and A. Ortony (Eds.), *Similarity and analogical reasoning* (pp. 21–59). New York: Cambridge University Press.

Rips, L. J., and Conrad, F. G. (1989). The folk psychology of mental activities. *Psychological Review, 96,* 187–207.

Rosch, E. (1975). Cognitive representations of semantic categories. *Journal of Experimental Psychology: General, 104,* 192–233.

Rosch, E., and Mervis, C. B. (1975). Family resemblances: Studies in the internal structure of categories. *Cognitive Psychology, 7,* 573–605.

Ross, B. H. (1984). Remindings and their effects in learning a cognitive skill. *Cognitive Psychology, 16,* 371–416.

Roth, E. M., and Shoben, E. J. (1983). The effect of context on the structure of categories. *Cognitive Psychology, 15,* 346–378.

Schank, R. C., Collins, G. C., and Hunter, L. E. (1986). Transcending inductive category formation in learning. *The Behavioral and Brain Sciences, 9*, 639–686.

Schweder, R. A. (1977). Likeness and likelihood in everyday thought: Magical thinking in judgments about personality. *Current Anthropology, 18*, 4.

Sebestyn, G. S. (1962). *Decision-making processes in pattern recognition*. New York: Macmillan.

Shepard, R. N. (1984). Ecological constraints on internal representation: Resonant kinematics of perceiving, imagining, thinking, and dreaming. *Psychological Review, 91*, 417–447.

Shepard, R. N., Hovland, C. I., and Jenkins, H. M. (1961). Learning and memorization of classifications. *Psychological Monographs, 75*, (13, Whole No. 517).

Smith, E. E., and Medin, D. L. (1981). *Categories and concepts*. Cambridge, MA: Harvard University Press.

Smith, E. E., Rips, L. J., and Medin, D. W. (1984). A psychological approach to concepts: Comments on Rey's 'Concepts and stereotypes.' *Cognition, 17*, 265–274.

Smith, E. E., Shoben, E. J., and Rips, L. J. (1974). Structure and processes in semantic memory: A featural model for semantic decisions. *Psychological Review, 81*, 214–241.

Sommers, F. (1971). Structural ontology. *Philosophia, 1*, 21–42.

Testa, T. J. (1974). Causal relationships and the acquisition of avoidance responses. *Psychological Review, 81*, 491–505.

Tulving, E. (1983). *Elements of episodic memory*. New York: Oxford University Press.

Tversky, A. (1977). Features of similarity. *Psychological Review, 84*, 327–352.

Watanabe, S. (1969). *Knowing and guessing: A formal and quantitative study*. New York: Wiley.

Wattenmaker, W. D., Dewey, G. I., Murphy, T. D., and Medin, D. L. (1986). Linear separability and concept learning: Context, relational properties, and concept naturalness. *Cognitive Psychology, 18*, 158–194.

Wattenmaker, W. D., Nakamura, G. V., and Medin, D. L. (1988). Relationships between similarity-based and explanation-based categorization. In D. Hilton (Ed.), *Contemporary science and natural explanation: Commonsense conceptions of causality* (pp. 205–241). Brighton, England: Harvester Press.

Winston, M. E., Chaffin, R., and Herrmann, D. (1987). A taxonomy of part-whole relations. *Cognitive Science, 11*, 417–444.

Wittgenstein, L. (1953). *Philosophical investigations* (G. E. M. Anscombe, trans.). Oxford, England: Blackwell.

2 'Emilie M. Roth and Edward J. Shoben
'The Effect of Context on the Structure of Categories'

Reprinted in full from: *Cognitive Psychology* **15**, 346–378 (1983)

An important aspect of text comprehension is the ability to form a coherent representation of the information provided. In order to form this representation, it is necessary to identify how the ideas presented in the different sentences are related, and to integrate them into a coherent whole (Haviland and Clark, 1974; Thorndike, 1976; Clark, 1975). One of the most common mechanisms for providing cohesion among the sentences in a text is the use of anaphoric reference, where a noun phrase is used to refer back to an entity introduced earlier in the text. An example is 'The children loved to play with their new *puppy*. Luckily, the *Collie* had a good temper and was very affectionate.' Understanding how people resolve such anaphoric references is one of the central issues in the study of text comprehension (Carpenter and Just, 1977; Garrod and Sanford, 1981; Hobbs, 1979; Sanford and Garrod, 1977). In this paper we address one aspect of this problem: how people use information from semantic memory in establishing the referent of an anaphoric expression. We focus particularly on the effect of context on the ease with which an exemplar can be identified as the referent of a category term.

There are several factors that influence the ease with which an anaphoric reference is established. One important factor is the availability of the concept that is being referred to. For example, an anaphoric reference can be established faster when the item being referred to occurs in the immediately preceding sentence (particularly in the immediately preceding clause) than if it occurs several sentences earlier (Carpenter and Just, 1977; Clark and Sengul, 1979). Similarly, concepts that are central to the theme of the text, or are otherwise linguistically foregrounded, are more easily identified as the referent of an anaphor than other concepts (Carpenter and Just, 1977).

A second important factor influencing the ease of establishing an anaphoric reference is the semantic relation between the item used to make the anaphoric reference and the concept it refers to. Anaphoric references are made in a variety of ways. In some cases the anaphor employs the same wording used when the concept was first introduced (e.g. 'John picked up the *toy*. The *toy* was brightly colored.'). More often, however, the wording is different. The anaphoric reference is likely to be made using either a pronoun (e.g., '*It* was brightly colored.') or a different noun phrase (e.g., 'The *ball* was brightly colored.'). When a different wording is used, information about the meaning of the words, and general knowledge about the situation described, need to be accessed in order to resolve the anaphoric reference (Clark, 1975; Hobbs, 1979). For the current example, in order to establish that the ball in the second sentence refers to the toy mentioned earlier, one must recognize that a ball can be a type of toy. Greater semantic relatedness between the two concepts leads to easier resolution of the anaphoric reference. This general result was shown in a series of studies conducted by Garrod and Sanford (1977) that are described below.

Garrod and Sanford (1977, 1981; Sanford and Garrod, 1977) have examined a number of semantic factors that influence the ease of establishing an anaphoric reference. Of particular interest is a study by Garrod and Sanford (1977) that demonstrates that the speed with which an anaphoric reference can be established depends on the semantic relatedness between the anaphor and the referent. In this study, subjects were presented with sets of three sentences. The first (context) sentence included a category term (e.g., 'The *trees* were shattered by the storm.'). The second (target) sentence included an anaphoric reference that served to specify a particular exemplar as the referent of the category term (e.g., 'The *oaks* were wrenched from the ground.'). The third sentence was a question requiring a yes/no response, that tested information presented in the first two sentences (e.g., 'Were the oaks pulled from the ground?'). The sentences were presented one at a time, and reading time for each individual sentence was recorded.

Garrod and Sanford varied how typical the exemplar mentioned in the second sentence was of the category mentioned in the first sentence.[1] For each set of sentences there was one typical exemplar and one atypical exemplar. For instance, in the example given above, 'oaks' (typical exemplar) and 'palms' (atypical exemplar) were used. The basic result they found was that reading time for the second sentence was faster if the instance was a typical exemplar of the category than if it was an atypical exemplar.

This result is interesting because it parallels the findings obtained in the semantic memory literature. In semantic memory experiments (e.g., Collins and Quillian, 1969; Lorch, 1981; Rips *et al.*, 1973) subjects determine if an exemplar is a member of a particular category. One of the most robust findings in this literature is that exemplars that are judged to be typical or good examples of a category are more rapidly confirmed as members of the category than less representative exemplars (Rips *et al.*, 1973; Rosch, 1973). For example, 'robin,' which is rated to be a good example of 'bird,' is verified to be a bird faster than 'turkey' or 'penguin,' which are rated to be poor members of the category. The fact that a typicality effect was obtained in this study led Garrod and Sanford to infer that part of the process of establishing an anaphoric reference includes a category membership verification procedure similar to the one studied in the semantic memory literature.

The results of the Garrod and Sanford study affirm the generality of the type of phenomena that have been studied in the semantic memory literature. Implicit category membership decisions occur in reading comprehension situations, and semantic variables that are known to affect category membership verification when the exemplar and the category term are presented in isolation continue to have an effect when the membership decision is embedded in a comprehension task. The results serve to emphasize that models of semantic memory (Collins and Loftus, 1975; Glass and Holyoak, 1975; McCloskey and Glucksberg, 1979; Smith *et al.*, 1974) that have been developed on the basis of the results of membership verification studies can have potentially broad explanatory power.

In the studies we report below, we explore further the extent to which the type of structural and processing assumptions made in semantic memory models can be extended to account for the implicit category membership decisions that occur during the process of understanding an anaphoric reference. We focus particularly on the typicality ordering of exemplars. As we observed earlier, exemplars of a category vary in the degree to which they are representative of the category term. When subjects are asked to rate exemplars in terms of how well they fit their idea or image of a category term, a graded typicality, or goodness-of-example (GOE) distribution, is generated which turns out to be an excellent predictor of category membership verification time (Rosch, 1975). To account for the variability in GOE, models of semantic memory generally assume that the attributes that are characteristic of typical exemplars (i.e., that occur frequently among typical exemplars) are included in the memory representation for the meaning of the category term. This assumption in turn implies that the typicality ordering should be relatively fixed across contexts, or at least should continue to exert a strong influence on category membership decisions across contexts. The experiments we report test this assumption.

The experiment conducted by Garrod and Sanford suggests that the typicality distribution obtained when category terms are presented in isolation does continue to apply even when a category term appears in the context of a sentence. However, Garrod and Sanford used relatively neutral context sentences that provided little information as to likely referents of the category term. If the context sentences contained information that restricted the set of likely referents, or otherwise altered the probability of various exemplars of the category, the results may have been different. For example, consider the sentence 'The bird walked across the barnyard.' 'Chicken' would seem to be more representative of 'bird' in this context than 'robin,' although in the absence of explicit context 'robin' is a more typical bird. If this context sentence were followed by the target sentence 'The chicken was larger than average,' comprehension time may be shorter than if it were followed by 'The robin was larger than average.' In the experiment we conducted, we specifically tested the effect of information content of the context sentence on the ease of establishing an anaphoric reference. We were particularly interested in determining to what degree the typicality ordering (typicality structure), observed in the absence of context, continues to affect the implicit category membership decisions that occur in understanding an anaphoric reference.

The fact that context can affect the representation of a term has been pointed out before (Anderson and Ortony, 1975; Anderson *et al.*, 1976; Barclay *et al.*, 1974; Barsalou, 1982; Bisanz *et al.*, 1978; Potter and Faulconer, 1979; Tabossi and Johnson-Laird, 1980). For example, Anderson *et al.* (1976) performed an experiment suggesting that context can result in a category representation that is more similar to an atypical category member than to a typical one. They presented subjects with sentences like 'The grocer stared at the fish in the bowl' and showed that atypical exemplars (e.g., goldfish) were better retrieval cues for the sentence than more typical exemplars (e.g., trout).

Although the results of these previous studies clearly demonstrate an effect of context, they are limited in several important respects. First, several of these studies have used a cued recall paradigm, making it impossible to determine whether context affected the representation of the concept at the time of comprehension or affected the retrieval of the concept during the recall portion of the task (Gumenick, 1979; McKoon and Ratcliff, 1980). Second, the studies have generally used sentences that place severe constraints on possible referents of the category term. Often there is only one possible referent, and, in many cases, the effects of context have been demonstrated using the most highly expected category referent. As a result, the studies provide little information about the distribution of likely referents of a category term in context. It is thus not possible to assess what relation exists, if any, between the GOE distribution observed in the absence of explicit context, and the distribution of likely referents of a category term in context. Third, none of the studies has examined the effect of typicality (as measured without explicit context) on category membership decisions made in the presence of context. It is consequently not possible to assess the extent to which typicality continues to influence category membership decisions in cases where context suggests an atypical exemplar of the category term as the most likely referent.

The present set of studies was specifically designed to examine the relation between the typicality structure that is obtained when category terms are presented in the absence of context and the representativeness distribution of exemplars that is generated when category terms are presented in context. The studies were conducted to determine the extent to which the structural and processing assumptions of current models of semantic memory can be extended to account for the type of implicit category membership decisions that occur in text comprehension.

Overview of the present experiments

The first study we report was conducted to provide unambiguous evidence that context can alter the relation between an examplar and a category term. The study employs the Garrod and Sanford paradigm to demonstrate that the ease with which an anaphoric reference between the exemplar and a category term is established depends on the context in which the category term is presented.

Once an effect of context was established, we examined the question of how context alters the degree of representativeness of exemplars of a category. It seems clear, on the basis of intuition, that one effect of context is to change which exemplar is most representative. In the barnyard example used earlier, *chicken* seems to be the bird that comes to mind most readily. However, it is not clear whether the category term presented in context continues to be associated with a graded distribution of representativeness, and if so, what determines the order of representativeness.

One possibility is that the category term in context leads to highly specific expectations as to its referent. In contrast to categories presented without explicit context, one's representation in context might indicate a specific exemplar rather than a graded distribution. For example, in the barnyard example, one's representation of *bird* might be that of a *chicken*. According to this view, which we will refer to as the *instantiation hypothesis*, chicken would be the only exemplar readily accepted as the referent of bird in that context. Although the instantiation hypothesis may accurately explain what occurs in highly constrained contexts that virtually restrict the set of possible referents to one (e.g., 'The monkey peeled and ate the yellow *fruit*.'), it is likely that in most cases the representation of a category term will be flexible enough readily to accept more than one possible referent of the category term. For example, in the barnyard example, we may consider chicken to be the best example, but we also judge other exemplars (duck, goose, turkey) as acceptable.

Given that a category term in context can produce a graded ordering of exemplars in terms of representativeness, what determines the representativeness ordering? We consider two possibilities. One possibility is that the representativeness distribution is based on similarity to the exemplar most strongly suggested by the context. In the barnyard example, chicken might serve as the category representation. Other exemplars would vary in representativeness according to their similarity to chicken. This account will be referred to as the *refocusing hypothesis*.

The refocusing hypothesis would seem to be able to account for context effects in many cases. Consider the sentence 'The musician tuned the strings of his instrument before playing the classical piece.' In this case we may readily think of a best example, violin, but we also would consider other examples as acceptable (viola, cello, bass, harp, etc.). This example is consistent with the refocusing hypothesis which assumes that context affects the representation of category terms by changing the prototype or best example, and by restricting the range of acceptable exemplars. According to this hypothesis, the new prototype is the example most strongly suggested by the context. Other exemplars that are acceptable referents of the category term in that context vary in representativeness according to their similarity to the new prototype. In the musician example, the set of acceptable exemplars is restricted to stringed instruments. Further, there is a clear grading in representativeness with *violin* as the most representative exemplar. The other exemplars appear to vary in representativeness according to their similarity to a violin. For example, *viola* would seem to be more representative than *harp*. This ordering is consistent with the refocusing hypothesis because viola is more similar to violin than harp is. A second possibility is that a graded GOE distribution is retained, but the entire GOE distribution is reordered on the basis of the constraints imposed by the context. Representativeness in this case would not be based on similarity to the best exemplar. This possibility will be referred to as the *restructuring hypothesis*. We will explore each of these possibilities in turn.

One way to represent the GOE distribution for a concept is as a multidimensional space (see Rips *et al.*, 1973, for a specific example), with representativeness determined by distance from some focal point. If one thinks of GOE in this way, then the effect of context, according to the refocusing hypothesis, is to shift the focus of the space to the exemplar most strongly suggested by the context. Representativeness is then a direct function of distance from this new point. The space itself does not change with context; only the prototype changes. An important implication of this hypothesis is that one can derive the entire GOE distribution for a concept in a given context simply by knowing which exemplar is most representative in that context, and the similarity relations in the original multidimensional space representation of the concept (obtained without explicit context).

Although the refocusing hypothesis is appealing, it is possible to come up with examples of effects of context that cannot be explained by it. For example, 'The square dance musician played his instrument very well' strongly suggests *fiddle* as the instrument. According to the refocusing hypothesis fiddle would serve as the category prototype in that context, and how representative other examplars were would depend on their similarity to a fiddle. However, a *viola* is quite similar to a fiddle (when no explicit context is given), but is a very unlikely exemplar in this context. In contrast, *accordion*, which is very different from a fiddle, seems more representative than viola. Thus, in this context, representativeness does not appear to be a function of similarity to the best exemplar.

The *square dance* example is consistent with the restructuring hypothesis, which assumes that the entire GOE distribution is reorganized on the basis of the constraints of the context. According to this hypothesis, GOE is a direct function of appropriateness in the context rather than a function of similarity to the best exemplar. Using the spatial analogy, one can describe the effect of context, according to the restructuring hypothesis, in one of two ways. First, context can be thought to shift the focus point in the space, or prototype, to some new point that represents a set of attributes suggested by the context. This point would not necessarily correspond to a particular exemplar. It could be an abstract prototype. Alternatively, context can be thought to alter the configuration of points in the space so that exemplars that are more representative of the concept in a particular context are positioned closer to the focus of the space. In either case, GOE would be a function of distance from the prototype or focus of the space. Since the prototype would not necessarily correspond to the most representative exemplar in the context, representativeness would not necessarily be a function of distance from this exemplar. Thus, in contrast to the refocusing hypothesis, the restructuring hypothesis does not predict that the GOE distribution for a concept in a given context can be determined by knowing the best exemplar in that context and the similarity relations in the original space.

Experiment 2 contrasts the refocusing and restructuring hypotheses. It establishes that category terms presented in context can be associated with graded GOE distributions and provides empirical support for the restructuring hypothesis. The third and final experiment employs a category verification time paradigm to investigate the process by which membership in a context-constrained category is determined. The experiment also examines whether the typicality of exemplars, as determined out of context, continues to influence verification time once context is introduced.

Experiment 1

Experiment 1 was conducted to demonstrate that context can change the relation between a category term and an exemplar at the time of comprehension. The experiment used the Garrod and Sanford (1977) paradigm. An effect of context was shown by comparing the time it took to establish an anaphoric reference between an exemplar and a category term when the category term was presented in different contexts.

The study compared the effects of three types of context sentences on the time to read and comprehend a target sentence. One type of context sentence (Bias+ context) provided information that made the exemplar specified in the target sentence a likely referent of the category term. A second type of context sentence (Bias− context) provided information that made the exemplar specified in the target sentence an unlikely referent. A third type of context sentence (Neutral context) provided little information that could be used to narrow the set of likely referents. In the Neutral context condition the category representation should be similar to the representation accessed when no explicit context is provided. Table 2.1 provides an example of each type of context sentence when the category is animal and the target exemplar is 'cow.'

The same target sentence was presented following one of each of the three types of context sentences. If context serves to shift the representation of a category term at the time of comprehension, causing a change in the representativeness of exemplars, then differences among context conditions should be reflected in target sentence reading time. If, with context, the representation used for a category term and an exemplar can become more closely related, then target sentence reading time should be faster in the Bias+ condition than in the Neutral condition. Similarly, if context can change a category representation to make it less closely related to an exemplar, then target reading time should be slower in the Bias− condition than in the Neutral context condition. This hypothesis was tested for both typical and atypical exemplars.

Table 2.1   Examples of the sentences used in Experiment 1

Target exemplar: Cow
Sentence:

1a.	Bias+ context	Stacy volunteered to milk the animal whenever she visited the farm.
1b.	Bias− context	Fran pleaded with her father to let her ride the animal.
1c.	Neutral context	Dorothy thought about the animal.
2.	Target	She was very fond of the cow.
3.	Test	She was fond of the animal.

Note: A trial consisted of sentences 1a, b, or c, 2, and 3.

Method

Design. Reading time for the same target sentence was compared following each of three context sentences (Bias+, Bias−, and Neutral context). The effect of the three context types was examined for both typical and atypical exemplars of categories. Different context and target sentences were used for the typical and atypical exemplars.

Subjects saw all target sentences in each of the three contexts; however, the items were spaced so that a target sentence appeared only once in each of three blocks. Moreover, within each block the three types of context sentences as well as the two levels of typicality were equally represented. The order in which the blocks were presented was counterbalanced across subjects. The items within a block were presented in a different random order for each subject.

Materials. A Bias+, a Neutral, and a Bias− context sentence were constructed for each of 30 typical and 30 atypical target exemplars. The context sentences referred to the name of a category to which the target exemplar belonged.

Bias+ context sentences strongly suggested the target exemplar as the likely referent of the category term. Bias− context sentences strongly suggested some other exemplar(s) of the category that had very different characteristics. This made the target exemplar an unlikely (though possible) referent of the category term in the Bias− sentence. The Neutral context sentences contained no information that would strongly suggest any particular exemplar.[2]

The context sentences were rated by a group of 26 undergraduates to determine how strongly they suggested the target exemplar. A 9-point scale was used where 1 meant the exemplar was not a possible referent of the category term in the context sentence, 5 meant the sentence was neutral with respect to the referent, and 9 meant the target exemplar was the only possible referent.

The mean suggestibility ratings for the Bias+ context sentences were 8.07 (SE = .07) for the typical exemplars and 7.93 (SE = .06) for the atypical exemplars. For the Neutral contexts they were 6.10 (SE = .11) for the typical exemplars and 5.41 (SE = .11) for the atypical exemplars. For the Bias− contexts, they were 3.02 (SE = .12) for the typical exemplars and 2.83 (SE = .14) for the atypical exemplars.

Typicality of the target exemplars was determined on the basis of ratings obtained from a separate group of 30 subjects. The instructions were similar to the ones described in Rosch (1975) with the exception that a 9-point scale was used (1 − very good exemplar). Mean typicality rating was 2.63 (SE = .14) for the typical exemplars and 4.53 (SE = .16) for the atypical exemplars.

For each target exemplar, a target sentence was constructed that made a reasonable follow-up sentence to each of the three context sentences. The sentence identified the target exemplar as the referent of the category term in the context sentence that preceded it.

For each pair of context and target sentences, a test sentence was constructed to serve as the basis of a true/false judgment. In half of the cases, the test sentences combined information presented in both the context and target sentences. In the other half it tested information presented in only one of the sentences. The test sentence was true in half of the cases. The inclusion of a test sentence ensured that subjects read the context and target sentences carefully.

Procedure. The sets of sentences were presented on an ADDS 970 terminal controlled by an IBM 1800 computer. At the start of each trial three asterisks, which served as focus points, appeared on the left side of the screen: one in the upper third, one in the center, and one in the lower third. When the subject pressed the space bar a context sentence appeared below the top asterisk. The subject read the sentence and then pressed the space bar. This caused the context sentence to be erased, and the target sentence to appear below the second asterisk. The subject read this sentence and then pressed the space bar causing the target sentence to be erased, and the test sentence to appear below the third asterisk. After reading the test sentence the subject pressed the 'true' key if the statement was consistent with the first two sentences and the 'false' key otherwise. The 'R' and 'O' letters served as response keys in all three response time studies reported. In all cases subjects used their dominant hand to respond 'true.' Reading time for each of the three sentences, as well as the response made to the test sentence, was recorded. If the response was incorrect an error message appeared.

The experiment was run in a single session. There were 10 practice trials followed by 180 experimental trials. The session lasted approximately 50 min. Up to five subjects were run simultaneously at individual terminals.

Subjects. Three participants made more than 15% errors on the test question and were excluded from the study. The remaining 42 undergraduates participated in partial fulfillment of an introductory psychology course requirement.

Results

The data of main interest are the reading times (RT) for the target sentences. Reading times longer than 4 standard deviations above the mean for the block (less than 1% of the data) as well as RTs on trials where the response was incorrect were removed. Error rates were low (6.0%) and correlated positively with the RTs for the test sentence.

The same target sentence appeared following a Bias+ context, a Neutral context, and a Bias− context. Mean RTs for the target sentence in each of the three contexts are presented in Table 2.2. As expected, the Bias+ context served to speed reading comprehension for both typical and atypical exemplars. Target sentences were read faster (72 msec) following a Bias+ context than following a Neutral context. The Bias− context slowed down RT for both typical and atypical exemplars. Target sentences were read 122 msec slower following a Bias− context than following a Neutral context. The context effect was significant overall (min $F'[2,186] = 20.2$, $p < .001$). In addition, both the facilitative effect of the Bias+ context (min $F'[1,188] = 5.38$, $p < .05$) and the inhibiting effect of the Bias− context (min $F'[1,186] = 15.79$, $p < .001$) were reliable. The only other significant effect was a main effect of blocks (min $F'[2,122] = 117.23$, $p < .001$) indicating an overall decrease in RT with blocks. None of the interactions with blocks approached significance.

The test sentence was included solely to ensure careful reading of the first two sentences. There was no effect of context on test sentence RT.

Table 2.2   Mean RTs (msec) for target sentence in Experiment 1

Target exemplar	Bias+ context	Neutral context	Bias− context
Typical exemplar	1986	2038	2186
Atypical exemplar	1980	2071	2167
Mean	1983	2055	2177

Discussion

The results of the study suggest that context can affect the relation between an exemplar and a category term. The context in which a category term was presented was found to affect how easily an anaphoric reference between an exemplar and the category term could be established. Comprehension time for the target sentence was fastest when the category term was presented in a Bias+ context. It was slowest when the category term appeared in a Bias− context sentence. This pattern of results suggests that context affects the representation for a category term. Bias+ contexts, which strongly suggest a particular exemplar, produce a category representation closely related to the target exemplar. Bias− contexts, which suggest an exemplar with different properties from the target exemplar, result in a category representation that is less related to the target exemplar.

Interestingly, the facilitation effect of Bias+ contexts and inhibition effect of Bias− contexts occurred for both typical and atypical exemplars. This result suggests that how closely related a category representation is to a particular exemplar is not fixed. It depends on context.

The results of the present study are not subject to the type of memory retrieval explanation that has been offered to account for the results of studies using a cued retrieval paradigm, and they therefore provide stronger evidence that context has its effect during the comprehension process.

Experiment 2

Experiment 1 established that context can alter how related an exemplar is to the representation of a category term. Experiment 2 was designed to examine more specifically how context alters the representativeness distribution of exemplars of a category. Two possible ways in which context could alter the representativeness distribution were outlined earlier. The predictions of the refocusing hypothesis and of the restructuring hypothesis are contrasted in Experiment 2.

According to the refocusing hypothesis, context serves to shift the prototype associated with a concept. The exemplar most strongly suggested by the context becomes the new prototype. The representativeness of all other exemplars is based on similarity to this prototype. Thus, in the example, 'Wendy loved to ride the *animal*' the prototype might be shifted to *horse* and other examples (pony, donkey, camel) would vary in representativeness according to their similarity to a horse.

One implication of the refocusing hypothesis is that contexts that suggest the same exemplar as the most likely referent of a category term should yield identical GOE distributions, because the new prototype for the category would be the same in all the contexts and GOE is determined by similarity to that prototype. In contrast, the restructuring hypothesis does not make this prediction. According to the restructuring hypothesis the entire GOE distribution is generated on the basis of the particular constraints of the context and not just the best exemplar. Consequently, contexts that suggest the same exemplar as the most likely referent of a category term need not always have identical GOE distributions.

Experiment 2 provides evidence against the refocusing hypothesis by demonstrating that contexts that suggest the same best exemplar do not necessarily yield identical GOE distributions. We generated pairs of context sentences that suggest the same exemplar as the most likely referent of a category term but produce opposite GOE orderings for two other exemplars. Sentences 1 and 2 in Table 2.3 provide an example of such a pair. Both sentences suggest coffee as the most likely referent of 'beverage.' However, in Sentence 1 *tea* is a more likely referent than *milk*, whereas the opposite is true in Sentence 2. Experiment 2a shows that pairs of context sentences such as these produce reliably different GOE orderings. Experiment 2b employs the Garrod and Sanford paradigm to show that the ratings accurately predict the speed with which an exemplar is identified as the referent of a category term in a context sentence.

Experiment 2a

The study obtained GOE ratings for context-constrained categories. The experiment used pairs of context sentences that suggest the same exemplar as the most likely referent of the category term (best exemplar), but suggest opposite GOE orderings for two other possible referents (target exemplars). For each sentence, subjects rated the best exemplar and each of the two target exemplars in terms of how well it fitted their idea of the category term in that context. The rating instructions used were analogous to the GOE instructions employed by Rosch (1975). It was predicted that the best exemplar would be rated to be most representative, but that there would also be reliable differences in GOE between the two target exemplars. In addition, it was predicted that the two sentences in each pair would produce opposite orderings of GOE for the two target exemplars.

Table 2.3   Example of a context sentence pair used in Experiment 2a and 2b

Best exemplar	Coffee
Similar exemplar	Tea
Dissimilar exemplar	Milk

Sentence 1: Congruent context
   During the midmorning break the two secretaries gossiped as
      they drank the beverage.
Sentence 2: Incongruent context
   Before starting his day, the truck driver had the beverage
      and a donut at the truck stop.

Note: In the case of Sentence 1 the similar exemplar is more representative than the dissimilar exemplar. The reverse is true in the case of Sentence 2.

Method

Materials. Fifty-three pairs of context sentences were constructed. Each member of a pair included the same category term and strongly suggested the same exemplar as the referent of that term (best exemplar). The context pairs were constructed so that two additional exemplars (target exemplars) were possible referents. The target exemplar that was the more likely referent of the category term in the first context was the less likely referent in the second context.

Design. Three types of normative data were collected. First, production frequency (PF) norms were collected to establish that both members of a pair of context sentences strongly suggested the same best exemplar. Second, representativeness norms were collected to establish that one target exemplar was more representative in the first context whereas the other exemplar was more representative in the second context. Third, similarity ratings were obtained to determine which of the two targets was more semantically similar to the best exemplar when no explicit context is provided.

Rating instructions and procedure

PF norms were obtained from two independent groups of subjects. Each group saw one of the two context sentences for each pair. Subjects were asked to write down next to each sentence the name of the category member that the sentence made them think of.

GOE ratings were obtained from an independent group of subjects. They were asked to rate, on a 9-point scale, how well a category member fitted their 'idea or image of what the category term refers to in the sentence,' where 1 meant it fitted very well and 9 meant it fitted very poorly. If they thought the exemplar was *not* a possible referent, they were instructed to put an X. GOE ratings were obtained for the best exemplar and the two target exemplars. Each example was rated independently.

Another group of subjects rated how similar in meaning each target exemplar was to the best exemplar of the corresponding context sentences. A 9-point scale was used where 9 meant the target exemplar was very similar in meaning to the best exemplar.

Subjects. Fifty-two students (two groups of 26) participated in the PF task. An additional 30 students provided GOE ratings and 26 more provided similarity ratings. All participated as part of an introductory psychology course requirement.

Results and discussion

The set of ratings was used to identify 24 pairs of context sentences where the two sentences strongly suggested the same best exemplar but resulted in opposite ordering of GOE ratings for the two target exemplars. The criteria for concluding that a pair of sentences strongly suggested the same best exemplar were that (1) more than 60% of the subjects named the same best exemplar in the PF task, and (2) each of the two target exemplars was named by fewer than 25% of the subjects.

The similarity ratings were used to identify which of the two target exemplars is more semantically similar to the best exemplar when the items are presented in isolation. The mean similarity rating for the more similar target exemplars (Similar Exemplar) was 6.64 (SE = .19). The mean similarity rating for the less similar target exemplars (Dissimilar Exemplar) was 5.12 (SE = .20).

Table 2.4 presents the mean representative ratings for the best exemplar and

Table 2.4   Mean GOE rating for 24 context sentence pairs identified in Experiment 2a

Context sentence	Best exemplar	Similar exemplar	Dissimilar exemplar
Congruent context	1.31 (.05)	3.23 (.20)	4.97 (.25)
Incongruent context	1.49 (.10)	5.39 (.19)	3.26 (.17)

Note: Standard error of the mean presented in parentheses.

each of the two target exemplars for each context sentence type. Congruent Context refers to the context sentences where the Similar Exemplar was more representative than the Dissimilar Exemplar. In this circumstance, the GOE ordering is consistent with the predictions of the refocusing hypothesis. Incongruent Context refers to the context sentences where the reverse was true.

As can be seen in Table 2.4, GOE ratings were graded. Not only was the best exemplar judged the most representative, but the two target exemplars differed in GOE as well. Although the target exemplars varied in representativeness, the subjects almost always agreed that all three exemplars were possible referents. In all cases at least 90% of the subjects indicated that the exemplar was a possible referent. These results suggest that context-dependent category representations can generate graded GOE distributions for category exemplars.

In addition, the results indicate that contexts that suggest the same exemplar as the referent of a category term need not result in similar GOE distributions. Contrary to the predictions of the refocusing hypothesis, the context sentences in each pair led to opposite GOE orderings of the target exemplars. An analysis of variance indicated that the reversal in GOE was reliable over subjects. This reversal was reflected in a significant interaction between context type (Congruent Context vs Incongruent Context) and target type (Similar Exemplar vs Dissimilar Exemplar) ($F[1,29] = 209.53$, $p < .001$). The difference in rated GOE between target exemplars was significant for both Congruent Context sentences ($F[1,29] = 84.01$, $p < .001$) and Incongruent Context sentences ($F[1,29] = 126.16$, $p < .001$). Significant effects were also obtained for context type ($F[1,29] = 12.37$, $p < .01$) and target type ($F[1,29] = 5.73$, $p < .05$). Both effects reflect the fact that the mean GOE rating for the less representative target exemplar was higher in Incongruent Contexts than in Congruent Contexts (see Table 2.4).

The results demonstrate that context-dependent category representations can generate graded GOE distributions. Subjects found the GOE rating instructions sensible and were able to agree on order of representativeness. These results suggest that the representation of concepts presented in context is similar in form to the representation of concepts presented in isolation. In both cases the representation results in a graded GOE distribution. The effect of context is to change the order of representativeness of the exemplars.

Experiment 2b

The results of Experiment 2a suggest that context-dependent category representations produce graded GOE distributions similar in form to the typicality distributions generated when category terms are presented in isolation. This conclusion rests on the assumption that the GOE ratings that were collected are analogous to typicality ratings obtained in the absence of explicit context. If this assumption is correct then the context-dependent GOE ratings obtained in Experiment 2a should predict the speed with which an exemplar is identified as a possible referent of a category term in a particular context. Experiment 2b used the Garrod and Sanford paradigm to test this prediction.

The experiment employed the 24 pairs of context sentences identified in Experiment 2a. Subjects read context sentences followed by target sentences that specified the referent of the category term. The exemplar specified was either the Similar Exemplar or the Dissimilar Exemplar. If GOE distributions for context-dependent category representations are analogous to typicality distributions, then reading time for the target sentence should be faster when the more representative exemplar is specified. In the case of Congruent Contexts, the Similar Exemplar is more representative than the Dissimilar Exemplar, therefore reading time should be faster when the target sentence specifies the Similar Exemplar. The opposite should occur in the case of Incongruent Context because in those contexts it is the Dissimilar Exemplar that is more representative.

Method

Design. Two types of contexts (Congruent Context and Incongruent Context) were factorially combined with two types of target exemplars (similar target and dissimilar target), where similarity refers to similarity to the best exemplar in the absence of context. Target sentence reading time was compared in the four conditions. The same target sentence frame was used across conditions.

The experiment was run in two sessions. In the first session a subject saw one of the target exemplars following a Congruent Context and the other exemplar following the corresponding Incongruent Context. In the second session the context/target pairings were switched. Each session was divided into two blocks. In each block the subject saw only one context sentence from each pair. The four conditions were equally represented in each block. The order in which the context/target combinations were presented was counterbalanced across subjects.

Materials. The experiment used the 24 pairs of context sentences and target exemplars identified in Experiment 2a. A target sentence frame was constructed for each pair of context sentences. The same target sentence frame was used for both target exemplars in both contexts. Test sentences were made up as described in Experiment 1.

Procedure. The procedure was the same as for Experiment 1, with the exception that the study was run in two sessions held 2 days apart. Each session consisted of 10 practice trials followed by 48 experimental trials and lasted approximately half an hour.

Subjects. Two participants who made more than 15% errors on the test question and one who had an extremely long mean RT (greater than four standard deviations above the mean) were excluded from the study. The remaining 40 undergratuates were students in an introductory course in psychology who were paid $4.50 for their participation.

Results and discussion

RTs longer than four standard deviations above the mean for the block (less than 1% of the data) as well as RTs on error trials were removed. Error rates were low (5.3%) and correlated positively with RTs for the test sentence.

Mean RTs for the target sentences are presented in Table 2.5. As expected, RT was faster when the target exemplar was more representative. This was true for both types of contexts. For Congruent Contexts, where the Similar Exemplar was more representative than the Dissimilar Exemplar, RT was 51 msec faster when the Similar Exemplar was specified. For Incongruent Contexts, where the Dissimilar Exemplar was more representative, RT was 92 msec faster when that exemplar was specified. This interaction between type of context and type of exemplar was significant (min F' [1,45] = 5.10, $p < .05$).

The difference in target sentence RT was significant for Incongruent Context sentences (min F' [1,48] = 4.75, $p < .05$) but not for Congruent Context sentences (min F' [1,39] = 1.02). The fact that representativeness had a larger, more reliable effect in the Incongruent condition was unexpected. One possible explanation is that the difference in representativeness was larger in that condition (see Table 2.4).

The only other significant effect on target sentence RT was a main effect of blocks (min F' [3,178] = 40.19, $p < .001$) reflecting a decrease in RT over blocks. There was no evidence of a main effect of semantic similarity of the target exemplar (min F' [1,56] = .54). There was no effect of context on test sentence RT.

The ratings from Experiment 2a predicted how easily an exemplar was identified as the referent of a category term. This provides supporting evidence that the ratings reflect differences in representativeness among members of context-constrained categories, just as differences in typicality ratings reflect differences in representativeness among members of categories presented in isolation.

Discussion

The results of Experiment 2 provide information about how context affects the representativeness distribution of exemplars of a category. Category terms presented in context resulted in a graded GOE distribution. In this respect the representation of category terms presented in context is similar to the category representations studied in the absence of explicit context. However, the order of representativeness is not necessarily the same in the two cases. In addition,

Table 2.5 Mean RTs (msec) for target sentence in Experiment 2b

Context sentence	Similar exemplar	Dissimilar exemplar	Difference
Congruent context	1914	1965	−51
Incongruent context	1987	1895	92

the results indicate that the order of representativeness in a context-constrained category is not determined by similarity to the exemplar most strongly suggested by the context. Thus, the effect of context cannot be explained by the refocusing hypothesis. The results are more consistent with the restructuring hypothesis.

The findings have implications for how context-dependent category representations might be represented within the framework of semantic memory models. In particular, they suggest that the change in category representation with context cannot be explained by assuming that the representation of the most strongly suggested exemplar is substituted for the representation of the category term. Instead it is necessary to assume that the entire GOE distribution is restructured on the basis of the constraints imposed by the context. Possible ways in which current models of semantic memory can explain such a reorganization are considered in the general discussion.

Experiment 3

Experiment 2 indicated that category terms presented in context produce graded GOE distributions similar in form (although not in content) to the typicality distributions obtained when category terms are presented in isolation. This result is encouraging from the point of view of attempting to extend the assumptions of semantic memory models to account for context effects, because it suggests that the representation of category terms presented in context may be similar in form to the representations of category terms presented in isolation. The purpose of Experiment 3 was to explore the possibility that the mental processes used to establish membership in a context-constrained category may be similar to the processes used to establish membership in a category presented in isolation as well.

Experiment 3 used a verification time paradigm. Subjects were asked to decide whether an exemplar was a possible referent of a category term in a context sentence; for example, whether *goat* was a possible referent of *animal* in the sentence 'Stacy went to milk the animal'. Response time (RT) was the measure of primary interest. It was assumed that RT reflected the time necessary to decide whether the exemplar was a member of the category, as it was constrained by the context.

The advantage of this verification time paradigm over the reading comprehension paradigm used in Experiments 1 and 2 is that it allowed examination of the mental operations involved in deciding that an exemplar does *not* belong to a context-constrained category. In half of the cases (false items) the exemplar presented was not a possible referent of the category term because it violated constraints imposed by the context. An example of such an item would be *bull*, which could not be the referent of *animal* in the milking context given above. The exemplars were, however, always members of the category mentioned in the context sentence. The question of interest was whether the pattern of response times for true and false items would conform to the pattern of results generally obtained in semantic memory studies where category terms are presented without explicit context.

One of the major findings in the semantic memory literature is that relatedness to the category representation influences the time it takes to verify category membership. In cases where the item is a category member (true items), higher relatedness (as measured by relatedness ratings, typicality ratings, or production frequency norms) leads to faster RTs (Collins and Quillian, 1969; Rips *et al.*, 1973; Rosch, 1973). For example, the true statement 'Roses are *flowers*' is confirmed more rapidly than 'Dandelions are *flowers*.' In cases where the item is not a category member (false items), higher relatedness generally leads to slower RTs. For example, 'Bats are *birds*' is more difficult to disconfirm than 'Chairs are *birds*.' Although there are some limits on the generality of the relatedness effect for falses (Glass *et al.*, 1979; Lorch, 1978; 1981) a positive relation between relatedness and RT generally holds (Collins and Quillian, 1972; Glass *et al.*, 1974; Meyer, 1970; Rips *et al.*, 1973; Wilkins, 1971).

Although current models of semantic memory vary widely in structural and processing assumptions, they generally account for the effect of relatedness on category verification time by assuming that the decision process takes into account evidence in favor of category membership and evidence against it. For example, feature comparison models (e.g., McCloskey and Glucksberg, 1979; Smith *et al.*, 1974), which represent concepts as sets of features or attributes, assume that category membership decisions are based on a comparison of the attributes of the two concepts involved. For true statements, the comparison process is facilitated by large numbers of matching attributes and inhibited by large numbers of mismatching attributes. The reverse is true for false statements. In this case a large overlap in attributes between the two concepts necessitates more time to complete the comparison process.

Network models (e.g., Collins and Loftus, 1975; Glass and Holyoak, 1975) represent concepts as nodes in an interconnected network. Unlike feature comparison models, network models assume that category membership information is stored explicitly as a superordinate link. Although these models place more emphasis on retrieval time in accounting for differences in category verification time, they also assume that category membership decisions take into account a variety of evidence. For example, in the Collins and Loftus (1975) model, category membership decisions are made by accessing and aggregating evidence in favor of and evidence against category membership until either a positive or negative threshold is reached. Attributes of the concepts are included as sources of evidence. Thus, most current models of semantic memory assume that category membership decisions involve a process whereby several component attributes are compared or evaluated.

If the mental processes used to verify membership in context-constrained categories are similar to the processes used to determine category membership in the absence of explicit context, then relatedness to the context-dependent category representation should influence verification time. For true items, verification time should be faster for exemplars that are related to the category representation than for exemplars that are unrelated. In the milking example, verification time should be faster for *cow* than for *goat* because *cow*

Table 2.6 An example of the type of item used in Experiment 3

Context sentence: The hunter shot at the 'bird' flying high overhead.

False items
    Related exemplar   Chicken
    Unrelated exemplar Penguin
True items
    Related exemplar   Duck
    Unrelated exemplar Crow

is generally considered to be more related to the category representation in this context than *goat* is.

A relatedness effect should also be observed for false items. In the case of falses, high relatedness between the exemplar and the context-dependent representation should lead to long RTs to decide that the exemplar is not a possible member of the category in that context. In the milking example, it should take longer to decide that *bull* is not a possible referent of *animal* in that context than that *bear* is not, because *bull* is generally considered to be more related to the category representation in that context than *bear* is.

Experiment 3 examined whether relatedness to a context-dependent category representation affects category verification for false items. The effect of relatedness was assessed by comparing response time for false items that were related to the category representation and false items that were unrelated. Table 2.6 provides a second example of the type of item used.

Method
    Design. Subjects were presented with context sentences, each followed by an exemplar of a category term mentioned in the sentence. The task was to determine whether the exemplar was a possible referent of the category term.

Four exemplars were associated with each context sentence. Two were possible referents (true items) and the other two were not (false items). For both the trues and the falses, one item (related exemplar) was more related to the category representation in the context than the other (unrelated exemplar). As a control, in half the contexts (standard ordering condition) the related exemplar for both true and false statements was a more typical member of the category (when presented in isolation) than the unrelated exemplar. The reverse was true in the other half (reverse ordering condition).

Each context sentence appeared four times, followed once by each of the four exemplars. The items were presented in four blocks, so that a sentence appeared only once per block. An equal number of related and unrelated trues and falses occurred in each block. Order of presentation was counterbalanced across subjects.

    Materials. Twenty context sentences were used. For each sentence, four exemplars of the category term mentioned in the sentence were selected. Two were possible referents of the category term; the others were not. The false items violated either explicitly mentioned constraints or constraints that could be validly inferred from the context sentence.

Relatedness ratings were collected to establish that the two true exemplars and the two false exemplars varied in relatedness to the context-dependent category representation. A 9-point scale was used, where 1 meant the exemplar was 'very similar' to the subject's 'idea or image of what the category term referred to in the sentence.' Mean relatedness for the true items in the standard ordering condition was 1.71 (SE = .13) and 4.58 (SE = .39) for the related and unrelated exemplars, respectively. In the reverse ordering condition it was 1.84 (SE = .16) and 3.78 (SE = .39), respectively. Mean relatedness for the false items in the standard ordering condition was 6.85 (SE = .28) and 8.27 (SE = .17) for the related and unrelated exemplars, respectively. In the reverse ordering condition it was 7.25 (SE = .26) and 8.23 (SE = .12), respectively. The true and false items were rated by independent groups of 24 subjects each.

The exemplars were also rated for typicality (when presented in isolation) by an independent group of 30 subjects. For both the trues and falses, related and unrelated exemplars were not significantly different in mean typicality, word length or word frequency (based on the Kučera and Francis [1967] norms).

To ensure that correct truth values were assigned to the items, additional subjects were asked whether the category terms in the context sentences could possibly refer to each of the four exemplars. Half of the items (one true and one false exemplar for each context sentence) was presented to each of two independent groups of 20 subjects. In all cases, at least 80% of the subjects agreed with the truth designation.

Procedure. The stimuli were presented on an ADDS 970 terminal controlled by an IBM 1800 computer. Subjects initiated a trial by pressing the space bar. This caused a context sentence to appear in which the category term was surrounded by single quotation marks. After reading the sentence, the subject pressed the space bar again causing the sentence to be erased. An 'X' which served as a focus point, appeared at the center of the screen. After 350 msec the 'X' was replaced by a category exemplar. Subjects were asked to indicate whether the exemplar could possibly be the referent of the category term in the sentence by pressing either the 'yes' or 'no' key.

If the response was correct, the next trial was initiated. Otherwise, the sentence and the exemplar were presented simultaneously and the subjects were informed of their response. They were asked to press 'yes' if they believed the response was correct and 'no' otherwise. It was explained that this was to find out whether they disagreed with the experimenters as to the correct response.

The experiment was run in a single session consisting of 20 practice followed by 80 experimental trials. The trials were presented in a different random order for each subject. The session lasted approximately 30 min.

Subjects. Twenty-five subjects participated in the RT study. One made more than 15% errors and was excluded. The remaining 24 subjects participated either in partial fulfillment of a course requirement or for a cash payment of $3.00. All were students of an introductory course in psychology.

Results

RT was the dependent variable of primary interest. RTs greater than four standard deviations above the grand mean (less than 1% of the data) and RTs on error trials were removed. Error rates correlated positively with RTs (see Tables 2.7 and 2.8). Trues and falses were analyzed separately.

The results of main interest are the RTs for false items, which are presented in Table 2.7. Overall, mean RT was 203 msec longer for related than for unrelated falses, min F' (1,30) = 6.78, $p < .05$. Although the difference was larger for contexts where the unrelated exemplar was more typical (275 vs

Table 2.7 Mean RT (msec) for false items in Experiment 3

Context sentence	Related exemplar	Unrelated exemplar	Difference
Standard ordering context	1520 (17)	1389 (4.6)	131 (12.4)
Reverse ordering context	1472 (5)	1197 (2.5)	275 (2.5)
Mean	1496 (11)	1293 (3.5)	203 (7.5)

Note: Mean percentage error in parentheses.

Table 2.8 Mean RT (msec) for true items in Experiment 3

Context sentence	Related exemplar	Unrelated exemplar	Difference
Standard ordering context	1101 (.4)	1704 (8.8)	−603 (−8.4)
Reverse ordering context	1188 (2.5)	1790 (10.0)	−602 (−7.5)
Mean	1144 (1.5)	1747 (9.4)	−603 (−7.9)

Note: Mean percentage error in parentheses.

121 msec), the interaction between type of exemplar (related vs unrelated) and type of context (standard ordering vs reversed ordering) was not reliable, min F' (1,22) = .30. The smaller difference in RT obtained in the standard ordering condition was due to a single item for which there was a large difference (800 msec) in the wrong direction. If this item is removed, the mean difference becomes 304 msec. No other effects approached significance.

Regression analyses indicated a strong relationship between relatedness and RT for false items ($r = -.73$, $t[38] = -6.58$, $p < .001$). RT increased as relatedness increased. The correlation is negative because low numbers indicate high relatedness. The correlation was not changed substantially when the effects of word frequency, word length, and typicality were partialled out ($r = -.74$, $t[35] = -6.51$, $p < .001$).

In contrast there was no evidence of an effect of typicality (when presented in isolation) on RT ($r = -.10$, $t[38] = -.62$). The correlation also did not differ reliably from zero when the effects of word frequency, word length, and relatedness were partialled out ($r = .20$, $t[35] = 1.21$, $p > .20$).

Mean RTs for the trues were also examined. These data are presented in Table 2.8. As expected, related exemplars were verified faster (603 msec) than unrelated exemplars (min F' [1,41] = 27.75, $p < .001$). No other effects approach significance.

Here again, regression analyses indicated a substantial relationship between relatedness and RT for the trues ($r = .82$, $t[38] = 8.83$, $p < .001$). RT decreased as relatedness increased (i.e., as mean relatedness rating became smaller). The correlation changed little when word length, word frequency, and typicality were partialled out ($r = .84$, $t[35] = 9.16$, $p < .001$). As in the case of the false items, there was no evidence of an effect of typicality (when presented in isolation) on RT for true items ($r = .23$, $t[38] = 1.46$, $p > .10$). The correlation remained unreliable when word length, word frequency, and relatedness were partialled out ($r = .16$, $t[35] = .96$).

The number of subjects in the experiment who indicated disagreement with the truth value assigned to a given item was also examined. Although the overall percentage disagreement was low, there were more disagreements for the unrelated trues than for the related trues (5.2 vs 1.1%). For the falses, there were more disagreements for the related exemplars (1.9 vs 1.5%). Because the number of disagreements was consistently higher in the conditions that were characterized by longer RTs, analyses of covariance were conducted to determine whether differences among conditions in number of disagreements accounted for the relatedness effects. For the false items there was still a significant main effect of relatedness when number of disagreements observed in the response time study was used as a covariate ($F[1,17] = 9.70$, $p < .01$). No other effects approached significance. Relatedness was also the only reliable effect for the trues ($F[1,17] = 23.49$, $p < .001$). The pattern of results was the same when the number of disagreements obtained from the independent group of subjects (see Materials section) was used as the covariate. Results reported for the regression analyses also remained virtually identical when frequency of disagreements in the RT study and in the norming study were partialled out.

Discussion
There were two important results of the study. Relatedness to the context-dependent category representation was found to affect verification time. For true items, high relatedness led to faster RT. For false items verification time was longer for related falses than for unrelated falses. This pattern of results is the same as the pattern obtained in standard semantic memory studies where category terms are presented in isolation. The fact that relatedness has a similar effect in both cases suggests that the process by which membership in a context-constrained category is established may be similar to the process by which membership is determined when the category term is presented in isolation. Although current models of semantic memory vary widely in structural and processing assumptions, they generally account for the effect of relatedness on category verification time for falses by assuming that the decision process takes into account evidence in favor of category membership and evidence against it. The relatedness effect observed in the present experiment suggests that a similar decision process may be used in determining membership in a context-constrained category. A second important result was that standard typicality measures (obtained in the absence of explicit context) had no effect on verification time for either trues or falses. Not only was there no reliable correlation between typicality and verification time, but there was actually a reversal of the typicality effect, in half of the cases. In the reverse ordering condition the true item that was more typical was verified more slowly than the less typical one. This typicality reversal strengthens the hypothesis that contextual information can completely restructure the GOE distribution. Once context is introduced, typicality, as determined in isolation, no longer plays an important role.

General discussion

Overview of results

Two main points can be drawn from the results of these studies. First, they indicate that the representativeness distribution associated with a category term undergoes a complete restructuring once context is introduced. Experiment 2 showed that the GOE ordering obtained when context is introduced cannot be derived from the semantic space representation obtained when a category term is presented in the absence of explicit context. Further, Experiment 3 indicated that the typicality ordering obtained without context no longer plays an important role once context is introduced. These results argue strongly against the existence of an invariant semantic space.

In addition, the results reveal a number of parallels between category terms presented in context and category terms presented in isolation. Experiment 2 showed that category terms presented in context can generate a graded GOE distribution similar in form to the typicality distribution obtained in the absence of context. This GOE distribution predicted reading time just as typicality predicts verification time in a category verification task. Further, Experiment 3 showed that relatedness to the representation of the category term in context predicts category membership verification time for both trues and falses, just as relatedness predicts membership verification time out of context.

These parallel results suggest that the typicality effects obtained in the absence of explicit context may in fact be a special case of a more general phenomenon: representativeness in a given context or situation is an important determiner of how easily an exemplar can be identified as a member of a category. The results call into question the assumption made in the semantic memory literature that membership verification time provides information about the fixed meaning representation stored in semantic memory for a category term. It appears instead that the results of membership verification studies reflect the category representation used in a particular context or situation.

Any adequate explanation of the results of these studies will need to account for the change in representativeness distribution brought about by context. It will also need to account for the effect of relatedness to the context-dependent category representation on verification time. In the next section we consider how models of semantic memory might account for these results. In the subsequent sections, we explore some alternative explanations that are not derived from existing semantic memory models.

Semantic memory models

Clearly, existing models of semantic memory will need to be extended in order to account for findings in context. In the past, these models have been evaluated in terms of their adequacy in accounting for the basic findings in the absence of explicit context, and they have not been developed to deal with the wide changes in representativeness that we have demonstrated. Nevertheless, there are several assumptions that these models could adopt to account for context-dependent results. These assumptions deal, generally, with the weighting of attributes and the relaxation of criteria for category membership. They are designed to explain the change in content of the category representation that appears to occur in the presence of context. Once a change in the content of the category representation is accounted for, the processing assumptions made by semantic memory models to account for the effect of typicality on category membership decision time could be directly extended to account for the effect of relatedness to the context-dependent category representation on verification time.

One general approach that might be adopted by these models is to allow context to alter the criteria for category membership. This change can occur either through a general revision of the criteria for membership or through a reweighting of the importance of various components (Smith, 1978; Tversky, 1977). These two operations are difficult to distinguish. For example, in the sentence 'The farm had many of the animals,' all animals typically found on a farm would be suitable candidates. In this case, context has restricted the set of good examples to a fairly well-defined subcategory.

Set-theory models (such as Smith *et al.*, 1974) might attempt to account for this kind of result in terms of the importance of various attributes. Features such as 'domesticated,' 'edible,' and 'eats grain' might take on added importance as these are features that are characteristic of farm animals but do not generally hold for other types of animals (e.g., predators). In the terminology of the Smith *et al.* model these features would become more defining.

Models of semantic memory that posit a network representation (Collins and Loftus, 1975; Anderson, 1976) might adopt a temporary change in activation pattern to explain the effect of context. According to these models, facilitation occurs through the spread of activation in the network. In the present example, the farm context enables activation to spread to those animal exemplars that have attributes that are related to farm (such as 'eats grain').

Although both of these modifications are plausible, they are also vague. Moreover, different contexts can make extensions of the models even more difficult. For example, in 'The hunter shot at the bird overhead,' the possible referents of bird range from duck (a good example) to crow (marginally acceptable) to pigeon (borderline anomalous) to penguin (clearly anomalous). In addition, there are other items such as 'clay pigeon' and 'rare flying penguin' that violate the technical criteria for 'bird,' but that nevertheless are possible instantiations of bird in this sentence.

In this circumstance it is more difficult to account for the results by altering the importance of individual features. One might argue that 'can fly' is a requirement, thereby rendering duck acceptable and penguin anomalous. However, this single change will not account for the lack of full acceptability of crow and pigeon. Other attributes that are characteristic of birds that are hunted such as 'large,' 'edible,' 'wild,' 'found in rural areas,' and perhaps even 'capable of being hunted' would have to be added to account fully for the gradient in representativeness. However, introducing complex features such as 'capable of being hunted' would entail a substantial deviation from the usual linguistic definition of a feature. An additional difficulty is that features that are generally considered to be highly defining for *bird*, such as 'living,' would have to be assigned a low weight in order to account for the acceptability of 'clay pigeon.'

The analysis of the last two sentences clearly indicates that the conception of a feature would have to undergo substantial change in order to account for the effect of context on the representativeness distribution. In addition, it seems clear that one's knowledge of the world would have to be involved in determining the particular feature configuration associated with a term in different contexts. For example, in the hunter context, the selection of features for bird would seem to be influenced by one's general knowledge of bird hunting. Were semantic memory models to adopt this approach to explain context effects, they would come to resemble schema models of comprehension more closely (Minsky, 1975; Rumelhart and Ortony, 1977; Schank and Abelson, 1977).

Bridging model

The semantic memory explanation places the locus of context effects at the point where the context sentence is comprehended. Differences in the ease with which an anaphoric reference between an exemplar and a category term is understood are assumed to reflect differences in the representation set up for the category term when the context sentence is understood. In the terminology of Clark (1975), the context effect is explained in terms of forward inferences. However, an alternative possibility is that the category representation remains the same in all cases, and that differences in comprehension time for the target sentence reflect differences in the complexity of the bridging inferences that need to be made to integrate the target exemplar with the information provided in the context sentence. In Clark's (1975) terminology this integration would be a backward inference. Several recent studies have demonstrated the importance of backward inference in language comprehension (Singer, 1979; Thorndike, 1976).

The model we consider is based on the concept of bridging introduced by Clark (1975). The model assumes that comprehension involves building a bridge between the anaphor and its referent. Thus, the task of the reader is to construct a scenario in which the specific term is a plausible instantiation of the general term. According to this model, duck is an acceptable instantiation for 'The hunter shot at the bird overhead' because one can easily construct a hunting trip scenario in which the object was to shoot ducks. Penguin is anomalous because it is difficult to generate a scenario in which a hunter would shoot penguins overhead.

Although this model seems quite plausible at first blush, it is not without problems. Like the other models, it is quite vague and does not specify how the bridge is constructed. Although one can make allusions to world knowledge as a data base from which the bridges are constructed, there is no specification as to why some bridges are easy and others are difficult. The model is thus quite vague. Without additional assumptions, the model also has some more specific difficulties. For example, it is not clear how to apply the model to the results of Experiment 3. The model has no mechanism by which to determine that some scenarios are 'false' in the sense of Experiment 3. One way in which to solve this problem is to view the true/false decision criterion as judgment of plausibility. In this way, one first constructs a bridge and then judges the plausibility of the scenario. Clark has argued that, although long, complex sequences of assumptions can be constructed (in principle) to link events to their antecedents, convention dictates that utterances/passages should require only short, direct bridges. Thus, judgments of plausibility could be made based on the length and complexity of the bridging inferences required. When the judged plausibility is far from the criterion, as in very likely completions or anomalous completions, the true/false judgment is rendered very quickly. This judgment is quite difficult, on the other hand, when judged plausibility is quite close to the criterion.

The model also has some difficulty with the results of Experiment 1. Without additional assumptions, the model does not predict that it is more difficult to form a bridge in the neutral context than in the Bias+ context. Using the example in Table 2.1, it should be relatively easy to form a bridge from 'Dorothy thought about the *animal*' to *cow*. Since the sentence provides few constraints on the type of animal or situation, any of a number of short bridges could be formed (e.g., she read about the cow, saw it on a farm, saw it at a fair). It is thus unclear why *cow* should be more readily accepted as the referent of animal in the Bias+ context 'Stacy volunteered to milk the *animal* whenever she visited the farm.' One solution might be to assume that having a large number of possible scenarios slows down the selection process (Sanford and Garrod, 1977; Schwanenflugel and Shoben, 1983); and in fact a similar assumption plays a major part in the last model we will consider.

Scope of exemplars model

One possible account of the comprehension of category terms in context is that people's expectations vary from specific to diffuse. To use the previous example, the context sentence 'Stacy volunteered to milk the animal whenever she visited the farm' results in fairly specific expectations. In this Bias+ context sentence, most people would be fairly certain that the animal in this sentence was a cow. Because their expectations are confirmed, the reading time for 'She was very fond of the cow' is quite rapid. Expectations are also quite specific in many of our Bias− contexts. 'Fran pleaded with her father to let her ride the animal' leads most people to expect that the animal is a horse. This expectation does not match with 'She was very fond of the cow,' resulting in a relatively long comprehension time. In contrast, whatever expectations are created in a neutral context, as in 'Dorothy thought about the animal,' are probably quite diffuse. Such neutral contexts place relatively little constraint on the set of plausible instantiations and thus it seems reasonable that readers would not commit themselves to a small set of expected exemplars prematurely. Thus, one can distinguish these context sentences by degree of commitment on the reader's part. For some sentences, the set of exemplars will be quite small (as in the Bias+ and the Bias− examples cited here). For other context sentences, the set will be quite large; that is, the context will not permit any significant narrowing of the set of exemplars that are members of the category.

This explanation has some similarity to Becker's (1980) verification model for lexical decisions in that the critical postulate concerns the size of the expected set. In both of the bias conditions, the set of acceptable exemplars is greatly reduced while no such reduction occurs in the neutral condition. To carry the analogy with Becker's model somewhat further, the target item is always in the set of expected items (albeit a large set) in the neutral condition, but it may or may not be in the expected set for the bias conditions. It typically will be in the set in the Bias+ condition, resulting in facilitation relative to the Neutral context because the set of exemplars to be searched is smaller in the Bias+ condition. Conversely, the target item will usually not be in the expected set in the Bias− condition, and consequently comprehension time will be inhibited relative to the neutral condition because the item is not in the expected set.

What this kind of model seems to capture is our intuitive feeling that we commit to one instantiation (or a very small set of alternatives) in some circumstances, but not in others. The amount of commitment depends on the amount of constraint provided by the context. 'At Thanksgiving, the bird on the platter looked delicious' provides a great deal of constraint, whereas 'The bird had a fungus on its wing' does not. Readers may commit heavily to turkey in the first sentence but make no commitment at all in the second. Presumably, expecting a target leads to more rapid comprehension (as opposed to comprehension with no expectation) if one's expectations prove correct and to less rapid comprehension if one's expectations are erroneous.

Despite the intuitive appeal of the model, it has some serious drawbacks as an account of the present experiments. Without additional assumptions, the model is unable to predict a GOE distribution for any of the contexts. For example, with only minimally constraining context, one might expect that subjects would be unwilling to commit to a small set of instantiations. Yet, in this circumstance, our results and those of Sanford and Garrod (1977) demonstrate conclusively that typical exemplars are comprehended more rapidly than atypical ones. Even in cases where one might be highly likely to commit to a particular reading, as in 'Mary served the bird on a platter at Thanksgiving dinner,' a grading in representativeness can still be found. For example, *goose* is a better example of bird in the Thanksgiving context than *quail* is. Without additional assumptions, the scope of exemplars model cannot explain such representativeness gradings.

A second problem of this approach is that it provides no mechanism by which to decide that a particular exemplar is false. In the Thanksgiving example, how does one know that *duck* is acceptable but *penguin* is not? Undoubtedly, one could add some assumptions about feature matching to the model, but the scope of the exemplars itself provides no adequate basis for a true/false decision.

Comprehension in context

None of these models is wholly adequate, and one might speculate that this inadequacy stems from the narrowness of each of the proposals. Each claims that only one process is involved in comprehending this type of anaphora in context. In fact, many processes may be involved depending on the circumstance. For example, in the context sentence 'The banker's wife wore her new fur coat to the opera,' *mink* is the best example, and one might anticipate only this instantiation. Additionally, the attributes luxurious, expensive, and conservative that are characteristic of furs worn by the wealthy might facilitate the acceptance of *sable* or *chinchilla* as the fur in question. Finally, *raccoon* might be acceptable but it might require a bridge, such as 'the banker's wife was eccentric.' Thus, this one example has invoked the major processes of each of the three classes of models that we have considered. The scope of exemplars model allowed us to come up with the best example, *mink*. The extended semantic memory models provided the criteria by which *sable* and *chinchilla* were accepted. Lastly, the bridging model provided the inference mechanism necessary for us to comprehend *raccoon*.

If this analysis is correct, then the proper question to ask is not which single process will account for comprehension in context, but which process will be used in which situation. For example, the present results indicate conclusively that instantiation (i.e., expecting a particular exemplar as the referent of a category term) is not universal. However, these results do not indicate that instantiation never occurs. At a minimum, it would seem that instantiation might occur when the context is very constraining, as when the bird under discussion is to be consumed at Thanksgiving dinner. More generally, one would like to specify how context might restrict the scope of exemplars. When we read, there are times when we have little idea what is coming next, and other times when we are quite sure what is coming. To take a limiting example, let us consider the situation in which we are reading a newswire that prints at a very slow rate (such as the rate of a Model 33 teletype). Often our frustration at the machine's slowness stems from our knowledge of what is coming next. For example 'At the White House, President . . . ' leads us all to expect Reagan as the next word. With the anaphoric references that we employed in our experiments, one is unlikely ever to be as certain, but the point is that one's certainty can vary. At this point we know very little about what makes one context highly constraining and another context minimally constraining. Finally, it is quite possible that different processes may be used in different anaphoras, or when the anaphor is the topic or comment of the sentence. Garrod and Sanford (1981) have provided some suggestive evidence on this last point, and Sanford and Garrod (1977) have compared processing where the category term appears in the second sentence with processing where the category term appears in the context sentence.

The results of the present studies suggest that our knowledge of category terms in isolation is unlikely to be terribly useful in addressing these issues. Typicality in the absence of context was not a good predictor of comprehension in constrained contexts. In these situations, it appears that the representation of the category term is quite different from the representation in the absence of explicit context. Despite this limitation, one should not conclude that the GOE structure in the absence of context is psychologically vacuous. On the contrary, as Sanford and Garrod (1977), Anderson *et al.* (1976), and our own Experiment 1 have shown, the GOE structure will predict performance in context when that context is not very constraining. The present studies indicate that these representations will not be accessed (or will be greatly modified) when the context in which a category term is presented restricts the set of possible referents of the term to a subset of exemplars that have properties that are not characteristic of most members of the category.

Notes

1 More precisely, Garrod and Sanford manipulated the instance dominance of the exemplars as measured by the Battig and Montague (1969) production frequency norms, which are highly correlated with typicality norms (Mervis *et al.*, 1976).
2 A listing of all the items used in the studies reported here can be found in Roth (1980).

References

Anderson, J. R. *Language, memory and thought*. Hillsdale, NJ: Erlbaum, 1976.
Anderson, R. C., and Ortony, A. On putting apples into bottles – A problem of polysemy. *Cognitive Psychology*, 1975, **7**, 167–180.
Anderson, R. C., Pichert, J. W., Goetz, E. T., Schallert, D. L., Stevens, K. V., and Trollip, S. R. Instantiation of general terms. *Journal of Verbal Learning and Verbal Behavior*, 1976, **15**, 667–679.
Barclay, J. R., Bransford, J. D., Franks, J. J., McCarrell, N. S., and Nitsch, K. Comprehension and semantic flexibility. *Journal of Verbal Learning and Verbal Behavior*, 1974, **13**, 471–481.
Barsalou, L. W. Context-independent and context-dependent information in concepts. *Memory and Cognition*, 1982, **10**, 82–93.
Battig, W. F., and Montague, W. E. Category norms for verbal items in 56 categories: A replication and extension of the Connecticut category norms. *Journal of Experimental Psychology Monograph*, 1969, **80** (3, Pt. 2).
Becker, C. A. Semantic context effects in visual word recognition: An analysis of semantic strategies. *Memory and Cognition*, 1980, **8**, 493–512.
Bisanz, G. L., LaPorte, R. E., Vesonder, G. T., and Voss, J. F. On the representation of prose: New dimensions. *Journal of Verbal Learning and Verbal Behavior*, 1978, **17**, 337–357.
Carpenter, P. A., and Just, M. A. Reading comprehension as the eyes see it. In M. A. Just and P. A. Carpenter (Eds.), *Cognitive processes in comprehension*. Hillsdale, NJ: Erlbaum, 1977.
Clark, H. H. Bridging. In R. Schank and B. Nash-Webber (Eds.), *Theoretical issues in natural language processing*. Proceedings of a conference at the Massachusetts Institute of Technology, Cambridge, 1975.
Clark, H. H., and Sengul, C. J. In search of referents for nouns and pronouns. *Memory and Cognition*, 1979, **7**, 35–41.

Collins, A. M., and Loftus, E. F. A spreading activation theory of semantic processing. *Psychological Review*, 1975, **82**, 407–428.

Collins, A. M., and Quillian, M. R. Retrieval time from semantic memory. *Journal of Verbal Learning and Verbal Behavior*, 1969, **8**, 240–248.

Collins, A. M., and Quillian, M. R. Experiments on semantic memory and language comprehension. In L. W. Gregg (Ed.), *Cognition in learning and memory*. New York: Wiley, 1972.

Garrod, S., and Sanford, A. J. Interpreting anaphoric relations: The integration of semantic information while reading. *Journal of Verbal Learning and Verbal Behavior*, 1977, **16**, 77–90.

Garrod, S., and Sanford, A. J. Bridging inferences and the extended domain of reference. In J. Long and A. Baddeley (Eds.), *Attention and performance IX*. Hillsdale, NJ: Erlbaum, 1981.

Glass, A. L., and Holyoak, K. J. Alternative conceptions of semantic memory. *Cognition*, 1975, **3**, 313–339.

Glass, A. L., Holyoak, K. J., and Kiger, H. I. Role of antonymy relations in semantic judgments. *Journal of Experimental Psychology: Human Learning and Memory*, 1979, **5**, 598–606.

Glass, A. L., Holyoak, K. J., and O'Dell, C. Production frequency and the verification of quantified statements. *Journal of Verbal Learning and Verbal Behavior*, 1974, **13**, 237–254.

Gumenik, W. E. The advantage of specific terms over general terms as cues for sentence recall: Instantiation or retrieval? *Memory and Cognition*, 1979, **7**, 240–244.

Haviland, S. E., and Clark, H. H. What's new? Acquiring new information as a process in comprehension. *Journal of Verbal Learning and Verbal Behavior*, 1974, **13**, 512–521.

Hobbs, J. R. Coherence and coreference. *Cognitive Science*, 1979, **3**, 67–90.

Kieras, D. Problems of reference in text comprehension. In M. A. Just and P. A. Carpenter (Eds.), *Cognitive processes in comprehension*. Hillsdale, NJ: Erlbaum, 1977.

Kučera, H., and Francis, W. N. *Computational analysis of present-day English*. Providence, RI: Brown Univ. Press, 1967.

Lorch, R. F., Jr. The role of two types of semantic information in the processing of false sentences. *Journal of Verbal Learning and Verbal Behavior*, 1978, **17**, 523–537.

Lorch, R. F., Jr. Effects of relation strength and semantic overlap on retrieval and comparison processes during sentence verification. *Journal of Verbal Learning and Verbal Behavior*, 1981, **20**, 593–610.

McCloskey, M., and Glucksberg, S. Decision processes in verifying category membership statements: Implications for models of semantic memory. *Cognitive Psychology*, 1979, **11**, 1–27.

McKoon, G., and Ratcliff, R. The comprehension processes and memory structures involved in anaphoric reference. *Journal of Verbal Learning and Verbal Behavior*, 1980, **19**, 668–682.

Mervis, C. B., Catlin, J., and Rosch, E. Relationships among goodness-of-example, category norms, and word frequency. *Bulletin of the Psychonomic Society*, 1976, **7**, 283–284.

Meyer, D. E. On the representation and retrieval of stored semantic information. *Cognitive Psychology*, 1970, **1**, 242–299.

Minsky, M. A framework for representing knowledge. In P. H. Winston (Ed.), *The psychology of computer vision*. New York: McGraw-Hill, 1975.

Potter, M. C., and Faulconer, B. A. Understanding noun phrases. *Journal of Verbal Learning and Verbal Behavior*, 1979, **18**, 509–521.

Rips, L. J., Shoben, E. J., and Smith, E. E. Semantic distance and the verification of semantic relations. *Journal of Verbal Learning and Verbal Behavior*, 1973, **12**, 1–20.

Rosch, E. On the internal structure of perceptual and semantic categories. In T. E. Moore (Ed.), *Cognitive development and acquisition of language*. New York: Academic Press, 1973.

Rosch, E. Cognitive representations of semantic categories. *Journal of Experimental Psychology: General*, 1975, **104**, 192–233.

Roth, E. M. *Context effects on the representation of meaning*. Unpublished doctoral dissertation, University of Illinois, 1980.

Rumelhart, D. E. and Ortony, A. The representation of knowledge in memory. In R. C. Anderson, R. J. Spiro, and W. E. Montague (Eds.), *Schooling and the acquisition of knowledge*. Hillsdale, NJ: Erlbaum, 1977.

Sanford, A. J., and Garrod, S. Memory and attention in text comprehension: The problem of reference. In R. S. Nickerson (Ed.), *Attention and performance VIII*. Hillsdale, NJ: Erlbaum, 1977.

Schank, R., and Abelson, R. *Scripts, plans, goals and understanding: An inquiry into human knowledge structures*. Hillsdale, NJ: Erlbaum, 1977.

Schwanenflugel, P. J., and Shoben, E. J. Differential context effects in the comprehension of abstract and concrete verbal materials. *Journal of Experimental Psychology: Learning, Memory and Cognition*, 1983, **9**(1), 82–102.

Singer, M. Processes of inference during sentence encoding. *Memory and Cognition*, 1979, **7**, 192–200.

Smith, E. E. Theories of semantic memory. In W. K. Estes (Ed.), *Handbook of learning and cognitive processes*. Potomac, MD: Erlbaum, 1978. Vol. 6.

Smith, E. E., Shoben, E. J., and Rips, L. J. Structure and process in semantic memory: A featural model for semantic decisions. *Psychological Review*, 1974, **81**, 214–241.

Tabossi, P., and Johnson-Laird, P. N. Linguistic context and priming of semantic information. *Quarterly Journal of Experimental Psychology*, 1980, **32**, 595–603.

Thorndike, P. W. The role of inferences in discourse comprehension. *Journal of Verbal Learning and Verbal Behavior*, 1976, **15**, 437–446.

Tversky, A. Features of similarity. *Psychological Review*, 1977, **84**, 327–352.

Wilkins, A. T. Conjoint frequency, category size and categorization time. *Journal of Verbal Learning and Verbal Behavior*, 1971, **10**, 382–385.

SECTION TWO
SHORT-TERM MEMORY

Editor's introduction

Over the last 30 or so years a wealth of evidence has accumulated in support of the idea that the brain contains independent modules for storing short- and long-term memories. Although there remain critics of this view (e.g., Crowder, 1989), the evidence from normal and brain-damaged populations is very strong. In the earliest models, such as the famous memory model of Atkinson and Shiffrin (1968), it was assumed that there existed a single short-term memory store through which information necessarily passed if it was to reach the long-term store. However, in seminal work in the 1970s, Alan **Baddeley** and Graham Hitch demonstrated that this simple conception could not be correct, and instead introduced the 'working memory' model in which short-term memory was split into a number of independent systems. Baddeley's chapter (Chapter 3) provides an up-to-date review of the evidence for this model. A good historical review of research on short-term memory can be found in Baddeley (1986) and discussions focusing more on its brain components are provided by Gathercole (1994) and Goldman-Rakic (1992).

References

Atkinson, R. C. and Shiffrin, R. M. (1968). Human memory: a proposed system and its control processes. In *The psychology of learning and motivation* (ed. K. W. Spence and J. T. Spence), Vol. 2, pp. 89–195, Academic Press, New York.

Baddeley, A. D. (1986). *Working memory*. Oxford University Press, Oxford.

Crowder, R. G. (1989). Modularity and dissociations in memory systems. In *Varieties of memory and consciousness: essays in honour of Endel Tulving* (ed. H. L. Roediger and F. I. M. Craik). Erlbaum, Hillsdale, NJ.

Gathercole, S. E. (1994). Neuropsychology and working memory: a review. *Neuropsychology*, 8, 494–505.

Goldman-Rakic, P. S. (1992). Working memory and the mind. *Scientific American*, 267(3), 72–79.

3   Alan D. Baddeley
'Is Working Memory Working?' The Fifteenth Bartlett Lecture

Reprinted in full from: *The Quarterly Journal of Experimental Psychology* **44A**, 1–31 (1992)

I am honoured and pleased to have been invited to give the Bartlett Lecture. I feel a particular debt of gratitude to Bartlett as he was instrumental in founding the Unit* in which I have spent most of my professional life, a Unit that embodied many of Sir Frederic's strengths, and which I hope continues to do so. When I arrived at the Unit as a young graduate research worker from University College London, Sir Frederic had already retired as Professor of Psychology and Director of the Unit. However, he still had a room at the Unit and maintained an interest in its activities, often bringing round visitors from abroad. In my own case my research stemmed from the attempt to design a postal code, and involved a series of very un-Bartlettian experiments on the learning of nonsense syllables, a perversion that Sir Frederic seemed to tolerate with a rather grandfatherly indulgence. Were he here today, I trust that he would at least approve of the fact that my lecture will contain relatively little work on nonsense material, while noting that I have not yet managed to kick the nonsense habit completely.

The topic of my lecture is a direct continuation of research on short-term memory that, although not pursued by Bartlett himself, owed much of its early development to Bartlett's students, Broadbent, Brown, and Conrad. I no longer use the term 'short-term memory', but I certainly regard my research on working memory as a continuation and elaboration of an existing tradition, rather than a rejection of old models for new, such as is occasionally suggested by colleagues who refer to the 'demise of short-term memory' (Crowder, 1982). Although disposable concepts may have their attractions, as will become clear, my own inclinations are towards attempting to build in durability and ease of maintenance.

While I was working on the long-term learning of sequences of nonsense syllables in an attempt to improve the design of codes, my supervisor Conrad was continuing to carry out work on the immediate recall of sequences of digits and letters, a problem that was prompted by developments in the field of telephony. These experiments included the classic studies whereby he demonstrated that when subjects remember sequences of visually presented consonants, their errors tend to be phonologically similar to the item they replace, with a misremembered 'B' being much more likely to be recalled as 'V' than as a visually similar item such as 'R' (Conrad, 1964). He then showed that sequences of similar-sounding consonants (e.g. 'P V T C G D') are considerably harder to recall than dissimilar sequences (e.g. 'R Y K W M Q') (Conrad and Hull, 1964).

* The Applied Psychology Unit, Cambridge. (Ed.)

Shortly after I finished my PhD, Conrad went off for a sabbatical year in Michigan, leaving me in charge of the various Post Office projects. Like the Sorcerer's Apprentice, I took advantage of the absence of my master to play with some of his magic, despite the fact that any links between acoustic similarity and the particular project I had been assigned were distinctly tenuous. Like the Sorcerer's Apprentice, I was bowled over by the experience and have, I am afraid, been doing experiments on acoustic similarity ever since. The experiments I carried out somewhat guiltily during Conrad's absence (Baddeley, 1966a, 1966b) were relevant to the issue of whether or not it was necessary to assume separate long- and short-term memory systems, and much of my subsequent research on memory has been concerned with related questions of memory fractionation.

When invited to give the Bartlett Lecture, it seemed sensible to talk about this problem, as it is one that has dominated my research. However, one of the drawbacks of working on the same topic for over 20 years is that, unless one has been spectacularly unproductive, it is very hard to cover it in one hour. Furthermore, any attempt to do so would prove extremely boring for those long-suffering members of the Society who have heard more about working memory than they would choose over the years. What I have not talked about, however, is the general philosophy behind my particular approach to theorizing. It is an approach that is strongly empirically driven, and as such contrasts with many of the currently very exciting developments stimulated by research in artificial intelligence, and perhaps most notably with the stimulating approach to modelling human memory that is associated with connectionist and parallel distributed processing (PDP) approaches. I would therefore like to begin by discussing broadly the philosophy underlying the Working Memory model, then going on to illustrate it by giving a brief overview of the model and some of the findings that have resulted from it. Finally I would like to talk about some new results and their possible implications.

A pragmatic approach to theory

On the whole, philosophies of science tend to be either prescriptive, purporting to tell the scientist what he should be doing, or descriptive, attempting to give an account of the process of scientific discovery. A number of controversies in the area seem to develop from a conflict between these two separate aims; that between Braithwaite (1953) and Toulmin (1953) in the 1950s is a case in point, as is much of the controversy aroused by the subsequent work of Kuhn (1970). In my own case, I used to be a convinced follower of Karl Popper's views with their emphasis on the importance of falsifiability in judging the value of scientific theories (Popper, 1959). Curiously enough, I managed to maintain such a position for many years before I noticed that it bore very little resemblance to the way in which I conducted science and abandoned the belief that I was indeed a Popperian.

I believe that many concepts and models may be extremely fruitful without being in the final analysis testable. Bartlett's concept of schema is a good example of this. Furthermore, in cognitive psychology at least, it is often possible to generate many parallel interpretations of phenomena, each of which is in principle testable, but where in practice we simply do not have adequate techniques to allow this differentiation.

An important part of the development of our subject is the search for techniques and methods that will increase our ability to choose among available theories. Our armoury of such techniques is, however, still very limited, and I suspect that if we took seriously the precept of dealing only with strictly testable theories, then we would have to abandon research on most of the important questions of cognitive psychology.

I shall try to make the case that such a view is too narrow, and to argue that simple qualitative models that do not readily give rise to crucial make-or-break predictions may nonetheless be very productive.

My own work is based on this approach to theory. Its most obvious feature is that it is empirically driven. I tend to develop a theory on the basis of experimental results, rather than set up an abstract theory and then find ways of testing it. Both methods are, of course, defensible, and my own choice simply reflects the fact that I enjoy doing experiments and have no skill in mathematical or computer modelling.

A second characteristic of my approach is that it tends to be phenomenon-driven, relying on a pattern of results from a number of relatively simple experiments, rather than the results of a smaller number of carefully designed parametric studies. This probably reflects both the area in which I work and also my personal style. The short-term memory area is rich in clear and robust phenomena, which can often be controlled in an almost all-or-none way by careful selection of material. I myself believe that we currently have only a relatively crude capacity to tease apart the components of cognition, and hence that we are on firmer ground dealing with clear binary results rather than opting for a sophisticated statistical analysis of a complex pattern of data. Again I suspect this may reflect my personal prejudice for experimental control rather than elegant statistical analysis (see Rubin, 1986, for an opposite view).

A third characteristic of my general approach to theory is a concern for the theory to be gradually cumulative rather than complete. This perhaps stems from an excessive preoccupation with the question of whether or not psychological research is cumulative, a question that seemed particularly pertinent during the 1960s, when the development of cognitive psychology was leading to a wholesale rejection of much of the behaviourally inspired work that had gone on in the previous 30 years. The tendency for psychology to be swept by successive fashions has encouraged my perhaps morbid preoccupation with continuity. I believe that earlier developments will influence our current thinking even if we are not directly aware of them, but I think that conscious awareness of the continuities is likely to be helpful in reducing to some extent the likelihood of repeating mistakes or continually re-inventing old concepts.

Finally, my particular approach to theory is strongly influenced by an interest in bridging the gap between the laboratory and the real world. For this, one needs simple, robust models. If those models can be applied across a wide range of practical situations, then so much the better. If one must choose between scope and precision, then my own temperamental choice is for breadth of application rather than detailed predictive power.

The four characteristics that I have outlined have all been presented broadly speaking as virtues. Needless to say, they may equally well be interpreted as vices. An excessive preoccupation with the collection of experimental data characterized the old stimulus-response (S-R) associationist approach to memory, which used to be termed 'verbal learning'. This approach tackled some fundamental and important questions but used a very narrow range of concepts and methods that proved, in my opinion, remarkably sterile, justifying the epithet Dustbowl Empiricism that was often applied to it. The tendency for cognitive psychology to be preoccupied with phenomena is also one that has been strongly criticized by Allen Newell (1974) in his influential paper 'You can't play twenty questions with nature and win'. My own concern with the phenomena of short-term memory (STM) suggests that I have a more optimistic view of the usefulness of such games with nature.

How about my concern that psychology should be cumulative? This could be criticized as leading to excessive conservatism. One might argue that cumulation is something that happens when you hit on the right approach, and that aiming for it directly is likely to lead to an unwillingness to abandon unsuccessful attempts, and hence delay subsequent progress.

Finally, one might suggest that a premature concern with applications is again likely to be counterproductive. A good illustration of this argument is I believe provided by work on face recognition, where early research was concerned with the very practical problem of improved eyewitness identification, and on the whole produced results that were disappointing (e.g. Baddeley and Woodhead, 1982), in contrast to the much more exciting and potentially applicable work that has since developed from a concerted attempt to gain a better theoretical understanding of the processes of face perception (Bruce, 1988). In fact, I think that it is much easier to argue the position that pure and applied research are mutually facilitative, but the argument that theoretical understanding should come first is certainly a defensible one (Banaji and Crowder, 1989).

To what extent, then, are the peculiar characteristics of my own approach to theorizing virtues and to what extent vices? I believe that on balance they represent a style of theorizing that works. For a theory to work, it should be capable of encompassing existing results, it should lead to the uncovering of other findings, and through this to its own modification and development. Finally, in my own case, I would like it to provide me with a simple, robust framework that allows me to tackle problems outside the laboratory as well as within. I would like to try to persuade you that on these criteria, the concept of working memory is working. In doing so I will give a brief account of the various components of the system, in each case following the account with a description of one area in which the model has extended in useful ways beyond the original findings.

Development of the Working Memory model

In 1958, John Brown published his research showing that material is forgotten within seconds if rehearsal is prevented – a finding that was echoed in North America by the development of the short-term forgetting paradigm by Peterson and Peterson (1959). These authors and others (e.g. Broadbent, 1958) suggested that their results reflected the operation of a limited-capacity short-term memory store that was fundamentally different from the system responsible for long-term learning and memory.

This view was countered by Melton (1963), who suggested that such findings were entirely compatible with a unitary view of memory in which forgetting was produced by the processes of interference described in the classic verbal learning literature. Melton's article stimulated a flurry of studies concerned to produce less equivocal evidence of the proposed dichotomy between long- and short-term memory. Probably the most influential evidence came from three sources.

The first evidence for separate memory systems came from the observation that a number of verbal memory tasks appear to have two components, one of which is relatively stable over time and was assumed to reflect long-term memory, whereas the other comprised a much less stable component that was attributed to short-term memory. The classic example of this dichotomy comes from the free-recall paradigm in which subjects are presented with a list of unrelated words and attempt to recall them in any order they wish. When recall is immediate, the last few items presented are very well recalled (the recency effect), in contrast to earlier items, which are much less likely to be recalled. If recall is delayed for a few seconds, with the subject being distracted by some intervening task such as counting, then the recency effect disappears, but recall of the earlier items is comparatively unaffected (Glanzer and Cunitz, 1966). One simple interpretation of these findings is to assume that the last few items are held in some form of short-term store, which is disrupted by the subsequent counting task. Equivalent recency effects were also shown in single-trial paired-associate learning (Peterson, 1966) and in serial probe recall (Waugh and Norman, 1965).

A second source of evidence for a dichotomy came from studies of coding in immediate and delayed serial recall. As mentioned earlier, Conrad and Hull (1964) showed that the immediate serial recall of items that were similar in sound, such as 'B D V T C' was consistently poorer than dissimilar sequences such as 'W K X Y R' (Conrad and Hull, 1964). Subsequent work using words indicated that the crucial factor was the phonological or acoustic similarity of the material. Sequences of words such as 'MAD, CAN, MAN, MAP, CAT' are consistently difficult, whereas sequences that were similar in meaning, such as 'HUGE, LONG, TALL, BIG, WIDE', or which were orthographically similar, such as 'ROUGH, BOUGH, COUGH, DOUGH, THROUGH', caused comparatively few problems (Baddeley, 1966a). In contrast, when subjects were required to learn sequences of ten such words under delayed recall conditions, phonological similarity ceased to be an important factor and was replaced in importance by similarity of meaning (Baddeley, 1966b).

Comparable results were obtained using paired-associate learning (Baddeley and Dale, 1966). A subsequent study by Kintsch and Buschke (1969) using a probed recall procedure showed that recency items were affected by acoustic similarity, whereas earlier items were sensitive to similarity of meaning.

A third source of evidence for a dichotomy came from neuropsychological results. More specifically, patients suffering from the classic amnesic syndrome were shown to be impaired in their performance on items that occurred early in the serial position curve but had normal recency. Although they showed very poor long-term memory as measured by paired-associate learning or recall of prose passages, they nevertheless showed normal memory span and, provided they were intellectually otherwise unimpaired, normal performance on the Peterson short-term forgetting task (Baddeley and Warrington, 1970). Shallice and Warrington (1970) identified patients who had the exact converse pattern of deficits, with grossly impaired memory span and Peterson performance coupled with apparently normal long-term learning.

By the late 1960s, the evidence appeared to be mounting in favour of a dichotomous view of memory. Models of short-term memory were proliferating but tended to have much in common and to resemble more or less closely the influential model proposed by Atkinson and Shiffrin (1968), which was itself a development and elaboration of an earlier model by Broadbent (1958). The Atkinson and Shiffrin model proposed three separate types of memory store. The briefest in duration were the sensory memory systems, which were associated with specific input modalities such as vision (iconic memory) and audition (echoic memory). These fed into a short-term store (STS) that had limited capacity and was essential for transferring information into and out of the larger capacity and more durable long-term store (LTS). Memory span, the recency effect in free recall, and performance on the Peterson task were all assumed to reflect the operation of the STS, which was assumed to function as a limited-capacity working memory. This store was capable of holding and manipulating information while subjects performed other more complex cognitive tasks such as learning, comprehending, and reading.

The Atkinson and Shiffrin model appeared initially to solve many of the problems of conceptualizing the memory system. It could account for most of the available data and appeared in addition to offer a detailed mathematical analysis of the underlying processes that seemed to promise considerable further development. However, in the 1970s it began to run into a number of problems (see Baddeley, 1990 for further discussion). It was particularly difficult for the model to accommodate the evidence from patients with STM deficits, as such a deficit should have led to gross impairment in long-term learning and to problems in cognitive performance in general. No such deficits occurred.

Graham Hitch and I decided to tackle this issue by attempting to simulate the effects of STM deficit through a dual-task technique. We tried to disrupt the operation of the short-term store by requiring our subjects to remember sequences of up to six digits at the same time as they were performing each of a range of tasks that were commonly assumed to depend on working memory for their adequate performance. In one study we presented our subjects with sequences of 16 unrelated words for immediate or delayed free recall. Subjects heard the 16 words, and were simultaneously presented visually with groups of nought, three, or six digits, which they were required to recall immediately. In another study the words were presented visually and the digits auditorily. Prediction from the Atkinson and Shiffrin model is clear — the digit span task should depend on the short-term store, with three digits using up a substantial amount of it and six digits, being near span, virtually wiping it out. This, in turn, should lead to a substantial impairment of performance on the earlier LTS items and a total abolition of the recency effect. The obtained results were quite different, with three digits causing no significant impairment, whereas six digits led to a moderate but significant impairment in the LTS part of the curve but had no influence on recency. The absence of any effect on recency is particularly hard to explain in terms of the model, as recency and span are both assumed to make massive demands on the same limited-capacity STS.

The presence of a significant but comparatively small effect of concurrent load on performance proved to be characteristic of other tasks that we studied, including reasoning and the comprehension of both visual and auditory prose (Baddeley and Hitch, 1974).

Insofar as our results showed an effect of concurrent digit span on a wide range of cognitive tasks, they supported the concept of a general working memory. However, the small magnitude of the effect and the total lack of an effect of concurrent span on recency suggested that the assumption of a unitary limited-capacity short-term store was unjustified. We proposed, instead, a multi-component Working Memory model controlled by a limited-capacity attentional system, which we termed the Central Executive. This is assumed to be supported by at least two active slave systems, the Articulatory or Phonological Loop that is responsible for maintaining and manipulating speech-based information and the Visuo-Spatial Scratchpad or Sketchpad, which holds and manipulates visuo-spatial information. In the section that follows, I describe some of the evidence that persuaded us to propose such a tripartite system, before going on to examine some of the subsequent applications of the model.

The Phonological Loop

This is assumed to comprise two subcomponents: (1) a phonological memory store, which can hold traces of acoustic or speech-based material — such traces are assumed to fade within about two seconds unless they are refreshed by means of (2) the process of articulatory subvocal rehearsal. This can serve two useful functions: maintaining the memory trace by subvocal rehearsal, and registering visually presented material by subvocal naming.

The model is supported by a network of empirical findings, each one of which is explicable in terms of a range of different models, but which together place substantial constraints on potential interpretations. I would argue that for our present state of knowledge, this style of theorizing has major advantages over the attempt to provide more detailed and quantitative models of individual isolated phenomena. It does not, of course, preclude such quantitative modelling in due course. The major phenomena that have led to the formulation of the Phonological Loop model are as follows.

1. The phonological similarity effect: As noted earlier, letters or words that are similar in sound lead to poorer immediate serial recall (Conrad and Hull, 1964). This is assumed to occur because the phonological store relies purely on a phonological code; similar codes present fewer discriminating features between items, leading to impaired retrieval and poorer recall.

2. The irrelevant speech effect: Immediate serial recall is also disrupted by the presentation of irrelevant spoken material. The disrupting effect is independent of the meaning of the irrelevant material, being as great when it is in a foreign language as when in the subject's native tongue. The disrupting material must, however, be speech-like; white noise has no effect, and non-vocal music produces a level of disruption in between that of noise and speech; sound intensity is not an important variable (Colle and Welsh, 1976; Salamé and Baddeley, 1982, 1989). It is assumed that irrelevant speech gains obligatory access to the phonological store and is thus able to corrupt the memory trace, leading to impaired recall.

3. The word-length effect: Immediate serial recall of words is inversely related to their spoken duration. This is assumed to occur because long words take longer to rehearse than do short words, allowing more time for the memory trace of earlier words to fade away before they can be revived through active rehearsal (Baddeley *et al.*, 1975). Word length has been shown to be responsible for consistent differences in digit span across languages; Ellis and Hennelly (1980) noted that the normative digit span for the Welsh-language version of the Wechsler Intelligence Scale for Children (WISC) were consistently poorer than the English language norms. They were able to demonstrate using bilingual native Welsh speakers that their span was better in English when measured in total number of digits but was equivalent when measured in total spoken time, as the Welsh digits took longer to say. When the use of the Articulatory Loop was disrupted by the requirement to suppress articulation, the difference disappeared. A similar relationship between spoken duration of digits and memory span has been demonstrated across a range of languages by Naveh-Benjamin and Ayres (1986).

It has also been suggested that the marked increase in digit span observed during childhood could be attributed to the change in rate of articulation. The increase in digit span closely parallels an increase in speech rate (Hitch and Halliday, 1983; Hulme *et al.*, 1984; Nicolson, 1981).

4. Articulatory suppression: When subjects are induced to suppress subvocal rehearsal by requiring them to utter a repeated irrelevant sound such as the word 'the', immediate memory span is reduced. The effects of irrelevant speech and acoustic similarity are removed when the material to be remembered is presented visually and articulation is suppressed. This is assumed to occur because suppression prevents the visually presented memory span items being registered in the phonological store; as the store is then irrelevant to performance, phonological similarity or the corruption of the store with irrelevant speech has no effect. Whether presentation is auditory or visual, articulatory suppression removes the word-length effect. Again this is assumed to occur because the word-length effect itself depends on the rate of subvocal rehearsal; if this is prevented then the variable is no longer relevant to performance (Baddeley *et al.*, 1984).

5. *STM patients*: With visual presentation, STM patients typically do not show either phonological similarity or word-length effects (Vallar and Baddeley, 1984; Vallar and Shallice, 1990). Such patients are assumed to have a defective phonological store, with the result that they gain no benefit from attempting the phonological storage of visually presented items, which are better recalled on the basis of other codes.

6. *Dysarthria and the Phonological Loop*: Normal phonological similarity and word-length effects can be found in patients who have suffered brain lesions leading to the loss of the power to articulate speech, coupled with unimpaired language processing (Baddeley and Wilson, 1985). Even more strikingly, Bishop and Robson (1989) have shown that congenitally dysarthric children may develop a comparatively normal Phonological Loop system, which shows evidence of phonological similarity and word-length effects. These results suggest that adequate rehearsal is not dependent on the capacity to articulate, presumably being based on the operation of some central command rather than on its peripheral operation.

The six sources of evidence reviewed suggest that the simple concept of a Phonological Loop has proved fruitful, not only in accounting for existing phenomena such as phonological similarity and articulatory suppression effects, but also in generating new findings in the area of the word-length effect and irrelevant speech, and through its application to both developmental and neuropsychological issues.

The Visuo-Spatial Sketchpad

Our work in this area began as an attempt to understand the role of visual imagery in verbal memory. Much of our work has used the technique devised by Brooks (1967) in which the subject is shown a 4 × 4 matrix, with one square marked as the starting square, and then required to listen to and repeat back sequences of sentences describing the location of digits 1–8. For example, a subject might hear the following:

> In the starting square put a 1, in the next square to the right put a 2, in the next square down put a 3, in the next square down put a 4, in the next square to the left put a 5, etc.

Subjects almost invariably remember the sentences by creating an imaginary path through the matrix, which they remember as a pattern, regenerating the sentences on the basis of the pattern. This strategy can be disrupted by the simple expedient of replacing the spatial adjectives, 'up', 'down', 'left', and 'right', with four non-spatial bipolar adjectives, namely, 'good', 'bad', 'weak', and 'strong'. Given a sequence like

In the starting square put a 1, in the next square to the good put a 2, in the next square to the weak put a 3, in the next square to the bad put a 4,

subjects tend to rely exclusively on rote verbal recall.

We showed that visuo-spatial tasks such as tracking a spot of light following a circular path on a pursuit rotor would disrupt performance on the spatial task, while having little effect on the verbal task. A subsequent study was concerned with the question of whether the disrupting effect of the pursuit rotor came from its visual or its spatial characteristics. Subjects were required to perform either a purely visual task involving judging the brightness of a field of light, or a non-visual spatial tracking task. This involved teaching the subject to keep the beam of a flashlight in contact with the bob of a swinging pendulum. The bob emitted a continuous tone unless the flashlight shone on it, in which case the tone became discontinuous. The subject was blindfolded and hence was required to use auditory cues to locate the position of the pendulum and to perform the tracking task. The results were clear in suggesting that for the Brooks' task spatial disruption by tracking was considerably greater than disruption from brightness judgements, whereas for the verbal recall task the opposite pattern occurred (Baddeley and Lieberman, 1980).

Our initial conclusions were that the memory system underlying performance on this task, which we termed the Visuo-Spatial Scratchpad or Sketchpad, was fundamentally spatial rather than visual in nature. However, subsequent work by Logie (1986) suggests that we have been over-generalizing on the basis of a single memory task. Logie used a paired-associate learning paradigm in which subjects under one condition were encouraged to use a pegword mnemonic. This involved learning rhyming imageable pegwords for each digit from 1 to 10 and forming an image of the pegword interacting with the items to be remembered. For example the pegword for one is 'bun', and if the first word were 'crocodile', then the subject might form the image of a crocodile with an enormous bun jammed between its jaws. Performance was compared with a condition in which the use of imagery was minimized by instruction and by rapid presentation. Logie found that a range of visual but relatively non-spatial tasks would interfere specifically with the use of the mnemonic. While the strongest disruption occurred when the subjects passively observed line drawings, significant impairment was found even when material as non-spatial as patches of colour were used. The effect of irrelevant patterns appears to be analogous to the effect of irrelevant speech on the Phonological Loop. Together with our own data using the Brooks paradigm, it suggests that the Sketchpad may have both visual and spatial components, a conclusion that was reached independently by Farah on the basis of neuropsychological evidence and data from psychophysiology (Farah *et al.*, 1988).

We have so far made rather less progress in understanding the Sketchpad than we have in the case of the Phonological Loop. I suspect there are three main reasons for this. (1) The first involves the greater complexity of the system, which does indeed appear to have both visual and spatial components, but components that are very difficult to tease apart experimentally.

(2) Neuropsychological evidence has so far had rather less impact on theorizing than it has in the case of verbal memory, although there are very welcome signs that this is starting to change, with evidence coming not only from the previously cited work by Farah but also from the identification of patients who appear to have very clear deficits in the functioning of the scratchpad system (e.g. Hanley *et al.*, 1991). (3) Finally, it is far less clear what mechanism underlies the process of the active rehearsal of visual imagery, playing the spatial equivalent to the role of subvocalization in verbal memory.

One possibility is that the rehearsal of images is based on the system involved in controlling eye movements. A series of as yet unpublished experiments suggests that voluntary saccadic eye movements differentially disrupt the spatial condition in the previously described Brooks memory task (see Baddeley, 1983, for a brief account of this work). However, eye movement control is itself complex, depending on different parts of the brain for different tasks, suggesting that this area will need a good deal of careful research before it is fully understood.

The Central Executive

This is assumed to be an attentional control system responsible for strategy selection and for the integration of information from other sources, including but not limited to the two previously described slave systems. While the proposed Working Memory model clearly demanded some such coordinating mechanism, early work concentrated almost exclusively on the simpler slave systems. It was assumed that these offered more tractable problems that formed an easier way into the complexities of a multi-component working memory. The Central Executive therefore represented an area of residual ignorance rather than a well-worked-out concept. Although I think that it is entirely defensible to concentrate initially on more tractable problems, attempting to work out peripheral modules before central coordination, by the mid-1980s I had clearly reached a point at which the yawning void of the Central Executive was becoming an embarrassment.

As many of the functions of the Executive were essentially attentional, it seemed sensible to look to the attentional literature for possible help. A review of the area by Donald Broadbent (1982) proved very timely and convinced me that the bulk of the work on attention, excellent though it was, offered little help in attempting to formulate the functioning of the Central Executive. Much of the work on attention has been concerned with perceptual selection (e.g. Broadbent, 1958; Posner, 1980; Treisman, 1988), whereas the Central Executive is essentially concerned with the attentional control of action. Fortunately, one model, that of Norman and Shallice (1980), was concerned with exactly this problem and has proved to offer an excellent candidate for a preliminary model of the Central Executive.

Norman and Shallice were concerned with two separate but related aspects of attentional control. Norman was principally interested in modelling slips of action such as those reported and analysed by Reason (1979), which may lead to minor social embarrassments or, on occasion, to major disasters (Norman,

1990). Shallice, on the other hand, was principally concerned with under-standing the breakdown of attentional control that is exhibited by patients suffering from the so-called frontal lobe syndrome. This can produce a bewildering and sometimes bizarre range of symptoms, including both rigid perseveration and its apparent opposite, excessive distractability.

The model assumes that on-going behaviour is controlled in two ways. Familiar and well-learned activities such as walking, driving, and talking depend on schemata that run off with relatively little demand for supervisory control. Where routine conflicts between well-learned tasks occur, they are settled by semi-automatic conflict resolution processes of the type that commonly feature in production system models of behaviour. The running of such schemata can, however, be overridden by a further mechanism, the supervisory attentional system or SAS. This comes into play when a situation arises in which the next stage is not obvious, or when a new high-priority stimulus occurs which needs to override the on-going behaviour. Shallice (1982) suggests that the SAS depends on the functioning of the frontal lobes. The model can be illustrated briefly by considering its capacity to account for slips of action and the paradoxical combination of rigidity and distractability found in the frontal lobe syndrome.

Consider a slip of action reported by Reason in which a respondent reports setting off for work in the morning, entering the garage to drive his car away, and finding himself sitting down and putting on his gardening boots. This can be explained on the assumption that the boots, which were part of the gardening gear kept in the garage, acted as a trigger for the chain of responses associated with preparing for gardening, and that this was able to override the earlier intention of getting into the car and driving it to work. Interestingly, patients suffering from the frontal lobe syndrome are particu-larly prone to this tendency, often showing a phenomenon known as utiliza-tion behaviour, whereby any object incidentally encountered will tend to be picked up and used, regardless of how appropriate the utilization is at the time. Hence given access to scissors and paper, the patient will tend to cut the paper (see Shallice and Burgess, 1991, for a more detailed account of this). It is the role of the SAS to maintain long-term goals and resist the distraction by stimuli that might otherwise trigger other conflicting behaviour. The weakness of the SAS in frontal patients leads to their vulnerability to such distractions.

In addition to maintaining goals, the SAS is responsible for overriding existing activities in order to achieve longer-term aims. This will include monitoring the outcome of current strategies and switching these when they cease to be fruitful. A good example of this occurs in retrieval from long-term memory, where the difficulties in utilizing a rich and flexible series of strategies tends to lead to poor performance on fluency tasks such as attempt-ing to generate as many animal names as possible. The problem does not lie in lack of stored information, as such patients can generate a large number of animals, given specific cues such as 'an animal with a hump' or 'an Australian animal with a large tail' (Baddeley and Wilson, 1988a). In searching auto-biographical memory, patients with the frontal lobe syndrome are prone to confabulation, sometimes producing bizarre memories with no foundation in fact, such as 'recalling' the death of a brother who is in fact still alive and visits the patient regularly (Baddeley and Wilson, 1986).

Adopting the Norman and Shallice model as the core of the Central Executive brought one unexpected bonus in the form of an explanation of some previously puzzling data on the capacity for random generation. When subjects are required to produce a random stream of letters at a rapid rate, their output deviates markedly from randomness, whether measured in terms of the frequency of individual letters or pairs of letters, or in the occurrence of alphabetic stereotypes such as 'A B' or 'Q R S' (Baddeley, 1966c) Redundancy and stereotype increase linearly with the logarithm of the rate of generation. When the number of alternatives is systematically varied, rate of generation decreases with set size up to about eight alternatives, at which point it levels off – a pattern very similar to that found in Hick's Law, where the loglinear relationship between number of alternatives and reaction time (RT) also holds only up to this point (Seibel, 1963). Finally, when subjects are required to generate letters at the same time as they are performing a card-sorting task at a paced rate of one response per 2 sec, the randomness of their output again decreases with the log of the number of sorting alternatives, suggesting that random generation is a good measure of the remaining capacity of the limited capacity processing system responsible for Hick's Law (Baddeley, 1966c).

These results allowed the original study to claim that the capacity for generating information was limited in very lawful ways, but it remained puzzling as to how this task should be theoretically interpreted. The Norman and Shallice model offers the following interpretation. Subjects are required to produce a sequence of letter names. There is one very strong schema or retrieval programme for doing so, namely reciting the alphabet. However, this would go diametrically against the second requirement, namely to keep the sequence as random as possible. The only way to achieve this, then, is for the SAS system to continually intervene so as to select new strategies, check that the output is suitably random, and then break up that strategy before it becomes too stereotyped. At slow rates such as one response every 4 sec, most subjects can perform this task very effectively; at faster rates of one or two items per second the task becomes increasingly demanding, presumably placing an ever greater strain on the capacity of the SAS to switch strategies and monitor outcome. In addition to providing a further illustration of the usefulness of the Norman and Shallice model, random generation offers a potential tool for loading the Central Executive as a secondary task.

Is Working Memory working?

The simple concept of a tripartite working memory system does, therefore, allow one to accommodate a relatively wide range of laboratory findings; it also seems to be applicable to some of the classic cognitive deficits found in neuropsychological patients. The model is, however, far from precise, and one might argue that it accounts for many of the data simply by being sufficiently imprecise to be adaptable to almost any result. It is certainly not a falsifiable theory in Popper's sense. I would argue, however, that given the complexity of cognitive functioning and our capacity to provide strong tests of models, direct and immediate experimental falsifiability is not a good criterion. Any model can be made falsifiable simply by making strong enough assumptions. Such assumptions would almost inevitably have to be made on a somewhat arbitrary basis, with the resulting danger that the predictions fail because the assumptions are incorrect, not because of the inappropriateness of the broad theoretical framework. How, then, should one evaluate theory, if not by precise experimental prediction?

My own view is that a theory is a tool that should serve two basic functions: (1) to give a reasonably economical and plausible account of existing findings; and (2) to facilitate new discoveries. These, in turn, may cause the theory to be modified, or possibly abandoned. On the whole, however, this should happen only if a better formulation is available, both in its capacity to account for existing data and in its capacity to produce new findings. I would argue that the Working Memory model has been shown to perform reasonably well on the first criterion of giving an economic account of existing data; to what extent has it generated new findings? I will begin by discussing the application of the model to a very general problem, that of analysing complex tasks.

Working Memory and chess

A major and continuing concern within cognitive psychology has been that of analysing the cognitive capacities that underlie complex real-world tasks. It was a prominent feature of the work of the Applied Psychology Unit when Bartlett was its director, and it continues to be an important component of the current APU. Adequate task analysis is likely to be necessary for selection and training of personnel, for understanding the conditions under which the task is likely to be performed well and conditions under which errors are probable. Finally, task analysis represents one way in which laboratory-based models of cognition can be tested for generality and validity.

The concept of Working Memory is beginning to be employed in this area: for example, Farmer *et al.* (1986) showed that articulatory suppression disrupted the performance of a verbal logical reasoning task but had little effect on the performance of the Manikin test, a visuo-spatial manipulation task initially devised to assist in pilot selection. The Manikin test, however, was clearly disrupted by a visuo-spatial task, which had no effect on verbal reasoning. Logie *et al.* (1988) showed that the Working Memory model could be used to analyse a complex computer game and to tease apart differences that occurred in the game following extensive practice. The results obtained using secondary tasks based on the Working Memory model were inconsistent with a simple unitary limited-capacity model and produced results that were not predictable on the basis of the rated difficulty of the component tasks, an approach that is commonly used in the practical analysis of complex skills.

A more recent application of the Working Memory model has been to the analysis of chess performance. Chess is a game that combines clear formal constraints with a degree of richness and complexity that has proved challenging both to the artificial intelligence field and to the cognitive psychologist (De Groot, 1965; Holding, 1985). One unresolved problem discussed by Holding (1985) is the nature of the representation underlying chess performance. One proposal is that the representation involves visual imagery, although attempts to provide support for this using self-ratings of imagery have proved unconvincing (Holding, 1985). Another possibility is that subjects use verbal representation, at least as an interim process in retaining and testing moves. Yet a third possibility is that the representation is abstract. My attention was drawn to this by Trevor Robbins, a very able player, and we agreed to investigate the point in collaboration with a number of undergraduates who chose to work in this area for their final-year research project.

Our first study (Robbins *et al.*, 1996) used the paradigm developed by De Groot (1965), which involves presenting the players with a series of positions from games taken from earlier tournaments and, after an exposure of 5 sec, requiring the subjects to attempt to reproduce the position on a second board. Subject were given 1 point for each correctly located piece, and they lost a point whenever a piece was mislocated. We tested subjects ranging in expertise from a rather average college club level to that of international grand master. De Groot had observed a direct relationship between the skill rating of his players and their memory performance, a finding that we replicated ($r = 0.624$, $p < 0.001$).

We investigated the nature of the underlying code by means of a secondary task procedure involving four conditions. Verbal coding was investigated by means of a condition involving articulatory suppression, in which subjects continuously uttered an irrelevant sound. The Central Executive was explored using random generation, with subjects being required to produce a random stream of letters at a rate of one every second. Visuo-spatial disruption occurred via the requirement to tap a series of keys in a pre-determined pattern. All three conditions were compared with a control condition in which the subject was unencumbered by any secondary task. Both strong and weak players show the same pattern of disruption, with articulatory suppression having no effect and both random generation and spatial processing causing a marked impairment (see Figure 3.1). Our results, therefore, suggest that verbal coding does not play an important role but that both the Visuo-Spatial Sketchpad and the Central Executive are necessary for adequate memory for chess positions.

A subsequent study moved away from memory and devised a task in which subjects were required to select the optimal next move. All the positions used had previously been analysed by experts who had agreed on the relative quality of the range of possible moves, allowing subjects' performance to be scored. We began by using exactly the same secondary task conditions as had been used in the previous study but found that random generation at a one-per-second rate totally disrupted performance. We therefore slowed the generation rate down to one every 2 sec. The pattern of results obtained was very similar to that found in the previous experiment – namely, no effect of

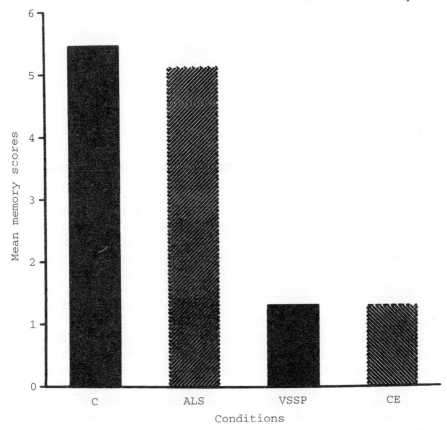

Figure 3.1 Effect of concurrent tasks on the recall of chess positions. C = Control, ALS = Articulatory Suppression, VSSP = Visuo-Spatial Sketchpad Suppression, CE = Central Executive disruption by random generation. (Data from Robbins *et al.*, 1996.)

articulatory suppression, together with very clear evidence of disruption from both the spatial and the random generation tasks.

A third experiment studied the capacity of players to make a rapid evaluation of position. Their task was simply to decide which player had the advantage from a brief glance at a complex middle game. The same three concurrent tasks were used, but in this case the pattern of performance was quite different, with none of the secondary tasks causing significant impairment.

We interpret our first two experiments as providing strong evidence against the use of verbal coding in chess, and in favour of a visuo-spatial code. Similar results have been obtained by Saariluoma (personal communication) using a broadly comparable paradigm. The Central Executive also seems to play a relatively important part in chess memory, presumably because of the need to organize the board into perceptual chunks and to retrieve these at recall. The role of the Central Executive in selecting the optimal move appears to be even more marked, as subjects were made quite unable to perform the task while generating letters at a rate of one per second and showed clear impairment even at the less demanding 2-sec rate. We interpret the lack of significant effect of secondary tasks in the third study as suggesting that the judgement of relative strength is performed at a relatively automatic pattern recognition level. This was, however, an unexpected result, and it clearly merits further investigation; we might expect, for example, that if subjects were allowed unlimited time, then they would attempt to use a more analytic approach to the position evaluation and paradoxically would then be more influenced by the concurrent random generation task, whereas rapid presentation will tend to force the use of a more automatic pattern recognition strategy.

The Central Executive in Alzheimer's disease

One major limitation in attempting to apply the concept of the Central Executive lies in its lack of specificity. However, it is possible to develop predictions from even simple models, gradually exploring the usefulness of the model at the same time as one is investigating the condition to which it is applied. A good example of this stems from our work on Alzheimer's disease, where the pattern of memory deficits suggested the possibility that the impairment lay with the operation of the Central Executive rather than the slave systems (Spinnler *et al.*, 1988).

Although the Central Executive is poorly specified, one of its crucial functions is assumed to be that of coordinating information from different sources. We decided therefore to test this in Alzheimer patients, using a paradigm in which we combined tasks loading on the Sketchpad and Phonological Loop. In order to avoid the complicating effects of general cognitive impairment, we adjusted the difficulty of the two tasks so as to match performance level across our three groups: namely, Alzheimer patients, normal elderly, and young subjects.

In one condition, we combined a pursuit tracking task, which had been adjusted so that subjects were performing at a level approximately 60% time-on-target, with a task in which the subjects repeated back digits adjusted to be approximately equivalent to their span. Under these conditions, the normal elderly and the young showed an equivalent amount of disruption when tracking and span were combined, whereas the Alzheimer patients were dramatically more impaired in the dual-task condition (Baddeley *et al.*, 1986).

A subsequent longitudinal study compared the performance of patients initially with their performance after 6 months and a year (Baddeley *et al*, 1991a). Performance on the individual tasks showed little sign of further decrement over a period of a year, but there was a consistent and marked impairment in performance on the combined tasks. Could this simply be due to task difficulty? This was tested in a second study in which difficulty was manipulated within-task by requiring the subjects to categorize words as belonging to one, two, or four categories. The larger the number of categories, the slower the response and the higher the error rate. When studied longitudinally, there was clear evidence of overall decrement in performance, but no evidence that this decline was any more marked for the difficult four-choice condition than for the easier one-choice (Baddeley *et al.*, 1991a).

Our results are therefore consistent with the hypothesis that the Central Executive is particularly sensitive to the effects of Alzheimer's disease. Such a conclusion has implications for understanding the nature of the disease, and furthermore suggests ways in which tests for the early diagnosis of the disease or its subsequent monitoring might be developed.

Imageability and the Visuo-Spatial Sketchpad

After many decades of neglect, the last 20 years have seen a major revival of interest in imagery. In the field of memory, much of the interest stemmed from Paivio's early work, which showed two things: that the best predictor of the ease of learning of a given word was its rated imageability or concreteness, and that instructions to form images facilitated learning. The efficacy of visual imagery mnemonics have been known since classical times, but it was only in the 1960s that its importance was acknowledged within the modern memory laboratory (Bower, 1970; Paivio, 1969). Paivio interpreted his data in terms of a dual coding hypothesis, suggesting that imageable words received both a verbal and a visual code, hence making them more readily retrieved and more resistant to forgetting.

We became interested in the possibility that the imageability effect might be mediated by the Visuo-Spatial Sketchpad. If this were the case, then a concurrent visual spatial task such as pursuit tracking should reduce the imageability advantage. We tested this in an experiment in which the subjects heard and then were tested on noun-adjective pairs that were either concrete, such as 'bullet–grey', or abstract, such as 'love–perfect'. Subjects learned and recalled such lists under either control conditions, or while performing a pursuit rotor tracking task. We expected that the tracking task would interfere with the setting up of a visual image and hence substantially reduce the advantage due to imageability. The results were clear-cut, with a massive advantage for the imageable words and a small but significant decrement due to tracking. There was, however, no suggestion that tracking differentially impaired retention of imageable pairs. We interpreted our results as indicating that the imageability effect represents the way in which the words are represented in semantic memory and is not dependent on the active visualization strategy of the subject (Baddeley *et al.*, 1973).

Others have reached a similar conclusion (e.g. Jones, 1988), but it could be argued that the reason we obtained disruptive effects in the earlier studies using the Brooks technique, but not in our verbal learning task, was because the latter involved long-term rather than short-term memory. We therefore conducted a further experiment in which we attempted to interfere with the active process of image formation in a long-term learning paradigm (Baddeley and Lieberman, 1980). Subjects were taught a location mnemonic whereby they were required to remember 10 words by imagining the relevant items located at 10 places along a walk through a University campus. The control condition involved presenting lists of 10 words rapidly but repeatedly so as to equate total presentation time but minimize the possibility of subjects using imagery. Once again subjects performed under either control conditions or while tracking. The results showed the expected advantage to the imagery mnemonic under control conditions, but the advantage disappeared completely when concurrent tracking was required. Our results, therefore, suggest that Paivio's two sources of evidence reflect very different processes, the imageability effect being dependent on the richness of representation of concrete words in semantic memory while the use of an imagery mnemonic depends upon the active manipulation of items within the Visuo-Spatial Sketchpad (Baddeley and Lieberman, 1980).

What use is the Phonological Loop?

As we saw earlier, the Phonological Loop seems to give a reasonably good account of a wide range of laboratory phenomena, mainly based on memory span procedures. The model appears to be able to explain the pattern of development of the span in children, to account for cross-linguistic findings, and to be applicable to the study of the breakdown of memory span performance in neuropsychological patients. Such patients do, however, provide a problem for the model: provided their deficit is limited to short-term phonological memory, they appear to have remarkably few problems in coping with everyday life. Shallice and Warrington's patient, J.B., was a successful secretary, and Vallar and Baddeley's patient, P.V., ran a shop, with few apparent problems other than the need to use pencil and paper to work out the customers' costs and change.

Such findings inevitably raise the question of what function is served by the Phonological Loop? To use Reason's rather colourful phrase, is the Phonological Loop anything more than 'a pimple on the face of cognition'? One obvious possibility is that the Loop plays an important role in language comprehension. Many models of comprehension have assumed a role for a temporary memory store (e.g. Clark and Clark, 1977), but the evidence remains equivocal. Most patients with STM deficits appear to show problems in understanding certain sentences, although doubt remains as to exactly how to characterize these, and the question remains as to whether the phonological store plays a role in normal sentence comprehension or serves only as a back-up for use when other processes become overloaded (see Vallar and Shallice, 1990, for a discussion of this issue). Indeed, at least one STM patient has been reported who is claimed to show no sentence comprehension deficit (Butterworth *et al.*, 1986), while in contrast patient T.B. showed a major disruption of the comprehension of sentences which appears to be a function of sentence length and memory load (Baddeley and Wilson, 1988b). With subsequent recovery of span, T.B. has shown an equivalent recovery in language comprehension capacity, although, interestingly, not of the capacity to perform certain tests of phonological awareness (Baddeley and Wilson, 1990). To summarize, although it seems likely that the Phonological Loop does play a role in comprehension, at least of complex sentences, there is no doubt that most STM patients show only minor comprehension difficulties under normal everyday conditions. This could either mean that the Loop is used only for back-up purposes, or else that most patients have sufficient residual Loop capacity to cope with most situations.

A second area in which phonological memory may be important is in that of learning to read. Reduced digit span is a prominent feature of the children suffering from developmental dyslexia (Jorm, 1983; Torgerson and Houck, 1980). As evidence for the importance of the Phonological Loop, however, such data are equivocal. On the one hand, there is controversy as to whether the association reflects a direct role of the Phonological Loop in learning to read, or the reverse effect of reading on span, or possibly the effect of a third variable such as phonological awareness on both of these (Ellis and Large, 1987). Furthermore, even if the Loop does prove to be causally involved in the acquisition of reading, it is hard to believe that the Loop evolved for this purpose, given the evolutionary recency of reading as a human skill. This relationship did, however, suggest the interesting possibility that the link between the Phonological Loop and reading might be through long-term phonological learning. This seemed initially unlikely, as one generally agreed feature of STM patients is that their long-term learning capacities are normal, whether tested using verbal or visual material (Basso *et al.*, 1982; Shallice and Warrington, 1970). However, the verbal memory tests used had typically employed meaningful words, which typically depend principally on semantic coding for their long-term memory (Baddeley, 1966b). We therefore decided to explore the role of the Phonological Loop in the acquisition of novel phonological material – namely, Russian vocabulary.

Our first experiment involved presenting patient P.V. with two learning tasks, the first involving associating pairs of words in her native language of Italian (e.g. 'cavallo–libro'), and the second requiring her to associate an Italian word with an unfamiliar Russian word (e.g. 'rosa–svieti'), with her performance being compared with that of a group of normal subjects matched for age and education (Baddeley *et al.*, 1988). As expected, the capacity of P.V. to learn pairs of meaningful words was entirely normal; in contrast, her capacity for learning novel phonological sequences was dramatically impaired. With auditory presentation, at the end of 10 trials the control subjects had all mastered the list of eight pairs, whereas P.V. had not acquired a single Russian item. In short, it appears to be the case that short-term phonological memory does indeed play a central role in long-term phonological learning.

This has not yet been replicated with other STM patients, but we have produced a similar though less dramatic effect in a study that used articulatory suppression to disrupt the use of the Phonological Loop in normal subjects, who were again learning either meaningful pairs of items or the vocabulary of an unfamiliar language; suppression had little or no effect on paired-associate learning, but caused substantial disruption of the new phonological learning (Papagno *et al.*, 1989; Papagno *et al.*, 1991).

These results encouraged us to explore the role of the Phonological Loop in the development of language in children. In one study, Susan Gathercole and I examined the memory capacities of children who had been classified as suffering from a specific language disability (Gathercole and Baddeley, 1990a). We found that these children had one particularly striking deficit – namely, that of repeating back unfamiliar non-words. On the sound-mimicry component of the Goldman–Fristoe–Woodcock auditory memory test, our 8-year-old children were performing at a level below that expected of 4-year-olds. This deficit was, on average, 2 years greater than the language deficit for which they had been selected.

We went on to explore the nature of this deficit in greater detail and were able to show that it did not appear to reflect either problems in language perception or production. These children appear to use the Phonological Loop system in the normal way, showing both similarity and word-length effects but performing at a significantly lower level than controls, whether these were matched on age and non-verbal intelligence, or comprised younger children of the same verbal intelligence. Our results were therefore consistent with the hypothesis of a reduced-capacity Phonological Loop, which was reflected in both the low non-word repetition score and in the delayed development of language.

Our evidence suggested therefore that a gross deficit in non-word repetition performance was associated with disordered language development; our next study was concerned with the extent to which the development of language in normal children was linked to non-word repetition performance and, by implication, the capacity of the Phonological Loop (Gathercole and Baddeley, 1989). We carried out a longitudinal study of children who had started school in Cambridge between the age of 4 and 5, and who at that time showed no evidence of the capacity to read. We measured their non-word repetition performance, together with non-verbal intelligence, using Raven's Matrices, and their vocabulary. This was tested using the appropriate sub-test of the British Picture Vocabulary Scale, which involves speaking a word to the child, who is then required to point to one of four pictures that corresponds to the spoken word. We then correlated performance on these various sub-tests, to see which was the best predictor of vocabulary.

The results obtained for these children on the initial test and on a re-test 1 and 2 years later are shown in Table 3.1. It is clear that non-word repetition is the best of the predictors and that it continues to explain a substantial proportion of the variance, even when the other variables such as age and intelligence are partialled out. It is of course possible that vocabulary leads to good non-word repetition, rather than the reverse. This can be tested using a cross-lagged correlation; if performance on vocabulary is the crucial factor, then there should be a high correlation between vocabulary performance in Year 1 and the subsequent performance of children on non-word repetition a year later. If, however, non-word repetition reflects the basic cause, then the correlation should be higher in the opposite direction. We observed that the correlation between age-4 performance on non-word repetition and age-5 vocabulary ($r = 0.597$) was significantly higher than the correlation between age-4 vocabulary and age-5 non-word repetition ($r = 0.415$), suggesting that it is more likely that good non-word repetition leads to good vocabulary than the reverse.

Table 3.1 Predictors of vocabulary score at ages 4, 5, and 6

	Age		
	4 years	*5 years*	*6 years*
Age	0.218*	0.007	0.154
Non verbal intelligence	0.388**	0.164	0.387**
Non-word repetition	0.525**	0.492**	0.532**

$*p < 0.05$; $**p < 0.01$

Table 3.2 Predictors of single word reading at ages 5 and 6

	Age	
	5 years	*6 years*
Age	0.135	0.171
Non-verbal intelligence	0.370**	0.368**
Vocabulary	0.222*	0.410**
Non-word repetition	0.382**	0.381**

$*p < 0.05$; $**p < 0.01$

Another way of asking the same question is to attempt an experimental simulation of vocabulary learning. We did this by selecting two groups of children who were matched for non-verbal intelligence but differed in non-word repetition performance. We then taught each group the names of a series of toy monsters; the names could either be familiar, such as 'Peter' and 'Michael', or novel such as 'Pichael' and 'Meter'. As predicted by the Phonological Loop hypothesis, the children who were poor in non-word repetition learnt more slowly – an effect that was particularly marked for the unfamiliar names (Gathercole and Baddeley, 1990b).

One of the reasons for suspecting a link between the Phonological Loop and long-term language learning came from the association between poor memory span and reading disability. Our longitudinal study has therefore been exploring the relationship between non-word repetition and reading. The picture we are finding appears to be somewhat more complex than that obtained with vocabulary acquisition. Table 3.2 shows the correlation between performance on the British Ability Score (BAS) reading test, in which subjects attempt to read out individual words and their age, non-verbal intelligence, vocabulary, and non-word repetition scores. It is clear, first of all, that a major predictor of reading performance is intelligence; however, the present data, and of course the occurrence of dyslexic children of normal or above-average intelligence, indicate that this is by no means the only factor. At age 5, non-word repetition is the best predictor, explaining a significant 6.7% of the variance in reading when intelligence and vocabulary have been partialled out ($p < 0.01$). By age 6 the pattern has changed somewhat, with vocabulary being a better predictor than non-word repetition. It is noteworthy, however, that non-word repetition at age 5 predicts reading a year later rather better ($r = 0.467$) than vocabulary at age 6 ($r = 0.410$).

Interpreting these results is, of course, complicated by the fact that vocabulary itself is affected by non-word repetition. However, if we take the conservative step of partialling out both intelligence and vocabulary before assessing the role of non-word repetition, our data indicate that this variable is particularly important about a year after our subjects begin to learn to read. Subsequent work (Gathercole *et al*, 1991) has replicated this pattern of results using a cross-section sample of children from another city, encouraging us in the view that the Phonological Loop plays an important role in this early stage of reading, which informal observation would suggest is concerned with the acquisition of the association between letters and sounds – a task that Byrne and Fielding-Barnsley (1989) have shown is an important factor in the early stages of acquiring reading. It is clear that children can learn to read by more than one route (Campbell and Butterworth, 1985), but we suspect that the usual and most effective method of reading acquisition places a major load on the Phonological Loop at this critical stage. However, it is clearly the case that many other factors are involved in reading acquisition, and we would certainly not wish to argue that the Phonological Loop is the only or even the principal determinant of reading performance for the average reader, although we suspect that a very severe impairment is likely to have a major effect on the development of reading.

Limitations of the current model of Working Memory

I began with the suggestion that models are tools that should both account for existing data and also stimulate the search for a wider and deeper understanding. Most tools eventually wear out or become obsolete; in the case of models they cease to be productive of new ideas, or they are unable to accommodate the new developments that occur. Hence a model that fitted the data perfectly but did nothing else would be unproductive, suggesting a field that is worked out. Such a model might serve the very useful function of summarizing the area until such time as it is incorporated within a more ambitious and extensive model. According to such a view, some of the most interesting and important features of a model are represented by its limitations, as these are potential growth points or, alternatively, issues that might indicate the need for alternative models to supplement or replace the original. I would therefore like to conclude by very briefly summarizing some of the limitations of the Working Memory model, considering each of the three major subcomponents in turn.

The Phonological Loop. This has probably proved to be the area that is most easily investigated as it is clearly modular and involves an extensively explored area of verbal memory. The simple two-component model gives a good qualitative account of a wide range of laboratory phenomena and has proved very fruitful in extrapolation to neuropsychological and developmental issues. The model in its current formulation, however, is too simple to allow more detailed predictions to be made. It is, for example, far from clear exactly how the irrelevant speech effect operates – why, for instance, it does not interact with phonological similarity, as both are assumed to influence the same phonological store (Salamé and Baddeley, 1986). The lack of interaction is not, of course, evidence against their influencing the same component, as the occurrence and nature of any such interaction would depend critically on the underlying memory processes. We have as yet no model of these, and it is unlikely that a satisfactory model will become available in the absence of a much more detailed quantitative model of the functioning of the phonological memory store.

Earlier models of memory using 1960s concepts of computer storage within specific locations seemed so unlikely as a model of memory storage that there appeared to be little immediate prospect of remedying this situation. I am, however, much more hopeful of the more recent developments in connectionist models, where the simulation of phonological information and in particular of serial order represents an area of considerable current interest. I would hope that the Phonological Loop would begin to attract the interest of workers in speech perception, whose quantitative modelling capabilities are considerably better than my own, and would see the empirical input from studies on short-term phonological memory as offering clues and placing constraints on subsequent models of language perception and processing (Baddeley *et al.*, 1991b).

The Visuo-Spatial Sketchpad. Our exploration of this subsystem is considerably less developed than that of the Phonological Loop. Questions still remain as to whether we should conceptualize it as a single system having both spatial and pictorial components, or whether quite separate subcomponents are involved. The nature of the rehearsal process in this system is also at present far from clear; the data from eye movements are suggestive, but at present not conclusive. Finally, we need to know more about the role of the Sketchpad in long-term learning and of the importance of this subsystem in everyday cognition.

The Central Executive. Understanding the executive control of human behaviour is clearly a major undertaking, and I must confess that the model of Working Memory has been stronger at acknowledging the problem than solving it. It seems extremely probable that the Central Executive will have a number of subcomponent systems and that untangling these will be very difficult. Indeed, it may prove to be the case that once the component processes have been identified, there will be no further need for the concept of a single executive, a position proposed by Barnard (1985). In the meantime, however, I would regard the concept as continuing to be useful, both in the negative sense of allowing the exploration of modular subsystems such as the Phonological Loop, without the requirement that the model accounts for everything, and in the positive sense of encouraging the direct exploration of executive processes. One important area of cognition that we have previously hinted might be associated with the Executive is that of conscious awareness. Techniques have now started to be developed that allow the exploration of the role of awareness in perception (e.g. Marcel, 1983) and long-term memory (Tulving, 1989). I am optimistic that the next few years may well see an expansion of research on the role of the Executive in consciousness (Teasdale, 1989).

So is Working Memory working? It does seem to account for a good deal of existing data and has in the past been very fruitful in generating new findings. It has allowed laboratory research to be applied to the practical problems of neuropsychological deficit and cognitive development, and it has certainly produced a range of further important questions, at least some of which we have some hope of answering. All things considered, then, I would suggest that the model is not yet ready for the breaker's yard.

References

Atkinson, R. C. and Shiffrin, R. M. (1968). Human memory: A proposed system and its control processes. In K. W. Spence (Ed.), *The psychology of learning and motivation: Advances in research and theory* (Vol. 2, pp. 89–195). New York: Academic Press.

Baddeley, A. D. (1966a). Short-term memory for word sequences as a function of acoustic, semantic and formal similarity. *Quarterly Journal of Experimental Psychology*, *18*, 362–365.

Baddeley, A. D. (1966b). The influence of acoustic and semantic similarity on long-term memory for word sequences. *Quarterly Journal of Experimental Psychology*, *18*, 302–309.

Baddeley, A. D. (1966c). The capacity for generating information by randomization. *Quarterly Journal of Experimental Psychology*, *18*, 119–129.

Baddeley, A. D. (1983). Working memory. *Philosophical Transactions of the Royal Society of London B*, *302*, 311–324.

Baddeley, A. D. (1990). *Human memory: Theory and practice.* London: Lawrence Erlbaum Associates Ltd.

Baddeley, A. D., Bressi, S., Della Sala, S., Logie R., and Spinnler, H. (1991a). The decline of working memory in Alzheimer's disease: A longitudinal study. *Brain*, *114*, 2521–2542.

Baddeley, A. D. and Dale, H. C. A. (1966). The effect of semantic similarity on retroactive interference in long- and short-term memory. *Journal of Verbal Learning and Verbal Behavior*, *5*, 417–420.

Baddeley, A. D., Grant, S., Wight, E., and Thomson, N. (1973). Imagery and visual working memory. In P. M. A. Rabbitt and S. Dornic (Eds.), *Attention and performance V* (pp. 205–217). London: Academic Press.

Baddeley, A. D. and Hitch, G. (1974). Working memory. In G. H. Bower (Ed.), *The psychology of learning and motivation* (Vol. 8). New York: Academic Press.

Baddeley, A. D., Lewis, V. J., and Vallar, G. (1984). Exploring the articulatory loop. *Quarterly Journal of Experimental Psychology*, *36*, 233–252.

Baddeley, A. D. and Lieberman, K. (1980). Spatial working memory. In R. S. Nickerson (Ed.), *Attention and performance VIII* (pp. 521–539). Hillsdale, NJ: Lawrence Erlbaum Associates, Inc.

Baddeley, A. D., Logie, R., Bressi, S., Della Sala, S., and Spinnler, H. (1986). Dementia and working memory. *Quarterly Journal of Experimental Psychology*, *38A*, 603–618.

Baddeley, A. D., Papagno, C., and Norris, D. (1991b). Phonological memory and serial order: A sandwich for TODAM. In W. Hockley and S. Lewandowsky (Eds.), *Relating theory and data* (pp. 175–194). Hillsdale, N.J.: Lawrence Erlbaum Associates.

Baddeley, A. D., Papagno, C., and Vallar, G. (1988). When long-term learning depends on short-term storage. *Journal of Memory and Language, 27*, 586–595.

Baddeley, A. D., Thomson, N., and Buchanan, M. (1975). Word length and the structure of short-term memory. *Journal of Verbal Learning and Verbal Behavior, 14*, 575–589.

Baddeley, A. D. and Warrington, E. K. (1970). Amnesia and the distinction between long- and short-term memory. *Journal of Verbal Learning and Verbal Behavior, 9*, 176–189.

Baddeley, A. D. and Wilson, B. (1985). Phonological coding and short-term memory in patients without speech. *Journal of Memory and Language, 24*, 490–502.

Baddeley, A. D. and Wilson, B. (1986). Amnesia, autobiographical memory and confabulation. In D. Rubin (Ed.), *Autobiographical memory* (pp. 225–252). New York: Cambridge University Press.

Baddeley, A. D. and Wilson, B. (1988a). Frontal amnesia and the dysexecutive syndrome. *Brain and Cognition, 7*, 212–230.

Baddeley, A. D. and Wilson, B. (1988b). Comprehension and working memory: A single case neuropsychological study. *Journal of Memory and Language, 27*, 479–498.

Baddeley, A. D. and Wilson, B. A. (1990). *Spontaneous recovery of impaired memory span: Does comprehension recover?* Paper presented at Manchester meeting of the Experimental Psychology Society.

Baddeley, A. D. and Woodhead, M. M. (1982). Depth of processing, context, and face recognition. *Canadian Journal of Psychology, 36*, 148–164.

Banaji, M. R. and Crowder, R. G. (1989). The bankruptcy of everyday memory. *American Psychologist, 44*, 1185–1193.

Barnard, P. (1985). Interacting cognitive subsystems: A psycholinguistic approach to short-term memory. In A. Ellis (Ed.), *Progress in the psychology of language* (Vol. 2, pp. 197–258). London: Lawrence Erlbaum Associates Ltd.

Basso, A., Spinnler, H., Vallar, G., and Zanobio, E. (1982). Left hemisphere damage and selective impairment of auditory-verbal short-term memory: A case study. *Neuropsychologia, 20*, 263–274.

Bishop, D. V. M. and Robson, J. (1989). Unimpaired short-term memory and rhyme judgement in congenitally speechless individuals: Implications for the notion of 'articulatory coding'. *Quarterly Journal of Experimental Psychology, 41A*, 123–141.

Bower, G. H. (1970). Analysis of a mnemonic device. *American Scientist, 58*, 496–510.

Braithwaite, R. (1953). *Scientific explanation.* Cambridge: Cambridge University Press.

Broadbent, D. E. (1958). *Perception and communication.* London: Pergamon Press.

Broadbent, D. E. (1982). Task combination and selective intake of information. *Acta Psychologica, 50*, 253–290.

Brooks, L. R. (1967). The suppression of visualization by reading. *Quarterly Journal of Experimental Psychology, 19*, 289–299.

Brown, J. (1958). Some tests of the decay theory of immediate memory. *Quarterly Journal of Experimental Psychology, 10*, 12–21.

Bruce, V. (1988). *Recognising faces.* London: Lawrence Erlbaum Associates Ltd.

Butterworth, B., Campbell, R., and Howard, D. (1986). The uses of short-term memory: A case study. *Quarterly Journal of Experimental Psychology, 38A*, 705–738.

Byrne, B. and Fielding-Barnsley, R. (1989). Phonemic awareness and letter knowledge in the child's acquisition of the alphabetic principle. *Journal of Educational Psychology, 81*, 313–321.

Campbell, R. and Butterworth, B. (1985). Phonological dyslexia and dysgraphia in a highly literate subject: A developmental case with associated deficits of phonemic processing and awareness. *Quarterly Journal of Experimental Psychology, 37A*, 435–476.

Clark, H. H. and Clark, E. V. (1977). *Psychology and language.* New York: Harcourt, Brace, Jovanovich.

Colle, H. A. and Welsh, A. (1976). Acoustic masking in primary memory. *Journal of Verbal Learning and Verbal Behavior, 15*, 17–32.

Conrad, R. (1964). Acoustic confusion in immediate memory. *British Journal of Psychology, 55*, 75–84.

Conrad, R. and Hull, A. J. (1964). Information, acoustic confusion and memory span. *British Journal of Psychology, 55*, 429–432.

Crowder, R. G. (1982). The demise of short-term memory. *Acta Psychologica, 50*, 291–323.

De Groot, A. D. (1965). *Thought and choice in chess.* New York: Basic Books.

Ellis, N. C. and Hennelly, R. A. (1980). A bilingual word-length effect: Implications for intelligence testing and the relative ease of mental calculation in Welsh and English. *British Journal of Psychology, 71*, 43–52.

Ellis, N. C. and Large, B. (1987). The development of reading: As you seek you shall find. *British Journal of Psychology, 78*, 1–28.

Farah, M. J., Hammond, K. M., Levine, D. N., and Calvanio, R. (1988). Visual and spatial mental imagery: Dissociable systems of representation. *Cognitive Psychology, 20*, 439–462.

Farmer, E. W., Berman, J. V. F., and Fletcher, Y. L. (1986). Evidence for a visuospatial scratch pad in working memory. *Quarterly Journal of Experimental Psychology, 38A*, 675–688.

Gathercole, S. and Baddeley, A. D. (1989). Evaluation of the role of phonological STM in the development of vocabulary in children: A longitudinal study. *Journal of Memory and Language, 28*, 200–213.

Gathercole, S. and Baddeley, A. (1990a). Phonological memory deficits in language-disordered children: Is there a causal connection? *Journal of Memory and Language, 29*, 336–360.

Gathercole, S. and Baddeley, A. (1990b). The role of phonological memory in vocabulary acquisition: A study of young children learning new names. *British Journal of Psychology, 81*, 439–454.

Gathercole, S. E., Willis, C., and Baddeley, A. D. (1991). Differentiating phonological memory and awareness of rhyme: Reading and vocabulary development in children. *British Journal of Psychology, 82*, 387–406.

Glanzer, M. and Cunitz, A. R. (1966). Two storage mechanisms in free recall. *Journal of Verbal Learning and Verbal Behavior, 5*, 351–360.

Hanley, J. R., Young, A. W., and Pearson, N. A. (1991). Impairment of the visuospatial sketch pad. *Quarterly Journal of Experimental Psychology, 43A*, 101–126.

Hitch, G. J. and Halliday, M. S. (1983). Working memory in children. *Philosophical Transactions of the Royal Society London B, 302*, 325–340.

Holding, D. H. (1985). *The psychology of chess skill.* Hillsdale, NJ: Lawrence Erlbaum Associates, Inc.

Hulme, C., Thomson, N., Muir, C., and Lawrence, A. (1984). Speech rate and the development of short-term memory span. *Journal of Experimental Child Psychology, 38*, 241–253.

Jones, G. V. (1988). Images, predicates, and retrieval cues. In M. Denis, J. Engelkamp, and J. T. E. Richardson (Eds.), *Cognitive and neuropsychological approaches to mental imagery* (pp. 89–98). Dordrecht: Martinus Nijhoff.

Jorm, A. F. (1983). Specific reading retardation and working memory: A review. *British Journal of Psychology*, 74, 311–342.

Kintsch, W. and Buschke, H. (1969). Homophones and synonyms in short-term memory. *Journal of Experimental Psychology*, 80, 403–407.

Kuhn, T. S. (1970). *The structure of scientific revolutions*. Chicago: Chicago University Press.

Logie, R. H. (1986). Visuo-spatial processing in working memory. *Quarterly Journal of Experimental Psychology*, 38A, 229–247.

Logie, R. H., Baddeley, A. D., Mane, A., Donchin, E. and Sheptak, R. (1988). Working memory in the acquisition of complex cognitive skills. In A. M. Colley and J. R. Beech (Eds.), *Cognition and action in skilled behaviour* (pp. 361–377). Amsterdam: Elsevier.

Marcel, A. J. (1983). Conscious and unconscious perception: Experiments on visual masking and word recognition. *Cognitive Psychology*, 15, 197–237.

Melton, A. W. (1963). Implications of short-term memory for a general theory of memory. *Journal of Verbal Learning and Verbal Behavior*, 2, 1–21.

Naveh-Benjamin, M. and Ayres, T. J. (1986). Digit span, reading rate, and linguistic relativity. *Quarterly Journal of Experimental Psychology*, 38, 739–751.

Newell, A. (1974). You can't play 20 questions with nature and win. In W. G. Chase (Ed.), *Visual information processing*. New York: Academic Press.

Nicolson, R. (1981). The relationship between memory span and processing speed. In M. P. Friedman, J. P. Das, and N. O'Connor (Eds.), *Intelligence and learning* (pp. 179–84). New York: Plenum Press.

Norman, D. A. (1990). The 'problem' with automation: Inappropriate feedback and interaction, not 'over-automation.' In D. E. Broadbent, J. T. Reason, and A. D. Baddeley, (Eds.), *Human factors in hazardous situations* (pp. 585–593). Oxford: Clarendon Press.

Norman, D. A. and Shallice, T. (1980). *Attention to action: Willed and automatic control of behavior*. University of California San Diego, CHIP Report 99.

Paivio, A. (1969). Mental imagery in associative learning and memory. *Psychological Review*, 76, 241–263.

Papagno, C., Baddeley, A. D., and Valentine, T. (1989). Memoria fonologica a breve termine e apprendimento verbale. *Archivio di Psicologia neurologia e Psichiatria*, 3, 542–557.

Papagno, C., Valentine, T., and Baddeley, A. D. (1991). Phonological short-term memory and foreign-vocabulary language learning. *Journal of Memory and Language*, 30, 331–347.

Peterson, L. R. (1966). Short-term verbal memory and learning. *Psychological Review*, 73, 193–207.

Peterson, L. R. and Peterson, M. J. (1959). Short-term retention of individual verbal items. *Journal of Experimental Psychology*, 58, 193–198.

Popper, K. (1959). *The logic of scientific discovery*. London: Hutchinson.

Posner, M. I. (1980). Orienting of attention: Seventh Bartlett Memorial Lecture. *Quarterly Journal of Experimental Psychology*, 32, 3–25.

Reason, J. T. (1979). Actions not as planned: The price of automatisation. In G. Underwood and R. Stevens (Eds.), *Aspects of consciousness, Volume 1: Psychological issues*. London: Academic Press.

Robbins, T. W., Anderson, E. J., Barker, D. R., Bradley, A. C., Fearnyhough, C., Henson, R., Hudson, S. R., and Baddeley, A. D. (1996). Working memory in chess. *Memory & Cognition*, 24, 83–93.

Rubin, D. C. (1986). *Autobiographical memory*. Cambridge: Cambridge University Press.

Salamé, P. and Baddeley, A. D. (1982). Disruption of short-term memory by unattended speech: Implications for the structure of working memory. *Journal of Verbal Learning and Verbal Behavior*, *21*, 150–164.

Salamé, P. and Baddeley, A. D. (1986). Phonological factors in STM: Similarity and the unattended speech effect. *Bulletin of the Psychonomic Society*, *24*, 263–265.

Salamé, P. and Baddeley, A. D. (1989). Effects of background music on phonological short-term memory. *Quarterly Journal of Experimental Psychology*, *41A*, 107–122.

Seibel, R. (1963). Discrimination reaction time for a 1023-alternative task. *Journal of Experimental Psychology*, *66*, 215–226.

Shallice, T. (1982). Specific impairments of planning. *Philosophical Transactions of the Royal Society London B*, *298*, 199–209.

Shallice, T. and Burgess, P. (1991). Higher-order cognitive impairments and frontal lobe lesions in man. In H. Levin, H. M. Eisenberg, and A. L. Benton (Eds.), *Frontal lobe function and injury* (pp. 125–138). Oxford: Oxford University Press.

Shallice, T. and Warrington, E. K. (1970). Independent functioning of verbal memory stores: A neuropsychological study. *Quarterly Journal of Experimental Psychology*, *22*, 261–273.

Spinnler, H., Della Sala, S., Bandera, R., and Baddeley, A. D. (1988). Dementia, ageing and the structure of human memory. *Cognitive Neuropsychology*, *5*, 193–211.

Teasdale, J. (1989). Daydreaming, depression and distraction. *The Psychologist*, *2*, 189–190.

Torgerson, J. K. and Houck, D. G. (1980). Processing deficiencies of learning-disabled children who perform poorly on the digit span test. *Journal of Educational Psychology*, *72*, 141–160.

Toulmin, S. (1953). *The philosophy of science*. London: Hutchinson.

Treisman, A. M. (1988). Features and objects: The 14th Bartlett Memorial Lecture. *Quarterly Journal of Experimental Psychology*, *40A*, 201–237.

Tulving, E. (1989). Memory: Performance, knowledge and experience. *European Journal of Cognitive Psychology*, *1*, 3–26.

Vallar, G. and Baddeley, A. D. (1984). Phonological short-term store, phonological processing and sentence comprehension: A neuropsychological case study. *Cognitive Neuropsychology*, *1*, 121–141.

Vallar, G. and Shallice, T. (Eds.) (1990). *Neuropsychological impairments of short-term memory*. Cambridge: Cambridge University Press.

Waugh, N. C. and Norman, D. A. (1965). Primary memory. *Psychological Review*, *72*, 89–104.

SECTION THREE
RELIABILITY OF MEMORY

Editor's introduction

One of the major applications of memory research concerns the accuracy and reliability of people's memories. For example, an understanding of the factors that affect memory accuracy is important in allowing us to judge how veridical an eyewitness's recollections of a crime or road accident are. One of the pioneers of laboratory research in this area was Elizabeth Loftus, who developed a simple technique, described in the **Loftus, Miller,** and **Burns** article (Chapter 4), for inducing errors in recall. Loftus and her colleagues have conducted numerous studies in which subjects see film or slides of an event such as a road accident and are then provided with a verbal description which includes an erroneous statement about the event. Loftus has argued that such 'misinformation' becomes integrated into the memory for the original event and creates false memories.

Findings emerging from this research area have been tremendously influential, but have also been controversial. **McCloskey** and **Zaragoza**'s article (Chapter 5) challenges Loftus *et al.*'s claim that misinformation becomes incorporated into the memory of the original event and have instead argued that the effects of misinformation can be explained by certain biases created in the experimental procedure. The issue of whether memories can be overwritten remains a contentious one. Further important contributions have been made by Chandler (1991), Payne *et al.* (1994), and Weingardt *et al.* (1995).

A number of studies have looked at memory enhancement techniques such as repeated testing and hypnosis. Recent contributions by Wheeler and Roediger (1992) and Dinges *et al.* (1992) are recommended.

A closely related topic that has been the subject of much publicity concerns 'recovered memories' associated with traumatic childhood events such as abuse. An excellent review is provided by Loftus (1993). Also recommended for further reading are studies of the long-term reliability of natural memories: see Neisser and Harsch (1992) and Bahrick *et al.* (1975).

References

Bahrick, H. P., Bahrick, P. O., and Wittlinger, R. P. (1975). Fifty years of memory for names and faces: a cross-sectional approach. *Journal of Experimental Psychology: General*, 104, 54–75.

Chandler, C. C. (1991). How memory for an event is influenced by related events: interference in modified recognition tests. *Journal of Experimental Psychology: Learning, Memory, and Cognition*, 17, 115–25.

Dinges, D. F., Whitehouse, W. G., Orne, E. C., Powell, J. W., Orne, M. T., and Erdelyi, M. H. (1992). Evaluating hypnotic memory enhancement (hypermnesia and reminiscence) using multitrial forced recall. *Journal of Experimental Psychology: Learning, Memory, and Cognition*, 18, 1139–47.

Loftus, E. F. (1993). The reality of repressed memories. *American Psychologist*, 48, 518–37.

Neisser, U. and Harsch, N. (1992). Phantom flashbulbs: false recollections of hearing the news about *Challenger*. In *Affect and accuracy in recall. Studies of 'flashbulb' memories* (ed. E. Winograd and U. Neisser), pp. 9–31. Cambridge University Press, New York.

Payne, D. G., Toglia, M. P., and Anastasi, J. S. (1994). Recognition performance level and the magnitude of the misinformation effect in eyewitness memory. *Psychonomic Bulletin and Review*, 1, 376–82.

Weingardt, K. R., Loftus, E. F., and Lindsay, D. S. (1995). Misinformation revisited: new evidence on the suggestibility of memory. *Memory and Cognition*, 23, 72–82.

Wheeler, M. A. and Roediger, H. L. (1992). Disparate effects of repeated testing: reconciling Ballard's (1913) and Bartlett's (1932) results. *Psychological Science*, 3, 240–5.

4   Elizabeth F. Loftus, David G. Miller and Helen J. Burns
'Semantic Integration of Verbal Information into a Visual Memory'

Reprinted in full from: *Journal of Experimental Psychology: Human Learning and Memory* 4, 19–31 (1978)

Almost two centuries ago, Immanuel Kant (1781/1887) spoke of the human tendency to merge different experiences to form new concepts and ideas. That tendency has crucial implications for one's ability to report his or her experiences accurately. When one has witnessed an important event, such as a crime or an accident, one is occasionally exposed to subsequent information that can influence the memory of that event. This occurs even when the initial event is largely visual and the additional information is verbal in nature (Loftus, 1975; Pezdek, 1977). For instance, in a previous study, subjects saw films of complex fast-moving events such as automobile accidents or classroom disruptions (Loftus, 1975). Immediately afterward, the subjects were asked a series of questions, some of which were designed to present accurate, consistent information (e.g., suggesting the existence of an object that did exist in the scene), while others presented misleading information (e.g., suggesting the existence of an object that did not exist in the original scene). Thus, a subject might have been asked, 'How fast was the car going when it ran the stop sign?' when a stop sign actually did exist (Experiment 1). Or the subject might have been asked, 'How fast was the white sports car going when it passed the barn while traveling along the country road?' when no barn existed (Experiment 3). These subjects were subsequently asked whether they had seen the presupposed objects. It was found that such questions increased the likelihood that subjects would later report having seen these objects. It was argued that the questions were effective because they contained information – sometimes consistent, sometimes misleading – which was integrated into the memorial representation of the event, thereby causing a reconstruction or alteration of the actual information stored in memory.

In these earlier experiments, the original event was presented visually, the subsequent information was introduced verbally via questionnaires, and the final test was also verbal in nature. In the present experiments, a recognition procedure was used; it involved showing a series of slides depicting a complex event and afterward exposing subjects to verbal information about the event. This study phase was followed by a recognition test in which the subjects were presented with target pictures identical to ones seen before and distractor pictures altered in some way. The first reason for this change was that if one subscribes to the view that verbal and visual information are stored separately, one could argue that Loftus' (1975) final test, being verbal in nature, helped subjects access the subsequent verbal information, thereby resulting in an incorrect response.

The second reason for using a recognition test procedure was that if recognition is assumed to be a relatively passive and simple process of matching stimuli to specific locations in a content-addressable storage system, one would expect a representation of the actual (or true) scene to result in a match, whereas an alteration would fail to match. In other words, if the original visual scene is stored in memory, presenting the subject with the original stimulus might result in a match between the memory representation and the stimulus. If the original scene had been transformed so that an altered version was stored in memory, presenting the subject with the original stimulus would not result in a match between the memorial representation and the stimulus.

These considerations motivated the present series of studies. Before turning to them, we describe a pilot study in some detail, since the materials and procedures were similar to those used in the remaining experiments.

Pilot experiment

In a pilot experiment (Loftus *et al.*, 1975), a series of 30 color slides, depicting successive stages in an auto–pedestrian accident, was shown to 129 subjects. The auto was a red Datsun seen traveling along a side street toward an intersection having a stop sign for half of the subjects and a yield sign for the remaining subjects. These two critical slides are shown in Figure 4.1. The remaining slides show the Datsun turning right and knocking down a pedestrian who is crossing at the crosswalk. Immediately after viewing the slides, the subjects answered a series of 20 questions. For half of the subjects, Question 17 was, 'Did another car pass the red Datsun while it was stopped at the stop sign?' The remaining subjects were asked the same question with the words 'stop sign' replaced by 'yield sign.' The assignment of subjects to conditions produced a factorial design in which half of the subjects received consistent or correct information, whereas the other half received misleading or incorrect information. All subjects then participated in a 20-min filler activity, which required them to read an unrelated short story and answer some questions about it. Finally, a yes–no recognition test was administered

Figure 4.1 Critical slides used in the acquisition series.

either immediately or 1 week later. The two critical slides (i.e., those containing the stop and yield signs) were randomly placed in the recognition series in different positions for different groups of subjects.

The results indicated that relative to the case in which consistent information is received, misleading information resulted in significantly fewer hits (correct recognitions of the slide actually seen) and slightly more false alarms (false recognitions of the slide not actually seen). With misleading information, the percentage of hits was 71 and the percentage of false alarms was 70, indicating that subjects had zero ability to discriminate the sign they actually saw from the sign they did not see.

Some aspects of the data from this study preclude a clear interpretation of the results and beg for a variation in design. Most of the subjects responded 'yes' to the slide shown first in the recognition series, even though the opposite sign had been seen and mentioned in the questionnaire. This indicates that the two critical slides are so similar that subjects failed to make any distinction between them. Perhaps when the second slide appeared, some subjects responded 'yes' again, thinking it was the same slide, while others felt obliged to respond 'no,' having already responded 'yes' to the earlier slide. For these reasons, a forced-choice recognition test seemed necessary, since it eliminates the problem of successive recognition tests and forces the subjects to discriminate between the two critical slides.

Overview of the experiments

In Experiment 1, subjects were presented with the acquisition series of slides, an intervening questionnaire, and a final forced-choice recognition test. It is shown that misleading information results in substantially less accurate responding than does consistent information. Next, we consider the possibility that subjects are simply agreeing with the information in their questionnaires, fully remembering what they actually saw. Experiment 2 was actually a demonstration designed to show that the results thus far cannot be explained simply by the demand characteristics of the procedure. In Experiment 3, we asked whether information presented verbally has a different effect depending on whether it is introduced immediately after the initial event (i.e., at the beginning of the retention interval) or just prior to the final test (i.e., at the end of the retention interval). It was found that misleading information has a greater impact when presented just prior to a recognition test rather than just after the initial event. Finally, we addressed the question of whether the verbally presented information actually results in a transformation of an existing representation or whether it is simply a supplementation phenomenon. To answer this issue, one needs to know whether the original sign entered memory in the first place. If not, then the subsequent verbal information may simply introduce a sign where none existed, supplementing the existing memorial representation. If the sign originally did get into memory, the subsequent information has caused either an alteration in the original representation (i.e., one sign replaced the other in memory) or the creation of a new, stronger representation that successfully competes with the original one, rendering the latter so dramatically suppressed as to be, for all intents and purposes, gone. Experiment 4, in conjunction with Experiment 3, indicates that the traffic sign is encoded by most subjects when they view the series of slides. Experiment 5 demonstrates the generality of the findings with other materials.

Experiment 1

Method

Subjects were 195 students from the University of Washington who participated in groups of various sizes. With a few exceptions, the procedure was similar to that used in the pilot experiment. The subjects saw the same series of 30 color slides, seeing each slide for approximately 3 sec. Approximately half of the subjects saw a slide depicting a small red Datsun stopped at a stop sign, whereas the remaining subjects saw the car stopped at a yield sign. Immediately after viewing the acquisition slides, the subjects filled out a questionnaire of 20 questions. For half of the subjects, Question 17 was, 'Did another car pass the red Datsun while it was stopped at the stop sign?' For the other half, the same question was asked with the words 'stop sign' replaced with 'yield sign.' Thus, for 95 subjects, the sign mentioned in the question was the sign that had actually been seen; in other words, the question contained consistent information. For the remaining 100 subjects, the question contained misleading information.

After completing the questionnaire, the subjects participated in a 20-min filler activity that required them to read an unrelated short story and answer some questions about it. Finally, a forced-choice recognition test was administered. Using two slide projectors, 15 pairs of slides were presented, each pair of slides being projected for approximately 8 sec. One member of each pair was old and the other was new. For each pair, the subjects were asked to select the slide that they had seen earlier. The critical pair was a slide depicting the red Datsun stopped at a stop sign and a nearly identical slide depicting the Datsun at a yield sign. The slides that the subjects actually saw varied in the left and right positions.

Results

The percentage of times a subject correctly selected the slide he or she had seen before was 75 and 41, respectively, when the intervening question contained consistent versus misleading information, $Z = 4.72$, $p < .001$. If 50% correct selection is taken to represent chance guessing behavior, subjects given consistent information performed significantly better than chance, $Z = 5.10$, $p < .001$, whereas those given misleading information performed significantly worse than chance, $Z = 1.80$, $p < .05$ (one-tailed test).

Experiment 2

Some time ago, Orne (1962) proposed that certain aspects of any psychological experiment may provide clues, or *demand characteristics*, that permit observant subjects to discern the experimental hypothesis. Obliging subjects may then try to confirm that hypothesis. In the context of the present paradigm, it is possible that some or all the subjects not only remembered what traffic sign they observed but also remembered what sign was presupposed on their questionnaire and then 'went along' with what they believed to be the experimental hypothesis and chose the sign from their questionnaire. A slightly different version of this position would argue that at the time of the final test, subjects said to themselves, 'I think I saw a stop sign, but my questionnaire said "yield sign," so I guess it must have been a yield sign.' Experiment 2 was designed to investigate this possibility.

Method

The method was similar to that of Experiment 1 with a few exceptions. Ninety subjects saw the slide series. Half of them saw a stop sign, and half a yield sign. Immediately after slides, the subjects filled out the questionnaire. For 30 subjects, the critical question was, 'Did another car pass the red Datsun while it was stopped at the intersection?' In other words, it did not mention a sign. For 30 other subjects, the critical question mentioned a stop sign, and for the remaining 30 it mentioned a yield sign. Thus, for one third of the subjects, the key question contained a true presupposition; for one third, the presupposition was false; and for the remaining one third, the question made no reference to a sign at all. A 20-min filler activity occurred, followed by a forced-choice recognition test.

Finally, the subject was given a 'debriefing questionnaire.' It stated,

The study in which you have just been involved was designed to determine the effects of subsequent information on eye-witness testimony. In the beginning, you saw a series of slides which depicted an accident. One of the slides contained either a stop sign or a yield sign. Later you were given a questionnaire. One of the questions on this questionnaire was worded to assume that you had seen either a stop sign or a yield sign or else it contained no information about what kind of sign you saw.

Please indicate which sign you think you saw and what was assumed on your questionnaire.

	My Questionnaire
I Saw	Mentioned
A stop sign	A stop sign
A yield sign	A yield sign
	No sign

This final debriefing questionnaire permitted a subject to claim, for example, that he or she had seen a stop sign but that the questionnaire had mentioned a yield sign. In other words, it gave the subjects the opportunity to be completely 'insightful' about their condition in the experiment.

Results

Of the 90 subjects who took the forced-choice recognition test, 53 chose the correct sign; 37 chose the incorrect sign. As in the previous experiment, accuracy depended on whether the subject had been given consistent, misleading, or no information on the intervening questionnaire. This relationship can be seen in Table 4.1.

Table 4.1   Data from Experiment 2

Information given	Incorrect subjects on forced-choice test		Correct subjects on forced-choice test	
	n	% correct on debriefing questionnaire	n	% correct on debriefing questionnaire
Consistent	9	22	21	52
Misleading	17	12	13	31
None	11	9	19	42
Weighted *M*		14		43

The subjects who chose the correct sign during the forced-choice test were more than three times as likely as incorrect subjects to be completely correct on the debriefing questionnaire. Overall, 43% of the subjects choosing the correct sign accurately responded to the debriefing questionnaire, whereas only 14% of the incorrect subjects were completely accurate, $Z = 2.96$, $p < .01$. Again, whether the subjects responded accurately to the debriefing questionnaire depended on whether they had been given consistent, misleading, or no information on their intervening questionnaires.

Of central concern was the performance of subjects who had been given misleading information and who had subsequently chosen incorrectly on their forced-choice test. For example, they saw a stop sign, read that it was a yield sign, and subsequently chose the yield sign on the forced-choice test. These subjects were the ones who may have been acting the way the experimenter wanted them to act. They may have been deliberately choosing the sign mentioned on their questionnaire although fully remembering what they saw. Yet, when given the debriefing questionnaire that afforded them the opportunity to say, 'I think I saw the stop sign, but my questionnaire said yield,' only 12% did so.

Experiment 3

The issue that motivated Experiment 3 was whether the information introduced subsequent to an event has a different impact when it is introduced immediately after the event than when it is introduced just prior to the final test. To determine this, we varied the time interval between the initial slides and the final forced-choice test. The intervening questionnaire was either presented immediately after the acquisition slides or it was delayed until just prior to the final test.

Method

Subjects were 648 students from the University of Washington who either participated for course credit or were paid for their participation. They participated in groups of various sizes.

The procedure was nearly identical to that used in Experiments 1 and 2, with the major variations being the retention interval and the time of the intervening questionnaire. Subjects saw each acquisition slide for approximately 3 sec. Half saw the key slide that contained a stop sign, and half saw a yield sign. A questionnaire was administered, followed by a forced-choice recognition test. The forced-choice test occurred after a retention interval of either 20 min, 1 day, 2 days, or 1 week, with 144 subjects tested at each interval. Half of the subjects at each retention interval answered the questionnaire immediately after viewing the acquisition slides (immediate questionnaire), and the other half answered it just before the final forced-choice test (delayed questionnaire). In addition, 72 subjects saw the slides, received the questionnaire immediately afterward, and immediately after that were given the forced-choice test. For purposes of analysis, we consider this group to have been tested at a retention interval of zero.[1]

Except at the zero retention interval, all subjects read a short, unrelated 'filler' story for 20 min and then answered some questions about it. Subjects who were given the immediate questionnaire completed the filler activity after answering the questionnaire. Subjects who were given the delayed questionnaire completed the filler activity after viewing the acquisition slides.

Question 17 on the questionnaire was the critical question. It mentioned either a stop sign, a yield sign, or no sign at all. Equal numbers of subjects received each version. Thus, one third of the subjects were given consistent information, one third were given misleading information, and one third were given no information at all relevant to a traffic sign.

In the final forced-choice recognition test, subjects were asked to choose the slide they had seen before and give a confidence rating from 1 to 3, where 1 indicated the subject was sure of the answer and 3 indicated a guess.

Results and discussion

Proportions of correct responses as a function of retention interval are displayed separately for subjects in different conditions in Figure 4.2. The data for subjects tested at a retention interval of zero appear twice in Figure 4.2, once under immediate questionnaire and once under delayed questionnaire, because the questionnaire occurred, by definition, both immediately after the slides and just prior to the final test. In a sense, it was both an immediate and a delayed questionnaire.

Before presenting statistical analyses, we shall point out some major observations. First, for both the immediate and delayed questionnaire, longer retention intervals led to worse performance. Type of information given also had an effect: relative to a control in which subjects were given no information, consistent information improved their performance and misleading information hindered it. The functions obtained when no relevant information was given show the usual forgetting over time. By 2 days, subjects were performing at chance level. Immediately after viewing the slides, however, there was relatively good memory for them (up to 87% correct).

The first analysis considered only the immediate-questionnaire data. A 5 (retention invervals × 3 (types of information) analysis of variance of the arc sine transformed proportions was conducted (Mosteller and Tukey, 1949, p. 189). All F tests reported here are with $MS_e = .01$ and $p < .01$, unless otherwise indicated. The analysis showed that longer retention intervals led

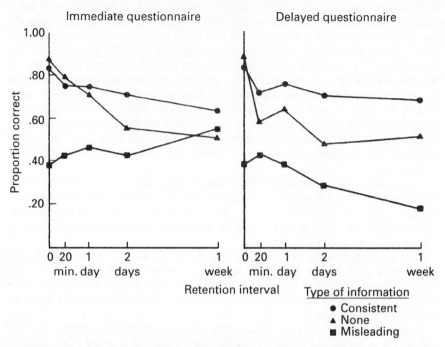

Figure 4.2 Proportion of correct responses as a function of retention interval displayed separately for subjects given an immediate questionnaire and subjects given a delayed questionnaire in Experiment 3. (The curve parameter is the type of information the subject received during the retention interval.)

to less accurate performance, $F(4, \infty) = 5.67$. Further, the type of information to which a subject was exposed affected accuracy, $F(2, \infty) = 50.19$, and there was an interaction between these factors, $F(8, \infty) = 5.19$. A test for monotonic trend for the subjects who were given consistent information yielded a significant trend, $F(1, \infty) = 10.38$. Similarly, the trend was significant for subjects given inconsistent and no information, $F(1, \infty) = 4.43$ and $F(1, \infty) = 43.13$, respectively.

The second analysis considered the data from subjects who received a delayed questionnaire. A 5 × 3 analysis of variance of the arc sine transformed proportions indicated that longer retention intervals led to less accurate performance, $F(4, \infty) = 13.37$. Type of information and the interaction were also significant, $F(2, \infty) = 90.91$, and $F(8, \infty) = 2.98$, respectively. Again, the monotonic trends for each of the three types of information also reached significance: $F(1, \infty) = 5.92$ for subjects given consistent information, 14.05 for inconsistent information, and 35.85 for no information (all *ps* < .05).

Consistent information. Not surprisingly, when a subject is exposed to information that essentially repeats information previously encoded, recognition performance is enhanced. With an immediate questionnaire, the visual and verbal repetitions are massed, whereas with a delayed questionnaire, they are spaced. Whereas in most memory tasks, successive repetitions affect memory less than do repetitions that are spaced apart in time (Hintzman, 1976), this outcome was not obtained in the present experiment. A popular explanation for the spacing effect is in terms of voluntary attention. The subject chooses to pay less attention to the second occurrence of an item when it closely follows the first occurrence than he does when the interval between the two is longer. In the present case, it appears as if the subject may have paid more attention to the second occurrence when it closely followed the first, resulting in memory enhancement that was able to survive longer retention intervals.

Misleading information. When misleading information occurs immediately after an event, it has a different effect than when it is delayed until just prior to the test. The immediate procedure results in a nearly monotonically increasing function, whereas the delayed procedure leads to a monotonically decreasing function. This result makes intuitive sense. When false information is introduced immediately after an event, it has its greatest impact soon. Therefore, when the test was immediate, such subjects performed well below chance. But after an interval of, say, 1 week, both the event and the misleading information apparently had faded such that the subject performed near chance levels. On the other hand, when the misleading information was delayed, it was able to influence the subjects' choice more effectively as the delay increased. Presumably, the weaker the original trace, the easier it is to alter.

To see more clearly the effects of an immediate versus a delayed questionnaire, we excluded the data for subjects tested at a retention interval of zero and collapsed the data over the four remaining retention intervals. The results of these computations are shown in Figure 4.3. The proportion correct is presented as a function of the type of information given, with the immediate versus delayed questionnaire data shown separately. It is again evident that the delayed questionnaire had a larger impact than the immediate one when the subjects were given misleading information: when misleading information was introduced immediately after the incident, 46% of the subjects were correct; however, when it was delayed until just prior to the final test, that percentage dropped to 31.5%, $Z = 2.06$, $p < .05$.

We should mention here that Dooling and Christiaansen (1977) have found a different effect of misleading information. They found that such information had a greater effect on memory distortion when it occurred before the retention interval rather than afterward. As these investigators rightfully point out, there are so many differences between their experimental paradigm and ours that it is difficult to essay a resolution of the difference in results. Our subsequent manipulation focuses on one particular detail of the material to be remembered, and a peripheral detail at that. In Dooling and Christiaansen's task, the subsequent information consists of the name of a famous person about whom subjects already have a great deal of knowledge stored in memory. Unfortunately, neither they nor we have been able to come up with an appealing hypothesis for why these paradigmatic differences should lead to different results.

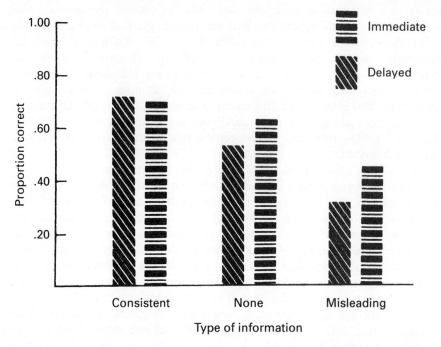

Figure 4.3 Proportion of correct responses for subjects given different types of information in Experiment 3. (Data for subjects given an immediate questionnaire are shown separately from data for those given a delayed questionnaire.)

Surprisingly, it appears that even when the questionnaire contained no information relevant to the traffic sign, performance on this key item was somewhat better when subjects were interrogated immediately after the event rather than later. Although this difference failed to reach significance by a Z test involving all four retention intervals, $Z = 1.41$, $.10 < p < .20$, it held up for those retention intervals that showed some memory performance above chance. For the 20-min and 1-day intervals, the immediate questionnaire had about a 15% advantage over the delayed. Perhaps the early questionnaire permitted the subjects to review the incident in order to answer questions about it, and in the course of this review, some of them refreshed their memory for the traffic sign even though they were not specifically queried on this detail.

Confidence ratings.   Recall that subjects indicated how confident they were in their responses, circling '1' if they felt certain and '3' if they were guessing. The rating '2' was used for intermediate levels of confidence. Figure 4.4 illustrates how these ratings varied as a function of the type of information a subject was exposed to, the timing of that information, and whether the response was correct or incorrect.

A $3 \times 2 \times 2$ unweighted-means analysis of variance (Winer, 1962, p. 241) was performed on all but the zero retention-interval data. This analysis included the 576 subjects who were unambiguously given either an immediate or a delayed questionnaire. The error for all F tests is .493, and $p < .01$ unless otherwise indicated.

Type of information affected confidence, $F(2, 564) = 9.15$, as did whether the subject responded correctly or incorrectly, $F(1, 564) = 23.64$; in other words, subjects were more confident if correct than if incorrect (1.92 vs. 2.18). The main effect of timing (whether the questionnaire was answered immediately or whether it was delayed) was not significant ($F < 1$). The Response Accuracy × Type of Information interaction was marginally significant, $F(2, 564) = 2.71, .05 < p < .10$, while the other two-way interactions were not ($Fs < 1$). Finally, the triple interaction reached significance, $F(2, 564) = 5.01$. It is evident from Figure 4.4 that a subject's confidence is boosted by being told anything, whether it is true or not. Further, delaying misleading information raises confidence in incorrect responses above the corresponding value associated with correct responses.

To summarize the major results, there appear to be two discernible consequences of exposing a subject to misleading information. First, the likelihood is lowered that a subject will correctly recognize the object previously seen. This is particularly true if the information is introduced just prior to the final test. Second, the misleading information affects a subject's confidence rating. Generally subjects are more confident of their correct responses than their incorrect ones. However, when exposed to delayed misleading information, they are less confident of their correct responses.

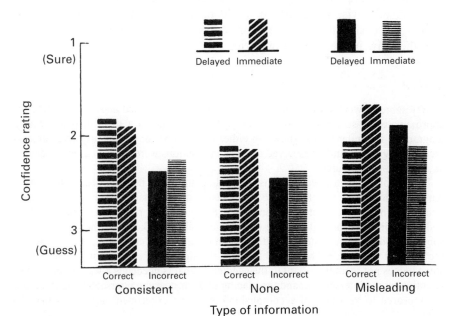

Figure 4.4 Mean confidence ratings as a function of type of information given, immediate versus delayed questionnaire, and correct versus incorrect responses in Experiment 3.

Experiment 4

Loftus (1975) argued that the information contained in a questionnaire influences subsequent choices because that information is integrated into an existing memorial representation and thereby causes an alteration of that representation. This view assumes that when a person sees the initial event, the items of interest are actually encoded at the time of viewing. In the context of the present stimuli, this position would hold that when a person sees a stop sign, for example, the sign gets into memory (i.e., is encoded). If a subsequent questionnaire reports that the sign was a yield sign, that information might, according to this view, enter the memory system and cause an alteration of the original representation. The subject can now be assumed to have a yield sign incorporated into his memorial representation of the event.

A question arises as to whether the stop sign actually got into memory in the first place. If it did not, then the subsequent verbal information may simply be introducing a sign where none existed. In other words, the existing memorial representation of the accident is simply supplemented. On the other hand, if the sign was encoded into memory, then the subsequent information may have caused what is functionally a transformation of the original representation. Thus, it is theoretically important to determine whether subjects attend to and/or encode the sign. A portion of the data from Experiment 3 suggests that people do. Notice in Figure 4.2 that when no information is contained in the questionnaire, subjects show some ability to discriminate the sign they saw from the one they did not, up to and including a retention inverval of 1 day. For these subjects, the sign must have been encoded, otherwise performance would have been at chance level. Experiment 4 was designed to provide a further test of whether subjects encoded the sign they saw in the acquisition series.

Method

Ninety subjects were shown the same series of slides described above, each slide for approximately 3 sec. Following the series, they were given a sheet of paper with a diagram on it similar to that shown in either Figure 4.5A or 4.5B. Forty-five subjects received Figure 5A and 45 received 5B. The instructions were to fill in as many details as could be remembered.

The reason for using two versions of the diagram stems from an observation made during a pilot study. Recall that the slides depict a red Datsun traveling along a side street toward an intersection. From there the car turns right and knocks over a pedestrian in the crosswalk. If the diagram contains no sketch of the car (5A), the subjects tend to concentrate their attention on details at the crosswalk, which is where the accident took place. They may have seen the sign at the corner, but do not draw it, since it does not seem important to the accident. What is needed is a way to focus their attention on the intersection, and the placing of a car near the intersection as in Figure 5B appeared to be a way of accomplishing this. The experiment lasted less than 10 min.

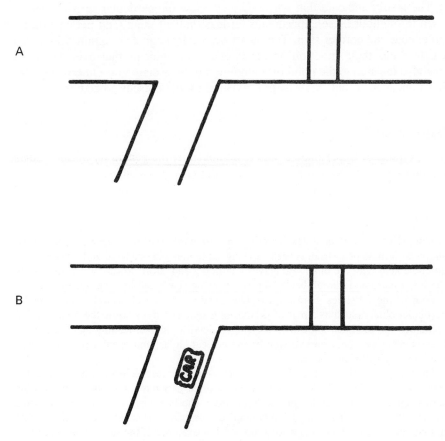

Figure 4.5 Diagrams used in Experiment 4.

Results

For purposes of analysis, we counted as correct the drawing made by any subject who either drew the sign he had seen or wrote its name. Over all, 45% of the subjects indicated the correct sign. Of those subjects given the outline without a car (Figure 4.5A), 36% correctly drew the stop sign, while 32% correctly drew the yield sign. Of those subjects given the outline with a car (Figure 4.5B), 60% correctly drew the stop sign, while 52% correctly drew the yield sign. An analysis of variance of the arc sine transformed proportions indicated that more subjects depicted a sign when a car was used to direct their attention to the intersection (Figure 5B) than when the diagram contained no car (5A), $F(1, \infty) = 19.94$, $MS_e = .01$. Whether the subject had actually seen a stop sign or a yield sign did not significantly affect the likelihood of drawing the correct sign, $F(1, \infty) = 1.51$, $MS_e = .01$, $p < .20$. The interaction also failed to reach significance ($F < 1$). Three of the 50 subjects who saw a yield sign incorrectly drew a stop sign in their diagram; none of the 'stop sign' subjects drew a yield sign.

The results indicate that when subjects view the particular series of slides used throughout these experiments, at least half of them (and perhaps more) do encode the correct sign. The data from subjects given diagram 5B (with a car to focus their attention on the intersection) indicate that over half have encoded the sign to the point of including it in their diagrams. Others may also have encoded it, but this was not revealed by the present procedure.

Experiment 5

The purpose of Experiment 5 was to demonstrate the generality of our studies beyond the single-stimulus pair used in the previous studies.

Method

A new series of 20 color slides depicting an auto–pedestrian accident was shown to 80 subjects. A male pedestrian is seen carrying some items in one hand and munching on an apple held with the other. He leaves a building and strolls toward a parking lot. In the lot, a maroon Triumph backs out of a parking space and hits the pedestrian.

Four of the 20 slides were critical. One version of each critical slide contained a particular object (such as a pair of skis leaning against a tree), while the other version contained the identical slide with a changed detail (a shovel leaning against a tree). Each subject saw only one version of the critical slides, and each critical slide was seen equally often across subjects.

Following the slides, which had been seen at a 3-sec rate, subjects completed a 10-min unrelated filler activity. Then they read a three-paragraph description of the slide series supposedly written by another individual who had been given much more time to view the slides. The description contained four critical sentences that either did or did not mention the incorrect critical object. For example, if the subject had seen skis leaning against a tree, his statement might include a sentence that mentioned 'the shovel leaning against the tree.' The statements were designed so that the mention or nonmention of a critical incorrect detail was counterbalanced over subjects for the four critical items.

After an interval of 10 min, subjects were given a forced-choice recognition test. Using two slide projectors, 10 pairs of slides were presented. The 4 critical pairs were randomly intermixed with the remaining filler pairs. One member of each pair had been seen before, whereas the other had not. The slides that the subject had actually seen varied in the left and right positions.

Results

The percentage of times a correct selection occurred was 55.3 when the intervening statement contained misleading information and 70.8 when it contained no information. For purposes of analysis, two proportions were calculated for each of the 4 critical slide pairs. One was the proportion of correct selections when misleading information had intervened, and the other, when no information had intervened. At t test for related measures indicated that the mean percentages (given above) were statistically different from each other, $t(3) = 9.34$, $SE_{diff} = 1.66$.

Discussion

The analysis of Experiment 5 permits us to generalize our findings beyond the single stop-sign–yield-sign stimulus pair. In the present experiment, subjects who saw a slide containing a particular detail, A, but who were given the information that the slide contained detail B, were subsequently more likely than control subjects to select on a forced-choice recognition test a slide containing B rather than a slide with A.

Note that even with misleading information, subjects were correct about 55% of the time, a figure that is much higher than the approximately 42% figure obtained with the stop–yield stimuli in Experiment 3 after a comparable retention interval. There is probably good reason for this. Any particular object, such as a shovel, can assume many forms. The particular shovel that any subject imagines while reading the story may not agree with the version shown during the recognition test. A subject can then successfully reject the slide containing the shovel, not because he or she recognizes the other slide (containing the skis) but because of not having seen the particular shovel presented during the recognition test.

With common traffic signs, this would not tend to happen. If a subject imagines a stop sign while answering a question that mentions a stop sign, the imagined sign will certainly match the stop sign that would be presented during the recognition test.

General discussion

When a person witnesses an important event, he or she is often exposed to related information some time afterward. The purpose of the present experiments was to investigate how the subsequent information influences memory for the original event.

In the pilot experiment, subjects saw a series of slides depicting an accident, and afterwards they were exposed to a questionnaire that contained either consistent or misleading information about a particular aspect of the accident. The misleading information caused less accurate responding on a subsequent yes–no recognition test. Similarly, in Experiment 1, misleading information resulted in poorer performance on a forced-choice recognition test. For example, in one condition, subjects saw a stop sign but a subsequent question suggested it was actually a yield sign. Some time later they were given a forced-choice test and asked to choose the sign they thought they had seen. Over half of these subjects incorrectly chose the yield sign.

It has been suggested that the reason this happens is that when the misleading information is presented, it is introduced into the memorial representation for the accident and causes an alteration of that representation. Another interpretation is that subjects are simply agreeing with the information contained in their questionnaires, even though they actually remember what they saw. This is a demand-characteristics explanation. Experiment 2 showed that when subjects were told that they might have been exposed to misleading information and were asked to state whether they thought they had, most of them persisted in claiming that they had seen the incorrect item.

A second interpretation of the forced-choice results is that the original sign information may not have been encoded in the first place. If it had not been encoded, then the subsequent question may have introduced a sign where none existed. In other words, the phenomenon may be one of supplementation. On the other hand, if the sign got into the original memory (i.e., was encoded), then the subsequent information caused either an alteration in the original representation or the creation of a new, stronger representation that competed with the original representation. Experiment 4 showed that at least half of the subjects encoded the initial sign to the point where it was included in a drawing they made of the incident.

The paradigm used throughout this research involves two critical time intervals: the time between the initial event and the presentation of subsequent information, and the time between the latter and the final test for recollection of the event. In Experiment 3, these intervals were examined. Subjects received their final test after a retention interval of 0 min, 20 min, 1 day, 2 days, or 1 week. The subsequent information was introduced either immediately after the initial event or just prior to the final test. The usual retention-interval results were observed: poorer performance after long intervals than after short ones. Of major interest was the finding that misleading information had a larger impact if presented just prior to a recognition test rather than just after the initial event.

We have noted two interpretations for our results, namely that either the subsequent information alters the original memory or both the original and the new information reside in memory, and the new competes with the old. Unfortunately, this extremely important issue cannot be resolved with the present data. Those who wish to maintain that the new information produces an alteration cannot prove that the earlier information will not one day spontaneously reappear. Those who wish to hold that new and old information both exist in memory will argue that a person who responds on the basis of new information alone does so because the proper retrieval cue or the right technique has not been used. The value of the present data lies in the fact that they clear up a number of alternative explanations for previously published phenomena. Furthermore, they indicate something about the conditions under which new information is more or less likely to affect accuracy.

The present work bears some resemblance to earlier work on the influence of verbal labels on memory for visually presented form stimuli. Much of the earlier work was designed to test the Gestalt hypothesis that progressive memory changes in the direction of a 'better' figure occur autonomously. Riley (1962), in an excellent review of that earlier literature, concluded that the hypothesis of autonomous change is probably not testable. Despite this drawback, the work on verbal labels was useful in revealing that reproductions and recognition memory (Carmichael *et al.*, 1932; Daniel, 1972) of simple forms were affected by the labels applied to those forms. The present work represents a much needed extension in that it reveals that these effects occur not only with artificial forms but also with highly naturalistic scenes under conditions that have a high degree of ecological validity. Further, the present work convincingly demonstrates both the integration of information from more than one source into memory and the use of that information to reconstruct a 'memory' that was never actually experienced.

Notes

1 A better design would have orthogonally varied the two critical intervals, namely, the interval between the slides and the questionnaire and the interval between the questionnaire and the recognition test. However, such a design would have required nearly three times as many subjects to obtain reasonably stable proportions in each cell, and the authors' colleagues were already becoming distressed at the rapidity with which these experiments were depleting the psychology department's subject pool. We doubt that any conclusions would be changed as a result of the fuller design.

References

Carmichael, L., Hogan, H. P., and Walter, A. A. An experimental study of the effect of language on the reproduction of visually perceived form. *Journal of Experimental Psychology*, 1932, *15*, 73–86.

Daniel, T. C. Nature of the effect of verbal labels on recognition memory for form. *Journal of Experimental Psychology*, 1972, *96*, 152–157.

Dooling, D. J., and Christiaansen, R. E. Episodic and semantic aspects of memory for prose. *Journal of Experimental Psychology: Human Learning and Memory*, 1977, *3*, 428–436.

Hintzman, D. L. Repetition and memory. In G. H. Bower (Ed.), *The psychology of learning and motivation* (Vol. 10). New York: Academic Press, 1976.

Kant, I. *Critique of pure reason* (Translated by J. M. D. Meiklejohn). London: George Bell, 1887. (Originally published, 1781.)

Loftus, E. F. Leading questions and the eyewitness report. *Cognitive Psychology*, 1975, *7*, 560–572.

Loftus, E. F., Salzberg, P. M., Burns, H. J., and Sanders, R. K. *Destruction of a visual memory by verbal information*. Paper presented at the annual meeting of the Psychonomic Society, Denver, November 1975.

Mosteller, F., and Tukey, J. W. The uses and usefulness of binomial probability paper. *Journal of the American Statistical Association*, 1949, *44*, 174–212.

Orne, M. T. On the social psychology of the psychological experiment: With particular reference to demand characteristics and their implications. *American Psychologist*, 1962, *17*, 776–783.

Pezdek, K. Cross-modality semantic integration of sentence and picture memory. *Journal of Experimental Psychology: Human Learning and Memory*, 1977, *3*, 515–524.

Riley, D. A. Memory for form. In L. Postman (Ed.), *Psychology in the making*. New York: Knopf, 1962.

Winer, B. J. *Statistical principles in experimental design*. New York: McGraw-Hill, 1962.

5   Michael McCloskey and Maria Zaragoza

'Misleading Postevent Information and Memory for Events: Arguments and Evidence against Memory Impairment Hypotheses'

Reprinted in full from: *Journal of Experimental Psychology: General* **114**, 1–16 (1985)

The claim that a person's memory for an event may be altered by information encountered after the event (e.g., Loftus, 1979a, 1979b; Loftus and Loftus, 1980) has rekindled interest in basic questions about forgetting and has contributed to the growing concern about the potential unreliability of eyewitness testimony. More generally, the claim has been influential in shaping current conceptions of memory, particularly the view that memory representations are highly mutable and often contain distortions or even gross inaccuracies.

The basis for the claim is a series of studies conducted by Elizabeth Loftus and her colleagues (e.g., Loftus, 1977; Loftus, 1979a; Loftus and Greene, 1980; Loftus *et al.*, 1978). In a typical study, subjects first view a sequence of slides depicting an event such as a traffic accident. The subjects then receive additional information about the event, such as a written narrative account of what took place. For subjects in the *misled* condition, the narrative provides misleading information about a detail from the slide sequence. For example, a stop sign that appeared in the slides might be described in the narrative as a yield sign. For subjects in the *control* condition, the narrative provides no specific information about the critical detail. Table 5.1 summarizes the design.

After presentation of the narrative, subjects in both conditions are given a two-alternative forced-choice recognition test on what they saw in the slides. For the question about the critical detail (e.g., What type of sign was at the intersection?), the choices are the item that was in the slides (stop sign), and the item presented to misled subjects as misleading postevent information (yield sign).

The consistent finding is that misled subjects perform more poorly than control subjects on the test question about the critical item. Loftus and her colleagues have interpreted this misleading information effect to mean that misleading information 'overwrites' or replaces the original information in the representation of the event, so that the original information is irrevocably lost from memory, (e.g., Loftus, 1979a, 1979b, 1981; Loftus and Loftus, 1980; Loftus *et al.*, 1978). Recently, several researchers (e.g., Bekerian and

Table 5.1 Design of a typical postevent information experiment

Condition	Slides	Narrative	Test
Control	Stop	—	Stop versus Yield
Misled	Stop	Yield	Stop versus Yield

Bowers, 1983; Christiaansen and Ochalek, 1983) have questioned this interpretation, contending that the original information is not lost from memory, but is merely rendered inaccessible (i.e., nonretrievable).

In this chapter we suggest that misleading postevent information has no effect on memory for the original event. In other words, we argue that misleading information neither erases original information nor renders it inaccessible. In developing this argument, we first show that the basic finding of poorer misled than control performance does not imply that misleading information causes any sort of memory impairment. In fact, we argue that the procedure used in previous studies is unsuited for assessing effects of misleading information on memory. We then introduce a more appropriate procedure, present several experiments using this procedure, and conclude from the results that presentation of misleading postevent information has no effect on subjects' ability to remember what they originally saw. Next, we review several recent postevent information studies that seem to conflict with our conclusion, showing that these studies do not in fact pose problems for our position. Finally, we discuss the implications of our conclusions for broader issues concerning the workings of memory.

The misleading information effect reconsidered

In this section we show that the misleading information effect does not imply that misleading postevent information impairs memory for the original event. In making this point we will continue to use the stop sign/yield sign experiment as an example. However, the argument we develop is a general one that applies to all of the studies demonstrating misleading information effects (e.g., Loftus, 1975, 1977; Loftus and Palmer, 1974).

Consider first how the subjects in the control group will perform on the recognition test. At the time of the test some of the control subjects will remember seeing a stop sign (i.e., they will be able to access information specifying that the sign was a stop sign). These subjects should uniformly choose the correct response on the test. However, some control subjects will not remember the sign, either because they never encoded it, or because they forgot it between the initial presentation and the test.[1] (Of course, any forgetting by control subjects can have nothing to do with the presentation of misleading information, because these subjects are not exposed to misleading information.) On the stop sign versus yield sign test, the control subjects who do not remember the stop sign will have to guess and therefore should be correct 50% of the time.[2]

Imagine a hypothetical situation in which 40% of the control subjects remember the stop sign and 60% do not. As shown in the upper portion of Table 5.2, the overall percentage correct for the control group in this situation should be 40% (all of the subjects who remember the stop sign) plus 30% (half of the subjects who do not remember the sign), or 70%.

The usual interpretation for the poorer performance in the misled condition than in the control condition is that the percentage of subjects who remember the original information is lower in the misled condition. In our example, this

Table 5.2 Expected test performance for control and misled conditions in a hypothetical situation

Memory state for original information	Percentage of subjects in memory state	Expected performance on test
	Control condition	
Remember	40%	100% correct
Don't remember	60%	50% correct
Total percentage correct		70% (40% + 30%)
	Misled condition	
Remember	40%	100% correct
Don't remember	60%	25% correct
Total percentage correct		55% (40% + 15%)
	Misled condition	
Remember	40%	75% correct
Don't remember	60%	25% correct
Total percentage correct		45% (30% + 15%)

interpretation would say that fewer than 40% of the misled subjects remembered the stop sign (because the misleading information 'erased' the stop sign representation, or rendered it inaccessible). It is certainly true that if fewer misled subjects than control subjects remember the original information, performance will be worse in the misled condition. However, even if the percentage of subjects who remember the original information is the same in both conditions, we still expect poorer performance in the misled condition.

Assume that the misleading information has no effect on the misled subjects's ability to remember what they originally saw, so that in the misled condition, as in the control condition, 40% of the subjects remember the stop sign and 60% do not. In addition, assume for the moment that the misled subjects who remember the stop sign will give the correct response on the test. Consider, though, the misled subjects who do not remember the stop sign. Will these subjects, like the corresponding control subjects, simply guess and so be correct 50% of the time? Clearly not. Subjects who do not remember what they saw – stop sign – but do remember what they read in the narrative – yield sign – will presumably choose the yield sign on the test and so will be systematically incorrect. Of course, subjects who remember neither the original information nor the misleading information will guess on the test. However, as long as any subjects who do not remember the stop sign do remember the yield sign, the overall level of performance for misled subjects who do not remember the original information will be lower than the corresponding control level of 50%. Consequently, performance will be worse in the misled condition than in the control condition.

The middle portion of Table 5.2 shows an example in which half of the misled subjects who do not remember the stop sign do remember the yield sign. In this example, the overall performance level for the misled condition is 55%, considerably below the control level of 70%.

Thus, even if misleading information has no effect on the subjects' ability to remember what they originally saw, performance will be worse in the misled condition than in the control condition. The reason is that misleading information will bias the responses of subjects who, for reasons unrelated to the presentation of misleading information, fail to remember what they originally saw. All that is required for the misleading information effect to occur is that (a) some subjects fail to remember the original information for reasons unrelated to the presentation of misleading information (this will be the case whenever control performance is below ceiling) and (b) some misled subjects who fail to remember the original information do remember the misleading information.

There is also another factor that may contribute to poorer misled than control performance even if misleading information has no effect on subjects' ability to remember the original information. We initially assumed that all of the misled subjects who remembered the original information would choose the correct response on the test. However, some subjects who remember both the original information (stop sign) and the misleading information (yield sign) may choose the latter on the test. For example, a subject who thinks that the slides showed a stop sign, but also thinks that the narrative described the sign as a yield sign, might reason that the experimenter who prepared the narrative must have known what was in the slides, and hence that the sign must have been a yield sign. Thus, misled subjects who remember the original information may be less than 100% correct on the test.

The lower portion of Table 5.2 revises the middle example to include this second potential source of misled–control differences not attributable to effects of misleading information on memory for the original event. It is assumed that half of the subjects who remember the original information also remember the misleading information and that half of the subjects who remember both pieces of information choose the incorrect alternative on the test. Under these assumptions the expected performance in the misled condition is 45% correct, much lower than the 70% expected for the control condition.

The finding of poorer performance in misled conditions than in control conditions does not, then, imply that presentation of misleading information impairs subjects' ability to remember what they originally saw.[3] The procedure used in previous studies is simply unsuited for determining whether misleading information impairs memory for the original event. In the following section we describe a modified procedure that permits clearer inferences about the effects of misleading information on memory.

The modified test procedure

The modified procedure is the same as the original procedure except for one crucial change in the recognition test phase. However, we will use a new example to explain the new procedure. Suppose that subjects first view a sequence of slides, one of which shows a man holding a hammer (the critical item). The subjects then read a narrative describing the event depicted in the slides. In the control condition the narrative gives no specific information

Table 5.3   The original test procedure and the modified test procedure

Condition	Slides	Narrative	Original test	Modified test
Control	Hammer	–	Hammer versus Screwdriver	Hammer versus Wrench
Misled	Hammer	Screwdriver	Hammer versus Screwdriver	Hammer versus Wrench

about the critical item. In the misled condition the narrative refers to the critical item as a screwdriver. After reading the narrative, the subjects are given a recognition test on what they saw in the slides.

The original test procedure requires subjects to choose between hammer, the originally seen item, and screwdriver, the item presented to the misled subjects as misleading information. In the modified test procedure, the misleading information (screwdriver) is not included as an option on the test. As shown in Table 5.3, subjects are asked instead to choose between the original item (hammer) and a new item (wrench). Unlike the original test procedure, the modified test procedure can be used to determine whether misleading information affects subjects' memory for what they initially saw. If misleading information impairs subjects' ability to remember the original information, then misled subjects should perform more poorly than control subjects. However, if misleading information does not affect memory for the original information, then the control and misled conditions should not differ.

Consider once again the hypothetical situation in which 40% of the subjects in both the control and misled conditions remember the original information (hammer) at the time of the test, and 60% do not. In the control condition all of the subjects who remember the original information should give the correct response on the modified test. The subjects who do not remember what they saw will have to guess, so that half should be correct. Thus, as shown in the top half of Table 5.4, the expected control performance is 40% + 30%, or 70%.

Consider now the subjects in the misled condition. Misled subjects who remember the original information should, like the corresponding control subjects, uniformly be correct on the modified test. The choices on the test are hammer and wrench; screwdriver is not an option. Thus, subjects who remember the original information – hammer – should choose the correct response on the test, whether or not they also remember the misleading information screwdriver.

Misled subjects who do not remember the original information should also perform like the corresponding control subjects. On a hammer versus wrench test, misled subjects who do not remember hammer must guess whether or not they remember the misleading information screwdriver. Thus, half of these subjects should be correct on the test. As shown in Table 5.4, in a situation where 40% of the misled subjects remember the original information and 60% do not, the expected performance is 40% + 30%, or 70%, the same as in the corresponding control condition.

In our implementation of the modified procedure the three versions of a

Table 5.4 Expected control and misled performance with the modified test procedure in a hypothetical situation

Memory state for original information	Percentage of subjects in memory state	Expected performance on test
Control condition		
Remember	40%	100% correct
Don't remember	60%	50% correct
Total percentage correct		70% (40% + 30%)
Misled condition		
Remember	40%	100% correct
Don't remember	60%	50% correct
Total percentage correct		70% (40% + 30%)

critical item (e.g., hammer, wrench, screwdriver) are chosen so that they are all approximately equal in similarity to one another. For example, the similarity of screwdriver to hammer is approximately the same as the similarity of screwdriver to wrench. Thus, a misled subject who does not remember the original information (hammer) but does remember the misleading information (screwdriver) should not be biased toward either of the test alternatives (hammer or wrench). In addition, complete counterbalancing is used. For example, when screwdriver is the misleading information and the test is hammer versus wrench, the correct answer (i.e., the originally seen item) is hammer for some subjects and wrench for others.

In Experiments 1–6 we use the modified test procedure to evaluate the claim that misleading information impairs subjects' ability to remember originally seen material.

Experiments 1–6

Experiments 1–6 differ only in minor details and are in essence six replications of a single experiment. Hence, we report all six experiments together. In each experiment, subjects saw a sequence of slides, read a postevent narrative, and took a written recognition test on what they saw in the slides. The slide sequence contained four critical items that were used to make a within-subjects misled–control manipulation. For each subject the narrative gave misleading information about two of the items, and no information about the other two. Thus, for each subject there were two misled items and two control items.

In each experiment two groups of subjects were tested. Subjects in the *original test* group were tested with the original test procedure to ensure that we could replicate the misleading information effect obtained in previous studies. Subjects in the *modified test* group were tested with the modified test procedure.

Method

Experiment 1

We first describe the method of Experiment 1 and then detail the changes made in Experiments 2–6.

   Subjects. Subjects were 120 undergraduate students at Johns Hopkins University and Towson State University. Sixty subjects were randomly assigned to each of two groups: the original test group and the modified test group.

   Stimuli. The slide sequence was a series of 79 color slides depicting an incident in which a maintenance man enters an office, repairs a chair, finds and steals $20 and a calculator, and leaves. The slide sequence included four critical slides, each showing one of the four critical items. For each critical slide three different versions were prepared. The critical items and the three versions of each were as follows: a coffee jar (Folgers, Maxwell House, Nescafé), a magazine (*Glamour*, *Vogue*, *Mademoiselle*), a soft drink can (Coca-Cola, Seven-Up, Sunkist Orange Soda), and a tool (hammer, wrench, screwdriver). For each critical item each version was presented to one-third of the subjects. For example, one-third of the subjects saw a hammer, one-third saw a wrench, and one-third saw a screwdriver.

   The narrative was a 735-word detailed description of the incident shown in the slides. For each subject the narrative presented misleading information about two of the critical items (misled items) and neutral information about the other two (control items). The assignment of critical items to misled and control conditions was counterbalanced across subjects. Specifically, each version of each critical item served as a control item for half of the subjects to whom it was presented and a misled item for the other half. For example, half of the subjects who saw a hammer in the slides received a narrative referring to it simply as a tool (control condition), and the other half received a narrative referring to it as a wrench or screwdriver (misled condition). Further, for each version of each critical item, the two alternative versions were used equally often as misleading information. For example, for subjects who saw a hammer and were then misled about this item, half received screwdriver as the misleading information, and half received wrench as the misleading information. Except for variations in reference to the critical items, the narrative was the same for all subjects.

   Procedure. Subjects were tested in groups of 4 to 20. As a rationale for the presentation of the slides and narrative, subjects were told that the experiment concerned intuitions about memory. The subjects were informed that they would see a slide sequence depicting an event, and would then read a written description of the event. The task, they were instructed, was to judge whether memory for the event would generally be better with the visual or the verbal mode of presentation. The subjects were told to pay careful attention to both the slides and the narrative.

   The subjects then (a) viewed the slide sequence at a presentation rate of 4s per slide, (b) performed a 10-min unrelated filler task, (c) read the narrative once at their own pace, (d) performed a second 10-min filler task, (e) answered two questions concerning their intuitions about memory and mode of presentation, and (f) completed a 36-item forced choice recognition test. The subjects were told to answer the questions solely on the basis of what they saw in the slides. The instructions indicated that for each question one of the two alternatives was correct.

   All test questions were sentences with a missing word and two alternatives. For example, for the tool critical item, the test question was 'The man slid the calculator beneath a _____ in his tool box.' Thirty-two of the thirty-six questions were fillers, and these were the same for all subjects. The remaining four questions consisted of one question for each of the four critical items. The four critical questions were the same for all subjects, except for variations in the response alternatives. The alternatives were dictated by the test condition (original test or modified test), the version of the item that appeared in the slides, and the version presented as misleading information. For example, for a subject in the modified test condition who saw a hammer in the slides and was presented with screwdriver as misleading information, the test alternatives were hammer and wrench. Across the experiment, the same test alternatives were used for both control and misled critical item questions. Thus, the control and misled conditions differed only in whether the subject received misleading information about an item. For each critical test question, the response alternatives were presented in one order (e.g., hammer, wrench) to half of the subjects, and in the other order (wrench, hammer) to the remaining half.

Experiments 2–6
Experiments 2–6 were identical to Experiment 1, with the following exceptions: (a) in Experiments 2–6 the slides were presented for 5 s each; (b) in Experiments 3–6 subjects read the narrative twice, and the filler task between the narrative and the test was eliminated; and (c) the number of filler items on the recognition test was 6 in Experiments 3 and 5, 16 in Experiment 4, and 32 in Experiment 6.

The number of subjects in the original and modified test groups also varied across experiments. For the modified test condition, the number of subjects was 84 in Experiments 2 and 6, and 72 in Experiments 3–5. For the original test condition, the number of subjects was 84 in Experiment 2, 48 in Experiments 3 and 5, 72 in Experiment 4, and 36 in Experiment 6. (Original test groups were included only to demonstrate the we could obtain a misleading information effect when we used the procedure that was used in previous studies. Large groups were not needed to obtain this effect, and so in some experiments we tested fewer subjects in the original test group than in the modified test group.)

Results

Tables 5.5 and 5.6 present for each of the six experiments the mean percentage correct for control and misled items in the original test and modified test conditions. The minor procedural variations among the six experiments had no discernible effect on the pattern of results in either the original or modified test condition. Hence, we will treat the experiments as six replications of a single study.

The results for the original test condition replicated the findings of previous studies. Averaging across the six experiments, the mean recognition test performance was 37% correct for misled items and 72% correct for control items. In each individual experiment a large misled–control difference was obtained.

Several t tests were performed with subjects as a random effect and with items as a random effect. (For the items analyses, the number of correct responses in the misled condition and the control condition was tabulated for each of the 12 individual versions of critical items: hammer, wrench, screwdriver, and so forth.) In the subjects analyses, the misled–control difference was reliable at the .001 level for each of the six experiments and when the data were collapsed across experiments ($ts \geq 4.0$). In the items

Table 5.5 Percent correct recognition in Experiments 1–6 for misled and control items in the original test condition

Experiment	Misled	Control	Difference
1	40	67	27
2	40	72	32
3	35	70	35
4	42	75	33
5	30	75	45
6	36	75	39
Mean	37	72	35

Table 5.6 Percent correct recognition in Experiments 1–6 for misled and control items in the modified test condition

Experiment	Misled	Control	Difference
1	66	71	5
2	71	77	6
3	77	73	−4
4	74	81	7
5	70	68	−2
6	71	77	6
Mean	72	75	3

analyses, the misled–control difference was reliable at or beyond the .01 level in each experiment and when the data were collapsed across experiments ($ts \geq 3.3$).

In the modified test condition, the pattern of results was quite different. Averaging across the six experiments, recognition test performance was 72% correct in the misled condition and 75% correct in the control condition. In the individual experiments, misled–control differences were consistently very small, ranging from −4% (4% better performance in the misled than in the control condition) to +7%. In subjects analyses and items analyses for the individual experiments, the misled–control difference never approached significance ($ts \leq 1.6$ $ps > .1$). The outcome was the same when the data were collapsed across experiments: $t(443) = 1.4$, $p > .1$, for the subjects analysis and $t(11) = 1.7$, $p > .1$, for the items analysis. Thus, with the modified test, performance in the misled condition did not differ from performance in the control condition.

We conclude from these results that misleading postevent information does not impair subjects' ability to remember what they originally saw. In other words, misleading information neither erases the original information nor renders it inaccessible.

Discussion

How does our conclusion accord with the results of previous studies? We have already shown that the misleading information effect obtained with the original test procedure does not imply that misleading information impairs memory for originally seen material. In the following sections we discuss several recent postevent information studies that appear to conflict with the conclusion we have drawn, showing that because of logical or methodological problems, these studies provide no basis for inferences concerning effects of misleading information on memory and hence pose no problems for our position.

The Weinberg, Wadsworth, and Baron (1983) study

Weinberg *et al.* used a recognition test similar to our modified test, but obtained a different result. Subjects in their study viewed a sequence of slides, one of which showed a yellow yield sign. Postevent information describing the sign as a yield sign (control condition) or a stop sign (misled condition) was then presented. The test consisted of a forced choice between a slide showing a yellow yield sign and a slide showing a red yield sign. Thus, as in our modified test, subjects chose between the originally seen item (yellow yield sign) and a new item (red yield sign). However, in contrast to our findings of no misled–control difference, Weinberg *et al.* found poorer performance in the misled condition (60% correct) than in the control condition (78% correct).

The Weinberg *et al.* results probably reflect not a memory impairment caused by misleading information, but rather an unfortunate choice of items coupled with a failure to counterbalance. Consider the subjects who at the time of the test did not remember what they originally saw. In the control condition these subjects had to guess; the postevent information (yield sign) provided no basis for choosing a particular test alternative. In the misled condition, however, the situation was different. Some misled subjects who did not remember the original information presumably remembered the misleading information (stop sign). Faced with a yellow yield sign versus red yield sign test, it seems likely that many of these subjects would choose the alternative most similar to a stop sign; that is, the red yield sign. Thus, among subjects who did not remember the original information, the misleading information may have created a bias toward selection of the incorrect test alternative. This response bias is simply a milder form of the bias in the original test procedure, where the misleading information is identical, and not merely similar, to the incorrect test alternative.

A bias of this sort will, of course, lead to poorer performance in the misled condition than in the control condition, even if the misleading information has no effect on subjects' ability to remember what they originally saw. Thus, the Weinberg *et al.* results can readily be interpreted without assuming that the misleading postevent information impaired subjects' memory for the original event.

Second-guess studies

In three experiments reported by Loftus (1979a), misled subjects were given a three-alternative forced choice in which the alternatives were the originally seen item (e.g., stop sign), the item presented as misleading information (e.g., yield sign), and a new item (e.g., no-parking sign). The subjects were asked to indicate their first choice and, on the assumption that this choice was wrong, their second guess. The purpose of the second guess was to determine whether any of the subjects who selected the misleading information on the first choice nevertheless had some memory for the original information.

In all three experiments second-guess performance among subjects who initially chose the misleading information was no better than chance. Loftus concluded from these results that none of the subjects who initially selected the misleading information remembered the original information and hence that presentation of misleading information caused original information to be forgotten.

A major problem with this reasoning concerns the leap from the first conclusion – that none of the subjects who initially chose the misleading information remembered the original information – to the second conclusion – that presentation of misleading information caused forgetting of the original information. The second conclusion follows from the first only if it can be assumed that some of the subjects who chose the misleading information on the first choice would have remembered the original information if they had not been misled. However, this 'would-have-remembered' assumption is not justified. Loftus and others have considered the assumption to be a self-evident consequence of the finding of poorer misled than control performance (in studies using the original test procedure). As we have shown, however, this finding does not necessarily mean that any misled subjects who selected the misleading information would have remembered the original information had they not been misled. A misled–control difference could be due entirely to biasing effects of the misleading information on the responses of subjects who, for reasons unrelated to the presentation of this information, did not remember the original information.

To justify the would-have-remembered assumption in a second-guess study, one would have to show that the misled–control difference on the first choice was too large to be accounted for entirely in terms of this response bias and therefore that some misled subjects who otherwise would have remembered the original information must have chosen the misleading information. However, no such demonstration was made in Loftus's second-guess studies. In fact, Loftus did not demonstrate any misled–control difference, because she did not report control-condition data. Thus, in the second-guess studies the set of subjects who initially chose the misleading information may have consisted entirely of subjects who, for reasons unrelated to the presentation of misleading information, did not remember the originally seen item. Consequently, chance performance among these subjects on the second guess does not imply that misleading information caused forgetting of the original information.

The failure to justify the would-have-remembered assumption takes a particularly dramatic form in one of the second-guess studies Loftus (1979a) reports. Subjects saw a slide sequence that included a traffic sign (e.g., a stop sign). One week later, the subjects were given misleading information about the sign (e.g., they were told it was a yield sign). A stop sign versus yield sign versus no-parking sign test was then given, and subjects were asked to indicate both first and second choices. Subjects who selected the misleading information on the first choice performed at chance on the second choice.

The problem with this study is that even before the misleading information was introduced, 1 week after presentation of the slides, all of the subjects may have forgotten the critical sign. In an experiment using the same slide sequence, Loftus *et al.* (1978, Experiment 3) found that control subjects tested 2 days after presentation of the slides performed at chance on recognition of the critical sign. If all of the subjects in the second-guess study had forgotten the critical sign before presentation of the misleading information, any subsequent test − including a second-choice test − would have shown no memory for the originally seen sign. Obviously, such results would not imply that the failure to remember the original sign had anything to do with presentation of misleading information.

The other two second-guess studies described by Loftus (1979a) have serious response bias problems. We will discuss only one of these studies because both have the same flaw. Subjects saw a slide sequence that included a man reading a book. Half of the subjects saw a yellow book, and the other half saw a blue book. Misleading information was then presented − subjects who saw a yellow book were told that it was blue, and subjects who saw a blue book were told that it was yellow. Finally, subjects were asked to indicate their first and second choices on a blue/green/yellow test. Of the subjects who initially chose the misleading information, only 23% chose correctly on the second choice; 77% selected the incorrect color (green). Because second-guess performance was not above chance, Loftus concluded that none of the subjects who initially chose the misleading color remembered the original color and therefore that the misleading color information caused forgetting of the original color.

As in the other second-guess studies, the second part of Loftus's conclusion − that the misleading color caused forgetting of the original color − is unwarranted because of the failure to justify the would-have-remembered assumption. However, in this study the first part of the conclusion − that none of the subjects who initially chose the misleading color remembered the original color − is also unwarranted, because of a response bias problem. Consider, for example, the subjects who saw a yellow book, were told it was blue, and selected blue as their first choice on the blue/green/yellow test. On the second guess these subjects must choose between green (incorrect) and yellow (correct). Any subjects who remember the original color yellow would probably choose correctly on the second choice. What, though, of the subjects who do not remember the original color? Some of these subjects presumably chose blue on the first choice because they remembered the misleading information. We would expect these subjects to show a strong tendency to choose the incorrect color green on the second choice: of the two choices (green and yellow) it is the closer to blue, the color they remember. Hence, subjects who do not remember the original color are likely to perform well below 50% correct. The fact that second-guess performance in Loftus's experiment was well below chance – 23% correct – clearly indicates that response biases of this sort were operating.

When subjects who do not remember the original information are biased toward the incorrect response on the second guess, overall second-guess performance may be at or below chance even if some of the subjects who initially selected the misleading information remember the original information. Thus, it cannot properly be concluded from the second-guess data that none of the subjects who initially chose the misleading color remembered the original color, or that presentation of misleading color information caused forgetting of the original color.

Warning studies

A 'warning' procedure has been used to ask whether misleading information causes original information to be lost from memory, or instead to be rendered inaccessible. Warning studies typically involve three conditions: a control condition, a misled condition, and a misled/warned condition. The control and misled conditions are the same as in a typical study using the original test procedure. The misled/warned condition is identical to the misled condition except that subjects are warned after presentation of misleading information. but before the test, that some (unspecified) details in the postevent information may have been inaccurate.

The rationale for the warning procedure is as follows: if misleading information merely renders the original information inaccessible, then the warning may somehow allow subjects to regain access to this information. A finding of better performance in the misled/warned condition than in the misled condition would imply that the proportion of subjects who could remember (i.e., access) the original information was higher in the former condition, and hence that the warning allowed some misled/warned subjects to recover original information rendered inaccessible by the misleading information. Equal performance in misled/warned and control conditions would imply that the proportion of subjects who remembered the original information was the same in both conditions, and hence that misleading information caused no loss of original information from memory.

This rationale is invalid because it assumes incorrectly that one can determine whether the proportion of subjects who remembered the original information in two conditions of a warning study was the same or different simply by comparing overall performance for the two conditions. The problems with this assumption become apparent when we consider the expected performance in each condition for subjects who remember the original information and subjects who do not (see Table 5.7).

Consider first the subjects who remember (i.e., can access) the original information. In the control condition these subjects should show perfect performance. In the misled condition their performance may be perfect (if all misled subjects who remember the original information choose the correct alternative on the test) or less than perfect (if some misled subjects who

Table 5.7 Expected performance for subjects who do and do not remember the original information

Memory for original information	Condition		
	Control	*Misled*	*Misled/Warned*
Remember	Perfect	Perfect or less than perfect	Perfect or less than perfect
Don't remember	Chance	Below chance	Above chance, chance, or below chance

remember both the original and the misleading information opt for the latter on the test).

In the misled/warned condition the performance of subjects who remember the original information may also be perfect or less than perfect. The warning should reduce any tendency of subjects who remember both the original and misleading information to choose the latter on the test. However, some subjects who remember both pieces of information might still respond incorrectly if, for example, they were unable to remember which item came from the slides and which came from the postevent information.

Consider now the subjects who do not remember the original information. In the control condition these subjects should perform at chance. In the misled condition performance should be below chance, because subjects who remember the misleading information but not the original information should systematically choose the misleading information on the test.

In the misled/warned condition the situation is more complex. Subjects who remember neither the original information nor the misleading information should perform at chance. Consider, though, the subjects who do not remember the original information but do remember the misleading information. Some of these subjects, because they have no recollection of the original information to contradict the misleading information, may opt to accept the misleading information in spite of the warning. These subjects will be uniformly incorrect. However, some subjects who remember the misleading information but not the original information may, because of the warning, reject the misleading information as possibly false. By rejecting an incorrect alternative, these subjects will perform above chance on the test. Depending on the relative proportions of subjects who accept the misleading information in spite of the warning and subjects who reject the misleading information, overall performance among misled/warned subjects who do not remember the original information may be above chance, at chance, or below chance.

The consequence of these considerations is that overall performance data for misled/warned, misled, and control conditions are uninformative with regard to effects of misleading information on memory for originally seen material. Whether or not misleading information causes original information to be lost from memory, and/or to become inaccessible, performance in the misled/warned condition may be worse than, equal to, or even better than performance in the control condition. Similarly, regardless of the effects of the misleading information, misled/warned performance may be better than or equal to misled performance.

This point can be made clear by examining the results of the available warning studies. We will consider only the two studies in which a warning was issued after presentation of misleading postevent information (Greene *et al.* 1982; Christiaansen and Ochalek, 1983). (Experiments in which a warning was given *before* presentation of misleading information – for example, Dodd and Bradshaw, 1980 – have generally not been considered relevant for determining whether misleading information affects memory for the original event, because a prior warning could improve test performance by leading subjects to ignore the misleading information when it is initially presented.)

Christiaansen and Ochalek emphasize the results of analyses focusing on a subset of their data, and we will discuss these results later. However, we will first consider the findings obtained when all of the data are taken into account. In both the Christiaansen and Ochalek study and the Greene *et al.* study, performance was better for misled/warned conditions than for misled conditions, although the difference was significant in only some comparisons. In the Christiaansen and Ochalek study, misled/warned performance was worse than control performance. (In the Greene *et al.* experiment, no control condition was included.)

The finding of better misled/warned than misled performance does not show that the warning allowed some misled/warned subjects to access original information rendered inaccessible by the misleading information, because several alternative interpretations of the result can be offered. To give just one example, the warning may have caused some misled/warned subjects who remembered the misleading information but not the original information to avoid the misleading information on the test, leading to better performance in the misled/warned condition than in the misled condition among subjects who did not remember the original information. The finding of poorer misled/warned than control performance is similarly uninformative.

Let us now consider the findings Christiaansen and Ochalek emphasize in their report. Subjects in their experiments viewed a slide sequence including four critical items. An initial multiple-choice test containing questions about the critical items was then presented. Two days later subjects read a narrative that contained misleading information (misled and misled/warned conditions) or neutral information (control condition) about all four critical items. After reading the narrative, misled/warned subjects were warned that a few unspecified details in the narrative were incorrect. All subjects were then given a final multiple-choice test that included questions about the four critical items.

The data Christiaansen and Ochalek focus on are the final-test responses for those critical-item questions that the subject answered correctly on the initial test (i.e., the test given before presentation of misleading information). When only initially accurate items were considered, performance was as good in the misled/warned condition as in the control condition.

Christiaansen and Ochalek argue from this result that misleading information renders original information inaccessible, but causes no loss of original information from memory. In fact, however, no clear conclusions can be drawn. Restricting the analysis of final-test data to those items that were answered correctly on the initial test should exclude some but not all of the subjects who, at the time of the final test, did not remember the original information. The procedure could not exclude subjects who did not remember the original information at the time of the initial test but selected the correct response by guessing, or subjects who forgot the original information between the initial test and the final test 2 days later. It is especially clear in Christiaansen and Ochalek's Experiment 2 that restricting the analysis to initially accurate items did not exclude all of the subjects who did not remember the original information; final-test performance on initially accurate items in the control condition was only 36% correct.

Because the final-test results for the initially accurate items included responses both from subjects who remembered the original information and from subjects who did not remember the original information, these results are subject to the interpretive problems discussed earlier. Thus, the finding of equal performance in the misled/warned and control conditions does not imply that the proportion of subjects who remembered the original information was the same in both conditions. As discussed earlier, the warning may cause some misled/warned subjects who do not remember the original information to avoid the misleading information on the test and so to perform better than at the chance performance expected for the corresponding control subjects. Consequently, overall misled/warned performance could be as good as overall control performance even if fewer misled/warned than control subjects remembered the original information.

Christiaansen and Ochalek attempt to counter this sort of objection, by presenting data to suggest that misled/warned subjects who failed to remember the original information did not avoid the misleading information on the test. Given these data, they argue, the finding of equal misled/warned and control performance does imply that misleading information caused no loss of information from memory. This argument is incorrect, because Christiaansen and Ochalek's assumptions do not explain the finding of equal misled/warned and control performance, but lead instead to a prediction of poorer misled/warned than control performance. If misled/warned subjects who fail to remember the original information do not avoid the misleading information on the test, these subjects will perform more poorly than the corresponding control subjects. In particular, misled/warned subjects who remember only the misleading information will choose the misleading information on the test and so will be systematically incorrect. Consequently, overall performance should be worse in the misled/warned condition even if the proportion of subjects who remember the original information is the same in this condition as in the control condition.

Thus, if we accept Christiaansen and Ochalek's assertion that misled/warned subjects who failed to remember the original information did not avoid the misleading information on the test, their results are anomalous. On the other hand, if we reject this assertion, the results are ambiguous. In either case the data do not allow inferences about effects of misleading postevent information on memory for the original event.

The Bekerian and Bowers (1983) study

Like Christiaansen and Ochalek, Bekerian and Bowers contend that presentation of misleading information does not erase original information, but merely renders it inaccessible. They argue as follows: in Loftus's studies, the recognition test items are presented in random order and not in the order in which the queried information occurred in the original slide sequence. Thus, the retrieval environment does not closely match the original encoding environment. The misleading information effect may occur because subjects are unable to access the original information effectively under these conditions and instead retrieve the postevent information. If the test reinstated the original encoding environment more fully, subjects might be able to access the original information effectively and misled subjects might perform as well as subjects who have not been misled.

To test this hypothesis, Bekerian and Bowers conducted an experiment in which subjects viewed a sequence of 24 slides that included a traffic sign (e.g., a stop sign) as the critical item. Some subjects received consistent postevent information (e.g., stop sign), and some received misleading information (e.g., yield sign). In the test phase subjects were shown 15 pairs of slides and asked to indicate for each pair which slide was present in the original sequence. Some subjects received the test items in random order (random test condition), whereas others received the items in the order in which they occurred in the original slide sequence (sequential test condition). The critical test item required subjects to choose between a stop sign and a yield sign.

In the random test condition performance on the critical test item was better for subjects given consistent postevent information (94% correct) than for subjects given misleading information (60% correct). However, in the sequential test condition, performance did not differ for subjects given consistent information (85% correct) and misleading information (87% correct). Bekerian and Bowers conclude from these results that presentation of misleading information did not cause the original information to be irrevocably lost, but merely rendered it inaccessible under the conditions of the random test.

This conclusion is not valid because Bekerian and Bowers' assumptions do not explain their results. In particular, the assumption that a sequential test allows the original information to be accessed as readily in the misled condition as in the consistent condition does not lead to a prediction of no difference between the two conditions on the sequential test. Bekerian and Bowers used the original test procedure; for the critical test question the alternatives were the originally seen item and the item presented to misled subjects as misleading information. As we have pointed out, when the original test procedure is used, poorer misled than control performance is expected even if misleading information has no effect on the subjects' ability to remember (i.e., access) the original information. This prediction applies to sequential as well as random tests. Hence, the Bekerian and Bowers sequential test results are anomalous. These results are all the more surprising in that the misled condition was compared not with a control condition in which the postevent information said nothing specific about the critical item, but rather with a consistent condition in which the postevent information gave a specific accurate description of the critical item. Thus, the misled subjects at best had a single source of reliable information about the critical item, whereas the consistent subjects had two different sources that could be relied upon.

Because the Bekerian and Bowers results are anomalous, we attempted to replicate these results with our stimulus materials. We used the same design and procedure as in the original test conditions of our other experiments, except in the test phase. Thus, we compared misled and control conditions instead of misled and consistent conditions.

In our test phase we made Bekerian and Bowers' manipulation for reinstating the encoding context even stronger. In the random test condition, eight pairs of test slides were presented in random order. In the sequential test condition, the entire original slide sequence was presented at test in the original order. The only difference between the original presentation and the test was that for eight of the positions in the sequence a pair of test slides was presented. Each test pair consisted of the slide from the original sequence and a distractor in which a detail had been changed. The eight test pairs — four concerning critical items and four fillers — were the same in the random and sequential test conditions. As in the Bekerian and Bowers study, the original test procedure was used. For each critical item, the alternatives were the original slide and a slide in which the critical item had been replaced with the item given to misled subjects as misleading postevent information. Eighty-four subjects were tested in each of the two test conditions.

As expected, our results were quite different from those of Bekerian and Bowers. In the random test condition, performance on critical-item questions was 41% correct for misled items and 70% correct for control items. In the sequential test condition the results were almost identical, 37% correct for misled items and 68% correct for control items. The misled–control difference was reliable, $F(1,166) = 60.9$, $p < .01$, but no other effects approached significance ($Fs < 1$). It is obvious from these results that the random versus sequential test manipulation had no effect on performance in either the misled condition or the control condition.

We suggest that our results and not Bekerian and Bowers' reflect the true state of affairs. Each mean in our study represents 168 data points, whereas in the Bekerian and Bowers study only 16–30 data points contributed to each mean. More important, our results are interpretable, whereas Bekerian and Bowers' findings are anomalous, regardless of what assumptions are made about effects of misleading information on memory for the original event. We conclude, therefore, that the Bekerian and Bowers results do not imply that for the misled subjects the original information was inaccessible under random test conditions and was made accessible by the use of a sequential test.

In summary, the findings of postevent information studies have consistently been taken to mean that misleading information impairs memory for the original event, either by erasing stored information about the event or by rendering this information inaccessible. We have shown, however, that because of logical problems with the procedures used, or methodological problems with the particular experiments reported, the results of previous studies provide no clear basis for conclusions about effects of misleading information on memory for originally seen material.

In contrast to previous findings, our modified test results can be brought to bear on questions concerning effects of misleading information on memory. These results strongly suggest that misleading information has no effect on a person's ability to remember the original event. Of course, our results cannot rule out the possibility that under some conditions misleading postevent information does affect memory for originally seen material. For example, our experiments, like virtually all previous postevent information studies, used a recognition test procedure. Hence, it remains an open question whether misleading information affects a person's ability to *recall* original information.

The recall–recognition issue is interesting in light of previous research on retroactive interference (RI). Traditional RI studies, like misleading postevent information experiments, examine the effects of subsequent information on memory for material presented earlier. It is not a foregone conclusion that the traditional RI studies, which for the most part involve paired-associate word lists, are relevant to situations involving memory for events. Nevertheless, it is interesting to note that RI is consistently obtained with recall procedures, but is typically weak or absent when recognition tests are used (for reviews, see, for example, Crowder, 1976; Postman and Underwood, 1973).

General discussion

We have presented arguments and evidence against the claim that misleading postevent information impairs memory for the original event. However, studies of postevent information have also led to a more general and see-mingly less controversial claim – the claim that information about an event obtained from various sources is integrated in memory into a single repre-sentation of the event (e.g., Loftus, 1979a; Loftus *et al.*, 1978). According to this claim, a person who attends a baseball game and later reads a newspaper story about the game constructs a single representation that incorporates both the information obtained through direct observation and the information from the story.

What is the evidence bearing on the integration claim? The misleading information effect obtained with the original test procedure demonstrates that postevent information can influence *responses* to questions about an event, However, interpretation of this finding requires virtually no specific assump-tions about the nature of the relevant memory representations or how these representations are accessed and used. The same is true of results showing that subjects' responses may be influenced by postevent information that does not directly contradict information from the original event (e.g. Loftus, 1975), and studies (e.g., Loftus, 1975, 1977) demonstrating that subjects may give test responses that represent a compromise between original information and postevent information (e.g., a response of *blue-green* when *blue* is the original information and *green* is the postevent information). These results simply illustrate the obvious point that original information, postevent information, or both, can be used as a basis for answering questions. The person who has both seen and read about a baseball game may answer questions about the game on the basis of his or her direct observations at the game, the newspaper story, or both, regardless of the precise nature of the game representation(s) or how they are retrieved.

Data from other experimental paradigms (e.g., Bransford and Franks, 1971; Carmichael *et al.*, 1932) are similarly uninformative. For example, the Carmichael *et al.* finding that verbal labels influence reproduction of line drawings has sometimes been taken as support for the integration view (e.g., Loftus, 1979a). However, like the results from the postevent information studies, this finding does not imply anything very specific about the representation or retrieval of information from the verbal labels or the drawings. A subject who remembers the label *eyeglasses* but recalls little about the appearance of the drawing so labeled will probably produce a drawing that looks more like eyeglasses than the original drawing, whether or not information provided by the label has in any sense been integrated in memory with information from the drawing.

What sorts of data would, then, support or disconfirm the integration claim? Consideration of this question leads quickly to the realization that what is meant by integration is not at all clear. One might suggest that the integration claim simply asserts that information from various sources is stored together in memory. Although this answer may be satisfying at an intuitive level, it loses much of its appeal when we ask, What does 'stored together in memory' mean? How, for instance, do items that are stored together behave differently from items that are stored separately? Unless we can answer these questions, we have succeeded only in exchanging one vague notion for another.

This is not to say that no specific interpretation of the integration claim can be conceived. On the contrary, the claim is so vague that several quite different interpretations can be imagined. For example, one possible interpretation is that information from various sources collectively acts as a single unit for purposes of retrieval, such that information from one source cannot be retrieved selectively. An alternative interpretation is that only a single version of each episode making up the event is maintained in memory (e.g., Loftus and Loftus, 1980). According to this view, if the baseball fan's observations at the game disagreed with the newspaper article on a particular point, only one of the two versions would be maintained in memory. A third interpretation is that stored propositions are not tagged with information about the source from which they were obtained. On this view, the baseball fan who remembers some episode from the game will have no knowledge of whether the stored information about the episode came from direct observation, the newspaper story, or both.

It is not our intention in this article to propose or evaluate specific interpretations of the integration claim. The interpretations we have mentioned are merely illustrative and are still insufficiently explicit. Our point is simply that the integration claim, as it typically appears in the memory literature, is so vague and ambiguous as to be virtually meaningless. Until the claim is made more specific, we cannot determine whether it is reasonable, what its implications are, or what sorts of data would serve to support or disconfirm it. If we are to progress in our understanding of human memory, we must relinquish vague claims of this sort in favor of specific proposals.

Notes

1 When we say that a subject cannot remember, or has forgotten, some piece of information, we simply mean that under the conditions of the test the subject cannot access the information in memory. It is irrelevant for our purposes whether the information that cannot be accessed has been lost from memory or is in memory but inaccessible. Similarly, when we say that a subject remembers some piece of information, we mean that under the conditions of the test the subject can access the information in memory.

2 We are assuming here that proper counterbalancing procedures have been used, so that overall performance will be about 50% correct for subjects who do not remember the sign even if there is a general bias toward choosing one of the signs – for example, the *stop sign* – among subjects who do not remember what they saw. However, the argument we will develop applies even if counterbalancing procedures have not been used and performance for subjects who do not remember the original sign is systematically above or below 50%.

3 In making this point, we have for simplicity assumed two discrete memory states (i.e., 'remembered' or 'not remembered') for original or misleading information. However, the arguments we developed (and those we make subsequently) are unaltered if we assume instead that subjects can have partial memory for original or misleading information.

References

Bekerian, D. A., and Bowers, J. M. (1983). Eyewitness testimony: Were we misled? *Journal of Experimental Psychology: Learning, Memory, and Cognition, 9,* 139–145.

Bransford, J. D., and Franks, J. J. (1971). The abstraction of linguistic ideas. *Cognitive Psychology, 2,* 331–350.

Carmichael, L., Hogan, H. P., and Walter, A. A. (1932). An experimental study of the effect of language on the reproduction of visually perceived form. *Journal of Experimental Psychology, 15,* 73–86.

Christiaansen, R. E., and Ochalek, K. (1983). Editing misleading information from memory: Evidence for the coexistence of original and postevent information. *Memory & Cognition, 11,* 467–475.

Crowder, R. G. (1976). *Principles of learning and memory.* Hillsdale, NJ: Erlbaum.

Dodd, D. H., and Bradshaw, J. M. (1980). Leading questions and memory: Pragmatic constraints. *Journal of Verbal Learning and Verbal Behavior, 21,* 207–219.

Greene, E., Flynn, M. S., and Loftus, E. F. (1982). Inducing resistance to misleading information. *Journal of Verbal Learning and Verbal Behavior, 21,* 207–219.

Loftus, E. F. (1975). Leading questions and the eyewitness report. *Cognitive Psychology, 7,* 560–572.

Loftus, E. F. (1977). Shifting human color memory. *Memory & Cognition, 5,* 696–699.

Loftus, E. F. (1979a). *Eyewitness testimony.* Cambridge, MA: Harvard University Press.

Loftus, E. F. (1979b). The malleability of memory. *American Scientist, 67,* 312–320.

Loftus, E. F. (1981). Mentalmorphosis: Alterations in memory produced by the mental bonding of new information to old. In J. Long and A. Baddeley (Eds.), *Attention and performance IX* (pp. 417–434). Hillsdale, NJ: Erlbaum.

Loftus, E. F. and Greene, E. (1980). Warning: Even memory for faces may be contagious. *Law and Human Behavior, 4,* 323–334.

Loftus, E. F. and Loftus, G. R. (1980). On the permanence of stored information in the human brain. *American Psychologist, 35,* 409–420.

Loftus, E. F., Miller, D. G., and Burns, H. J. (1978). Semantic integration of verbal information into a visual memory. *Journal of Experimental Psychology: Human Learning and Memory, 4,* 19–31.

Loftus, E. F. and Palmer, J. E. (1974). Reconstruction of automobile destruction: An example of the interaction between language and memory. *Journal of Verbal Learning and Verbal Behavior, 13,* 585–589.

Postman, L., and Underwood, B. J. (1973). Critical issues in interference theory. *Memory & Cognition, 1,* 19–40.

Weinberg, H. I., Wadsworth, J., and Baron, R. S. (1983). Demand and the impact of leading questions on eyewitness testimony. *Memory & Cognition, 11,* 101–104.

SECTION FOUR
NEUROPSYCHOLOGY OF MEMORY

Editor's introduction

The theoretical analysis of memory has been enormously influenced by findings from memory-impaired individuals. Numerous causes of brain damage in humans are associated with amnesia, and in animals lesions to specific brain areas may dramatically impair memory. Without any doubt the most famous single-case history of an amnesic concerns 'H.M.,' who was operated on by Dr William Scoville in 1953 for the relief of intractable epilepsy. In an experimental operation, Scoville removed substantial parts of H.M.'s temporal lobes bilaterally, and although this was successful in terms of relieving H.M.'s seizures, it rendered him profoundly amnesic. **Corkin**'s article (Chapter 6) provides a detailed review of the pattern of memory deficits in H.M.

One of the key findings to have emerged from research on human amnesia is that the observed memory impairments may be selective. Thus although H.M. may be unable to remember for any length of time events that have happened to him, he is able to acquire certain perceptual and cognitive skills at a normal rate. This sort of observation led Cohen and Squire (1980) to propose a distinction between *declarative* and *procedural* memory. Declarative memory refers to memory for facts and events and is assumed to be impaired in the classic amnesic syndrome. Procedural (or 'nondeclarative') memory, on the other hand, refers to memory for procedures and skills and is hypothesized to be intact in anterograde amnesia. **Squire, Knowlton** and **Musen**'s chapter (Chapter 7) presents a thorough review of the evidence for this and other memory distinctions, drawing on data from both humans and animals. Squire *et al.* also describe the evidence connecting the hippocampus with declarative memory.

The literature on the neuropsychology of memory is vast, but important topics for further reading are: evidence from functional imaging studies of brain localization (Shallice *et al.*, 1994), the brain processes governing memory consolidation (McClelland *et al.*, 1995; McGaugh, 1990), the brain regions associated with different forms of procedural memory (Soliveri *et al.*, 1992), and the neuropsychology of working memory (Gathercole, 1994).

References

Cohen, N. J. and Squire, L. R. (1980). Preserved learning and retention of pattern-analyzing skill in amnesia: dissociation of knowing how and knowing that. *Science*, 210, 207–10.

Gathercole, S. E. (1994). Neuropsychology and working memory: a review. *Neuropsychology*, 8, 494–505.

McClelland, J. L., McNaughton, B. L., and O'Reilly, R. C. (1995). Why there are complementary learning systems in the hippocampus and neocortex: insights from the successes and failures of connectionist models of learning and memory. *Psychological Review*, 102, 419–57.

McGaugh, J. L. (1990). Significance and remembrance: the role of neuro-modulatory systems. *Psychological Science*, 1, 15–25.

Shallice, T., Fletcher, P., Frith, C. D., Grasby, P., Frackowiak, R. S. J., and Dolan, R. J. (1994). Brain regions associated with acquisition and retrieval of verbal episodic memory. *Nature*, 368, 633–5.

Soliveri, P., Brown, R. G., Jahanshahi, M., and Marsden, C. D. (1992). Procedural memory and neurological disease. *European Journal of Cognitive Psychology*, 4, 161–93.

6   Suzanne Corkin

'Lasting Consequences of Bilateral Medial Temporal Lobectomy: Clinical Course and Experimental Findings in H.M.'

Reprinted in full from: *Seminars in Neurology* **4**, 249–259 (1984)

Dedicated to William Beecher Scoville, M.D. 1906–1984

The attention that has been devoted to the patient H.M. in terms of number of hours of evaluation and amount of journal and book space probably exceeds that devoted to any other single case. This circumstance is due to the unusual purity and severity of his amnesic syndrome, to its well-documented anatomical substrate, to the relatively static nature of his condition, and to his being a willing and cooperative subject. This article provides an overview of the history, 31-year postoperative clinical course, and neuropsychologic findings in this 58-year-old man.

History

Preoperative clinical course

H.M. was born in 1926. He was the only child of working-class parents. The hospital birth was apparently normal, but no details of the procedure are available. His development was said to have been unremarkable until age 7 years when he was knocked down by a bicycle. (Note that H.M.'s age at the time of this injury was given as 9 in an earlier report;[1] the correction was made following a subsequent conversation with his mother.) He sustained a laceration in the left supraorbital region, and was unconscious for 5 minutes. It should be noted, too, that three first cousins on his father's side of the family had epilepsy. H.M. experienced his first minor seizure at age 10 years, and his first major seizure on his 16th birthday. He still remembers that he was riding in the car with his parents at the time of the latter event, but states that it was his 15th birthday. He dropped out of high school because the other boys teased him about his seizures. After a 2 year interval, however, he entered a different high school and graduated in 1947, at age 21. In high school, he took the 'practical' course, in preference to the 'commercial' or 'college' course, and states that he took as little mathematics as possible because he did not care for it. He was a member of the Science Club and was fond of guns, hunting and roller skating.

After high school, he worked on an assembly line and also held a job as a motor-winder until his seizures incapacitated him to the extent that he could no longer perform his duties. At that time, he was having on the average 10 *petit mal* seizures per day and 1 major seizure per week. Unsuccessful attempts had been made over a 10-year period to control these seizures with large doses of anticonvulsant medications, including Dilantin, phenobarbital, Tridione, and Mesantoin. The frequency and severity of the attacks ultimately led H.M. and his family to consider a brain operation. The proposal to do a radical experimental operation was discussed with them on several occasions before the decision to proceed was reached.

Brain operation

In 1953, when H.M. was 27 years old, Dr. William Beecher Scoville performed a bilateral medial temporal lobe resection.[2] He approached the brain through two 1.5-inch supraorbital trephine holes. By inserting a flat brain spatula through each hole, he was able to elevate both frontal lobes, thereby exposing the tips of the temporal lobes. They in turn were retracted laterally in order to permit access to the medial surfaces, where electrocorticography was carried out in order to assess the activity of the uncus, amygdala, and hippocampus – structures that are often implicated in epilepsy. There was no clear-cut evidence of an epileptic focus in this region. An incision was then made that bisected the tips of the temporal lobes, and he resected the medial half of the tip of each temporal lobe. Next, Dr. Scoville removed by suction all of the gray and white matter medial to the temporal horns of the lateral ventricles, sparing the temporal neocortex almost entirely. The removal was bilateral, and it is said to have extended 8 cm back from the tips of the temporal lobes. It included the prepyriform gyrus, uncus, amygdala, hippocampus, and parahippocampal gyrus, and must have produced an interruption of some of the white matter leading to and from the temporal lobes (Figure 6.1). H.M. was awake and talking during the operation.

Five pieces of excised brain tissue underwent gross neuropathologic study. Microscopic examination of three of them, taken from one uncus and both amygdalae, found them to be without inflammation or scarring.

Postoperative clinical course

The operation reduced the frequency of H.M.'s major seizures to the point where now his attacks are infrequent, and he may be free of generalized convulsions for as long as a year. The minor seizures persist; they are atypical *petit mal* attacks that do not noticeably disturb him. His current seizure medications are Dilantin, 100 mg three times daily, and Mysoline, 250 mg three times daily. The reduction in seizure frequency is juxtaposed against the unexpected handicap produced by the resection: since the time of his operation, H.M. has had a profound anterograde amnesia that is especially salient because his overall intelligence and neurologic status are relatively well-preserved. H.M.'s global amnesia has put marked limitations on his daily activities and accomplishments. Once the harmful effects of bilateral medial temporal lobectomy were recognized, Dr. Scoville campaigned widely against its use.[3]

Living situation and daily activities
After his operation, H.M. returned home to live with his mother and father. His daily activities included accompanying his mother on errands, helping

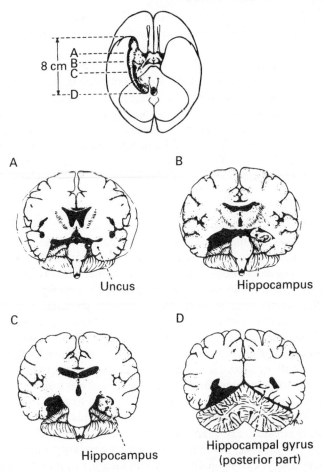

Figure 6.1 These cross-sections of human brain were prepared by Dr Lamar Roberts to show the extent of H.M.'s resection. For didactic purposes, the resection is shown on the right side of the brain, and the intact structures on the left side of the brain, but note that the lesion is bilateral. At the top is a drawing of the base of the brain that shows where the cross-sections are taken from. Level A = uncus; level B = anterior hippocampus; the amygdala would be in a section between A and B, but is not shown; level C = more posterior hippocampus; level D = parahippocampal gyrus at the posterior limits of the resection (from Scoville and Milner, 1957).

with household chores, mowing the grass, watching television, and doing crossword puzzles. His father, whom H.M. resembles both physically and in his gentle, passive nature, died in 1967. Beginning in that year, H.M. attended a rehabilitation workshop on a daily basis for about 10 years. There, he performed simple, repetitive tasks, went on field trips, and also worked in this protective setting as a handyman. H.M. and his mother lived by themselves until 1974, when owing to his mother's advanced age, they went to live with a relative. Three years later, H.M.'s mother was admitted to a nursing home. Then, in 1980, because the relative who cared for him was terminally ill, H.M. moved to the nursing home where he currently resides (though not the one where his mother was living). His mother died in 1980 at age 94.

Currently, H.M. is assisted with his bath or shower, but dresses himself with the clothes that are laid out for him. He is reminded to shave, brush his teeth, and comb his hair. He spends much of his time doing difficult crossword puzzles and watching television. He also participates in the daily activities of the nursing home, such as poetry reading, crafts projects, games, and entertainment. His appetite is good, and he is reported to sleep well, but all-night electroencephalogram (EEG) recordings reveal that he wakes up often because of sleep apnea.

Motivation and affect
One of H.M.'s most striking characteristics is that he rarely complains about anything. In 1968, his mother stated that 'the trouble with H. is that he doesn't complain – ever. There could be something quite seriously wrong with him, but you would have to guess.' At the nursing home, when H.M. is observed to be acting differently, the nurses question him by running through a list of possible complaints, such as toothache, headache, stomachache, until they hit upon the correct one. He will not spontaneously say for example, 'I have a headache,' causing one to wonder whether he knows what is wrong. Similarly, he does not ask for food or beverages, and unless questioned, does not say that he is hungry, full, or tired. He sometimes asks to go to the bathroom, however. H.M. appears to be content at all times, and is always agreeable and cooperative to the point that if, for example, he is asked to sit in a particular place, he will do so indefinitely. The rare exceptions to this placid demeanor occur when H.M. is stressed. For example, during the time that H.M. and his mother lived with their relative, his mother's constant nagging would cause H.M. to become very angry. Occasionally, he would kick her in the shin or hit her with his glasses. More recently, another patient in the nursing home apparently liked to annoy H.M. by calling him names, criticizing him, and disturbing his Bingo card. Her behavior angered H.M. to the point that he would shake the sides of his bed and walk around in circles. As soon as he was distracted, his anger would dissipate immediately. Since this woman's discharge from the nursing home, H.M. has not had any such outbursts. He is described as even-tempered and well-behaved; he does not throw objects, swear, or hit. Moreover, his sense of humor is often evident, as it was the day that Dr. Harvey Sagar and H.M. walked out of a testing room into the hall, allowing the door to close behind them. Dr. Sagar commented to H.M., 'I'm wondering whether I left my keys inside the room.' H.M. replied, 'At least you'll know where to find them!'

After H.M.'s father died, his mother believed that H.M. was depressed, and concern for him motivated her to enroll him in the rehabilitation workshop mentioned above. When she died 4 years later, the staff at the nursing home where H.M. lives observed that his grief was mild. He told them what a nice woman she had been and that she had taken care of him all his life. He sometimes remembers that his parents are dead and mentions that he is all alone. His adjustment to all of the changes in his personal relationships and living situation has been smooth.

H.M. appears to have no interest in sexual relationships, as indicated by the absence of conversation on sexual topics and by his failure to seek sexual satisfaction. He does not flirt, he has never had a girlfriend, and he does not masturbate, as far as his caretakers have been able to determine. Hyposexuality is sometimes associated with temporal-lobe lesions, and thus it is tempting to speculate that H.M.'s sexual indifference is attributable to the brain operation; it may be due to other factors, however. Preoperative testing by a clinical psychologist, Dr. Liselotte K. Fisher, led her to conclude that H.M. had difficulty in his sexual adjustment. Moreover, anticonvulsant therapy produces elevated sex hormone binding globulin levels which are associated with reduced plasma total testosterone, raised luteinizing hormone levels, and sexual dysfunction.[4] Thus, the sexual disorder may have been present before the operation, and it may be due at least in part to drug-induced hormonal abnormalities. Further study of sex hormone patterns is warranted in H.M.

Physical examination

We have documentation of H.M.'s medical history since 1966; he has been free of major illnesses. Information relevant to his neurologic status is described below.

Neurologic examination

During the postoperative years that we have followed up H.M. his neurologic status has remained stable. Neurologic examination in 1984 revealed an ataxia of gait, polyneuropathy, and a left ulnar neuropathy. These signs are identical to those found in 1966, except for progression of the polyneuropathy since 1970 and the appearance of the ulnar neuropathy in 1977. The relative absence of neurologic deficit is surprising when one considers the nature and extent of the abnormal conditions that coexist in H.M.'s brain. In this man, six factors contribute to the total cerebral disorder: the long-standing neural abnormality that produced his frequent major and minor seizures; the lasting deleterious effects of repeated seizure activity; the effects of long-term use of anticonvulsant medications; the substantial loss of brain tissue due to bilateral medial temporal lobe resection; the cortical and subcortical neuronal loss that normally occurs throughout life; and the chemical counterparts of the presumed morphologic changes.

Laboratory tests

Urinalysis and routine blood tests show no consistent abnormality apart from a mild red cell macrocytosis, which is probably due to Dilantin therapy. The 1984 EKG tracing is within normal limits. In addition, urine testosterone, blood testosterone, free cortisol, and adrenocorticotropin levels measured in

1980 were all normal. These findings are of interest because there are numerous corticosterone receptors in the hippocampus, and this structure is involved in the control of glucocorticoid secretion,[5] and because the hippocampus sends extensive projections to the hypothalamus.[6]

A contrast-enhanced computed tomography (CT) scan was performed in 1984 on a GE 9800 scanner at the Massachusetts General Hospital. The use of

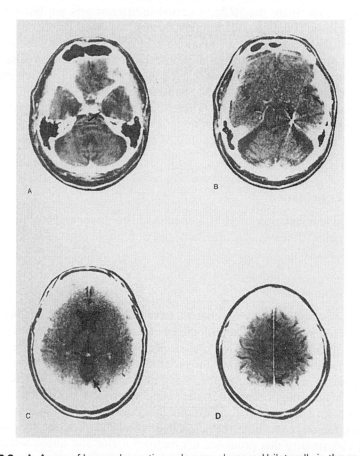

Figure 6.2   A: Areas of lower absorption value are observed bilaterally in the region of the medial aspects of the temporal lobes anteriorly. The changes are more prominent on the left side (arrow). These areas of low absorption value are consistent with partial volume averaging of tissue loss due to the surgical resection. B: Mild to moderate tissue loss is seen in the Sylvian cistern on the left. These changes could be secondary to the surgical removal of tissue in the medial temporal lobes. The linear streaking more posteriorly is due to artifact from a surgical clip. C: The Sylvian cistern (arrow) is not well filled out by the superior cerebellar vermis, indicating atrophy of this structure. The cerebellum shows marked, diffuse atrophy. The ventricles are enlarged, consistent with the patient's age. D: The changes laterally, over the convexity, are consistent with the patient's age. The cortical sulci are prominent bilaterally, especially medially, in the interhemispheric fissure. Whether these changes reflect some secondary alteration in the region of the cingulate gyrus cannot be determined.

this current generation scanner made it possible for the first time to visualize H.M.'s medial temporal-lobe lesions. Other evidence of the resection was dilation of the temporal horns of both lateral ventricles. Additional findings included cerebellar atrophy, possibly associated with long-term Dilantin treatment, and mild cortical atrophy, as is sometimes seen in a 58-year-old person (Figure 6.2). These findings are in agreement with those obtained in 1978.

An EEG performed in 1978 showed a large amount of bilateral and diffuse seizure activity. The most prominent finding was that of wave and spike activity that was symmetrical and maximal in the frontal regions, and polyspike and wave activity in sleep. There was some slow activity in the temporal regions, which was greater on the left, but in that area only fragments of low amplitude spike activity were seen.

Neuropsychologic evaluation

The information about H.M. described up to this point provides a background against which to consider the objective neuropsychologic test results. These findings serve two purposes: they illustrate the purity of H.M.'s amnesic syndrome, and they provide answers to a variety of questions about the organization of human memory systems. Now that H.M. is 58 years old, a new question has arisen: will the aging process proceed normally in his brain, or will the symptoms of aging be accelerated in an already damaged structure? The experimental findings summarized here in brief have either been described in detail previously in separate research reports or will be the basis for future articles.

Sensory and sensorimotor function

Visual field testing was carried out in 1966, 1970, and 1984 using the Tübingen perimeter.[7] H.M.'s visual fields are normal, as are most other visual functions tested, including prism adaptation (Held, unpublished data), masking and metacontrast (Schiller, unpublished data), and perception of spiral after-effects. The single exception is his contrast sensitivity function, which is slightly reduced for his age (Nissen and Corkin, unpublished data). Because he viewed the stimuli through the upper lens of his bifocals, and because the correction may not have been optimal, testing will be repeated with H.M. wearing full frame glasses with the proper correction.

H.M.'s performance on a series of olfactory tasks indicated a dissociation of function: he is able to detect weak odors compared with distilled-deionized water, to appreciate odor intensity, and to adapt normally to strong odors.[8] Discrimination, matching, and identification tasks, however, reveal that he is severely impaired in the perception of odor quality. This disorder is not surprising because the resection invaded primary olfactory cortex in the uncus, and because retraction of the frontal lobes during the operation might have damaged the orbitofrontal cortex, olfactory bulb, or olfactory tracts.

Nevertheless, these structures must have been at least partially spared in order to support the residual olfactory capacities demonstrated in H.M.

Since 1962, we have documented H.M.'s peripheral neuropathy on his hands and forearms with quantitative measures of somatosensory function, including pressure sensitivity, two-point discrimination, point localization, position sense, thermal discrimination and pain sensitivity.[9,10] On these tests, H.M. has mild to moderate deficits bilaterally, although his performance is variable and sometimes even falls within the normal range. His grip strength shows little fluctuation; in 1983, it was 70.3 pounds on the left, and 72.3 pounds on the right. H.M. appears to be right-handed, but he states that in second grade he was forced to switch his writing hand from left to right. On tests of repetitive finger tapping and visuomotor coordination,[11] H.M.'s score for the two hands are comparable, and at the bottom of the normal range for his age. The exception is the Thurstone tapping test, in which his scores for the bimanual condition are markedly impaired; this abnormality is probably attributable at least in part to his cerebellar atrophy. His performance on a test of repetitive fine finger movement[12] is asymmetric, with the left hand markedly inferior to the right, even on unimanual conditions. This finding suggests some interference with the primary motor cortex or other part of the pyramidal system, presumably in the right hemisphere.[13,14] The sensorimotor deficit revealed in the laboratory is also apparent in his daily activities. For example, the staff at the rehabilitation workshop noted some clumsiness in working with his hands, although the quality of his work was said to have been excellent.

Overall intelligence

The Wechsler-Bellevue scale was administered to H.M. on seven occasions, including an examination the day before his operation by Dr. Liselotte K. Fisher (Table 6.1). Postoperative testing also included the Wechsler memory scale (WMS); the discrepancy between the memory quotient (MQ) and the full scale IQ rating provides a crude index of the severity of global amnesia, although marked IQ–MQ differences can occur for other reasons, such as severe verbal memory impairment. Overall IQ ratings have been consistently in the average range, whereas performance IQ ratings fall in the average to superior ranges. Individual subtest scores vary considerably: preoperatively H.M.'s equivalent weighted score on the arithmetic subtest was 1, reflecting his dislike of mathematics; the postoperative arithmetic scores ranged from 4 to 7. Object assembly and digit symbol were both 7 preoperatively, but all other scores were above 10. On postoperative testing, the object assembly score has risen to 12 and 13, but the digit symbol scores remain low, perhaps reflecting the effects of medication. The full scale IQ ratings cover the average and bright normal ranges, and all are at least 35 points above the memory quotient, indicating an inferiority of memory function to overall intelligence. A more sensitive index of memory impairment, however, is performance on delayed recall of verbal (WMS logical memory and associate learning) and nonverbal (WMS visual reproduction) material.[15] On both tasks,

Table 6.1 The amnesic patient H.M.: Wechsler intelligence scale and memory scale results (1953–1983)

Date	Age	Test	Verbal IQ	Performance IQ	Full scale IQ	Memory quotient	Delayed recall	
							Verbal (deficit ≤11)	Nonverbal (deficit ≤7)
Preop								
1953	27	W-B I	101	106	104	*	*	*
Postop								
1955	29	W-B I	107	114	112	67	*	*
1962	36	W-B II	109	125	118	64	1	0
1977	51	W-B I	107	126	118	74	5	0
1978	52	W-B II	91	104	98	63	1	0
1980	54	W-B II	97	108	104	64	1	0
1983	57	W-B II	97	115	108	64	0	0

* Not assessed

H.M. is severely impaired on all occasions (see Table 6.1). More detailed studies of specific memory capacities are cited below.

A comparison of the 1977 and 1983 test results indicates that H.M.'s verbal IQ rating has dropped 10 points, his performance IQ rating 11 points, and his full scale IQ rating 10 points (see Table 6.1). In normal aging, IQ test performance is maintained until after age 70,[16] so that H.M.'s losses, though not dramatic, may reflect premature aging produced by his multiple neural abnormalities. The manifestation of this process could be a decrease in the number of neurons, in the number of receptor sites, or in the efficiency of the remaining neurons. Alternatively, transneuronal degeneration in the limbic system, a rare cause of progressive intellectual loss, could underlie H.M.'s slight deterioration.[17]

Language capacities

H.M. is able to appreciate puns and linguistic ambiguities,[18] and although he does not usually initiate conversations himself, when someone begins a conversation with him, he talks readily and in general communicates effectively. Nevertheless, his language functions are now minimally impaired. Clinically, he has a slight anomia, but on the Boston naming test,[19] he scores in the normal range (Huff, unpublished data). Although he also achieves perfect scores on six subtests of the Minnesota test for differential diagnosis of aphasia – three reflecting receptive language capacities and three expressive language capacities – this test is relatively easy, and on more challenging language tests, he is less accurate. Thus, on the token test of language comprehension,[20] he achieves 34 of 36 and 32 of 36 correct on separate occasions (deficit ≤ 33), and on the reporter's test of language production,[21] he succeeds on 19 of 26 and 23 of 26 items (deficit ≤ 24). His spelling is poor, although this disorder may have antedated the brain operation. In addition, he is clearly impaired on tests of semantic and symbolic verbal fluency [11,22] (Nissen, unpublished data). Because other cognitive functions of the frontal lobes are preserved in H.M. (see later), it is believed that the fluency deficit is not related to frontal-lobe dysfunction, but rather reflects an alteration in more general cognitive capacities. Studies of language in aging and Alzheimer's disease reveal that performance on tests of verbal fluency is compromised early in the succession of cognitive changes.[23] H.M.'s mild language disorder, therefore, may be age-related. One of the issues of interest is the extent to which this deficit influences his performance on memory tests.[24]

Spatial and perceptual capacities

O'Keefe and Nadel[25] proposed a model of hippocampal function in which the hippocampus is concerned with context-dependent memory. They provided evidence that the hippocampal system develops objective spatial representations, and for the human hippocampus they postulated that an analogous mapping of linguistic information also occurs. We were initially resistant to this notion because of certain preserved spatial capacities in H.M., but a review of his performance on a wide range of spatial tests that do not rely heavily on memory function indicates that some spatial capacities are compromised, whereas others are not: deficits are revealed on the hidden figures test,[11,26,27] visual locomotor mazes,[28] copy of the Rey-Osterrieth figure,[29] and the body schema test.[28] He is similarly thwarted when given a floor plan of the MIT Clinical Research Center to use as a map and asked to walk the route from one room to another. In contrast, H.M.'s performance is exceptionally good on two other spatial tasks and two complex perceptual tasks, the block design subtest of the Wechsler-Bellevue scale, a modified version of Hebb's triangular blocks test,[29] the Mooney faces test,[30] and the McGill picture anomalies.[15] Moreover, his recognition of fragmented line drawings from the Gollin incomplete-pictures test is normal,[24,30] and he shows savings from one test session to the next: in 1962, 1980, 1982, and 1983, his respective error scores were 21, 16, 8, and 7. He is also able to draw an accurate floor plan of the house where he lived during the postoperative years from 1960 to 1974, showing all the rooms in their proper location. He believes that he still lives there and can recognize the floor plan, drawn by someone else, when it is presented with four foils (distractors). In the nursing home where he lives, he can find his way from the ground floor to his room, which is one flight up. These latter two instances of preserved spatial capacities occur in environments where H.M. has had thousands of learning trials, however. Because patients with right temporal lobe lesions are often impaired on the complex spatial tasks that H.M. performs efficiently,[15,31,32] the distinction between the tests on which he succeeds and those on which he fails may reflect a contrasting specialization of the temporal neocortex and medial temporal lobe structures, respectively.

Frontal lobe capacities

The constellation of symptoms observed in H.M. may be contrasted with that seen in patients with less pure amnesias due to ruptured anterior communicating artery aneurysm or to Korsakoff's syndrome; they show frontal lobe dysfunctions that are believed to contribute to the memory impairment.[33-35] Specifically, they fail to show release from proactive interference, and are poor at judging the temporal order of events and at problem solving. Unlike these patients, H.M. shows preservation of the cognitive functions of the frontal lobes, aside from verbal fluency discussed above. Thus, on six of seven administrations of the Wisconsin card sorting test,[36] he has achieved more than three categories; on the seventh occasion, his Dilantin level was in the toxic range, and understandably he did not achieve any sorting categories. H.M. makes few perseverative errors, and he shows normal release from proactive interference (Cohen, unpublished data). Moreover, his test quotient on the Porteus maze test[37] has gone up from 110 in 1977 to 126 in 1983. The number of qualitative errors is abnormally high, but they are attributable to awkwardness in reorienting his hand, and not to a predilection for rule breaking.

Selective attention

Because of the importance of attention for the conscious remembering that takes place in conventional memory tests, it was important to determine whether H.M.'s memory impairment is accompanied by an attentional disorder. One way in which we probe for such a deficit is to ask whether detection of a stimulus is faster when it is in the expected position than when it is in the unexpected position. On a visual simple reaction time task,[38] H.M. responds more slowly than control subjects, but demonstrates normal effects of spatial and temporal expectancy, indicating that his selective attention is unaffected (Nissen and Corkin, unpublished data).

Classical conditioning

Classical conditioning has been attempted only once with H.M., but without success because the unconditioned stimulus, a shock delivered to the right ankle, did not elicit the expected increase in galvanic skin response (Kimura, unpublished data). This kind of experiment should be pursued with H.M., however, using discrete striated muscle responses because of the reports that cerebellar lesions in animals permanently abolish classical conditioning of such responses with aversive unconditioned stimuli,[39] and because of the finding that the hippocampus plays a role in such conditioning.[40] H.M. does show an electrodermal response to white noise, which habituates during a testing session. In this paradigm, he shows savings several hours and one day later (Merker and Pastel, unpublished data).

Recent-memory capacities

Immediate memory

A consistent finding with H.M. since 1955 has been the preservation of his immediate memory capacities. His digit span increased postoperatively, and since then his immediate memory span for both digits and block patterns has been borderline normal.[24,41] Nevertheless, his forward digit span was 6 through 1977, and dropped to 5 in each of 4 subsequent years, indicating a small deterioration of immediate memory function. Decay in short-term memory is normal, as measured by both recognition[42] and recall tasks[24] (see also Corsi).[41] H.M.'s initial acquisition of complex visual stimuli, color photographs of scenes and objects from magazines, is also unimpaired (Grove, unpublished data). Thus, H.M. is able to register new information; his striking disability becomes apparent when his immediate memory span is exceeded, if only by a single item,[41,43] when distraction is introduced during retention intervals,[31] and with the mere lapse of time if the material cannot be rehearsed verbally.[44,45]

Long-term memory

A striking feature of H.M. is the stability of his symptoms during the 31 postoperative years. He still exhibits a profound anterograde amnesia, and does not know where he lives, who cares for him, or what he ate at his last meal. His guesses as to the current year may be off by as much as 43 years, and, when he does not stop to calculate it, he estimates his age to be 10 to 26 years less than it is. In 1982, he did not recognize a picture of himself that had been taken on his 40th birthday in 1966. Nevertheless, he has islands of remembering, such as knowing that an astronaut is someone who travels in outer space, that a public figure named Kennedy was assassinated, and that rock music is 'that new kind of music we have.' The following pieces of anecdotal evidence illustrate the severity of his anterograde amnesia and provide some examples of the information that he has been able to recall.

In July 1973, H.M. could not identify Watergate, John Dean, or San Clemente, in spite of the fact that he watched the news on television every night. He did not know who the President was, but when told that his name began with an 'N,' H.M. said 'Nixon.' When H.M. was asked whether he could tell the examiner anything about Skylab, he replied, 'I think, uh, of a docking place in space.' When asked how many people were in Skylab, he correctly said 'three,' but was not confident of his answer because he immediately added, 'But then I had an argument with myself, then, was it three or five?' In response to the question, 'What's it like to move around up there?' he said, 'Well, they have weightlessness . . . I think of magnets to hold them on metal parts so they . . . won't float off away, and to hold them there so they can move around themselves and stay in one area, and they won't move away unvoluntarily (sic).' In 1980, he erroneously stated that a hippie is a dancer, that Howard Cosell does the news on television, and that Barbara Walters is a singer. However, he correctly said that 'grass' could refer to drugs or marijuana, that Raymond Burr plays the part of a detective on television, and that Archie Bunker calls his son-in-law 'Meathead.' He is comfortable dealing with the products of new technology, such as computerized tests and portable radios with headphones. These anecdotes indicate that although H.M.'s fund of general knowledge is meager, it is not void.

The severity and pervasiveness of H.M.'s memory disorder have been documented repeatedly by his performance on a wide variety of neuropsychologic tests. For example, delayed recall is impaired whether the stimuli are stories, verbal paired associates, digit strings, new vocabulary words, drawings, nonverbal paired associates, block patterns, songs, common objects, or object locations[24,41,46] (Corkin and Sullivan, unpublished data; Cohen, Gabrieli, and Corkin, unpublished data). Further, H.M. does not benefit from the use of visual imagery in paired-associate learning,[47] and he is unable to learn the correct path from start to finish in both visual and tactual stylus mazes[48,49] unless the number of turns is within his immediate memory span.[30] H.M. is also impaired on continuous recognition of words, nonsense syllables, numbers, geometric drawings, and nonsense shapes,[50] and on forced-choice recognition of faces, houses, words, and tonal sequences (Corkin, unpublished data). Although the pattern of memory deficits in H.M. resembles that seen after unilateral temporal lobectomy coupled with hippocampectomy, the magnitude of H.M.'s losses are more marked than those typically seen after unilateral excisions.[51]

In the face of H.M.'s profound anterograde amnesia, it is impressive that certain classes of memory function are preserved. The first hint of a residual learning capacity was Milner's 1962 report that H.M.'s error and time scores on a mirror-drawing task decreased over 3 days of training, despite his being unaware that he had done the task before.[52] Later experiments provided further evidence of his ability to acquire new motor skills.[49,53] More recent studies make it clear, however, that the domain of preserved learning was formulated too narrowly as motor learning. Thus, H.M. can also acquire certain perceptual skills, such as reading of briefly presented words and mirror reading[54] (Cohen and Corkin, unpublished data), and the cognitive skills required to solve the Tower of Hanoi puzzle.[55,56] Other evidence of preserved learning is that H.M. shows the biasing effects of experience with words, while at the same time being unable to recall that experience. For example, H.M. is shown a word, such as 'DEFINE,' and asked to indicate how much he likes or dislikes it on a 1 to 5 scale. Next, he is given the stem 'DEF' and asked to say the first word that comes to mind. Here he typically responds with the previously experienced word, even though it is not the most frequent completion of the stem 'DEF' when biasing is absent. In contrast, he fails dramatically on subsequent recall and recognition testing with the same words (Gabrieli, Cohen, and Corkin, unpublished data).

In summary, H.M.'s impaired performance on traditional tests of delayed recall and recognition memory is in marked contrast to his normal performance on tests of motor, perceptual, and cognitive skill learning and on measures of biasing effects of experience with words. Among the various dichotomies that have been proposed to account for such findings, the distinction between procedural learning (knowing how) and declarative learning (knowing that) is perhaps the most appropriate to conceptualize the kind of knowledge that is spared in H.M. and the kind that is preserved.[57] Declarative knowledge appears to require medial temporal lobe structures bilaterally for its expression; procedural knowledge is independent of that system.

Remote-memory capacities

In an effort to explore some of H.M.'s premorbid memories in a natural environment, Dr. Neal Cohen and I accompanied H.M. to his 35th high school reunion in 1982. A number of his classmates remembered him and greeted him warmly; one woman even gave him a kiss. As far as we could determine, however, H.M. did not recognize anyone's face or name. But he was not alone in this respect. We met a woman who claimed that she too did not know anyone in the room. Clearly, she and H.M. were the exceptions in this regard, but her comment reminds us that as people age they also forget. Thus, in evaluating H.M.'s remote memory function with objective tests, it has been important to compare his performance with that of age-matched control subjects.

In 1968, Milner *et al.*[30] reported that H.M.'s retrograde amnesia was restricted to about 2 years preceding the operation. This conclusion was based upon information from the neurosurgeon's office notes and on post-operative interviews with H.M. and his mother. Recently, objective tests have been used to probe the limits of H.M.'s remote memory for public and personal events.[58,59] The new data confirm the finding that H.M.'s remote memory impairment is temporally limited, but they extend the limits of the deficit back to 1942, 11 years before the medial temporal lobe resection. The public events tests measure recall of famous tunes, verbal recognition of public events, and recall and recognition of famous scenes. In the famous tunes test (Marslen-Wilson, unpublished data), subjects hear samples of 48 tunes from the 1920s to the 1960s, and are asked to provide the titles. H.M.'s ability to name famous tunes is below the normal range for the 1930s, 1940s, and 1960s. A comparison of H.M.'s performance with that of two other amnesic patients suggests that the severity of the remote memory loss may be related to the severity of their anterograde amnesia. Errors in dating famous tunes were defined as the difference between the subject's dating and the actual date. Normal control subjects have an equal number of over-shoots and undershoots, as does a patient with global amnesia secondary to encephalitis, although he is less accurate. H.M., in contrast, has a tendency to attribute most tunes to the 1940s so that he systematically overshoots in the 1920s and 1930s, and systematically undershoots in the 1950s and 1960s. On the verbal recognition test of public events,[60] there are 88 questions about events from the 1940s through the 1970s. On this test, H.M.'s performance is normal for the 1940s, borderline for the 1950s, and clearly impaired for the 1960s and 1970s. A comparison of these results with those for other amnesic patients suggests that the extent in time of the retrograde loss is related to the duration of the amnesic syndrome. The postencephalitic patient who had been amnesic for 26 years is impaired, whereas two other patients who had been amnesic for 10 years and 1 year, respectively, both performed normally. Items for the famous scenes test were selected because they depict an event that cannot be deduced from the picture itself. There are four pictures at each of five decades from the 1940s through the 1980s. In the recall test, subjects are first asked whether they have seen the picture before. They are then given 1 minute to describe the content and action in the picture, and what event it depicts. If the subject omits important details, they are probed for by specific questions. Finally, subjects are asked, 'When was the picture taken?' A content score and a dating score are given for each picture. On the recall test, H.M.'s content scores are impaired for all decades except the 1940s, and his dating scores are impaired at all decades tested. The number of datings per decade is also noted, the actual number for each decade being four. Reminiscent of the famous tunes test, H.M. preferentially chooses the 1940s and 1950s at the expense of the 1960s through 1980s: his dating is shifted into his nonamnesic time period. It is striking that with this preference for the 1940s and 1950s, H.M. is still impaired in dating 1940s and 1950s items. Similar findings are obtained with the famous scenes recognition test.

The personal events test is a modified version of the Crovitz personal remote memory test.[58,59,61] Here, subjects are given eight concrete nouns, one at a time, and are asked to relate some personally experienced event cued by each noun, from any period of their life, and to state when the event took place. In order to establish the consistency of the memory, an attempt is made to invoke the same memory a day later, and to assess its content and dating. Day one and day two memories are scored from 0 to 3, according to their specificity. On this task, a perfect score is 30, and all subjects perform efficiently. A drop from day one to day two means either that the subject could not produce the day one memory on day two at all, or that the day two memory was less specific. H.M. and one other amnesic patient show a slight drop from day one to day two. Every time that a subject gives a memory that is specific enough to be scored 3, he is asked to date that memory. Normal control subjects and three amnesic patients who have been amnesic for from 1 to 26 years produce memories across their life span up to their current age. In contrast, H.M.'s memories are all from age 16 years or younger, even though his operation took place at age 27. It is important to note that his major seizures began at age 16, however. This absence of memories over age 16 replicates our previous results (Cohen and Corkin, unpublished data). Consistent with this finding are the observations that H.M. does not remember the end of World War II, nor his high school graduation, both of which occurred after his 16th birthday and before his operation. The fact that H.M. produces no memories after age 16 is not evidence that he is unable to do so. He was therefore given the same words again and asked to relate memories only after the age of 16. Because the task becomes more difficult for everyone when responses are restricted to a particular time period, H.M.'s performance was compared with the performance of another amnesic patient whose responses were similarly constrained. The results indicate that H.M.'s total score is about half of what it was in the unconstrained condition, and poorer than the scores of the other amnesic patients in the constrained condition; that the memories that he does give are for ages 17 and 18 only, and when he is asked to redate these memories the same day and the next day, he dates three of the four below age 16; and that the consistency of memories from day one to day two is practically 0, again in contrast to his unconstrained performance and to the constrained performance of the other patient. These experiments, taken together, provide clear evidence that H.M.'s remote memory impairment extends from the present time back to age 16, 11 years before the operation that resulted in the severe anterograde amnesia. There are at least three factors that may account for this finding. First, there is likely to be a retrograde amnesia covering a period of years before the operation. This impairment would be a true loss of previously established memories. Second, there may also be an anterograde component due to the occurrence of seizures and the toxic doses of anticonvulsant medications prescribed to prevent them. This condition could have interfered with the acquisition of new information. Third, another factor may be a progressive deterioration of remote memories over the years due to impoverished rehearsal secondary to retrograde amnesia, anterograde amnesia, or both.

Comment

H.M.'s legacy to cognitive science and brain science has been to provide evidence relevant to distinctions between memory systems and among amnesias of different etiologies based upon the selective preservation or disturbance of specific capacities. H.M. shows a sparing of immediate but not lasting memory function, of skill learning and priming effects but not learning of facts and events, and of remote memories up to 11 years before operation but not after that. These findings suggest that processes in the storage of immediate memories are biologically independent of those underlying memories that endure, and that the acquisition of skills and priming effects is not supported by medial temporal-lobe structures, whereas the remembrance of people and episodes is. Further, H.M.'s preservation of immediate memory capacity and span and his temporally limited remote memory loss distinguish him from patients with Korsakoff's syndrome and patients with Alzheimer's disease, who do show deficits in immediate memory, as well as in remote memory across all time periods examined.[24,62,63] The additional deficits seen in Korsakoff's syndrome and Alzheimer's disease are in part related to the more extensive pathologic changes in the brain. Results from patients with a variety of brain pathologies are needed to understand the neurology of memory.

In 1984, 31 years after H.M. underwent bilateral medial temporal lobectomy, research with this patient continues to provide new insights into the cognitive and biologic processes that constitute normal human learning and memory. Neuroscientists of present and future generations are indebted to H.M. for his ongoing contributions to our knowledge. We should also recognize the neurosurgeon Dr. Scoville for encouraging research with H.M., and for publicizing it himself in an effort to ensure that, in the patient group to which H.M. belongs, N = 1.

References

1. Scoville, W. B. and Milner, B. Loss of recent memory after bilateral hippocampal lesions. J Neurol Neurosurg Psychiatry 20, 11–21, 1957.
2. Scoville, W. B., Dunsmore, R. H., Liberson, W. T., Henry, C. E. and Pepe, A. Observations of medial temporal lobotomy and uncotomy in the treatment of psychotic states. Proc Assoc Res Nerv Ment Dis 31, 347–69, 1953.
3. Scoville, W. B. Amnesia after bilateral mesial temporal-lobe excision: Introduction to Case H.M. Neuropsychologia 6, 211–3, 1968.
4. Toone, B. K., Wheeler, M. and Fenwick, P. B. C. Sex hormone changes in male epileptics. Clin Endocrinol 12, 391–5, 1980.
5. McEwen, B. Glucocorticoids and hippocampus: Receptors in search of a function. In Current Topics in Neuroendocrinology, Vol 2. Ganten D., Pfaff D. (eds): Berlin: Springer, 1982, pp. 23–43, 1982.
6. Poletti, C. E. and Sujatanond, M. Evidence for a second hippocampal efferent pathway to hypothalamus and basal forebrain comparable to fornix system: A unit study in the awake monkey. J Neurophysiol 44, 514–531, 1980.

7. Aulhorn, E. and Harms, H. Visual perimetry. In Jameson, E. and Hurvich, L. H. (eds): Handbook of Sensory Physiology, VII. New York: Springer, 1972.

8. Eichenbaum, H., Morton, T. H., Potter, H. and Corkin, S. Selective olfactory deficits in Case H.M. Brain 106, 459–72, 1984.

9. Corkin, S., Milner, B. and Rasmussen, T. Somatosensory thresholds: Contrasting effects of postcentral-gyrus and posterior parietal-lobe excisions. Arch Neurol 23, 41–58, 1970.

10. Hebben, N., Corkin, S., Eichenbaum, H. and Shedlack K. Diminished ability to interpret and report internal states after bilateral medial temporal resection: Case H.M. Behavioral Neuroscience 99, 1031–9, 1985.

11. Thurstone, L. L. A Factorial Study of Perception. Chicago: University Press, 1944.

12. Corkin, S., Growdon, J. H., Sullivan, E. V. and Rosen, T. J. Dissociation of sensorimotor functions in Alzheimer's disease. Unpublished MS.

13. Bucy, P. C. Neurology, 4th ed. Springfield, M. A. 1949: Thomas, 1949.

14. Brinkman, J. and Kuypers, H. G. J. M. Cerebral control of contralateral and ipsilateral arm, hand, and finger movements in the split-brain rhesus monkey. Brain 96, 653–74, 1973.

15. Milner, B. Psychological defects produced by temporal-lobe excision. Res Public Assoc Res Nerv Ment Dis 36, 244–57, 1958.

16. Doppelt, J. E. and Wallace, W. L. Standardization of the Wechsler adult intelligence scale for older persons. J Abnorm Soc Psychol 51, 213–30, 1955.

17. Torch, W. C., Hirano, A. and Solomon, S. Anterograde transneuronal degeneration in the limbic system: Clinical-anatomical correlation. Neurology 27, 1157–63, 1977.

18. Lackner, J. R. Observations on the speech processing capabilities of an amnesic patient: Several aspects of H.M.'s language function. Neuropsychologia 12, 199–207, 1974.

19. Kaplan, E., Goodglass, H. and Weintraub, S. The Boston Naming Test, experimental edition. Boston: Lea & Febinger, 1978.

20. DeRenzi, E and Vignolo, L. A. The token test: A sensitive test to detect receptive disturbances in aphasics. Brain 85, 655–78, 1962.

21. DeRenzi, E. and Ferrari, C. The reporter's test: A sensitive test to detect expressive disturbances in aphasics. Cortex 14, 279–93, 1978.

22. Newcombe, F. Missile Wounds of the Brain. London: Oxford University Press, 1969.

23. Huff, F. J., Corkin, S., Growdon J. J. Anomia in Alzheimer's disease: Associated cognitive deficits. Soc Neurosci Abstr 9, 94, 1983.

24. Corkin, S. Some relationships between global amnesia and the memory impairments in Alzheimer's disease. In Corkin, S., Davis, K. L., Growdon, J. H., Usdin, E. and Wurtman R. J. (eds): Alzheimer's disease: a report of progress in research. New York: Raven Press, 1982.

25. O'Keefe, J. and Nadel, L. The Hippocampus as a Cognitive Map. Oxford: Clarendon Press, 1978.

26. Teuber, H-L. and Weinstein, S. Ability to discover hidden figures after cerebral lesions. Arch Neurol Psychiatry 76, 369–79, 1956.

27. Corkin, S. Hidden figures test performance: Lasting effects of unilateral penetrating head injury and transient effects of bilateral cingulotomy. Neuropsychologia 17, 585–605, 1979.

28. Semmes, J., Weinstein, S., Ghent L. and Teuber, H-L. Correlates of impaired orientation in personal and extrapersonal space. Brain 86, 747–72, 1963.

29. Hebb, D. O. Organization of Behavior. New York: John Wiley and Sons, p 278, 1949.
30. Milner, B., Corkin, S. and Teuber, H-L. Further analysis of the hippocampal amnesic syndrome: 14-year follow-up study of H.M. Neuropsychologia 6, 215–34, 1968.
31. Milner, B. Disorders of memory after brain lesions in man. Neuropsychologia 6, 175–9, 1968.
32. Lansdell, H. C. Effect of extent of temporal lobe ablations on two lateralized deficits. Physio Behav 3, 271–3, 1968.
33. Cohen, N. J. and Corkin, S. Chronic global amnesia after ruptured aneurysms of the anterior communicating artery. Soc Neurosci Abstr 8, 25, 1982.
34. Squire, L. R., Cohen, N. J. and Zola-Morgan, S. Comparisons among forms of amnesia: Some deficits are unique to Korsakoff's syndrome. Soc Neurosci Abstr 8, 24, 1982.
35. Winocur, G., Kinsbourne, M., Moscovitch, M. The effect of cueing on release from proactive interference in Korsakoff amnesic patients. J Exp Psychol [Hum Learn] 7, 56–65, 1981.
36. Milner, B. Effects of different brain lesions on card sorting. Arch Neurol 9, 90–100, 1963.
37. Porteus, S. D. Porteus Maze Test. Palo Alto, CA: Pacific Books, 1965.
38. Posner, M. I., Nissen, M. J. and Ogden W. C. Attended and unattended processing modes: The role of set for spatial location. In Pick, H. L. Jr. and Saltzman, E. (eds): Modes of Perceiving and Processing Information. Hillsdale, NJ: Erlbaum, 1978.
39. McCormick, D. A., Lavond, D. G., Clark, G. A., Kettner, R. E. et al. The engram found? Role of the cerebellum in classical conditioning of nictitating membrane and eyelid responses. Bull Psychonomic Soc 18, 103–5, 1984.
40. Solomon, P. R., Vander Shaaf, E. R., Nobre, A. C., Weisz, D. J. and Thompson, R. F. Hippocampus and trace conditioning of the rabbit's nictitating membrane response. Soc Neurosci Abstr 9, 645, 1983.
41. Corsi, P. Human memory and the medial temporal region of the brain. Unpublished doctoral dissertation, McGill University, 1972.
42. Wickelgren, W. A. Sparing of short-term memory in an amnesic patient: Implications for a strength theory of memory. Neuropsychologia 6, 235–44, 1968.
43. Drachman, D. A. and Arbit, J. Memory and the hippocampal complex. Arch Neurol 15, 52–61, 1966.
44. Prisko, L. Short-term memory in focal cerebral damage. Unpublished doctoral dissertation, McGill University, 1963.
45. Milner, B. Memory and the medial temporal regions of the brain. In Biology of Memory. New York: Academic Press, 1970, pp. 29–50, 1970.
46. Smith, M. L. and Milner, B. The role of the right hippocampus in the recall of spatial location. Neuropsychologia 19, 781–93, 1981.
47. Jones, M. K. Imagery as a mnemonic aid after left temporal lobectomy: Contrast between material-specific and generalized memory disorders. Neuropsychologia 12, 21–30, 1974.
48. Milner, B. Visually guided maze learning in man: Effect of bilateral hippocampal, bilateral frontal, and unilateral cerebral lesions. Neuropsychologia 3, 317–38, 1965.
49. Corkin, S. Tactually guided maze learning in man: Effects of unilateral cortical excisions and bilateral hippocampal lesions. Neuropsychologia 3, 339–51, 1965.
50. Penfield, W. and Milner, B. Memory deficit produced by bilateral lesions in the hippocampal zone. Arch Neurol Psychiatry 79, 475–97, 1958.
51. Milner, B. and Kimura, D. Dissociable visual learning defects after unilateral

temporal lobectomy in man. Paper presented at the 35th annual meeting of the Eastern Psychological Association, Philadelphia, April, 1964.

52. Milner, B. Les troubles de la memoire accompagnant des lesions hippocampiques bilaterales. In Physiologie de l'Hippocampe. Paris: Centre National de la Recherche Scientifique, pp. 257–72, 1962.
53. Corkin, S. Acquisition of motor skill after bilateral medial temporal-lobe excision. Neuropsychologia 6, 255–64, 1968.
54. Nissen, M. J., Cohen, N. J. and Corkin, S. The amnesic patient H. M.: Learning and retention of perceptual skills. Soc Neurosci Abstr 7, 235, 1981.
55. Cohen, N. J. and Corkin, S. Normal learning of the Tower of Hanoi puzzle despite amnesia. Unpublished ms.
56. Cohen, N. J. and Corkin, S. The amnesic patient H. M.: Learning and retention of a cognitive skill. Soc Neurosci Abstr 7, 235, 1981.
57. Cohen, N. J. and Squire, L. Preserved learning and retention of pattern-analyzing skill in amnesia: Dissociation of knowing-how and knowing-that. Science, 210, 207–10, 1980.
58. Corkin, S., Cohen, N. J. and Sagar, H. J. Memory for remote personal and public events after bilateral medial temporal lobectomy. Soc Neurosci Abstr 9, 28, 1983.
59. Sagar, H. J., Cohen, N. J. and Corkin, S. Dissociations among processes in remote memory. To be presented at the Conference on Memory Dysfunctions, New York Academy of Sciences, June, 1984.
60. Squire, L. R. Remote memory as affected by aging. Neuropsychologia 12, 429–35, 1974.
61. Crovitz, H. F. and Shiffman, H. Frequency of episodic memories as a function of their age. Bull Psychonomic Soc 4, 517–8, 1974.
62. Butters, N. and Cermak, L. S. Alcoholic Korsakoff's Syndrome. New York: Academic Press, 1980.
63. Cohen, N. J. and Squire, L. R. Retrograde amnesia and remote memory impairment. Neuropsychologia 19, 337–56, 1981.

7 Larry R. Squire, Barbara Knowlton and Gail Musen
'The Structure and Organization of Memory'

Reprinted in full from: *Annual Review of Psychology* **44**, 453–495 (1993)

Introduction

A major goal of psychology is to understand the underlying organization of cognition – that is, to develop formal accounts of cognitive processes, information flow, and representations. Ultimately, one wants to understand cognition not just as an abstraction, or in terms that are simply plausible or internally consistent. Rather, one wants to know as specifically and concretely as possible how the job is actually done. It is often said, working from logical considerations alone, that in describing the function of a complex device one can separate consideration of its formal operations (the software) from consideration of the mechanisms used to implement the operations (the hardware). In the history of cognitive psychology it has been traditional to separate psychological theory from neurobiological detail. Until recently, this approach could be justified by the fact that relevant neurobiological information was simply not available. Yet it is increasingly true that the domains of psychology and neuroscience are reinforcing each other and working hand in hand (Kandel and Squire, 1992). Neuroscience has become relevant and useful for elucidating the structure and organization of cognition.

Here we consider recent work on learning and memory from a combined psychology-neuroscience point of view. We focus on the characteristics of various forms of memory, their relationship to each other, and how they are organized in the brain. Although work with normal human subjects has been vital to this line of inquiry, our discussion draws especially on neuropsychological studies of memory-impaired patients and related studies with experimental animals. For recent reviews that emphasize work with normal subjects, see Hintzman (1990), Richardson-Klavehn and Bjork (1988), Schacter *et al.*, (1993), and Tulving (1991).

Short-term memory

One of the oldest and most widely accepted ideas about memory is that short-term memory (STM) can be usefully distinguished from long-term memory (LTM) (James, 1890; Waugh and Norman, 1965; Glanzer and Cunitz, 1966; Atkinson and Shiffrin 1968). That this distinction is prominently reflected in the organization of brain systems is demonstrated by the fact that amnesic patients have intact STM, despite severely impaired LTM (Baddeley and Warrington, 1970; Drachman and Arbit, 1966; Milner, 1971). A recent study of amnesic patients has made this proposition even more secure (Cave and Squire, 1992a). Verbal STM was assessed with seven separate administrations of the standard digit span test in order to obtain a more precise measure of STM than has previously been available. In addition, nonverbal STM was assessed with four tests, including a test of STM for spatial information. Amnesic patients with hippocampal formation damage had the same average digit span as normal subjects (6.8 digits) and performed entirely normally on the other tests. Thus, STM is independent of LTM and independent of the structures and connections damaged in amnesia.

An important development has been the separation of STM and LTM in experimental animals, which raises the possibility of investigating the biological basis of STM. In one compelling study (Wright *et al.*, 1985), the same recognition memory test consisting of four sequentially presented colored slides was given to pigeons, monkeys, and humans. (The humans viewed patterns from a kaleidoscope, and the pigeons and monkeys viewed pictures.) After a variable delay interval, a probe item was presented that on half the trials matched one of the four list items. Subjects made one response if the probe matched a list item, another if it did not. All three species exhibited primacy and recency effects as indicated by U-shaped serial position functions in which the first and fourth items in the list were remembered better than the second and third items. (The primacy effect refers to the superiority of the first item, and the recency effect refers to the superiority of the last item.) Pigeons exhibited a U-shaped serial position function at delay intervals of 1 and 2 sec, monkeys at delays of 1–10 sec, and humans at delays of 10–60 sec. At shorter delays than these, the primacy effect was absent. At longer delays, the recency effect was absent. The results for all three species require two distinct memory processes – e.g. a transient STM to account for the short-lived recency effect and, to account for the primacy effect, a longer-lasting LTM that emerges as retroactive interference decays during the delay interval.

A strong parallel between humans and experimental animals is also indicated by the finding that hippocampal lesions in rats eliminate the primacy portion of the serial position curve but not the recency portion (Kesner and Novak, 1982), just as occurs in amnesic patients (Baddeley and Warrington, 1970; Milner, 1978). Finally, monkeys with large medial temporal lobe lesions were entirely normal at relearning postoperatively the trial-unique delayed nonmatching to sample task (Mishkin and Delacour, 1975) with a delay interval of 1 sec between the sample and the choice (Overman, 1990). In contrast, a severe impairment in performance was observed at longer delays. This finding is noteworthy because the usefulness of the delayed nonmatching to sample task for studying memory in monkeys was questioned recently, precisely because this task has not always distinguished STM and LTM (Ringo, 1991). This issue was subsequently considered more fully (Alvarez-Royo *et al.*, 1992). Monkeys with medial temporal lobe lesions exhibited impaired memory at long retention delays and normal memory at short retention delays, when the delay intervals were presented in mixed order. Moreover, the normal monkeys and the monkeys with lesions exhibited a statistically significant group X retention delay interaction, which could be demonstrated whether the data were analyzed using a percentage correct measure, a d' (discriminability) measure, or an arcsine transform. Thus, the work with monkeys is fully consistent with the facts of human amnesia and provides an additional illustration of the separation between STM and LTM.

The traditional view of the distinction between STM and LTM has been that the systems operate serially (Atkinson and Shiffrin, 1968; Glanzer and Cunitz, 1966; Waugh and Norman, 1965). Information initially enters STM and subsequently becomes incorporated into a more stable LTM. This view was challenged some years ago (Shallice and Warrington, 1970; Warrington and Shallice, 1969) on the basis of findings from a carefully studied patient (K.F.). Following a left parietal injury from a motorcycle accident, K.F. had a severely deficient verbal STM, as reflected by a digit span of one item, but nevertheless exhibited normal verbal LTM as measured, for example, by paired-associate learning of words and word-list learning. This pattern of findings led to the proposal that information may not need to enter STM before reaching LTM because the inputs to these two systems are arranged in parallel (Shallice and Warrington, 1970; Weiskrantz, 1990).

As the result of newer work, the findings from patient K.F. can now be understood fully without postulating parallel STM and LTM stores. STM has come to be viewed as a diverse collection of temporary capacities that are distributed across multiple, separate processing modules (Baddeley and Hitch, 1974; Goldman-Rakic, 1987; Monsell, 1984; Squire, 1987). In this view, auditory-verbal STM is a temporary storage system only for phonologically coded information. If one supposes that STM and LTM are serially organized, then one would expect a deficit in auditory-verbal STM to result in a corresponding deficit in LTM, but only to the extent that tests of LTM also depend critically on phonological analysis of verbal material. Findings from recent studies support this perspective.

Baddeley and his colleagues studied a patient (P.V.) who had suffered a cerebrovascular accident involving the left perisylvian region (Baddeley *et al.*, 1988). The patient appeared to have a deficit in STM similar to that of patient K.F. Thus, her auditory digit span was two items, but prose recall and free recall of word lists were intact. Yet, when tests of LTM were specially devised that required P.V. to depend on phonological analysis at the time of learning (e.g. visual or auditory presentation of foreign language word pairs that would be difficult to learn by forming semantic associations), performance was distinctly impaired.

Related evidence on this point came from studies of 4- to 6-year-old normal children who were selected according to their repetition ability for single nonwords. Children who had low repetition scores for nonwords also had difficulty in a LTM task involving the learning and retention of arbitrary, unfamiliar names for toys (Gathercole and Baddeley, 1990). Finally, articulatory suppression (whereby subvocal rehearsal is discouraged by requiring subjects to perform an interfering task) impaired the long-term learning of Russian vocabulary in normal adult subjects but not the learning of native language paired associates (Papagno *et al.*, 1991). These findings all suggest that a deficit in short-term phonological memory leads to a deficit in LTM when the long-term learning also depends on phonological information.

Accordingly, the findings from patients K.F., P.V., and other similar patients with impaired verbal STM can be understood as a selective deficit in one component of STM, and a correspondingly selective deficit in LTM for information that is ordinarily processed by the defective STM component. Such a deficit leaves other components of STM available for the establishment of LTM. This perspective thus holds to the traditional view that STM grades into LTM and is essential for its formation.

Long-term memory

Declarative memory

One important insight to emerge recently is that LTM is not a single entity but is composed of several different components, which are mediated by separate brain systems. Precursors to this idea can be found in many earlier writings (for reviews, see Schacter, 1987; Squire, 1987), but it became the subject of wide interest beginning only in the early 1980s as the result of experimental findings with normal adult subjects, amnesic patients, and experimental animals (see, e.g., Cohen and Squire, 1980; Graf *et al.*, 1984; Jacoby and Witherspoon, 1982; Malamut *et al.*, 1984; Tulving *et al.*, 1982; Warrington and Weiskrantz, 1982; for two important earlier proposals, see Hirsh, 1974; O'Keefe and Nadel, 1978). The major distinction is between conscious memory for facts and events and various forms of nonconscious memory, including skill and habit learning, simple classical conditioning, the phenomenon of priming, and other instances where memory is expressed through performance rather than by recollection (see the section below on Nondeclarative Memory).

Studies of amnesic patients have provided particularly strong evidence for this distinction. These patients fail conventional memory tasks that involve, for example, recall or recognition but nevertheless perform entirely normally on a wide variety of other tasks. Although various terms have been used to describe these kinds of memory, the terms have remarkably similar meanings. Declarative memory (explicit memory, relational memory) is a brain-systems construct, referring to memory that is dependent on the integrity of the hippocampus and anatomically related structures in the medial temporal lobe and diencephalon (Squire and Zola-Morgan, 1991; Zola-Morgan and Squire, 1993). Nondeclarative (implicit) memory is a heterogeneous collection of separate abilities that can be additionally dissociated from each other (Butters *et al.*, 1990; Heindel *et al.*, 1989, 1991). These memory abilities depend on brain systems outside of the medial temporal lobe and diencephalon.

A number of important questions have been raised about whether distinctions between kinds of memory can be defined and established outside of the experimental contexts in which they were first developed. For example, the distinction between declarative and nondeclarative (or explicit and implicit) emphasizes the notion of conscious recollection, which is not useful when considering learning and memory in nonhuman animals. It has therefore been important to ask whether terms like declarative and nondeclarative have meaning independent of the concept of conscious recollection and independent of an empirically determined list of what amnesic patients can and cannot do. Recent work has helped to free these terms from such potential circularity by showing that different kinds of memory have different characteristics (for additional discussion see Sherry and Schacter, 1987; Squire, 1992a).

Declarative memory is fast, it is not always reliable (i.e. forgetting and retrieval failure can occur), and it is flexible in the sense that it is accessible to multiple response systems. Nondeclarative memory is slow (priming is an exception), reliable, and inflexible – that is, the information is not readily expressed by response systems that were not involved in the original learning. Two important experiments have illustrated that declarative and nondeclarative memory differ in flexibility. In the first experiment (Eichenbaum *et al.*, 1989), rats with damage to the hippocampal system were trained concurrently on two separate odor discrimination tasks (A+B−, C+D−) that they could eventually perform about as well as normal rats. Thus, both normal rats and rats with lesions came to choose odor A when it was presented in the odor pair

AB and odor C when it was presented in the odor pair CD. However, a transfer task showed that something different had been learned by the two groups. Specifically, when rats were presented with recombined odor pairs (AD or CB), the normal rats tended to choose odor A, performing about as well as on the regular learning trials. That is, they were not disrupted by the new combination of stimuli; they were able to use relational information about the odors in a flexible way. In contrast, the rats with lesions behaved as if they were confronting a new problem and performed near chance. In their case, it appeared that the kind of knowledge that had been acquired was inaccessible when the original learning event was not precisely repeated.

A similar result was obtained with monkeys who had lesions of the hippocampus or related structures (Saunders and Weiskrantz, 1989). Monkeys first learned which pairs of four objects were rewarded (e.g. AB+ and CD+) and which were not (e.g. AC− and BC−). Specifically, normal monkeys and monkeys with lesions were given a series of two-choice discrimination tasks in which a positive object pair was always presented together with a negative pair (e.g. AB+ and AC−). In this way, monkeys were required to respond on the basis of both objects in each pair (e.g. object A was correct when it appeared with object B but not when it appeared with object C). In a subsequent transfer task, monkeys were tested to determine what they had learned about the associations. One element of a previously rewarded pair was first presented (e.g. object A), and monkeys were immediately given a choice between two other objects (in this example, objects B and C). The normal monkeys selected object B, which had been part of the two-element, rewarded pair (AB), on 70% of the trials; but the monkeys with lesions performed at chance. Thus, what the operated monkeys had learned about the object-reward associations was bound to the original learning situation.

This issue has been addressed to some extent in studies of human learning and memory. In one study, amnesic patients who had gradually (and abnormally slowly) learned computer programming commands had difficulty applying their knowledge to new situations and difficulty answering open-ended questions about what they had learned (Glisky *et al.*, 1986a). In another study, in which much less training was given, amnesic patients acquired a limited ability to complete sentences in response to cue words (cued recall) (Shimamura and Squire, 1988). In this case, it was shown that the knowledge acquired by the patients was as flexible, as accessible to indirect cues, and as available to awareness as the knowledge acquired by normal subjects. A likely possibility is that these patients relied on residual declarative memory to learn the sentences, while the patients who learned computer commands acquired the information as procedural memory for programming skills. Hyperspecificity appears to be a property of nondeclarative memory (also see Tulving and Schacter, 1990), not a property of whatever information amnesic patients are able to acquire. When tasks are amenable to declarative memory strategies, amnesic patients will attempt to learn with their impaired declarative memory system, and whatever they succeed in remembering will be flexible and accessible to awareness.

Episodic and semantic memory

Episodic and semantic memory are two types of declarative memory (Tulving, 1983, 1991). Episodic memory refers to autobiographical memory for events that occupy a particular spatial and temporal context, and semantic memory refers to general knowledge about the world. Both types of memory are declarative, in the sense that retrieval of information is carried out explicitly and subjects are aware that stored information is being accessed. While it is agreed that episodic memory is severely impaired in amnesia and dependent on the integrity of the brain system damaged in amnesia, the relationship between semantic memory and this brain system has not been so clear. Amnesic patients do have great difficulty acquiring semantic knowledge (Glisky *et al.*, 1986 a, 1986b; Kovner *et al.*, 1983), but they can typically succeed to some extent after much repetition. In one report (Tulving *et al.*, 1991), a severely amnesic patient (K.C.) eventually learned to complete arbitrary three-word sentences during a large number of training trials distributed over many months. This occurred despite the apparent absence of any memory at all for specific episodes.

An issue that remains to be addressed is whether episodic memory can truly be absent altogether, in the presence of gradually successful semantic learning, or whether semantic learning succeeds by building on residual episodic memory. Even a small amount of residual episodic memory might, in the fullness of time and after sufficient repetition, develop into serviceable semantic knowledge. When memory is impaired, the ability to acquire new semantic knowledge through repetition will always exceed the ability to acquire episodic memory, because episodic memory is by definition unique to time and place and cannot be repeated (see Ostergaard and Squire, 1990).

One proposal is that episodic and semantic memory are dissociated in amnesia (Cermak, 1984; Kinsbourne and Wood, 1975; Parkin, 1982). For example, it has been proposed that amnesia selectively affects episodic memory, that semantic learning is fully intact in amnesia, and that the advantage of normal subjects over amnesic patients in tests of semantic learning is due to the fact that normal subjects can perform these tests by drawing on episodic memory (Tulving, 1991). By this view, repeated exposure to factual material can lead gradually and directly to long-term memory storage without requiring the participation of the brain system damaged in amnesia. A problem with this view is that amnesic patients have difficulty with factual information even when the contribution of episodic retrieval is unlikely. Thus, they fail remote memory questions about past public events that occurred more than a decade before the onset of amnesia (Squire *et al.*, 1989). This deficit would appear to reflect a failure of semantic memory because it is unlikely that normal subjects gain their advantage over amnesic patients on such remote memory tests by using episodic memory to answer the questions. Can episodic memory materially contribute to one's ability to identify Sara Jane Moore (the woman who attempted the assassination of President Ford) or to recall what dance the Peppermint Lounge was famous for (the Twist)?

A second difficulty turns on the question of how memory systems in humans relate to memory systems in nonhuman animals. If semantic memory is independent of the brain system damaged in amnesia, then experimental animals should be affected by damage to this brain system only to the extent that they use episodic memory to perform tasks. The difficulty is that rats, monkeys, and other animals are severely impaired on a wide variety of memory tasks following damage to the hippocampus and related structures (for reviews, see Sutherland and Rudy, 1989; Squire, 1992a), and the tasks that are affected involve much more than is usually intended by the term episodic memory (e.g. maze tasks and object recognition tasks). Indeed, episodic memory is usually considered to be either unavailable to nonhuman animals altogether or analogous to particular forms of trial-dependent memory (Olton, 1985; Tulving, 1985). Thus, one must suppose either that animals use episodic memory extensively, or that in animals some kinds of memory other than episodic memory depend on the hippocampus and related structures.

If the distinction between episodic and semantic memory is not relevant to the function of the brain system damaged in amnesia, the distinction is no less interesting or important. One possibility is that both episodic and semantic memory depend on the brain system damaged in amnesia (i.e. the hippocampus and related structures) and that episodic memory additionally depends on the integrity of the frontal lobes. Patients with frontal lobe damage, who are not amnesic, exhibit a phenomenon termed source amnesia (Janowsky *et al.*, 1989c). Source amnesia refers to loss of information about when and where a remembered item was acquired (Evans and Thorn, 1966; Schacter *et al.*, 1984; Shimamura and Squire, 1987). Thus, source amnesia amounts to a loss of autobiographical involvement with recollected material – i.e. a disturbance of episodic memory. It is important to note that amnesic patients who commit source errors can subsequently demonstrate by multiple-choice testing that they have as much knowledge about the learning event as amnesic patients who do not commit source errors (Shimamura and Squire, 1991). Thus, source amnesia appears to reflect a loss of episodic memory, related to frontal lobe dysfunction, which reflects a disconnection between facts and their contexts.

If episodic memory were understood in this way, a number of points would be clarified. First, the biological validity of the distinction between episodic memory and semantic memory is based on the greater contribution that frontal lobe function makes to episodic memory, compared to semantic memory. Second, episodic memory is available to nonhuman animals in a limited way, in the sense that animals do not acquire or express information about past events in the same way that people do – i.e. as recollections of past personal happenings. According to this view, the difference between human episodic memory and that of animals is attributable to the greater size and complexity of the human frontal lobe.

Third, episodic memory can be virtually absent in some severely amnesic patients who can still accomplish some semantic learning (e.g. patient K.C.). Such a condition depends in part on source amnesia, pursuant to frontal lobe pathology, which is superimposed on a severe difficulty in acquiring information about both facts and events. This view suggests two possibilities: (1) patients more amnesic that K.C., but without frontal lobe damage, might be unable to accomplish semantic learning as well as patient K.C.; (2) severely amnesic patients might be able to accomplish some semantic learning as well as a corresponding degree of learning about single past events, albeit at an impaired level, provided they were tested with a method that does not require source memory and is not sensitive to frontal lobe pathology. For example, patients could be tested with multiple-choice methods that asked about what occurred in a specific event without requiring that the patients be able to place themselves autobiographically within the episode.

The brain system supporting declarative memory

During the past decade, an animal model of human amnesia was established in the monkey (Mishkin, 1982; Squire and Zola-Morgan, 1983; Mahut and Moss, 1984). Cumulative work with monkeys based on this animal model, together with findings from rats and new information from memory-impaired patients, has identified in broad outline the structures and connections important for declarative memory. Damage within the medial temporal lobe or the medial thalamus is sufficient to cause severe memory impairment. Within the medial temporal lobe, the important structures are the hippocampus and adjacent, anatomically related cortex (i.e. entorhinal, perirhinal, and parahippocampal cortices) (Squire and Zola-Morgan, 1991). Within the diencephalon, the most important structures are in the medial thalamus: the anterior thalamic nucleus, the mediodorsal nucleus, and connections to and from the medial thalamus that lie within the internal medullary lamina. The medial thalamus receives well-described projections from several anatomical components of the medial temporal lobe. It is not clear whether or not the mammillary nuclei (MN) make an important separate contribution to memory functions, although damage to MN has sometimes been reported to produce a small degree of memory impairment (for reviews, see Markowitsch, 1988, Victor *et al.*, 1989; Zola-Morgan and Squire, 1993).

Both the medial temporal lobe and the medial thalamus project to the frontal lobe, thereby providing a route by which recollections can be translated into action. Damage to the frontal lobe does not itself cause amnesia (Janowsky *et al.*, 1989a); but frontal lobe pathology markedly affects cognition (Levin *et al.*, 1991), and it substantially alters the nature of the memory impairment when it occurs together with damage to the medial temporal lobe or medial thalamus (Shimamura *et al.*, 1991).

Transient amnesic conditions leave patients permanently unable to remember the events that occurred while they were amnesic (Kritchevsky *et al.*, 1988). This shows that the medial temporal/diencephalic system is required at the time of learning if an enduring and retrievable long-term (declarative) memory is to be established. How long after learning this brain system remains essential can in principle be determined by examining the phenomenon of retrograde amnesia. In particular, one wants to know which periods are lost from the period before amnesia began. In practice, it has been difficult to settle this matter with memory-impaired patients. First, the moment when amnesia begins is often difficult to establish. Second, there is usually considerable uncertainty about the precise locus and extent of damage in the particular patients being studied. Third, studies of remote memory in patients necessarily rely on retrospective methods and imperfect tests. Despite these difficulties, something useful has been learned about retrograde amnesia through quantitative studies of memory-impaired patients. More recently, the matter has been clarified by prospective studies of retrograde amnesia in mice, rats, and monkeys.

Time-limited function of the brain system supporting declarative memory

The characteristics of retrograde amnesia vary enormously across different patients and patient groups. For one patient (R.B.), in whom the damage was restricted to the CA1 region of the hippocampus, retrograde amnesia was limited to perhaps 1 or 2 years prior to the onset of amnesia (Zola-Morgan *et al.*, 1986). Other patients exhibit temporally graded memory loss covering one to two decades (Squire *et al.*, 1989). Still other patients, usually ones with severe impairment, exhibit retrograde amnesia that appears extensive and ungraded, covering most of adult life (for reviews, see Butters and Stuss, 1989; Squire, 1992a). One possibility is that the extent of retrograde memory loss is related simply to the severity of amnesia and to the extent of damage within the medial temporal/diencephalic system. By this view, extended, ungraded retrograde memory loss represents an extreme condition on a continuum of severity. This alternative seems unlikely, because the severity of anterograde amnesia and the severity of remote memory impairment are not always correlated (Barr *et al.*, 1990; Shimamura and Squire, 1986; Kopelman, 1989) and because the severely amnesic patient H.M. is capable of recalling well-formed episodic memories from his early life (Sagar *et al.*, 1985). Many of the patients who have been reported to have extended, ungraded remote memory impairment have damage outside of the medial temporal lobe and medial thalamus. Thus, another possibility is that temporally graded retrograde amnesia occurs when damage is limited to the medial temporal lobe or medial thalamus and that extended, ungraded loss occurs only when there is damage outside this system.

Retrograde amnesia exhibits quite similar characteristics in medial temporal lobe amnesia and diencephalic amnesia (Squire *et al.*, 1989). The amnesia reflects a loss of usable knowledge, not a loss of accessibility that can be compensated for by providing repeated retrieval opportunities. Moreover, there are no compelling demonstrations that retrograde amnesia can be remediated by simple changes in the test procedures (e.g. asking patients to complete a famous name from a few letters instead of matching the name to a photograph (see Squire *et al.*, 1990).

Retrograde amnesia can in one sense be described as a retrieval deficit. This description fits the observation that most lost memories return following transient amnesia (Benson and Geschwind, 1967; Squire *et al.*, 1975). Yet, in another sense this description does not capture the nature of the impairment. First, memories acquired just prior to the amnesic episode cannot be recovered. Second, it is not clear that lost memories would return so fully if the system remained dysfunctional for a long time. Third, recent treatments of the medial temporal/diencephalic brain system favor a role for the system in establishing long-term memory that does not fit easily either a storage or a retrieval interpretation (Eichenbaum *et al.*, 1992; Halgren, 1984; McNaughton and Nadel, 1990; Milner, 1989; Rolls, 1990; Teyler and Discenna, 1986; Squire, 1992a). For example, the system has been proposed as the storage site for a summary sketch, a conjunction, or an index; and it has been proposed that one critical event is the induction of long-term potentiation (LTP) in the hippocampus at the time of learning.

Prospective studies with experimental animals have addressed long-standing questions concerning the precise shape of retrograde amnesia gradients (see Squire *et al.*, 1984). In one study, monkeys learned 100 object pairs prior to removal of the hippocampal formation (Zola-Morgan and Squire, 1990). Twenty object pairs were learned at each of five preoperative periods (16, 12, 8, 4, and 2 weeks). After surgery, memory was tested by presenting all 100 objects in a mixed order for a single trial. Normal monkeys remembered objects learned recently better than objects learned 12–16 weeks earlier. Operated monkeys exhibited the opposite pattern, remembering objects learned remote from surgery significantly better than objects learned recently. Moreover, memory for remotely learned object pairs was entirely normal. Similar temporal gradients of retrograde amnesia have recently been demonstrated for rats acquiring a context-dependent fear response at different times prior to hippocampal damage (Kim and Fanselow, 1992), for rats acquiring a food preference prior to hippocampal or diencephalic damage (Winocur, 1990), and for mice acquiring maze habits at different times prior to damage of entorhinal cortex (Cho *et al.*, 1991).

These results show that the medial temporal/diencephalic memory system is not a repository of long-term memory. Indeed, in each of the animal experiments it was possible to identify a time after learning when damage to this system had no effect on memory for what had been learned. Thus, information that initially depends on the medial temporal/diencephalic system can eventually become independent of it. Initially, this system participates in the storage and retrieval of declarative memory. As time passes after learning, a process of consolidation and reorganization occurs such that a more permanent memory is established that is independent of the system. Permanent storage is likely to occur in neocortex where information is first processed and held in short-term memory.

A more specific version of this idea states that the medial temporal/ diencephalic memory system initially binds together the distributed sites in neocortex that together represent the memory of a whole event (Zola-Morgan and Squire, 1990). This low-capacity, fast system permits the acquisition and storage of representations involving arbitrarily different elements, and for a period it provides a basis for retrieving the full representation, even when a partial cue is presented. As time passes, the burden of long-term memory storage is assumed fully by neocortex. The time course of consolidation will vary depending on the species, the strength of initial learning, and the rate of forgetting. The changes can be expected to continue during a significant portion of the lifetime of a memory.

The development of declarative memory

When the notion of multiple memory systems was first developed, it provided a new way to think about the phenomenon of infantile amnesia – i.e. the relative unavailability of memories for events that occurred before the third year of life. The traditional view, as influenced by psychoanalytic theory (Freud, 1962), has been that memories are acquired in infancy but are later repressed or become otherwise inaccessible (Neisser, 1962; White and Pillemer, 1979). Another possibility, based on notions about multiple memory systems, is that the memory system that supports declarative memory develops late and that declarative (conscious) memories are simply not formed early in life (Bachevalier and Mishkin, 1984; Douglas, 1975; Nadel and Zola-Morgan, 1984; Overman, 1990; Schacter and Moscovitch, 1984).

This newer idea initially found support in the fact that the delayed non-matching to sample task, which in adult humans and nonhuman primates depends on the integrity of medial temporal/diencephalic memory structures, is performed poorly by infant monkeys (Bachevalier and Mishkin, 1984) and by human infants (Diamond, 1990; Overman, 1990). By contrast, habit learning, which does not depend on this same brain system, is possible in monkeys as early as 3 months of age (Bachevalier, 1990). Moreover, many of the tasks that can support learning and memory in infants younger than 1 year can be construed as implicit memory tasks, i.e. as tasks of habituation, conditioning, and skill learning (see Schacter and Moscovitch, 1984).

However, recent data have cast doubts on this view (for discussion, see Diamond, 1990). One focus of interest has been the visual paired-comparison task (Fantz, 1964; Fagan, 1970), in which two identical items are presented together followed later by presentation of a familiar item and a novel item. Infants as young as 5 months of age tend to look more at the new item than the old item, thus providing a spontaneous measure of their memory for the previously encountered item. What kind of memory is exhibited here? Does visual paired-comparison depend on implicit (nondeclarative) memory or does it reflect early-developing declarative memory?

There are two relevant findings. First, performance on the visual paired-comparison task is severely impaired in infant monkeys with large bilateral medial temporal lobe lesions (Bachevalier, 1990). Second, performance on this task is also severely impaired in human amnesic patients (McKee and Squire, 1993). Thus, performance on this task is dependent on the medial temporal/diencephalic structures that are essential for declarative memory. It therefore seems reasonable to suppose that successful performance on the visual paired-comparison task reflects an early capacity for declarative memory. If so, the medial temporal/diencephalic memory system must be functional early in life, and its absence or slow development cannot account for infantile amnesia. The view that declarative memory is available early in life is also consistent with recent demonstrations of long-term-recall-like memory abilities in human infants (Baillargeon and DeVos, 1991; Bauer and Mandler, 1989; Mandler, 1990; Meltzoff, 1985). For example, infants younger than 1 year will reproduce actions involving toys, even 1 day after viewing a single demonstration of the actions by the experimenter.

If some degree of declarative memory is available to infants, what accounts for infantile amnesia? Recent evidence from nonhuman primates suggests that inferotemporal cortex, a higher-order visual association area in neocortex, is functionally immature early in life and less mature than medial temporal lobe structures (Bachevalier, 1990; Bachevalier *et al.*, 1986). Thus, what limits the formation and persistence of declarative memory may be not the maturation of the medial temporal/diencephalic structures that are essential for declarative memory, but rather the gradual maturation of the neocortical areas that are served by these structures and that are believed to be the repositories of long-term memory. This perspective provides points of contact between a neural account of infantile amnesia and accounts founded in cognitive psychology that emphasize the gradual maturation of cognition, the emergence of strategies for organizing information, the development of language, and the growth of individual identity (Neisser, 1962; White and Pillemer, 1979; Nelson, 1988).

Can the brain system supporting declarative memory be subdivided?

Do the anatomical components of the medial temporal/diencephalic memory system make similar or different contributions to memory? Although it is entirely reasonable, and even likely, that specialization exists within this large system, it has been difficult to find compelling evidence for this idea (for two points of view, see Parkin [1984] and Victor *et al.*, [1989]). For many years there was confusion on this point. Patients with Korsakoff's syndrome, an example of diencephalic amnesia, differ behaviorally in a number of respects from other amnesic patients, including those with medial temporal lobe lesions. However, it is now clear that amnesic patients with Korsakoff's syndrome typically have frontal lobe pathology (Jacobson and Lishman, 1987; Shimamura *et al.*, 1988). Their frontal lobe pathology produces certain symptoms that are not essential to memory impairment itself and that can also be found in patients with frontal lobe lesions who are not globally amnesic. For example, frontal lobe pathology produces difficulty in making temporal order judgments (Meudell *et al.*, 1985; Milner, 1971; McAndrews and Milner, 1991; Squire, 1982), it impairs metamemory (Janowsky *et al.*, 1989b; Shimamura and Squire, 1986), and it produces source amnesia (Janowsky *et al.*, 1989c, Schacter *et al.*, 1984). While these findings concerning the frontal lobes are important, they do not speak to possible differences in the contributions of diencephalic or medial temporal lobe structures to memory function.

Forgetting rates

With respect to diencephalic and medial temporal lobe brain structures, one early suggestion was that both regions are essential for establishing long-term memory but that medial temporal lobe damage is associated with rapid forgetting (of whatever information enters long-term memory) and that diencephalic damage is associated with a normal rate of forgetting (Huppert and Piercy, 1979; Squire, 1981). However, the case for medial temporal lobe damage rested on data from a single patient (H.M.), and subsequent testing of the same patient has not confirmed the original impression (Freed *et al.*, 1987). In support of these later results, patients with Alzheimer's disease, who have severe memory impairment and prominent pathology in the medial temporal lobe, also exhibited a normal rate of forgetting within long-term memory (Kopelman, 1985).

It has recently been possible to study forgetting rates in amnesic patients with confirmed medial temporal lobe lesions or diencephalic lesions (McKee and Squire, 1992), using the same procedure used in the original study by Huppert and Piercy (1979). The two groups of patients saw 120 colored pictures, each for 8 sec, and normal subjects saw the same pictures for 1 sec each. This procedure resulted in all three groups' performing equivalently at a 10-min retention delay. The important finding was that performance was also equivalent at retention delays of 2 hours and 1 day. Thus, the two amnesic groups exhibited equivalent (and apparently normal) rates of forgetting. The available data favor the idea that the medial temporal lobe and diencephalic structures damaged in amnesia are part of a single memory system. While it is likely that the two regions make different contributions to the function of the system, convincing evidence for this idea has yet to be demonstrated.

Spatial memory

The medial temporal/diencephalic memory system, and more commonly the hippocampus proper, has sometimes been considered particularly important for spatial memory (O'Keefe and Nadel, 1978). This idea originated in electrophysiological data from rats showing that cells in the hippocampus respond selectively when the animal is in a particular place (Ranck, 1973); and also in hippocampal lesion studies, which demonstrated striking deficits in rats performing spatial memory tasks. However, hippocampal cells respond to many properties of the stimulus environment besides spatial location (Berger and Thompson, 1978; Eichenbaum *et al.*, 1986; Wible *et al.*, 1986), and hippocampal lesions impair memory on a variety of nonspatial tasks, including odor-discrimination learning in rats (Eichenbaum *et al.*, 1988), configural learning in rats (Sutherland and Rudy, 1989), object discrimination and delayed nonmatching to sample in monkeys (Zola-Morgan *et al.*, 1989), and numerous human memory tests that assess retention of recently learned facts and events (Mayes, 1988; Squire, 1987). These considerations show clearly that the function of the hippocampus is not exclusively spatial, but the question remains whether the hippocampus and related limbic/dien-cephalic structures are more important for spatial memory than for other kinds of memory.

One approach has been to assess the status of spatial memory in human amnesia. In one study (Shoqeirat and Mayes, 1991) subjects were presented with 16 nameable shapes arranged in a 7×7 grid. The scores of amnesic patients and control subjects were matched on a recognition task for the shapes by increasing the number of presentations given to the patients and by decreasing the delay between study and test. Under these conditions, the amnesic patients performed worse than the control subjects both on tests of free recall for the shapes and on tests of incidental recall for their spatial locations. In a second study (Mayes *et al.*, 1991), subjects were shown words in one of the four corners of a computer screen and instructed to remember the words and their locations. Amnesic patients and control subjects were matched on a recognition task for the words by requiring the amnesic patients to retain a shorter list of words, by providing them longer exposure to each word, and by using a shorter retention delay between study and test. Under these conditions, the amnesic patients performed worse than the control subjects in recollecting the locations of the words they had seen.

A complicating feature of these two experiments is that spatial and non-spatial memory were confounded with recall and recognition memory. Also, whenever a match is forced between amnesic patients and control subjects based on just one data point and using just one measure of memory, it is possible that amnesic patients would perform poorly on many other measures. Further, some spatial tasks might be failed because they approximate tests of source memory – e.g. tests in which spatial location provides important context for what is to be remembered. Finally, a recent study of human amnesia found only proportionate impairments of spatial memory relative to recall and recognition memory, using variations of the same tasks just described (MacAndrew and Jones, 1993). An additional complication is that many of the amnesic patients in these studies had frontal lobe pathology, which can especially affect recall performance and can cause source amnesia (Janowsky *et al.*, 1989a; Janowsky *et al.*, 1989c; Jetter *et al.*, 1986).

In another study, object name recall, object name recognition, and object location memory were tested in patients with confirmed damage to the diencephalon or the hippocampal formation (Cave and Squire, 1991). Amnesic patients and normal subjects were matched on both recall and recognition by testing amnesic patients after a 5-min delay and different groups of control subjects after delays from 5 min to 5 weeks. The main finding was that, when the recall and recognition performance of amnesic patients was matched to the recall and recognition performance of control subjects, spatial memory per-formance was equivalent in the two groups. Taken together, the available data in humans do not provide strong support for the idea that the hippocampus, or other components of the medial temporal/diencephalic memory system, are especially involved in spatial memory. A reasonable alternative is that spatial memory is simply a good example of a broader class of (declarative, rela-tional) memory abilities that are dependent on the integrity of this system (also see Eichenbaum *et al.*, 1992; Squire and Cave, 1991).

This issue was also explored in monkeys with lesions of the posterior medial temporal lobe that included the hippocampus, the parahippocampal gyrus, and the posterior entorhinal cortex (Parkinson *et al.*, 1988). The monkeys were severely impaired in forming associations between objects and places. In addition, they were more severely impaired on this object-place association task than on a recognition memory task for objects (delayed nonmatching to sample). A comparison group with lesions of the anterior medial temporal lobe, which included the amygdala and underlying perirhinal cortex, performed about as well on the recognition task as the monkeys with hippocampal formation lesions, but were only mildly impaired on the spatial task.

Although more work is needed, these results can be interpreted in the light of recent information concerning the anatomical projections from neocortex to the anterior and posterior portions of the medial temporal lobe. Parietal cortex, which processes spatial information, projects posteriorly to parahippocampal cortex but not anteriorly to perirhinal cortex. Inferotemporal cortex, which processes visual pattern information, projects more strongly to perirhinal cortex than to parahippocampal cortex (Suzuki *et al.*, 1991). The perirhinal and parahippocampal cortices provide nearly two-thirds of the input to entorhinal cortex, which in turn originates most of the afferent projections to the hippocampus. On the basis of these considerations, spatial memory functions may be associated more with parahippocampal cortex than with perirhinal cortex. Accordingly, posterior medial temporal lobe lesions (i.e. lesions that include parahippocampal cortex) would be expected to disrupt spatial memory more than anterior lesions. By this view, although a specialization for spatial memory might exist in the parahippocampal cortex, and a specialization for visual memory in the perirhinal cortex, no such specialization should be found in the entorhinal cortex or in the hippocampus itself, because these structures receive convergent projections from both the perirhinal and parahippocampal cortices.

Recall and recognition

Another important question about the function of the brain system that supports declarative memory is whether it is equivalently involved in the two fundamental processes of recall and recognition. By one view, recall and recognition are closely linked functions of declarative memory (Tulving, 1983; Hayman and Tulving, 1989). Alternatively, recall has been proposed to depend on declarative memory, while recognition depends partly on declarative memory and partly on increased perceptual fluency – i.e. priming (Gardiner, 1988; Jacoby, 1983; Mandler, 1980). By this view, subjects can detect the facility with which they process a test item and can attribute this improved fluency to the fact that the item was recently presented.

Evidence relevant to this issue could come from the study of amnesia, because amnesia spares priming while severely impairing declarative memory. Accordingly, if recognition performance is supported significantly by implicit (nondeclarative) memory, amnesic patients should perform disproportionately better on recognition tests than on recall tests, in comparison to normal subjects. Two early studies that examined this issue (Hirst *et al.*, 1986, 1988) reported that amnesic patients exhibited disproportionate sparing of recognition memory. In these studies, recall and recognition performance were compared at a single performance level.

In another study, amnesic patients and control subjects were compared across a range of retention intervals (15 sec to 8 weeks), and performance was assessed independently by recall, recognition, and confidence ratings for the recognition choices (Haist *et al.*, 1992). The results were that recall and recognition were proportionately impaired in the patients, and their confidence ratings were commensurate with the level of impaired performance.

It is not entirely clear what accounts for the different findings by Hirst and his colleagues concerning the relative status of recall and recognition in amnesia. When an attempt was made to reproduce the experimental conditions from the second of these studies (Hirst *et al.*, 1988), the findings were not replicated (Haist *et al.*, 1992). The explanation may lie in differences in the locus of pathology in the patient populations and differences in the pattern of cognitive deficits present in addition to memory impairment. For example, some of the patients in the studies by Hirst *et al.*, (1988) became amnesic from a condition that produces signs of frontal lobe dysfunction, and frontal lobe pathology can affect recall performance more than recognition performance (Janowsky *et al.*, 1989a; Jetter *et al.*, 1986).

The available findings provide little support for the view that recognition memory differs from recall in depending importantly on processes like priming that are intact in amnesia. Some behavioral findings with normal subjects have been taken as evidence that recognition memory regularly and typically depends on priming (i.e. increased fluency). However, the results appear to support this idea only indirectly, and recognition is usually not considered in relation to recall (Graf and Mandler, 1984; Jacoby and Dallas, 1981; Mandler, 1980; Gardiner, 1988; Gardiner and Java, 1990; Johnston *et al.*, 1985; also, see Jacoby [1991] for a different method of assessing in normal subjects the separate contributions of intentional and automatic processes [recollection and familiarity] to recognition performance). While one cannot rule out a possible contribution of priming-like phenomena to recognition performance under some conditions, another possibility is that implicit (nondeclarative) memory does not ordinarily contribute to performance on the typical recognition memory task. That is, when a recently encountered percept is encountered again, perceptual fluency will be operating and detection will be improved, but these effects need not contribute to overt judgments concerning whether the percept is familiar, in the sense of having been presented previously. Johnston *et al.* (1991) have also concluded that the contribution of perceptual fluency to recognition memory may occur under limited conditions, perhaps when explicit (declarative) memory is weak. More work is needed to understand the dissociations that have been demonstrated in normal recognition memory performance, the implications of these dissociations for conscious and nonconscious forms of memory, and the relationship between recognition performance and free recall.

In summary, the idea developed here is that limbic/diencephalic brain structures are equivalently involved in recall and recognition. Recall and recognition are no doubt different in important ways, and the differential contribution of other brain structures, including the frontal lobe, to recall and recognition will be important in understanding the difference. For example, recognition memory would be expected to depend on processes that can be dissociated from other components of memory processing. Thus, recognition memory should be dissociable from the component of recall that depends on the contribution of the frontal lobe. The experiments reviewed here suggest simply that implicit (nondeclarative) memory probably does not typically support recognition memory performance, at least no more than it also contributes to free recall.

Nondeclarative memory

Whereas declarative memory is a brain systems construct, a form of memory that is reflected in the operation of an anatomically real neural system and its interaction with neocortex, nondeclarative (or implicit) memory includes several forms of learning and memory abilities and depends on multiple brain systems. Although it is too early to develop a classification scheme for all the nondeclarative forms of memory, one can tentatively distinguish among skills and habits, some forms of conditioning, and the phenomena of priming. Information is emerging about the neural basis of these major types, and this information can be expected to be relevant to the problem of classification.

Skills and habits

Skills are procedures (motor, perceptual, and cognitive) for operating in the world; habits are dispositions and tendencies that are specific to a set of stimuli and that guide behavior. Under some circumstances, skills and habits can be acquired in the absence of awareness of what has been learned and independently of long-term declarative memory for the specific episodes in which learning occurred. However, many skill-like tasks are also amenable to declarative learning strategies. For example, if a task is sufficiently simple and the information being acquired becomes accessible to awareness, then performance can be enhanced by engaging declarative memory strategies. Examples are available of human learning tasks that result in both declarative and nondeclarative knowledge (Willingham *et al.*, 1989), and of tasks that are learned nondeclaratively by monkeys but declaratively by humans (pattern discrimination and the 24-hour concurrent discrimination task; Zola-Morgan and Squire, 1984; Malamut *et al.*, 1984; Squire *et al.*, 1988). Accordingly, identifying the varieties of nondeclarative memory is not straightforward. The most compelling examples have come from dissociations in normal human subjects, findings of fully intact performance in otherwise severely amnesic patients, and findings of fully normal performance in experimental animals with lesions of the hippocampus or related structures.

The earliest evidence that skill learning can proceed independently of long-term declarative memory came from the finding that the severely amnesic patient H.M. was capable of day-to-day improvement on a mirror-drawing task, despite being unable to remember that he had practiced the task (Milner, 1962). Later, it was demonstrated that perceptuomotor learning can occur at an entirely normal rate in amnesia (Brooks and Baddeley, 1976). During the past decade, it has become clear that motor-skill learning is a small subset of a much broader category of skill-based abilities that also include perceptual and cognitive skills. The perceptual skills that have now been found to be fully intact in human amnesia include mirror reading (Cohen and Squire, 1980), speeded reading of normal text (Musen *et al.*, 1990), speeded reading of repeated nonwords (Musen and Squire, 1991), the ability to resolve random-dot stereograms (Benzing and Squire, 1989), and adaptation-level effects based on sampling sets of weights (Benzing and Squire, 1989).

One particularly interesting group of experiments has demonstrated implicit learning of a sequence of regularly repeating spatial locations (Cleeremans and McClelland, 1991; Lewicki *et al.*, 1987; Stadler, 1989; Nissen and Bullemer, 1987) or words (Hartman *et al.*, 1989). The evidence that the learning was implicit is that subjects improved their performance (a) in the absence of awareness that a sequence had been presented; or (b) in the absence of the ability to generate the sequence at the completion of testing. In this case, the sequence was presented once again, and subjects attempted to predict each successive element in the sequence before it appeared. In one study (Nissen and Bullemer, 1987) it was also shown that amnesic patients could acquire the sequence at a normal rate. If the sequence tasks are complex enough, they can be attention demanding in the sense that learning is impeded by requiring subjects to perform a competing task (Nissen and Bullemer, 1987). Alternatively, simpler versions of such tasks may be acquired automatically without requiring attention (Cohen *et al.*, 1990).

One reason for identifying these tasks as skill-based is that patients with Huntington's disease, who have pathological, degenerative changes in the neostriatum, have been found to be deficient in many of these tasks, including mirror reading (Martone *et al.*, 1984), adaptation-level effects (Heindel *et al.*, 1991), and sequence learning (Knopman and Nissen, 1991). In two of the studies just cited, the patients with Huntington's disease performed better than other memory-impaired patients on conventional tasks of recognition memory.

Some tasks that are neither perceptual nor motor can also be acquired implicitly. For example, cognitive tasks have been studied in which subjects attempt to achieve and then maintain a specific target value across trials. On each trial, the response needed to achieve the target value is determined algorithmically by current task conditions. When the relationship is sufficiently obscure, and not amenable to easy discovery or memorization, subjects improve their performance despite having little or no understanding of what they have done (Berry and Broadbent, 1984). For example, one task asked subjects to achieve a target level of production in a fictitious sugar factory by determining how many workers should be hired on each trial. In this case, subjects learned the mapping function that related the level of sugar production on the previous trial to the target value. Amnesic patients were entirely intact at the early stages of this task, although normal subjects eventually acquired declarative knowledge about the task structure and out-performed the patients (Squire and Frambach, 1990). The important finding is that early-stage acquisition of skilled behavior can sometimes proceed inde-pendently of verbal mediation and declarative knowledge.

There are other ways in which subjects can apparently learn regularities in their environment implicitly and then reveal what they have learned in their judgments or choices. In one notable study (Lewicki, 1986a), normal subjects saw a few photographs of women, some with short hair and some with long hair. Hair length was systematically associated with narratives that described the women as either kind or capable. (These terms did not appear in the narratives.) A few minutes later, subjects decided (yes or no) whether new photographs depicted someone who was 'kind' or, in other cases, 'capable.' Reaction times for yes and no decisions were slower when subjects judged photographs of women whose hair length had previously been associated with the corresponding attribute than when they judged photographs that were discordant with the attribute. It was suggested that processing time is increased whenever subjects have information available about the relevant covariation. In addition to these findings for reaction time, subjects more often judged photographs of women as 'kind' or 'capable' when hair length had been associated with the corresponding narrative than when it had been associated with the other narrative. However, these effects were rather small and were not consistently observed across experiments. Nevertheless, the finding that subjects indicated no awareness that hair length was linked to any attributes raises the possibility that whatever was learned about the covariance between physical features and attributes was learned indepen-dently of declarative knowledge. However, in these and similar experiments (Lewicki, 1989b) it is difficult to rule out a threshold interpretation based on weak declarative memories that are more or less accessible depending on how memory is tested. For example, in the hair-length experiment, the results could mean simply that as declarative memory weakens, the ability to make judgments based on the learned relationships between stimuli will usually remain in evidence after the ability to report the relationships has reached chance levels.

Artificial grammar learning is an extensively studied problem domain in which subjects acquire knowledge through multiple presentations of unique material. Subjects see letter strings (e.g. BFZBZ) in which the letter order is determined by a finite-state rule system. After the letter strings are presented, subjects are told for the first time that the letter strings were in fact all determined by a complex set of rules. Subjects then attempt to classify new items as being either consistent (grammatical) or inconsistent (nongramma-tical) with these rules. Reber (1967, 1989), who introduced this paradigm, suggested that the learning is implicit and independent of conscious access to the training items. For example, subjects can usually provide little informa-tion about the basis for their judgments, and telling subjects beforehand about the existence of the rules does not improve classification performance

(Reber, 1976; Dienes *et al.*, 1991). Another point of view has been that artificial grammar learning is based on conscious application of declarative knowledge that is weak and imperfect (Dulany *et al.*, 1984; Perruchet and Pacteau, 1990). In support of this idea, it has been shown that the ability of subjects to recognize grammatically valid fragments of letter strings (bigrams and trigrams) was sufficient to account for their classification performance (Perruchet and Pacteau, 1990).

This issue was clarified by the finding that amnesic patients, who were much poorer than normal subjects at recognizing which letter strings had been presented, were nevertheless able to classify letter strings (grammatical vs nongrammatical) as well as normal subjects (Knowlton *et al.*, 1992). This finding supports the view that artificial grammar learning is implicit, and it appears to rule out the idea that the learning is based on consciously accessible rules, declarative memory for permissible letter groups, or direct and conscious comparisons with letter strings that are stored in declarative memory.

Although these possibilities can probably be excluded, several other possibilities remain for how implicit learning of artificial grammars could occur: the implicit acquisition of abstract rules (Reber, 1989; Mathews *et al.*, 1989), analogic comparisons to individual test items based on acquired (but implicit) associations between the test items and the grammatical category (Brooks and Vokey, 1991; Vokey and Brooks, 1992), or the acquisition of implicit associations between letter groups (chunks) and the grammatical category (Servan-Schreiber and Anderson, 1990).

The ability to classify is more commonly based on natural categories, like chairs and birds, where class membership is defined by experience with exemplars rather than by fixed rules (Rosch, 1973). In this case, too, a number of possible mechanisms have been proposed by which category-level knowledge is achieved (for reviews, see Estes, 1988, 1991; Smith and Medin, 1981). One possibility is that category-level knowledge is acquired in the form of knowledge about prototypes (a representative instance) or knowledge of the statistical characteristics of groups of exemplars, and that this knowledge is represented distinctly from knowledge about the exemplars themselves (Fried and Holyoak, 1984; Posner and Keele, 1968; Reed, 1972). Another possibility is that category-level knowledge has no special status but is derivative from item memory (Brooks, 1978; Hintzman, 1986; Medin and Schaffer, 1978; Nosofsky, 1984). By this view, knowledge about prototypes emerges as a property of the way in which items are stored. Specifically, a test item will be recognized as a good representative of a category because it shares many features with items in storage. Exemplar-based models of category learning can account for important aspects of classification performance such as the ability of subjects to identify the prototype more accurately than the items that were actually presented, even when subjects did not see the prototype itself and when the prototype itself is not actually represented.

A third possibility is illustrated by connectionist models in which the elements of the model are neither features nor items but homogeneous units that can vary in the strengths of their connections with each other (Estes, 1991; Gluck and Bower, 1988; McClelland and Rumelhart, 1985; see the section below on Conditioning). In such models, knowledge about prototypes emerges naturally during the learning process as a result of the fact that multiple instances are stored in a distributed fashion within the network. Models that combine elements of these approaches have also been proposed (e.g. exemplar-based connectionist models [Kruschke, 1992; Nosofsky *et al.*, 1992]).

Preliminary findings with amnesic patients suggest that prototype learning proceeds in parallel with and independently of declarative memory for specific instances (Knowlton and Squire, 1992). If so, it cannot be the case that prototype knowledge is derived from or is in any way dependent on long-term declarative memory for individual instances. Whereas limbic/diencephalic brain structures support memory for individual instances, a different brain system may support the development of category-level knowledge.

One possibility is that learning based either on rules (e.g. artificial grammar learning) or natural categories (e.g. prototype learning) is best classified as habit learning. In both cases, category learning can be viewed as the acquisition of implicit associations between items or features and a category. A growing body of evidence from studies with experimental animals, reviewed below, suggests that the neural substrates of habit learning are different from those of declarative memory.

Neural evidence for distinguishing skills and habits from declarative memory

Recent work suggests that the brain structures important for acquiring skills and habits involve the corticostriatal system – i.e. projections from the neocortex to the caudate and putamen. Patients with Parkinson's disease, who have striatal dysfunction as the result of primary pathology in the substantia nigra pars compacta, were impaired on a cognitive skill task but intact at the declarative memory tasks of recall and recognition (Saint-Cyr *et al.*, 1988). Recent results for the delayed nonmatching to sample task and the 24-hour concurrent discrimination task, two memory tasks developed for the monkey, have been especially illuminating. Delayed nonmatching to sample is a test of recognition memory, in which the monkey attempts to select in a two-choice test the object that was *not* presented recently. New pairs of objects are used for each trial. Monkeys initially learn to perform the task across a short delay interval and are then tested at increasing delays that can be 10 min or even longer. In the 24-hour concurrent discrimination task, monkeys are presented with 20 pairs of objects for one trial each day. One of the objects in each pair is always correct. Learning in this task occurs gradually in about 10 days.

In humans, both these tasks are learned declaratively – i.e. subjects memorize the material to be learned – and performance is impaired in amnesic patients (Squire *et al.*, 1988). In monkeys, the findings are quite different. Both tasks are impaired by damage to inferotemporal cortex (area TE), a higher-order visual area in neocortex that is essential for processing information about visually presented objects (Mishkin, 1982; Phillips *et al.*, 1988). However, the two tasks can be differentiated in an important way. Performance on delayed nonmatching to sample is impaired by large medial temporal lobe lesions (Mishkin, 1978; Squire and Zola-Morgan, 1991), but monkeys with these same lesions learn the 24-hour concurrent discrimination task about as well as normal animals (Malamut *et al.*, 1984). In contrast, the 24-hour concurrent task is impaired by damage to the tail of the caudate nucleus, which is a target of cortical projections from area TE, but performance on delayed nonmatching to sample is not affected (Wang *et al.*, 1990).

Thus, an interaction between visual area TE and limbic/diencephalic areas is critical for visual recognition memory, but an interaction between TE and the neostriatum is critical for the 24-hour concurrent task. The results are similar for two-choice, visual pattern-discrimination learning, which is unaffected by large medial temporal lobe lesions (Zola-Morgan and Squire, 1984) but is impaired by lesions of the caudate nucleus (Divak *et al.*, 1967). These differential effects have been interpreted in terms of two qualitatively different memory systems, a system that supports cognitive (or declarative) memory and a second system, involving the caudate and putamen, that supports noncognitive habit memory (Mishkin *et al.*, 1984; Phillips *et al.*, 1988).

A similar distinction was drawn on the basis of work with rats (Packard *et al.*, 1989). A win-shift task, which required animals to remember which arms of a radial maze had been recently visited, was impaired by fornix lesions but not by caudate lesions. Conversely, a win-stay task that required animals to visit arms that were marked by a light was impaired by caudate lesions but not by fornix lesions.

It is tempting to relate these habit-like tasks to habit learning in humans. A complication is that win-stay tasks and the 24-hour concurrent discrimination task are readily learned by humans using their well-developed declarative memory strategies, particularly when the rules governing reward contingencies are simple ones (Squire *et al.*, 1988). It is significant that patients with Huntington's disease are impaired on a number of skill-like tasks involving motor responses, but neuropsychological studies are needed with habit-like tasks that have no motor component. The ability to relate findings from experimental animals and humans should improve as it becomes possible to define tasks in terms of what strategies are being used to learn them rather than in terms of the logical structure of the tasks (see the section, above, on Long-term Memory: Declarative Memory).

Conditioning

Learning of simple conditioned responses of the skeletal musculature or conditioned autonomic responses occurs normally in experimental animals despite complete removal of the hippocampus (Solomon and Moore 1975; Caul *et al.*, 1969). Moreover, amnesic patients exhibit progressive learning and 24-hour retention of a conditioned eyeblink response, despite inability to describe the apparatus or what it had been used for (Weiskrantz and Warrington, 1979; Daum *et al.*, 1989). Thus, although conditioning in humans has been reported to require awareness of the conditioned stimulus–unconditioned stimulus contingency (Marinkovic *et al.*, 1989), the successful conditioning that has been observed in amnesic patients and in decerebrate animals (Norman *et al.*, 1977) suggests that awareness is not always necessary for conditioning to occur. However, until control subjects are tested to determine whether the learning in amnesic patients is entirely normal, the possibility remains that an essential part of conditioned performance in humans is due to declarative knowledge about the structure of the task. If so, the limbic/diencephalic structures important for declarative memory could play some role. In any case, other brain structures and connections are known to be critically important (see Thompson [1988] and Lavond *et al.*, [1993] for eyeblink conditioning; LeDoux [1987] for fear conditioning; Dunn and Everitt [1988] for taste aversion learning).

Limbic/diencephalic structures are not essential when experimental animals acquire a simple conditioned response – i.e. when a single CS and US are used in a standard delay paradigm, CS onset occurs about 250 msec prior to US onset, and CS and US offset occur together. However, these structures are important for more complex conditioning procedures such as reversal of conditioned discriminations (Berger and Orr, 1983), occasion setting (Ross *et al.*, 1984), trace conditioning (Moyer *et al.*, 1990), or when configural (Sutherland and Rudy, 1989) or contextual cues (Winocur *et al.*, 1987) are used. An examination of these and other paradigms in human amnesic patients should help to identify fundamental aspects of declarative memory.

Some recent work on classification learning in human subjects has been inspired by theories of animal conditioning. In one paradigm, subjects performed a medical diagnosis task in which each of four different symptoms was probabilistically associated across trials with each of two fictitious diseases (Gluck and Bower, 1988; Shanks, 1990). On each trial, subjects were presented with a 'patient' who exhibited one, two, three, or four symptoms in any combination and tried to guess which disease the 'patient' had. In this case, performance could be modeled by a connectionist network that learned according to the Rescorla–Wagner rule, as derived from studies of associative learning in animals (Rescorla and Wagner, 1972). Thus, subjects could be viewed as learning to associate each symptom with one of the diseases in much the same way that a CS gradually becomes associated with a US (for other connectionist models of classification learning, see Kruschke, 1992; Nosofsky *et al.*, 1992).

Other experiments with human subjects using similar tasks have demonstrated the phenomena of blocking, overshadowing, and conditioned inhibition (Chapman and Robbins, 1990; Gluck and Bower, 1988; Shanks, 1991). These phenomena can be understood as resulting from competition among cues for associative strength. According to theories derived from animal conditioning, very predictive cues will successfully compete for the available associative strength at the expense of less predictive cues. Because the framework developed in animal conditioning accounts for these phenomena, and because simple forms of animal conditioning are known to occur independently of limbic/diencephalic brain structures, it is reasonable to expect that human learning of associations between features and categories will also occur independently of these brain structures (so long as the associative rules cannot easily be discovered and memorized).

Although some examples of human classification learning can be illuminated by theories of classical conditioning, the similarities between classification learning and classical conditioning should not be pushed too far. In terms of neural organization, the cerebellum is essential for classical conditioning of skeletal musculature (Thompson, 1988; Lavond *et al.*, 1993), perhaps because precise timing of responses is needed (Ivry and Baldo, 1992). For conditioned emotional responses, the amygdala is important. In contrast, when subjects must learn the predictive value of two or more cues, and the predictive relationship is not easily discovered, such learning is probably better viewed as another example of habit learning, just as has been suggested for artificial grammar learning and prototype learning. If so, the neostriatum may be an important substrate for classification learning.

Priming

Priming refers to an improved facility for detecting or identifying perceptual stimuli based on recent experience with them. Priming is currently the most intensively studied example of nondeclarative memory, and a number of reviews are available that consider this topic in some detail (Richardson-Klavehn and Bjork, 1988; Shimamura, 1986; Schacter, 1990; Schacter *et al.*, 1993; Tulving and Schacter, 1990). The discussion here identifies the key features of priming and considers the phenomenon in the context of brain systems. In a typical experiment, subjects see lists of words, pictures of objects, or nonverbal materials such as novel objects or line drawings. Subsequently, subjects are tested with both old and new items and asked to name words or objects, to produce items from fragments, or to make rapid decisions about new and old items. The finding is that performance is better for old than for new items.

Two lines of evidence show that priming is dissociable from and independent of declarative memory. First, manipulations in normal subjects that markedly affect the strength of declarative memory, such as variations in the extent of elaborative processing carried out at the time of encoding, have little or no effect on priming (for review, see Schacter *et al.*, 1993). Second, several examples of priming have been shown to be fully intact in amnesic patients, including word priming as measured by word-stem completion, perceptual identification, and lexical decision (Cermak *et al.*, 1985; Graf *et al.*, 1984; Smith and Oscar-Berman, 1990), visual object priming (Cave and Squire, 1992b), and priming of novel objects or line patterns (Gabrieli *et al.*, 1990; Musen and Squire, 1992; Schacter *et al.*, 1991). Amnesic patients provide a favorable way to establish the distinction between priming and declarative memory, because amnesic patients are impaired on conventional recall and recognition tests. If declarative memory significantly supports priming, then amnesic patients should be impaired on tests that measure priming. Finally, it has also been pointed out that measures of priming and measures of declarative memory often exhibit statistical independence

(Tulving and Schacter, 1990), but this criterion for making inferences about the independence of memory systems has been questioned by a number of authors (Hintzman and Hartry, 1990; Ostergaard, 1992; Shimamura, 1985).

An early view, based especially on work with amnesic patients, was that priming involves the activation of pre-existing memory representations (Diamond and Rozin, 1984; Cermak *et al.*, 1985, 1991). However, a number of studies with amnesic patients have now demonstrated robust and intact priming of nonwords as well as nonverbal material such as novel objects and line drawings that have no pre-existing representations (Haist *et al.*, 1991; Musen and Squire, 1992; Schacter *et al.*, 1991; Squire and McKee, 1992; for other recent studies involving normal subjects, see Bentin and Moscovitch, 1988; Kersteen-Tucker, 1991; Musen and Treisman, 1990; Schacter *et al.*, 1991). An exception appears to be the priming of nonwords on lexical-decision tasks, which is weak even in normal subjects (Bentin and Moscovitch, 1988; Verfaellie *et al.*, 1991; for a report that nonword lexical-decision priming occurs in normal subjects but not in amnesic patients, see Smith and Oscar-Berman, 1990).

One of the striking features of priming is that it can sometimes be extraordinarily long-lasting. Word-stem completion priming, which was among the first well-studied examples of priming, disappears within 2 hours, at least when multiple completions are available for each word stem (Squire *et al.*, 1987). In contrast, in normal subjects priming of object naming is still present 6 weeks after a single exposure to a picture (Mitchell and Brown, 1988); and word-fragment completion priming, when only one solution is available for each fragment, has been demonstrated in normal subjects after a delay of 16 months (Sloman *et al.*, 1988). The question of how long priming persists is complicated by the possibility that tests for priming can be contaminated by declarative memory strategies. A contribution from declarative memory has been ruled out in one case by the finding of fully intact object-naming priming in amnesic patients, even 7 days after a single exposure to pictures (Cave and Squire, 1992b). Thus, stimuli can result in long-lasting effects on performance that are supported independently of the limbic/diencephalic structures important for declarative memory.

Presentation of stimuli can also influence preferences and judgments about the stimuli, even when the stimuli are exposed so briefly that they cannot later be recognized (Bonnano and Stillings, 1986; Kunst-Wilson and Zajonc, 1980; Mandler *et al.*, 1987). A related phenomenon is that subjects are more likely to judge a proper name as famous if the name has been encountered previously. Dividing attention during the initial presentation of famous and nonfamous names markedly reduced recognition memory scores but had no effect on the fame-judgment effect (Jacoby *et al.*, 1989). Moreover, amnesic patients exhibited the fame-judgment effect at full strength (Squire and McKee, 1992). These results suggest that priming not only improves the ability to identify stimuli but can also alter judgments about the stimuli.

The kinds of priming discussed so far are perceptual in the sense that the effects are pre-semantic and highly determined by the specific perceptual features of the originally presented item. For example, when pictures of objects are presented and subjects are asked to name them as quickly as possible, the priming effect is greatly attenuated by changing the orientation of the object, adding shading to the object, or changing from one example of an object to another example that has the same name (Bartram, 1974; Biederman and Cooper, 1991a; Cave and Squire 1992b). Also, in word-priming tasks, priming can be attenuated by changes in sensory modality from study to test and by changes in the voice of the speaker (Graf *et al.*, 1985; Jacoby and Dallas, 1981; Schacter and Church, 1992). Finally, priming effects are sometimes reduced by changes in type case or other surface features of words, although such effects are not always obtained (see Schacter *et al.*, 1993).

Although priming effects are highly specific, the representation that supports priming does not retain all the perceptual information in the stimulus. For example, changes in size or left–right mirror reflection of objects did not affect priming, despite the fact that these same changes significantly affected performance on tests of declarative memory (Biederman and Cooper, 1991b, 1992; Cooper *et al.*, 1992). Because declarative memory was sensitive to these stimulus features, it is difficult to explain priming as depending on the same process or system that supports declarative memory.

Priming effects can also occur on tests that require semantic or conceptual processing, but these effects can be dissociated from and are likely quite different from perceptual priming (Srinivas and Roediger, 1990; Tulving and Schacter, 1990). For example, conceptually driven priming depends on the extent of elaborative encoding at the time of study (Hamann, 1990). Nevertheless, this kind of priming is also independent of declarative memory, as demonstrated by the fact that amnesic patients are fully intact at tests of free-association priming (Shimamura and Squire, 1984) and priming of category exemplars (Gardner *et al.*, 1973; Graf *et al.*, 1985; Schacter, 1985).

There has also been interest in whether associative priming effects can occur for previously unrelated pairs of items (Graf and Schacter, 1985; Moscovitch *et al.*, 1986). Recent work suggests that the most commonly studied paradigm (word-stem completion priming using novel associates as cues) does not yield associative priming in severely amnesic patients (Cermak *et al.*, 1988; Mayes and Gooding, 1989; Schacter and Graf, 1986; Shimamura and Squire, 1989). Although the phenomenon as a whole can be dissociated from declarative memory in normal subjects (see Schacter *et al.*, 1993), the initial formation of novel associations probably places a critical demand on declarative memory (Shimamura and Squire, 1989). In addition, the rapid (one-trial) formation of implicit associations between unrelated word pairs (using a paradigm based on reading speed; Moscovitch *et al.*, 1986) has proven difficult to demonstrate within implicit memory (Musen and Squire, 1993).

Some information has recently become available about the neural basis of perceptual priming. In divided visual-field studies with normal subjects, word-stem completion priming was greater when word stems were presented to the right hemisphere rather than to the left (Marsolek *et al.*, 1992). This effect was obtained if and only if the study and test items were in the same sensory modality and in the same type case. Thus, the right cerebral hemisphere appears to be more effective than the left at supporting form-specific components of perceptual priming. The left hemisphere may support more abstract components of perceptual priming – e.g. the priming that survives type-case changes and modality changes. These results suggest that the two hemispheres contribute to priming in different ways, and that the results of priming studies can be expected to differ depending on which hemisphere is dominant in performing the task.

A recent study using positron emission tomography (PET) has provided direct evidence for the involvement of right posterior cortex in word priming (Squire *et al.*, 1992). Study and test items were presented visually and always in uppercase letters. During word-stem completion priming there was a significant reduction of cerebral blood flow in right extrastriate cortex, in the region of the lingual gyrus, in comparison to a baseline condition in which subjects also completed word stems but none of the possible word completions had been presented for study. This finding suggests a simplifying hypothesis for perceptual priming: after a word has been presented for study, less neural activity is subsequently required to process the same stimulus. The right posterior cortical locus identified by PET in this study is precisely the same region that in earlier studies was activated by the visual features of words (Petersen *et al.*, 1990). Words, nonwords, letter strings, and letter-like shapes were all effective at activating this locus.

The PET findings count against earlier proposals that a left-hemisphere word-form area is the locus of word priming (Schacter, 1990; Tulving and Schacter, 1990). More likely, left or right posterior cerebral cortex is important depending on whether priming is based on more abstract or more form-specific mechanisms. Indeed, we suggest that perceptual priming may occur in any of the more than 30 cortical areas known to be involved in visual information processing (Felleman and Van Essen, 1991). Which areas are involved in any particular case would depend on the extent of the match between study and test materials and task demands. Indeed, this diversity of cortical areas potentially relevant to priming may help to explain why so many dissociations have been found among different kinds of verbal priming tests (Keane *et al.*, 1991; Srinivas and Roediger, 1990; Witherspoon and Moscovitch, 1989).

Priming is presumably adaptive because animals evolved in a world where stimuli that are encountered once are likely to be encountered again. Perceptual priming improves the speed and fluency by which organisms interact with familiar stimuli. For example, in the case of visual priming, the posterior visual cortex becomes more efficient at processing precisely those stimuli that have been processed recently. This plasticity occurs well before information reaches the limbic/diencephalic structures important for declarative memory.

Perspective

This review has considered several kinds of memory as well as the distinct brain systems that support them. It has sometimes been proposed that distinctions between kinds of memory are best understood as reflecting the different processes that can be used to access a common memory trace (Blaxton, 1989; Jacoby, 1988; Masson, 1989; Roediger, 1990). When discussion of this issue is limited to priming, the matter can seem difficult to settle (see Schacter, 1990). For example, the same single words can be remembered intentionally, or they can be produced in a priming paradigm. However, when discussion of memory is broadened to include the learning of skills and habits, and conditioning phenomena, the data favor a systems perspective over a processing perspective (for discussion of points of contact between these two views, see Roediger, 1990; Schacter, 1992; Tulving and Schacter, 1990). Indeed, it cannot even be assumed that long-term storage of declarative and nondeclarative memories ocurs in the same brain region. Declarative memories require the reciprocal anatomical connections that enable the neocortex to interact with the hippocampus and related structures, and the neocortex is thought to be the final repository of declarative memory. Skills and habits depend on corticostriatal projections, and these projections are not reciprocated by return projections to neocortex from the neostriatum. Accordingly, one possibility is that the storage of information underlying skills and habits occurs at the synapses between cortical neurons and neurons in the neostriatum.

The findings from PET also strongly endorse a brain-systems orientation. Word-stem completion priming was supported significantly by right extrastriate visual cortex. Intentional recall of words using word stems as cues engaged the right hippocampal region significantly more than the priming condition did. (The priming condition also engaged the hippocampal region more than the above-mentioned baseline condition did. Because subjects became aware of the link between word stems and study words during the priming task, some explicit visual recognition probably occurred as the word stems were presented, even though the performance measure in the priming task does not itself depend on declarative memory.)

Recent studies of event-related potentials (ERPs) also suggest that different brain regions are involved in word recall and recognition on the one hand and word priming on the other (Paller, 1990; Paller and Kutas, 1992). For example, the ERP associated with intentional recognition had a different scalp distribution and a different latency from the ERP associated with perceptual identification priming (Paller and Kutas, 1992).

It has been noted previously that the finding of task dissociations in normal subjects is an insufficient basis on which to postulate two or more memory systems (Roediger, 1990; Schacter, 1992). Indeed, as several authors have noted (Graf *et al.*, 1984; Jacoby, 1991; Roediger, 1990; Schacter, 1990; Squire, 1992b), the proper emphasis is on the processes and strategies that subjects use, not the tasks used to measure memory. Moreover, to support hypotheses about multiple memory systems, evidence is needed that is independent of dissociation experiments. This kind of evidence has come from findings in experimental animals and neurological patients where the contributions to performance of anatomically defined brain systems can be evaluated directly. For example, a consideration of this evidence has led us in this review to suggest that superficially different tasks including artificial grammar learning and classification learning in human subjects, the 24-hour concurrent discrimination task in monkeys, and win-stay, lose-shift maze tasks in rodents all depend on similar underlying computations and might usefully be categorized together under the generic heading of habit learning.

One difficulty with the processing view is that it has been stated rather abstractly, so that it is sometimes difficult to appreciate what would count for or against it. A difficulty with the systems view is that the definition of the term 'system' is uncertain, and it is not always clear from studies of normal subjects when behavioral findings justify postulating a separate memory system. The concept of brain systems, while not entirely free of problems itself, provides a more concrete and in the end a more satisfying basis for thinking about memory systems. This is because a long tradition of anatomical and physiological work on the structure and organization of the brain has concerned itself with the identification and study of separable neural systems, sometimes independently of or in advance of any understanding of their functional significance.

This kind of information provides powerful convergent evidence that becomes extremely compelling when a function identified and characterized from psychological data appears to map onto a neural system that has been defined previously by anatomical and physiological criteria. Indeed, this is approximately what has happened in the case of limbic/diencephalic structures (for declarative memory), the neostriatum (for skills and habits), and the cerebellum (for some forms of conditioning). In any case, it should be clear that the issue is not a philosophical or semantic one about whether a processing or systems view provides the best research approach. The issue is about how memory is actually organized and how the brain accomplishes learning and memory.

A fundamental issue that so far has yielded little biological information concerns the nature and locus of long-term declarative representations. However, one can find a few clues and identify some guiding principles. The brain is highly specialized and differentiated, and it is organized such that different regions of neocortex carry out parallel computations on many different dimensions of external stimuli. Memory for an event, even memory for a single object, is stored in component parts and in a distributed fashion across geographically separate parts of the brain (Mishkin, 1982; Squire, 1987). Although direct evidence is not available, permanent information storage is thought to occur in the same processing areas that are engaged during learning. By this view, long-term memory is stored as outcomes of processing operations and in the same cortical regions that are involved in the perception and analysis of the events and items to be remembered.

Available information about the organization and structure of knowledge systems suggests a surprising degree of specialization in how information is stored. Cortical lesions in humans can produce remarkably selective losses of category-specific knowledge – e.g. loss of the ability to comprehend the names of small 'indoor' objects with relative preservation of the names of large 'outdoor' objects; or loss of knowledge about inanimate, man-made objects with relative preservation of knowledge about foods and living things (Damasio, 1990; Farah *et al.*, 1991; Hart *et al.*, 1985; Warrington and

Shallice, 1984; Yamadori and Albert, 1973). It has been proposed that these specializations can be understood in terms of the nature of the interaction between the perceiver and objects in the world during the time that objects are learned about (Damasio, 1990; Farah and McClelland, 1991; Warrington and McCarthy, 1987). By this view, the sensory modality that is relevant to learning about an item and the nature of the relevant information (physical or functional) will influence the locus of information storage. For example, information based especially on physical features such as shape and color (e.g. gems, animals) will be stored in different loci from information based more on manual interaction and an understanding of function (e.g. tools and furniture).

What is needed is a way to access neurons within the networks that actually represent long-term declarative knowledge, so that the locus and organization of representations can be studied directly. There are abundant examples, from single-cell recordings of neurons in the temporal lobe of awake monkeys, where neurons change their activity rather quickly in response to behaviorally relevant stimuli (Fuster and Jervey, 1981; Miller *et al.*, 1991; Riches *et al.*, 1991). However, it is difficult to know in these cases what kind(s) of memory the neurons might be involved in. Particularly in experiments that require retention of newly acquired information across delays of less than a minute, neurons that respond either during the delay or when test stimuli are presented at the end of the delay could be related to short-term memory or priming. The question is how would one determine whether or not a neuron being recorded from were part of a network representing information in long-term declarative memory?

One promising approach is suggested by a recent study of paired-associate learning in the awake monkey (Sakai and Miyashita, 1991). During extended training, monkeys learned 12 pairs of computer-generated patterns. On each trial, a monkey observed one of the pictures (the cue) and then 4 sec later selected its associate from among two patterns. A reward was delivered if a correct response occurred within 1.2 sec. Neurons were found in the anterior temporal cortex that responded strongly to one of the pictures when that picture served as a cue in the paired-associate test. These same neurons were found to exhibit increased activity during the 4-sec delay on trials when the associate of that picture served as a cue. These neurons were termed 'pair-recall' neurons. Thus, neurons acquired information about the specific pairings of the patterns that were used, and they exhibited activity related to the process of stimulus recall.

These results should make it possible to pursue several interesting experimental questions. Does development of pair-specific neuronal activity require a contribution from the limbic/diencephalic brain system that is essential for declarative memory? What would be the effect of inactivating circuitry within the hippocampus or inactivating efferent projections from entorhinal cortex to neocortex? If the limbic/diencephalic system proved essential, then should pair-recall neurons be viewed as belonging to a network that represents long-term declarative memory of the associations? What is the role of the limbic/diencephalic system in the acquisition of pair-specific activity, its maintenance, and its expression? In other words, how does the limbic/diencephalic system interact with neocortex during learning, consolidation, and retrieval? If it becomes feasible, using this or some other paradigm, to observe directly the development of cortical plasticity related to declarative memory, one can expect the entire discussion of memory systems to be raised to a new level.

In the span of just a few years, the field of memory research has moved from a rather monolithic view of long-term memory to a view that distinguishes several kinds of memory. One system involves limbic/diencephalic structures, which in concert with neocortex provide the basis for conscious recollections. This system is fast, phylogenetically recent, and specialized for one-trial learning – e.g. for the rapid acquisition of associations, propositions, or items in a context. The system is fallible in the sense that it is sensitive to interference and prone to retrieval failure. It is also precious, giving rise to the capacity for personal autobiography and the possiblity of cultural evolution.

Other kinds of memory have also been identified – e.g. those involved in skills and habits, priming, conditioning, and perhaps the ability to acquire category-level generic knowledge. Such memories can be acquired, stored, and retrieved without the participation of the limbic/diencephalic brain system. These forms of memory are phylogenetically early, they are reliable and consistent, and they provide for myriad, nonconscious ways of responding to the world. In no small part, by virtue of the nonconscious status of these forms of memory, they create much of the mystery of human experience. Here arise the dispositions, habits, and preferences that are inaccessible to conscious recollection but that nevertheless are shaped by past events, influence our behavior, and are a part of who we are.

References

Alvarez-Royo, P., Zola-Morgan, S., Squire, L. R. 1992. Impairment of long-term memory and sparing of short-term memory in monkeys with medial temporal lobe lesions: a response to Ringo. *Behav. Brain Res.* 52: 1–5

Atkinson, R. C., Shiffrin, R. M. 1968. Human memory: a proposed system and its control processes. In *Psychology of Learning and Motivation, Advances in Research and Theory*, ed. K. W. Spence, J. T. Spence, pp. 89–195. New York, Academic

Bachevalier, J. 1990. Ontogenetic development of habit and memory formation in primates. See Diamond 1990, pp. 457–84

Bachevalier, J., Mishkin, M. 1984. An early and a late developing system for learning and retention in infant monkeys. *Behav. Neurosci.* 98: 770–78

Bachevalier, J., Ungerleider, L. G., O'Neill, J. B., Friedman, D. P. 1986. Regional distribution of [3H]naloxone binding in the brain of a newborn rhesus monkey. *Dev. Brain Res.* 25: 302–8

Baddeley, A. D., Hitch, G. J. 1974. Working memory. In *The Psychology of Learning and Motivation, Advances in Research and Theory*, ed. G. H. Bower, pp. 47–90. New York, Academic Press

Baddeley, A. D., Papagno, C., Vallar, G. 1988. When long-term learning depends on short-term storage. *J. Mem. Lang.* 27: 86–95

Baddeley, A. D., Warrington, E. K. 1970. Amnesia and the distinction between long and short-term memory. *J. Verbal Learn. Verbal Behav.* 9: 176–89

Baillargeon, R., DeVos, J. 1991. Object permanence in young infants, further evidence. *Child Dev.* 62: 1227–46

Barr, W. B., Goldberg, E., Wasserstein, J., Novelly, R. A. 1990. Retrograde amnesia following unilateral temporal lobectomy. *Neuropsychologia* 28: 243–56

Bartram, D. J. 1974. The role of visual and semantic codes in object naming. *Cogn. Psychol.* 6: 325–56

Bauer, P. J., Mandler, J. M. 1989. One thing follows another: effects of temporal structure on 1- to 2-year-olds' recall of events. *Dev. Psychol.* 25: 197–206

Benson, D. F., Geschwind, N. 1967. Shrinking retrograde amnesia. *J. Neurol. Neurosurg. Psychiatry* 30: 539–44

Bentin, S., Moscovitch, M. 1988. The time course of repetition effects for words and unfamiliar faces. *J. Exp. Psychol., Gen.* 117: 148–60

Benzing, W., Squire, L. R. 1989. Preserved learning and memory in amnesia, intact adaptation-level effects and learning of stereoscopic depth. *Behav. Neurosci.* 103: 548–60

Berger, T. W., Orr, W. B. 1983. Hippocampectomy selectively disrupts discrimination reversal learning of the rabbit nictitating membrane response. *Behav. Brain Res.* 8: 49–68

Berger, T. W., Thompson, R. F. 1978. Neuronal plasticity in the limbic system during classical conditioning in the rabbit nictitating membrane response. I. The hippocampus, *Brain Res.* 145: 323–46

Berry, D., Broadbent, D. 1984. On the relationship between task performance and associated verbalizable knowledge. *Q. J. Exp. Psychol.* 36A: 209–31

Biederman, I., Cooper, E. E. 1991a. Priming contour deleted images: evidence for intermediate representations in visual object recognition. *Cogn. Psychol.* 23: 393–419

Biederman, I., Cooper, E. E. 1991b. Evidence for complete translational and reflectional invariance in visual object priming. *Perception.* 20: 585–93

Biederman, I., Cooper, E. E. 1992. Size invariance in visual object priming. *J. Exp. Psychol.: Hum. Percept. Perform.* 18: 121–33

Blaxton, T. A. 1989. Investigating dissociations among memory measures, support for a transfer appropriate processing framework. *J. Exp. Psychol.: Learn. Mem. Cogn.* 15: 657–68

Bonnano, G. A., Stillings, N. A. 1986. Preference, familiarity, and recognition after repeated brief exposures to random geometric shapes. *Am. J. Psychol.* 99: 403–15

Brooks, D. N., Baddeley, A. 1976. What can amnesic patients learn? *Neuropsychologia* 14: 111–22

Brooks, L. R. 1978. Nonanalytic concept formation and memory for instances. In *Cognition and Categorization*, ed. E. Rosch, B. B. Lloyd, pp. 169–211. New York, Wiley

Brooks, L. R., Vokey, J. R. 1991. Abstract analogies and abstracted grammars, comments on Reber (1989) and Mathews *et al.* (1989). *J. Exp. Psychol.: Gen.* 120: 316–23

Butters, N., Heindel, W. C., Salmon, D. P. 1990. Dissociation of implicit memory in dementia, neurological implications. *Bull. Psychonomic Soc.* 28: 359–66

Butters, N., Stuss, D. T. 1989. Diencephalic amnesia. In *Handbook of Neuropsychology*, ed. F. Boller, J. Grafman, pp. 107–48. Amsterdam, Elsevier

Caul, W. F., Jarrard, L. E., Miller, R. E., Korn, J. H. 1969. Effects of hippocampal lesions on heart rate in aversive classical conditioning. *Physiol. Behav.* 4: 917–22

Cave, C. B., Squire, L. R. 1991. Equivalent impairment of spatial and nonspatial memory following damage to the human hippocampus. *Hippocampus* 1: 329–40

Cave, C. B., Squire, L. R. 1992a. Intact verbal and nonverbal short-term memory following damage to the human hippocampus. *Hippocampus* 2: 151–63

Cave, C. B., Squire, L. R. 1992b. Intact and long-lasting repetition priming in amnesia. *J. Exp. Psychol.: Learn. Mem. Cogn.* 18: 509–20

Cermak, L. S. 1984. The episodic-semantic distinction in amnesia. See Squire and Butters, 1984, pp. 55–62

Cermak, L. S., Bleich, R. P., Blackford, S. P. 1988. Deficits in implicit retention of new associations by alcoholic Korsakoff patients. *Brain Cogn.* 7: 312–23

Cermak, L. S., Talbot, N., Chandler, K., Wolbarst, L. R. 1985. The perceptual priming phenomenon in amnesia. *Neuropsychologia* 23: 615–22

Cermak, L. S., Verfaellie, M., Milberg, W., Letourneau, L., Blackford, S. 1991. A further analysis of perceptual identification priming in alcoholic Korsakoff patients. *Neuropsychologia* 29: 725–36

Chapman, G. B., Robbins, S. J. 1990. Cue interaction in human contingency judgement. *Mem. Cogn.* 18: 537–45

Cho, Y. H., Beracochea, D., Jaffard, R. 1991. Temporally graded retrograde and anterograde amnesia following ibotenic entorhinal cortex lesion in mice. *Soc. Neurosci. Abstr.* 17: 1045

Cleeremans, A., McClelland, J. L. 1991. Learning the structure of event sequences. *J. Exp. Psychol.: Gen.* 120: 235–53

Cohen, A., Ivry, R. I., Keele, S. W. 1990. Attention and structure in sequence learning. *J. Exp. Psychol.: Learn. Mem. Cogn.* 16: 17–30

Cohen, N. J., Squire, L. R. 1980. Preserved learning and retention of pattern analyzing skill in amnesia: dissociation of knowing how and knowing that. *Science* 210: 207–10

Cooper, L. A., Schacter, D. L., Ballesteros, S., Moore, C. 1992. Priming and recognition of transformed three-dimension objects, effects of size and reflection. *J. Exp. Psychol.: Learn. Mem. Cogn.* 18: 43–57

Damasio, A. R. 1990. Category-related recognition defects as a clue to the neural substrates of knowledge. *Trends Neurosci.* 13: 95–98

Daum, I., Channon, S., Canavar, A. 1989. Classical conditioning in patients with severe memory problems. *J. Neurol. Neurosurg. Psychiatry* 52: 47–51

Diamond, A. 1990. Rate of maturation of the hippocampus and the developmental progression of children's performance on the delayed non-matching to sample and visual paired comparison tasks. In *The Development and Neural Bases of Higher Cognitive Functions*, ed. A. Diamond, pp. 394–426. New York, NY Acad. Sci.

Diamond, R., Rozin, P. 1984. Activation of existing memories in anterograde amnesia. *J. Abnorm. Psychol.* 93: 98–105

Dienes, Z., Broadbent, D., Berry, D. 1991. Implicit and explicit knowledge bases in artificial grammar learning. *J. Exp. Psychol.: Learn. Mem. Cogn.* 17: 875–87

Divak, J., Rosvold, H. E., Szwarcbart, M. K. 1967. Behavioral effects of selective ablation of the caudate nucleus. *J. Comp. Physio. Psychol.* 63: 184–90

Douglas, R. J. 1975. The development of hippocampal function: implications for theory and for therapy. In *The Hippocampus: Neurophysiology and Behavior*, ed. L. Isaacson, K. H. Pribram, pp. 327–61. New York, Plenum

Drachman, D. A., Arbit, J. 1966. Memory and the hippocampal complex. II. Is memory a multiple process? *Arch. Neurol.* 15: 52–61

Dulany, D. E., Carlson, R. A., Dewey, G. I. 1984. A case of syntactical learning and judgment: how conscious and how abstract? *J. Exp. Psychol.: Gen.* 113: 541–55

Dunn, L. T., Everitt, B. J. 1988. Double dissociations of the effects of amygdala and insular cortex lesions on conditioned taste aversion, passive avoidance, and neophobia in the rat using the excitotoxin ibotenic acid. *Behav. Neurosci.* 102: 3–23

Eichenbaum, H., Fagan, A., Mathews, P., Cohen, N. J. 1988. Hippocampal system dysfunction and odor discrimination learning in rats: impairment or facilitation depending on representational demands. *Behav. Neurosci.* 102: 331–39

Eichenbaum, H., Kuperstein, M., Fagan, A., Nagode, J. 1986. Cue-sampling and goal-approach correlates of hippocampal unit activity in rats performing an odor discrimination task. *J. Neurosci.* 7: 716–32

Eichenbaum, H., Mathews, P., Cohen, N. J. 1989. Further studies of hippocampal representation during odor discrimination learning. *Behav. Neurosci.* 103: 1207–16

Eichenbaum, H., Otto, T., Cohen, N. J. 1992. The hippocampus – What does it do? *Behav. Neurol. Biol.* 57: 2–36

Estes, W. K. 1988. Human learning and memory. In *Stevens' Handbook of Experimental Psychology*, ed. R. D. Atkinson, R. Herrnstein, G. Lindzey, R. D. Luce, pp. 352–415. New York, Wiley

Estes, W. K. 1991. Cognitive architectures from the standpoint of an experimental psychologist. *Annu. Rev. Psychol.* 42: 1–28

Evans, F. J., Thorn, W. A. F. 1966. Two types of posthypnotic amnesia, recall amnesia and source amnesia. *Int. J. Clin. Exp. Hypnosis* 14: 162–79

Fagan, J. F. 1970. Memory in the infant. *J. Exp. Child Psychol.* 9: 217–26

Fantz, R. L., 1964. Visual experience in infants. Decreased attention to familiar patterns relative to novel ones. *Science* 146: 668–70

Farah, M. J., McClelland, J. L. 1991. A computational model of semantic memory impairment: modality specificity and emergent category specificity. *J. Exp. Psychol.: Gen.* 120: 339–57

Farah, M. J., McMullen, P. A., Meyer, M. M. 1991. Can recognition of living things be selectively impaired? *Neuropsychologia* 29: 185–93

Felleman, D., Van Essen, D. 1991. Distributed hierarchical processing in primate cerebral cortex. *Cerebral Cortex* 1: 1–47

Freed, D. M., Corkin, S., Cohen, N. J. 1987. Forgetting in H. M.: a second look. *Neuropsychologia* 25: 461–71

Freud, S. 1962. *Three Essays on the Theory of Sexuality*, pp. 125–273. New York, Basic Books (Originally published 1905)

Fried, L. S., Holyoak, K. J. 1984. Induction of category distributions: a framework for classification learning. *J. Exp. Psychol.: Learn. Mem. Cogn.* 10: 234–57

Fuster, J. M., Jervey, J. P. 1981. Inferotemporal neurons distinguish and retain behaviorally relevant features of visual stimuli. *Science* 212: 952–55

Gabrieli, J. D. E., Milberg, W., Keane, M. M., Corkin, S. 1990. Intact priming of patterns despite impaired memory. *Neuropsychologia* 28: 417–27

Gardiner, J. M. 1988. Recognition failures and free-recall failures: implications for the relation between recall and recognition. *Mem. Cogn.* 16: 446–51

Gardiner, J. M., Java, R. I. 1990. Recollective experience in word and nonword recognition. *Mem. Cogn.* 18: 23–30

Gardner, H., Boller, F., Moreines, J., Butters, N. 1973. Retrieving information from Korsakoff patients: effects of categorical cues and reference to the task. *Cortex* 9: 165–75

Gathercole, S. E., Baddeley, A. D. 1990. The role of phonological memory in vocabulary acquisition: a study of young children learning new names. *Br. J. Psychol.* 81: 439–54

Glanzer, M., Cunitz, A. R. 1966. Two storage mechanisms in free recall. *J. Verbal Learn. Verbal Behav.* 5: 351–60

Glisky, E. L., Schacter, D. L., Tulving, E. 1986a. Computer learning by memory-impaired patients: acquisition and retention of complex knowledge. *Neuropsychologia* 24: 313–28

Glisky, E. L., Schacter, D. L., Tulving, E. 1986b. Learning and retention of computer-related vocabulary in memory-impaired patients: method of vanishing cues. *J. Clin. Exp. Neuropsychol.* 8: 292–312

Gluck, M. A., Bower, G. H. 1988. From conditioning to category learning: an adaptive network model. *J. Exp. Psychol.: Gen.* 117: 227–47

Goldman-Rakic, P. S. 1987. Circuitry of primate prefontal cortex and regulation of behavior by representational memory. In *Handbook of Physiology*, ed. V. B. Mountcastle, F. Plum, S. R. Geiger, pp. 373–418. Bethesda, MD, Am. Physiol. Soc.

Graf, P., Mandler, G. 1984. Activation makes words more accessible, but not necessarily more retrievable. *J. Verbal Learn. Verbal Behav.* 23: 553–68

Graf, P., Schacter, D. L. 1985. Implicit and explicit memory for new asociations in normal and amnesic subjects. *J. Exp. Psychol.: Learn. Mem. Cogn.* 11: 501–18

Graf, P., Shimamura, A. P., Squire, L. R. 1985. Priming across modalities and priming across category levels: extending the domain of preserved function in amnesia. *J. Exp. Psychol.: Learn. Mem. Cogn.* 11: 386–96

Graf, P., Squire, L. R., Mandler, G. 1984. The information that amnesic patients do not forget. *J. Exp. Psychol.: Learn. Mem. Cogn.* 10: 164–78

Haist, F., Musen, G., Squire, L. R. 1991. Intact priming of words and nonwords in amnesia. *Psychobiology* 19: 275–85

Haist, F., Shimamura, A. P., Squire, L. R. 1992. On the relationship between recall and recognition memory. *J. Exp. Psychol.: Learn. Mem. Cogn.* 18: 691–702

Halgren, E. 1984. Human hippocampal and amygdala recording and stimulation, evidence for a neural model of recent memory. See Squire and Butters 1984, pp. 165–82

Hamann, S. B. 1990. Level-of-processing effects in conceptually driven implicit tasks. *J. Exp. Psychol.: Learn. Mem. Cogn.* 16: 970–77

Hart, J., Berndt, R. S., Caramazza, A. 1985. Category-specific naming deficit following cerebral infarction. *Nature* 316: 439–40

Hartman, M., Knopman, D. S., Nissen, M. J. 1989. Implicit learning of new verbal associations. *J. Exp. Psychol.: Learn. Mem. Cogn.* 15: 1070–82

Hayman, C. A. G., Tulving, E. 1989. Contingent dissociation between recognition and fragment completion: the method of triangulation. *J. Exp. Psychol.: Learn. Mem. Cogn.* 15: 220–24

Heindel, W. C., Salmon, D. P., Butters, N. 1991. The biasing of weight judgments in Alzheimer's and Huntington's disease: a priming or programming phenomenon? *J. Clin. Exp. Neuropsychol.* 13: 189–203

Heindel, W. C., Salmon, D. P., Shults, C. W., Walicke, P. A., Butters, N. 1989. Neuropsychological evidence for multiple implicit memory systems: a comparison of Alzheimer's, Huntington's, and Parkinson's disease patients. *J. Neurosci.* 9: 582–87

Hintzman, D. 1986. Schema abstraction in a multiple-trace memory model. *Psychol. Rev.* 93: 411–28

Hintzman, D. 1990. Human learning and memory: connections and dissociations. *Annu. Rev. Psychol.* 41: 109–39

Hintzman, D., Hartry, A. L. 1990. Item effects in recognition and fragment completion: contingency relations vary for different subsets of words. *J. Exp. Psychol.: Learn. Mem. Cogn.* 16: 955–69

Hirsh, R. 1974. The hippocampus and contextual retrieval from memory: A theory. *Behav. Biol.* 12: 421–44

Hirst, W., Johnson, M. K., Phelps, E. A., Risse, G., Volpe, B. T. 1986. Recognition and recall in amnesics. *J. Exp. Psychol.: Learn. Mem. Cogn.* 12: 445–51

Hirst, W., Johnson, M. K., Phelps, E. A., Volpe, B. T. 1988. More on recognition and recall in amnesics. *J. Exp. Psychol.: Learn. Mem. Cogn.* 14: 758–62

Huppert, F. A., Piercy, M. 1979. Normal and abnormal forgetting in organic amnesia: effect of locus of lesion. *Cortex* 15: 385–90

Ivry, R., Baldo, J. 1992. Is the cerebellum involved in learning and cognition? *Curr. Opin. Neurobiol.* 2: 212–16

Jacobson, R. R., Lishman, W. A. 1987. Selective memory loss and global intellectual deficits in alcoholic Korsakoff's syndrome. *Psychol. Med.* 17: 649–55

Jacoby, L. L. 1983. Remembering the data: analyzing interactive processes in reading. *J. Verbal Learn.: Verbal Behav.* 22: 485–508

Jacoby, L. L. 1988. Memory observed and memory unobserved. In *Remembering Reconsidered: Ecological and Traditional Approaches to the Study of Memory,* ed. U. Neisser, E. Winograd, pp. 145–177. Cambridge, Cambridge Univ. Press

Jacoby, L. L. 1991. A process dissociation framework: separating automatic from intentional uses of memory. *J. Mem. Lang.* 30: 513–41

Jacoby, L. L., Dallas, M. 1981. On the relationship between autobiographical memory and perceptual learning. *J. Exp. Psychol.: Learn. Mem. Cogn.* 3: 306–40

Jacoby, L. L., Witherspoon, D. 1982. Remembering without awareness. *Can. J. Psychol.* 32: 300–24

Jacoby, L. L., Woloshyn, V., Kelley, C. M. 1989. Becoming famous without being recognized: unconscious influences of memory produced by dividing attention. *J. Exp. Psychol.: Gen.* 118: 115–25

James, W. 1890. *Principles of Psychology.* New York, Holt.

Janowsky, J. S., Shimamura, A. P., Kritchevsky, M., Squire, L. R. 1989a. Cognitive impairment following frontal lobe damage and its relevance to human amnesia. *Behav. Neurosci.* 103: 548–60

Janowsky, J. S., Shimamura, A. P., Squire, L. R. 1989b. Memory and metamemory: comparisons between patients with frontal lobe lesions and amnesic patients. *Psychobiology.* 17: 3–11

Janowsky, J. S., Shimamura, A. P., Squire, L. R. 1989c. Source memory impairment in patients with frontal lobe lesions. *Neuropsychologia* 27: 1043–56

Jetter, W., Poser, U., Freeman, R. B. Jr., Markowitsch, J. H. 1986. A verbal long-term memory deficit in frontal lobe damaged patients. *Cortex* 22: 229–42

Johnston, W. A., Dark, W. J., Jacoby, L. L. 1985. Perceptual fluency and recognition judgments. *J. Exp. Psychol.: Learn. Mem. Cogn.* 11: 3–11

Johnston, W. A., Hawley, K. J., Elliot, M. G. 1991. Contribution of perceptual fluency to recognition judgments. *J. Exp. Psychol.: Learn. Mem. Cogn.* 17: 210–23

Kandel, E. R., Squire, L. R., 1992. Cognitive neuroscience. *Curr. Opin. Neurobiol.* 2: 143–45

Keane, M. M., Gabrieli, J. D. E., Fennema, A. C., Growdon, J. H., Corkin, S. 1991. Evidence for a dissociation between perceptual and conceptual priming in Alzheimer's disease. *Behav. Neurosci.* 105: 326–42

Kersteen-Tucker, Z. 1991. Long-term repetition priming with symmetrical polygons and words. *Mem. Cogn.* 19: 37–43

Kesner, R. P., Novak, J. M. 1982. Serial position curve in rats: role of the dorsal hippocampus. *Science* 218: 173–75

Kim, J. J., Fanselow, M. S. 1992. Modality-specific retrograde amnesia of fear. *Science* 256: 675–77

Kinsbourne, M., Wood, F. 1975. Short-term memory processes and the amnesic syndrome. In *Short-term Memory*, ed. D. Deutsch, J. A. Deutsch, pp. 258–91. New York, Academic Press

Knopman, D. S., Nissen, M. J. 1991. Procedural learning is impaired in Huntington's disease: evidence from the serial reaction time task. *Neuropsychologia* 29: 245–54

Knowlton, B. J., Ramus, S. J., Squire, L. R. 1992. Intact artificial grammar learning in amnesia: dissociation of classification learning and explicit memory for specific instances. *Psychol. Sci.* 3: 172–79

Knowlton, B. J., Squire, L. R. 1992. Intact prototype learning by amnesic patients: evidence for parallel learning of item-specific and general information. *Soc. Neurosci. Abstr.* 18: 386

Kopelman, M. D. 1985. Rates of forgetting in Alzheimer type dementia and Korsakoff's syndrome. *Neuropsychologia* 23: 623–38

Kopelman, M. D. 1989. Remote and autobiographical memory, temporal context memory and frontal atrophy in Korsakoff and Alzheimer patients. *Neuropsychologia* 27: 437–60

Kovner, R., Mattis, S., Goldmeier, E. 1983. A technique for promoting robust free recall in chronic organic amnesia. *J. Clin. Neuropsychol.* 5: 65–71

Kritchevsky, M., Squire, L. R., Zouzounis, J. 1988. Transient global amnesia: characterization of anterograde and retrograde amnesia. *Neurology* 38: 213–19

Kruschke, J. K. 1992. ALCOVE: an exemplar-based connectionist model of category learning. *Psychol. Rev.* 99: 22–44

Kunst-Wilson, W. R., Zajonc, R. B. 1980. Affective discrimination of stimuli that cannot be recognized. *Science* 207: 557–58

Lavond, D. G., Kim, J. J., Thompson, R. F. 1993. Mammalian brain substrates of aversive classical conditioning. *Annu. Rev. Psychol.* 44: 317–42

LeDoux, J. E. 1987. Emotion. In *Handbook of Physiology: The Nervous System v. Higher Functions of the Nervous System*, ed. F. Plum, pp. 419–60. Betheda, MD, Am. Physiol. Soc.

Levin, H. S., Eisenberg, H. M., Benton, A. L. 1991. *Frontal Lobe Function and Dysfunction*, New York, Oxford Univ. Press

Lewicki, P. 1986a. Processing information about covariations that cannot be articulated. *J. Exp. Psychol.: Learn. Mem. Cogn.* 12: 135–46

Lewicki, P. 1986b. *Nonconscious Social Information Processing*, pp. 130–72. New York, Academic Press

Lewicki, P., Czyzewska, M., Hoffman, H. 1987. Unconscious acquisition of complex procedural knowledge. *J. Exp. Psychol.: Learn. Mem. Cogn.* 13: 523–30

MacAndrew, S. B. G., Jones, G. V. 1993. Spatial memory in amnesia: evidence from Korsakoff patients. *Cortex* 29: 235–49

Mahut, M., Moss, M. 1984. Consolidation of memory: the hippocampus revisited. See Squire and Butters 1984, pp. 297–315

Malamut, B. L., Saunders, R. C., Mishkin, M. 1984. Monkeys with combined amygdalohippocampal lesions succeed in object discrimination learning despite 24-hour intertrial intervals. *Behav. Neurosci.* 98: 759–69

Mandler, G. 1980. Recognizing: the judgment of previous occurrence. *Psychol. Rev.* 87: 252–71

Mandler, G., Nakamura, Y., Van Zandt, B. J. S. 1987. Nonspecific effects of exposure on stimuli that cannot be recognized. *J. Exp. Psychol.: Learn. Mem. Cogn.* 13: 646–48

Mandler, J. M. 1990. Recall of events by preverbal children. See Diamond 1990, pp. 485–516

Marinkovic, K., Schell, A. M., Dawson, M. E. 1989. Awareness of the CS-UCS contingency and classical conditioning of skin conductance responses with olfactory CSs. *Biol. Psychol.* 29: 39–60

Markowitsch, H. 1988. Diencephalic amnesia: a reorientation towards tracts? *Brain Res. Rev.* 13: 351–70

Marsolek, C. J., Kosslyn, S., Squire, L. R. 1992. Form-specific visual priming in the right cerebral hemisphere. *J. Exp. Psychol.: Learn. Mem. Cogn.* 18: 492–508

Martone, M., Butters, N., Payne, P. 1984. Dissociations between skill learning and verbal recognition in amnesia and dementia. *Arch. Neurol.* 41: 965–70

Masson, M. E. J. 1989. Fluent reprocessing as an implicit expression of memory for experience. In *Implicit Memory: Theoretical Issues,* ed. S. Lewandowsky, J. C. Dunn, K. Kirsner, pp. 123–38. Hillsdale, NJ, Erlbaum

Mathews, R. C., Buss, R. R., Stanley, W. B., Blanchard-Fields, F., Cho, J. R., *et al.* 1989. The role of implicit and explicit processes in learning from examples: a synergistic effect. *J. Exp. Psychol.: Learn. Mem. Cogn.* 15: 1083–1100

Mayes, A. R. 1988. *Human Organic Memory Disorders,* New York, Oxford Univ. Press

Mayes, A. R., Gooding, P. 1989. Enhancement of word completion priming in amnesics by cuing with previously novel associates. *Neuropsychologia* 27: 1057–72

Mayes, A. R., Meudell, P., MacDonald, C. 1991. Disproportionate intentional spatial memory impairments in amnesia. *Neuropsychologia* 29: 771–84

McAndrews, M. P., Milner, B. 1991. The frontal cortex and memory for temporal order. *Neuropsychologia* 29: 849–60

McClelland, J. L., Rumelhart, D. E. 1985. Distributed memory and the representation of general and specific information. *J. Exp. Psychol.: Gen.* 114: 159–88

McKee, R., Squire, L. R. 1992. Equivalent forgetting rates in long-term memory for diencephalic and medial temporal lobe amnesia. *J. Neurosci.* 12: 3765–72

McKee, R., Squire, L. R. 1993. On the development of declarative memory. *J. Exp. Psychol.: Learn. Mem. Cognit.* 19: 397–404

McNaughton, B. L., Nadel, L. 1990. Hebb-Marr networks and the neurobiological representation of action in space. In *Neuroscience and Connectionist Theory*, ed. M. Gluck, D. Rumelhart, pp. 1–63. Hillsdale, NJ, Erlbaum

Medin, D. L., Schaffer, M. M. 1978. Context theory of classification learning. *Psychol. Rev.* 85: 207–38

Meltzoff, A. N. 1985. Immediate and deferred imitation in fourteen- and twenty-month-old infants. *Child Dev.* 56: 62–72

Meudell, P. R., Mayes, A. R., Ostergaard, A., Pickering, A. 1985. Recency and frequency judgments in alcoholic amnesics and normal people with poor memory. *Cortex* 21: 487–511

Miller, E. K., Li, L., Desimone, R. 1991. A neural mechanism for working and recognition memory in inferior temporal cortex. *Science* 254: 1377–79

Milner, B. 1962. Les troubles de la mémoire accompagnant des lésions hippocampiques bilatérales. In *Physiologie de l'hippocampe*, pp. 257–72. Paris, Cent. Natl. Rech. Sci.

Milner, B. 1971. Interhemispheric differences in the localization of psychological processes in man. *Br. Med. Bull.* 27: 272–77

Milner, B. 1978. Clues to the cerebral organization of memory. In *Cerebral Correlates of Conscious Experience, INSERM Symposium*, ed. P. A. Buser, A. Rougeul-Buser, pp. 139–53. Amsterdam, Elsevier

Milner, P. M. 1989. A cell assembly theory of hippocampal amnesia. *Neuropsychologia* 27: 23–30

Mishkin, M. 1978. Memory in monkeys severely impaired by combined but not by separate removal of amygdala and hippocampus. *Nature* 273: 297–98

Mishkin, M. 1982. A memory system in the monkey. *Philos. Trans. R. Soc. London Ser.* B298: 85–92

Mishkin, M., Delacour, J. 1975. An analysis of short-term visual memory in the monkey. *J. Exp. Psychol.: Anim. Behav.* 1: 326–34

Mishkin, M., Malamut, B., Bachevalier, J. 1984. Memories and habits: two neural systems. In *Neurobiology of Learning and Memory*, ed. G. Lynch, J. L. McGaugh, N. M. Weinberger, pp. 65–77. New York, Guilford

Mitchell, D. B., Brown, A. S. 1988. Persistent repetition priming in picture naming and its dissociation from recognition memory. *J. Exp. Psychol.: Learn. Mem. Cogn.* 14: 213–22

Monsell, S. 1984. Components of working memory underlying verbal skills, a 'distributed capacities' view. In *International Symposia on Attention and Performance*, ed. H. Bouma, D. Bonnhuis, 10, 327–50. Hillsdale, NJ: Erlbaum

Moscovitch, M., Winocur, G., McLachlan, D. 1986. Memory as assessed by recognition and reading time in normal and memory impaired people with Alzheimer's disease and other neurological disorders. *J. Exp. Psychol.: Gen.* 115: 331–47

Moyer, J. R., Deyo, R. A., Disterhoft, J. F. 1990. Hippocampectomy disrupts trace eye-blink conditioning in rabbits. *Behav. Neurosci.* 204: 243–52

Musen, G., Shimamura, A. P., Squire, L. R. 1990. Intact text-specific reading skill in amnesia. *J. Exp. Psychol.: Learn. Mem. Cogn.* 6: 1068–76

Musen, G., Squire, L. R. 1991. Normal acquisition of novel verbal information in amnesia. *J. Exp. Psychol.: Learn. Mem. Cogn.* 17: 1095–1104

Musen, G., Squire, L. R. 1992. Nonverbal priming in amnesia. *Mem. Cogn.* 20: 441–48

Musen, G., Squire, L. R. 1993. On the implicit learning of novel associations by amnesic patients and normal subjects. *Neuropsychology* 7: 119–35

Musen, G., Treisman, A. 1990. Implicit and explicit memory for visual patterns. *J. Exp. Psychol.: Learn. Mem. Cogn.* 16: 127–37

Nadel, L., Zola-Morgan, S. 1984. Infantile amnesia: a neurobiological perspective. In *Infant Memory*, ed. M. Moscovitch, pp. 145–72. New York, Plenum

Neisser, U. 1962. Cultural and cognitive discontinuity. In *Anthropology and Human Behavior*, ed. T. E. Gladwin, W. Sturtevant. Washington, DC, Anthropol. Soc.

Nelson, K. 1988. The ontogeny of memory for real events. In *Remembering Reconsidered: Ecological and Traditional Approaches to the Study of Memory*, ed. U. Neisser, E. Winograd, pp. 244–77. New York, Cambridge Univ. Press

Nissen, M. J., Bullemer, P. 1987. Attentional requirements of learning: evidence from performance measures. *Cogn. Psychol.* 19: 1–32

Norman, R. J., Buchwald, J. S., Villablanca, J. R. 1977. Classical conditioning with auditory discrimination of the eyeblink reflex in decerebrate cats. *Science* 196: 551–53

Nosofsky, R. M. 1984. Choice, similarity, and the context theory of classification. *J. Exp. Psychol.: Learn. Mem. Cogn.* 10: 104–14

Nosofsky, R. M., Kruschke, J. K., McKinley, S. C. 1992. Combining exemplar-based category representations and connectionist learning rules. *J. Exp. Psychol.: Learn. Mem. Cogn.* 18: 211–33

O'Keefe, J., Nadel, L. 1978. *The Hippocampus as a Cognitive Map*. London, Oxford Univ. Press

Olton, D. S. 1985. Memory: neuropsychological and ethopsychological approaches to its classification. In *Perspectives on Learning and Memory*, ed. L. Nilsson, T. Archer, pp. 95–118. Hillsdale, NJ: Erlbaum

Ostergaard, A. L. 1992. A method for judging measures of stochastic dependence: further comments on the current controversy. *J. Exp. Psychol.: Learn. Mem. Cogn.* 18: 413–20

Ostergaard, A. L., Squire, L. R. 1990. Childhood amnesia and distinctions between forms of memory. *Brain Cogn.* 14: 127–33

Overman, W. H. 1990. Performance on traditional matching to sample, non-matching to sample, and object discrimination tasks by 12- to 32-month-old-children: a developmental progression. See Diamond 1990, pp. 365–94

Packard, M. G., Hirsh, R., White, N. M. 1989. Differential effects of fornix and caudate nucleus lesions on two radial maze tasks: evidence for multiple memory systems. *J. Neurosci.* 9: 1465–72

Paller, K. A. 1990. Recall and stem-completion priming have different electrophysiological correlates and are modified differentially by directed forgetting. *J. Exp. Psychol.: Learn. Mem. Cogn.* 16: 1021–32

Paller, K. A., Kutas, M. 1992. Brain potentials during memory retrieval: neurophysiological support for the distinction between conscious recollection and priming. *J. Cogn. Neurosci.* 4: 375–91

Papagno, C., Valentine, T., Baddeley, A. 1991. Phonological short-term memory and foreign-language vocabulary learning. *J. Mem. Lang.* 30: 331–47

Parkin, A. J. 1982. Residual learning capability in organic amnesia. *Cortex* 18: 417–40

Parkin, A. J. 1984. Amnesic syndrome: a lesion-specific disorder. *Cortex* 20: 479–508

Parkinson, J. K., Murray, E., Mishkin, M. 1988. A selective mnemonic role for the hippocampus in monkeys: memory for the location of objects. *J. Neurosci.* 8: 4159–67

Perruchet, P., Pacteau, C. 1990. Synthetic grammar learning: implicit rule abstraction or explicit fragmentary knowledge? *J. Exp. Psychol.: Gen.* 119: 264–75

Petersen, S. E., Fox, P. T., Snyder, A. Z., Raichle, M. E. 1990. Activation of extrastriate and frontal cortical areas by visual words and word-like stimuli. *Science* 249: 1041–44

Phillips, R. R., Malamut, B. L., Bachevalier, J., Mishkin, M. 1988. Dissociation of the effects of inferior temporal and limbic lesions on object discrimination learning with 24-h intertrial intervals. *Behav. Brain Res.* 27: 99–107

Posner, M. I., Keele, S. W. 1968. On the genesis of abstract ideas. *J. Exp. Psychol.* 77: 353–63

Ranck, J. B. 1973. Studies on single neurons in dorsal hippocampal formation and septum in unrestrained rats. *Exp. Neurol.* 41: 461–531

Reber, A. S. 1967. Implicit learning of artificial grammars. *J. Verbal Learn.: Verbal Behav.* 6: 855–63

Reber, A. S. 1976. Implicit learning of synthetic languages, the role of instructional set. *J. Exp. Psychol.: Hum. Learn. Mem.* 2: 88–94

Reber, A. S. 1989. Implicit learning and tacit knowledge. *J. Exp. Psychol.: Gen.* 3: 219–35

Reed, S. K. 1972. Pattern recognition and categorization. *Cogn. Psychol.* 3: 382–407

Rescorla, R. A., Wagner, A. R. 1972. A theory of Pavlovian conditioning: variations in the effectiveness of reinforcement and non-reinforcement. In *Classical Conditioning II, Current Theory and Research*, ed. A. H. Black, W. F. Prokasy, pp. 64–99. Orlando, FL, Academic

Richardson-Klavehn, A., Bjork, R. A. 1988. Measures of memory. *Annu. Rev. Psychol.* 39: 475–543

Riches, I. P., Wilson, F. A. W., Brown, M. W. 1991. The effects of visual stimulation and memory on neurons of the hippocampal formation and the neighboring parahippocampal gyrus and inferior temporal cortex of the primate. *J. Neurosci.* 11: 1763–979

Ringo, J. L. 1991. Memory decays at the same rate in macaques with and without brain lesions when expressed in d' or arcsine terms. *Behav. Brain Res.* 42, 123–34.

Roediger, H. L. 1990. Implicit memory: retention without remembering. *Am. Psychol.* 45: 1043–56

Rolls, E. 1990. Principles underlying the representation and storage of information in neuronal networks in the primate hippocampus and cerebral cortex. In *Introduction to Neural and Electronic Networks*, ed. S. F. Zornetzer, J. L. Davis, C. Lau, pp. 73–90. San Diego, CA, Academic Press

Rosch, E. H. 1973. On the internal structure of perceptual and semantic categories. In *Cognitive Development and the Acquisition of Language*, ed. T. E. Moore, pp. 111–44, New York, Academic Press

Ross, R. T., Orr, W. B., Holland, P. C., Berger, T. W. 1984. Hippocampectomy disrupts acquisition and retention of learned conditional responding. *Behav. Neurosci.* 98: 211–25

Sagar, H. H., Cohen, N. J., Corkin, S., Growdon, J. M. 1985. Dissociations among processes in remote memory. In *Memory Dysfunctions*, ed. D. S. Olton, E. Gamzu, S. Corkin, pp. 533–35. New York, NY Acad. Sci.

Saint-Cyr, J. A., Taylor, A. E., Lang, A. E. 1988. Procedural learning and neostriatal dysfunction in man. *Brain* 111: 941–59

Sakai, K., Miyashita, Y. 1991. Neural organization for the long-term memory of paired associates. *Nature* 354: 152–55

Saunders, R. C., Weiskrantz, L. 1989. The effects of fornix transection and combined fornix transection, mammillary body lesions and hippocampal ablations on object-pair association memory in the rhesus monkey. *Behav. Brain Res.* 35: 85–94

Schacter, D. L. 1985. Priming of old and new knowledge in amnesic patients and normal subjects. *Ann. NY Acad. Sci.* 444: 44–53

Schacter, D. L. 1987. Implicit memory: history and current status. *J. Exp. Psychol.: Learn. Mem. Cogn.* 13: 501–18

Schacter, D. L. 1990. Perceptual representation systems and implicit memory, toward a resolution of the multiple memory systems debate. See Diamond 1990, pp. 543–71

Schacter, D. L. 1992. Understanding implicit memory: a cognitive neuroscience approach. *Am. Psychol.* 47: 559–69

Schacter, D. L., Chiu, C.-Y. P., Ochsner, K. N. 1993. Implicit memory: a selective review. *Annu. Rev. Neurosci.* 16: 159–82

Schacter, D. L., Church, B. 1992. Auditory priming: implicit and explicit memory for words and voices. *J. Exp. Psychol.: Learn. Mem. Cogn.* 18: 915–30

Schacter, D. L., Cooper, L. A., Tharan, M., Rubens, A. B. 1991. Preserved priming of novel objects in patients with memory disorders. *J. Cogn. Neurosci.* 3: 118–31

Schacter, D. L., Graf, P. 1986. Preserved learning in amnesic patients: perspectives on research from direct priming. *J. Clin. Exp. Neuropsychol.* 8: 727–43

Schacter, D. L., Harbluk, J. L., McLachlan, D. R. 1984. Retrieval without recollection: an experimental analysis of source amnesia. *J. Verbal Learn.: Verbal Behav.* 23: 593–611

Schacter, D. L., Moscovitch, M. 1984. Infants, amnesics, and dissociable memory systems. In *Infant Memory*, ed. M. Moscovitch, pp. 173–216. New York, Plenum

Servan-Schreiber, E., Anderson, J. R. 1990. Learning artificial grammars with competitive chunking. *J. Exp. Psychol.: Learn. Mem. Cogn.* 16: 592–608

Shallice, T., Warrington, E. K. 1970. Independent functioning of verbal memory stores: a neuropsychological study. *Q. J. Exp. Psychol.* 22: 261–73

Shanks, D. R. 1990. Connectionism and the learning of probabilistic concepts. *Q. J. Exp. Psychol.* 42A: 209–37

Shanks, D. R. 1991. Categorization by a connectionist network. *J. Exp. Psychol.: Learn. Mem. Cogn.* 17: 433–43

Sherry, D. F., Schacter, D. L. 1987. The evolution of multiple memory systems. *Psychol. Rev.* 94: 439–54

Shimamura, A. P. 1985. Problems with the finding of stochastic independence as evidence for multiple memory systems. *Bull. Psychon. Soc.* 23: 506–8

Shimamura, A. P. 1986. Priming effects in amnesia: evidence for a dissociable memory function. *Q. J. Exp. Psychol.* 38A: 619–44

Shimamura, A. P., Janowsky, J. S., Squire, L. R. 1991. What is the role of frontal lobe damage in memory disorders? In *Frontal Lobe Functioning and Dysfunction*, ed. H. D. Levin, H. M. Eisenberg, A. L. Benton, pp. 173–95. New York, Oxford Univ. Press

Shimamura, A. P., Jernigan, T. L., Squire, L. R. 1988. Korsakoff's syndrome: radiological (CT) findings and neuropsychological correlates. *J. Neurosci.* 8: 4400–10

Shimamura, A. P., Squire, L. R. 1984. Paired-associate learning and priming effects in amnesia: a neuropsychological analysis. *J. Exp. Psychol.: Gen.* 113: 556–70

Shimamura, A. P., Squire, L. R. 1986. Memory and metamemory: a study of the feeling of knowing phenomenon in amnesic patients. *J. Exp. Psychol.: Learn. Mem. Cogn.* 12: 452–60

Shimamura, A. P., Squire, L. R. 1987. A neuropsychological study of fact memory and source amnesia. *J. Exp. Psychol.: Learn. Mem. Cogn.* 13: 464–73

Shimamura, A. P., Squire, L. R. 1988. Long-term memory in amnesia, cued recall, recognition memory, and confidence ratings. *J. Exp. Psychol.: Learn. Mem. Cogn.* 14: 763–70

Shimamura, A. P., Squire, L. R. 1989. Impaired priming of new associations in amnesia. *J. Exp. Psychol.: Learn. Mem. Cogn.* 15: 721–28

Shimamura, A. P., Squire, L. R. 1991. The relationship between fact and source memory: Findings from amnesic patients and normal subjects. *Psychobiology* 19: 1–10

Shoqeirat, M. A., Mayes, A. R. 1991. Disproportionate incidental spatial memory and recall deficits in amnesia. *Neuropsychologia* 29: 749–69

Sloman, S. A., Hayman, C. A. G., Ohta, N., Law, J., Tulving, E. 1988. Forgetting in primed fragment completion. *J. Exp. Psychol.: Learn. Mem. Cogn.* 14: 223–39

Smith, E. E., Medin, D. L. 1981. *Categories and Concepts*, Cambridge, MA, Harvard Univ. Press

Smith, M. E., Oscar-Berman, M. 1990. Repetition priming of words and pseudowords in divided attention in amnesia. *J. Exp. Psychol.: Learn. Mem. Cogn.* 16: 1033–42

Solomon, P. R., Moore, J. W. 1975. Latent inhibition and stimulus generalization of the classically conditioned nictitating membrane response in rabbits *(Oryctolagus cuniculus)* following dorsal hippocampal ablation. *J. Comp. Physiol. Psychol.* 89: 1192–203

Squire, L. R. 1981. Two forms of human amnesia, an analysis of forgetting. *J. Neurosci.* 1: 635–40

Squire, L. R. 1982. Comparisons between forms of amnesia: some deficits are unique to Korsakoff's syndrome. *J. Exp. Psychol.: Learn. Mem. Cogn.* 8: 560–71

Squire, L. R. 1987. *Memory and Brain*, New York, Oxford Univ. Press

Squire, L. R. 1992a. Memory and the hippocampus: a synthesis from findings with rats, monkeys and humans. *Psychol. Rev.* 99: 195–231

Squire, L. R. 1992b. Declarative and nondeclarative memory: multiple brain systems supporting learning and memory. *J. Cogn. Neurosci.* 4: 232–43

Squire, L. R., Butters, N., eds. 1984. *Neuropsychology of Memory.* New York, Guilford

Squire, L. R., Cave, C. B. 1991. The hippocampus, memory, and space. *Hippocampus* 1: 329–40

Squire, L. R., Cohen, N. J., Nadel, L. 1984. The medial temporal region and memory consolidation: a new hypothesis. In *Memory Consolidation*, ed. H. Weingartner, E. Parker, pp. 185–210. Hillsdale, NJ, Erlbaum

Squire, L. R., Frambach, M. 1990. Cognitive skill learning in amnesia. *Psychobiology* 18: 109–17

Squire, L. R., Haist, F., Shimamura, A. P. 1989. The neurology of memory: quantitative assessment of retrograde amnesia in two groups of amnesic patients. *J. Neurosci.* 9: 828–39

Squire, L. R., McKee, R. 1992. Influence of prior events on cognitive judgments in amnesia. *J. Exp. Psychol.: Learn. Mem. Cogn.* 18: 106–15

Squire, L. R., Ojemann, J. G., Miezin, F. M., Petersen, S. E., Videen, T. O., Raichle, M. E. 1992. Activation of the hippocampus in normal humans: a functional anatomical study of memory. *Proc. Natl. Acad. Sci. USA* 89: 1837–41

Squire, L. R., Shimamura, A. P., Graf, P. 1987. The strength and duration of priming effects in normal subjects and amnesic patients. *Neuropsychologia* 25: 195–210

Squire, L. R., Slater, P. C., Chace, P. M. 1975. Retrograde amnesia: temporal gradient in very long-term memory following electroconvulsive therapy. *Science* 187: 77–79

Squire, L. R., Zola-Morgan, S. 1983. The neurology of memory: the case for correspondence between the findings for man and non-human primate. In *The Physiological Basis of Memory*, ed. J. A. Deutsch, pp. 199–268. New York, Academic Press

Squire, L. R., Zola-Morgan, S. 1991. The medial temporal lobe memory system. *Science* 253: 1380–86

Squire, L. R., Zola-Morgan, S., Cave, C. B., Haist, F., Musen, G., Suzuki, W. A. 1990. Memory: organization of brain systems and cognition. *Cold Spring Harbor Symp.: Quant. Biol.* 55: 1007–23

Squire, L. R., Zola-Morgan, S., Chen, K. 1988. Human amnesia and animal models of amnesia: performance of amnesic patients on tests designed for the monkey. *Behav. Neurosci.* 11: 2110–21

Srinivas, K., Roediger, H. L. I. 1990. Classifying implicit memory tests: category association and anagram solution. *J. Mem. Lang.* 29: 389–413

Stadler, M. A. 1989. On learning complex procedural knowledge. *J. Exp. Psychol.: Learn. Mem. Cogn.* 15: 1061–69

Sutherland, R. W., Rudy, J. W. 1989. Configural association theory: the role of the hippocampal formation in learning, memory and amnesia. *Psychobiology* 17: 129–44

Suzuki, W., Zola-Morgan, S., Squire, L. R., Amaral, D. G. 1991. Lesions of the perirhinal and parahippocampal cortices in monkeys produce a modality general and long lasting memory impairment. *Soc. Neurosci. Abstr.* 21: 399

Teyler, T. J., Discenna, P. 1986. The hippocampal memory indexing theory. *Behav. Neurosci.* 100: 147–54

Thompson, R. F. 1988. The neural basis of basic associative learning of discrete behavioral responses. *Trends Neurosci.* 11: 152–55

Tulving, E. 1983. *Elements of Episodic Memory.* Oxford, Oxford Univ. Press

Tulving, E. 1985. How many memory systems are there? *Am. Psychol.* 40: 385–98

Tulving, E. 1991. Concepts in human memory. *In Memory, Organization and Locus of Change,* ed. L. R. Squire, N. M. Weinberger, G. Lynch, J. L. McGaugh, pp. 3–32. New York, Oxford Univ. Press

Tulving, E., Hayman, C. A. G., MacDonald, C. A. 1991. Long-lasting perceptual priming and semantic learning in amnesia: a case experiment. *J. Exp. Psychol.: Learn. Mem. Cogn.* 17: 595–617

Tulving, E., Schacter, D. L. 1990. Priming and human memory systems. *Science* 247: 301–6

Tulving, E., Schacter, D. L., Stark, H. 1982. Priming effects of word-fragment completion are independent of recognition memory. *J. Exp. Psychol.: Learn. Mem. Cogn.* 8: 336–42

Verfaellie, M., Cermak, L. S., Letourneau, L., Zuffante, P. 1991. Repetition effects in a lexical decision task: the role of episodic memory in alcoholic Korsakoff patients. *Neuropsychologia* 29: 641–57

Victor, M., Adams, R. D., Collins, C. 1989. *The Wernicke-Korsakoff Syndrome and Related Neurological Disorders Due to Alcoholism and Malnutrition.* Philadelphia: Davis. 2nd ed.

Vokey, J. R., Brooks, L. R. 1992. Salience of item knowledge in learning artifical grammars. *J. Exp. Psychol.: Learn. Mem. Cogn.* 18: 328–44

Wang, J., Aigner, T., Mishkin, M. 1990. Effects of neostriatal lesions on visual habit formation in rhesus monkeys. *Soc. Neurosci. Abstr.* 16: 617

Warrington, E. K., McCarthy, R. A. 1987. Categories of knowledge: further fractionations and an attempted integration. *Brain* 110: 1273–96

Warrington, E. K., Shallice, T. 1969. The selective impairment of auditory verbal short-term memory. *Brain* 92: 885–96

Warrington, E. K., Shallice, T. 1984. Category specific semantic impairments. *Brain* 107: 829–54

Warrington, E. K., Weiskrantz, L. 1982. Amnesia: a disconnection syndrome? *Neuropsychologia* 20: 233–48

Waugh, N. C., Norman, D. A. 1965. Primary memory. *Psychol. Rev.* 72: 89–104

Weiskrantz, L. 1990. Problems of learning and memory: one or multiple memory systems? *Philos. Trans. R. Soc. London Ser. B* 329: 99–108

Weiskrantz, L., Warrington, E. K. 1979. Conditioning in amnesic patients. *Neuropsychologia* 17: 187–94

White, S. H., Pillemer, D. B. 1979. Childhood amnesia and the development of a socially accessible memory system. In *Functional Disorders of Memory,* ed. J. F. Kihlstrom, F. J. Evans, pp. 29–47. Hillsdale, NJ: Erlbaum

Wible, C. G., Findling, R. L., Shapiro, M., Lang, E. J., Crane, S., et al. 1986. Mnemonic correlates of unit activity in the hippocampus. *Brain Res.* 399: 97–110

Willingham, D. B., Nissen, M. J., Bullemer, P. 1989. On the development of procedural knowledge. *J. Exp. Psychol.: Learn. Mem. Cogn.* 15: 1047–60

Winocur, G. 1990. Anterograde and retrograde amnesia in rats with dorsal hippocampal or dorsomedial thalamic lesions. *Behav. Brain Res.* 38: 145–54

Winocur, G., Rawlins, J. N. P., Gray, J. A. 1987. The hippocampus and conditioning to contextual cues. *Behav. Neurosci.* 101: 617–27

Witherspoon, D., Moscovitch, M. 1989. Stochastic independence between two implicit memory tasks. *J. Exp. Psychol.: Learn. Mem. Cogn.* 15: 22–30

Wright, A. A., Santiago, H. C., Sands, S. F., Kendrick, D. F., Cook, R. G. 1985. Memory processing of serial lists by pigeons, monkeys and people. *Science* 229: 287–89

Yamadori, A., Albert, M. L. 1973. Word category aphasia. *Cortex* 9: 112–25

Zola-Morgan, S., Squire, L. R. 1984. Preserved learning in monkeys with medial temporal lesions: sparing of motor and cognitive skills. *J. Neurosci.* 4: 1072–85

Zola-Morgan, S., Squire, L. R. 1990. The primate hippocampal formation: evidence for a time-limited role in memory storage. *Science* 250: 288–90

Zola-Morgan, S., Squire, L. R. 1993. The neuroanatomy of memory. *Annu. Rev. Neurosci.* 16: 547–63

Zola-Morgan, S., Squire, L. R., Amaral, D. G. 1986. Human amnesia and the medial temporal region: enduring memory impairment following a bilateral lesion limited to field CA1 of the hippocampus. *J. Neurosci.* 6: 2950–67

Zola-Morgan, S., Squire, L. R., Amaral, D. G. 1989. Lesions of the hippocampal formation but not lesions of the fornix or the mammillary nuclei produce long-lasting memory impairment in monkeys. *J. Neurosci.* 9: 898–913

relating to meaning
in language something

SECTION FIVE
ENCODING AND RETRIEVAL

Editor's introduction

According to a recent literature search (Roediger, 1993), the most cited article on memory in the last 25 or so years is Craik and Lockhart's famous 1972 paper 'Levels of processing: a framework for memory research'. That paper presented the argument that the key factor determining whether a memory is retained or not is the depth to which the original event was encoded. Craik and Lockhart argued, for example, that a list of words would be well-retained if the words are processed semantically but would be only poorly retained if the processing focused on their perceptual attributes. An enormous amount of evidence has subsequently been marshalled in support of this claim, but at the same time clear violations are often seen. The key problem with the levels-of-processing view is that it concentrates on encoding at the expense of an adequate consideration of retrieval processes. Tulving's chapter (Chapter 8) presents a review of the status of the levels-of-processing theory, but more importantly relates it to the principle of *encoding specificity*. This principle creates a fusion between encoding and retrieval. The crucial claim (p. 202) is the idea that 'specific encoding operations performed on what is perceived determine what is stored, and what is stored determines what retrieval cues are effective in providing access to what is stored.' Towards the end of his chapter, Tulving describes the transfer-appropriate processing theory of memory, originally proposed by Morris *et al.* (1977), which is the focus of **Blaxton**'s elegant experimental study (Chapter 10). This is the idea that memory will be successful to the extent that the operations performed at retrieval recapitulate those performed at encoding.

From the encoding specificity principle, it follows that an item of semantic knowledge should not act successfully as a retrieval cue for episodic memory. Thus a distinction between semantic and episodic memory is a strong corollary of Tulving's position. The articles by **McKoon** *et al.* (Chapter 9) and by Blaxton concentrate on the semantic/episodic distinction. McKoon *et al.* review the evidence in favour of this distinction and argue that it is poorly specified and, compared to the procedural/declarative distinction (see Chapter 7), only weakly supported by experimental evidence. Blaxton directly pits the predictions derived from the semantic/episodic theory against those derived from a transfer-appropriate processing perspective and obtains support for the latter. Overall, these chapters emphasize the interactions between encoding and retrieval operations and argue for a view of memory as a *skill*. What is remembered is the set of operations performed in a study episode, and those operations leave behind a procedural residue in the same way that practice at hitting a tennis ball does.

A thorough review of the levels of processing framework has been produced by Lockhart and Craik (1990). For a critical analysis of the encoding specificity principle, see Santa and Lamwers (1974). An alternative theory of encoding and retrieval, the 'generate-recognize' theory, is discussed by Watkins and Gardiner (1979). Finally the relationship between recognition and recall has been the subject of a good deal of theoretical dispute: see Flexser and Tulving (1978) and Hintzman (1992).

References

Craik, F. I. M. and Lockhart, R. S. (1972). Levels of processing: a framework for memory research. *Journal of Verbal Learning and Verbal Behavior*, 11, 671–84.

Flexser, A. J. and Tulving, E. (1978). Retrieval independence in recognition and recall. *Psychological Review*, 85, 153–71.

Hintzman, D. L. (1992). Mathematical constraints and the Tulving-Wiseman law. *Psychological Review*, 99, 536–42.

Lockhart, R. S. and Craik, F. I. M. (1990). Levels of processing: a retrospective commentary on a framework for memory research. *Canadian Journal of Psychology*, 44, 87–112.

Morris, C. D., Bransford, J. D. and Franks, J. J. (1977). Levels of processing versus transfer appropriate processing. *Journal of Verbal Learning and Verbal Behavior*, 16, 519–33.

Roediger, H. L (1993). Learning and memory: progress and challenge. In *Attention & Performance XIV: Synergies in experimental psychology, artificial intelligence, and cognitive neuroscience* (ed. D. E. Meyer and S. Kornblum), pp. 509–28. MIT Press, Cambridge, MA.

Santa, J. L. and Lamwers, L. L. (1974). Encoding specificity: fact or artifact. *Journal of Verbal Learning and Verbal Behavior*, 13, 412–23.

Watkins, M. J. and Gardiner, J. M. (1979). An appreciation of generate-recognize theory of recall. *Journal of Verbal Learning and Verbal Behavior*, 18, 687–704.

8   Endel Tulving
'Relation between Encoding Specificity and Levels of Processing'

Reprinted in full from: *Levels of Processing in Human Memory* (ed. L. S. Cermak and F. I. M. Craik, 1979)

In this chapter I review the concepts of encoding specificity and levels of processing and discuss the relation between them. The main point of the chapter is that these two sets of ideas are converging on a common fundamental orientation toward phenomena of episodic memory. In this orientation, recollection of an event is a joint function of information stored in memory about the event (the trace) and the information available to the rememberer at the time of attempted retrieval (the cue). Whether or not recollection succeeds depends on the compatibility of the two kinds of information. The major challenge to memory theory lies in the description and understanding of the relation between trace information and retrieval information that underlies remembering of events. Factors such as depth of encoding and distinctiveness or elaboration of memory traces are a part of such description and play a partial role in the attempts to gain such understanding; they need not be considered separately from, or in addition to, the compatibility relation between the trace and the cue.

Encoding specificity

The set of ideas we now know under the label of 'encoding specificity' originated in experimental work designed to illuminate the problem of effectiveness of retrieval cues. The original experiment produced results that were interpreted as suggesting that

> specific retrieval cues facilitate recall if and only if the information about them and about their relation to the to-be-remembered words is stored at the same time as the information about the membership of the to-be-remembered words in a given list.
>
> (Tulving and Osler, 1968, p. 599)

The 'if and only if' clause in this suggestion was meant to imply a rejection of the then-popular and strongly held belief that one word could serve as an aid for the retrieval of another solely by virtue of the pre-experimental relation between them. Under the impact of the results of other experiments and the general acceptance of the idea that words and word-events could be usefully conceptualized as bundles of features or collections of attributes (Bower, 1967; Underwood, 1969), the encoding specificity hypothesis was formulated in more general terms. Thus, for instance, 2 years later we found it more convenient to suggest that 'a specific encoding format of the to-be-remembered item seems to constitute a prerequisite for the effectiveness of any particular retrieval cue' (Thomson and Tulving, 1970, p. 255); we defined the encoding specificity hypothesis as a proposition that 'retrieval of event information can only be effected by retrieval cues corresponding to a part of the total encoding pattern representing the perceptual cognitive registration of the occurrence of the event [p. 261].' We wanted to emphasize the fact that the subjects' task was one of remembering the *event* of a word's occurrence in a particular list and that it was stored information about the word-event, rather than about the target word as such, that was critical for cue effectiveness. The phrase, 'the total encoding pattern representing the perceptual cognitive registration' of the event was meant to convey the impression that more was involved in studying a to-be-remembered word than just strengthening, or activating, or adding an occurrence tag to the word's pre-experimental representation in memory, although the wording of the idea might have left something to be desired.

In 1973 Donald Thomson and I proposed the encoding specificity principle, asserting that 'only that can be retrieved that has been stored, and that how it can be retrieved depends on how it was stored' (Tulving and Thompson, 1973, p. 359); or, in somewhat more elaborate terms, that 'specific encoding operations performed on what is perceived determine what is stored, and what is stored determines what retrieval cues are effective in providing access to what is stored [p. 369].' The formulation of the encoding specificity principle is not greatly different from the wording of the encoding specificity hypothesis, although it makes a bit more explicit the dependence of the memory trace on the encoding operations and hence the relation between encoding and retrieval conditions; the difference between the two has to do with their status in the ongoing enterprise of attempting to make sense of the empirical facts. The encoding specificity hypothesis is testable, and it gains or loses credibility depending on experimental outcomes. In order to test the hypothesis, however, the experimenter must know or assume, on whatever basis, exactly what has been encoded in any particular study instance. Such knowledge is not always available; indeed, it is frequently the object of inquiry. This is where the encoding specificity principle enters the picture. We can assume that the encoding specificity hypothesis is in fact true and that a retrieval cue is effective only to the extent that its informational contents match those of the trace; we can then make inferences about what has been encoded, or about the memory trace, on the basis of observed effectiveness of different retrieval cues. In either case – treating encoding specificity as a hypothesis or as a principle – the only facts are provided by observations about the effectiveness of different retrieval cues, whereas two things are unknown – the properties of the trace and the validity of the encoding specificity hypothesis. In order to relate all three principal components of the logical structure of the retrieval situation, we must make some sort of an assumption about one of the two unknown factors. When we use encoding specificity as a hypothesis, we make an assumption about the trace; when we use it as a principle, we make an assumption about the validity of the hypothesis.

Experimental evidence relevant to the evaluation of the encoding specificity hypothesis is derived from a particular type of experiment. The general characteristics of the class of experiments include the requirements that the subject variables and learning materials be held constant in all conditions of the experiment and that both the study (encoding) and test (retrieval) conditions be manipulated in an orthogonal design. The Tulving and Osler (1968) experiment can serve both as an example of a typical encoding specificity experiment and as a source of critical data. Only a part of the complete design is described here, the part relevant to our present purpose.

In the experiment, subjects studied, on a single trial, a list of 24 cue–target pairs and were then tested for their ability to recall the target items in the presence of cues. The cues were either the same that they had seen at the time of study or they were 'new,' not encountered before in the experiment. There were two encoding conditions: (a) target word accompanied by cue A, or (b) target word accompanied by cue B. These two encoding conditions were crossed with two retrieval conditions: (a) cue A presented, or (b) cue B presented. Cues A and B were single words that in free associations elicited the target words as a primary response with a probability of 0.01. Two cue words corresponding to any given target word were selected according to normative data and were assigned to the two sets, A and B, on a random basis. Thus, the target words were identical in all four experimental conditions, the cues were equivalent in the two sets, and the relation between the cues and targets in both sets was also equivalent. These features of the design are important in determining the inferences to be drawn from the experimental results.

The results of the experiment, in the form of mean proportions of words recalled, are shown in Table 8.1. The data show a strong 'crossover' type interaction between encoding and retrieval conditions: when the retrieval cue matched the encoding cue, subjects recalled 62% of the target words, whereas the mismatch between retrieval cues and encoding cues produced a recall rate of approximately 30%. (This latter figure was lower than free recall of target words in the two encoding conditions considered here, as shown by other experimental conditions not described here.)

There are four general conclusions that can be drawn from these data. First, the results clearly show that no absolute answer can be given to the question of which of the two encoding conditions was 'better,' or produced a stronger memory trace, or led to more efficient remembering. Any answer to such a question must necessarily be qualified by the observed interaction between encoding and retrieval conditions and can only be given in relation to a

Table 8.1 Probability of recall as a function of encoding and retrieval conditions (Tulving and Osler, 1968)

Encoding cue	Retrieval cue	
	A	*B*
A	0.62	0.29
B	0.33	0.62

particular retrieval condition. *The 'goodness' of a particular encoding operation depends on the nature of the cues present at the time of retrieval.*

Second, no absolute answer can be given to the question of which of the two retrieval cues, A or B, was more effective. This question, too, can be answered only relative to a particular encoding condition. *Effectiveness of a cue, with respect to a particular target item, depends on the conditions under which the target item was encoded.*

Third, on the unassailable assumption that cue A has more information in common with the trace of the A–T (T for target) pair of studied items than with the trace of the B–T pair, we can say that the probability of successful retrieval of the target item is a monotonically increasing function of informational overlap between the information present at retrieval and the information stored in memory. *Successful recollection of an event depends on the compatibility between the trace and the cue.*

Fourth, since the cues, targets, and the pre-experimental (semantic) relations were either identical or equivalent in all four experimental conditions, the observed systematic variability in the effectiveness of retrieval cues cannot be attributed to pre-experimentally established relations between cue and target words; it must be determined by processes occurring in the study episode. *The compatibility relation between the trace and the cue, as a necessary condition of recollection of an event, is determined by specific encoding operations at the time of study and not by the properties of cues and target items, and their relations, in semantic memory.*

I would like to propose these four conclusions as defining the essence of the notion of encoding specificity. The central ideas are: (a) the necessity of stipulating *both* encoding and retrieval conditions when describing data or making theoretical inferences from them; (b) the futility of trying to understand processes of remembering, either in general or in any specific situation, in terms of only the encoding or storage processes or only in terms of retrieval processes; and (c) the pivotal role played by phenomena demonstrating *interactions* between encoding and retrieval conditions in shaping theoretical ideas about memory.

Levels of processing

An interesting feature of psychological thought about memory throughout history has been its preoccupation with the first stage of remembering – that is, acquisition and retention of memorial knowledge, or encoding and storage of mnemonic information. Explaining memory usually has meant explaining how knowledge is acquired and retained, or how information is encoded and stored. There has generally been little concern with the problem of how memorial knowledge affects conscious awareness or behaviour, or how the stored information is used. Thus, the second stage of remembering – that is, utilization of stored information, or ecphory, activation of latent memory traces – had received scant attention until only about a decade ago.

The essence of the set of ideas known as 'levels of processing' initially also was that memory is a by-product of perception and that goodness of retention of a learned item depends on the conditions under which it was studied. Craik and Lockhart (1972), for instance, proposed that the durability of the memory trace is determined by the depth or level at which stimulus items are processed: 'Trace persistence is a function of depth of analysis, with deeper levels of analysis associated with more elaborate, longer lasting, and stronger traces [p. 675].' True to tradition, there was little concern with how the acquired information was utilized, that is, how it was retrieved. It is true that Craik and Lockhart also mentioned the importance of retrieval factors; however, it seems fair to say that at least in the early days of the levels-of-processing era, these factors were not of central interest.

In a typical levels-of-processing experiment, subject variables and pre-experimental characteristics of to-be-remembered items are held constant, and the manner in which the learners study to-be-remembered items is varied by manipulating orienting tasks, learning instructions, the context of target items, the learners' expectations about the nature of the retention test, and in other similar ways. It is assumed that these manipulations induce the learner to engage in different mental activities at the time of study, or that they induce the memory system to perform different encoding operations upon the input, resulting in qualitatively different memory traces of to-be-remembered events. It is the characteristics of these traces – depth, spread, elaboration, etc. – that determine how well the item or event is remembered.

The idea that retention depends on how the to-be-remembered material is studied is a familiar one in psychology. For instance, Woodworth (1938), discussing problems in connection with the topic of 'memory for form,' mentions G. E. Müller's theory, according to which 'the memory trace weakens or disintegrates and loses the distinctive characteristics of the original figure, except that a characteristic which was emphasized in perception will persist longer than other characteristics and so be accentuated in the reproduction [p. 81].' Woodworth's (1938) own restatement of Müller's theory includes the following proposition:

> The same objective figure can be seen in a variety of ways according to the features that stand out or are emphasized in perception. What stands out may be either a detail or a character of the whole figure. Both stand out in the common learning process of schema-with-correction. Besides the features specially emphasized, [the observer] may be more or less aware of other details and peculiarities of the figure . . . The theory . . . assumes a true process of forgetting; the trace weakens or dies out; features which were barely noticed die out more rapidly than those that were emphasized [p. 81].

What is novel and surprising about the elaboration of these old ideas in contemporary research are two facts. First, the same kinds of processes that underlie 'emphasizing' of various features of the to-be-remembered complex form also seem to be operating in the 'perception' of extremely familiar words when they serve as target items in a memory experiment. The well-known experiments from the Minnesota laboratories (e.g., Hyde and Jenkins, 1969, 1973; Jenkins, 1974; Till and Jenkins, 1973; Walsh and Jenkins, 1973) have shown that free recall of a word can depend greatly on the orienting task in which a subject engages at the time of study. These results suggest that different orienting tasks result in 'emphasizing' different features even when the features are not *perceptually* identifiable and distinguishable as they are in the case of complex figures. The classical conception of words was that they were mental or behavioral atoms, basic units not further divisible into components; even today there exist theories in which different words are represented as different nodes in an associative network and in which individual nodes are activated in an all-or-none manner. Second, the effects of encoding operations can be very large. For instance, in some of the experiments described by Craik and Tulving (1975), free recall as well as recognition varied over a range from less than 20% to 70% or 80%, even though all 'classical' learning variables were held constant. Variations in performance of this magnitude are difficult to achieve through the manipulation of classical variables such as study time or meaningfulness or ability of subjects; in levels-of-processing experiments, they are brought about by differences in encoding conditions within a few seconds per item. In terms of the sheer magnitude of the effects, encoding operations must be regarded as among the most important determinants of memory performance.

The common theme of levels-of-processing experiments that I am emphasizing here, manifested in large differences in recall or recognition of unitary linguistic units as a function of encoding operations, has emerged over the last few years. Initially the theoretical concerns of the leading proponents of levels-of-processing ideas were somewhat different. For instance, Hyde and Jenkins (1969) presented their experimental findings in the context of the theoretical problem of the locus of organizational effects in free recall. The question was whether organization is determined by certain processes at the time of storage or whether it manifests itself because of what happens at the time of recall. Similarly, Craik and Lockhart (1972) developed their ideas about levels of processing as a theoretical alternative to models of memory postulating separate short-term and long-term memory stores. Neither of these issues, locus of organization or usefulness of the distinction between short-term and long-term stores, is of any great interest to anyone now, whereas experimental work and theoretical speculation about the basic theme of levels of processing still seem to be gathering momentum.

As mentioned earlier, early levels-of-processing experiments involved the manipulation of encoding conditions and the measurement of memory performance in one and the same retention test. Thus, for instance, all of the experiments of Jenkins and his associates (e.g., Hyde and Jenkins, 1969, 1973; Till and Jenkins, 1973; Walsh and Jenkins, 1973) have employed the free-recall test. Similarly, Craik and his associates (e.g., Craik, 1973, 1977; Craik and Tulving, 1975; Moscovitch and Craik, 1976) have usually assessed the effects of encoding operations by free recall or recognition. The logical structure of these experiments is the same as that of one-half of a typical encoding specificity experiment: encoding conditions are manipulated while retrieval conditions are held constant. For instance, the data in the first column of Table 8.1, showing the results of the Tulving and Osler (1968) experiment, can be thought of as demonstrating the effects of an encoding operation defined in terms of the particular cue present at the study of the to-be-remembered word. In this somewhat limited view, the encoding conditions exerted a large effect on retention performance.

The problem with the interpretation of the data from typical levels-of-processing experiments is twofold. First, as long as the experiment demonstrates only different retention performances in a single test, resulting from different kinds of orienting tasks, instructions, or contexts, it would be perfectly logical to argue that encoding operations constitute just another way of influencing the strength of the memory trace. Such an experiment cannot provide any evidence in support of the contention that different encoding operations create *qualitatively different* memory traces, an idea central to the current levels-of-processing view. The many terms and ideas now used to interpret levels-of-processing experiments – depth, spread, degree of elaboration, uniqueness, distinctiveness, congruity, meaning, and the like – could be replaced with a single concept such as the strength of the memory trace without any dramatic loss of explanatory power. The second problem is that describing the results of levels-of-processing experiments in terms of the relation between properties of memory traces and probability of retention neglects the critical role played by the retrieval information. When the consequences of some orienting task are said to be the establishment of 'deep' or 'elaborate' memory traces, and it is argued that such traces endure over a longer period of time than those less deep or elaborate, the implicit assumption is that the nature of conditions at the time of the test does not matter.

The emphasis on the importance of retrieval conditions in the encoding specificity approach and the initial neglect of these factors in the levels-of-processing approach created an obvious discrepancy, if not a conflict, between these two broad frameworks for the study of memory. Now, however, they seem to be converging on the same set of basic ideas shaped by the data from the same kind of experiment. Moscovitch and Craik (1976), for instance, have conducted three experiments to study the relations between retrieval and encoding in a levels-of-processing framework. They pointed out that inasmuch as measured memory performance is 'influenced by retrieval factors as well as by encoding operations' [p. 447], the explanation of memory processes suggested by the levels-of-processing framework is incomplete. Another series of experiments by Fisher and Craik (1977) was designed to test the hypothesis that the correlation between encoding operations and retention performance reflects differential compatibility of trace and cue information rather than differential durability of traces. In these experiments, encoding conditions were crossed with retrieval conditions, exactly as in encoding specificity experiments. The results showed that 'the retention levels associated with a particular type of encoding were not fixed, but depended heavily on the type of retrieval cue used' (Fisher and Craik, 1977, p. 709). Such an interaction between encoding and retrieval conditions can be appropriately interpreted in terms of qualitative differences in memory traces resulting from different types of encoding; it is not readily reconciled with the notion of unidimensional strength of memory traces.

The initial concern of encoding specificity was with the conditions determining the effectiveness of retrieval cues, whereas the initial thrust of the levels-of-processing approach was directed at the importance of encoding conditions. The more recent levels-of-processing experiments, as we have just seen, are indistinguishable from encoding specificity experiments, and so are the basic beliefs held by theorists representing these two points of view. In the process of convergence, however, some new issues have emerged that have opened the door to a fresh debate. We consider two such issues, but first we must take a closer look at the experimental evidence that has pointed to the critical importance of the interaction between encoding conditions and retrieval processes.

Encoding/retrieval interactions

There are, as we saw earlier in this chapter, four general conclusions that could be drawn from a simple demonstration experiment such as the one described by Tulving and Osler (1968). The most important of these for what follows later in the paper is the third one: successful recollection of an event depends on the compatibility between the trace and the cue. But the first two conclusions are also relevant: one cannot make any general statements about 'goodness' of encoding operations or about effectiveness of retrieval cues; only relative statements are permissible. The fourth conclusion, concerning the role of specific encoding operations as compared with semantic properties of cues and to-be-remembered items, is of less immediate concern in the present context, since all theorists now accept and make active use of the distinction between pre-experimental and experimentally created (or semantic and episodic) components of memory, although they may differ in the details of the manner in which the two kinds of information are conceptualized (see, for instance, Anderson, 1976; Anderson and Ortony, 1975; Crowder, 1976; Kintsch, 1974; Tulving, 1976).

The results of the Tulving and Osler (1968) experiment in some sense were perfectly obvious and hence perhaps trivial; all they showed was that one word can serve as a retrieval cue for another one if an association is formed between them and not otherwise. The generality of the conclusions drawn from the results of such an experiment, therefore, may be questionable. The results of some experiments that I next briefly describe serve to demonstrate that the same general pattern of results can also be obtained with materials and under conditions where the reasons for the outcomes are somewhat less obvious and hence also less trivial. Among other things, they show that encoding conditions determine the effectiveness of retrieval cues even when the cues are strongly related to the to-be-remembered items already before the experiment. The results also show that the compatibility relation between traces and cues that is all-important for successful recollection of the event is created at the time of study of the to-be-remembered material, and that whatever compatibility exists between the cue and the to-be-remembered item otherwise is of no direct relevance.

The first experiment we consider is Experiment 2 reported by Thomson and Tulving (1970). The to-be-remembered items (response words from free-association norms) were presented for study either: (a) singly, one item at a time, with the subjects expecting a free recall test; or (b) as members of cue-target pairs of the same kind as those used in the Tulving and Osler (1968) experiment, with the subjects expecting to be tested with the cues seen at the time of input. The three retrieval conditions, crossed with the two study conditions, were: (a) no specific cues, that is, free recall; (b) the intralist 'weak' cues presented in one of the encoding conditions; and (c) 'strong extralist cues,' words not encountered by the subjects in the experiment, but strongly associated with target words in semantic memory. The study list was presented once, at the rate of 3 sec/target word, and the retention test was given immediately following the presentation of appropriate recall instructions.

The results, in terms of mean proportions of words recalled, are presented in Table 8.2. Comparing no-cue and weak-cue retrieval conditions, or weak-cue and strong-cue conditions, we observe strong interactions. The most important result is that the strong extralist cues considerably facilitate recall following encoding of single to-be-remembered items in anticipation of free recall (0.68 vs 0.49), but they do not at all help recall following study of target items in the company of weak cues, under conditions where subjects expected to be tested with weak cues (0.23 vs 0.30). Thus, effectiveness of cue words strongly associated with target words in *semantic* memory depends greatly on the conditions of *episodic encoding* of target words. Conversely, 'goodness' of encoding depends on cue conditions at retrieval.

The second set of data come from Experiment 1 described by Tulving and Thomson (1973). Actually, only one-half of the data come from that experiment – the other half being imaginary, based on data from other experiments in which the same kinds of materials were used. What is again important here is the overall pattern of the data rather than any particular single data point. In the experiment, subjects saw and studied the same kind of list that had been used in the Thomson and Tulving experiments, pairs of weak cues and corresponding target words. The subjects were induced to encode the pairs in the expectation that the recall of the target words would be tested with their weak cues. After the presentation of the list, subjects were asked to produce *free associations* to strong *extralist* associates of target words; many of the

Table 8.2 Probability of recall as a function of encoding and retrieval conditions (Thomson and Tulving, 1970, Exp. 2)

Encoding cue	Retrieval cue		
	None	*Weak*	*Strong*
None	0.49	0.43	0.68
Weak	0.30	0.82	0.23

words thus produced indeed were copies of the to-be-remembered target words. Subjects then were asked to perform a recognition test on these free associations, under instructions to try to identify the to-be-remembered words from the studied list. After they had finished with this 'subject-produced' recognition test, they proceeded to take a cued-recall test in which the weak cues they had seen in the study list were presented as aids to retrieval of target words. Thus, there were two test situations – recognition and cued recall – or two kinds of cues – copy cues and list cues – given after the encoding of the to-be-remembered item in the presence of weak semantic associates. The imaginary condition, the results of which are indicated in parentheses in Table 8.3, is one in which the subjects see the same to-be-remembered items, but in the absence of any list cues, and in anticipation of, say, a free-recall test. Following this presentation, the subjects are again tested with copy cues, in a recognition test, or with the (now extralist) weak associates. The latter of these two test conditions was a part of the design of the Thomson and Tulving (1970) experiments, and we have a pretty good basis for estimating the results in this condition; the results for the recognition test following the 'free-recall' encoding are based on an unpublished experiment done in the Toronto laboratories by Judith Sutcliffe.

The results of this experiment are shown in Table 8.3. Again, there is a strong interaction between encoding and retrieval conditions. The weak retrieval cue, not at all surprisingly, is more effective following the encoding of the target item in the presence of these cues, whereas the copy cue, rather surprisingly, is not only more effective following 'free-recall' encoding than 'weak-cue' encoding, but is also considerably less effective than the weak cue following 'weak-cue' encoding. The overall pattern is very similar to that shown in Table 8.1, despite the fact that one of the cues was the copy of the target item. For reasons of parsimony, I would like to suggest that the interpretation and meaning of this pattern of results are identical with those of the Tulving and Osler (1968) results discussed earlier, including the conclusion about the critical importance of the compatibility of (episodically encoded) traces and retrieval cues.

The third set of data come from an experiment by Bobrow and Light, as described by Bower (1970). Subjects saw a list of 44 ambiguous nouns, each accompanied by an adjective specifying a particular meaning of the noun. Under one condition of study, the adjectives specified the meaning of the nouns in such a fashion that the nouns fell into eight large taxonomic categories (e.g., *chirping*–CARDINAL, *homing*–PIGEON; *lamb*–CHOP,

Table 8.3 Probability of recall as a function of encoding and retrieval conditions (Tulving and Thomson, 1973, Exp. 1)

Encoding cue	Retrieval cue	
	Weak	Copy
(None)	(0.45)	(0.80)
Weak	0.63	0.24

Table 8.4 Probability of recall as a function of encoding and retrieval conditions (Bobrow and Light, as reported by Bower, 1970)

Encoding condition	Retrieval cue	
	None	Category name
Category	0.39	0.55
Unrelated	0.27	0.20

Table 8.5 Probability of recall as a function of encoding and retrieval conditions (Fisher and Craik, 1977, Exp. 1)

Encoding condition	Retrieval cue		
	Rhyme	Category	Sentence
Rhyme	0.40	0.15	0.10
Category	0.43	0.81	0.50
Sentence	0.29	0.46	0.78

roast–HAM), whereas in the other list, the adjective defined the meanings of the nouns in such a fashion that the nouns were unrelated to one another (e.g., *church*–CARDINAL, *stool*–PIGEON; *karate*–CHOP, *theatrical*–HAM). There were two conditions of recall: free recall, or cued recall with the category names appropriate to the categories of the first encoding condition as cues.

The results are summarized in Table 8.4. The interaction between encoding conditions and retrieval cues is again apparent: category names of to-be-remembered words were effective cues after the corresponding category encoding, but ineffective after 'unrelated' encoding.

The next experiment we consider is Experiment 1 by Fisher and Craik (1977). Subjects saw 72 concrete nouns and answered questions about them. One-third of the questions were about rhymes, another third about category membership, and the remaining third about the word fitting into a sentence. Answers to the questions were either 'yes' or 'no.' The six encoding conditions (three kinds of questions and two kinds of answers) were crossed with three retrieval conditions, defined by the presentation of the same three classes of retrieval cues used as questions at the time of study.

Table 8.5 shows the recall of words whose encoding questions were answered affirmatively at the time of study. Proportions of words recalled in the cells along the negative diagonal represent conditions where the retrieval cues were the same cues that the subjects encountered at input, whereas the off-diagonal cells represent data from conditions in which extra-list cues were presented. The important point here again is the strong interaction between encoding and retrieval conditions: The 'goodness' of encoding depends on the type of cue used at retrieval, and the effectiveness of cues varies with the encoding conditions.

There are other experiments in which interactions between encoding and retrieval conditions have been described (e.g., Anderson *et al.*, 1976; Barclay *et al.*, 1974; Morris *et al.*, 1977; Moscovitch and Craik, 1976; Nelson, 1979; Nelson *et al.*, 1974; Tulving and Watkins, 1975), but those briefly described here illustrate the main features of such experiments. Many different kinds of cues – rhyming words, category names, strong associates, and even literal copies of targets – can vary widely in their effectiveness, depending on how the target words were stored in memory; conversely, different kinds of encoding operations performed on the input – relating the target to a cue word, interpreting its meaning depending on a biasing adjective, considering the target word as a member of a particular category, interpreting it within a sentence frame – lead to differential recovery of the to-be-remembered items, depending on exactly what retrieval information is available. In short, over a considerable range of experimental conditions, empirical facts show that remembering of events is determined by the interaction between encoding and retrieval; the concordant theoretical conclusion holds that success of recollection of an event depends on the congruence or compatibility between trace information and retrieval information.

In the experiments we have just considered, this interaction manifests itself in an unmistakable form. But we must assume that the processes responsible for the interaction are the same in all situations, including those in which its consequences are not apparent. It makes no sense to assume that the basic principles of memory are different depending on the design of the experiment. It is obviously possible to do experiments in which some of the basic principles are not permitted to manifest themselves, but it does not mean that they are not operative in those situations. For these reasons it makes good sense to assume that the recollection of an event is always determined by the compatibility relation between encoding and retrieval conditions, or the trace information and the cue information. This is the basic premise, accepted by both the encoding specificity and levels-of-processing views of memory, with which all analyses of processes of memory must begin.

Depth of encoding and trace/cue compatibility

An appropriate relation between the trace and the cue – we have referred to it as compatibility – is obviously a critical determinant of recollection. But is anything else critical, too? More specifically, is it necessary to be concerned with properties of memory traces or retrieval cues separately from, or in addition to, the compatibility relation between them? In this section we consider two possible answers to this question.

One answer has been given by Fisher and Craik (1977), who hold that a complete account of remembering must include a reference to the depth of processing or the resulting trace in addition to the reference to the relation between encoding operations and retrieval cues. In their words, 'both the qualitative nature of the encoding and the degree of compatibility between encoding and cue are apparently necessary to give an adequate account of memory processes [p. 710],' and 'no one factor in isolation – the type of encoding, the type of cue, or the compatibility between encoding and cue – is by itself sufficient to describe performance [p. 710].'

Another answer to the earlier question, which I find preferable, is that once we accept the proposition that retrieval of a memory is determined by the compatibility between trace and cue information, there is no need to postulate anything in addition about the relevance of encoding, trace, or retrieval factors. Thus, I would like to argue that the compatibility of trace and retrieval information 'in isolation,' to use Fisher and Craik's expression, would be sufficient to provide an understanding of memory performance. This position is more parsimonious than Fisher and Craik's, which postulates two factors; it should be explored first and rejected only if it is contrary to empirical facts. For the time being, the insistence on the importance of either the trace or the cue properties separately, in addition to considering their compatibility relation, appears to be logically superfluous; it may also mislead theorists into the traditional preoccupation with trace properties as such, a preoccupation that may have prevented us from making faster progress with understanding of memory.

Fisher and Craik (1977) found support for their conclusion that both compatibility between trace and cue and the depth of the trace were important in three kinds of findings yielded by their experiments. First, as illustrated by the data in Table 8.5, subjects' performance was higher following semantic encoding than rhyme encoding, even when the retrieval conditions were said to be 'optimal' – that is, when rhyme-encoded target words were tested with rhymes as cues and associatively encoded target words were tested with their intralist associates as cues. These are the experimental conditions represented by the cells along the negative diagonal in Table 8.5. I return to the concept of 'optimal retrieval conditions' later in this chapter; here I would only like to point out that it is incorrect to assume that nominal identity between encoding and retrieval conditions is equivalent to 'optimal' retrieval conditions.

The other two important findings come from Fisher and Craik's (1977) Experiment 3. In this experiment, subjects studied target words either in the presence of rhyming context words (e.g., CAT studied in the context of *hat*) or in the presence of associatively related words (CAT studied in the context of *dog*). Crossed with these two encoding conditions (rhyming encoding and associative encoding) were three kinds of retrieval cues: (a) 'identical' cues, the same context words that accompanied the target words in the study list (*hat* as cue after *hat*–CAT encoding and *dog* as cue after *dog*–CAT encoding); (b) 'similar' cues, consisting of extralist cues related to the target words along the same dimension that was biased by the encoding situation (e.g., extralist cue *mat* after *hat*–CAT encoding and extralist cue *lion* after *dog*–CAT encoding); and (c) 'different' cues, consisting of extralist words related to the target word along the dimension that was not biased at the time of encoding (e.g., cue word *lion* given for the target word CAT encoded in the rhyming condition, and the cue word *mat* given for the target word CAT encoded in the context of *dog* in the associative condition).

The results of this experiment are reproduced in Table 8.6. These results contain two important findings. First, the level of performance in the experi-

Table 8.6 Probability of recall as a function of encoding condition and encoding/retrieval similarity (Fisher and Craik, 1977, Exp. 3)

Encoding condition	Encoding/retrieval similarity		
	Identical	Similar	Different
Rhyme	0.24	0.18	0.16
Associate	0.54	0.36	0.22

mental conditions defined by rhyme encoding and 'identical' encoding/retrieval similarity (0.24) was essentially the same as the level of performance in the condition in which associative encoding was combined with 'different' encoding/retrieval similarity (0.22). Since the 'similarity' between the cue and the encoding condition must have been higher in the former condition than in the latter, identical recall probability suggests the presence of a factor other than encoding/retrieval (or target/cue) similarity. This other factor, according to Fisher and Craik, is the depth of the initial encoding.

The second important finding contained in the data in Table 8.6, according to Fisher and Craik, is the fact that the *superiority* of associative over rhyme encoding was positively correlated with the degree of *similarity* between the encoding context and the retrieval cue: as encoding/retrieval similarity is reduced from 'identical' through 'similar' to 'different,' the difference between associative and rhyming encoding conditions becomes progressively smaller – from 0.30 to 0.18 to 0.06. Fisher and Craik conclude that 'the beneficial effects of similarity between encoding context and cue are greatest with deep, semantic encodings' [p. 709]; it is this interaction between the level of processing (or the nature of the trace) and the degree of similarity between encoding and retrieval conditions that is taken as evidence that the type of encoding (the type of trace) is important in addition to the trace/cue similarity.

The conclusions that Fisher and Craik have drawn from their findings are logically perfectly consistent with their data. The problem is that the findings are also perfectly logically consistent with two other sets of conclusions that are different from Fisher and Craik's. One is that the other important factor besides the trace/cue compatibility is defined by the retrieval conditions; the other is that it is not necessary to specify any additional factors and that the probability of retrieval always depends only on the nature of the relation between the trace information and the retrieval information.

To illustrate how the first of these two alternative conclusions follows from the data, we take the results of Fisher and Craik's (1977) Experiment 3 from Table 8.6 and rearrange them as shown in Table 8.7. Here one variable is still the similarity between encoding and retrieval conditions, whereas the other variable now is the type of retrieval cue, either rhyme or associate. This arrangement is also perfectly consistent with the design of Fisher and Craik's experiment, but the conclusions we would draw from the data are now quite different. First, we notice that the levels of performance are quite similar in two experimental conditions: one in which the 'similar' encoding/retrieval is

Table 8.7 Probability of recall as a function of type of retrieval cue and encoding/retrieval similarity (Fisher and Craik, 1977, Exp. 3)

Encoding/retrieval similarity	Retrieval cue	
	Rhyme	Associate
Identical	0.24	0.54
Similar	0.18	0.36
Different	0.22	0.16

combined with the rhyme cue (0.18), and the other in which the 'different' encoding/retrieval is combined with the associate (0.16). On this basis we could argue that since the trace/cue similarity was greater in the former than in the latter condition, the virtual identity of outcomes suggests that there is another important factor that contributes to performance, namely the type of retrieval cue.

The second important conclusion that follows from the results tabulated in Table 8.7 is that there is apparently an interaction between type of retrieval cue and similarity of cue to encoding context, since the superiority of associative over rhyme cue is greater at higher degrees of similarity.

Thus, on the basis of the data from Fisher and Craik's (1977) Experiment 3, summarized in Table 8.7, we can conclude that both type of retrieval cue and similarity of cue to encoding context play major roles in determining the level of recall. This last statement is very similar to the one made by Fisher and Craik to the effect that the results of their Experiment 3 confirm that 'both type of encoding and similarity of cue to encoding context play a major role in determining the level of recall' [p. 708].

The point of the exercise we have just concluded is very simple: there is no way of deciding on empirical or logical grounds whether one has to specify encoding conditions or the nature of retrieval cues *in addition to* describing the relation between the two as a determinant of remembering. If one finds that recall is higher with cue X presented after X-encoding than with cue Y after Y-encoding, one can only say that remembering is more likely in the former situation than in the latter, and try to understand the difference in terms of whatever ideas seem useful. But one cannot say that X-encoding is in any sense superior to Y-encoding, since such an assertion about the effect of one component violates the logic of the observed interaction; it would be equally correct, or equally incorrect, to say that X retrieval cues are more powerful than Y cues.

Granted that experimental results of the kind described by Fisher and Craik cannot be used to distinguish between encoding and retrieval conditions as a factor to be specified in addition to the trace/cue compatibility, would it at least be possible to argue that one of these two factors – either the type of encoding or the type of retrieval cue – must be specified in addition to the trace/cue relation in a complete account of remembering? I would like to suggest that the answer to this question is 'no.' Fisher and Craik's (1977) findings are logically consistent with our second alternative conclusion, namely that probability of recall is always determined only by the compatibility between the trace information and the retrieval information. If one accepts this conclusion, any insistence on the importance of encoding or retrieval conditions outside the relation between the two makes little sense. The results of Fisher and Craik's (1977) experiments, such as those shown in Tables 8.5, 8.6 and 8.7, can parsimoniously be regarded as showing that in some experimental conditions the compatibility between the trace information and the retrieval information was greater than in others. Thus, for instance, the appropriate interpretation of the data in Table 8.5 is that the compatibility was about the same in category/category and sentence/sentence conditions and higher in these two conditions than in the rhyme/rhyme condition. Similarly, if we are willing to make an assumption about the linearity of the relation between trace/cue compatibility and proportions of target items recalled, we could say, on the basis of the data in Table 8.6, that the difference in the compatibility between associate/identical condition and rhyme/identical condition was greater than the difference between associate/different and rhyme/different conditions. But neither in these two instances, nor in any other imaginable one, are there any logical grounds for making inferences about the superiority or inferiority of different kinds of encoding conditions, their resultant memory traces, or the nature of retrieval information.

It may be useful to consider some simple analogies to the situation in which the successful recollection of an event depends on the compatibility between the trace information and the retrieval information. One such analogy is provided by lock and key: whether or not a lock can be operated or activated by a certain key depends on the compatibility between the two. The compatibility can be specified by describing both the lock and the key, and in a certain sense, of course, it is the properties of these two objects that determine their compatibility relation. Yet, once we know that a particular lock is or is not compatible with a particular key, any further statements that we might make about either of them are irrelevant to the question of whether the activation of the lock is possible under the conditions specified.

In the lock-and-key analogy, it is difficult to see how the specification of anything other than the appropriate relation between two entities adds anything to the description of the relation and its consequences. In a similar vein, there is no need to try to speculate about the properties of memory traces or retrieval cues separately from, or in addition to, the relation between them. If we want to understand why recollection of event E_1 is easier than that of E_2, we must know why the compatibility between the trace and retrieval information is greater for E_1 than E_2. Knowing something about the properties of the memory traces in these two cases is useful only insofar as it helps to specify the trace/cue compatibility. It does not matter how we describe memory traces – whether in terms of depth, spread, elaboration, uniqueness, distinctiveness, or what not. In the relativity view here proposed, these terms are meaningful and useful only to the extent that they help us specify the extent to which retrieval information in any particular situation is compatible with the information stored about an event.

I should mention parenthetically that a few years ago I wrote a paper

(Tulving, 1974) in which I argued that ideas about cue-dependent forgetting were as useful, if not more so, than ideas about trace-dependent forgetting. The general conclusion I offered in that paper – that forgetting is best thought of in terms of inadequate or insufficient cues – no longer appears acceptable. It seems to make more sense now to think about forgetting, too, in terms of the relation between the properties of the memory trace and the characteristics of the (functional) retrieval cue.

Transfer-appropriate processing?

The arguments I have been advancing here against the idea that retention depends on the depth of processing or properties of the memory trace in addition to the trace/cue relation are very similar to the thoughts expressed by Morris *et al.* (1977). These authors, too, question the usefulness of making general statements about the 'goodness' of different types of processing and suggest that the value of any processing task must be assessed relative to the demands of the test situation. They base their criticisms of the conventional levels-of-processing ideas on the results of three experiments that show that a 'shallow' orienting task (making rhyming judgments about words) leads to a higher performance than a 'deep' task (making semantic judgments) *if* performance is measured in a recognition test requiring subjects to make use of information about phonetic properties of seen words. Morris *et al.* propose an alternative to the levels-of-processing framework for interpreting these results, referring to it as 'transfer-appropriate processing.' The basic idea is that the value of particular acquisition activities depends on particular goals and purposes.

In light of what I have said in this chapter, I am obviously very sympathetic to the ideas of Morris *et al.*, but I do have some reservations about what these authors have to say about 'appropriate' and 'inappropriate' tests or 'optimal' and 'nonoptimal' situations for assessing what the learner has learned. Once we are agreed that no absolute statements about efficacy of learning conditions are possible and that performance always depends on, and can only be understood in terms of, the relation between encoding and retrieval conditions (or the trace/cue relation), it is not obvious exactly what is gained by talking about 'right' and 'wrong' test situations. I think that the traditional research into memory erred by not paying enough attention to retrieval processes and their relation to the products of acquisition, with subjects almost always tested with 'training stimuli'; now we should not slip back into the error of insisting that subjects be tested in the 'appropriate' or 'optimal' situation. Such a practice would not fit with the emerging relativity theory of remembering.

It may be useful to distinguish between two possible questions that can be asked about a learner in a learning situation:

1 How well or to what extent has the learner acquired some particular information that he or she did not possess before?
2 Exactly what information has the learner acquired in the situation?

Both questions are perfectly legitimate, meaningful, and worth pursuing; the second question logically includes, and goes beyond, the first. The initial levels-of-processing experiments addressed the first question; to address the second, they now have been extended to include different test situations. Morris *et al.* (1977) also recommend using designs of experiments in which two or more encoding conditions are crossed with (two or more) retrieval conditions. Depending on the choice of the latter, such an extended experiment can provide information relevant to both questions. Thus, if we do wish to find out exactly what the learner has learned in a given learning episode, it will hardly do to test the subject only in what the experimenter *thinks* is the 'appropriate' or 'optimal' situation; it is necessary to test the subject in many ways, with many queries and many probes.

An added difficulty characterizes concepts such as 'test-appropriate strategies' (Lockhart *et al.*, 1976, p. 91), 'optimization of retrieval conditions' (Fisher and Craik, 1977; Moscovitch and Craik, 1976), and 'optimal test situations' (Morris *et al.*, 1977). Optimal retrieval conditions must exist in an abstract sense, perhaps like absolute zero in physics, but they will never be realized in either the real world or the laboratory. To claim that a particular retrieval situation with respect to a to-be-remembered item encoded in a particular manner is optimal implies that there are no other retrieval cues that could be more effective. Surely we know enough about these things now not to want to make such claims. Not so long ago, it was generally believed that recognition was the most sensitive test of retention and that if a copy cue failed, no other cue could provide access to the trace of a to-be-remembered item. Now recognition failure of recallable words is a well-known fact (e.g., Rabinowitz *et al.*, 1977; Tulving and Wiseman, 1975). We also know of conditions where a cue that a subject has not seen in the list (an extralist cue) is more effective than a cue that has been paired with a to-be-remembered item (an intralist retrieval cue), a fact demonstrated by Anderson *et al.* (1976). Fisher and Craik (1977, p. 705) referred to the situation where a word was encoded in a rhyme context and tested with a rhyme cue as the 'optimal retrieval context,' pointing out that performance in this situation was much lower than that provided by appropriately cued 'deeper' encodings. As we saw earlier, this was one of the critical findings that led Fisher and Craik to postulate depth of encoding as a second important factor determining the level of retention. But we know, without having to do a special experiment, that a rhyme-encoded word could be more readily retrieved with the aid of a copy cue than a rhyme cue; this fact means that the condition labeled *optimal* is not so in fact. Finally, in the Morris *et al.* (1977) experiment, subjects did better in the rhyming recognition test after the rhyming encoding task than after the semantic task. This does not mean, however, that the retrieval information was more appropriate or optimal in the former condition than in the latter. Subjects in the semantic encoding condition in the Morris *et al.* experiment would have been capable of picking out the correct words on the rhyming recognition test as well or better than the subjects in the rhyming encoding group if they had been given more appropriate retrieval information, for instance, semantic or copy cues. It is not true that subjects in the Morris *et al.*

rhyming encoding groups learned something that subjects in the semantic encoding groups did not; the results of the experiments show only that retention performance depends on the compatibility between encoding and retrieval conditions.

Despite these reservations about the set of ideas under the label of transfer-appropriate processing, I find Morris *et al.* quite correct in their major criticism of the early levels-of-processing point of view: semantic orienting tasks do not provide inherently stronger memory traces than do nonsemantic orienting tasks. The same objection to the levels-of-processing ideas has been voiced by Nelson (1979), backed by a good deal of convincing evidence.

If remembering depends on the relation between encoding and retrieval conditions, or the compatibility of trace and cue, then the problem for theory is to explain the variability in the efficacy of these relations. Why does one relation between encoding and retrieval produce a higher level of performance than another relation? To say that the trace/cue compatibility is greater in one case than another may well describe the situation, but it does not explain it.

Since this particular form of the problem is of relatively recent origin, there are few directly relevant ideas in the literature. Most theoretical ideas about encoding processes and levels-of-processing phenomena have been directed at the question of the interpretation of differences in the 'goodness' of different encoding operations. Just about the only idea that theorists have about the relation between encoding and retrieval conditions is that the nominal identity of these conditions somehow constitutes optimal conditions of remembering. This idea, as I have suggested, is demonstrably wrong. Its replacement with better insights remains a problem for future research.

Uniqueness of traces and retrieval cues

One final matter should be mentioned. Many attempts at explanation of encoding effects have been based on the idea that a memory trace can be more readily retrieved, or 'found' in the store, if it is different from other traces. Terms such as *discrimination, differentiation*, and *uniqueness* express this idea; and others, such as *elaboration*, and *richness*, are motivated by the same set of considerations. For instance, the thought that there is something 'inherently' superior in semantic as compared with, say, phonetic encoding can be rationalized by assuming that if not always, then at least frequently, semantic encodings result in richer, more unique, more elaborate, or more readily discriminable memory traces than does phonetic encoding. So, what about uniqueness?

Moscovitch and Craik (1976) have suggested that the concept of uniqueness might be regarded as alternative to the idea of depth; deep encodings are unique, whereas shallow encodings are less readily discriminable from one another. This suggestion merits careful thought. There is at least one sense in which a concept such as uniqueness, however labeled, may be important even if we believe in the primacy of the relation between encoding and retrieval as a determinant of remembering. It requires, however, that we think of uniqueness not as an alternative to depth of processing, but rather as an orthogonal dimension.

Given the possibility or existence of different encoding operations, the assertion about the critical role played by the relation between encoding and retrieval conditions, like all scientific ·hypotheses, is based on the (implicit) assumption of the *ceteris paribus* clause: the assertion does not imply that other variables or conditions could not affect the probability of recollection of an event. One such variable is similarity of items in a to-be-remembered collection. If an item I_1 is encoded in situation E_x, then its retrievability in situation R_x may well vary with the number of other similar items $I_2, I_3 \ldots I_n$ in the list. This is the classical phenomenon of associative interference, or its modern equivalent of 'cue overload.' In this case, we can describe the situation by saying that the 'uniqueness' of encoded I_1 varies as a function of a variable that is independent of the encoding situation E_x, retrieval condition R_x, and the relation between the two; and in this sense the uniqueness of the trace of an event can be said to be determined by at least two orthogonal factors – the encoding operation performed on I_1 at input and the presence of other related items $I_2, I_3, \ldots I_n$ in the same collection. These ideas are discussed and illuminated in some detail by Eysenck (1979).

What I am saying is rather mundane: it is possible to entertain the hypothesis that characteristics of the memory trace depend both on what the to-be-remembered item is and what encoding operations have been performed on it at the time of its appearance. Hence uniqueness of the trace also is determined by two factors – the similarity of the target item to others and the similarity between the encoding operations performed on all the items in a set. Whether the two factors can be usefully conceptualized as converging into one and the same underlying dimension of uniqueness, however labeled, or whether it is necessary to keep the two factors apart in thinking about problems of encoding and retrieval is something we cannot say at the present time. The problem is important and undoubtedly will come under experimental and theoretical scrutiny. For the time being, we will do well to keep an open mind about it.

References

Anderson, J. R. *Language, memory and thought.* Hillsdale, N.J.: Lawrence Erlbaum Associates, 1976.
Anderson, R. C., and Ortony, A. On putting apples into bottles – A problem of polysemy. *Cognitive Psychology*, 1975, 7, 167–180.
Anderson, R. C., Pichert, J. W., Goetz, E. T., Schallert, D. L., Stevens, K. V., and Trollip, S. R. Instantiation of general terms. *Journal of Verbal Learning and Verbal Behavior*, 1976, 15, 667–679.
Barclay, J. R., Bransford, J. D., Franks, J. J., McCarrell, N. S., and Nitsch, K. Comprehension and semantic flexibility. *Journal of Verbal Learning and Verbal Behavior*, 1974, 13, 471–481.
Bower, G. H. A multicomponent theory of the memory trace. In K. W. Spence and

J. T. Spence (Eds.), *The psychology of learning and motivation* (Vol. 1). New York: Academic Press, 1967.

Bower, G. H. Organizational factors in memory. *Cognitive Psychology*, 1970, *1*, 18–46.

Craik, F. I. M. A 'levels of analysis' view of memory. In P. Pliner, L. Krames, and T. M. Alloway (Eds.), *Communication and affect: Language and thought*. New York: Academic Press, 1973.

Craik, F. I. M. Depth of processing in recall and recognition. In S. Dornic (Ed.), *Attention and performance VI*. Hillsdale, N.J.: Erlbaum, 1977.

Craik, F. I. M., and Lockhart, R. S. Levels of processing: A framework for memory research. *Journal of Verbal Learning and Verbal Behavior*, 1972, *11*, 671–684.

Craik, F. I. M., and Tulving, E. Depth of processing and the retention of words in episodic memory. *Journal of Experimental Psychology: General*, 1975, *104*, 268–294.

Crowder, R. G. *Principles of learning and memory*. Hillsdale, N.J.: Erlbaum, 1976.

Eysenck, M. W. Depth, elaboration and distinctiveness. In L. S. Cermak and F. I. M. Craik (Eds.), *Levels of processing in human memory* (pp. 89–118). Hillsdale, N.J.: Erlbaum, 1979.

Fisher, R. P., and Craik, F. I. M. The interaction between encoding and retrieval operations in cued recall. *Journal of Experimental Psychology: Human Learning and Memory*, 1977, *3*, 701–711.

Hyde, T. S., and Jenkins, J. J. Differential effects of incidental tasks on the organization of recall of a list of highly associated words. *Journal of Experimental Psychology*, 1969, *82*, 472–481.

Hyde, T. S. and Jenkins, J. J. Recall for words as a function of semantic, graphic, and syntactic orienting tasks. *Journal of Verbal Learning and Verbal Behavior*, 1973, *12*, 471–480.

Jenkins, J. J. Can we have a theory of meaningful memory? In R. L. Solso (Ed.), *Theories in cognitive psychology: The Loyola Symposium*. Hillsdale, N.J.: Erlbaum, 1974.

Kintsch, W. *The representation of meaning in memory*. Hillsdale, N.J.: Erlbaum, 1974.

Lockhart, R. S. Craik, F. I. M. and Jacoby, L. Depth of processing, recognition and recall. In J. Brown (Ed.), *Recall and recognition*. London: Wiley, 1976.

Morris, C. D., Bransford, J. D., and Franks, J. J. Levels of processing versus transfer appropriate processing. *Journal of Verbal Learning and Verbal Behavior*, 1977, *16*, 519–533.

Moscovitch, M., and Craik, F. I. M. Depth of processing, retrieval cues, and uniqueness of encoding as factors in recall. *Journal of Verbal Learning and Verbal Behavior*, 1976, *15*, 447–458.

Nelson, D. L. Remembering pictures and words: Appearance, significance and name. In L. S. Cermak and F. I. M. Craik (Eds.), *Levels of processing in human memory* (pp. 45–76). Hillsdale, N.J.: Erlbaum, 1979.

Nelson, D. L., Wheeler, J. W. J., Borden, R. C. and Brooks, D. H. Levels of processing and cuing: Sensory versus meaning features. *Journal of Experimental Psychology*, 1974, *103*, 971–977.

Rabinowitz, J. C., Mandler, G., and Barsalou, L. W. Recognition failure: Another case of retrieval failure. *Journal of Verbal Learning and Verbal Behavior*, 1977, *16*, 639–663.

Thomson, D. M. and Tulving, E. Associative encoding and retrieval: Weak and strong cues. *Journal of Experimental Psychology*, 1970, *86*, 255–262.

Till, R. E., and Jenkins, J. J. The effects of cued orienting tasks on the free recall of words. *Journal of Verbal Learning and Verbal Behavior*, 1973, *12*, 489–498.

Tulving, E. Cue-dependent forgetting. *American Scientist*, 1974, *64*, 74–82.

Tulving, E. Ecphoric processes in recall and recognition. In J. Brown (Ed.), *Recall and recognition*. London: Wiley, 1976.

Tulving, E., and Osler, S. Effectiveness of retrieval cues in memory for words. *Journal of Experimental Psychology*, 1968, *77*, 593–601.

Tulving, E., and Thomson, D. M. Encoding specificity and retrieval processes in episodic memory. *Psychological Review*, 1973, *80*, 352–373.

Tulving, E., and Watkins, M. J. Structure of memory traces. *Psychological Review*, 1975, *82*, 261–275.

Tulving, E., and Wiseman, S. Relation between recognition and recognition failure of recallable words. *Bulletin of the Psychonomic Society*, 1975, *6*, 79–82.

Underwood, B. J. Attributes of memory. *Psychological Review*, 1969, *76*, 559–573.

Walsh, D. A., and Jenkins, J. J. Effects of orienting tasks on free recall in incidental learning: 'Difficulty,' 'effort,' and 'process' explanations. *Journal of Verbal Learning and Verbal Behavior*, 1973, *12*, 481–488.

Woodworth, R. S. *Experimental psychology*. New York: Holt, 1938.

---

9   Gail McKoon, Roger Ratcliff and Gary S. Dell
'A Critical Evaluation of the Semantic–Episodic Distinction'

Reprinted in full from: *Journal of Experimental Psychology: Learning, Memory, and Cognition* **12**, 295–306 (1986)

It has long been recognized by psychologists and philosophers that experience leaves its effect on the mind in the form of both specific memories for events and knowledge that is not tied to such events (see Herrmann, 1982, for a review). The distinction was eloquently brought to the attention of cognitive psychologists by Tulving in 1972. Tulving distinguished between episodic memory, which records events directly experienced by the subject, and semantic memory, which stores general knowledge of the world.

The purpose of this article is to examine recent updates of the episodic–semantic distinction proposed by Tulving (1983, 1984). The distinction has proved highly influential in the field: from 1972 to 1984 Tulving's original article (1972) received more than 500 citations in the Social Science Citation Index. The distinction is appealing because it allows one to distinguish between two forms of memory that seem intuitively different phenomenologically, and to distinguish between two domains of research, each with its own tasks and variables.

As well as having these heuristic uses, the distinction has been used to interpret a large range of data. On the face of it, it makes sense that newly learned episodes should be organized differently and have different characteristics from semantic knowledge. For example, Tulving (1983) proposed that semantic information is highly interconnected and organized, relatively permanent, and context independent, whereas episodic information was less well organized, highly susceptible to forgetting, and context dependent. Thus it was possible to interpret experimental results concerning context effects, forgetting, retrieval, and so on in terms of the distinction. In addition, it appeared possible to extend the distinction to neuropsychological data concerning amnesia and brain damage. When the ability to form new autobiographical memories is lost, yet old memories are retained, it could be said that the episodic system is damaged while the semantic system is intact. In sum, Tulving's distinction is of great heuristic and pragmatic use. However, an evaluation of the theoretical and empirical status of the distinction, as presented in this article, leads to the conclusion that the case for the distinction is weak.

In the 1983 version of the distinction, Tulving adds a number of new features that were not discussed in the original 1972 article. Tulving (1983) provides a list of diagnostics that are meant to discriminate between episodic memory and semantic memory, and suggests a larger framework in which there are two more memory systems – lexical memory and procedural memory. He also lists a series of experimental results that are intended to support the episodic–semantic distinction. In the 1984 version, Tulving suggests that episodic memory is embedded in semantic memory, rather than being a separate system from semantic memory. He also provides some new support for the distinction.

We criticize Tulving's proposals in three main ways. First, we argue that the episodic–semantic distinction is not well enough defined to be empirically testable and that many of the diagnostics and experimental results are questionable as support for the distinction. Second, we consider in detail the results from experiments cited by Tulving (1983) as evidence for the distinction and present counterarguments and additional data to show that the results are inconclusive. Third, we point out that even if the distinction were successful in providing a basis for separability of experimental effects, the task would remain of modeling the processes that operate within each memory system. Labeling effects as semantic or episodic does *not* provide a theoretical explanation, but only a categorization. Although there are significant single-store models (e.g., Anderson, 1983), the episodic–semantic debate has not led to any significant development of dual-store models.

In the respect that the episodic–semantic distinction is described by a list of distinguishing features and empirical results, it can be compared to the distinction between long-term and short-term memory. A useful description of the short-term/long-term distinction has been provided by Craik and Lockhart (1972), who lay out clearly the bases for the distinction, and then point out its weaknesses and suggest an alternative theory. For the short-term/long-term distinction, the distinguishing features of short-term memory were said to be a mainly phonemic code, relatively fast forgetting, and limited capacity, whereas the features of long-term memory were a mainly semantic code, slow (or no) forgetting, and unlimited capacity. These features summarized a large body of data from a variety of experiments, and testing this distinction involved finding new variables (e.g., rate of presentation) that, on theoretical grounds, should affect one memory system but not the other. If such a variable did affect one system and not the other, then the result was taken to be consistent with the distinction. But if experimental separation was not achieved, then theoretical or empirical work was required to resolve the difficulty. In the end, in the mid-1970s, the difficulties overcame the distinction. For example, it was found that codes in short-term memory could be visual, articulatory, or semantic and that forgetting rate and capacity were variable, depending on methods of measurement. In light of recent critiques of levels of processing, we do not want to force a final decision about the distinction between short- and long-term memories. But we do want to make clear that it was possible to falsify the particular short-term/long-term model that was developed by the early 1970s because the model was well-formulated enough to present testable hypotheses and because it was based on a large body of consistent data.

The situation with respect to the episodic–semantic distinction is quite different. The body of data on which the distinction is based is not large. In his chapter on empirical evidence for the distinction, Tulving (1983) cites only a small number of results from experimental work with normal adults. Although there are now neurophysiological data, the distinction was originally based on experimental results from cognitive psychology, and these results do not provide a large data base either for the distinction itself or for the attribution of specific features to one or the other of the two memory systems. In addition, these results appear serendipitous in their relevance to the distinction, a point to be taken up in the Discussion section of this article. Another way in which the episodic–semantic distinction suffers in comparison to the short-term/long-term distinction is that it is not well-formulated enough to present clearly testable hypotheses. This is because of diagnostic features that are not clearly defined and because of complexities involved in possible interactions between the episodic, semantic, lexical, and procedural systems.

These points are taken up in the next sections of the article. First, diagnostic features listed by Tulving (1983, Chapter 3) are reviewed and considered with respect to empirical evidence. Second, the empirical and neurological evidence cited by Tulving (1983, 1984) as directly relevant to the distinction is reviewed. Finally, Tulving's 1984 position is discussed.

Diagnostic features

In the following discussion, features that seem to be aspects of the same phenomenon are grouped together, and features of application (e.g., semantic but not episodic memories are applied in education) are not considered because they are not relevant to deciding about the status of episodic and semantic memories as separate systems.

*Definitional features: reference, veridicality, temporal coding,
retrieval query, and retrieval report*

Episodic memory has the following characteristics: reference is to oneself; events are believed veridical because they happened to oneself; information is organized temporally; queries are with respect to oneself; and events are 'remembered.' Semantic memory is characterized by the following attributes: reference, queries, and veridicality are with respect to general knowledge; information is not organized by temporal order; and events are 'known.' All of these features are true by definition of episodic and semantic memories: it is difficult to see any way of testing them that would speak to the reality of the episodic–semantic distinction independently of this definition. In other words, for example, if episodic memory were not temporally organized, it would not be episodic memory.

The definitional features appear unambiguous and also unchanged since Tulving's (1972) original proposal of the episodic–semantic distinction. But even these features are open to confusion. Although intuition suggests that overlearned personal events (e.g., 'the first time I . . .') should be part of permanent semantic knowledge, they would have to remain, by definition, part of episodic knowledge.

Characteristics of contents: source, registration, and units

According to Tulving (1983, p. 31), the split between episodic and semantic memories allows one to 'separate the remembering of a personal episode from the knowlege of its "semantic" contents.' This separation is difficult to understand because it is not clear what kind of semantic information is included in an episodic trace. According to Tulving, direct perception is the source of episodic information, and the units are 'events.' In contrast, registration of semantic information requires that the content be understood and related to existing knowledge (Tulving, 1983, p. 37). Tulving (1983) states that a 'mere sensation' (p. 36) can be the source of information registered in the episodic system, but at the same time, the sensation can be so meaningless as to go unrecorded in the semantic system. These diagnostics raise a series of interrelated questions. Are events in episodic memory not related to existing knowledge? Do the events not contain information about the referents of the objects involved in the events? The events of episodic memory are said to be propositional, but that term usually involves abstract properties; what would such properties be in episodic memory? How is the beginning and the end of an event known, if not by reference to the event's meaning? Unless we can understand exactly what semantic information is allowed into episodic memory, the characteristics of contents become less than diagnostic for distinguishing episodic and semantic memory.

Organization, inferential capability, and access

Organization of knowledge in the episodic system is supposed to be temporal, and episodic memory is supposed to have little inferential capability. Access for episodic information is supposed to be deliberate or conscious, whereas access for semantic information is supposed to be automatic. These features are considered together here because a series of experiments by McKoon and Ratcliff (1979, 1980a, 1980b, 1986; Ratcliff and McKoon, 1978, 1981a, 1981b) call them jointly into question.

McKoon and Ratcliff's experiments invovled priming with newly learned information. Sentences or pairs of words were presented for study and then pairs of words were presented for test (lexical decision or recognition). The first word of a test pair was a prime, and the second word of the pair was the target. The extent to which the prime facilitated the response to the target relative to a control condition was the amount of priming. One result from these experiments shows that the organization of textual information is not solely temporal; instead, the organization is based on meaning (and so must be the result of inference processes). For example, when a sentence like 'The pauper chopped wood and lugged water' was studied, there were equal amounts of priming between *wood* and *pauper* and between *water* and *pauper*, and less priming between *wood* and *water*. So Ratcliff and McKoon (1978) argued that the first two pairs were equally closely connected in memory, reflecting an organization based on meaning, not the temporal order of the words in the sentence.

The same kinds of priming experiments also show that access to newly learned information can be automatic (McKoon and Ratcliff, 1979; Ratcliff and McKoon, 1981a, 1981b). In these experiments, a response was required only to the target, not the prime, so that the delay between presentation of prime and target could be controlled. Priming effects between words from the same studied pair or sentence were found even when the delay between prime and target was as short as 100 ms, and when the probability that prime and target would come from the same studied sentence or pair was very low. These two criteria (taken from Posner and Snyder, 1975) show that access to the newly learned information was automatic. (With respect to access, it should also be pointed out that access to information in semantic memory is sometimes very slow and strategic, as evidenced by the time required to think of a 'fruit beginning with the letter K.')

In sum, primed effects with newly learned information show organization based on meaning and show automatic access, neither of which should be found with episodic information according to Tulving (1983). One possible response to these findings might be to argue that priming reflects associations in semantic memory, not episodic memory. However, two of the experiments cited by Tulving (1983) as providing direct evidence for the episodic–semantic distinction are studies that attribute priming effects to episodic memory (Herrmann and Harwood, 1980; McKoon and Ratcliff, 1979). Either it must be that these studies do not provide support for the distinction (because priming results reflect semantic information) or it must be that information in episodic memory can be organized on nontemporal bases and be accessed automatically.

Retrieval mechanisms and context dependence

Tulving (1983, p. 48) speculates that retrieval mechanisms might be different in episodic and semantic memory. Such a speculation contrasts sharply with other recent work. The kinds of measures that are used for data bases in investigations of retrieval (e.g., accuracy, reaction time, and growth of accuracy as a function of retrieval time) are the same for episodic and semantic memory, and many recent models of retrieval have been applied both to semantic and episodic information. For example, search models have been applied to recognition (Sternberg, 1969) and to semantic memory (Meyer, 1970), as has a model proposed by Atkinson and Juola (1973; Smith *et al.*, 1974). A sequential sampling retrieval process has also been used for both recognition (Pike *et al.*, 1977; Ratcliff, 1978) and semantic memory (Collins and Loftus, 1975; McCloskey and Glucksberg, 1979; Ratcliff and McKoon, 1982). In fact, taking all modeling efforts together, we would suggest that the similarities between semantic and episodic retrieval far outweigh the differences, and that there is little evidence for separation of the two systems on the basis of retrieval.

Tulving's specific suggestion regarding the differences in retrieval is that retrieval from the episodic system 'takes the form of a synergistic combination of the information stored in the episodic system and the information provided by the cognitive environment of the remember' (Tulving, 1984, p. 225). In contrast, retrieval from semantic memory is said to occur 'relatively independently of the nature of the instigating cue' (p. 225). Despite Tulving's use of the qualifier 'relatively,' he seems to be arguing that retrieval context plays only a small role in the semantic system. Taken at face value, the data show otherwise, as 20 years of research on the effect of context on word recognition (e.g., Tulving and Gold, 1963), lexical ambiguity (e.g., Tanenhaus *et al.*, 1979), and retrieval of semantic facts (e.g., Muter, 1978) have shown. Both Muter (1978) and Neely and Payne (1983) have used procedures in which direct comparisons can be drawn between context effects on the retrieval of episodic and semantic information and found that the effects are quantitatively similar. Results also show that proportion of recallable words recognized plotted against proportion recognized (Tulving and Wiseman, 1975) falls on the same function for both episodic and semantic tasks (Muter, 1978). So the effect of context on retrieval does not appear to provide a useful diagnostic for distinguishing episodic from semantic memory.

Vulnerability

Tulving (1983) argues that episodic memory is more vulnerable (subject to forgetting) than semantic memory. The problem with testing this conjecture is that it is difficult to arrange an experimental procedure in which episodic and semantic memories are equated on dimensions such as degree of learning, difficulty of material, and so on. However, in the one case that comes closest to achieving such control, that is with amnesic subjects, forgetting appears to occur at the same rate for episodic and semantic information. Zola-Morgan *et al.* (1983) showed that for a variety of kinds of amnesia, remote memory impairments were parallel for public (largely semantic) and personal (episodic) events. Also, Cohen (1983) has summarized work with H. M. that showed equivalent deficits for newly learned episodic information and semantic information (e.g., public figures; Marslen-Wilson and Teuber, 1975).

Recollective experience, affect, and artificial intelligence

According to Tulving (1983, p. 48), remembered events 'belong to the rememberer' and have a 'definite affective tone,' all of which are present to a greater degree in episodic memory than in semantic memory. Basically, we agree, but we attribute the difference to the content of the memories, not to separate stores. Episodic memories have a warm, personal quality essentially by definition, whereas semantic memories, such as the fact that a canary is a bird, are usually impersonal (but see Morton and Bekerian's [1984] discussion of this point). We do not agree, however, when Tulving speculates that episodic memory, unlike semantic memory, is impossible in a computer. When Winograd's (1972) robot responds to the question, 'When did you pick up the green pyramid?' with 'While I was stacking up the red cube . . . , ' it is retrieving information about 'personal' events from its past. It actually did stack up the red cube a short time before. Perhaps Tulving's point is that the robit is not really *consciously* recalling the action of stacking, and that it is the machine's lack of subjective experience that disqualifies it from having an episodic memory. If so, then the point seems to be that episodic retrieval is conscious. However, as we mentioned earlier, experimental evidence indicates that episodic information can be retrieved automatically and hence independently of consciousness (Posner, 1978).

Interactions between memory systems

The episodic–semantic distinction is not well defined in several respects, all pointed out by Tulving himself (1983). One complicating factor is the addition of the procedural and lexical memory systems, which are assumed to interact with the semantic and episodic systems. Procedural memory is memory for the particular operations involved in performing a task, and it is contrasted with the propositional episodic and semantic systems. With the inclusion of procedural memory into the system, 'it is possible that data discrepant with the episodic–semantic distinction can be accounted for in terms of procedural memory' (Tulving, 1983, p. 10). But then, it could be argued, perhaps data consistent with the episodic–semantic distinction could also be accounted for by the procedural/propositional distinction, rendering the separation of episodic and semantic systems unnecessary. A similar problem arises with lexical memory. Although, as Tulving points out, little thought has gone into understanding the relationship between the lexical, episodic, and semantic systems, still the existence of the lexical system provides another way of explaining away data discrepant with the episodic–semantic distinction.

Summary

The important diagnositc features can be divided into content features (source, registration, units) and process features (organization, inference, access, retrieval, and forgetting). With respect to content features, we find it difficult to understand how semantic content is allowed into episodic memory in such a way as to preserve the episodic–semantic distinction. With respect to process features, we find that most evidence about processes does not support a distinction between episodic and semantic memories. In fact, access, organization, retrieval, susceptibility to forgetting, and dependence on context all appear, from empirical evidence, to be similar for episodic and semantic information.

Empirical evidence

Tulving (1983, 1984) presents a number of experimental findings (with normal adult subjects) that in his view speak directly to the issue of the separation of episodic and semantic memories. These are findings by Anderson and Ross (1980), Herrmann and Harwood (1980), Shoben *et al.* (1978), McKoon and Ratcliff (1979), Kihlstrom (1980), Underwood *et al.* (1978), and a series of results that compare word identification and recognition (Jacoby and Dallas, 1981; Jacoby and Witherspoon, 1982; Tulving *et al.*, 1982). Each of these is discussed in turn in the sections that follow.

In general, the findings can be divided into two sets: those that were originally presented as attacks on the episodic–semantic distinction and those that Tulving (1983, 1984) has cited in support of the distinction. Tulving has countered those meant as attacks by arguing either that the findings are irrelevant to the distinction or that the findings do, in fact, support the distinction. Findings that Tulving believes support the distinction take the form of dissociations. A dissociation occurs if a single variable affects performance in an episodic task differently from the way it affects performance in a semantic task.

We criticize Tulving's interpretations in three ways. First, episodic–semantic theory is not well enough specified to allow predictions of which variables or experiments will be relevant to the distinction and which will not. Second, for experiments in which dissociation is obtained, there often exist similar experiments in which the same dissociation is not obtained. Third, for some findings, Tulving's interpretations have no more plausibility than interpretations that assume only a single-store system. These problems are illustrated in the sections that follow.

Anderson and Ross (1980)

Anderson and Ross designed their experiments to show that episodic and semantic memories were not functionally independent. Subjects were asked to learn sentences about, for example, spaniels and dogs, and then were asked to verify whether a spaniel is a dog. The general question was whether response time in the semantic task (verification) would be affected by the newly learned (episodic) information. Specifically, Anderson and Ross thought that presentation of the sentence 'A spaniel is a dog' would facilitate verification of the same sentence, but that presentation of 'interfering' sentences such as 'A spaniel retrieves a ball' would slow verification of 'A spaniel is a dog' (predictions derived from their single-memory [Adaptive Control of Thought] (ACT) theory). Although the results of the experiments were complicated (by 'false' verification items and by practice effects), effects of the newly learned information on verification were observed. However, the expected interference effect did not appear (for 'true' items). Anderson and Ross explained this failure by assuming an implicit rehearsal process; when studying 'A spaniel retrieves a ball,' subjects rehearsed the fact that a spaniel is a dog. Such rehearsal led to facilitation that counteracted interference effects. Anderson and Ross concluded that with the addition of this explanation for the failure to obtain interference effects, their single-memory theory (ACT) could account for the results of their experiments and that models assuming separate episodic and semantic memories could not account for the results in any obvious way.

In connection with this discussion, it should be noted that interference effects of newly learned information on semantic verification have been found in other experiments. Both Lewis and Anderson (1976) and Peterson and Potts (1982) have shown that learning new facts about a famous person slows verification time for previously known facts.

In contrast to Anderson and Ross (1980), Tulving (1983) does not propose a theory to account for the effects of episodic information on semantic verification. Instead, he suggests that these effects are 'largely irrelevant to the problem of the distinction between episodic and semantic memory' (p. 82) and may reflect the procedural memory system. The problem illustrated here is the lack of a method for deciding whether a particular effect speaks to the semantic–episodic distinction. On the one hand, Anderson and Ross (1980) found effects that they used to support a single-store model. On the other hand, Tulving (1983) attributes those same effects to the procedural memory system. This lack of agreement contrasts sharply with the situation with the short-term/ long-term distinction, in which there were relatively precise methods for deciding whether particular experimental results spoke to the distinction.

Shoben, Wescourt, and Smith (1978)

Shoben *et al.* (1978) presented results that they argued supported the episodic– semantic distinction. They used two tasks, recognition and verification, involving the same sentences as materials. One variable was the relatedness of the predicate to the subject in a sentence. For verification, the second variable was the number of different sentences, each with a different predicate, tested about a particular subject noun. For recognition, the second variable was the number of different sentences, each with a different predicate, that were learned about a particular noun. Shoben *et al.* assumed that the second variable was the same for verification and recognition, and, following previous usage in recognition research, labeled it 'fanning.' They found that amounts of fanning (number of different sentences) affected response time in recognition but not verification. They also found that relatedness affected verification response times but not recognition response times. So they argued for a dissociation: semantic memory, reflected in the verification task, and episodic memory, reflected in recognition, were subject to different variables.

This interpretation has been criticized by Anderson and Ross (1980), McKoon and Ratcliff (1979), and McCloskey and Santee (1981). First, both Anderson and Ross and McCloskey and Santee point to problems with the way Shoben *et al.* operationalized the fanning variable and argue that a single-store model such as ACT can well account for the different effects of the different implementations of the variable in the two tasks. Second, the finding that relatedness has no effect in an episodic task is countered by other findings that semantic variables do have effects in episodic tasks (e.g., McCloskey and Santee, 1981; Lewis and Anderson, 1976). Also for Shoben *et al.*'s particular experiment, relatedness effects in recognition are *not* predicted by the single-store model, ACT (Anderson and Ross, 1980). Finally, a general point to be made is that whether a single- or dual-store model is assumed, an explanation still must be provided for the different results in the two tasks. As McKoon and Ratcliff (1979) noted, even the explanation put forward by Shoben *et al.* (1978) seems consistent with either kind of model. For effects of relatedness, Shoben *et al.* assumed that information about the meanings of words was used in verification, whereas information about their occurrence was used in recognition. Certainly, both kinds of information would be present in a single-store memory system. Similarly, for effects of fanning, they assumed that different amounts of information were involved in the processes of recognition and verification, an assumption that could be incorporated into a single-store model.

Tulving (1983, p. 86) responds to criticisms of the results of Shoben *et al.* (1978) by pointing to the 'separate and different explanations of the effects of the two independent variables,' and suggesting that the episodic–semantic distinction provides 'a unifying framework within which the individual explanations might be integrated.' However, at the present time, we do not see any way in which this framework contributes toward the individual explanations or a unification of them or toward relating these results to other empirical findings. The results of experiments like Shoben *et al.*'s cannot be used to support either single- or dual-store models unless detailed predictions from the two models can be made.

McKoon and Ratcliff (1979)

When McKoon and Ratcliff (1979) published their experiments, they interpreted them as providing evidence against the episodic–semantic distinction. However, Tulving (1983) finds instead that they support the distinction.

McKoon and Ratcliff (1979) used two different tasks, lexical decision and recognition. For both tasks, subjects studied pairs of words. Then, in recognition test lists, they were asked to distinguish words that had been studied from words that had not been studied, whereas in lexical decision test lists, they were asked to distinguish words (some of which had been studied) from nonwords. The variable for both tasks was the relationship involved in priming between two words presented sequentially in the test lists. The prime and target words were related semantically (e.g., 'green grass'), episodically (e.g. the pair 'city grass' was studied), or both (e.g., the pair 'green grass' was studied).

McKoon and Ratcliff (1979) argued that recognition and lexical decision were prototypical tasks for episodic and semantic information, respectively, so that, if there were separate memory systems, semantic information should not lead to priming in recognition and episodic information should not lead to priming in lexical decision. In fact, these priming effects were obtained, and McKoon and Ratcliff (1979) interpreted them as providing evidence against a dual-store system.

Tulving (1983), on the other hand, reinterpreted McKoon and Ratcliff's (1979) results as evidence for a dissociation between episodic and semantic memories. Because, according to Tulving (1983), in McKoon and Ratcliff's experiments, response times for primed words were a function of kind of priming (semantic, episodic, or both) in recognition but not in lexical decision, their data exhibit a dissociation and so support the episodic–semantic distinction. However, there are several problems with this argument. First, the result that primed response times are not a function of kind of priming for lexical decision may be a floor effect on reaction time; the 0.53-s reaction times obtained for primed lexical decision responses may be the minimum possible under the specific experimental conditions used. Second, for semantically primed response times in lexical decision, Tulving (1983) used the condition in which target words were from the pairs of words studied. It might be more reasonable to use the semantic priming condition in which the target words had not been studied and thus avoid any contamination from episodic memory. If one uses this condition for an estimate of semantic priming in lexical decision, primed response time does vary as a function of type of priming, going from 0.56 s for semantic priming to 0.54 s for episodic priming and 0.53 s for semantic plus episodic priming. Although these differences are small (only approaching significance, $p = .11$), the direction of the effect is the same as for the recognition data. Third, in recognition, the semantic priming condition was different from the other priming conditions in that the prime word did not appear in the studied list of words. This means that the prime required a negative response whereas the primes in the other conditions required positive responses like the targets. So the semantic priming condition was open to the well-known problems with sequential effects; these effects were evidenced by a 20% error rate in this condition, compared with 3% and 6% error rates in the other two priming conditions. In sum, given these problems, it is clear that McKoon and Ratcliff's data do not neatly provide a dissociation between episodic and semantic memories.

Recently, Neely and Durgunoglu (1985) have further investigated semantic and episodic priming in lexical decision and recognition. They held study conditions constant for the two tasks and varied only test conditions in an effort to ensure that no other variable was confounded with the type of task (although, of course, this does not guarantee equivalent processing in retrieval; once subjects are presented with different tasks, they may employ different strategies or use different kinds of information). Neely and Durgunoglu (1985) found that an episodic prime facilitated responses in recognition but not lexical decision and that a semantic prime inhibited responses in recognition but had little effect in lexical decision. These results are different from the results obtained by McKoon and Ratcliff (1979), although it may be that the difference can be accounted for by the differences in procedures. But the point Neely and Durgunoglu wish to make is that with their procedures, they find dissociative episodic and semantic priming effects in the episodic and semantic tasks. They note that this dissociation might support the episodic–semantic distinction, although they acknowledge that episodic priming in lexical decision has been obtained by McKoon and Ratcliff (1979, 1986) and by other experiments in their own laboratory (Durgunoglu and Neely, 1987). More importantly for our purposes in this article, they also acknowledge that the distinction supported by their results may be one of retrieval processes within a single-store system rather than a distinction between two separate storage systems.

Recognition-identification studies (Jacoby and Witherspoon, 1982; Jacoby and Dallas, 1981; Tulving, Schacter, and Stark, 1982)

Several experiments have shown that studying a word increases performance on a later semantic memory task involving that word (identification), but that the amount of the benefit is not correlated with performance in a *yes–no* recognition task. For example, Jacoby and Witherspoon (1982) found that studying a word enhances the probability of identifying it when it is presented very briefly, and that this probability is independent of the probability of recognizing that the word had been studied. In a related study, Jacoby and Dallas (1981) found that varying whether the subject's attention was directed toward the appearance, the sound, or the meaning of the word affected recognition accuracy, but not identification accuracy. Tulving *et al.* (1982) found independence between recognition performance and performance in a fragment-completion task. Their subjects studied a list of low-frequency words such as AARDVARK and were later given a *yes/no* recognition test for the words. They were also given word fragments such as A—D—RK to complete. Probability of successful completion of a word was independent of the recognition judgment for that word. This was true for both old and new words.

In these experiments the occurrence of some event (the study of a word) had independent effects on an episodic task (recognition) and a semantic task (identifying a word under conditions of limited stimulus information). According to Tulving (1983) these dissociation effects support the episodic–semantic distinction. There are two points that we can make in response. The first is that it is not at all clear that word identification involves semantic memory. Depending on the taste of the theorist, one could implicate procedural or lexical memory. Our second point is that even if we grant that word identification involves semantic memory, the two-store position does not account for the finding that the effects of prior study in identification and recognition are sometimes not independent. For example, Jacoby and Witherspoon (1982) find that with pseudoword items, recognition and identification are positively related. Why do the memory systems act as if they are separate with some stimuli, but not others?

Underwood, Boruch, and Malmi (1978)

Tulving (1983, 1984) cites the Underwood *et al.* finding of low correlations between individual subjects' performance in episodic and semantic tasks as support for the distinction. Underwood *et al.* obtained intercorrelations of performance on 33 different measures of memory performance, five of which were designated as semantic memory tasks: judging word frequencies; vocabulary; spelling; and two Scholastic Aptitude Test (SAT) measures, SAT-verbal and SAT-math. Although the semantic memory tasks were only weakly correlated with most of the episodic tasks, there were some low correlations within the semantic group as well. The SAT-math was correlated with SAT-verbal (.31) but not with any of the other semantic tasks (.08, .09, and .08, for the remaining tasks, respectively). In fact, SAT-math was more correlated with the group of episodic tasks labeled serial learning (.19 and .24), memory span (.13, .24, .27), and interference susceptibility (.36). The high intercorrelations among semantic tasks were restricted to the lexical memory tasks of vocabulary, spelling, and SAT-verbal, a group that also correlated with paired associate and serial learning performance, albeit at a somewhat lower level. In short, the structure of the intercorrelations seems to be much more complex than a simple episodic–semantic division would imply. Furthermore, the tasks labeled semantic are not semantic in the way usually meant in semantic memory research. Thus, conclusions drawn from this research have little to say about the episodic–semantic distinction.

Herrmann and Harwood (1980)

The next experimental result used by Tulving (1983) to support the episodic–semantic distinction comes from a paper by Herrmann and Harwood (1980). They designed their experiment to address the question of whether semantic information affects the retrieval of episodic information. Of course, it might be that semantic information could be encoded as part of an episodic trace (although, as discussed above, we are not sure of Tulving's position on this). And, when semantic information was encoded as part of an episodic trace, it would affect the retrieval of that trace. But the important question addressed by Herrmann and Harwood (1980) was whether semantic information not involved in encoding would affect retrieval.

Subjects in Herrmann and Harwood's (1980) experiment studied lists of categorized words and then were presented with pairs of words for a recognition test (responding 'old' if both words had been studied, 'new' if neither had been studied, and 'mixed' for one old and one new word). The key results were those for pairs in which neither word had been studied. When other members of the categories had been studied, then response times were faster if the two words came from the same category than from different categories. But when other members of the categories had not been studied, same-category and different-category response times were equal. Herrmann and Harwood (1980) and Tulving (1983) interpreted these results by saying that the semantic variable, category membership, had an effect on the episodic task, recognition, when category information was likely to have been encoded in episodic memory during study, but not otherwise, and Tulving (1983) used these results as support for the distinction between the episodic and semantic memory systems.

This support is of questionable value, however, because of the lack of generality of Herrmann and Harwood's (1980) results. McKoon *et al.* (1985) have found results that are not in agreement with those of Herrmann and Harwood (1980). McKoon *et al.* designed their experiments with the same goal as Herrmann and Harwood (1980), namely, to investigate whether semantic information affects the retrieval of episodic information. In some respects, the McKoon *et al.* experiments were similar to the Herrmann and Harwood (1980) experiment; for example, subjects studied categorized lists and were tested for recognition of items from those lists. But there were also procedural differences; in McKoon *et al.*'s experiments, study time per item was shorter, and items were tested for recognition individually rather than in pairs. With these differences in procedure, McKoon *et al.* found that for test items whose categories had not been studied, response time was faster for an item preceded by another item from the same category than for an item preceded by an item from a different category. So, McKoon *et al.* argued that the semantic variable, category membership, did affect performance in the episodic task even when the semantic information could not have been encoded into memory during study.

What can be concluded from these two seemingly contradictory sets of results? One possibility is that semantic information does, in fact, affect retrieval of episodic information. The reason that Herrmann and Harwood (1980) failed to find this effect is that it is small (about 36 ms in one of McKoon *et al.*'s experiments), smaller than the standard error (53 ms) in Herrmann and Harwood's experiments. This possibility is given some credibility because another effect that Herrmann and Harwood failed to find, facilitation for same-versus-different-category mixed pairs, has been found by Neely *et al.* (1983), with somewhat different procedures.

The other possible reason for the differences between the results obtained by McKoon *et al.* (1985) and by Herrmann and Harwood (1980) is the different procedures that were used. If this is the case, then the problem for the episodic–semantic distinction is to explain why the procedural differences led to the different results. This point echoes our contention that the episodic–semantic distinction offers little basis for deciding between two experiments, one that supports the distinction and one that does not.

The conclusion that semantic information does affect recognition receives support from recent work by Dosher (1984). In her experiments, subjects studied pairs of words. One pair might include the word *dog*, another pair the word *cat*. Then subjects were tested for recognition of pairs, using a response signal procedure in which subjects were required to respond immediately upon a signal given at various delays after the test pair was presented. When subjects were asked to recognize whether the words *dog–cat* were studied as a pair, they tended to respond positively early in processing. Only later in processing (after 600 or 700 ms) was that tendency suppressed so that there was a greater proportion of correct, negative responses. The interpretation favored by Dosher is that semantic information is initially retrieved, then later suppressed. This finding, like the McKoon *et al.* (1985) findings, argues that well-known associations are used in recognition even though these associations were not studied during the encoding phase of the experiments.

Kihlstrom (1980)

Tulving (1983) describes Kihlstrom's (1980) experiment as showing a dissociation between performance on semantic and episodic tasks that supports the episodic–semantic distinction. The episodic task was free recall of a list of words that had been learned under hypnosis, with subjects instructed to forget the list when they awakened. The semantic task was free association, where the stimuli were words likely to elicit the learned list words as primary associates. Subjects highly susceptible to hypnosis recalled almost none of the words, whereas subjects of low to medium susceptibility recalled 86% of the words. But in free association, there were only small differences across the groups of subjects; thus there was a dissociation between performance on the free recall and free association tasks.

Using this dissociation to support the episodic–semantic distinction, as Tulving (1983) does, ignores other cases in which performance on an episodic task was not affected by instructions to subjects to forget the material learned while hypnotized. For example, Graham and Patton (1968) found that a group of subjects hypnotized during learning of a list showed just as much retroactive inhibition from that list as did a normal group of subjects. Such data cannot be ignored; either they argue against the episodic–semantic distinction, or the distinction must account for the difference in results with the different episodic tasks.

Conclusion

The experiments cited by Tulving (1983, 1984) as support for the episodic–semantic distinction (and discussed and criticized above) follow the logic of dissociation. Roediger (1984) has questioned the use of dissociation results as support for separate systems on several grounds. For example, a dissociation might equally well reflect different processes as different systems (Tulving and Bower, 1974), and it is difficult to know for which of the many dissociations that could be found experimentally new memory systems should be proposed. Tulving replies to Roediger (1984) with the statement that 'dissociations represent a necessary but not a sufficient condition for different memory systems' (Tulving, 1984, p. 260). In addition to the experimental dissociations, experiments involving different brain states and studies of pathological cases must be considered. In the next section of the article, we discuss the several different kinds of evidence from these sources.

Evidence from studies of brain activity and pathology

Effects of drugs

The drug studies cited by Tulving (1984) as support for the episodic–semantic distinction obtained dissociations between performance levels on episodic and semantic tasks. In the first study, an alcohol study (Hashtroudi *et al.*, 1984), there were two episodic tasks, recall and recognition, and the semantic task was fragment completion. Recall was degraded for intoxicated subjects relative to normal subjects, but fragment completion was not different for the two groups. This would be evidence for the episodic–semantic distinction, except that recognition performance (as measured by d') was also not different for the two groups. Thus, by the logic of dissociation, it would be just as reasonable to argue for the existence of two episodic systems as for separate episodic and semantic systems (see Roediger, 1984, for a similar argument).

In the second study cited by Tulving (1984), level of blood alcohol affected recognition performance but not performance on word fragment completion (Parker *et al.*, 1983). But, in state-dependent research, changing a subject's brain state with moderate doses of a drug often does *not* affect recognition (Eich, 1980), and so, without a detailed explanation of the differences between the Parker *et al.* and other studies, this dissociation is not convincing as evidence for the episodic–semantic distinction.

Blood flow and evoked potential studies

Wood *et al.* (1980) have shown that patterns of regional cerebral blood flow, an index of neural activity, differ for a recognition task and a semantic classification task. Tulving (1983) has noted the caveats offered by Wood *et al.*, for example, that the two tasks differ on many other dimensions such as difficulty, but still has added the blood flow study to his list of evidence (Tulving, 1984). Baddeley (1984) has further criticized the use of this study as a way of separating episodic and semantic memory by noting that it is possible that any two tasks will differ in blood flow patterns and by posing this question: Would one assume different physical systems for each task?

Clearly what is needed is a systematic study of the blood flow method before it can be taken as evidence for the episodic–semantic distinction. It seems that this is not likely because of the cost of such methods, so we can only take this study as intriguing rather than as strong evidence for a separation of systems.

In like manner, Tulving (1984) cites a statement by Sanquist *et al.* (1980) that suggests that the late positive component of the evoked potential is much different in a recognition task than in a judgment task. The conclusion that Sandquist *et al.* draw is that the late positive component indexes processes associated with stimulus recognition. However, we make the same argument as for the blood flow study and that is that much more work needs to be done before this finding can be used as evidence for an episodic–semantic distinction. For example, if the late positive component only indexed recognition and not recall, there would be no evidence for the episodic–semantic distinction. However, if a range of semantic and episodic tasks of varying degrees of difficulty produced a systematic difference in the late positive component as a function of episodic versus semantic task, this would provide quite strong evidence for a separation of systems.

Amnesia

Results from studies of amnesia seem to hold an important place in the debate about episodic and semantic memory. Tulving has provided a wide range of evidence (1983; see also Schacter and Tulving, 1982) from amnesia studies to support the episodic–semantic distinction, all of which takes the form of finding dissociations such that amnesia affects episodic memory but not semantic memory. However, there are a number of other positions held by students of amnesia. The most popular position at present is that what is spared in amnesia is procedural memory; so, for example, normal performance by amnesics on word fragment completion, perceptual identification, motor tasks such as mirror image tracing and pursuit rotor, jigsaw puzzles, the tower of Hanoi problem, mirror reading, and long-term facilitation in lexical decision are all attributed to an intact procedural system (e.g., Baddeley, 1984; Cohen, 1983; Graf *et al.*, 1984; Moscovitch, 1982).

In a related but slightly different theoretical characterization of the amnesic syndrome, Warrington and Weiskrantz (1982) attribute the amnesic deficit to the disconnection of a 'dynamic cognitive mediational memory system' (responsible for the manipulation, interrelation, and storage of information) from the semantic system. They distinguish this view from a strict episodic–semantic view because of experimental findings that amnesic subjects show some retention in paired associate learning, especially for highly associated pairs such as *milk–cow* or *walk–run* and for pairs made up of rhyming words. The fact that amnesics show paired-associate learning that is little different from normal performance under some conditions and the fact that performance is sometimes improved when pre-existing knowledge is involved lead to the rejection of a strict episodic–semantic interpretation.

The view of Warrington and Weiskrantz (1982) is quite similar to Wickelgren's (1979) more detailed theory of chunking and consolidation. Wickelgren proposes that chunking (or forming new nodes) is the critical process involved in cognitive learning and that amnesia results from damage to the system (the hippocampal-limbic arousal system) that allows the formation of new nodes. Although the details of the theory are quite different from those proposed by Warrington and Weiskrantz (1982), there is a marked similarity between the two in terms of a global explanation of the deficit.

One critical set of investigations concerns the ability of amnesics to access semantic and episodic information learned prior to their becoming amnesic. Tulving argues that only prior episodic memories have been lost. Cermak and O'Connor (1983) have presented the case of one subject (S. S.) who seems to show an absence of any preamnesic episodic memory. The subject, an expert on lasers, shows excellent semantic knowledge (he is able to read technical reports on new laser research and explain them as he reads), but he is unable to retain the new knowledge. More importantly for the present discussion, Cermak and O'Connor argue that the subject shows no episodic memory for personal events prior to the onset of amnesia. Although the subject is able to produce much information about his childhood and young adult life, he seems unable to focus on individual specific episodes in which he participated, and so Cermak and O'Connor seem to argue that the anecdotes are actually part of semantic memory and that the subject has lost the episodic system. In contrast to Cermak and O'Connor's findings with this subject, both Baddeley and Wilson (1983) and Zola-Morgan *et al.* (1983) have found amnesics' memories for preamnesia personal events to be unimpaired, despite their difficulties with postamnesia memories.

Another case of amnesia that seems to show a loss of episodic memory for events prior to amnesia has been reported by Schacter and Tulving (1982). Although semantic knowledge was intact, this patient appeared to have completely lost all his memory for personal events, including his name, home, occupation, and family except for a very few islands of childhood memory. However, there is an inconsistency in interpretation of the syndromes displayed by this patient and the patient reported by Cermak and O'Connor (1983) as evidence for the episodic–semantic distinction. Cermak and O'Connor's patient showed considerable memory for episodic events that were termed as 'equivalent to one's being able to recount a family story more because it had become family folklore than because it was truly remembered.' If such memories are to be classified as semantic, as Cermak and O'Connor classified them, then the patient studied by Schacter and Tulving, who had lost all personal memories, had lost these kinds of semantic memories and would no longer show a strict episodic–semantic dissociation. On the other hand, if it were assumed that what Schacter and Tulving's patient had lost was episodic memory and not semantic memory, then Cermak and O'Connor's patient could not be said to have lost all of the episodic memory but only selective aspects of episodic memory.

Although much of the research on amnesia seems to have important implications for the episodic–semantic distinction, at a detailed level, the picture can be complicated. In general, Tulving has used results from the study of amnesia like those mentioned above to support the case for a distinction between episodic and semantic memory systems. But we agree with Baddeley (1984) that this interpretaion appears to represent a minority view and that the distinction that seems to have garnered most support is a procedural/declarative distinction (which Tulving also accepts). Although we would not go as far as Crowder (1982) and claim that we have learned nothing about normal functioning from the study of amnesia, we do have some sympathy for Crowder's view that analyses of amnesia reflect, at a lag, the attitudes currently fashionable toward general forgetting theory.

Tulving's 1984 position: episodic memory embedded within semantic memory

Recently, *The Behavioral and Brain Sciences* published a series of critical reviews of Tulving's 1983 book. Among these were papers that evaluated the episodic–semantic distinction. These critiques were followed by a reply from Tulving in which he acknowledged difficulties with his previous views and, as a result of some of the points made in the critiques as well as changes in his own thinking, suggested a major modification of his position on the episodic–semantic distinction. The new position is that episodic memory is a distinct but interactive subsystem embedded within semantic memory. Although Tulving did not commit himself with complete certainty to this position, it nevertheless deserves attention.

One critical question to ask about the new position is how it differs from the old one. First, Tulving (1984) notes that an embedded episodic system differs from a separate one in that the embedded system would not be able to function independently of the semantic system. Since we had difficulty imagining how an episodic system could function on its own, we find the new position more to our liking on this point. Second, Tulving states that embedding the episodic system in the semantic system allows for the generation of episodic inferences using inferential capacities of semantic memory (see McCauley's, 1984, comments on this point). Again, given our earlier discussion of the need for inferencing with both episodic and semantic information, we prefer the new position. Third, the new view of the distinction focuses, according to Tulving, on episodic memory as a 'higher,' and developmentally and phylogenetically later, subsystem of semantic memory. This is an intriguing possibility. However, evidence for it must await a clearer exposition of how we could tell whether infants and nonhumans possess episodic memory. Fourth, the new position predicts that amnesic syndromes should involve impairment in (a) episodic memory only or (b) episodic and semantic memory, but not (c) semantic memory only. We do think that this prediction is more likely to be confirmed than that from the old view, in which amnesia was predicted to be purely episodic in nature. As discussed earlier, amnesia does seem to involve both semantic and episodic information.

With respect to the problems we have raised with the episodic–semantic distinction, we can see many problems that the new version of the distinction does not address. First, all of the criticisms of Tulving's use of experimental results to support the distinction still seem to apply because the distinction still does not provide a procedure for predicting under what conditions a dissociation should occur. Experimental results that show particular dissociations can still be countered with other results that do not show those dissociations. Second, although the content features of episodic memory are less problematic because an embedded episodic system could more easily be understood to contain semantic information and allow inferencing, the features of processing still raise difficulties. For example, is the organization of episodic information temporal, as Tulving (1983) originally claimed, or can it be semantic? Can access to episodic memory, originally said to be strategic, now be automatic? Are retrieval processes for episodic and semantic information the same or different? In general, what does it mean for episodic memory to be embedded in semantic memory?

One way in which Tulving (1984) attempts to answer this question is with an analogy to the visual system. Although some aspects of the structure of the visual system support the idea that Tulving seems to have in mind, there are a number of subsystems that range from having different kinds of information carried by the same neural pathways (motion vs form: Lennie, 1980; Van Essen and Maunsell, 1983) to different kinds of information being completely integrated (motor plus visual information: Baker and Berthold, 1977). Thus it seems that an appeal to the nature of the visual system allows one the freedom to interpret the episodic and semantic systems in ways that range from highly interactive through to almost independent.

Another way to interpret the embeddedness view is that it is close to a single-store view. We, in fact, see little difference between an interactive embeddedness view and a single-store view. However, we expect that Tulving and other dual-store theorists will disagree and assert that an important distinction is still present in the embeddedness view. The source of this anticipated disagreement would be that Tulving's position has a very high 'albedo.' The theorist can easily see his or her own position reflected when regarding Tulving's. In the absence of an explicit theory of the relation between the encoding, storage, and retrieval of episodic and semantic information, this state of affairs will prevail. In the final section of the article, we elaborate on the need for such a theory.

Discussion

Our criticisms of the episodic–semantic distinction have covered both the features of the distinction and the empirical evidence for it. We find that the features do not separate the two memory systems in a clear, testable fashion. In addition, we have concluded that the experimental and neuropsychological evidence for the distinction is weak. Most of this evidence involves dissociations, and our comments can be summarized by three points regarding Tulving's use of dissociative evidence.

1. For many of the experimental and neuropsychological dissociations cited as support for the distinction, we have pointed to very similar experiments or cases in which no dissociation between episodic and semantic memory was found.
2. In a few cases of dissociation between an episodic and semantic task, we have pointed to related cases in which two episodic tasks dissociated from each other, one behaving exactly like the semantic task.
3. For some of the evidence, we (and others) have suggested that no true dissociation is present, and thus the results are consistent with a single-store view.

In general, the use of dissociation evidence will be problematic as long as the episodic–semantic distinction lacks a set of principles that allow one to decide what evidence does and does not address the distinction. In the absence of these principles to guide the selection of evidence, dissociations can be gleaned from the literature wherever they are found, and cases in which no dissociation or the wrong dissociation is found can be ignored. As Hintzman (1984, p. 241) points out, 'If one wants to claim that a dissociation outcome supports the episodic–semantic distinction, one must show that the dissociation is predicted by theory that embodies the distinction.' We think that a theory could take the form of either an explicit model of memory that encompasses both episodic and semantic information, or, less ambitiously, a framework for organizing independent variables, so that each variable's predicted effect (or lack thereof) on the episodic and semantic systems is derived directly from the features of the distinction. At present this is not the case. For example, what feature of the distinction leads to Shoben *et al.*'s (1978) fan effect in an episodic task, but not in a semantic task? Along with this framework, it would be important to specify the relative contributions of the episodic, semantic, and other systems to particular experimental tasks. For example, what system is primarily involved in fragment completion? In the absence of a specific theory, we see no way in which the status of the episodic–semantic distinction can be clarified.

At this point, it may be worth considering whether the current situation in memory research is such that the episodic–semantic distinction is theoretically useful even though problematic. For example, it might be that there is no other theory that is not equally problematic. Although it is not within the scope of this article to provide an alternative, we should point out that there does exist one alternative theory that is well developed and accounts for a number of phenomena with a unified semantic–episodic store, and that is Anderson's (1983) ACT theory. As mentioned above, ACT accounts for the results of Shoben *et al.* (1978), Anderson and Ross (1980), and the experiments showing activation of semantic information in episodic tasks and the automatic activation of episodic information. ACT could as well explain much of the amnesia data, because declarative (propositional) knowledge is treated differently from procedural knowledge. For the separate episodic–semantic view to provide an equally useful theoretical framework, it would need to be much more specific. Although it would not have to be at the level of specificity of ACT, it would at least have to provide a description at the level of the qualitative aspects of Atkinson and Shiffrin's (1968) model of long- and short-term memory. Atkinson and Shiffrin's model (as well as others) encompassed both short- and long-term processes, and the features that separated the stores were closely tied to experimental variables. For example, it was agreed that differences in coding between the stores (phonemic vs semantic) could be tested by varying the semantic and (or) phonological similarity of the words to be remembered.

To conclude, we do not think that more progress will be made toward an understanding of memory for semantic and episodic information until more theoretical work is done. The episodic–semantic distinction is an interesting idea that has had much heuristic value for interpreting and generating data over the past 14 years. Now it needs theoretical development.

References

Anderson, J. R. (1983). *The architecture of cognition*. Cambridge, MA: Harvard University Press.

Anderson, J. R. and Ross, B. H. (1980). Evidence against a semantic–episodic distinction. *Journal of Experimental Psychology: Human Learning and Memory*, *6*, 441–465.

Atkinson, R. C. and Juola, J. F. (1973). Factors influencing speed and accuracy of word recognition. In S. Kornblum (Ed.), *Attention and performance* (Vol. 6, pp. 583–612). New York: Academic Press.

Atkinson, R. C. and Shiffrin, R. M. (1968). Human memory: A proposed system and its control processes. In K. W. Spence and J. T. Spence (Eds.), *The psychology of learning and motivation* (Vol. 2, pp. 89–105). New York: Academic Press.

Baddeley, A. D. (1984). Neuropsychological evidence and the semantic/episodic distinction. Commentary on Tulving, E., Précis of *Elements of episodic memory*. *Behavioral and Brain Sciences*, *7*, 238–239.

Baddeley, A., and Wilson, B. (1983). *Differences among amnesia and between amnesics: The role of single case methodology in theoretical analysis and practical treatment*. Paper presented at Princeton Symposium on Amnesia, Princeton, NJ.

Baker, R., and Berthold, A. L. (1977). *The control of gaze by brain stem neurons*. New York: Elsevier.

Cermak, L. S. and O'Connor, M. (1983). The anterograde and retrograde retrieval ability of a patient with amnesia due to encephalitis. *Neuropychologia*, *21*, 213–234.

Cohen, N. J. (1983). Preserved learning capacity in amnesia: Evidence for multiple memory systems. In N. Butters and L. Squire (Eds.), *The neuropsychology of memory* (pp. 83–103). New York: Guilford Press.

Collins, A. M., and Loftus, E. F. (1975). A spreading-activation theory of semantic processing. *Psychological Review*, *82*, 407–428.

Craik, F. I. M., and Lockhart, R. S. (1972). Levels of processing: A framework for memory research. *Journal of Verbal Learning and Verbal Behavior*, *11*, 671–684.

Crowder, R. G. (1982). General forgetting theory and the locus of amnesia. In L. S. Cermak, (Ed.), *Human memory and amnesia*. (pp. 33–42). Hillsdale, NJ: Erlbaum.

Dosher, B. A. (1984). Discriminating pre-experimental (semantic) from learned (episodic) associations: A speed-accuracy study. *Cognitive Psychology*, *16*, 519–555.

Durgunoglu, A. Y. and Neely, J. H. (1987). On obtaining episodic priming in a lexical decision task following paired associate learning. *Journal of Experimental Psychology: Learning, Memory, and Cognition, 13,* 206–222.

Eich, J. E. (1980). The cue-dependent nature of state-dependent retrieval. *Memory & Cognition, 8,* 157–173.

Graf, P., Squire, L. R., and Mandler, G. (1984). The information that amnesic patients do not forget. *Journal of Experimental Psychology: Learning, Memory, and Cognition, 10,* 164–178.

Graham, K. R., and Patton, A. (1968). Retroactive inhibition, hypnosis, and hypnotic amnesia. *International Journal of Clinical Experimental Hypnosis, 16,* 68–74.

Hashtroudi, S., Parker, E. S., Delisi, L. E., and Wyatt, R. J. (1984). Intact retention in acute alcohol amnesia. *Journal of Experimental Psychology: Learning, Memory, and Cognition, 10,* 156–163.

Herrmann, D. J. (1982). The semantic–episodic distinction and the history of long-term memory typologies. *Bulletin of the Psychonomic Society, 20,* 207–210.

Herrmann, D. J., and Harwood, J. R. (1980). More evidence for the existence of separate semantic and episodic stores in long-term memory. *Journal of Experimental Psychology: Human Learning and Memory, 6,* 467–478.

Hintzman, D. L. (1984). Episodic versus semantic memory: A distinction whose time has come – and gone? Commentary on Tulving, E., Précis of *Elements of episodic memory. Behavioral and Brain Sciences, 7,* 240–241.

Jacoby, L. L., and Dallas, M. (1981). On the relationship between autobiographical memory and perceptual learning. *Journal of Experimental Psychology: General, 3,* 306–340.

Jacoby, L. L., and Witherspoon, D. (1982). Remembering without awareness. *Canadian Journal of Psychology, 36,* 300–324.

Kihlstrom, J. F. (1980). Posthypnotic amnesia for recently learned material: Interactions with 'episodic' and 'semantic' memory. *Cognitive Psychology, 12,* 227–251.

Lennie, P. (1980). Parallel visual pathways: A review. *Vision Research, 20,* 561–594.

Lewis, C., and Anderson, J. (1976). Interference with real-world knowledge. *Cognitive Psychology, 8,* 311–335.

Marslen-Wilson, W. D., and Teuber, H. L. (1975). Memory for remote events in anterograde amnesia: Recognition of public figures from newsphotographs. *Neuropsychologia, 13,* 353–364.

McCauley, R. N. (1984). Inference and temporal coding in episodic memory. Commentary on Tulving, E., Précis of *Elements of episodic memory. Behavioral and Brain Sciences, 7,* 246–247.

McCloskey, M., and Glucksberg, S. (1979). Decision processes in verifying category membership statements: Implications for models of semantic memory. *Cognitive Psychology, 11,* 1–37.

McCloskey, M., and Santee, J. (1981). Are semantic memory and episodic memory distinct systems? *Journal of Experimental Psychology: Human Learning and Memory, 7,* 66–71.

McKoon, G., and Ratcliff, R. (1979). Priming in episodic and semantic memory. *Journal of Verbal Learning and Verbal Behavior, 18,* 463–480.

McKoon, G., and Ratcliff, R. (1980a). The comprehension processes and memory structures involved in anaphoric reference. *Journal of Verbal Learning and Verbal Behavior, 19,* 668–682.

McKoon, G., and Ratcliff, R. (1980b). Priming in item recognition: The organization of propositions in memory for text. *Journal of Verbal Learning and Verbal Behavior, 1,* 369–386.

McKoon, G., and Ratcliff, R. (1986). Automatic activation of episodic information in a semantic memory task. *Journal of Experimental Psychology: Learning, Memory, and Cognition, 12,* 108–115.

McKoon, G., Ratcliff, R., and Dell, G. S. (1985). The role of semantic information in episodic retrieval. *Journal of Experimental Psychology: Learning, Memory, and Cognition, 11,* 742–751.

Meyer, D. E. (1970). On the representation and retrieval of stored semantic information. *Cognitive Psychology, 1,* 242–299.

Morton, J., and Bekerian, D. A. (1984). The episodic/semantic distinction: Something worth arguing about. Commentary on Tulving, E., Précis of *Elements of episodic memory: Behavioral and Brain Sciences, 7,* 247–248.

Moscovitch, M. (1982). Multiple dissociations of function in amnesia. In L. S. Cermak (Ed.), *Human memory and amnesia* (pp. 337–70). Hillsdale, NJ: Erlbaum.

Muter, P. (1978). Recognition failure of recallable words in semantic memory. *Memory & Cognition, 6,* 9–12.

Neely, J. H., and Durgunoglu, A. (1985). Dissociative episodic and semantic priming effects in episodic and semantic memory. *Journal of Memory and Language, 24,* 466–489.

Neely, J. H., and Payne, D. G. (1983). A direct comparison of recognition failure rates for recallable names in episodic and semantic memory tests. *Memory & Cognition, 11,* 161–171.

Neely, J. H., Schmidt, S. R., and Roediger, H. L. (1983). Inhibition from related primes in recognition memory. *Journal of Experimental Psychology: Learning, Memory, and Cognition, 9,* 196–211.

Parker, E. S., Schoenberg, R., Schwartz, B. S, and Tulving, E. (1983). Memories on the rising and falling blood alcohol curve. *Bulletin of the Psychonomic Society, 21,* 363.

Peterson, S. B., and Potts, G. R. (1982). Global and specific components of information integration. *Journal of Verbal Learning and Verbal Behavior, 21,* 403–420.

Pike, R., Dalgleish, L., and Wright, J. (1977). A multiple-observations model for response latency and the latencies of correct and incorrect responses in recognition memory. *Memory & Cognition, 5,* 580–589.

Posner, M. I. (1978). *Chronometric exploration of mind.* Hillsdale, NJ: Erlbaum.

Posner, M. I., and Snyder, C. R. (1975). Attention and cognitive control. In R. L. Solso (Ed.), *Information processing and cognition* (pp. 55–85). Hillsdale, NJ: Erlbaum.

Ratcliff, R. (1978). A theory of memory retrieval. *Psychological Review, 85,* 59–108.

Ratcliff, R., and McKoon, G. (1978). Priming in item recognition: Evidence for the propositional structure of sentences. *Journal of Verbal Learning and Verbal Behavior, 17,* 403–417.

Ratcliff, R., and McKoon, G. (1981a). Automatic and strategic priming in recognition. *Journal of Verbal Learning and Verbal Behavior, 20,* 204–215.

Ratcliff, R., and McKoon, G. (1981b). Does activation really spread? *Psychological Review, 88,* 454–462.

Ratcliff, R., and McKoon, G. (1982). Speed and accuracy in the processing of false statements about semantic memory. *Journal of Experimental Psychology: Learning, Memory, and Cognition, 8,* 16–36.

Roediger, H. L. (1984). Does current evidence from dissociation experiments favor the episodic/semantic distinction? Commentary on Tulving, E., Précis of *Elements of episodic memory. Behavioral and Brain Sciences, 7,* 252–254.

Sanquist, T. F., Rohrbaugh, J. W., Syndulko, K., and Lindsley, D. B. (1980). Electrocortical signs of levels of processing: Perceptual analysis and recognition memory. *Psychophysiology, 17,* 568–576.

Schacter, D., and Tulving E. (1982). Memory, amnesia, and the episodic/semantic distinction. In R. L. Isaacson and N. E. Spear (Eds.), *Expression of knowledge* (pp. 33–65). New York: Plenum Press.

Shoben, E. J., Wescourt, K. T., and Smith, E. E. (1978). Sentence verification, sentence recognition, and the semantic–episodic distinction. *Journal of Experimental Psychology: Human Learning and Memory*, *4*, 304–317.

Smith, E. E., Shoben, E. J., and Rips. L. J. (1974). Structure and process in semantic memory: A featural model for semantic decisions. *Psychological Review*, *81*, 214–241.

Sternberg, S. (1969). Memory-scanning: Mental processes revealed by reaction-time experiments. *American Scientist*, *57*, 421–457.

Tanenhaus, M. K., Leiman, J. M., and Seidenberg, M. S. (1979). Evidence for multiple stages in the processing of ambiguous words in syntactic contexts. *Journal of Verbal Learning and Verbal Behavior*, *18*, 427–440.

Tulving, E. (1972). Episodic and semantic memory. In E. Tulving and W. Donaldson (Eds.), *Organization of memory* (pp. 381–403). New York: Academic Press.

Tulving, E. (1983). *Elements of episodic memory*. New York: Oxford University Press.

Tulving, E. (1984). Précis of *Elements of episodic memory*. *Behavioral and Brain Sciences*, *7*, 223–268.

Tulving, E., and Bower, G. H. (1974). The logic of memory representations. In G. H. Bower (Ed.), *The psychology of learning and motivation* (Vol. 8., pp. 265–301). New York: Academic Press.

Tulving, E., and Gold, C. (1963). Stimulus information and contextual information as determinants of tachistoscopic recognition of words. *Journal of Experimental Psychology*, *66*, 319–327.

Tulving, E., Schacter, D. L., and Stark, H. A. (1982). Priming effects in word-fragment completion are independent of recognition memory. *Journal of Experimental Psychology: Learning, Memory, and Cognition*, *8*, 336–341.

Tulving, E., and Wiseman, S. (1975). Relation between recognition and recognition failure of recallable words. *Bulletin of the Psychonomic Society*, *6*, 79–82.

Underwood, B. J., Boruch, R. F., and Malmi, R. A. (1978). Composition of episodic memory. *Journal of Experimental Psychology: General*, *107*, 393–419.

Van Essen, D. C. and Maunsell, J. H. R. (1983). Hierarchical organization and functional streams in the visual cortex. *Trends in Neuroscience*, *6*, 370–375.

Warrington, E. K., and Weiskrantz, L. (1982). Amnesia: A disconnection syndrome? *Neuropsychologia*, *20*, 233–248.

Wickelgren, W. A. (1979). Chunking and consolidation: A theoretical synthesis of semantic networks, configuring in conditioning, S–R cognitive learning, normal forgetting, the amnesic syndrome, and the hippocampal arousal system. *Psychological Review*, *86*, 44–60.

Winograd, T. (1972). *Understanding natural language*. New York: Academic Press.

Wood, F., Taylor, B., Penny, R., and Stump, D. (1980). Regional cerebral blood flow response to recognition memory versus semantic classification tasks. *Brain and Language*, *9*, 113–122.

Zola-Morgan, S., Cohen, N. J., and Squire, L. R. (1983). Recall of remote-episodic memory in amnesia. *Neuropsychologia*, *21*, 487–500.

10 Teresa A. Blaxton

'Investigating Dissociations among Memory Measures:
Support for a Transfer-Appropriate Processing Framework'

Reprinted in full from: *Journal of Experimental Psychology:
Learning, Memory, and Cognition* **15**, 657–668 (1989)

Recently many researchers have investigated findings in which performance on one memory measure is uncorrelated, or dissociated, from performance on one or more other memory tests. For example, subjects can show evidence of learning from prior experience on some measure such as savings or repetition priming even though the demonstration of that learning is not accompanied by the conscious recollection of the original learning episode (e.g., Jacoby and Witherspoon, 1982). Investigation of these dissociations is important both for purposes of predicting patterns of performance on specific memory tests and for understanding memory function in general.

The current interest in dissociations among memory measures has its origins in experiments performed with amnesic subjects. As an illustration, consider results reported by Warrington and Weiskrantz in 1970 (Experiment 2). They presented amnesic and matched control subjects with a list of five-letter words three times prior to testing them on one of several types of memory tasks. These tasks included standard measures of free recall and yes/no recognition, and a task in which subjects identified words when given word fragments in which each individual letter had been visually degraded. Results showed that although recall and recognition performance for amnesics was inferior to that of controls, amnesics did show evidence of learning in that the two groups were equally likely to identify previously studied items when given word fragments. That is, amnesics' performance on fragment identification was dissociated from that on the recall and recognition tests. Similar findings have been reported elsewhere with amnesic subjects (see Shimamura, 1986, for a review).

Perhaps what makes these dissociations so interesting is that they are often observed in studies testing normal subjects (see Richardson-Klavehn and Bjork, 1988, and Schacter, 1987, for extensive reviews). Some of the most compelling evidence for dissociations among memory measures was reported by Jacoby (1983). During an initial phase of experimentation, subjects either read or generated a target word in one of three conditions (Experiments 1 through 3). In a no-context condition, subjects saw a neutral stimulus (XXX) followed by a target (*cold*) which they read aloud. In a context condition a target was read aloud but was preceded by an antonym (hot–*cold*). Finally, subjects in a generate condition produced a target from an antonym cue (hot–???). Following this initial phase, subjects were given either a recognition or perceptual identification test in which the task was to say words aloud following very brief (35-ms) presentations. Priming was evidenced in perceptual identification when studied words were more likely to be identified than nonstudied words.

The results obtained for recognition performance replicated the generation effect reported by Slamecka and Graf (1978) in that generated items were better recognized. In addition, recognition performance in the context condition was superior to that in the no-context condition but worse than that in the generate condition. Performance on the perceptual identification test, on the other hand, actually showed a reversal of this trend. The probability of identification for items in the no-context condition was higher than that in the context condition, which, in turn, was superior to performance in the generate condition. Thus, the dissociation between perceptual identification and recognition was so strong as to result in a complete reversal of the generation effect in perceptual identification.

Theoretical accounts

There have been two families of theoretical accounts offered to explain dissociations such as those obtained by Jacoby (1983). The first of these is based on distinctions between memory tasks, namely that some tasks require recollecton of the original learning episode for their completion, whereas others do not. Tulving (1972) adopted the terms *episodic* and *semantic* to distinguish between the memory tasks typically used in experimental settings. A task is said to tap the episodic system if its completion requires the recollection of a particular event with its temporal–spatial relations to other episodes. In contrast, semantic memory tasks rely on world knowledge rather than the retrieval of specific episodes.

A dichotomy similar to the episodic–semantic memory distinction is the classification of tasks as being either explicit or implicit (e.g., Graf and Schacter, 1985). A memory test such as recognition or recall is said to be explicit in that the subject explicitly thinks back to the study episode in order to perform the task. In contrast, tasks such as word fragment completion and perceptual identification may be thought of as implicit because they are performed without any explicit reference to prior study.

At times, the episodic–semantic and implicit–explicit distinctions have been discussed as if they reflect more than just differences in characteristics among memory tasks. In the case of the episodic–semantic distinction, differences obtained in performance of these tasks have been interpreted as evidence that they actually tap different underlying memory systems (e.g., Tulving, 1983, 1985, 1986). Taking Jacoby's (1983) results as an example, the differential effects of generating versus reading items on semantic (implicit) perceptual identification and episodic (explicit) recognition performance are explained in terms of the tasks tapping separate memory systems.

A second theoretical account of dissociations among memory measures focuses less on the memory tasks themselves than on the match in mental operations performed at study and test. The premise is that memory performance will be improved to the degree that the types of operations performed at study overlap with those required at test. This principle has been referred to as *transfer-appropriate processing* (e.g., Morris *et al.*, 1977), encoding specificity (e.g., Tulving and Thomson, 1973), and most simply as a processing account (e.g., Roediger and Blaxton, 1987b; Roediger *et al.*, 1989).

As an illustration of how the processing account may be used to explain dissociations, consider again the study conditions in Jacoby's (1983) experiments. In all cases the subject produced a target word (e.g., *cold*), but the way in which this was achieved varied across conditions. In the no-context condition the subject simply read the target aloud from analysis of its physical features in the absence of any semantic cues that might prime its representation in memory. Jacoby referred to this type of processing as 'data driven' because subjects relied on processing of the physical features of the presented stimulus in order to say the target aloud.

In contrast, when instructed to produce the antonym of the cue *hot* in the generate condition, the subject could not say *cold* by analyzing the physical stimulus itself because cold was not even presented. Instead, the subject had to use the antonym cue to retrieve the target *cold* from memory. Thus Jacoby argued that the processing required in the generate condition was more 'conceptually driven' in that the production of *cold* was driven by processing of the related concept *hot* by the rule to produce opposites. Processing in the context condition was thought to involve a combination of both data-driven and conceptually driven processing.

With regard to the memory tests, Jacoby suggested that perceptual identification of isolated words was primarily a data-driven task. Items were presented very briefly in the absence of any semantic cues, and subjects had to rely on the analysis of physical features of the words in order to identify them at time of test. In contrast, processing on the recognition test was said to be more conceptually driven in that subjects could rely on analysis of meaning in order to make familiarity decisions.

Levels of performance on Jacoby's (1983) memory tests as a function of study condition were governed by the transfer-appropriate processing account. That is, performance on the data-driven perceptual identification test was best in the no-context condition because subjects did more data-driven processing in the no-context condition at study than in the other conditions. Analyzing the physical features of items at study transferred well to a test requiring similar analysis. Likewise, performance levels on the recognition test reflected the fact that having to produce items in the generate condition required a preponderance of conceptually driven processing at input.

Logic of the present experiments

From the foregoing discussion it is clear that a clean comparison is needed between the memory systems account and transfer-appropriate processing as explanations for dissociations among memory measures. This has not been possible so far because no one has employed an experimental design that uses the right combination of memory tasks. Experiments demonstrating dissociations have compared one explicit task with one implicit task, one episodic task with one semantic task, or one data-driven task with one conceptually driven task, depending upon one's choice of terms. In these cases the type of task (episodic/explicit vs semantic/implicit) was perfectly confounded with the type of processing the task requires (data-driven vs conceptually driven). In almost every case, an episodic conceptually driven task such as recognition or recall has been compared with a semantic data-driven test such as word completion or perceptual identification (e.g., Graf and Mandler, 1984; Jacoby and Dallas, 1981).

In order to correct this confounding, one needs an experimental design that simultaneously investigates the effects of study variables on at least four types of memory tasks: episodic data-driven, episodic conceptually driven, semantic data-driven, and semantic conceptually driven. If data from all four types of tests are compared in a single experiment, a judgment can be rendered as to which distinction is more important in determining memory performance. That is, one may classify memory tests according to memory system and type of processing required, introduce a study manipulation, and then see which theory best accounts for the pattern of results obtained. If dissociation patterns are divided according to memory system, that approach will be favored. On the other hand, if dissociations occur between data-driven and conceptually driven tasks, a processing account will be supported.

In order to implement this design it was necessary to adopt procedures for assigning tests to the categories just described. Tasks whose completion requires recollection of the original study episode can be designated as episodic (or explicit), whereas tasks which can be performed on the basis of general knowledge without reference to any specific time and place may be classified as semantic (or implicit). The method employed for classifying tasks as being either data driven or conceptually driven draws on the procedures introduced by Jacoby (1983). The effects of Jacoby's (1983) study conditions (which were replicated as nearly as possible) were compared on several memory tests in Experiment 1. To anticipate, any test showing better performance in the no-context (or read) condition that in the generate condition was operationally defined as being data driven, whereas any test showing better performance in the generate than in the no-context condition was classified as being conceptually driven. Note that no claim is being made that these tasks are *completely* data driven or conceptually driven. Rather, tasks are thought of as involving a preponderance of one type of processing or the other. Converging validation for these classifications was obtained in Experiments 2 and 3 with different study manipulations.

Experiment 1

As previously stated, the purpose of the present series of experiments was to separate the effects of the memory system tapped by a test from effects produced by the type of processing required by that test. As may be seen in Figure 10.1, several tests were assigned to each of the four cells in this matrix for Experiment 1. One of these was a semantic test in which subjects answered general knowledge questions. It was thought that this test would primarily involve conceptually driven processing in that the semantic information provided in the question itself would prime the answer in memory. On the other hand, it is doubtful that any data-driven analysis of the physical features of the question could aid in producing the desired response.

A semantic memory test of word fragment completion such as the one used by Tulving *et al.* (1982) was also employed.[1] Previous findings by Roediger and Blaxton (1987a) have shown that this task is sensitive to such manipulations as the match between typography and modality of target items between study and test. Fragment completion performance is greatest in these cases when the physical features of the stimulus encountered during study are preserved at time of test. On the basis of these findings, it was believed that word fragment completion involves data-driven processing. Thus, both the general knowledge and the fragment completion tests were classified as semantic memory tasks because both could be performed without reference to the original study episode, but they were thought to differ in the types of processing they required.

With regard to the left hand side of the matrix presented in Figure 10.1, three tests of episodic memory were used. One of these was a standard free recall test. Because no data at all are presented on free recall tests, it was reasoned that any responses produced must derive from conceptually driven processing. A second test was semantic cued recall, in which subjects were presented with words that were semantically related (but not physically similar) to studied items. Because the cue words were similar in meaning to target items, this task was expected to be conceptually driven.

A third episodic graphemic cued recall test was employed in which subjects were given cue words that were physically, but not semantically, similar to studied items (e.g., *eager* as a cue for eagle). To use the cues for recall effectively, subjects were assumed to focus on the physical attributes of the

		Memory system	
		Episodic	Semantic
Type of processing	Data-driven	Graphemic cued recall	Word fragment completion
	Conceptually driven	Free recall Semantic cued recall	General knowledge

Figure 10.1 Design of Experiment 1, including the types of memory tasks employed.

cues and to ignore their semantic content. For this reason, the graphemic cued recall test was included as a candidate for the data-driven episodic memory cell. Thus, the free recall, semantic cued recall, and graphemic cued recall tests were thought to differ in terms of the types of processing they required, even though they were all episodic memory tasks.

Method

Subjects. The subjects were 60 Purdue University undergraduates who participated in the experiment in partial fulfillment of an introductory psychology course requirement.

Memory tests and study materials. The first of the five memory tasks was a general knowledge test in which students answered questions such as 'What was the name of Armstrong and Aldrin's lunar module?' (answer *Eagle*). The second was a word fragment completion test in which subjects filled in the missing letters of fragments to form complete words (e.g., E — G — E for *eagle*). Also included was a standard free recall test in which subjects wrote down any words they could remember from the study phase in any order they chose. On two cued recall tests subjects were given a list of words and told to use them as cues to help them remember previously studied items. Subjects taking the semantic cued recall test were told that the cues were related in meaning to studied items (e.g., *falcon* was a cue for *eagle*). In contrast subjects taking the graphemic cued recall test were told that the cues were similar in physical appearance but not in meaning to studied items (e.g., *eager* was presented as a cue for *eagle*).

A set of 126 words was assembled for use as stimulus materials in the experiment. For each of these items a general knowledge question, word fragment, semantic cue, and graphemic cue were created so that the same items were tested on all five memory tests. Norming procedures carried out before the experiment showed that the average nonstudied completion rate for fragments and general knowledge questions was 25%, thus ensuring that priming effects as a result of previous study could be easily detected.

Items to be presented as cues on the cued recall test were pretested for their effectiveness by having subjects search through two separate lists containing targets and cues and match them either for semantic or graphemic similarity. An item was chosen as a cue for a target word if pretesting showed a 90% or better agreement rate among subjects from this matching exercise. A sample list of stimulus materials along with their word fragments, general knowledge questions, semantic cues, and graphemic cues appears in Table 10.1.

Design and counterbalancing. The 126 items were arbitrarily divided into two base lists of 63 words each. Each subject saw one of these base lists during study, and the remaining base list words appeared as nonstudied items on the memory tests. (Of course, no items were presented at time of test for free recall.)

Subjects studied items in three conditions before taking a memory test. In the no-context condition, items were preceded by the neutral stimulus *XXX*. In the context condition, target words were preceded by semantically related primes (e.g., *hawk* before *eagle*). Finally, in the generate condition subjects generated target items when given a semantically related word and single letter cue (e.g., *hawk–e:* for *eagle*). (Note that these conditions differ slightly from those used by Jacoby, 1983, in that he used antonym cues in the context and generate conditions and did not supply the initial letter of the target word in the generate condition.) Each subject was given only one

Table 10.1 Sample study and test items used in the present experiments

Target	Word fragment	Graphemic cue	Semantic cue	General knowledge question
bashful	B_SH_U_	bushel	timid	Which of the seven dwarfs comes first alphabetically?
cheetah	_H__T_H	cheetohs	jaguar	What is the fastest animal on earth?
cologne	C___GN_	colony	fragrance	What German city is famous for the scent it produces?
computer	C__PU___	commuter	processor	What is a Univac 1?
copper	C_PP__	chopper	bronze	What metal makes up 10% of yellow gold?
freckle	F_EC__E	fickle	birthmark	What appears when the sun activates your melanocytes?
metropolis	M_T___OL_S	acropolis	township	In what fictional city did Clarke Kent and Lois Lane live?
plague	P__GU_	vague	epidemic	What disease was called the 'Black Death'?
treason	_RE__ON	treasure	disloyalty	For what crime were the Rosenbergs executed?
universe	__IV__SE	unversed	cosmos	What was the Big Bang said to have created?

type of memory test, and 12 subjects were tested on each different memory test. Study condition was manipulated within subjects, whereas type of test was a between-subjects factor

Each base list was divided into three subgroups of 21 items, and each subject studied one of these subgroups in each of the three input conditions. Items were always studied in the same order, and order of study conditions was counterbalanced in blocks in such a way that across subjects each condition appeared in each study list position equally often. Order of presentation of subgroups of items studied first was always the subgroup to be tested first, and so on. However, the actual ordering of items within a given subgroup was different at study and test. New items on a test were taken from the corresponding subgroups of the nonstudied base list so that all subjects in a particular memory test group received the same test regardless of which base list they had studied earlier. The only difference was that the studied target items for half of the subjects were the nonstudied items for the remaining subjects and vice versa.

The construction of the cued recall tests was slightly different from that just described. As was true for the fragment completion and general knowledge tasks, half of the cues on the graphemic and semantic cued recall tests corresponded to nonstudied items. In addition, half of the target items were cued with the 'wrong' type of cue. Taking the graphemic cued recall test as an example, half of the studied items were indeed cued with graphemically similar items, but half were cued with words that were semantically related to studied targets. Subjects in the graphemic cued recall group were nevertheless instructed that the cues were similar to studied items only in terms of physical features and that any apparent similarities in meaning were to be ignored. This construction allowed the same study lists and tests to be administered to all subjects in the graphemic and semantic cued recall groups, with the only difference between tests being the instructions (cf. Neely and Payne, 1983). Two forms of each test were constructed in such a way that an item cued with a semantic cue on one test was cued with a graphemically similar item on the other. Across subjects all items were cued equally often with graphemic and semantic cues.

Procedure. Subjects were tested individually. They were told that they would study a series of words and that they would later receive a memory test, although the nature of the test was not specified. Prior to studying items in the no-context condition, subjects were informed that they would be seeing alternating slides of *XXX*s and words, with the words to be read aloud. Before viewing the context condition, subjects were told that they would read a word silently before reading each related (target) word aloud. Finally, for the generate condition, subjects were instructed to read the context word silently and then produce a related word beginning with the initial letter provided on the next (target) slide. Subjects were given examples of study pairs in each of these conditions prior to study.

Slides were presented for 5 s each. There was a short (30-s) pause between blocks of items as the experimenter changed the slide tray and read the instructions for the next study condition to the subject. The task in the generate study condition was somewhat difficult in that subjects failed to produce targets on roughly 10% of the trials. When a subject was unable to produce the intended target word, the experimenter said the target aloud at the end of the 5-s interval.

Upon completion of the study phase, each subject was given a memory test. In the general knowledge group, the experimenter read questions aloud to each subject, and the subject recorded his or her answer on a test sheet. Subjects were told that the answer to a question would never be included in the wording of that question. Subjects were given 20 s to answer each question before going to the next item. In the word fragment completion task, subjects were given test sheets containing word fragments and were again given a maximum of 20 s to solve each item. Subjects used a cover sheet so as to avoid looking ahead to new items and were instructed not to go back to an item once it had been passed. Subjects in both the general knowledge and word fragment groups were given practice with three nonstudied items on the tasks before the test.

In the free recall group, subjects were given a blank sheet of paper and told to write any words they could remember reading aloud during the first part of the experiment. The free recall test lasted 10 min. Subjects in both cued recall groups were told to use the words presented on their test sheets as cues to help them remember studied items. The nature of the relation between the cues and targets was explained, and examples were given prior to testing. Subjects were also informed that some of the items on a given test sheet would not be similar to any items they had studied and that they were free to make guesses if they were unsure of an answer. Cued recall subjects paced themselves through the test, with the restriction that they not spend more than 20 s on any given item.[2] This entire procedure lasted 25 min for the free recall group and 1 hour for all other groups.

Results and discussion

Proportion correct as a function of type of task and study condition are presented in Table 10.2. The results obtained for the different memory tests fell into two distinct groupings. The free recall, general knowledge, and semantic cued recall tests showed the typical generation effect with better performance in the generate than in the no-context condition. In contrast, the word fragment completion and graphemic cued recall tests showed the opposite pattern of results. Note that the three tests expected to be conceptually driven did indeed show the most benefit from prior conceptually driven processing, whereas the tasks offered as candidates for the data-driven cells

Table 10.2 Proportion correct as a function of study condition and type of test in Experiment 1

Type of test	Study condition			
	Generate	Context	No context	Nonstudied
Conceptually driven				
Free recall	.30	.16	.19	
General knowledge	.50	.38	.33	.25
Semantic cued recall	.67	.46	.51	.04
Data-driven				
Word fragment completion	.46	.62	.75	.27
Graphemic cued recall	.34	.40	.45	.06

were both enhanced more from prior data driven than conceptually driven processing.

Statistical analyses confirmed these general observations. First, an analysis of variance (ANOVA) was performed on the data from each group, assessing the differences among study conditions. Differences between individual cells were examined by using least significant difference (LSD) tests. After this, another ANOVA including data from nonstudied items was then used where appropriate to examine differences between the studied and nonstudied conditions.

Free recall. As may be seen in Table 10.2, free recall subjects recalled more items that had been studied in the generate than in the no-context condition. This observation was supported by the finding of a significant main effect of study manipulation in the free recall group, $F(2, 22) = 8.18$, $MS_e = 0.0834$. (All significance levels are set at $p < .05$). Performance levels were higher in the generate than in either the context or no-context conditions, which did not differ, LSD = .06. Using the rule for classifying memory tasks described above, free recall was operationally defined as being conceptually driven because performance was greater when subjects generated, rather than read, study items.[3]

General knowledge. A similar pattern of results was observed in the general knowledge group. There was a main effect of study manipulation, $F(2, 22) = 5.28$, $MS_e = 0.0185$. With an LSD of .09, performance was better in the generate than in either the context or no-context conditions, which yielded statistically equivalent performance levels. Thus, the general knowledge task was operationally defined as being conceptually driven.

There was also an overall priming effect in the general knowledge group, with subjects answering more questions corresponding to studied than to nonstudied items in all study conditions, $F(3, 33) = 8.99$, $MS_e = 0.0152$, LSD = .08. This finding indicates that the general knowledge test was not insensitive to priming in the no-context and context conditions. Rather, there was just a larger priming effect in the generate condition as compared with these other two conditions.

Semantic cued recall. Although the semantic cues used on the test were pretested for their effectiveness, subjects sometimes recalled a target by using a cue that had originally been intended to cue another item. For instance, the word *retailer* was intended to cue *merchant* but by coincidence was also a good cue for *salesman*. Items were scored as being correctly recalled if they were semantically related to the cue beside which they were written. The results obtained by using this scoring criterion did not differ from those observed by using a 'strict' criterion in which only experimenter-defined cue-target pairings were accepted.

Performance on the semantic cued recall test was much like that observed for the free recall and general knowledge tests. First, performance in the generate condition was better than that observed in either the context or no-context conditions. An ANOVA showed a main effect of study condition, $F(2, 22) = 6.70$, $MS_e = 0.0190$. With an LSD of .09, performance levels in the generate condition were higher than those in the context or no-context conditions, which did not differ. An ANOVA including data from nonstudied items showed that performance in all study conditions was far superior to that obtained for nonstudied items, $F(3, 33) = 57.73$, $MS_e = 0.0137$, LSD = .08, showing that guessing played only a very minor role in performance levels. The findings for semantic cued recall were thus similar to those of free recall and general knowledge in that better memory performance was obtained for those items that were generated rather than read at study. Given these results, the semantic cued recall test was operationally defined as being a conceptually driven memory test.

Word fragment completion. The reader will see in Table 10.2 that the generation effect obtained in the first three tests was reversed on the fragment completion test. Word fragment completion was operationally defined as a data-driven task because subjects were better able to complete fragments for items that had been studied in the no-context than in the generate condition. This observation was supported by an ANOVA showing a main effect of study condition, $F(2, 22) = 24.26$, $MS_e = 0.0010$. Performance in the no-context condition was superior to that in the context condition, which, in turn, was better than that observed in the generate condition (LSD = .07). Also of interest was the finding that completion performance for studied items was superior to that for nonstudied items regardless of study condition. An ANOVA including data from nonstudied items showed that this priming effect was indeed reliable, $F(3, 33) = 56.00$, $MS_e = 0.0093$, LSD = .07.

Graphemic cued recall. As with the semantic cued recall test, it happened that some of the graphemic cues turned out to be useful for items other than those for which they were originally intended. For example, *volume* sometimes cued the response *valium* on the test although it was originally matched to the target *vacuum*. Items were thus judged to be correctly recalled when they matched with a pretested cue or when they had at least 50% of their letters in common with the cue word. In such cases *valium* would be scored as being correctly recalled because the cue word *volume* has 4/6 (i.e., more than 50%) of *valium*'s letters. The findings obtained by using this scoring criterion did not differ qualitatively from those observed using a 'strict' criterion in which only experimenter-defined correspondences between cues and targets were accepted.

An ANOVA showed a main effect of study condition, $F(2, 22) = 5.81$, $MS_e = 0.0061$. With an LSD of .06, levels of performance in the no-context and context conditions exceeded that in the generate condition, although these two conditions did not differ statistically from each other. Of further interest was the fact that superior recall was obtained in all study conditions relative to nonstudied items $F(3, 33) = 54.91$, $MS_e = 0.0099$, LSD = .07. This pattern of results parallels that obtained for word fragment completion and suggests that graphemic cued recall involves data-driven processing.

These results clearly show that distinguishing among memory systems is not a useful index in accounting for the dissociations obtained in Experiment 1. For instance, although two episodic tasks – free recall and cued recall with semantic cues – did show the same pattern of results, performance on the graphemic cued recall test showed exactly the opposite pattern. Likewise, the results observed for the two semantic tasks of general knowledge and word fragment completion were dissociated from one another.

Whereas a memory systems approach was not effective in accounting for the data presented in Table 10.2, a transfer-appropriate processing account shows more promise. The two tests proposed as candidates for the data-driven cells in Figure 10.1 did indeed show larger priming effects for items studied under conditions requiring data-driven processing. The *a priori* intuitions guiding the selection of conceptually driven tasks proved to be sound as well. However, converging evidence for the validity of these assignments of memory tasks to processing categories is needed before the processing account may be invoked to explain the present results. The purpose of Experiment 2 was to marshall this converging evidence by using a different study manipulation.

Experiment 2

It has been known for some years that modality of presentation can affect memory in immediate recall paradigms. This modality effect is characterized by a recall advantage for auditory compared with visual presentation for the last few items in the learning list (see Crowder, 1976). With regard to paradigms in which memory tests are delayed, however, the conventional wisdom has been that study modality generally produces either very small effects or no effects at all on memory (but see Gardiner and Gregg, 1979). To illustrate, modality of presentation has been shown to produce no effects in standard free recall experiments in which visually and auditorily presented items are recalled with equal likelihood (e.g., Graf *et al.*, 1985).

In contrast to the failure to find substantial modality effects in explicit memory paradigms, experiments employing other dependent measures have shown that modality can be an important factor in memory performance. For instance, Nelson and McEvoy (1979) had subjects study four-letter words presented either auditorily or visually before taking one of two types of visually cued recall tests. The first of these involved the presentation of an item's semantic category label as a cue for recall (e.g., *coin* as a cue for *dime*). In the second, subjects were cued with the last three letters of the studied items (e.g., *ime* as a cue for *dime*). The results of interest showed that performance on the category label test was unaffected by the modality manipulation. However, subjects were more likely to recall words given their last three letters if the words had been studied visually rather than auditorily. That is, performance on the three-letter cued recall test (which is rather similar to the graphemic cued recall test used in the present experiments) was best when the physical features of the test stimuli were presented in the same modality as study, whereas the other episodic recall test was unaffected by this manipulation. These results suggest that tasks requiring extensive processing of physical features, as opposed to semantic information, are sensitive to changes in modality between study and test.

In a similar vein, Roediger and Blaxton (1987a) had subjects study words presented either visually or auditorily before taking a fragment completion test. Test items were always presented visually, and it was found that fragment completion performance was enhanced for visually, as compared with auditorily, studied items. Analogous effects have been observed for perceptual identification (e.g., Clarke and Morton, 1983; Jacoby and Dallas, 1981; Kirsner *et al.*, 1983), lexical decision tasks (e.g., Kirsner *et al.*, 1983; Kirsner and Smith, 1974), and word stem completion tasks (Graf *et al.*, 1985).

Both the memory systems and the processing accounts offer explanations for these findings. If tasks are sorted by memory system, it would appear that episodic tasks such as recall and recognition are not as sensitive to changes in modality between study and test as are semantic memory tasks like word fragment completion. On the other hand, the processing account predicts that changes in modality between study and test will affect data-driven, but not conceptually driven, test performance. Experiment 2 provided a test of these two accounts.

Method

   Subjects. Sixty-eight subjects participated in the experiment in partial fulfillment of an introductory course requirement.
   Design and procedure. The materials and tests were the same as those employed in Experiment 1. Two extra study items were added so that a total of 128 items were used. Sixty-four items were presented to each subject for study, half in the auditory and half in the visual modality. Items were blocked by condition and always presented in the same order, with order of study condition counterbalanced across subjects. Each subject saw all 128 items at test, half studied and half nonstudied (except on the free recall test, where no items were presented). Study condition was manipulated within subjects, whereas type of test was a between-subjects factor.
   Subjects were tested individually. In the visual modality condition, subjects silently read words one at a time as they appeared on slides. In the auditory condition, subjects listened on a prerecorded tape in which words were read aloud in a female voice. All items were presented at a rate of 5 s each. Twelve subjects were assigned to each of the free recall, general knowledge, and word fragment completion groups, and 16 subjects were tested in the semantic and graphemic cued recall test groups. All other aspects of the procedure were the same as in Experiment 1.

Results and discussion

Conceptually driven memory tasks. As may be seen in the top portion of Table 10.3, none of the conceptually driven memory tests were affected by the manipulation of study modality. An ANOVA for the free recall data showed no effect of study manipulation, $F(1, 11) < 1$. The same was true for data from the general knowledge and semantic cued recall groups (both $Fs < 1$). An analysis for the general knowledge group, including data from the nonstudied conditions, was significant, $F(2, 22) = 10.63$, $MS_e = 0.0065$, indicating priming for both auditorily and visually studied items as compared with nonstudied items. With an LSD of .05, it was found that subjects were more likely to answer a general knowledge question if the answer had been presented during study than if it had not. A similar result was obtained for the semantic cued recall data, $F(2, 30) = 41.51$, $MS_e = 0.014$, LSD = .07.

Data driven memory tests. Although no effects of study modality were observed for the conceptually driven memory tests, this manipulation did affect data-driven test performance. An ANOVA including data from the studied conditions in the word fragment completion group showed a significant effect of study modality, $F(1, 11) = 8.22$, $MS_e = 0.0069$, with more fragments completed from the visual than from the auditory study condition. The same pattern was observed for graphemic cued recall, $F(1, 15) = 6.37$, $MS_e = 0.0292$. Significant priming effects of studied compared with nonstudied test conditions were obtained in addition to these effects of study modality. An ANOVA for the word fragment group, including data from the nonstudied test items, showed that fragments corresponding to studied items were more likely to be completed than those for nonstudied words, $F(2, 22) = 39.13$, $MS_e = 0.0073$. With an LSD of .06, both the auditory and visual study conditions showed higher performance levels than did the nonstudied condition. Again, an analogous result was observed for graphemic cued recall performance, $F(2, 30) = 33.92$, $MS_e = 0.0202$, LSD = .08. Thus, although performance on conceptually driven tests was unaffected by the modality manipulation, data-driven test performance was highest when items were both studied and tested in the same (visual) modality.

The findings obtained in Experiment 2 are not readily handled by a memory

Table 10.3 Proportion correct as a function of study condition and type of test in Experiment 2

Type of test	Study condition		
	Auditory	Visual	Nonstudied
Conceptually driven			
Free recall	.26	.22	
General knowledge	.38	.37	.24
Semantic cued recall	.35	.36	.03
Data-driven			
Word fragment completion	.40	.50	.20
Graphemic cued recall	.31	.46	.05

systems approach. Although dissociations were indeed obtained between episodic and semantic tasks, there were dissociations within a single memory system as well. For instance, the modality manipulation failed to affect either episodic free recall or semantic cued recall but did affect the episodic task of graphemic cued recall. Similarly, match between study and test modality enhanced semantic word fragment completion performance but produced no effect on the semantic test of general knowledge performance. There seems to be limited utility, then, in drawing distinctions between memory systems that tests might tap in explaining these dissociations.

On the other hand, a transfer-appropriate processing account provides a good framework for interpreting these data. First, note that these findings offer converging evidence that the memory tasks are validly assigned to data-driven and conceptually driven categories. As was expected, data-driven, but not conceptually driven, task performance was affected by the manipulation of presentation modality between study and test. That is, fragment completion and graphemic cued recall performance were both enhanced when the physical features of test items most closely matched those encountered during study, indicating that these tasks require data-driven processing. In contrast, a match in modality between study and test did not enhance general knowledge or semantic cued recall performance, presumably because those tasks rely more on analysis of meaning than physical attributes of stimulus material. Thus the assignment of tasks into data-driven and conceptually driven categories held up under a set of study manipulations other than those used in Experiment 1, and the pattern of results again indicates that dissociations occurred between tasks requiring different types of processing. Dissociations among memory tasks were examined further in Experiment 3 with a different set of study manipulations.

Experiment 3

One of the variables manipulated in Experiment 3 was match in typography between study and test. Prior demonstrations indicate that some tasks such as word fragment completion (e.g., Gardiner, 1988; Roediger and Blaxton, 1987a), tachistoscopic recognition (Clarke and Morton, 1983; Jacoby and Hayman, 1987), and recognition of typography as well as semantic content (e.g., Kolers and Ostry, 1974) are sensitive to this manipulation.

The transfer-appropriate processing framework predicts that data-driven fragment completion and graphemic cued recall performance should be enhanced when items are both studied and tested in the same typography because the instantiation of processes used to analyze physical features of stimuli overlaps on those two occasions. On the other hand, the data-driven processing engaged in at test is different from that done at study when typography is not held constant, thus reducing the benefit of prior study. Because conceptually driven tasks are not affected by analysis of physical features, this manipulation should not affect semantic cued recall or general knowledge performance.

Unlike the processing account, the memory systems approach does not make any specific predictions about the direction of effects produced by the typography manipulation. Instead, the distinction simply predicts that tasks within a memory system will be affected in the same manner by a given variable. That is, episodic free recall, semantic cued recall, and graphemic cued recall performance should show similar patterns of results. Likewise, the semantic fragment completion and general knowlege tasks should be affected in the same way by the experimental variables.

In addition to the typography factor, the design of Experiment 3 included a very different manipulation: namely that of imagery instructions given at study. Much research has shown that memory on such tasks as free recall, cued recall with semantic cues, and recognition is enhanced when subjects are instructed to form images of item referents during study. It is not known how fragment completion, graphemic cued recall, or the general knowledge task will be affected by this manipulation.

According to the transfer-appropriate processing account, forming an image of an item's referent is a conceptually driven process that should enhance performance of tasks such as free recall, semantic cued recall, and general knowledge. The formation of images does not aid in the processing of physical features of the stimulus word itself, however, and so is not predicted to differentially affect data-driven task performance (see Durgunoglu and Roediger, 1987). As with the typography manipulation, the memory systems approach makes the simple prediction that tasks within a given memory system should be similarly affected by instructions to form images during study. Because it is already known that free recall and semantic cued recall are enhanced by instructions to form images, one should expect that graphemic cued recall will show this same effect. The direction of the effect of this manipulation on semantic tasks of fragment completion and general knowledge, however, remains unspecified.

Method

Subjects. One hundred and twelve Purdue undergraduates were tested in the experiment in partial fulfillment of an introductory course requirement. Sixteen subjects were tested on each of the free recall, general knowledge, and fragment completion tasks, whereas thirty-two subjects were assigned to each of the semantic and graphemic cued recall groups.

Design and procedure. Materials and counterbalancing procedures were the same as those used in previous experiments. Each subject studied one base list of 64 items before receiving one of the five memory tests. Items were presented in four blocks of 16 items each. Two of these blocks were studied with instructions to form mental images of the items' referents, whereas two were presented with no special study instruction. Crossed with this was a factor of typography whereby half of the words were presented in lowercase italic type, and the other half were shown in uppercase elite typography. This manipulation was realized at test by a variation in the typography of printed questions on the general knowledge test, cued words on the two cued recall tests, and fragments on the word fragment completion task. Half of the studied items were tested in the typography in which they had been studied, and half in the other typography. Two forms of each test (except free recall) were constructed in such a way that an item presented in uppercase elite typography on one form of the test was presented in lowercase italic on the other form.

Subjects were tested in groups of four or fewer. In all conditions, subjects read words silently as they were presented singly on slides for 5 s each. Prior to the imagery blocks, subjects were told to form images of each item's referent as it was presented. For the no-imagery instruction blocks, subjects were told that they should simply pay attention and not form images. Within each of these blocks, subjects were instructed that half of the items would be presented in uppercase elite typeface, whereas half would be in lowercase italic. Following study, each subject received one of the five memory tests and was given instructions identical to those used in the previous experiments.

Results and discussion

Conceptually driven memory tests. Results for the general knowledge, semantic cued recall, and free recall tests are presented in Table 10.4. ANOVAS including data from nonstudied items revealed that priming was obtained in all conditions for studied as compared with nonstudied items both for the general knowledge task, $F(2, 15) = 25.41$, $MS_e = 0.0114$, LSD = .06, and the semantic cued recall test, $F(2, 31) = 42.72$, $MS_e = 0.0187$, LSD = .05. Main effects of imagery instruction reflected the fact that priming was greater in the imagery than in the no-imagery conditions for general knowledge, $F(1, 15) = 14.35$, $MS_e = 0.0286$; semantic cued recall, $F(1, 31) = 21.46$, $MS_e = 0.0321$; and free recall, $F(1, 15) = 20.07$, $MS_e = 0.0184$. This result replicates imagery

Table 10.4 Performance as a function of study instruction, study typography, and test typography for conceptually driven memory tasks in Experiment 3

Typography at study and test	Study instruction		Nonstudied	
	Imagery	No imagery	TT	PL
	Free recall			
E	.31	.16		
I	.29	.14		
	General knowledge			
EE	.48	.34		
II	.48	.34	E	.25
EI	.50	.38	I	.25
IE	.50	.41		
	Semantic cued recall			
EE	.31	.15		
II	.22	.18	E	.05
EI	.28	.15	I	.06
IE	.25	.17		

Note: The first letter in each entry indicates either uppercase elite (E) or lowercase italic (I) typography at study, whereas the second indicates the test typography. Thus, in the EE condition, for example, items were both studied and tested in uppercase elite typeface. TT = test typography; PL = performance level.

effects reported elsewhere for what now may be thought of as conceptually driven memory tasks (e.g., Yuille, 1983).

The match in typeface between study items and test questions failed to produce any effects, however. There was no main effect of test typography for free recall, $F(1, 15) = 1.58$, $MS_e = 0.0111$, general knowledge, or semantic cued recall, (both $Fs < 1$). Similarly, no main effects were observed for typography of studied items either for general knowledge ($F < 1$) or for semantic cued recall, $F(1, 31) = 1.26$, $MS_e = 0.0186$. Likewise, there were no interactions between study and test typography on either of these tests. Thus, there was no hint that performance on the conceptually driven tasks was affected by the typography in which either study or test cues were presented.

Data-driven memory tests. Results obtained in the word fragment completion and graphemic cued recall tasks are presented in Table 10.5. An ANOVA performed on the data from the word fragment completion test revealed that priming was obtained in all studied conditions relative to nonstudied conditions, $F(2, 15) = 26.83$, $MS_e = 0.0266$, LSD = .06. The same was true for graphemic cued recall, $F(2, 31) = 42.64$, $MS_e = 0.0151$, LSD = .07. No main effects of imagery instruction were observed for either word fragment completion ($F < 1$) or graphemic cued recall, $F(1, 31) = 2.39$, $MS_e = 0.0450$. Nevertheless, there were reliable Imagery × Test Typography × Study Typography interactions in both groups, $F(1, 15) = 6.87$, $MS_e = 0.0225$, for fragment completion and $F(1, 31) = 6.67$, $MS_e = 0.0348$, for graphemic cued recall. These interactions were due to the fact that performance rates were lower in the no-imagery conditions in which typographies mismatched than in any of the other conditions (which did not differ among themselves).

Put another way, it may be seen in Table 10.5 that the formation of images

Table 10.5 Performance as a function of study instruction, study typography, and test typography for data-driven memory tasks in Experiment 3

| Typography at study and test | Study instruction | | Nonstudied | |
	Imagery	No imagery	TT	PL
	Word fragment completion			
EE	.56	.60		
II	.60	.62	E	.27
EI	.60	.49	I	.26
IE	.59	.49		
	Graphemic cued recall			
EE	.25	.30		
II	.27	.26	E	.05
EI	.26	.17	I	.05
IE	.28	.17		

Note: The first letter in each entry indicates either uppercase elite (E) or lowercase italic (I) typography at study, whereas the second indicates the test typography. Thus, in the EE condition, for example, items were both studied and tested in uppercase elite typeface. *TT* = test typography; *PL* = performance level.

during study did aid performance relative to conditions in which no images were formed, but only when the typography of the test cues did not match those presented during study. Indeed, with an LSD of .09 for fragment completion and .08 for graphemic cued recall, performance in both the EE and II conditions exceeded that of the EI and IE cells[4] in the no-imagery conditions, even though no differences were obtained among any of the other conditions.

The memory systems approach does little to aid in the interpretation of the findings obtained in Experiment 3. As in the previous experiments, the problem is that dissociations were obtained within, as well as between, memory systems. For example, the typography manipulation affected episodic graphemic cued recall but not the other two episodic tasks. In addition, the imagery manipulation greatly enhanced general knowlege but did not produce a main effect in word fragment completion believed to tap the same (semantic) memory system. Taken together with findings of Experiments 1 and 2, these results suggest that invoking a classification of memory systems does not satisfactorily account for dissociations among memory measures.

The analysis of these data in terms of a transfer-appropriate processing framework is more promising. The processing account accurately predicted the following findings: (a) performance on conceptually driven memory tasks was enhanced in the imagery compared with the no-imagery conditions; (b) conceptually driven task performance was unaffected by the typography manipulation; and (c) data-driven task performance was enhanced under conditions in which study and typography matched relative to conditions in which study and test cues were presented in different typefaces.

The one surprising result in Experiment 3 was the Imagery × Study × Test Typography interaction obtained in the data-driven memory tests. That is, in conditions where the typefaces of cues were different at study and test, performance was higher in the imagery than in the no-imagery conditions. This suggests that, depending upon the experimental conditions, both fragment completion and graphemic cued recall may be aided by either data-driven or conceptually driven processing during study. Performance levels in the imagery conditions were fairly constant across typography manipulations for both tasks. Within the no-imagery conditions where typography matched between study and test, performance levels were as high as in the imagery conditions. In the no-imagery conditions where typographies mismatched, subjects could rely neither on prior elaborative processing nor on appropriate data-driven processing. Thus, performance levels were substantially lower in those conditions than in any others.

Perhaps the most important aspect of the interactions just described is that they refine one's thinking about the processing account. Specifically, these results suggest that the distinction between data-driven and conceptually driven memory tasks does not represent a dichotomy, but rather characterizes two endpoints of a continuum. That is, a memory test which relies predominantly on data-driven processing could have some conceptually driven components as well, and vice versa. To take an intuitively appealing example, consider results obtained with recognition tests. Although Jacoby's (1983) results suggest that recognition is conceptually driven, findings reported elsewhere (e.g., Masson, 1984) indicate that it is sensitive to analysis of physical features of study and test cues. For this reason recognition might be thought of as lying more toward the center of the data-driven/conceptually driven continuum than out on the conceptually driven endpoint (see Johnston *et al.*, 1985; Mandler, 1980).

Indeed, the findings of all of the experiments reported in this article support this assertion to some extent in that priming was obtained in all studied as compared with nonstudied conditions. For instance, recall that data-driven test performance was better when subjects had previously read targets in the absence of context rather than generating them in Experiment 1. Nevertheless, prior generation did produce priming relative to nonstudied conditions on the data-driven tests. If it were truly the case that there was no transfer from the conceptually driven processing done in generation to performance of the data-driven tests, performance levels in the generate conditions would have been equivalent to that for nonstudied items. Similar arguments for transfer may be made with respect to the results obtained in Experiment 2.

General discussion

As was stated at the outset, a finding of central interest to memory theorists is the fact that performance on different memory measures is sometimes uncorrelated, or dissociated. The present experiments were designed to examine dissociations among five different memory tasks. Across experiments it was shown that study manipulations such as instructions to generate rather than to read target items (Experiment 1) or to form mental images of item referents (Experiment 3) enhanced performance on free recall, semantic cued recall, and general knowledge tasks more than on data-driven tasks. By the same token, analysis of physical features of items in the absence of semantic context (Experiment 1) and the preservation of such physical features as modality (Experiment 2) and typography (Experiment 3) between study and test were beneficial to fragment completion and graphemic cued recall but not to the three conceptually driven tasks.

A transfer-appropriate processing framework accounts for these results in that performance on data-driven tests relying on the analysis of physical features was improved when those features were similar at study and test. On the other hand, conceptually driven tasks benefitted most from elaborative processing of meaning during study. A similar analysis may be applied to other dissociations reported in the memory literature (e.g., Clarke and Morton, 1983; Hashtroudi *et al.*, 1988; Jacoby, 1983; Jacoby and Dallas, 1981; Jacoby and Witherspoon, 1982; Tulving *et al.*, 1982; Winnick and Daniel, 1970).

Unlike the processing approach, the alternative view that dissociations between tasks are attributable to the operation of different memory systems does not fare so well in handling these data. A memory systems account would predict that tasks tapping the same system should generally be affected in a similiar manner by the manipulation of experimental factors. In the past, some of the best arguments for the distinction were based on the fact that independent variables produced differential effects on episodic and semantic memory performance (e.g., Tulving, 1983, Chapter 5; but see Tulving, 1986). This type of account works for experiments in which memory performance on only one episodic and one semantic task is examined and found to be dissociated (e.g., Jacoby and Dallas, 1981, Experiments 1, 2, and 2a). However, in experimental designs such as those employed in the present experiments, where performance on multiple episodic and semantic tasks is compared using the same study manipulations and target items, one is able to observe dissociations between two tasks tapping the same system (see Roediger, 1984). For example, it was shown that episodic performance on free recall and semantic cued recall tests was dissociated from graphemic cued recall performance. Likewise, performance on semantic memory tests of word fragment completion and general knowledge was dissociated as well.

There have been additional reports of similar dissociations between two episodic tasks (e.g., Arbuckle and Katz, 1976; Balota and Neely, 1980; Fisher and Craik, 1977; Stein, 1978) and between two semantic memory tasks (e.g., Balota and Chumbley, 1984). Dissociations between two tasks that tap the same memory system would seem to undermine seriously the utility of the memory systems approach in accounting for dissociations among tasks tapping different systems.

In addition to providing the better fit to data obtained in the present experiments, the transfer-appropriate processing framework embodies other characteristics that make it preferable to the memory systems approach. The process distinction not only accounted for, but actually predicted, precise patterns of results obtained in the present experiments. The power to predict the direction of dissociations among memory measures is a marked advance over the offerings of other accounts which simply predict 'differences' among tasks. Furthermore, the processing approach provides an explanation of why variables produce effects on some tasks and not others, whereas the memory systems account has been found to be lacking in this regard (see McKoon *et al.*, 1986).

Although the transfer-appropriate processing framework is the preferred account for the results obtained in the present studies, it is not without its problems. In a practical sense, there is the difficulty of determining what types of processing are required by the memory tasks in question. In the present experiments, a bootstrapping technique was employed whereby memory tasks were operationally defined as conceptually driven or data driven on the basis of their response to Jacoby's (1983) study manipulations: namely reading versus generating material. Following this initial step, converging evidence for the validity of these classifications was obtained by using manipulations of modality, typography, and imagery instructions. With the exception of the imagery manipulation in Experiment 3, the patterns of results obtained were precisely in line with *a priori* predictions made by the processing account.

Even with these operations, the results from Experiment 3 suggested that some tasks will not always fall cleanly into either the data-driven or conceptually driven categories. That is, word fragment completion and graphemic cued recall behaved like data-driven tests until it was shown that they benefitted from prior conceptually driven processing under some conditions in which no transfer from appropriate data driven processing was possible (i.e., in conditions in which typography was switched between study and test). As was argued in the discussion of Experiment 3, these findings suggest that the conceptually driven/data-driven process distinction might best be viewed as a continuum rather than a dichotomy. That is, although there may be tasks that strictly involve either conceptually or data-driven processing, others may involve a mixture of the two. Such a formulation suggests many possibilities for further investigation. For example, the task of determining where memory tests rank in relation to one another along the continuum is an obvious place to begin. Perhaps more interestingly, one could attempt to manipulate task performance so that it is data driven under some conditions and more conceptually driven under others. Whatever form these future experiments take, it is certain that they will provide useful insights into dissociations among memory measures, thus contributing in important ways to our understanding of memory functions.

Notes

1 Fragment completion was classified as semantic because performance of this task does not depend upon the recollection of a prior learning episode. Some might argue that fragment completion also involves a procedural component. Arguments may be made for and against each of these views, but the fact remains that whether the task is semantic or procedural, it is certainly not episodic.

2 The graphemic cued recall task was a difficult one for some subjects. Even though practice items had been given during the instructions, some subjects in the graphemic cued recall group initially had to be reminded to use the words printed on the test sheet as graphemic, not semantic, cues. Once any initial confusion had been cleared up, however, the subjects proceeded smoothly through the test.

3 The failure to obtain better performance in the context than in the no-context condition in free recall may be attributed to the fact that subjects in the context condition had twice the memory load of those in the no-context condition; that is, they saw twice the number of words at study. Because the same is true for the generate relative to the no-context condition, the finding of superior performance in the generate condition is all the more compelling.

4 EE = studied and tested in uppercase elite; II = studied and tested in lowercase italic; EI = studied in uppercase elite and tested in lowercase italic; IE = studied in lowercase italic and tested in uppercase elite.

References

Arbuckle, T. Y., and Katz, W. A. (1976). Structure of memory traces following semantic and nonsemantic orientation tasks in incidental learning. *Journal of Experimental Psychology: Human Learning and Memory, 2,* 362–369.

Balota, D. A., and Chumbley, J. I. (1984). Are lexical decisions a good measure of lexical access: The role of word frequency in the neglected decision stage? *Journal of Experimental Psychology: Human Perception and Performance, 10,* 340–357.

Balota, D. A., and Neely, J. H. (1980). Test-expectancy and word-frequency effects in recall and recognition. *Journal of Experimental Psychology: Human Learning and Memory, 6,* 576–587.

Clarke, R., and Morton, J. (1983). Cross modality facilitation in tachistoscopic word recognition. *Quarterly Journal of Experimental Psychology, 35A,* 79–96.

Crowder, R. G. (1976). *Principles of learning and memory.* Hillsdale, NJ: Erlbaum.

Durgunoglu, A., and Roediger, H. L. (1987). Test differences in accessing bilingual memory. *Journal of Memory and Language, 26,* 377–391.

Fisher, R. P., and Craik, F. I. M. (1977). The interaction between encoding and retrieval operations in cued recall. *Journal of Experimental Psychology: Human Learning and Memory, 3,* 701–711.

Gardiner, J. M. (1988). Generation and priming effects in word-fragment completion. *Journal of Experimental Psychology: Learning, Memory, and Cognition, 14,* 495–501.

Gardiner, J. M., and Gregg, V. H. (1979). When auditory memory is not overwritten. *Journal of Verbal Learning and Verbal Behavior, 18,* 705–719.

Graf, P., and Mandler, G. (1984). Activation makes words more accessible, but not necessarily more retrievable. *Journal of Verbal Learning and Verbal Behavior, 23,* 553–568.

Graf, P., and Schacter, D. (1985). Implicit and explicit memory for new associations in normal and amnesic subjects. *Journal of Experimental Psychology: Learning, Memory, and Cognition, 11,* 501–518.

Graf, P., Shimamura, A. P., and Squire, L. R. (1985). Priming across modalities and category levels: Extending the domain of preserved function in amnesia. *Journal of Experimental Psychology: Learning, Memory, and Cognition, 11,* 386–396.

Hashtroudi, S., Ferguson, S. A., Rappold, V. A., and Crosniak, L. D. (1988). Data driven and conceptually driven processes in partial word identification and recognition. *Journal of Experimental Psychology: Learning, Memory, and Cogntion, 14,* 749–757.

Jacoby, L. L. (1983). Remembering the data: Analyzing interactive processes in reading. *Journal of Verbal Learning and Verbal Behavior, 22,* 485–508.

Jacoby, L. L., and Dallas, M. (1981). On the relationship between autobiographical memory and perceptual learning. *Journal of Experimental Psychology: General, 3,* 306–340.

Jacoby, L. L., and Hayman, C. A. G. (1987). Specific visual transfer in word identification. *Journal of Experimental Psychology: Learning, Memory, and Cognition, 13,* 456–463.

Jacoby, L. L., and Witherspoon, D. (1982). Remembering without awareness. *Canadian Journal of Psychology, 36,* 300–324.

Johnston, W. H., Dark, V. J., and Jacoby, L. L. (1985). Perceptual fluency and recognition judgments. *Journal of Experimental Psychology: Learning, Memory, and Cognition, 11,* 3–11.

Kirsner, K., Milech, D., and Standen, P. (1983). Common and modality-specific processes in the mental lexicon. *Memory & Cognition, 11,* 621–630.

Kirsner, K., and Smith, M. C. (1974). Modality effects in word identification. *Memory & Cognition, 2,* 637–640.

Kolers, P. A., and Ostry, D. J. (1974). Time course of loss of information regarding pattern analyzing operations. *Journal of Verbal Learning and Verbal Behavior, 13,* 599–612.

Mandler, G. (1980). Recognizing: The judgment of previous occurrence. *Psychological Review, 87,* 252–271.

Masson, M. E. J. (1984). Memory for the surface structure of sentences: Remembering with and without awareness. *Journal of Verbal Learning and Verbal Behavior, 23,* 579–592.

McKoon, G., Ratcliff, R., and Dell, G. S. (1986). A critical evaluation of the semantic–episodic distinction. *Journal of Experimental Psychology: Learning, Memory, and Cognition, 12,* 295–306.

Morris, C. D., Bransford, J. D. and Franks, J. J. (1977). Levels of processing versus transfer appropriate processing. *Journal of Verbal Learning and Verbal Behavior, 16,* 519–533.

Neely, J. H., and Payne, D. G. (1983). A direct comparison of recognition failure rates for recallable names in episodic and semantic memory tests. *Memory & Cognition, 11,* 161–171.

Nelson, D. L., and McEvoy, C. L. (1979). Effects of retention interval and modality on sensory and semantic trace information. *Memory & Cognition, 7,* 257–262.

Richardson-Klavehn, A., and Bjork, R. A. (1988). Measures of memory. *Annual Review of Psychology, 39,* 475–543.

Roediger, H. L. (1984). Does current evidence from dissociation experiments favor the episodic/semantic distinction? *Behavioral and Brain Sciences, 7,* 252–254.

Roediger, H. L., and Blaxton, T. A. (1987a). Effects of varying modality, surface features, and retention interval on priming in word fragment completion. *Memory & Cognition, 15,* 379–388.

Roediger, H. L., and Blaxton, T. A. (1987b). Retrieval modes produce dissociations in memory for surface information. In D. S. Gorfein and R. R. Hoffman (Eds.), *Memory and learning: The Ebbinghaus Centennial Conference* (pp. 349–379). Hillsdale, NJ: Erlbaum.

Roediger, H. L., Weldon, M. S., and Challis, B. A. (1989). Explaining dissociations between implicit and explicit measures of retention: A processing account. In H. L. Roediger III and F. I. M. Craik (Eds.), *Varieties of memory and consciousness: Essays in honor of Endel Tulving* (pp. 3–41). Hillsdale, NJ: Erlbaum.

Schacter, D. L. (1987). Implicit memory: History and current status. *Journal of Experimental Psychology: Learning, Memory, and Cognition, 13,* 501–518.

Shimamura, A. P. (1986). Priming effects in amnesia: Evidence for a dissociable memory function. *Quarterly Journal of Experimental Psychology, 38A,* 619–644.

Slamecka, N. J., and Graf, P. (1978). The generation effect: Delineation of a phenomenon. *Journal of Experimental Psychology: Human Learning and Memory, 4,* 592–604.

Stein, B. S. (1978). Depth of priming re-examined: The effects of precision of encoding and test appropriateness. *Journal of Verbal Learning and Verbal Behavior, 17,* 165–174.

Tulving, E. (1972). Episodic and semantic memory. In E. Tulving and W. Donaldson (Eds.), *Organization of memory* (pp. 381–403). New York: Academic Press.

Tulving, E. (1983). *Elements of episodic memory.* New York: Oxford University Press.

Tulving, E. (1985). How many memory systems are there? *American Psychologist, 40,* 385–398.

Tulving, E. (1986). What kind of a hypothesis is the distinction between episodic and semantic memory? *Journal of Experimental Psychology: Learning, Memory, and Cognition, 12,* 307–311.

Tulving, E., Schacter, D. L., and Stark, H. A. (1982). Priming effects in word-fragment completion are independent of recognition memory. *Journal of Experimental Psychology: Learning, Memory, and Cognition, 8,* 336–342.

Tulving, E., and Thomson, D. M. (1973). Encoding specificity and retrieval processes in episodic memory. *Psychological Review, 80,* 352–373.

Warrington, E. K., and Weiskrantz, L. (1970). Amnesic syndrome: Consolidation or retrieval? *Nature (London), 228,* 628–630.

Winnick, W. A., and Daniel, S. A. (1970). Two kinds of response priming in tachistoscopic recognition. *Journal of Experimental Psychology, 84,* 74–81.

Yuille, J. C. (Ed.) (1983). *Imagery, memory, and cognition: Essays in honor of Allan Paivio.* Hillsdale, NJ: Erlbaum.

SECTION SIX
MODELS OF MEMORY

Editor's introduction

A major advance has been seen in the last few years in the construction of formal models of memory. These are precisely specified models, often running as computer simulations, which attempt to account for memory performance across a range of situations and tasks, and their abilities and weaknesses have provided some important insights into the nature of memory processes. Many of the best-known formal models, such as the Search of Associative Memory model of Gillund and Shiffrin (1984), are largely unconstrained by the known properties of the brain but are instead conceived of as functional models. In contrast, *parallel distributed processing* (or 'connectionist') models, such as the one described by **McClelland** and **Rumelhart** (Chapter 11), are deeply constrained by knowledge of the ways in which information is processed in the brain. Such models store information in a distributed fashion across networks of simple but highly interconnected processing units, with excitation and inhibition passing in parallel along the connections between the units.

These models have dramatically changed the way in which researchers think about memory. For example, the problem of content addressability – the problem of accessing a memory on the basis of part of its content – is dealt with in an extremely elegant and natural way by connectionist models, whereas it poses a significant problem to more traditional symbolic models. A good discussion of the general properties of connectionist representations is provided by van Gelder (1991).

Parallel distributed processing models of memory have not been without their critics, however. Ratcliff (1990), for example, has demonstrated some severe limitations in the recognition memory performance of McClelland and Rumelhart's model, and the problem of 'catastrophic forgetting' has been much explored. This refers to the finding that many connectionist models suffer near-total forgetting of a set of memories when a subsequent set is encoded. A discussion of this problem, together with an exploration of some possible ways of avoiding it, is provided by Lewandowsky (1991), and a more recent connectionist memory model is presented by Chappell and Humphreys (1994).

Non-connectionist models of memory also continue to be studied. The interested reader is referred to specific models described in Hintzman (1986), Lewandowsky and Murdock (1989), Nosofsky (1992), and

Shiffrin and Steyvers (1997). Raaijmakers and Shiffrin (1992) provide an accessible review of the major current models.

References

Chappell, M. and Humphreys, M. S. (1994). An auto-associative neural network for sparse representations: analysis and application to models of recognition and cued recall. *Psychological Review*, 101, 103–28.

Gillund, G. and Shiffrin, R. M. (1984). A retrieval model for both recognition and recall. *Psychological Review*, 91, 1–67.

Hintzman, D. L. (1986). 'Schema abstraction' in a multiple-trace memory model. *Psychological Review*, 93, 411–28.

Lewandowsky, S. (1991). Gradual unlearning and catastrophic interference: a comparison of distributed architectures. In *Relating theory and data: essays on human memory in honor of Bennet B. Murdock* (ed. W. E. Hockley and S. Lewandowsky), pp. 445–76. Erlbaum, Hillsdale, NJ.

Lewandowsky, S. and Murdock, B. B. (1989). Memory for serial order. *Psychological Review*, 96, 25–57.

Nosofsky, R. M. (1992). Exemplar-based approach to relating categorization, identification, and recognition. In *Multidimensional models of perception and cognition* (ed. F. G. Ashby), pp. 363–93. Erlbaum, Hillsdale, NJ.

Raaijmakers, J. G. W. and Shiffrin, R. M. (1992). Models for recall and recognition. *Annual Review of Psychology*, 43, 205–34.

Ratcliff, R. (1990). Connectionist models of recognition memory: constraints imposed by learning and forgetting functions. *Psychological Review*, 97, 285–308.

Shiffrin, R. M. and Steyvers, M. (1997). A model for recognition memory: REM – retrieving efficiently from memory. *Psychonomic Bulletin and Review*, 4, 145–66.

van Gelder, T. (1991). What is the 'D' in 'PDP'? A survey of the concept of distribution. In *Philosophy and connectionist theory* (ed. W. Ramsey, S. P. Stich, and D. E. Rumelhart), pp. 33–59. Erlbaum, Hillsdale, NJ.

11 James L. McClelland and David E. Rumelhart
'Distributed Memory and the Representation of General and Specific Information'

Reprinted in full from: *Journal of Experimental Psychology: General* **114**, 159–188 (1985)

In the late 1960s and early 1970s a number of experimenters, using a variety of different tasks, demonstrated that subjects could learn through experience with exemplars of a category to respond better – more accurately, or more rapidly – to the prototype than to any of the particular exemplars. The seminal demonstration of this basic point comes from the work of Posner and Keele (1968, 1970). Using a categorization task, they found that there were some conditions in which subjects categorized the prototype of a category more accurately than the particular exemplars of the category that they had previously seen. This work, and many other related experiments, supported the development of the view that memory by its basic nature somehow abstracts the central tendency of a set of disparate experiences, and gives relatively little weight to the specific experiences that gave rise to these abstractions.

Recently, however, some have come to question this 'abstractive' point of view, for two reasons. First, specific events and experiences clearly play a prominent role in memory and learning. Experimental demonstrations of the importance of specific stimulus events even in tasks which have been thought to involve abstraction of a concept or rule are now legion. Responses in categorization tasks (Brooks, 1978; Medin and Shaffer, 1978), perceptual identification tasks (Jacoby, 1983a, 1983b; Whittlesea, 1983), and pronunciation tasks (Glushko, 1979) all seem to be quite sensitive to the congruity between particular training stimuli and particular test stimuli, in ways which most abstraction models would not expect.

At the same time, a number of models have been proposed in which behavior which has often been characterized as *rule-based* or *concept-based* is attributed to a process that makes use of stored traces of specific events or specific exemplars of the concepts or rules. According to this class of models, the apparently rule-based or concept-based behavior emerges from what might be called a conspiracy of individual memory traces or from a sampling of one from the set of such traces. Models of this class include the Medin and Shaffer (1978) context model, Hintzman's (1983) multiple trace model, and Whittlesea's (1983) episode model. This trend is also exemplified by our interactive activation model of word perception (McClelland and Rumelhart, 1981; Rumelhart and McClelland, 1981, 1982), and an extension of the interactive activation model to generalization from exemplars (McClelland, 1981).

One feature of some of these exemplar-based models troubles us. Many of them are internally inconsistent with respect to the issue of abstraction. Thus, though our word perception model assumes that linguistic rules emerge from a conspiracy of partial activations of detectors for particular words, thereby eliminating the need for abstraction of rules, the assumption that there is a single detector for each word implicitly assumes that there is an abstraction process that lumps each occurrence of the same word into the same single detector unit. Thus, the model has its abstraction and creates it too, though at slightly different levels.

One logically coherent response to this inconsistency is to simply say that each word or other representational object is itself a conspiracy of the entire ensemble of memory traces of the different individual experiences we have had with that unit. We will call this view the *enumeration of specific experiences* view. It is exemplified most clearly by Jacoby (1983a, 1983b), Hintzman (1983), and Whittlesea (1983).

As the papers just mentioned demonstrate, enumeration of specific experiences can work quite well as an account of quite a number of empirical findings. However, there still seems to be one drawback. Such models seem to require an unlimited amount of storage capacity, as well as mechanisms for searching an almost unlimited mass of data. This is especially true when we consider that the primitives out of which we normally assume one experience is built are themselves abstractions. For example, a word is a sequence of letters, or a sentence is a sequence of words. Are we to believe that all of these abstractions are mere notational conveniences for the theorist, and that every event is stored as an extremely rich (obviously structured) representation of the event, with no abstraction?

In this article, we consider an alternative conceptualization: a distributed, superpositional approach to memory. This view is similar to the separate enumeration of experiences view in some respects, but not in all. On both views, memory consists of traces resulting from specific experiences; and on both views, generalizations emerge from the superposition of these specific memory traces. Our model differs, though, from the enumeration of specific experiences in assuming that the superposition of traces occurs at the time of storage. We do not keep each trace in a separate place, but rather we superimpose them so that what the memory contains is a composite.

Our theme will be to show that distributed models provide a way to resolve the abstraction–representation of specifics dilemma. With a distributed model, the superposition of traces automatically results in abstraction though it can still preserve to some extent the idiosyncrasies of specific events and experiences, or of specific recurring subclasses of events and experiences.

We will begin by introducing a specific version of a distributed model of memory. We will show how it works and describe some of its basic properties. We will show how our model can account for several recent findings (Salasoo *et al.*, 1985; Whittlesea, 1983) on the effects of specific experiences on later performance, and the conditions under which functional equivalents of abstract representations such as prototypes or logogens emerge. The discussion considers generalizations of the approach to the semantic–episodic distinction and the acquisition of linguistic rule systems, and considers reasons for preferring a distributed-superpositional memory over other models.

Previous, related models. Before we get down to work, some important credits are in order. Our distributed model draws heavily from the work of Anderson (e.g., 1977, 1983; Anderson *et al.*, 1977; Knapp and Anderson, 1984) and Hinton (1981a). We have adopted and synthesized what we found to be the most useful aspects of their distinct but related models, preserving (we hope) the basic spirit of both. We view our model as an exemplar of a class of existing models whose exploration Hinton, Anderson, Kohonen (e.g., Kohonen, 1977; Kohonen *et al.*, 1981), and others have pioneered. A useful review of prior work in this area can be obtained from Anderson and Hinton (1981) and other articles in the volume edited by Hinton and Anderson (1981). Some points similar to some of these we will be making have recently been covered in the papers of Murdock (1982) and Eich (1982), though the distributed representations we use are different in important ways from the representations used by these other authors.

Our distributed model is not a complete theory of human information processing and memory. It is a model of the internal structure of some components of information processing, in particular those concerned with the retrieval and use of prior experience. The model does not specify in and of itself how these acts of retrieval and use are planned, sequenced, and organized into coherent patterns of behavior.

A distributed model of memory

General properties

Our model adheres to the following general assumptions, some of which are shared with several other distributed models of processing and memory.

Simple, highly interconnected units. The processing system consists of a collection of simple processing units, each interconnected with many other units. The units take on activation values, and communicate with other units by sending signals modulated by weights associated with the connections between the units. Sometimes, we may think of the units as corresponding to particular representational primitives, but they need not. For example, even what we might consider to be a primitive feature of something, like having a particular color, might be a pattern of activation over a collection of units.

Modular structure. We assume that the units are organized into modules. Each module receives inputs from other modules, the units within the module are richly interconnected with each other, and they send outputs to other modules. Figure 11.1 illustrates the internal structure of a very simple module, and Figure 11.2 illustrates some hypothetical interconnections between a number of modules. Both figures grossly underrepresent our view of the numbers of units per module and the number of modules. We would imagine that there would be thousands to millions of units per module and many hundreds or perhaps many thousands of partially redundant modules in anything close to a complete memory system.

The state of each module represents a synthesis of the states of all of the modules it receives inputs from. Some of the inputs will be from relatively

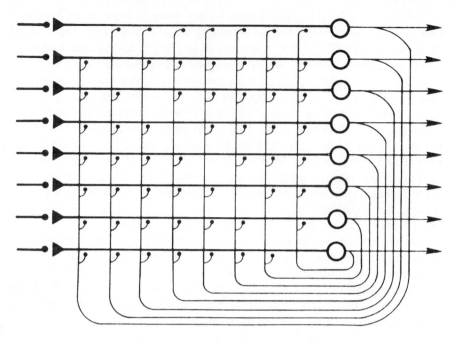

Figure 11.1 A simple information processing module, consisting of a small ensemble of eight processing units. (Each unit receives inputs from other modules [indicated by the single input impinging on the input line of the node from the left; this can stand for a number of converging input signals from several nodes outside the module] and sends outputs to other modules [indicated by the output line proceeding to the right from each unit]. Each unit also has a modifiable connection to all the other units in the same module, as indicated by the branches of the output lines that loop back onto the input lines leading into each unit. All connections, which may be positive or negative, are represented by dots.)

more sensory modules, closer to the sensory end-organs of one modality or another. Others will come from relatively more abstract modules, which themselves receive inputs from and send outputs to other modules placed at the abstract end of several different modalities. Thus, each module combines a number of different sources of information.

Mental state as pattern of activation. In a distributed memory system, a mental state is a pattern of activation over the units in some subset of the modules. The patterns in the different modules capture different aspects of the content of the mental states in a partially overlapping fashion. Alternative mental states are simply alternative patterns of activation over the modules. Information processing is the process of evolution in time of mental states.

Units play specific roles within patterns. A pattern of activation only counts as the same as another if the same units are involved. The reason for this is that the knowledge built into the system for recreating the patterns is built into the set of interconnections among the units, as we will explain later. For a pattern to access the right knowledge it must arise on the appropriate

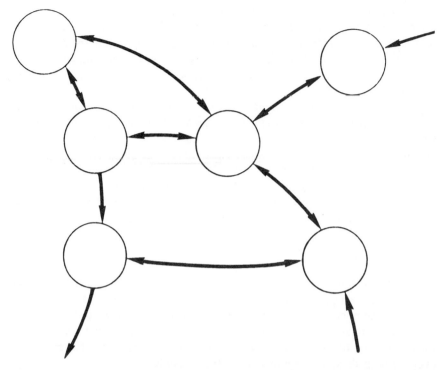

Figure 11.2 Diagram showing several modules and interconnections among them. (Arrows between modules simply indicate that some of the nodes in one module send inputs to some of the nodes in the other. The exact number and organization of modules is, of course, unknown; the figure is simply intended to be suggestive.)

units. In this sense, the units play specific roles in the patterns. Obviously, a system of this sort is useless without sophisticated perceptual processing mechanisms at the interface between memory and the outside world, so that similar input patterns arising at different locations in the world can be mapped into the same set of units internally. Such mechanisms are outside the scope of this article (but see Hinton, 1981b; McClelland, 1985).

Memory traces as changes in the weights. Patterns of activation come and go, leaving traces behind when they have passed. What are the traces? They are changes in the strengths or *weights* of the connections between the units in the modules.

This view of the nature of the memory trace clearly sets these kinds of models apart from traditional models of memory in which some copy of the 'active' pattern is generally thought of as being stored directly. Instead of this, what is actually stored in our model is changes in the connection strengths. These changes are derived from the presented pattern, and are arranged in such a way that, when a part of a known pattern is presented for processing, the interconnection strengths cause the rest of the pattern to be reinstated. Thus, although the memory trace is not a copy of the learned pattern, it is something from which a replica of that pattern can be recreated. As we already said, each memory trace is distributed over many different connections, and each connection participates in many different memory traces. The traces of different mental states are therefore superimposed in the same set of weights. Surprisingly enough, as we will see in several examples, the connections between the units in a single module can store the information needed to complete many different familiar patterns.

Retrieval as reinstatement of prior pattern of activation. Retrieval amounts to partial reinstatement of a mental state, using a cue which is a fragment of the original state. For any given module, we can see the cues as originating from outside of it. Some cues could arise ultimately from sensory input. Others would arise from the results of previous retrieval operations fed back to the memory system under the control of a search or retrieval plan. It would be premature to speculate on how such schemes would be implemented in this kind of a model, but it is clear that they must exist.

Detailed assumptions

In the rest of our presentation, we will be focusing on operations that take place within a single module. This obviously oversimplifies the behavior of a complete memory system because the modules are assumed to be in continuous interaction. The simplification is justified, however, in that it allows us to focus on some of the basic properties of distributed memory that are visible even without these interactions with other modules.

Let us look, therefore, at the internal structure of one very simple module, as shown in Figure 11.1. Again, our image is that in a real system there would be much larger numbers of units. We have restricted our analysis to small numbers simply to illustrate basic principles as clearly as possible; this also helps to keep the running time of simulations in bounds.

Activation values. The units take on activation values which range from −1 to +1. Zero represents in this case a neutral resting value, toward which the activations of the units tend to decay.

Inputs, outputs, and internal connections. Each unit receives input from other modules and sends output to other modules. For the present, we assume that the inputs from other modules occur at connections whose weights are fixed. In the simulations, we treat the input from outside the module as a fixed pattern, ignoring (for simplicity) the fact that the input pattern evolves in time and might be affected by feedback from the module under study. Although the input to each unit might arise from a combination of sources in other modules, we can lump the external input to each unit into a single real valued number representing the combined effects of all components of the external input. In addition to extra-modular connections, each unit is connected to all other units in the module via a weighted connection. The weights on these connections are modifiable, as described later. The weights can take on any real values, positive, negative, or 0. There is no connection from a unit onto itself.

The processing cycle. Processing within a module takes place as follows. Time is divided into discrete ticks. An input pattern is presented at some point in time over some or all of the input lines to the module and is then left on for several ticks, until the pattern of activation it produces settles down and stops changing.

Each tick is divided into two phases. In the first phase, each unit determines its net input, based on the external input to the unit and activations of all the units at the end of the preceding tick modulated by the weight coefficients which determine the strength and direction of each unit's effect on every other.

For mathematical precision, consider two units in our module, and call one of them unit i, and the other unit j. The input to unit i from unit j, written i_{ij} is just

$$i_{ij} = a_j w_{ij},$$

where a_j is the activation of unit j, and w_{ij} is the weight constant modulating the effect of unit j on unit i. The total input to unit i from all other units internal to the module, i_i, is then just the sum of all of these separate inputs:

$$i_i = \sum_j i_{ij}.$$

Here, j ranges over all units in the module other than i. This sum is then added to the *external* input to the unit, arising from outside the module, to obtain the net input to unit i, n_i:

$$n_i = i_i + e_i,$$

where e_i is just the lumped external input to unit i.

In the second phase, the activations of the units are updated. If the net input is positive, the activation of the unit is incremented by an amount proportional to the distance left to the ceiling activation level of $+1.0$. If the net input is negative, the activation is decremented by an amount proportional to the distance left to the floor activation level of -1.0. There is also a decay factor which tends to pull the activation of the unit back toward the resting level of 0.

Mathematically, we can express these assumptions as follows: For unit i, if $n_i > 0$,

$$\dot{a}_i = En_i (1 - a_i) - Da_i.$$

If $n_i \leq 0$,

$$\dot{a}_i = En_i[a_i - (-1)] - Da_i.$$

In these equations, E and D are global parameters which apply to all units, and set the rates of excitation and decay, respectively. The term a_i is the activation of unit i at the end of the previous cycle, and $\dot{a}_i$ is the change in a_i; that is, it is the amount added to (or, if negative, subtracted from) the old value a_i to determine its new value for the next cycle.

Given a fixed set of inputs to a particular unit, its activation level will be driven up or down in response until the activation reaches the point where the incremental effects of the input are balanced by the decay. In practice, of course, the situation is complicated by the fact that as each unit's activation is changing it alters the input to the others. Thus, it is necessary to run the simulation to see how the system will behave for any given set of inputs and any given set of weights. In all the simulations reported here, the model is allowed to run to 50 cycles, which is considerably more than enough for it to achieve a stable pattern of activation over all the units.

Memory traces. The memory trace of a particular pattern of activation is a set of changes in the entire set of weights in the module. We call the whole set of changes an *increment* to the weights. After a stable pattern of activation is achieved, weight adjustment takes place. This is thought of as occurring simultaneously for all of the connections in the module.

The delta rule. The rule that determines the size and direction (up or down) of the change at each connection is the crux of the model. The idea is often difficult to grasp on first reading, but once it is understood it seems very simple, and it directly captures the goal of facilitating the completion of the pattern, given some part of the pattern as a retrieval or completion cue.

To allow each part of a pattern to reconstruct the rest of the pattern, we simply want to set up the internal connections among the units in the module so that when part of the pattern is presented, activating some of the units in the module, the internal connections will lead the active units to tend to reproduce the rest. To do this, we want to make the internal input to each unit have the same effect on the unit that the external input has on the unit. That is, given a particular pattern to be stored, we want to find a set of connections such that the internal input to each unit from all of the other units matches the external input to that unit. The connection change procedure we will describe has the effect of moving the weights of all the connections in the direction of achieving this goal.

The first step in weight adjustment is to see how well the module is already doing. If the network is already matching the external input to each unit with the internal input from the other units, the weights do not need to be changed. To get an index of how well the network is already doing at matching its excitatory input, we assume that each unit i computes the difference Δ_i between its external input and the net internal input to the unit from the other units in the module:

$$\Delta_i = e_i - i_i.$$

In determining the activation value of the unit, we added the external input together with the internal input. Now, in adjusting the weights, we are taking the difference between these two terms. This implies that the unit must be able to aggregate all inputs for purposes of determining its activation, but it must be able to distinguish between external and internal inputs for purposes of adjusting its weights.

Let us consider the term Δ_i for a moment. If it is positive, the internal input is not activating the unit enough to match the external input to the unit. If negative, it is activating the unit too much. If zero, everything is fine and we do not want to change anything. Thus, Δ_i determines the magnitude and direction of the overall change that needs to be made in the internal input to unit i. To achieve this overall effect, the individual weights are then adjusted according to the following formula:

$$\dot{w}_{ij} = S\Delta_i a_j.$$

The parameter S is just a global strength parameter which regulates the overall magnitude of the adjustments of the weights; $\dot{w}_{ij}$ is the change in the weight to i from j.

We call this weight modification rule the *delta rule*. It has all the intended consequences; that is, it tends to drive the weights in the direction of the right values to make the internal inputs to a unit match the external inputs. For example, consider the case in which Δ_i is positive and a_j is positive. In this case, the value of Δ_i tells us that unit i is not receiving enough excitatory input, and the value of a_j tells us that unit j has positive activation. In this case, the delta rule will increase the weight from j to i. The result will be that the next time unit j has a positive activation, its excitatory effect on unit i will be increased, thereby reducing Δ_i.

Similar reasoning applies to cases where Δ_i is negative, a_j is negative, or both are negative. Of course, when either Δ_i or a_j is 0, w_{ij} is not changed. In the first case, there is no error to compensate for; in the second case, a change in the weight will have no effect the next time unit j has the same activation value.

What the delta rule can and cannot do. The delta rule is a continuous variant of the perceptron convergence procedure (Rosenblatt, 1962), and has been independently invented many times (see Sutton and Barto, 1981, for a discussion). Its popularity is based on the fact that it is an error-correcting rule, unlike the Hebb rule used until recently by Anderson (1977; Anderson *et al.*, 1977). A number of interesting theorems have been proven about this rule (Kohonen, 1977; Stone, 1986). Basically, the important rule is that, for a set of patterns which we present repeatedly to a module, if there is a set of weights which will allow the system to reduce Δ to 0 for each unit in each pattern, this rule will find it through repeated exposure to all of the members of the set of patterns.

It is important to note that the existence of a set of weights that will allow Δ to be reduced to 0 is not guaranteed, but depends on the structure inherent in the set of patterns which the model is given to learn. To be perfectly learnable by our model, the patterns must conform to the following *linear predictability constraint:*

Over the entire set of patterns, the external input to each unit must be predictable from a linear combination of the activations of every other unit.

This is an important constraint, for there are many sets of patterns that violate it. However, it is necessary to distinguish between the patterns used inside the model, and the stimulus patterns to which human observers might be exposed in experiments, as described by psychologists. For our model to work, it is important for patterns to be assigned to stimuli in a way that will allow them to be learned.

A crucial issue, then, is the exact manner in which the stimulus patterns are encoded. As a rule of thumb, an encoding which treats each dimension or aspect of a stimulus separately is unlikely to be sufficient; what is required is a *context-sensitive* encoding, such that the representation of each aspect is colored by the other aspects. For a full discussion of this issue, see Hinton *et al.*, 1986).

Decay in the increments to the weights. We assume that each trace or increment undergoes a decay process, though the rate of decay of the increments is assumed to be much slower than the rate of decay of patterns of activation. Following a number of theorists (e.g., Wickelgren, 1979), we imagine that traces at first decay rapidly, but then the remaining portion becomes more and more resistant to further decay. Whether it ever reaches a point where it is no longer decaying at all we do not know. The basic effect of this assumption is that individual inputs exert large short-term effects on the weights, but after they decay the residual effect is considerably smaller. The fact that each increment has its own temporal history increases the complexity of computer simulations enormously. In all of the particular cases to be examined, we will therefore specify simplified assumptions to keep the simulations tractable.

Illustrative examples

In this section, we describe a few illustrative examples to give the reader the feel for how we use the model, and to illustrate key aspects of its behavior.

Storage and retrieval of several patterns in a single memory module. First we consider the storage and retrieval of two patterns in a single module of 8 units. Our basic aim is to show how several distinct patterns of activation can all be stored in the same set of weights, by what Lashley (1950) called a kind of algebraic summation, and not interfere with each other.

Before the first presentation of either pattern, we start out with all the weights set to 0. The first pattern is given at the top of Table 11.1. It is an arrangement of +1 and −1 inputs to the 8 units in the model. (In Table 11.1, the 1s are suppressed in the inputs for clarity.) When we present the first pattern to this module, the resulting activation values simply reflect the effects of the inputs themselves because none of the units are yet influencing any of the others.

Then, we teach the module this pattern by presenting it to the module 10 times. Each time, after the pattern of activation has had plenty of time to settle

Table 11.1 Behavior of an 8-unit distributed memory module

Case	Input or response for each unit							
Pattern 1								
The pattern:	+	−	+	+	−	+	+	−
Response to pattern before learning	+.5	−.5	+.5	+.5	−.5	+.5	+.5	−.5
Response to pattern after 10 learning trials	+.7	−.7	+.7	+.7	−.7	+.7	+.7	−.7
Test input (incomplete version of pattern)	+	−	+	+	−	+		
Response	+.6	−.6	+.6	+.6	−.6	+.6	−.4	−.4
Test input (distortion of pattern)	+	−	+	+	−	+	+*	+*
Response	+.6	−.6	+.6	+.6	−.6	+.6	+.1	+.1
Pattern 2								
The pattern:	+	+	−	−	−	+	+	+
Response to pattern with weights learned for Pattern 1	+.5	+.7	−.5	−.5	−.5	+.5	+.7	+.5
Response to pattern after 10 learning trials	+.7	+.7	−.7	−.7	−.7	+.7	+.7	+.7
Retest of response to Pattern 1	−.7	−.7	+.7	+.7	+.7	+.7	−.7	−.7

down, we adjust the weights. The next time we present the complete pattern after the 10 learning trials, the module's response is enhanced, compared with the earlier situation. That is, the activation values are increased in magnitude, owing to the combined effects of the external and internal inputs to each of the units. If we present an incomplete part of the pattern, the module can complete it; if we distort the pattern, the module tends to drive the activation back in the direction it thinks it ought to have. Of course, the magnitudes of these effects depend on parameters; but the basic nature of the effects is independent of these details.

Figure 11.3 shows the weights our learning procedure has assigned. Actual numerical values have been suppressed to emphasize the basic pattern of excitatory and inhibitory influences. In this example, all the numerical values are identical. The pattern of + and − signs simply gives the pattern of pairwise correlations of the elements. This is as it should be to allow pattern enhancement, completion, and noise elimination. Units which have the same activation in the pattern have positive weights, so that when one is activated it will tend to activate the other, and when one is inhibited it will tend to inhibit the other. Units which have different activations in the pattern have negative weights, so that when one is activated it will inhibit the other and vice versa.

What happens when we present a new pattern, dissimilar to the first? This is illustrated in the lower portion of Table 11.1. At first, the network responds to it just as though it knew nothing at all: the activations simply reflect the direct effects of the input, as they would in a module with all 0 weights. The reason is simply that the effects of the weights already in the network cancel each other out. This is a result of the fact that the two patterns are maximally

Pattern 1

+ − + − + + − −

Pattern 2

+ + − − − + − +

Weights for Pattern 1

	1	2	3	4	5	6	7	8
1		−	+	−	+	+	−	−
2	−		−	+	−	−	+	+
3	+	−		−	+	+	−	−
4	−	+	−		−	−	+	+
5	+	−	+	−		+	−	−
6	+	−	+	−	+		−	−
7	−	+	−	+	−	−		+
8	−	+	−	+	−	−	+	

Weights for Pattern 2

	1	2	3	4	5	6	7	8
1		+	−	−	−	+	−	+
2	+		−	−	−	+	−	+
3	−	−		+	+	−	+	−
4	−	−	+		+	−	+	−
5	−	−	+	+		−	+	−
6	+	+	−	−	−		−	+
7	−	−	+	+	+	−		−
8	+	+	−	−	−	+	−	

Composite weights for both patterns

	1	2	3	4	5	6	7	8
1				−−		++	−−	
2			−−		−−			++
3		−−			++			−−
4	−−					−−	++	
5		−−	++					−−
6	++			−−			−−	
7	−−			++		−−		
8		++	−−		−−			

Figure 11.3 Weights acquired in learning Pattern 1 and Pattern 2 separately, and the composite weights resulting from learning both. (The weight in a given cell reflects the strength of the connection from the corresponding column unit to the corresponding row unit. Only the sign and relative magnitude of the weights are indicated. A blank indicates a weight of 0; + and − signify positive and negative, with a double symbol, ++ or −−, representing a value twice as large as a single symbol, + or −.)

dissimilar from each other. If the patterns had been more similar, there would not have been this complete cancellation of effects.

Now we learn the new pattern, presenting it 10 times and adjusting the weights each time. The resulting weights (Figure 11.3) represent the sum of the weights for Patterns 1 and 2. The response to the new pattern is enhanced, as shown in Table 11.1. The response to the old, previously learned pattern is not affected. The module will now show enhancement, completion, and noise elimination for both patterns, though these properties are not illustrated in Table 11.1.

Thus, we see that more than one pattern can coexist in the same set of weights. There is an effect of storing multiple patterns, of course. When only one pattern is stored, the whole pattern (or at least, a pale copy of it) can be retrieved by driving the activation of any single unit in the appropriate direction. As more patterns are stored, larger subpatterns are generally needed to specify the pattern to be retrieved uniquely.

Learning a prototype from exemplars

In the preceding section, we considered the learning of particular patterns and showed that the delta rule was capable of learning multiple patterns, in the same set of connections. In this section, we consider what happens when distributed models using the delta rule are presented with an ensemble of patterns that have some common structure. The examples described in this section illustrate how the delta rule can be used to extract the structure from an ensemble of inputs, and throw away random variability.

Let us consider the following hypothetical situation. A little boy sees many different dogs, each only once, and each with a different name. All the dogs are a little different from each other, but in general there is a pattern which represents the typical dog: each one is just a different distortion of this prototype. (We are not claiming that the dogs in the world have no more structure than this; we make this assumption for purposes of illustration only.) For now we will assume that the names of the dogs are all completely different. Given this experience, we would expect that the boy would learn the prototype of the category, even without ever seeing any particular dog which matches the prototype directly (Posner and Keele, 1968, 1970; Anderson, 1977, applies an earlier version of a distributed model to this case). That is, the prototype will seem as familiar as any of the exemplars, and he will be able to complete the pattern corresponding to the prototype from any part of it. He will not, however, be very likely to remember the names of each of the individual dogs though he may remember the most recent ones.

We model this situation with a module consisting of 24 units. We assume that the presentation of a dog produces a visual pattern of activation over 16 of the units in the hypothetical module (the ninth through twenty-fourth, counting from left to right). The name of the dog produces a pattern of activation over the other 8 units (Units 1 to 8, counting from left to right).

Each visual pattern, by assumption, is a distortion of a single prototype. The prototype used for the simulation simply had a random series of +1 and −1 values. Each distortion of the prototype was made by probabilistically flipping the sign of randomly selected elements of the prototype pattern. For each new distorted pattern, each element has an independent chance of being flipped, with a probability of .2. Each name pattern was simply a random sequence of +1s and −1s for the 8 name units. Each encounter with a new dog is modeled as a presentation of a new name pattern with a new distortion of the prototype visual pattern. Fifty different trials were run, each with a new name pattern–visual pattern pair.

For each presentation, the pattern of activation is allowed to stabilize, and then the weights are adjusted as before. The increment to the weights is then allowed to decay considerably before the next input is presented. For simplicity, we assume that before the next pattern is presented, the last increment decays to a fixed small proportion of its initial value, and thereafter undergoes no further decay.

What does the module learn? The module acquires a set of weights which is continually buffeted about by the latest dog exemplar, but which captures the prototype dog quite well. Waiting for the last increment to decay to the fixed residual yields the weights shown in Figure 11.4.

Prototype pattern:

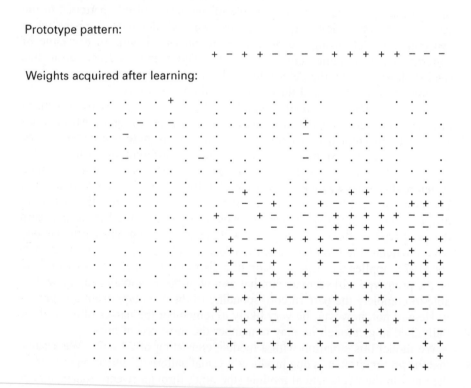

Weights acquired after learning:

Figure 11.4 Weights acquired in learning from distorted exemplars of a prototype. (The prototype pattern is shown above the weight matrix. Blank entries correspond to weights with absolute values less than .01; dots correspond to absolute values less than .06; pluses or minuses are used for weights with larger absolute values.)

These weights capture the correlations among the values in the prototype dog pattern quite well. The lack of exact uniformity is due to the more recent distortions presented, whose effects have not been corrected by subsequent distortions. This is one way in which the model gives priority to specific exemplars, especially recent ones. The effects of recent exemplars are particularly strong, of course, before they have had a chance to decay. The module can complete a prototype quite well, and it will respond more strongly to the prototype than to any distortion of it. It has, however, learned no particular relation between this prototype and any name pattern, because a totally different random association was presented on each trial. If the pattern of activation on the name units had been the same in every case (say, each dog was just called *dog*), or even in just a reasonable fraction of the cases, then the module would have been able to retrieve this shared name pattern from the prototype of the visual pattern and the prototype pattern from the name.

Multiple, nonorthogonal prototypes. In the preceeding simulation we have seen how the distributed model acts as a sort of signal averager, finding the central tendency of a set of related patterns. In and of itself this is an important property of the model, but the importance of this property increases when we realize that the model can average several different patterns in the same composite memory trace. Thus, several different prototypes can be stored in the same set of weights. This is important, because it means that the model does not fall into the trap of needing to decide which category to put a pattern in before knowing which prototype to average it with. The acquisition of the different prototypes proceeds without any sort of explicit categorization. If the patterns are sufficiently dissimilar, there is no interference among them at all. Increasing similarity leads to increased confusability during learning, but eventually the delta rule finds a set of connection strengths that minimizes the confusability of similar patterns.

To illustrate these points, we created a simulation analog of the following hypothetical situation. Let us say that our little boy sees, in the course of his daily experience, different dogs, different cats, and different bagels. First, let's consider the case in which each experience with a dog, a cat, or a bagel is accompanied by someone saying *dog*, *cat*, or *bagel*, as appropriate.

The simulation analog of this situation involved forming three *visual* prototype patterns of 16 elements, two of them (the one for dog and the one for cat) somewhat similar to each other ($r = .5$), and the third (for the bagel) orthogonal to both of the other two. Paired with each visual pattern was a name pattern of eight elements. Each name pattern was orthogonal to both of the others. Thus, the prototype visual pattern for cat and the prototype visual pattern for dog were similar to each other, but their names were not related.

Stimulus presentations involved presentations of distorted exemplars of the name–visual pattern pairs to a module of 24 elements like the one used in the previous simulation. This time, both the name pattern and the visual pattern were distorted, with each element having its sign flipped with an independent probability of .1 on each presentation. Fifty different distortions of each name–visual pattern pair were presented in groups of three consisting of one distortion of the dog pair, one distortion of the cat pair, and one distortion

Table 11.2 Results of tests after learning the dog, cat, and bagel patterns

Case	Name units								Visual pattern units																	
Pattern for dog prototype	+	−	+	+	−	+	+	−	+	−	−	−	+	+	+	+	+	−	−	−	−	+	−	−		−3
Response to dog name	+5	−4	+4	−5	+5	−4	+4	−4	+3	−4	+4	+4	−4	−4	−4	+4	+4	+3	+4	+4	−4	−4	−4	−4	−4	−3
Response to dog visual pattern																										
Pattern for cat prototype	+	+	−	+	+				+	−	+	+	−	−	−	−	+	−	+	+	−	+	+	+		+
Response to cat name	+5	+4	−5	+4	+4	−4	−4		+4	−3	+4	+4	−4	−3	−3	−4	+4	−4	+4	+4	−4	−4	+4	+4	−4	+4
Response to cat visual pattern																										
Pattern for bagel prototype	+	−	−	+	+				+	+	−	+	−	+	+	−	+	−	+	+	+	+	+	+		−
Response to bagel name	+4	−4	−4	+4	+4	−4	−4	+4	+3	+4	−4	+4	−4	−4	+4	+4	−4	−4	+4	+3	+4	+4	+4	+4	+4	−4
Response to bagel visual pattern																										

Note: Decimal points have been suppressed for clarity; thus, an entry of +4 represents an activation value of +.4.

of the bagel pair. Weight adjustment occurred after each presentation, with decay to a fixed residual before each new presentation.

At the end of training, the module was tested by presenting each name pattern and observing the resulting pattern of activation over the visual nodes, and by presenting each visual pattern and observing the pattern of activation over the name nodes. The results are shown in Table 11.2. In each case, the model reproduces the correct completion for the probe, and there is no apparent contamination of the cat pattern by the dog pattern, even though the visual patterns are similar to each other.

In general, pattern completion is a matter of degree. One useful measure of pattern completion is the dot product of the pattern of activation over the units with the pattern of external inputs to the units. Because we treat the external inputs as +1s and −1s, and because the activation of each node can only range from +1 to −1, the largest possible value the dot product can have is 1.0. We will use this measure explicitly later when considering some simulations of experimental results. For getting an impression of the degree of pattern reinstatement in the present cases, it is sufficient to note that when the sign of all of the elements is correct, as it is in all of the completions in Table 11.2, the average magnitude of the activations of the units corresponds to the dot product.

In a case like the present one, in which some of the patterns known to the model are correlated, the values of the connection strengths that the model produces do not necessarily have a simple interpretation. Though their sign always corresponds to the sign of the correlation between the activations of the two units, their magnitude is not a simple reflection of the magnitude of their correlation, but is influenced by the degree to which the model is relying on this particular correlation to predict the activation of one node from the others. Thus, in a case where two nodes (call them i and j) are perfectly correlated, the strength of the connection from i to j will depend on the number of other nodes whose activations are correlated with j. If i is the only node correlated with j, it will have to do all the work of predicting j, so the weight will be very strong; on the other hand, if many nodes besides i are correlated with j, then the work of predicting j will be spread around, and the weight between i and j will be considerablly smaller. The weight matrix acquired as a result of learning the dog, cat, and bagel patterns (Figure 11.5) reflects these effects. For example, across the set of three prototypes, Units 1 and 5 are perfectly correlated, as are Units 2 and 6. Yet the connection from 2 to 5 is stronger than the connection from 1 to 4 (these connections are asterisked in Figure 11.5). The reason for the difference is that 2 is one of only three units which correlate perfectly with 5, whereas Unit 1 is one of seven units which correlate perfectly with 4. (In Figure 11.5, the weights do not reflect these contrasts perfectly in every case, because the noise introduced into the learning happens by chance to alter some of the correlations present in the prototype patterns. Averaged over time, though, the weights will conform to their expected values.)

Thus far we have seen that several prototypes, not necessarily orthogonal, can be stored in the same module without difficulty. It is true, though we do

Prototypes:

```
Dog:   + - + - + - + -      + - + + - - - - + + + + + - - -

Cat:   + + - - + + - -      + - + + - - - - + - + - + + - +

Bagel: + - - + + - - +      + + - + - + + - + - - + + + + -
```

Weights:

```
        -1 -1  +2*-1    -1    +3        +5 -2 -1    -3 +2 -1        +2        -1
              -2  -1 +4*        +1 -1              -1 -1 +1 -1 -1    -3 -1     -3 +3
     -1 -2  -1      +5              +1    +1 -1 -1 -1    -1 +4    +1    -5    -1
           -1    -1    -1 +2    -1 +3 -3        +2 +3        -1 -2    -1 +1 +3
     +3 -1 -1                +1        -1    +3 -3        -2 +2        +1 +3 +1 -1 -1
     -1 +5 -3            -2    -1 -1    -1    -1        -1 -2 +1 -5 -1 +2 -1 +5
     -1    +3 -1 -1 -2          +1        -1    +1    +4        -1 -2
     -1 -1 -1 +2        -1    -1 +3 -2 -1    +3 +3    -1 -1 -3 +1 -1 +3 +3


     +3   -1 -1 +2 -1 -1            +3 -2        -3 +2    +1    +3 +1    -1
     -1 -1 -1 +3    -1    +3        -3 -1    +3 +3 +1 -1 -2 -2 +1 -1    +2
     +1 +1 +1 -3            -2    +1 -3        -1 -3 -3        +1 +3 -1    -1 -2 +2
     +2 -1 -1 -1 +3    -1    +3 -1 +1    -2 -1    -2 +2 -1        +2 +1 -1
     -2 +1 +1    -2 +1 +1 +1    -3        -3        +1 +2 -3        -1 -2 -1 +1
       -1    +2 -1        +2    -1 +2 -2    +1    +2 +1 -1    -3    -1    +2
     -1 -1 -1 +2    -1 -1 +2        +2 -3        +3    +1        -3    -1    +3
     -2 +1 +1 +1 -3        +1 +1    -2 +1 -1 -3 +3        -2 +1 -1 -1 -3 -1 +1
     +3    -1    +2    -1        +2        +3 -3        -3    -1 +1    +3 +1 -1 -1
           +5 -1 -1 -1 +4 -1            +1    -3 +1        +1    -1 -5 -1 -1
       +1    -2    +1 +1 -3    +1 -2 +2 +1 -1 -3 -3 -1    +1    -2        -3 +1
     +1 -5 +2 +1 +1 -5 +3            -2 +1 -1 +1        +1 +1 -2    +1 -2 +1 -3
     +2 -1 -1    +3 -1        +2    +1 +2 -2        -3 +2    +1
       +3 -4 +1    +3 -4 +1    +1    -1        +1 +1    +1 -5 -1 -3        +1 +2
         +2 -1    -1        -1 +2 -3        +2 +2        -1 -3        +1
     -1 +3 -2 -1 -1 +5 -3        -1 +3    +1 -1        -1      +1 -2    +3 -1
```

Figure 11.5 Weights acquired in learning the three prototype patterns shown. (Blanks in the matrix of weights correspond to weights with absolute values less than or equal to .05. Otherwise the actual value of the weight is about .05 times the value shown; thus +5 stands for a weight of +.25. The gap in the horizontal and vertical dimensions is used to separate the name field from the visual pattern field.)

not illustrate it, that the model has more trouble with the cat and dog visual patterns earlier on in training, before learning has essentially reached asymptotic levels as it has by the end of 50 cycles through the full set of patterns. And, of course, even at the end of learning, if we present as a probe a part of the visual pattern, if it does not differentiate between the dog and the cat, the model will produce a blended response. Both these aspects of the model seem generally consistent with what we should expect from human subjects.

Category learning without labels. An important further fact about the model is that it can learn several different visual patterns, even without the benefit of distinct identifying name patterns during learning. To demonstrate this we repeated the previous simulation, simply replacing the name patterns with 0s. The model still learns about the internal structure of the visual patterns, so that, after 50 cycles through the stimuli, any unique subpart of any one of the patterns is sufficient to reinstate the rest of the corresponding pattern correctly. This aspect of the model's behavior is illustrated in Table 11.3. Thus, we have a model that can, in effect, acquire a number of distinct categories, simply through a process of incrementing connection strengths in response to each new stimulus presentation. Noise, in the form of distortions in the patterns, is filtered out. The model does not require a name or other guide to distinguish the patterns belonging to different categories.

Coexistence of the prototype and repeated exemplars. One aspect of our discussion up to this point may have been slightly misleading. We may have given the impression that the model is simply a prototype extraction device. It is more than this, however; it is a device that captures whatever structure is present in a set of patterns. When the set of patterns has a prototype structure, the model will act as though it is extracting prototypes; but when it has a different structure, the model will do its best to accommodate this as well. For example, the model permits the coexistence of representations of prototypes with representations of particular, repeated exemplars.

Consider the following situation. Let us say that our little boy knows a dog next door named Rover and a dog at his grandma's house named Fido. And let's say that the little boy goes to the park from time to time and sees dogs, each of which his father tells him is a dog.

The simulation-analog of this involved three different eight-element name patterns, one for Rover, one for Fido, and one for Dog. The visual pattern for Rover was a particular randomly generated distortion of the dog prototype pattern, as was the visual pattern for Fido. For the dogs seen in the park, each one was simply a new random distortion of the prototype. The probability of flipping the sign of each element was again .2. The learning regime was otherwise the same as in the dog–cat–bagel example.

At the end of 50 learning cycles, the model was able to retrieve the visual pattern corresponding to either repeated exemplar (see Table 11.4) given the associated name as input. When given the Dog name pattern as input, it retrieves the prototype visual pattern for dog. It can also retrieve the appropriate name from each of the three visual patterns. This is true, even though the visual pattern for Rover differs from the visual pattern for dog by only a single element. Because of the special importance of this particular element, the weights from this element to the units that distinguish Rover's name pattern from the prototype name pattern are quite strong. Given part of a visual pattern, the model will complete it; if the part corresponds to the prototype, then that is what is completed, but if it corresponds to one of the repeated exemplars, that exemplar is completed. The model, then, knows both the prototype and the repeated exemplars quite well. Several other sets of prototypes and their repeated exemplars could also be stored in the same module, as long as its capacity is not exceeded; given large numbers of units per module, a lot of different patterns can be stored.

Table 11.3 Results of tests after learning the dog, cat, and bagel patterns without names

Case	Input or response for each visual unit																
Dog visual pattern																	
Probe	+	−	+	+	+	−	−	−	−	+	+	+	+	+	+	−	−
Response	+3	−3	+3	+3	+3	−3	−4	−3	−3	+6	+5	+6	+5	+3	−2	−3	−2
Cat visual pattern																	
Probe	+	−	+	+	−	−	−	−	+	+	+	−	−	+	+	+	+
Response	+3	−3	+3	+3	+3	−3	−3	−3	+6	−5	−5	+6	−5	+3	+2	−3	+2
Bagel visual pattern																	
Probe	+	+	+	−	+	+	−	+	+	−	−	−	+	+	+	+	−
Response	+2	+3	+3	−4	+3	+3	−3	+3	+6	−6	−6	−6	+6	+3	+3	+3	−3

Table 11.4 Results of tests with prototype and specific exemplar patterns

Case	Input or response for each unit																						
	Name units								Visual pattern units														
Pattern for dog prototype	+	−	+	−	+	−	+	−	+	−	+	+	−	−	−	+	+	+	+	+	+	−	−
Response to prototype name									+4	−5	+3	+3	−4	−3	−3	+3	+3	+4	+4	+3	+4	−3	−4
Response to prototype visual pattern	+5	−4	+4	−4	+5	−4	+4	−4															
Pattern for 'Fido' exemplar	+	−	−	−	+	−	−	−	+	(−)	+	−	+	+	+	+	+	+	+	+	+	−	−
Response to Fido name									+4	−4	−4	+4	−4	−4	+4	−4	−4	+4	+4	+4	+4	−4	−4
Response to Fido visual pattern	+5	−5	−3	−5	+4	−5	−3	−5															
Pattern for 'Rover' exemplar	+	−	−	+	+	+	−	+	+	(+)	+	−	+	+	+	+	+	+	+	+	+	−	(+)
Response to Rover name									+4	+5	+4	+4	−4	−4	−4	+4	+4	+4	+4	+4	−4	−4	−4
Response to Rover visual pattern	+4	−4	−2	+4	+4	+4	−2	+4															

Let us summarize the observations we have made in these several illustrative simulations. First, our distributed model is capable of storing not just one but a number of different patterns. It can pull the central tendency of a number of different patterns out of the noisy inputs; it can create the functional equivalent of perceptual categories with or without the benefit of labels; and it can allow representations of repeated exemplars to coexist with the representation of the prototype of the categories they exemplify in the same composite memory trace. The model is not simply a categorizer or a prototyping device; rather, it captures the structure inherent in a set of patterns, whether it be characterizable by description in terms of prototypes or not.

The ability to retrieve accurate completions of similar patterns is a property of the model which depends on the use of the delta learning rule. This allows both the storage of different prototypes that are not completely orthogonal and the coexistence of prototype representations and repeated exemplars.

Simulations of experimental results

Up to this point, we have discussed our distributed model in general terms and have outlined how it can accommodate both abstraction and repesentation of specific information in the same network. We will now consider, in the next two sections, how well the model does in accounting for some recent evidence about the details of the influence of specific experiences on performance.

Repetition and familiarity effects

When we perceive an item – say a word, for example – this experience has effects on our later performance. If the word is presented again, within a reasonable interval of time, the prior presentation makes it possible for us to recognize the word more quickly, or from a briefer presentation.

Traditionally, this effect has been interpreted in terms of units that represent the presented items in memory. In the case of word perception, these units are called *word detectors* or *logogens*, and a model of repetition effects for words has been constructed around the logogen concept (Morton, 1979). The idea is that the threshold for the logogen is reduced every time it *fires* (that is, every time the word is recognized), thereby making it easier to fire the logogen at a later time. There is supposed to be a decay of this priming effect with time, so that eventually the effect of the first presentation wears off.

This traditional interpretation has come under serious question of late, for a number of reasons. Perhaps paramount among the reasons is the fact that the exact relation between the specific context in which the priming event occurs and the context in which the test event occurs makes a huge difference (Jacoby, 1983a, 1983b). Generally speaking, nearly any change in the stimulus – from spoken to printed, from male speaker to female speaker, and so forth – tends to reduce the magnitude of the priming effect.

These facts might easily be taken to support the enumeration of specific experiences view, in which the logogen is replaced by the entire ensemble of experiences with the word, with each experience capturing aspects of the specific context in which it occurred. Such a view has been championed most strongly by Jacoby (1983a, 1983b).

Our distributed model offers an alternative interpretation. We see the traces laid down by the processing of each input as contributing to the composite, superimposed memory representation. Each time a stimulus is processed, it gives rise to a slightly different memory trace: either because the item itself is different or because it occurs in a different context that conditions its representation. The logogen is replaced by the set of specific traces, but the traces are not kept separate. Each trace contributes to the composite, but the characteristics of particular experiences tend nevertheless to be preserved, at least until they are overridden by cancelling characteristics of other traces. And the traces of one stimulus pattern can coexist with the traces of other stimuli, within the same composite memory trace.

It should be noted that we are not faulting either the logogen model or models based on the enumeration of specific experiences for their physiological implausibility here, because these models are generally not stated in physiological terms, and their authors might reasonably argue that nothing in their models precludes distributed storage at a physiological level. What we are suggesting is that a model which proposes explicitly distributed, superpositional storage can account for the kinds of findings that logogen models have been proposed to account for, as well as other findings which strain the utility of the concept of the logogen as a psychological construct. In the discussion section we will consider ways in which our distributed model differs from enumeration models as well.

To illustrate the distributed model's account of repetition priming effects, we carried out the following simulation experiment. We made up a set of eight random vectors, each 24 elements long, each one to be thought of as the prototype of a different recurring stimulus pattern. Through a series of 10 training cycles using the set of eight vectors, we constructed a composite memory trace. During training, the model did not actually see the prototypes, however. On each training presentation it saw a new random distortion of one of the eight prototypes. In each of the distortions, each of the 24 elements had its value flipped with a probability of .1. Weights were adjusted after every presentation, and then allowed to decay to a fixed residual before the presentation of the next pattern.

The composite memory trace formed as a result of the experience just described plays the same role in our model that the set of logogens or detectors play in a model like Morton's or, indeed, the interactive activation model of word perception. That is, the trace contains information which allows the model to enhance perception of familiar patterns, relative to unfamiliar ones. We demonstrate this by comparing the activations resulting from the processing of subsequent presentations of new distortions of our eight familiar patterns with other random patterns with which the model is not familiar. The pattern of activation that is the model's response to the input is stronger, and grows to a particular level more quickly, if the stimulus is a new distortion of an old pattern than if it is a new pattern. We already observed this general enhanced response to exact repetitions of

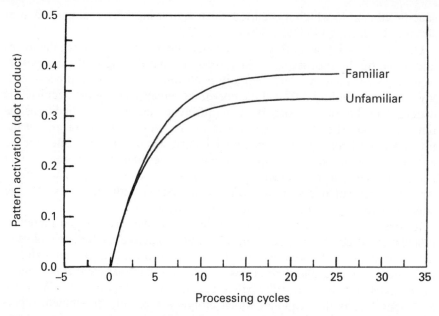

Figure 11.6 Growth of the pattern of activation for new distortions of familiar and unfamiliar patterns. (The measure of the strength of the pattern activation is the dot product of the response pattern with the input vector. See text for explanation.)

familiar patterns in our first example (see Table 11.1). Figure 11.6 illustrates that the effect also applies to new distortions of old patterns, as compared with new patterns, and illustrates how the activation process proceeds over successive time cycles of processing.

Pattern activation and response strength. The measure of activation shown in the Figure 11.6 is the dot product of the pattern of activation over the units of the module times the stimulus pattern itself, normalized for the number n of elements in the pattern: for the pattern j we call this expression α_j. The expression α_j represents the degree to which the actual pattern of activation on the units captures the input pattern. It is an approximate analog to the activation of an individual unit in models which allocate a single unit to each whole pattern.

To relate these pattern activations to response probabilities, we must assume that mechanisms exist for translating patterns of activation into overt responses measurable by an experimenter. We will assume that these mechanisms obey the principles stated by McClelland and Rumelhart (1981) in the interactive activation model of word perception, simply replacing the activations of particular units with the α measure of pattern activation.

In the interactive activation model, the probability of choosing the response appropriate to a particular unit was based on an exponential transform of a time average of the activation of the unit. This quantity, called the *strength* of the particular response, was divided by the total strength of all alternatives (including itself) to find the response probability (Luce, 1963). One complica-

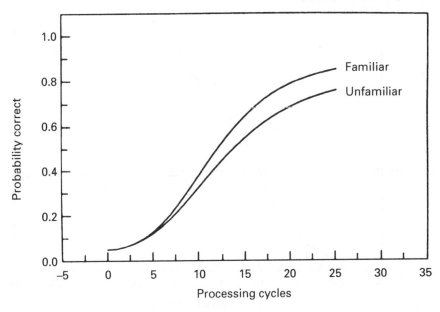

Figure 11.7 Simulated growth of response accuracy over the units in a 24-unit module, as a function of processing cycles, for new distortions of previously learned patterns compared with new distortions of patterns not previously learned.

tion arises because of the fact that it is not in general possible to specify exactly what the set of alternative responses might be for the denominator. For this reason, the strengths of other responses are represented by a constant C (which stands for the competition). Thus, the expression for the probability of choosing the response appropriate to pattern j is just $p(r_j) = e^{k\bar{\alpha}_j}/C + e^{k\bar{\alpha}_j}$, where $\bar{\alpha}_j$, represents the time average of α_j, and k is a scaling constant.

These assumptions finesse an important issue: namely the mechanism by which a pattern of activation gives rise to a particular response. A detailed discussion of this issue will appear in Rumelhart and McClelland (1986). For now, we wish only to capture basic properties any actual response selection mechanism must have: it must be sensitive to the input pattern, and it must approximate other basic aspects of response selection behavior captured by the Luce (1963) choice model.

Effects of experimental variables on time-accuracy curves. Applying the assumptions just described, we can calculate probability of correct response as a function of processing cycles for familiar and unfamiliar patterns. The result, for a particular choice of scaling parameters, is shown in Figure 11.7. If we assume performance in a perceptual identification task is based on the height of the curve at the point where processing is cut off by masking (McClelland and Rumelhart, 1981), then familiarity would lead to greater accuracy of perceptual identification at a given exposure duration. In a reaction time task, if the response is emitted when its probability reaches a particular threshold activation value (McClelland, 1979), then familiarity would lead to speeded responses. Thus, the model is consistent with the

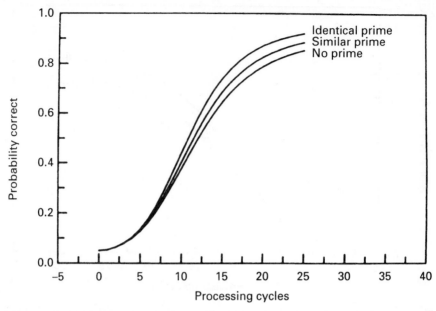

Figure 11.8   Response probability as a function of exposure time for patterns preceded by identical primes, similiar primes, or no related prime.

ubiquitous influence of familiarity both on response accuracy and speed, in spite of the fact that it has no detectors for familiar stimuli.

But what about priming and the role of congruity between the prime event and the test event? To examine the issue, we carried out a second experiment. Following learning of eight patterns as in the previous experiment, new distortions of half of the random vectors previously learned by the model were presented as primes. For each of these primes, the pattern of activation was allowed to stabilize, and changes in the strengths of the connections in the model were then made. We then tested the model's response to (a) the same four distortions; (b) four new distortions of the same patterns; and (c) distortions of the four previously learned patterns that had not been presented as primes. There was no decay in the weights over the course of the priming experiment; if decay had been included, its main effect would have been to reduce the magnitude of the priming effects.

The results of the experiment are shown in Figure 11.8. The response of the model is greatest for the patterns preceded by identical primes, intermediate for patterns preceded by similar primes, and weakest for patterns not preceded by any related prime.

Our model, then, appears to provide an account, not only for the basic existence of priming effects, but also for the graded nature of priming effects as a function of congruity between prime event and test event. It avoids the problem of multiplication of context-specific detectors which logogen theories fall prey to, while at the same time avoiding enumeration of specific experiences. Congruity effects are captured in the composite memory trace.

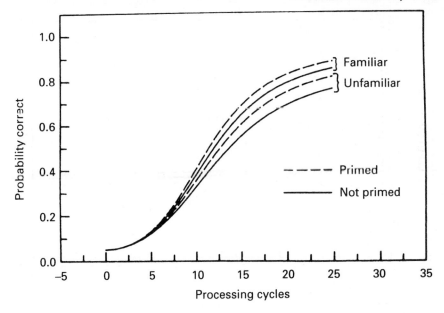

Figure 11.9 Response to new distortions of primed, unfamiliar patterns, unprimed, familiar patterns, primed, unfamiliar patterns, and unprimed, unfamiliar patterns.

The model also has another advantage over the logogen view. It accounts for repetition priming effects for unfamiliar as well as familiar stimuli. When a pattern is presented for the first time, a trace is produced just as it would be for stimuli that had previously been presented. The result is that, on a second presentation of the same pattern, or a new distortion of it, processing is facilitated. The functional equivalent of a logogen begins to be established from the very first presentation.

To illustrate the repetition priming of unfamiliar patterns and to compare the results with the repetition priming we have already observed for familiar patterns, we carried out a third experiment. This time, after learning eight patterns as before, a priming session was run in which new distortions of four of the familiar patterns and distortions of four new patterns were presented. Then, in the test phase, 16 stimuli were presented: new distortions of the primed, familiar patterns; new distortions of the unprimed, familiar patterns; new distortions of the primed, previously unfamiliar patterns; and finally, new distortions of four patterns that were neither primed nor familiar. The results are shown in Figure 11.9. What we find is that long-term familiarity and recent priming have approximately additive effects on the asymptotes of the time–accuracy curves. The time to reach any given activation level shows a mild interaction, with priming having slightly more of an effect for unfamiliar than for familiar stimuli.

These results are consistent with the bulk of the findings concerning the effects of pre-experimental familiarity and repetition in the recent series of experiments by Feustel *et al.* (1983) and Salasoo *et al.* (1985). They found

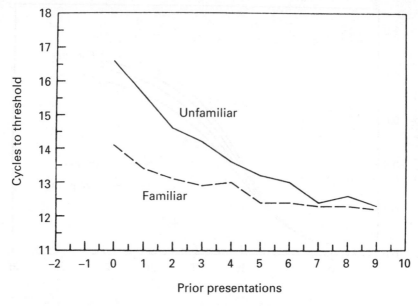

Figure 11.10   Time to reach a fixed-accuracy criterion (60% correct) for previously familiar and unfamiliar patterns, as a function of repetitions.

that pre-experimental familiarity of an item (word vs nonword) and prior exposure had this very kind of interactive effect on exposure time required for accurate identification of all the letters of a string, at least when words and nonwords were mixed together in the same lists of materials.

A further aspect of the results reported by Salasoo *et al.* is also consistent with our approach. In one of their experiments, they examined threshold for accurate identification as a function of number of prior presentations, for both words and pseudowords. Although thresholds were initially elevated for pseudowords, relative to words, there was a rather rapid convergence of the thresholds over repeated presentations, with the point of convergence coming at about the same place on the curve for two different versions of their perceptual identification task (Salasoo *et al.*, 1985, Figure 7). Our model, likewise, shows this kind of convergence effect, as illustrated in Figure 11.10.

The Feustel *et al.* (1983) and Salasoo *et al.* (1985) experiments provide very rich and detailed data that go beyond the points we have extracted from them here. We do not claim to have provided a detailed account of all aspects of their data. However, we simply wish to note that the general form of their basic findings is consistent with a model of the distributed type. In particular, we see no reasons to assume that the process by which unfamiliar patterns become familiar involves the formation of an abstract, logogen-like unit separate from the episodic traces responsible for repetition priming effects.

There is one finding by Salasoo *et al.* (1985) that appears to support the view that there is some special process of unit formation that is distinct from the priming of old units. This is the fact that after a year between training and testing, performance with pseudowords used during training is indistinguishable from performance with words, but performance with words used during training shows no residual benefit compared with words not previously used. The data certainly support the view that training experience made the pseudo-words into lasting perceptual units, at the same time that it produced transitory priming of existing units. We have not attempted to account for this finding in detail, but we doubt that it is inconsistent with a distributed model. In support of this, we offer one reason why repetition effects might seem to persist longer for pseudowords rather than for words in the Salasoo *et al.* experiment. For pseudowords, a strong association would be built up between the item and the learning context during initial training. Such associations would be formed for words, but because these stimuli have been experienced many times before and have already been well learned, smaller increments in connection strength are formed for these stimuli during training, and thus the strength of the association between the item and the learning context would be less. If this view is correct, we would expect to see a disadvantage for pseudowords relative to words if the testing were carried out in a situation which did not reinstate the mental state associated with the original learning experience, because for these stimuli much of what was learned would be tied to the specific learning context: such a prediction would appear to differentiate our account from any view which postulated the formation of an abstract, context-independent logogen as the basis for the absence of a pseudoword decrement effect.

Representation of general and specific information

In the previous section, we cast our distributed model as an alternative to the view that familiar patterns are represented in memory either by separate detectors or by an enumeration of specific experiences. In this section, we show that the model provides alternatives to both abstraction and enumeration models of learning from exemplars of prototypes.

Abstraction models were originally motivated by the finding that subjects occasionally appeared to have learned better how to categorize the prototype of a set of distorted exemplars than the specific exemplars they experienced during learning (Posner and Keele, 1968). However, pure abstraction models have never fared very well, because there is nearly always evidence of some superiority of the particular training stimuli over other stimuli equally far removed from the prototype. A favored model, then, is one in which there is both abstraction and memory for particular training stimuli.

Recently, proponents of models involving only enumeration of specific experiences have noted that such models can account for the basic fact that abstraction models are primarily designed to account for — enhanced response to the prototype, relative to particular previously seen exemplars, under some conditions — as well as failures to obtain such effects under other conditions (Hintzman, 1983; Medin and Shaffer, 1978). In evaluating distributed models, it is important to see if they can do as well. Anderson (1977) has made important steps in this direction, and Knapp and Anderson (1984) have shown how their distributed model can account for many of the details of the Posner–Keele experiments. Recently, however, two sets of findings have been put forward which appear strongly to favor the enumeration of specific experiences view, at least relative to pure abstraction models. It is important, therefore, to see how well our distributed model can do in accounting for these kinds of effects.

The first set of findings comes from a set of studies by Whittlesea (1983). In a large number of studies, Whittlesea demonstrated a role for specific exemplars in guiding performance on a perceptual identification task. We wanted to see whether our model would demonstrate a similar sensitivity to specific exemplars. We also wanted to see whether our model would account for the conditions under which such effects are not obtained.

Whittlesea used letter strings as stimuli. The learning experiences subjects received involved simply looking at the stimuli one at a time on a visual display and writing down the sequence of letters presented. Subjects were subsequently tested for the effect of this training on their ability to identify letter strings bearing various relations to the training stimuli and to the prototypes from which the training stimuli were derived. The test was a perceptual identification task; the subject was simply required to try to identify letters from a brief flash.

The stimuli Whittlesea used were all distortions of one of two prototype letter strings. Table 11.5 illustrates the essential properties of the sets of training and test stimuli he used. The stimuli in Set Ia were each one step away from the prototype. The Ib items were also one step from the prototype and one step from one of the Ia distortions. The Set IIa stimuli were each two steps from the prototype, and one step from a particular Ia distortion. The Set IIb items were also two steps from the prototype, and each was one step from one of the IIa distortions. The Set IIc distortions were two steps from the prototype also, and each was two steps from the closest IIa distortion. Over the set of five IIc distortions, the A and B subpatterns each occurred once in each position, as they did in the case of the IIa distortions. The distortions in Set III were three steps from the prototype, and one step from the closest member of Set IIa. The distortions in Set V were each five steps from the prototype.

Whittlesea ran seven experiments using different combinations of training and test stimuli. We carried out simulation analogs of all of these experiments, plus one additional experiment that Whittlesea did not run. The main difference between the simulation experiments and Whittlesea's actual experiments was that he used two different prototypes in each experiment, whereas we only used one.

The simulation used a simple 20-unit module. The set of 20 units was divided into five submodules, one for each letter in Whittlesea's letter strings. The prototype pattern and the different distortions used can be derived from the information provided in Table 11.5.

Each simulation experiment began with null connections between the units. The training phase involved presenting the set or sets of training stimuli analogous to those Whittlesea used, for the same number of presentations. To avoid idiosyncratic effects of particular orders of training stimuli, each

Table 11.5 Schematic description of stimulus sets used in simulations of Whittlesea's experiments

Prototype	Stimulus set						
	Ia	*Ib*	*IIa*	*IIb*	*IIc*	*III*	*V*
PPPPP	APPPP	BPPPP	ABPPP	ACPPP	APCPP	ABCPP	CCCCC
	PAPPP	PBPPP	PABPP	PACPP	PAPCP	PABCP	CBCBC
	PPAPP	PPBPP	PPABP	PPACP	PPAPC	PPABC	BCACB
	PPPAP	PPPBP	PPPAB	PPPAC	CPPAP	CPPAB	ABCBA
	PPPPA	PPPPB	BPPPA	CPPPA	PCPPA	BCPPA	CACAC

Note: The actual stimuli used can be filled in by replacing P with $+-+-$; A with $++--$; B with $+--+$; and C with $++++$. The model is not sensitive to the fact the same subpattern was used in each of the five slots.

experiment was run six times, each with a different random order of training stimuli. On each trial, activations were allowed to settle down through 50 processing cycles, and then connection strengths were adjusted. There was no decay of the increments to the weights over the course of an experiment.

In the test phase, the model was tested with the sets of test items analogous to the sets Whittlesea used. As a precaution against effects of prior test items on performance, we simply turned off the adjustment of weights during the test phase.

A summary of the training and test stimuli used in each of the experiments, of Whittlesea's findings, and of the simulation results are shown in Table 11.6. The numbers represent relative amounts of enhancement in performance as a result of the training experience, relative to a pretest baseline. For Whittlesea's data, this is the per letter increase in letter identification probability between a pre- and posttest. For the simulation, it is the increase in the size of the dot product for a pretest with null weights and a posttest after training. For comparability to the data, the dot product difference scores have been doubled. This is simply a scaling operation to facilitate qualitative comparison of experimental and simulation results.

A comparison of the experimental and simulation results shows that wherever there is a within-experiment difference in Whittlesea's data, the simulation produced a difference in the same direction. (Between-experiment comparisons are not considered because of subject and material differences which render such differences unreliable.) The next several paragraphs review some of the major findings in detail.

Some of the comparisons bring out the importance of congruity between particular test and training experiences. Experiments 1, 2, and 3 show that when distance of test stimuli from the prototype is controlled, similarity to particular training exemplars makes a difference both for the human subjects and in the model. In Experiment 1, the relevant contrast was between Ia and Ib items. In Experiment 2, it was between IIa and IIc items. Experiment 3 shows that the subjects and the model both show a gradient in performance with increasing distance of the test items from the nearest old exemplar.

Experiments 4, 4', and 5 examine the status of the prototype and other test

Table 11.6 Summary of perceptual identification experiments with experimental and simulation results

Whittlesea's experiment	Training stimulus set(s)	Test stimulus sets	Experimental results	Simulation results
1	Ia	Ia	.27	.24
		Ib	.16	.15
		V	.03	−.05
2	IIa	IIa	.30	.29
		IIc	.15	.12
		V	.03	−.08
3	IIa	IIa	.21	.29
		IIb	.16	.14
		IIc	.10	.12
4	IIa	P	–	.24
		Ia	.19	.21
		IIa	.23	.29
		III	.15	.15
4′	Ia	P	–	.28
		Ia	–	.24
		IIa	–	.12
5	IIa, b, c	P	–	.25
		Ia	.16	.21
		IIa	.16	.18
		III	.10	.09
6	III	Ia	.16	.14
		IIa	.16	.19
		III	.19	.30
7	IIa	IIa	.24	.29
		IIc	.13	.12
		III	.17	.15

stimuli closer to the prototype than any stimuli actually shown during training. In Experiment 4, the training stimuli were fairly far away from the prototype, and there were only five different training stimuli (the members of the IIa set). In this case, controlling for distance from the nearest training stimuli, test stimuli closer to the prototype showed more enhancement than those farther away (Ia vs III comparison). However, the actual training stimuli nevertheless had an advantage over both other sets of test stimuli, including those that were closer to the prototype than the training stimuli themselves (IIa vs Ia comparison).

In Experiment 4′ (not run by Whittlesea) the same number of training stimuli were used as in Experiment 4, but these were closer to the prototype. The result is that the simulation shows an advantage for the prototype over the old exemplars. The specific training stimuli used even in this experiment do influence performance, however, as Whittlesea's first experiment (which used the same training set) shows (Ia–Ib contrast). This effect holds both for the subjects and for the simulation. The pattern of results is similar to the findings of Posner and Keele (1968), in the condition where subjects learned six exemplars which were rather close to the prototype. In this condition, their subjects' categorization performance was most accurate for the prototype, but more accurate for old than for new distortions, just as in this simulation experiment.

In Experiment 5, Whittlesea demonstrated that a slight advantage for stimuli closer to the prototype than the training stimuli would emerge, even with high-level distortions, when a large number of different distortions were used once each in training, instead of a smaller number of distortions presented three times each. The effect was rather small in Whittlesea's case (falling in the third decimal place in the per letter enhancement effect measure), but other experiments have produced similar results, and so does the simulation. In fact, because the prototype was tested in the simulation, we were able to demonstrate a monotonic drop in performance with distance from the prototype in this experiment.

Experiments 6 and 7 examine in different ways the relative influence of similarity to the prototype and similarity to the set of training exemplars, using small numbers of training exemplars rather far from the prototype. Both in the data and in the model, similarity to particular training stimuli is more important than similarity to the prototype, given the sets of training stimuli used in these experiments.

Taken together with other findings, Whittlesea's results show clearly that similarity of test items to particular stored exemplars is of paramount importance in predicting perceptual performance. Other experiments show the relevance of these same factors in other tasks, such as recognition memory, classification learning, and so forth. It is interesting to note that performance does not honor the specific exemplars so strongly when the training items are closer to the prototype. Under such conditions, performance is superior on the prototype or stimuli closer to the prototype than the training stimuli. Even when the training stimuli are rather distant from the prototype, they produce a benefit for stimuli closer to the prototype, if there are a large number of distinct training stimuli each shown only once. Thus, the dominance of specific training experiences is honored only when the training experiences are few and far between. Otherwise, an apparent advantage for the prototype, though with some residual benefit for particular training stimuli, is the result.

The congruity of the results of these simulations with experimental findings underscores the applicability of distributed models to the question of the nature of the representation of general and specific information. In fact, we were somewhat surprised by the ability of the model to account for Whittlesea's results, given the fact that we did not rely on context-sensitive encoding of the letter string stimuli. That is, the distributed representation we assigned to each letter was independent of the other letters in the string. However, a context-sensitive encoding would prove necessary to capture a larger ensemble of stimuli.

Whether a context-sensitive encoding would produce the same or slightly different results depends on the exact encoding. The exact degree of overlap of the patterns of activation produced by different distortions of the same prototype determines the extent to which the model will tend to favor the prototype relative to particular old exemplars. The degree of overlap, in turn, depends on the specific assumptions made about the encoding of the stimuli. However, the general form of the results of the simulation would be unchanged: when all the distortions are close to the prototype, or when there is a very large number of different distortions, the central tendency will produce the strongest response; but when the distortions are fewer, and farther from the prototype, the training exemplars themselves will produce the strongest activations. What the encoding would effect is the similarity metric.

In this regard, it is worth mentioning another finding that appears to challenge our distributed account of what is learned through repeated experiences with exemplars. This is the finding of Medin and Schwanenflugel (1981). Their experiment compared ease of learning of two different sets of stimuli in a categorization task. One set of stimuli could be categorized by a linear combination of weights assigned to particular values on each of four dimensions considered independently. The other set of stimuli could not be categorized in this way; and yet, the experiment clearly demonstrated that linear separability was not necessary for categorization learning. In one experiment, linearly separable stimuli were less easily learned than a set of stimuli that were not linearly separable but had a higher degree of intra-exemplar similarity within categories.

At first glance, it may seem that Medin and Schwanenflugel's experiment is devastating to our distributed approach, because our distributed model can only learn linear combinations of weights. However, whether a linear combination of weights can suffice in the Medin and Schwanenflugel experiments depends on how patterns of activation are assigned to stimuli. If each stimulus dimension is encoded separately in the representation of the stimulus, then the Medin and Schwanenflugel stimuli cannot be learned by our model. But if each stimulus dimension is encoded in a context-sensitive way, then the patterns of activation associated with the different stimuli become linearly separable again.

One way of achieving context sensitivity is via separate enumeration of traces. But it is well known that there are other ways as well. Several different kinds of context-sensitive encodings which do not require separate enumeration of traces, or the allocation of separate nodes to individual experiences, are considered in Hinton (1981a), Hinton *et al.* (1986), and Rumelhart and McClelland (1986).

It should be noted that the motivation for context-sensitive encoding in the use of distributed representations is captured by but by no means limited to the kinds of observations reported in the experiment by Medin and Schwanenflugel. The trouble is that the assignment of particular context-sensitive encodings to stimuli is at present rather *ad hoc*: there are too many different possible ways it can be done to know which way is right. What is needed is a principled way of assigning distributed representations to patterns of activation. The problem is a severe one, but really it is no different from the problem that all models face, concerning the assignment of representations to stimuli. What we can say for sure at this point is that context-sensitive encoding is necessary, for distributed models or for any other kind.

Discussion

Until very recently, the exploration of distributed models was restricted to a few workers, mostly coming from fields other than cognitive psychology. Although in some cases, particularly in the work of Anderson (1977; Anderson *et al.*, 1977; Knapp and Anderson, 1984), some implications of these models for our understanding of memory and learning have been pointed out, they have only begun to be applied by researchers primarily concerned with understanding cognitive processes *per se*. The present contribution, along with the articles by Murdock (1982) and Eich (1982), represents what we hope will be the beginning of a more serious examination of these kinds of models by cognitive psychologists. For they provide, we believe, important alternatives to traditional conceptions of representation and memory.

We have tried to illustrate this point here by showing how the distributed approach circumvents the dilemma of specific trace models. Distributed memories abstract even while they preserve the details of recent, or frequently repeated, experiences. Abstraction and preservation of information about specific stimuli are simply different reflections of the operation of the same basic learning mechanism.

The basic points we have been making can, of course, be generalized in several different directions. Here we will mention two: the relation between episodic and semantic memory (Tulving, 1972) and the representations underlying the use of language.

With regard to episodic and semantic memory, our distributed model leads naturally to the suggestion that semantic memory may be just the residue of the superposition of episodic traces. Consider, for example, representation of a proposition encountered in several different contexts, and assume for the moment that the context and content are represented in separate parts of the same module. Over repeated experience with the same proposition in different contexts, the proposition will remain in the interconnections of the units in the propositon submodule, but the particular associations to particular contexts will wash out. However, material that is only encountered in one particular context will tend to be somewhat contextually bound. So we may not be able to retrieve what we learn in one context when we need it in other situations. Other authors (e.g., Anderson and Ross, 1980) have recently argued against a distinction between episodic and semantic memory, pointing out interactions between traditionally episodic and semantic memory tasks. Such findings are generally consistent with the view we have taken here.

Distributed models also influence our thinking about how human behavior might come to exhibit the kind of regularity that often leads linguists to postulate systems of rules. We have recently developed a distributed model of a system that can learn the past tense system of English, given as inputs pairs of patterns, corresponding to the phonological structure of the present and past tense forms of actual English verbs (Rumelhart and McClelland,

1986). Given plausible assumptions about the learning experiences to which a child is exposed, the model provides a fairly accurate account of the time course of acquisition of the past tense (Brown, 1973; Ervin, 1964; Kuczaj, 1977).

In general distributed models appear to provide alternatives to a variety of different kinds of models that postulate abstract, summary representations such as prototypes, logogens, semantic memory representations, or even linguistic rules.

Why prefer a distributed model?

The fact that distributed models provide alternatives to other sorts of accounts is important, but the fact that they are sometimes linked rather closely to the physiology often makes them seem irrelevant to the basic enterprise of cognitive psychology. It may be conceded that distributed models describe the *physiological substrate* of memory better than other models, but why should we assume that they help us to characterize human information processing at a more abstract level of description? There are two parts to the answer to this question. First, though distributed models may be approximated by other models, on close inspection they differ from them in ways that should have testable consequences. If tests of these consequences turn out to favor distributed models – and there are indications that in certain cases they will – it would seem plausible to argue that distributed models provide an importantly different description of cognition, even if it does take the phenomena somewhat closer to the physiological level of analysis. Second, distributed models alter our thinking about a number of aspects of cognition at the same time. They give us a whole new constellation of assumptions about the structure of cognitive processes. They can change the way we think about the learning process, for example, and can even help shed some light on why and how human behavior comes to be as regular (as bound by rules and concepts) as it seems to be. In this section we consider these two points in turn.

A different level, or a different description? Are distributed models at a different level of analysis from cognitive models, or do they provide a different description of cognition? We think the answer is some of both. Here we focus primarily on underscoring the differences between distributed and other models.

Consider, first, the class of models which state that concepts are represented by prototypes. Distributed models approximate prototype models, and under some conditions their predictions converge, but under other conditions their predictions diverge. In particular, distributed models account both for conditions under which the prototype dominates and conditions under which particular exemplars dominate performance. Thus, they clearly have an advantage over such models, and should be preferred as accounts of empirical phenomena.

Perhaps distributed models are to be preferred over some cognitive level models, but one might argue that they are not to be preferred to the correct cognitive level model. For example, in most of the simulations discussed in this article, the predictions of enumeration models are not different from the predictions of our distributed model. Perhaps we should see our distributed model as representing a physiological plausible implementation of enumeration models.

Even here, there are differences, however. Though both models superimpose traces of different experiences, distributed models do so at the time of storage, while enumeration models do so at the time of retrieval. But there is no evidence to support the separate storage assumption of enumeration models. Indeed, most such models assume that performance is always based on a superimposition of the specific experiences. Now, our distributed model could be rejected if convincing evidence of separate storage could be provided, for example, by some kind of experiment in which a way was found to separate the effects of different memory experiences. But the trend in a number of recent approaches to memory has been to emphasize the ubiquity of interactions between memory traces. Distributed models are essentially constructed around the assumption that memory traces interact by virtue of the nature of the manner in which they are stored, and they provide an explanation for these interactions. Enumeration models, on the other hand, simply assume interactions occur and postulate separate storage without providing any evidence that storage is in fact separate.

There is another difference between our distributed model and the enumeration models, at least existing ones. Our distributed model assumes that learning is an *error-correcting* process, whereas enumeration models do not. This difference leads to empirical consequences which put great strain on existing enumeration models. In existing enumeration models, what is stored in memory is simply a copy of features of the stimulus event, independent of the prior knowledge already stored in the memory system. But there are a number of indications that what is learned depends on the current state of knowledge. For example, the fact that learning is better after distributed practice appears to suggest that more learning occurs on later learning trials, if subjects have had a chance to forget what they learned on the first trial. We would expect such effects to occur in an error-correcting model such as ours.

The main point of the foregoing discussion has been to emphasize that our distributed model is not simply a plausible physiological implementation of existing models of cognitive processes. Rather, the model is an alternative to most, if not all, existing models, as we have tried to emphasize by pointing out differences between our distributed model and other models which have been proposed. Of course this does not mean that our distributed model will not turn out to be an exact notational variant of some particular other model. What it does mean is that our distributed model must be treated as an alternative to — rather than simply an implementation of — existing models of learning and memory.

Interdependence of theoretical assumptions. There is another reason for taking distributed models seriously as psychological models. Even in cases where our distributed model may not be testably distinct from existing models, it does provide an entire constellation of assumptions which go together as a package. In this regard, it is interesting to contrast a distributed model with a model such as John Anderson's ACT* model (J. R. Anderson, 1983). One difference between the models is that in ACT* it is productions rather than connection strengths that serve as the basis of learning and memory. This difference leads to other differences: in our model, learning occurs through connection strength modulation, whereas in ACT* learning occurs through the creation, differentiation, and generalizaton of productions. At a process level the models look very different, whether or not they make different empirical predictions. Learning in our distributed model is an automatic consequence of processing based on information locally available to each unit whose connections are changing; in ACT*, learning requires an overseer that detects cases in which a production has been misapplied, or in which two productions with similar conditions both fit the same input, to trigger the differentiation and generalization processes as appropriate.

Similar contrasts exist between our distributed model and other models; in general, our model differs from most abstractive models (that is, those that postulate the formation of abstract rules or other abstract representations) in doing away with complex acquisition mechanisms in favor of a very simple connection strength modulation scheme. Indeed, to us, much of the appeal of distributed models is that they do not already have to be intelligent in order to learn, like some models do. Doubtless, sophisticated hypothesis testing models of learning such as those which have grown out of the early concept identification work of Bruner *et al.* (1956) or out of the artificial intelligence learning tradition established by Winston (1975) have their place, but for many phenomena, particularly those that do not seem to require explicit hypothesis formation and testing, the kind of learning mechanism incorporated in our distributed model may be more appropriate.

Two final reasons for preferring a distributed representation are that it leads us to understand some of the reasons why human behavior tends to exhibit such strong regularities. Some of the regularity is due to the structure of the world, of course, but much of it is a result of the way in which our cultures structure it; certainly the regularity of languages is a fact about the way humans communicate that psychological theory can be asked to explain. Distributed models provide some insight both into why it is beneficial for behavior to be regular, and how it comes to be that way.

It is beneficial for behavior to be regular, because regularity allows us to economize on the size of the networks that must be devoted to processing in a particular environment. If all experiences were completely random and unrelated to each other, a distributed model would buy us very little – in fact it would cost us a bit – relative to separate enumeration of experiences. An illuminating analysis of this situation is given by Willshaw (1981). Where a distributed model pays off, though, is in the fact that it can capture generalizations. Enumeration models lack this feature. There are, of course, limits on how much can be stored in a distributed memory system, but the fact that it can abstract extends those limits far beyond the capacity of any system relying on the separate enumeration of experiences, whenever abstraction is warranted by the ensemble of inputs.

We have just explained how distributed models can help us understand why it is a good thing for behavior to exhibit regularity, but we have not yet indicated how they help us understand how it comes to be regular. But it is easy to see how distributed models tend to impose regularity. When a new pattern is presented, the model will impose regularity by dealing with it as it has learned to deal with similar patterns in the past; the model automatically generalizes. In our analysis of past tense learning (Rumelhart and McClelland, 1986), it is just this property of distributed models which leads them to produce the kinds of over-regularizations we see in language development; the same property, operating in all of the members of a culture at the same time, will tend to produce regularizations in the entire language.

Conclusion

The distributed approach is in its infancy, and we do not wish to convey the impression that we have solved all the problems of learning and memory simply by invoking it. Considerable effort is needed on several fronts. We will mention four that seem of paramount importance. (a) Distributed models must be integrated with models of the overall organization of information processing, and their relation to models of extended retrieval processes and other temporally extended mental activities must be made clear. (b) Models must be formulated which adequately capture the structural relations of the components of complex stimuli. Existing models do not do this in a sufficiently flexible and open-ended way to capture arbitrarily complex propositional structures. (c) Ways must be found to take the assignment of patterns of activation to stimuli out of the hands of the modeler, and place them in the structure of the model itself. (d) Further analysis is required to determine which of the assumptions of our particular distributed model are essential and which are unimportant details. The second and third of these problems are under intensive study. Some developments along these lines are reported in a number of recent papers (Ackley *et al.*, 1985; McClelland, 1985; Rumelhart and Zipser, 1985).

Although much remains to be done, we hope we have demonstrated that distributed models provide distinct, conceptually attractive alternatives to models involving the explicit formation of abstractions or the enumeration of specific experiences. Just how far distributed models can take us toward an understanding of learning and memory remains to be seen.

References

Ackley, D., Hinton, G. E., and Sejnowski, T. J. (1985). Boltzmann machines: Constraint satisfaction networks that learn. *Cognitive Science*, 9, 147–169.

Anderson, J. A. (1977). Neural models with cognitive implications. In D. LaBerge and S. J. Samuels (Eds.), *Basic processes in reading: Perception and comprehension*. Hillsdale, NJ: Erlbaum.

Anderson, J. A. (1983). Cognitive and psychological computation with neural models. *IEEE Transactions on Systems, Man, and Cybernetics, SMC-13*, 799–815.

Anderson, J. A., and Hinton, G. E. (1981). Models of information processing in the brain. In G. E. Hinton and J. A. Anderson (Eds.), *Parallel models of associative memory*. Hillsdale, NJ: Erlbaum.

Anderson, J. A., Silverstein, J. W., Ritz, S. A., and Jones, R. S. (1977). Distinctive features, categorical perception, and probability learning: Some applications of a neural model. *Psychological Review, 84*, 413–451.

Anderson, J. R. (1983). *The architecture of cognition*. Cambridge, MA: Harvard.

Anderson, J. R., and Ross, B. H. (1980). Evidence against a semantic-episodic distinction. *Journal of Experimental Psychology: Human Learning and Memory, 6*, 441–465.

Brooks, L. R. (1978). Nonanalytic concept formation and memory for instances. In E. Rosch and B. B. Lloyd (Eds.), *Cognition and categorization*. Hillsdale, NJ: Erlbaum.

Brown, R. (1973). *A first language*. Cambridge, MA: Harvard University Press.

Bruner, J. S., Goodnow, J. J., and Austin, G. A. (1956). *A study of thinking*. New York: Wiley.

Eich, J. M. (1982). A composite holographic associative retrieval model. *Psychological Review, 89*, 627–661.

Ervin, S. (1964). Imitation and structural change in children's language. In E. Lenneberg (Ed.), *New directions in the study of language*. Cambridge, MA: MIT Press.

Feustel, T. C., Shiffrin, R. M., and Salasoo, A. (1983). Episodic and lexical contributions to the repetition effect in word identification. *Journal of Experimental Psychology: General, 112*, 309–346.

Glushko, R. J. (1979). The organization and activation of orthographic knowledge in reading aloud. *Journal of Experimental Psychology: Human Perception and Performance, 5*, 674–691.

Hinton, G. E. (1981a). Implementing semantic networks in parallel hardware. In G. E. Hinton and J. A. Anderson (Eds.), *Parallel models of associative memory*. Hillsdale, NJ: Erlbaum.

Hinton, G. E. (1981b). A parallel computation that assigns canonical object-based frames of reference. *Proceedings of the Seventh International Joint Conference in Artificial Intelligence* (pp. 683–685). Vancouver, British Columbia, Canada.

Hinton, G. E., and Anderson, J. A. (Eds.). (1981). *Parallel models of associative memory*. Hillsdale, NJ: Erlbaum.

Hinton, G. E., McClelland, J. L., and Rumelhart, D. E. (1986). Distributed representations. In D. E. Rumelhart and J. L. McClelland (Eds.), *Parallel distributed processing: Explorations in the microstructure of cognition. Volume I: Foundations*. Cambridge, MA: MIT Press.

Hintzman, D. (1983). *Schema abstraction in a multiple trace memory model*. Paper presented at conference on 'The priority of the specific.' Elora, Ontario, Canada.

Jacoby, L. L. (1983a). Perceptual enhancement: Persistent effects of an experience. *Journal of Experimental Psychology: Learning, Memory, and Cognition, 9*, 21–38.

Jacoby, L. L. (1983b). Remembering the data: Analyzing interactive processes in reading. *Journal of Verbal Learning and Verbal Behavior, 22*, 485–508.

Knapp, A., and Anderson, J. A. (1984). Theory of categorization based on distributed memory storage. *Journal of Experimental Psychology: Learning, Memory, and Cognition, 10*, 616–637.

Kohonen, T. (1977). *Associative memory: A system-theoretical approach*. Berlin: Springer-Verlag.

Kohonen, T., Oja, E., and Lehtio, P. (1981). Storage and processing of information in distributed associative memory systems. In G. E. Hinton and J. A. Anderson (Eds.), *Parallel models of associative memory*. Hillsdale, NJ: Erlbaum.

Kuczaj, S. A., II. (1977). The acquisition of regular and irregular past tense forms. *Journal of Verbal Learning and Verbal Behavior, 16*, 589–600.

Lashley, K. S. (1950). In search of the engram. *Society for Experimental Biology Symposium No. 4: Physiological Mechanisms in Animal Behavior* (pp. 478–505). London: Cambridge University Press.

Luce, R. D. (1963). Detection and recognition. In R. D. Luce, R. R. Bush, and E. Galanter (Eds.), *Handbook of Mathematical Psychology: Vol. I*. New York: Wiley.

McClelland, J. L. (1979). On the time-relations of mental processes: An examination of systems of processes in cascade. *Psychological Review, 86*, 287–330.

McClelland, J. L. (1981). Retrieving general and specific information from stored knowledge of specifics. *Proceedings of the Third Annual Meeting of the Cognitive Science Society* (pp. 170–172). Berkeley, CA.

McClelland, J. L. (1985). Putting knowledge in its place: A framework for programming parallel processing structures on the fly. *Cognitive Science, 9*, 113–146.

McClelland, J. L., and Rumelhart, D. E. (1981). An interactive activation model of the effect of context in perception, Part I. An account of basic findings. *Psychological Review, 88*, 375–407.

Medin, D., and Schwanenflugel, P. J. (1981). Linear separability in classification learning. *Journal of Experimental Psychology: Human Learning and Memory, 7*, 355–368.

Medin, D. L., and Shaffer, M. M. (1978). Context theory of classification learning. *Psychological Review, 85*, 207–238.

Morton, J. (1979). Facilitation in word recognition: Experiments causing change in the logogen model. In P. A. Kolers, M. E. Wrolstal, and H. Bouma (Eds.), *Processing visible language I*. New York: Plenum.

Murdock, B. B. (1982). A theory for the storage and retrieval of item and associative information. *Psychological Review, 89*, 609–626.

Posner, M. I., and Keele, S. W. (1968). On the genesis of abstract ideas. *Journal of Experimental Psychology, 77*, 353–363.

Posner, M. I., and Keele, S. W. (1970). Retention of abstract ideas. *Journal of Experimental Psychology, 83*, 304–308.

Rosenblatt, F. (1962). *Principles of neurodynamics*. Washington, DC: Spartan.

Rumelhart, D. E., and McClelland, J. L (1981). Interactive processing through spreading activation. In A. M. Lesgold and C. A. Perfetti (Eds.), *Interactive Processes in Reading*. Hillsdale, NJ: Erlbaum.

Rumelhart, D. E., and McClelland, J. L. (1982). An interactive activation model of the effect of context in perception, Part II. The contextual enhancement effect and some tests and extensions of the model. *Psychological Review, 89*, 60–94.

Rumelhart, D. E., and McClelland, J. L. (1986). On learning the past tense of English verbs. In J. L. McClelland and D. E. Rumelhart (Eds.), *Parallel distributed processing: Explorations in the microstructure of cognition. Volume II: Psychological and Biological Models*. Cambridge, MA: MIT Press.

Rumelhart, D. E., and Zipser, D. (1985). Competitive learning. *Cognitive Science, 9*, 75–112.

Salasoo, A., Shiffrin, R. M., and Feustel, T. C. (1985). Building permanent memory codes: Codificaton and repetition effects in word identification. *Journal of Experimental Psychology: General. 114*, 50–77.

Stone, G. (1986). An analysis of the delta rule and the learning of statistical associations. In D. E. Rumelhart and J. L. McClelland (Eds.), *Parallel distributed processing: Explorations in the microstructure of cognition. Vol. 1. Foundations.* Cambridge, MA: MIT Press.

Sutton, R. S., and Barto, A. G. (1981). Toward a modern theory of adaptive networks: Expectation and prediction. *Psychological Review, 88*, 135–170.

Tulving, E. (1972). Episodic and semantic memory. In E. Tulving and W. Donaldson (Eds.), *Organization of Memory.* New York: Academic Press.

Whittlesea, B. W. A. (1983). *Representation and generalization of concepts: The abstractive and episodic perspectives evaluated.* Unpublished doctoral dissertation, MacMaster University.

Wickelgren, W. A. (1979). Chunking and consolidation: A theoretical synthesis of semantic networks, configuring in conditioning, S-R versus cognitive learning, normal forgetting, the amnesic syndrome, and the hippocampal arousal system. *Psychological Review, 86*, 44–60.

Willshaw, D. (1981). Holography, associative memory, and inductive generalization. In G. E. Hinton and J. A. Anderson (Eds.), *Parallel models of associative memory.* Hillsdale, NJ: Erlbaum.

Winston, P. H. (1975). Learning structural descriptions from examples. In P.H. Winston (Ed.), *The psychology of computer vision.* Cambridge, MA: Harvard.

SECTION SEVEN
MEMORY AND CONSCIOUSNESS

Editor's introduction

Probably the major new issue in memory research over the last 15 or so years has been the investigation of the relationship between memory and consciousness. We tend to assume that although the processes controlling remembering may be largely unconscious, memories themselves are things that we are fully conscious of. But many studies have now demonstrated that memories can express themselves unconsciously or implicitly. **Schacter**'s review (Chapter 12) on implicit memory describes some of the major ways in which implicit memories can be manifested and explores some of the key theoretical claims that have come from this body of research. As Schacter points out, the existence of implicit memory was in fact acknowledged in the nineteenth century by Ebbinghaus and other early experimental psychologists; however, an explosion of interest took place in the 1980s. The distinction between implicit and explicit memory bears strong connections to the procedural/declarative distinction described in Section Four.

Since Schacter's review was published, research in this area has been heavily influenced by a new procedure devised by Larry Jacoby and his colleagues. In this *process dissociation procedure*, the contributions of unconscious and conscious memory can be precisely measured by comparing subjects' performance in two memory tasks which differ according to whether or not the subject is trying intentionally to exclude recollected information from an earlier study phase. This procedure has generated a wealth of compelling results but has also been very controversial. The interested reader should consult Jacoby *et al.* (1993) for a description of the procedure, and Curran and Hintzman (1995) for a discussion of some of its pitfalls.

Another substantial literature relates to the involvement of consciousness in learning. Studies of *implicit learning* ask whether subjects can acquire knowledge of some complex domain without becoming aware of that knowledge. For reviews of this interesting topic, see Berry and Dienes (1993) and Shanks and St John (1994).

References

Berry, D. C. and Dienes, Z. (1993). *Implicit learning: theoretical and empirical issues*. Erlbaum, Hove.

Curran, T. and Hintzman, D. L. (1995). Violations of the independence assumption in process dissociation. *Journal of Experimental Psychology: Learning, Memory, and Cognition*, 21, 531–47.

Jacoby, L. L., Toth, J. P., and Yonelinas, A. P. (1993). Separating conscious and unconscious influences of memory: measuring recollection. *Journal of Experimental Psychology: General*, 122, 139–54.

Shanks, D. R. and St John M. F. (1994). Characteristics of dissociable human learning systems. *Behavioral and Brain Sciences*, 17, 367–447.

12 Daniel L. Schacter
'Implicit Memory: History and Current Status'

Reprinted in full from: *Journal of Experimental Psychology: Learning, Memory, and Cognition* **13**, 501–518 (1987)

Psychological studies of memory have traditionally relied on tests such as free recall, cued recall, and recognition. A prominent feature of these tests is that they make explicit reference to, and require conscious recollection of, a specific learning episode. During the past several years, however, increasing attention has been paid to experimental situations in which information that was encoded during a particular episode is subsequently expressed without conscious or deliberate recollection. Instead of being asked to try to remember recently presented information, subjects are simply required to perform a task, such as completing a graphemic fragment of a word, indicating a preference for one of several stimuli, or reading mirror-inverted script; memory is revealed by a facilitation or change in task performance that is attributable to information acquired during a previous study episode. Graf and Schacter (1985, 1987; Schacter and Graf, 1986a, 1986b) have labeled this type of memory *implicit memory*, and have used the term *explicit memory* to refer to conscious recollection of recently presented information, as expressed on traditional tests for free recall, cued recall, and recognition.

Recent cognitive and neuropsychological research has demonstrated a variety of striking dissociations between implicit and explicit memory and has shown that under certain conditions, implicit and explicit memory can be entirely independent of one another. These observations have raised fundamental questions concerning the nature and composition of memory, questions that will have to be addressed by any satisfactory theory of memory. The purposes of this article are to present an historical survey of observations concerning implicit memory, to review modern experimental studies and theoretical analyses, with particular emphasis on recent work in cognitive psychology and neuropsychology, and to suggest directions for future research.

Before the historical survey is initiated, two points regarding the terms implicit and explicit memory should be clarified. First, I use these terms in the manner suggested by Graf and Schacter (1985). Implicit memory is revealed when previous experiences facilitate performance on a task that does not require conscious or intentional recollection of those experiences; explicit memory is revealed when performance on a task requires conscious recollection of previous experiences. Note that these are *descriptive* concepts that are primarily concerned with a person's psychological experience at the time of retrieval. Accordingly, the concepts of implicit and explicit memory neither refer to, nor imply the existence of, two independent or separate memory systems. The question of whether implicit and explicit memory depend on a single underlying system or on multiple underlying systems is not yet resolved, as will be discussed later in this article. Second, the term *implicit memory* resembles two more familiar terms from the psychological literature: unconscious memory (e.g., Freud and Breuer, 1966; Prince, 1914) and unaware memory or memory without awareness (e.g., Eriksen, 1960; Jacoby and Witherspoon, 1982). These two terms have been used to describe phenomena that will be referred to here with the term *implicit memory*. The main reason for adopting *implicit memory* in favor of either *unconscious memory* or *unaware memory* has to do with the conceptual ambiguity of the latter two terms. The terms *unconscious* and *unaware* have a large number of psychological meanings and implications (e.g., Bowers, 1984; Ellenberger, 1970; Eriksen, 1960), many of which do not apply to the phenomena of interest here. Although the term *implicit* is not entirely free of conceptual ambiguity, it is less saturated with multiple and possibly misleading meanings than are *unconscious* or *unaware*.

Implicit memory: an historical survey

This section considers ideas and observations concerning implicit memory contributed by philosophers, psychologists, neurologists, psychiatrists, and others from the seventeenth century until the middle of the twentieth century. Unless otherwise stated, these investigators did not actually use the term *implicit memory* in their writings. They did, however, describe and discuss situations in which memory for recent experiences was expressed in the absence of conscious recollection. I sometimes use the phrase *implicit memory phenomena* in reference to these observations. This is done purely for purposes of expositional clarity and should not be seen as an attempt to put present concepts in the minds of past observers.

Philosophical analyses: Descartes, Leibniz, and Maine de Biran

It is widely recognized that both Plato and Aristotle commented extensively about the nature of memory, but both appear to have been concerned exclusively with explicit memory. During the Middle Ages, St. Augustine and St. Thomas Aquinas had a great deal to say about explicit retrieval and search processes, but I have not found any discussion of implicit memory in their writings.

The first clear reference to an implicit memory phenomenon appears to have been made by Descartes in his 1649 *The Passions of the Soul* (cited by Perry and Laurence, 1984), in which he observed that a frightening or aversive childhood experience may 'remain imprinted on his [the child's] brain to the end of his life' without 'any memory remaining of it afterwards' (Haldane and Ross, 1967, p. 391). Descartes did not, however, elaborate on the philosophical consequences of this phenomenon. In 1704, Gottfried Wilhelm Leibniz developed a systematic doctrine that both allowed for and made reference to implicit memory (Leibniz, 1916). He emphasized the importance of 'insensible' or 'unconscious' perceptions: ideas of which we are not consciously aware, but which do influence behavior. Leibniz explicitly claimed that people may have 'remaining effects of former impressions without remembering them,' and that '. . . often we have an extraordinary facility for conceiving certain things, because we formerly conceived them, without remembering them' (1916, p. 106). Although Leibniz's ideas concerning unconscious perceptions were later championed by several students and followers, they constituted a minority view during the eighteenth century, owing largely to the predominance of the British associationists. Locke, Hume, Mill, Brown, Hartley and others discussed memory at considerable length, but their analysis was restricted entirely to the domain of explicit memory; they had virtually nothing to say about implicit memory. Darwin (1794, p. 12) distinguished between *involuntary* and *voluntary* recollection, but both of these concepts were used in reference to explicit memory phenomena.

The first philosopher after Leibniz to systematically discuss phenomena of implicit memory was a French philosopher known by the surname Maine de Biran. Though virtually unknown today, he published an important treatise in 1804 entitled *The Influence of Habit on the Faculty of Thinking* (Maine de Biran, 1929). Like others before him, Maine de Biran believed that the analysis of habit was central to an understanding of human thought and behavior. Unlike others, however, Maine de Biran elucidated a feature of habit that had not been discussed previously in philosophical or scientific analyses: after sufficient repetition, a habit can eventually be executed *automatically* and *unconsciously* without awareness of the act itself or of the previous episodes in which the habit was learned. Thus, he observed that repeated actions are eventually executed with 'such promptitude and facility that we no longer perceive the voluntary action which directs them and we are absolutely unaware of the source that they have' (p. 73). The most striking feature of Maine de Biran's system, however, was his delineation and detailed discussion of three different types of memory: mechanical, sensitive, and representative. The first two types are driven by habit and are involved in the largely unconscious or implicit expression of repeated movements (mechanical) and feelings (sensitive); the third type (representative) is involved in conscious recollection of ideas and events (pp. 156–157). Thus, according to Maine de Biran,

If signs [in Maine de Biran's system, a *sign* is a motor response code] are absolutely empty of ideas or separated from every representative effect, from whatever cause this isolation may arise, recall is only a simple repetition of movements. I shall call this faculty for it *mechanical* memory. When the . . . recall of the sign is accompanied or immediately followed by the clear appearance of a well circumscribed idea, I shall attribute to it *representative memory*. If the sign expresses an affective modification, a feeling or even a fantastic image whatsoever, a vague, uncertain concept, which cannot be brought back to sense impressions . . . the recall of the sign . . . will belong to *sensitive memory*. (p. 156)

Maine de Biran's scheme represents the first clear articulation of what we might now call a *multiple memory system* interpretation of differences between implicit and explicit memory. Although it is alleged that Maine de Biran influenced the thinking of both Pierre Janet and Henri Bergson (Ellenberger, 1970), his ideas went almost entirely unrecognized outside of France. Most subsequent nineteenth-century philosophers did not systematically discuss the implicit expressions of memory that were so central to Maine de Biran's view. One exception was Johann Friedrich Herbart, who in 1816 introduced the notion that 'suppressed ideas,' which are unable to exceed the threshold of conscious awareness, can nevertheless influence conscious thinking (Herbart, 1896). The next systematic contributions were made by nineteenth-century scientists who approached the issue from the standpoint of biology and physiology.

Middle nineteenth century: unconscious cerebration and organic memory

It is now widely recognized that various nineteenth-century thinkers were concerned with the general problem of unconscious mental processing (cf. Ellenberger, 1970; Perry and Laurence, 1984). One of the most prolific of them was the British physiologist William Carpenter, who invoked the term *unconscious cerebration* to refer to mental activity that occurs outside of awareness (Carpenter, 1874). To support this idea, Carpenter marshalled clinical and anecdotal observations which demonstrated that the effects of recent experiences could be expressed without conscious awareness of those experiences. For example, drawing on observations of automatic writing (writing that appears to occur involuntarily while a subject is in a hypnotic or similar state), he claimed that 'It is a most remarkable confirmation of this view [unconscious cerebration], that ideas which have passed out of the *conscious* memory, sometimes express themselves in *involuntary muscular movements*, to the great surprise of the individuals executing them . . .' (1874, pp. 524–525). To Carpenter, the striking lack of autobiographical recognition of awareness that characterized implicit memory phenomena highlighted the critical role of such awareness in normal memory:

> Without this recognition, we should live in the present alone; for the reproduction of past states of consciousness would affect us only like the succession of fantasies presented to us in the play of the imagination . . . I am satisfied that I am the person to whom such and such experiences happened yesterday or a month, or a year, or twenty years ago; because I am not only conscious at the moment of the ideas which represent those experiences, but because I recognize them as the revived representations of my past experiences. (1874, p. 455)

Carpenter's concept of unconscious cerebration and consequent interest in implicit memory derived from a more general attempt to relate physiology and psychology. A similar integrative effort was made by the Viennese physiologist Ewald Hering, who in 1870 introduced the idea of *organic* or *unconscious* memory (Hering, 1920). Hering criticized earlier writers for restricting their analyses to conscious or explicit memory: 'The word ''memory'' is often understood as though it meant nothing more than our faculty of intentionally reproducing ideas or series of ideas' (1920, p. 68). Hering argued that it is necessary to consider unconscious memory, which is involved in involuntary recall, the development of automatic and unconscious habitual actions, and even in the processes of ontogenetic development and heredity. Although this last aspect of Hering's analysis clearly lies outside the domain of the present concerns, his psychological analyses of involuntary recall and the development of automaticity shared much in common with the earlier ideas of Maine de Biran. Following Hering's lead, a large number of psychologists, biologists, and others developed ideas concerning organic memory and its relation to what they referred to as conscious memory (see Schacter, 1982, Chapter 7).

Late nineteenth and early twentieth centuries: systematic empirical and theoretical developments

Toward the end of the nineteenth century, systematic empirical and theoretical analyses of implicit memory emerged in five different areas: 'psychical' research, neurology, psychiatry, philosophy, and experimental psychology.

Psychical research. Although modern practitioners might be reluctant to admit it, a good case can be made that nineteenth-century psychical researchers were the first to document implicit memory phenomena on the basis of controlled empirical observation. Two major 'implicit memory tests' were used: crystal ball gazing and automatic writing. Both procedures were characterized by the main feature of an implicit memory test: when performing these tasks, subjects made no explicit reference to a specific past event; they either reported what they 'saw' in the crystal or wrote whatever came to mind. Although the purpose of these procedures was to document phenomena such as telepathy and clairvoyance, several investigators reported that fragmentary representations of past experiences, devoid of any familiarity or autobiographical reference, frequently appeared during crystal gazing and automatic writing.

In an anonymously authored article in the *Journal of the Society for Psychical Research* (Miss X, 1889), it was reported that information that had been registered unconsciously (i.e., without attention) during the recent past often surfaced as an unfamiliar 'vision' during crystal gazing. On the basis of this observation, the author questioned 'spiritual' interpretations of crystal visions:

> It is easy to see how visions of this kind, occurring in the age of superstition, almost irresistibly suggested the theory of spirit-visitation. The percipient, receiving information which he did not recognize as already in his own mind, would inevitably suppose it to be derived from some invisible and unknown source external to himself. (p. 513)

In studies of automatic writing, several investigators described the emergence of knowledge acquired during past episodes which subjects were not aware that they possessed and that seemed foreign to their conscious personalities

(Binet, 1890; Prince, 1914). On the basis of his own experiments with automatic writing, Barkworth (1891) concluded that 'nothing is ever really forgotten, though the bygone memories evoked by pencil, or crystal, may appear so new and strange that we fail to recognize them as ever having been included in our experience' (p. 29).

Neurology. In 1845, the British physician Robert Dunn described the case of a woman who became amnesic after a near drowning and a long period of unconsciousness. During her amnesic state, the woman learned how to make dresses, even though she apparently did not explicitly remember that she had made any dresses:

> She applied herself closely to her new occupation and abandoned altogether the old one. Still she had no recollection from day to day what she had done, and every morning began something new unless her unfinished work was placed before her. (1845, p. 588)

Dunn did not discuss the theoretical implications of his observations.

Perhaps the first investigator to document implicit memory phenomena in neurological cases of amnesia and to delineate their theoretical implications was Sergei Korsakoff (1889). In one of his two classic papers describing the amnesic syndrome that now bears his name, Korsakoff observed that '. . . although the patient was not aware that he preserved traces of impressions that he received, those traces however probably existed and had an influence in one way or another on the course of ideas, at least in unconscious intellectual activity' (1889, p. 512). Korsakoff provided several insightful observations to support this notion. For example, he described a patient whom he had given an electrical shock. Though this patient did not explicitly remember being given any shocks, when Korsakoff showed him a case that contained the shock apparatus, 'he told me that I probably came to electrify him, and meanwhile I knew well that he had only learned to know that machine during his illness' (p. 512). Korsakoff went on to argue that amnesic patients retained 'weak' memory traces that could affect behavior unconsciously, but were not 'strong' enough to enter conscious memory. He emphasized that his observations had important implications for psychologists:

> We notice that a whole series of traces which could in no way be restored to consciousness, neither actively nor passively, continue to exist in unconscious life, continue to direct the course of ideas of the patients, suggesting to him some or other inferences and decisions. That seems to me to be one of the most interesting peculiarities of the disturbance about which we are speaking. (p. 518)

Over 20 years later, Claparède (1911/1951) reported observations that were similar to Korsakoff's, although they are somewhat better known today. Claparède described the now famous example of an amnesic woman who refused to shake hands with him after he pricked her with a pin, even though she did not explicitly remember that Claparède had done so. Claparède interpreted this implicit expression of memory in terms of a disconnection between the ego and the memory trace. At about the same time, Schneider (1912, cited in Parkin, 1982) reported experiments in which he demonstrated that amnesic patients required progressively less information across learning trials to identify fragmented pictures, even though patients did not explicitly remember having seen the pictures before.

Psychiatry. Seminal observations concerning implicit memory were reported in the late 1880s and early 1890s by Pierre Janet and by Sigmund Freud, partly in collaboration with Joseph Breuer. For both Janet and Freud, the critical phenomena were observed in patients suffering hysterical amnesia as a result of emotional trauma. Although these patients could not explicitly remember the traumatic events, their memories of them were expressed indirectly (implicitly) in various ways. Janet (1893), for example, described a case in which a woman became amnesic after being mistakenly informed by a man who appeared suddenly in her doorway that her husband had died. Even though she subsequently could not consciously remember this incident, she 'froze with terror' whenever she passed the door that the man had entered. In a later article, Janet (1904) described a woman who had become amnesic following the death of her mother. Though she could not consciously remember any of the events surrounding her mother's death, she experienced 'hallucinations' that preserved the contents of those events. After describing numerous other cases of implicit memory in hysteric patients, Janet concluded that hysterical amnesia consists of two key factors: '1. the inability of the subject to evoke memories consciously and voluntarily, and 2. the automatic, compelling, and untimely activation of these same memories' (1904, p. 24). He theorized that hysteria was attributable to a pathological process of dissociation that interfered with the ability to synthesize memories into the 'personal consciousness.'

Freud's observations on hysteria were similar to Janet's insofar as he emphasized that traumatic memories, inaccessible to consciousness, were expressed unconsciously by the patient as hysterical symptoms (see Freud and Breuer, 1966, for relevant cases). Although Freud later changed this view (Ellenberger, 1970), he never abandoned the idea that unconscious memories exert powerful influences on behavior.

Both Janet and Freud emphasized the role of unconscious or implicit memory in psychopathology. The American psychiatrist Morton Prince clearly delineated the importance of implicit memory for normal cognitive function. In *The Unconscious* (1914), Prince drew together numerous observations of implicit memory from work with hysterical patients, hypnosis, dreams, and automatic writing, in which '. . . memories of the forgotten experiences [are expressed] without awareness therefore on the part of the personal consciousness' (p. 13). Noting that '. . . memories may be made to reveal themselves, without inducing recollection, at the very moment when the subject cannot voluntarily recall them' (p. 63), Prince concluded that '. . . a conscious experience that has passed out of mind may not only recur again as conscious memory, but may recur subconsciously below the threshold of awareness' (p. 8). These observations, Prince argued, demonstrate that experiences that are not available to conscious or voluntary recall nevertheless influence cognition and behavior in everyday life:

> In normal life ideas of buried experiences of which we have no recollection intrude themselves from time to time and shape our judgments and the current of our thoughts without our realizing what has determined our mental processes. We have forgotten the source of our judgments, but this forgetfulness does not affect the mechanism of the process. (p. 68)

Philosophy. The major philosophical contribution to the analysis of implicit memory was made by Henri Bergson. In *Matter and Memory* (1911), he argued that 'The past survives under two distinct forms: first, in motor mechanisms; secondly, in independent recollections' (p. 87). The first form of memory involves gradual learning of habits and skills and does not entail explicit reference to any specific past events; a learned habit '. . . bears upon it no mark which betrays its origin and classes it in the past; it is part of my present . . .' (p. 91). Bergson's second form of memory, recollection, entails explicit remembering of 'memory-images' that represent specific events from one's past. Although this view is clearly reminiscent of Maine de Biran, Bergson did not actually discuss or even reference Maine de Biran's views anywhere in *Matter and Memory*.

Experimental psychology. Experimental psychologists paid relatively little attention to implicit memory phenomena in the late nineteenth and early twentieth centuries. Even though there was a large and thriving field in this post-Ebbinghausian era (cf. Schacter, 1982, Chapter 8), most practitioners did not distinguish between explicit and implicit memory. Several exceptions, however, can be identified. Ebbinghaus (1885) himself acknowledged that not all effects of memory are expressed in conscious awareness (1885, p. 2). He also made a relevant empirical contribution, noting that savings were observed over a 24-hour retention interval for items that he did not consciously remember having studied before (pp. 58–59; see Slamecka, 1985a, 1985b; Tulving, 1985b). This intriguing observation was not systematically followed up by Ebbinghaus or others. Ebbinghaus' savings paradigm, in which memory is tested by relearning previously studied lists, can be viewed more generally as an implicit memory test; explicit recollection of a prior episode or list is not called for during relearning (Slamecka, 1985b). Indeed, Ebbinghaus noted that one advantage of the savings method was that it could provide evidence for the existence in memory of information that could not be recollected consciously (1885, p. 8). Of course, numerous subsequent investigators used the savings method to analyze learning and transfer of training. Although there is a sense in which 'the entire literature on transfer of training may be perceived as the study of implicit memory' (Slamecka, 1985b, p. 499), researchers did not view it as such and did not elaborate any distinctions like the one between implicit and explicit memory.

After Ebbinghaus, three lines of experimental investigation were concerned with certain aspects of implicit memory. First, Thorndike conducted a large number of experiments that, he claimed, demonstrated that subjects could learn various rules without conscious awareness of them or explicit memory for them (Thorndike and Rock, 1934; see Irwin *et al.*, 1934, for methodological criticisms). Second, Poetzl reported in 1917 that unreported features of subliminally exposed pictures appeared in subjects' subsequent imagery and dreams, even though they did not remember these features and were allegedly unaware of them at the time of stimulus exposure (see Poetzl, 1960). Poetzl's experiments, however, were characterized by serious methodological deficiencies (Dixon, 1981; Erdelyi, 1970). Third, studies of hypnotic phenomena by Clark Hull (1933) and his students provided numerous demonstrations of implicit memory for skills, conditioned responses, and facts acquired during hypnosis. Hull's description of the quality of recall by hypnotic subjects resembled Claparède's and Korsakoff's earlier observations of organic amnesia: 'In such cases they stated that the name seemed to come from ''nowhere'' and was not accompanied by any recollection that the character or syllable had ever been encountered before' (1933, p. 134).

One further contribution from experimental psychology ought to be noted. In *Outline of Psychology* (1924), William McDougall became the first investigator to use the terms *implicit* and *explicit* with reference to the different ways in which memory can be expressed. He distinguished between explicit recognition, which involves conscious recollection of a past event, and implicit recognition, which involves a change in behavior that is attributable to a recent event yet contains no conscious recollection of it or explicit reference to it (1924, pp. 308–309).

Summary of historical survey

Four general points can be made regarding the historical survey. First, observations of implicit memory were reported across a broad range of tasks, subjects, and conditions. Perhaps the richest sources of implicit memory phenomena were the clinical observations made by Claparède, Freud, Janet, Korsakoff, Prince and others. With the exception of Prince, these clinicians did not set out with the specific aim of distinguishing between forms of memory. Nevertheless, they were insightful observers who recognized clearly that the phenomena they described had important implications for theories of normal and abnormal mental function. Indeed, there were relatively few investigators who explicitly raised the issue of whether different forms of memory could be distinguished and then went on to report original empirical observations; Ebbinghaus and Prince should be counted prominently among them. A second, related point is that most empirical observations either were anecdotal, were made under relatively uncontrolled clinical conditions, or were reported in experiments that lacked methodological rigor. Thus, even though the early observers reported phenomena that are broadly similar to those of interest today, methodological inadequacies limit the degree to which they bear directly on contemporary theoretical concerns. Third, there were only a few attempts to develop theoretical accounts of the dissociations that had been observed. The most popular idea was that implicit memory phenomena were produced by memory traces that are too 'weak' to exceed the threshold of strength or activation needed for explicit memory (Herbart, 1896; Leibniz, 1916; Korsakoff, 1889; Prince, 1914). As will be shown later, recent experimental work has provided grounds for rejecting this view. However, several other ideas were advanced, including the multiple-memories view of Maine de Biran and Bergson, and the notion of a dissociation between memory traces and the 'self' articulated by Claparède and Janet. Fourth, the various investigators who were concerned with implicit memory phenomena exhibited little or no knowledge of each other's work. This circumstance is perhaps not surprising, because observations of implicit memory were made in disparate fields of study.

Modern research on implicit memory

Let us now consider research concerning implicit memory from the 1950s to the present. Data from five different though partly overlapping research areas will first be reviewed: savings during relearning, effects of subliminally encoded stimuli, learning and conditioning without awareness, repetition priming, and preserved learning in amnesic patients. This review is followed by a consideration of contemporary theoretical approaches to implicit memory.

Savings during relearning

As noted earlier, it is possible to view the phenomenon of savings during relearning as an index of implicit memory, in the sense that relearning a previously studied list does not require explicit reference to a prior learning episode, although the influence of the prior episode is revealed by savings (cf. Slamecka, 1985b). However, little of the voluminous research on savings has addressed the question of whether subjects do indeed rely on explicit memory for prior learning episodes when relearning a list, so it is not entirely clear what savings studies tell us about implicit memory. The most directly pertinent evidence has been provided by Nelson (1978), who has shown savings for items that are neither recalled nor recognized, which thereby suggests that savings can occur in an entirely implicit manner.

Effects of subliminally encoded stimuli

The controversy concerning subliminal perception is well known to experimental psychologists (Dixon, 1971). Although early experiments purporting to demonstrate subliminal perception were severely criticized (Eriksen, 1960), recent studies using a variety of new experimental techniques have supplied more convincing evidence that stimuli that are not represented in subjective awareness (Cheesman and Merikle, 1986) are nevertheless processed to high levels by the perceptual system (e.g., Cheesman and Merikle, 1986; Dixon, 1981; Fowler *et al.*, 1981; Marcel, 1983; see Holender, 1986, for a methodological critique). More relevant to the present concerns, several studies have purported to show that stimuli that are not consciously perceived, and hence cannot be explicitly remembered, influence subsequent behavior and performance on tasks that do not require conscious recollection of the subliminal stimulus, such as free association (Haber and Erdelyi, 1967; Shevrin and Fritzler, 1968) and imaginative story and fantasy productions (Giddan, 1967; Pine, 1960). However, questions regarding interpretation of these results have been raised (Dixon, 1981; Erdelyi, 1970).

The foregoing experiments did not systematically examine the relation between implicit and explicit memory for subliminally exposed stimuli. However, recent studies have demonstrated implicit memory for subliminal or briefly exposed stimuli under conditions in which subjects exhibit little or no explicit memory. Kunst-Wilson and Zajonc (1980) showed subjects geometric shapes at exposure durations that they contended were too brief (1 ms) to permit conscious perception. Explicit memory for the shapes, as indexed by forced-choice recognition performance, was at chance. However, subjects demonstrated implicit memory by showing a reliable preference for the previously exposed shapes on a test in which they rated which of two shapes – one old, one new – they liked better. Similar results have been reported by Seamon *et al.* (1983) and Wilson (1979). Mandler *et al.* showed that brief stimulus exposures that yield chance levels of recognition memory can influence nonaffective stimulus judgments (i.e., brightness). Bargh and Pietromonaco (1982) examined the effects of subliminal exposures to 'hostile' words (e.g., unkind, thoughtless) on a subsequent impression formation task. Subjects who had been given subliminal exposures to hostile words later rated a target person more negatively than did those who had not received such prior exposure, even though explicit recognition of the hostile words was at the chance level. Bargh *et al.* (1986) observed similar implicit effects following subliminal exposure to various other types of words. Lewicki (1985) found that after subliminal exposure to adjective-noun pairs (e.g., *old–tree*) subjects tended to choose the previously exposed adjective in response to questions concerning how they 'felt' about the noun (e.g., *Is a tree big or old?*).

A recent study by Eich (1984) that used a different method to attenuate conscious perception of target materials yielded data consistent with the foregoing results. Eich used an auditory divided-attention task in which homophones were presented on the unattended channel together with words intended to bias the low frequency interpretation of the homophone (e.g., *taxi–FARE*). Subjects subsequently showed no explicit memory for the homophones on a *yes/no* recognition test. However, when required to spell the target words, subjects provided the low frequency spelling of the homophones more often than in baseline conditions, thereby demonstrating implicit memory for the unattended information.

Learning and conditioning without awareness

In learning-without-awareness studies, subjects allegedly learn rules or contingencies without awareness of learning them and, hence, without explicit memory for them (cf. Greenspoon, 1955; Thorndike and Rock, 1934). The phenomenon was studied extensively during the 1950s in multi-trial learning experiments in which subjects were reinforced for making specific responses or types of responses. Several investigators reported that subjects who were unaware of the reinforcement-response contingency provided the reinforced response with increasing frequency across trials, but others pointed to the lack of appropriate methods for determining subjects' awareness of the reinforcement-response contingency (for review, see Eriksen, 1960). Studies that used more rigorous methods for assessing awareness reported some positive evidence of learning without awareness (Giddan and Eriksen, 1959; Krieckhaus and Eriksen, 1960), as did research in which the reinforcement-response contingency was thoroughly disguised (Rosenfeld and Baer, 1969; see also Nisbett and Wilson, 1977). However, many negative observations were also reported (Brewer, 1974).

In related research, several investigators presented evidence that subjects could acquire various types of classically conditioned responses without awareness of conditioning contingencies (cf. Adams, 1957; Lacey and Smith, 1954), but assessment of awareness was often insufficient (Brewer, 1974). Along these same lines, research concerning the phenomenon of subception (Lazarus and McCleary, 1951) indicated that an experimentally acquired conditioned response, revealed by the galvanic skin response to nonsense syllables that had been accompanied by shock, could be subsequently elicited by brief exposures to the nonsense syllables, even though subjects did not detect the presence of the syllables. Although some questions and criticisms were raised about interpretations of the subception phenomenon, the finding that a conditioned response could sometimes be elicited by an unreported stimulus was not challenged (Eriksen, 1960, pp. 287–288).

Recent evidence concerning rule or contingency learning without awareness has been reported in a series of experiments by Reber and his colleagues concerning a phenomenon that they call *implicit learning* (e.g., Reber, 1976; Reber *et al.*, 1985; see also Brooks, 1978; Gordon and Holyoak, 1983; McAndrews and Moscovitch, 1985). In these studies, subjects were presented with letter strings that were organized according to various rules of a synthetic grammar. Reber and his associates reported that subjects learned to identify grammatically correct strings even when they were not consciously or explicitly aware of the appropriate rules (for critique and discussion, see Dulany *et al.*, 1984, 1985; Reber *et al.*, 1985). Using a somewhat different procedure, Lewicki (1986) showed that contingencies between different features of stimulus information influenced latencies to respond to questions regarding the contingent features, even though none of the subjects could explicitly state the nature of the contingency.

Repetition priming effects

Most of the recent work in cognitive psychology that can be characterized as implicit memory research has been concerned with the phenomenon of direct or repetition priming (cf. Cofer, 1967): facilitation in the processing of a stimulus as a function of a recent encounter with the same stimulus. Repetition priming has been observed on a variety of tests that do not make explicit reference to a prior study episode. The tests most commonly used in priming research are *lexical decision, word identification*, and *word stem* or *fragment completion*. On the lexical decision test (e.g., Forbach *et al.,* 1974; Scarborough *et al.,* 1979), subjects are required to state whether or not a particular letter string constitutes a legal word; priming is reflected by a decreased latency in the making of a lexical decision on the second presentation of a letter string relative to the first. On the word identification test (also referred to as *tachistoscopic identification* or *perceptual identification*; e.g., Feustel *et al.,* 1983; Jacoby and Dallas, 1981; Neisser, 1954), subjects are given a brief exposure (e.g., 30 ms) to a stimulus and then attempt to identify it. Priming on this task is indicated by an increase in the accuracy of identifying recently exposed items relative to new items or by a decrease in the amount of exposure time necessary to identify recently exposed items. On word completion tests (e.g., Graf *et al.,* 1982; Tulving *et al.,* 1982; Warrington and Weiskrantz, 1974), subjects are either given a word *stem* (e.g., tab — for table) or *fragment* (e.g., –ss–ss —for assassin) and are instructed to complete it with the first appropriate word that comes to mind. Here, priming is reflected by an enhanced tendency to complete test stems or fragments with words exposed on a prior study list. Other priming tests include reading of transformed script (Kolers, 1975, 1976; Masson, 1984), face identification (Bruce and Valentine, 1985; Young *et al.,* 1986), and free association (Storms, 1958; Williamsen *et al.,* 1965).

The current interest in repetition priming derives from two distinct and at times independent areas of investigation. The first area grew out of research on word recognition and lexical organization. The general purpose of these studies was to use the pattern of priming effects observed on tasks such as word identification and lexical decision as a basis for making inferences about the nature of lexical access and representation (cf. Morton, 1979; Murrell and Morton, 1974; Scarborough *et al.,* 1979). This line of research has yielded a number of useful findings about performance on implicit memory tests. Several investigators who attempted to distinguish between modality-specific and modality-nonspecific components of lexical organization by examining the effect of auditory–visual modality shifts on the magnitude of repetition priming reported little or no priming of tachistosopic identification (e.g. Kirsner and Smith, 1974; Kirsner *et al.,* 1983) and lexical decision performance (e.g., Kirsner *et al.,* 1983; Scarborough *et al.,* 1979) following an auditory study presentation. A number of studies have compared repetition priming of real words and nonwords, and have generally found that nonwords show either no priming or smaller amounts of priming than real words (Forbach *et al.,* 1974; Forster and Davis, 1984; Kirsner and Smith, 1974; Scarborough *et al.,* 1977), although robust priming of nonwords has been observed under some experimental conditions (Feustel *et al.,* 1983; Salasoo *et al.,* 1985).

Several studies have demonstrated that priming of word identification performance occurs for morphologically similar words (e.g., exposure to *seen* facilitates identification of *sees*; Murrell and Morton, 1974), but not for visually similar words (*seen* does not facilitate *seed*; Murrell and Morton, 1974; see also Osgood and Hoosain, 1974) or phonologically similar words (*frays* does not facilitate *phrase*; Neisser, 1954). In an important study, Winnick and Daniel (1970) examined word identification performance following three types of study conditions: reading a familiar word from a visual presentation of it, generation of the word from a picture of it, or generation of the word from its definition. They observed significant priming on the word identification task following visual presentation but observed no priming in either of the generation conditions. By contrast, they found that free recall of words in both generation conditions was considerably higher than in the read condition. Although Winnick and Daniel did not set out to compare implicit and explicit memory, their results revealed a sharp dissociation between these two forms of memory (for similar results, see Jacoby, 1983b).

The second line of investigation concerned with priming effects was initiated in the context of research on episodic memory. It was stimulated largely by Warrington and Weiskrantz's (1968, 1974) work on amnesia, which will be reviewed in the next section. Their experiments demonstrated that amnesic patients showed excellent retention when required to complete three-letter stems of recently presented words, despite their inability to remember the prior occurrence of the words on a *yes/no* recognition test. Several investigators examined whether similar dissociations could be produced in normal subjects by manipulation of appropriate experimental variables (e.g., Graf *et al.*, 1982; Jacoby and Dallas, 1981; Tulving *et al.*, 1982), and thereby initiated systematic comparison of performance on implicit and explicit memory tests. Data generated by this line of investigation indicate that repetition priming effects on implicit memory tests can be experimentally dissociated from explicit recall and recognition in a number of ways.

First, several studies have demonstrated that variations in level or type of study processing have differential effects on priming and remembering, in conformity with the finding first reported by Winnick and Daniel (1970). For instance, Jacoby and Dallas (1981) showed subjects a list of familiar words and had them perform a study task that required elaborative processing (e.g., answering questions about the meaning of target words) or did not require elaborative processing (e.g., deciding whether or not a word contains a particular letter). Memory for the words was subsequently assessed with *yes/no* recognition and word identification tests. As expected on the basis of many previous experiments (cf. Craik and Tulving, 1975), explicit memory was influenced by type of study processing: recognition performance was higher following elaborative study tasks than non-elaborative study tasks. Implicit memory, however was unaffected by the study task manipulation; priming effects on word identification performance were about the same following the elaborative and non-elaborative processing tasks. Graf *et al.* (1982) reported a similar pattern of results by using free recall as an index of explicit memory and stem completion as an index of implicit memory. More recently, Graf and Mandler (1984) found dissociable effects of a study-task manipulation on implicit and explicit memory when test cues were identical (i.e., three-letter word stems) and only instructions were varied. When subjects were told to use the stems to try to remember study-list words (explicit memory instructions), more items were recalled following elaborative study processing than following non-elaborative study processing. However, when subjects were instructed to write down the first word that came to mind in response to a test stem (implicit memory instructions), type of study task did not affect the amount of priming observed. Schacter and McGlynn (1989) assessed implicit memory for common idioms (e.g., SOUR—GRAPES) with a free-association test (e.g., SOUR–?) in which subjects wrote down the first word that came to mind, and assessed explicit memory with a cued-recall test in which the same cue was provided and subjects were instructed to try to remember the appropriate study-list target. Implicit memory was invariant across several elaborative and non-elaborative study tasks that significantly influenced explicit memory.

A second type of dissociation between implicit and explicit memory involves the effect of study-test changes in modality of presentation and other types of surface information. As was noted earlier, priming effects on lexical decision and word identification tests are significantly reduced by study-test modality shifts (Clarke and Morton, 1983; Kirsner *et al.*, 1983; Kirsner and Smith, 1974). Jacoby and Dallas (1981) compared the effects of modality shifts on implicit (word identification) and explicit (*yes/no* recognition) tasks. They found that changing modality of presentation from study (auditory) to test (visual) severely attenuated priming effects on word identification performance but had little or no effect on recognition performance. Graf *et al.* (1985) reported that priming effects on the stem completion task were reduced by a study-test modality shift, whereas cued-recall performance was not significantly influenced by this manipulation, and Roediger and Blaxton (1987) found that priming of word-fragment completion performance was attenuated by modality shifts even though free recall and recognition performance were largely unaffected. Along the same lines, several studies have shown that within the visual modality, priming effects on lexical decision, fragment completion, and reading tasks are highly sensitive to study-test changes of various types of surface information (Kolers, 1975, 1976; Roediger and Blaxton, 1987; Roediger and Weldon, 1987; Scarborough *et al.*, 1979), whereas recall and recognition are either unaffected or slightly affected by such changes.

A third kind of evidence for implicit/explicit dissociations comes from studies that have manipulated retention interval. On both word fragment completion (Komatsu and Ohta, 1984; Tulving *et al.*, 1982) and word identification tests (Jacoby and Dallas, 1981), priming effects persist with little change across delays of days and weeks, whereas recognition memory declines across the same delays. In other situations, however, priming of word stem completion (Graf and Mandler, 1984; Graf *et al.*, 1984; Shimamura and Squire, 1984) and lexical decision (Forster and Davis, 1984) has proved to be a relatively transient phenomenon, decaying across delays of minutes and hours over which explicit remembering persists. Fourth, recent studies indicate that manipulations of retroactive and proactive interference that significantly impair explicit recall and recognition do not influence priming effects on either word stem completion (Graf and Schacter, 1987) or word fragment completion (Sloman *et al.*, 1988). A fifth and final type of evidence for dissociation between priming and remembering is the finding of statistical independence between performance on recognition tests and tests of word fragment completion (Tulving *et al.*, 1982), word stem completion (Graf and Schacter, 1985), homophone spelling (Eich, 1984; Jacoby and Witherspoon, 1982), prototype identification (Metcalfe and Fisher, 1986), and reading of mirror-inverted script (Kolers, 1976). In these experiments, successful performance on an implicit memory test was uncorrelated with success or failure on an explicit memory test.

Taken together, the foregoing studies provide impressive evidence that priming effects on implicit memory tests differ substantially from explicit recall and recognition. Other studies, however, have revealed several similarities between priming and remembering. First, under certain conditions manipulations of retention interval have parallel effects on priming effects and explicit memory (Jacoby, 1983a; Schacter and Graf, 1986a; Sloman *et al.*, 1988). Second, Jacoby (1983a) has shown that manipulating list context at the time of test, which is known to affect recognition memory, also affects performance on the word identification task: identification performance was higher when 90% of tested words came from a previously studied list than when only 10% did. Third, both implicit and explicit memory are influenced by newly acquired associations between unrelated word pairs. On a variety of implicit memory tests, including word stem completion (Graf and Schacter, 1985, 1987; Schacter and Graf, 1986a, 1986b), lexical decision (McKoon and Ratcliff, 1979, 1986), and reading of degraded word pairs (Moscovitch *et al.*, 1986), more priming is observed when a target word is tested in the context of its study-list cue than when it is tested alone or in the presence of some other cue. Fourth, this phenomenon of *implicit memory for new associations* (cf. Graf and Schacter, 1985) resembles explicit remembering of new associations insofar as it depends on some degree of elaborative processing at the time of study. For example, Schacter and Graf observed associative effects on word completion performance after subjects had performed study tasks that required them to elaborate semantic links between two unrelated words, such as generating sentences or reading meaningful sentences (e.g., *The injured* OFFICER *smelled the* FLOWER). When subjects engaged in study tasks that prevented elaboration of semantic relations, such as comparing the number of vowels and consonants in the target words or reading anomalous sentences (e.g., *The dusky* COW *multiplied the* EMPLOYER), implicit memory for new associations was not observed. Schacter and McGlynn (1989), using free association and cued recall tests, also found that both implicit and explicit memory for newly acquired associations depends on elaborative study processing. A fifth type of evidence showing a relation between implicit and explicit memory was reported by Johnston *et al.* (1985). They demonstrated that processes subserving implicit memory can affect performance on an explicit memory task: recently studied words that were identified quickly on a word identification test were more likely to be given a recognition judgment of 'old' than were more slowly identified words. These similarities between implicit and explicit memory have a number of implications that will be discussed later when alternative theoretical accounts of implicit memory are compared.

Implicit memory in amnesia

The amnesic syndrome, which is produced by lesions to the medial temporal and diencephalic regions of the brain (e.g., Moscovitch, 1982; Rozin, 1976; Squire, 1986; Weiskrantz, 1985), is characterized by normal perceptual, linguistic, and intellectual functioning together with an inability to remember explicitly recent events and new information. Amnesic patients are seriously impaired on standard tests of explicit recall and recognition, and they perform disastrously in real-life situations that require explicit remembering, such as recollecting actions and events during a round of golf (Schacter, 1983). Beginning with the previously discussed clinical observations of Korsakoff (1889) and Claparède (1911/1951), instances of implicit memory by amnesic patients have been documented widely. Most modern studies of implicit memory in amnesia can be classified into two broad categories: skill learning or repetition priming.

Research on skill learning in amnesia was initiated by Milner and Corkin and their colleagues in the 1960s. They demonstrated that the profoundly amnesic patient H. M. could acquire motor skills such as pursuit rotor and mirror tracing, even though he did not remember explicitly that he had previously performed the task (Milner, 1962; Milner *et al.*, 1968). Robust learning of motor skills has been observed in various other amnesic patients (e.g., Butters, 1987; Eslinger and Damasio, 1986; Starr and Phillips, 1970). Amnesic patients have also exhibited normal or near-normal learning of perceptual and cognitive skills, including reading of mirror-inverted script (Cohen and Squire, 1980; Moscovitch, 1982), puzzle solving (Brooks and Baddeley, 1976), rule learning (Kinsbourne and Wood, 1975), and serial pattern learning (Nissen and Bullemer, 1987), despite their failure to remember explicitly that they had previously performed the skills. Similar dissociations have been observed in drug-induced amnesia (Nissen *et al.*, 1987) and multiple-personality amnesia (Nissen *et al.*, 1988).

The second major area of research on implicit memory in amnesia, concerned with repetition priming effects, was initiated by the important series of experiments conducted by Warrington and Weiskrantz (1968, 1970, 1974, 1978). They found that amnesic patients could show normal retention of a list of familiar words when tested with word stem or fragment cues, whereas these same patients were profoundly impaired on free recall and recognition tests. Indeed, Warrington and Weiskrantz (1968) noted that patients often did not remember that they had been shown any study-list items and treated the fragment test as a kind of 'guessing game.' In subsequent research using the fragment cueing procedure, amnesic patients' performance was sometimes impaired with respect to that of control subjects (e.g., Squire *et al.*, 1978).

It is now clear that whether or not amnesic patients show normal retention when tested with word fragments and various other cues depends critically on the implicit/explicit nature of the test. For example, Graf *et al.* (1984) demonstrated that when subjects were given explicit memory instructions – that is, they were told to use word stems as cues for *remembering* previously studied words – amnesics were impaired with respect to controls. By contrast, when subjects were given implicit memory instructions – that is, they were told to complete the stems with the first word that comes to mind – amnesics and controls showed comparable amounts of priming (see also Graf *et al.*, 1985). In an early and often overlooked study, Gardner *et al.* (1973) presented Korsakoff's syndrome amnesics and controls with a categorized word list. When subjects were subsequently given category cues and asked to respond with the first category member that came to mind, both amnesics and controls showed equivalent amounts of priming. When asked to remember list items in response to category cues, amnesics were impaired with respect to controls (see also Graf *et al.*, 1985; see Kihlstrom, 1980, for priming of category production performance in hypnotic amnesia). Schacter (1985) found that amnesic patients showed normal priming effects after studying a list of common idioms (e.g., SOUR—GRAPES) and then writing down the first word that came to mind on a free-association test (e.g., SOUR—?). Amnesics were impaired, however, when instructed to try to use the same cues to remember study-list targets. Shimamura and Squire (1984) obtained a similar pattern of results with highly related paired associates (e.g., TABLE—CHAIR). On the basis of these studies, it seems reasonable to conclude that normal retention of a list of familiar items by amnesic patients occurs only when implicit tests are used. Consistent with this observation, amnesic patients have shown normal priming effects on various other implicit memory tests, including lexical decision (Moscovitch, 1982), perceptual identification (Cermak *et al.*, 1985), and homophone spelling (Jacoby and Witherspoon, 1982; for more extensive review, see Schacter and Graf, 1986b; Shimamura, 1986).

In most of the priming experiments discussed thus far, study materials consisted of items with integrated or unitized pre-existing memory representations, such as common words, linguistic idioms, or highly related paired associates. Recently, several investigators have examined whether amnesic patients show normal priming or implicit memory for novel information that does not have any pre-existing representation as a unit in memory, such as nonwords or unrelated paired associates. The results thus far have been mixed. Cermak *et al.* (1985) found that amnesic patients do not show priming of nonwords on a perceptual identification task, and Diamond and Rozin (1984) obtained similar results when implicit memory was tested with three-letter stems. Using a word completion test, Graf and Schacter (1985) and Schacter and Graf (1986b) found that some amnesic patients – those with relatively mild memory disorders – showed normal implicit memory for a newly acquired association between unrelated words, whereas severely amnesic patients did not show implicit memory for new associations. Moscovitch *et al.* (1986) assessed implicit memory with a task that involved reading degraded pairs of unrelated words, and observed normal implicit memory for new associations in patients with severe memory disorders. McAndrews *et al.* 1987 investigated implicit memory for new information by presenting subjects with novel, difficult-to-comprehend sentences (e.g., *The haystack was important because the cloth ripped*), and requiring them to generate cues that rendered the sentences comprehensible (e.g., *parachute*). They found that severely amnesic patients' ability to generate the correct cues was facilitated substantially by a single prior exposure to the cue-sentence pair, despite their complete lack of explicit memory for the sentences and cues.

The foregoing studies indicate that amnesic patients can show priming effects for newly acquired information, but they also suggest that such effects depend on the type of implicit memory test that is used and, in some instances, on the severity of amnesia. Another important issue concerning priming in amnesic patients concerns the duration of the phenomenon. Several investigators have reported that priming of word completion performance in amnesic patients is a relatively transient phenomenon, lasting only a few hours (Diamond and Rozin, 1984; Graf *et al.*, 1984; Rozin, 1976; Squire *et al.*, 1987). By contrast, McAndrews *et al.* (1987) found that severely amnesic patients showed robust priming on their sentence puzzle task after a 1-week retention interval. These observations suggest that the duration of priming in amnesic patients may depend on the way that implicit memory is assessed and the nature of the target information.

In addition to skill learning and repetition priming phenomena, amnesic patients have also exhibited dissociations between implicit and explicit memory in various other situations. Schacter *et al.* (1984) demonstrated that amnesic patients could learn some fictitious information about people (e.g., *Bob Hope's father was a fireman*), but could not remember explicitly that they had just been told the information (see also Schacter and Tulving, 1982; Shimamura and Squire, 1987). Similarly, Luria (1976) observed that an amnesic patient produced bits and pieces of recently presented stories, even though he did not remember being told any stories. Glisky *et al.* (1986) showed that a densely amnesic patient could learn to program a microcomputer despite the patient's persistent failure to remember explicitly that he had ever worked on a microcomputer. Johnson *et al.* (1985) found that amnesics acquired preferences for previously exposed melodies, Crovitz *et al.* (1979) demonstrated that amnesics could spot a hidden figure more quickly after a single exposure to it, and Weiskrantz and Warrington (1979) reported evidence of classical conditioning in amnesic patients – in all cases, with little or no explicit recollection of the experimental materials and of the learning episode itself.

Summary of contemporary studies

The research reviewed in the preceding five sections indicates that implicit memory has been documented across different tasks, materials, and subject populations. Although it is clear that a wide variety of phenomena can all be grouped together under the rather general heading of *implicit memory*, it is equally clear that there are differences among these diverse phenomena. One difference that may be significant theoretically concerns whether implicit memories are *accessible* or *inaccessible* explicitly – that is, whether or not information that is expressed implicitly can, under certain conditions, be remembered explicitly. Several studies have found substantial implicit memory when explicit recognition is at the chance level and explicit recall is at or close to the floor, thereby suggesting that the implicitly expressed information is inaccessible explicitly (e.g., Bargh and Pietromonaco, 1982; Eich, 1984; Graf *et al.*, 1982, 1984; Kunst-Wilson and Zajonc, 1980; Lewicki, 1986; McAndrews *et al.*, 1987; Squire *et al.*, 1985). These findings come either from studies of amnesic patients or from experiments in which normal subjects are prevented from encoding target materials in a fully conscious or elaborative manner. By contrast, in studies of normal subjects that allow elaborative encoding of target materials, implicitly expressed information is generally accessible explicitly. For example, normal subjects who produce a previously studied word on a completion test following elaborative encoding are able to consciously remember having studied the word if an explicit recall test is given, whereas a densely amnesic patient who produces a recently studied word on a completion test cannot under any circumstances consciously or explicitly remember having studied the word.

The observation that many implicit memory phenomena in normal subjects fall into the category of 'accessible explicitly' raises questions concerning the extent to which, and sense in which, such phenomena should be considered implicit. That is, if normal subjects *can* remember target information explicitly under appropriate test conditions, how can we be sure that they do not remember explicitly on a nominally implicit memory test? Some investigators have attempted to disguise the fact that previously presented items appear on a test by presenting an implicit memory task as one of several filler tasks during a retention interval, and by testing only a small proportion of previously studied items (e.g., Graf *et al.*, 1984; Jacoby, 1983a; Schacter and Graf, 1986a). The point of these procedures is to prevent subjects from catching on concerning the nature of the test, or at least to discourage the use of explicit memory strategies. It seems quite likely, however, that subjects will 'clue in' concerning the nature of the test once they have been exposed to, or have successfully produced, a number of list items. Nevertheless, the fact that several studies have shown differential effects of experimental variables on implicit and explicit memory tasks when identical test cues were provided, and only the implicit/explicit nature of test instructions were varied (e.g., Graf and Mandler, 1984; Schacter and Graf, 1986a), suggests that subjects do not deliberately use explicit memory strategies on implicit memory tasks. If subjects did use such strategies, we would expect to observe parallel effects of experimental variables when the same cues are provided on implicit and explicit tasks.

However, the foregoing considerations indicate only that it is possible to prevent intentional or *voluntary* explicit memory from influencing performance on implicit memory tests. It is possible that some instances of what appear to be implicit memory may be better described as *involuntary* explicit memory: cases in which a test cue leads to an unintentional but fully conscious and explicit 'reminding' of the occurrence of a prior episode (cf. Ross, 1984). The possibility of confusing implicit memory with involuntary explicit memory would appear to be greatest in experiments with normal subjects that permit elaborative encoding of target materials. At present, we know little about the relation between implicit memory and involuntary explicit memory, but future research and theorizing should be directed toward this issue.

Another difference among the various implicit memory phenomena concerns whether or not target information acquired during a study episode is represented directly in consciousness at the time of test. For example, in repetition priming studies, the target material (i.e., *assassin*) is represented in consciousness at the time of test, such as when the subject completes a test fragment with a previously studied item. By contrast, in other situations target content is not represented in consciousness at the time of test, yet influences performance *indirectly*. For example, when subjects performing an impression-formation task rate a target person more negatively because of subliminal exposure to hostile words that cannot be recalled (e.g., Bargh and Pietromonaco, 1982), or when subjects make classification responses on the basis of rules that they cannot articulate (e.g., Lewicki, 1986; Reber, 1976), the influence of acquired information on implicit memory is indirect. Although we do not know whether direct and indirect expressions of implicit memory differ in theoretically significant ways, the issue has been previously overlooked and may be worth exploring in future studies.

The foregoing considerations also highlight the fact that we presently lack well-specified criteria for assessing whether subjects are explicitly aware of previous experiences at the time of test (Tulving, 1985c). Similar issues concerning criteria for determining awareness have been debated extensively in the literature on perception and learning without awareness (e.g., Cheesman and Merikle, 1986; Eriksen, 1960; Nisbett and Wilson, 1977), and memory researchers would do well to attempt to incorporate some of the lessons from these investigations into research on implicit memory.

Theoretical accounts of implicit memory

In view of the diversity of phenomena that can be grouped under the rubric of implicit memory, it is perhaps not surprising that no single theory has addressed, much less accounted for, all or even most of the observations discussed in this article. Rather, different theoretical views have been advanced to accommodate different subsets of the data. However, one general idea that can be rejected on the basis of recent research is the threshold view discussed in the historical section. The finding that implicit memory is unaffected by experimental variables that have large effects on explicit memory, and that performance on implicit tests is often statistically independent of performance on explicit tests, is inconsistent with a threshold model in which implicit and explicit tests differ only in their sensitivity to the strength of memory traces. In this section, three more viable theoretical approaches to implicit memory phenomena are considered, which are referred to, respectively, as *activation, processing,* and *multiple memory system* accounts. Each of these views has been concerned primarily with repetition priming effects and with dissociations observed in amnesic patients.

Activation views hold that priming effects on implicit memory tests are attributable to the temporary activation of pre-existing representations, knowledge structures, or logogens (e.g., Graf and Mandler, 1984; Mandler, 1980; Morton, 1979; Rozin, 1976). Activation is assumed to occur automatically, independently of the elaborative processing that is necessary to establish new episodic memory traces. An activated representation readily 'pops into mind' on an implicit memory test, but it contains no contextual information about an item's occurrence as part of a recent episode and therefore does not contribute to explicit remembering of the episode.

Processing views seek to understand differences between implicit and explicit memory by explicating the nature of and relations between encoding and retrieval processes or procedures (e.g., Craik, 1983; Jacoby, 1983a, 1983b; Moscovitch *et al.*, 1986; Roediger and Blaxton, 1987; Witherspoon and Moscovitch, 1989). Such views assume that both implicit and explicit memory rely on newly established episodic representations, and portray differences between them in terms of interactions between features of encoded representations and different demands posed by implicit and explicit tests. The best articulated version of this view relies on the distinction between *conceptually driven* processes and *data-driven* processes (Jacoby, 1983b; Roediger and Blaxton, 1987). Conceptually driven processes reflect subject-initiated activities such as elaborating, organizing, and reconstructing; data-driven processes are initiated and guided by the information or data that are presented in test materials. Although both explicit and implicit tests can have data-driven and conceptually driven components, it is argued that explicit memory tests typically draw primarily on conceptually driven processes, whereas implicit tests typically draw primarily on data-driven processes. Performance dissociations between implicit and explicit tests are thus attributed to differences between conceptually driven and data-driven processes.

Multiple memory system interpretations ascribe differences between implicit and explicit memory to the different properties of hypothesized underlying systems. For example, Squire and Cohen (1984) argued that conscious or explicit recollection is a property of, and supported by, a *declarative* memory system that is involved in the formation of new representations or data structures. By contrast, implicit memory phenomena such as learning of skills and repetition priming effects are attributed to a *procedural* system in which memory is expressed by on-line modification of procedures or processing operations. The distinction between episodic and semantic memory (Tulving, 1972, 1983) has also been invoked to account for dissociations on implicit and explicit tests (e.g., Cermak *et al.*, 1985; Kinsbourne and Wood, 1975; Parkin, 1982; Schacter and Tulving, 1982; Tulving, 1983). The episodic memory system is viewed as the basis for explicit remembering of recent events, whereas semantic memory is seen as responsible for performance on tasks such as word completion, lexical decision, and word identification, which require subjects to make use of pre-existing knowledge of words and concepts. A variety of other multiple memory system views have also been put forward (e.g., Johnson, 1983; O'Keefe and Nadel, 1978; Schacter and Moscovitch, 1984; Warrington and Weiskrantz, 1982).

Each of these three approaches is consistent with certain features of existing data and has difficulty accommodating others. Activation views account for the finding that priming of pre-existing representations does not depend on elaborative processing (e.g., Graf *et al.*, 1982; Jacoby and Dallas, 1981) and that under certain conditions, priming decays rapidly in both normals and amnesics (Cermak *et al.*, 1985; Diamond and Rozin, 1984; Graf *et al.*, 1984; Graf and Mandler, 1984; Shimamura and Squire, 1984; Squire *et al.*, 1987). Activation accounts are also consistent with the finding that some severely amnesic patients who show normal priming of items with pre-existing memory representations (e.g., familiar words, idioms) do not show normal priming of nonwords or unrelated paired associates (Cermak *et al.*, 1985; Diamond and Rozin, 1984; Schacter, 1985; Schacter and Graf, 1986b). However, an activation view does not readily accommodate those cases in which amnesic patients do show implicit memory for new information (Graf and Schacter, 1985; McAndrews *et al.*, 1987; Moscovitch *et al.*, 1986), and has difficulty accounting for the effect of newly acquired associations on implicit memory tests in normal subjects (Graf and Schacter, 1985, 1987; McKoon and Ratcliff, 1979, 1986; Schacter and Graf, 1986a, 1986b; see Mandler, 1989, for discussion). The activation notion is also inconsistent with the persistence of facilitation on certain implicit memory tests over days, weeks, and months in normal subjects (Jacoby, 1983a; Jacoby and Dallas, 1981; Komatsu and Ohta, 1984; Schacter and Graf, 1986a; Sloman *et al.*, 1988; Tulving *et al.*, 1982) and amnesic patients (Crovitz *et al.*, 1979; McAndrews *et al.*, 1987).

The strengths and weaknesses of the conceptual versus data-driven processing view are a virtual mirror image of those of the activation view. With its heavy emphasis on an episodic basis of implicit memory, this notion accounts well for observations of persistence, associative effects, contextual sensitivity, and study–test interactions (see Jacoby, 1983b; Roediger and Blaxton, 1987, for elaboration). However, it is less able to handle the findings on short-lived activation, dependence of some priming effects on pre-existing representations in amnesic patients, and differences between priming of new and old representations in normals (cf. Feustel *et al.*, 1983; Schacter and Graf, 1986a). This view also has difficulty accounting for the finding that implicit memory for newly acquired associations, as indexed by performance on the stem completion task, depends on some degree of elaborative study processing (e.g., Schacter and Graf, 1986a). Because it has been argued that elaborative study processing should not affect performance on data-driven implicit memory tasks such as stem completion (e.g., Roediger and Weldon, 1987), the finding that some aspects of performance on an implicit test are elaboration dependent is puzzling. It is also important to note that this view does not speak directly to the key feature of implicit memory phenomena: the absence of conscious recollection of a prior experience at the time of test. That is, it is not clear why data-driven processing should be associated with lack of explicit recollection of a prior experience, whereas conceptually driven processing is generally associated with conscious recollection of a prior experience (see Jacoby, 1984, for relevant discussion).

The strengths and weaknesses of multiple memory system views differ somewhat from the foregoing. The procedural/declarative view has been primarily applied to phenomena observed in amnesic patients. The strength of this view is that it provides a straightforward account of *normal* perceptual-motor skill learning in amnesics who lack conscious recollection of prior episodes: skill learning is assumed to depend on a procedural memory system that is spared in amnesic patients, but does not provide a basis for explicit remembering. It has also been suggested that procedural memory is responsible for priming effects (Cohen, 1984; Squire, 1986). However, recent evidence indicates that priming and skill learning can be dissociated experimentally (Butters, 1987). This hypothesis also cannot readily account for amnesic patients' failure to show priming for nonwords: if priming reflects the modification of procedures used to encode target stimuli, it should occur for both old and new information. Moreover, amnesic patients show implicit memory in situations in which it is unlikely that performance is mediated by the procedural system. For example, amnesics can retrieve newly acquired facts and vocabulary even though they have no explicit recollection of having learned the information (Glisky *et al.*, 1986; Schacter *et al.*, 1984). It does not seem reasonable to attribute the implicit memory observed here to the procedural system, because learning of new facts is allegedly the responsibility of declarative memory (Squire and Cohen, 1984).

Proponents of the episodic–semantic distinction can account for some priming phenomena by postulating that performance on completion and identification tests depends upon activation of the semantic memory system, whereas explicit recall and recognition depend on episodic memory. This account would then be characterized by similar strengths and weaknesses to the activation view discussed earlier. Several other difficulties in applying the episodic–semantic distinction to implicit memory phenomena have been discussed elsewhere (McKoon *et al.*, 1986; Roediger and Blaxton, 1987; Schacter and Tulving, 1982; Squire and Cohen, 1984; Tulving, 1983, 1986).

The foregoing considerations indicate that although each of the three main theoretical views accommodates certain aspects of the data, no single theoretical position accounts satisfactorily for all of the existing findings concerning implicit memory.

Implicit memory: future directions

To conclude the chapter, I will first summarize key issues that need to be addressed in implicit memory research; I will then consider briefly a related domain of inquiry which may provide fruitful perspectives on implicit memory and suggest new directions for research.

Empirical and theoretical extensions of implicit memory research

One of the most striking features of the historical survey and review of current research is the sheer diversity of implicit memory phenomena that have been observed. The fact that implicit memory has been observed across a wide variety of tasks and subject populations has both empirical and theoretical implications. On the empirical side, it seems clear that a critical task for future research is to delineate systematically the similarities and differences among the various implicit memory tests that have been used. Within the domain of repetition priming, for example, it would be desirable to explore further the relations among word stem and fragment completion, word identification, lexical decision, free association, and other implicit memory tasks; each of these tests may be tapping different aspects of implicit memory (cf. Witherspoon and Moscovitch, 1989). Such research could help to clarify a number of unresolved issues. Consider, for example, the time course of repetition priming effects on implicit memory tests. It was noted earlier that activation views are consistent with findings of rapid decay of priming. However, the meaning of *rapid decay* varies widely, from seconds or minutes in some lexical decision paradigms (e.g., Forster and Davis, 1984) to several hours in stem completion paradigms (e.g., Diamond and Rozin, 1984; Graf and Mandler, 1984). Moreover, as discussed previously, priming in fragment completion, word identification, and other implicit memory paradigms can persist for days, weeks, and months (Jacoby, 1983a; McAndrews *et al.*, 1987; Schacter and Graf, 1986a; Sloman *et al.*, 1988; Tulving *et al.*, 1982). To understand these differences in the time course of priming, researchers will need a better understanding of the nature of the information and processes tapped by different implicit memory tests.

It would also be desirable to attempt to relate the findings from priming studies to observations concerning implicit memory in other paradigms, such as implicit rule learning. One area that appears particularly promising concerns the role of implicit memory in affective and social phenomena such as mood states (Bowers, 1984), fears and phobias (Jacobs and Nadel, 1985), impression formation (Bargh and Pietromonaco, 1982), and self-conceptions (Markus and Kunda, 1986). As revealed in the historical section, many striking implicit memory phenomena were reported by investigators concerned with the role of unconscious influences in affective states (e.g., Freud, Janet), and experimental studies of this issue could provide key insights into the functions of implicit memory. A second, related area that has not yet been fully exploited concerns the role of implicit memory in functional amnesias. A few investigators have examined implicit memory in hypnosis (Kihlstrom, 1980, 1984; Williamsen *et al.*, 1965), multiple personality (Nissen *et al.*, 1988), and alcohol and drug intoxication (Hashtroudi *et al.*, 1984; Nissen *et al.* 1988), but much work remains to be done. Third, research concerning the development of implicit memory in young and old populations is needed. Schacter and Moscovitch (1984) argued that infants and very young children may be capable of implicit memory only. However, there has been virtually no research that has explored the issue directly.

Several studies have reported that older adults show intact repetition priming (Graf and Schacter, 1985; Light *et al.*, 1986) but little else is known about the relation between aging and implicit memory.

On the theoretical side, the diversity of implicit memory phenomena suggests that attempts to account for all relevant observations with a single construct or dichotomy will probably not be entirely successful. As was evident in the discussion of theoretical alternatives, no single position convincingly handles all relevant data. Accordingly, it is worth entertaining the idea that there are multiple sources of implicit memory phenomena. For example, Schacter and Graf (1986b) argued that automatic, relatively short-lived priming effects depend on activation of pre-existing representations, whereas longer-lasting, elaboration-dependent effects may be based on specific components of newly created episodic representations (see also Schacter and Graf, 1986a; Forster and Davis, 1984). Similarly, it is possible that some implicit memory phenomena, such as perceptual-motor skill learning in amnesic patients, reflect the operation of a memory system that is distinct from the system subserving explicit recall and recognition, whereas other implicit memory phenomena, such as associative effects on word completion performance, depend on components of the same system that subserves recall and recognition. Unfortunately, firm criteria for distinguishing between multiple-system and single-system accounts do not exist, although some possibilities have been discussed (cf. Sherry and Schacter, 1987; Tulving, 1985a). Nevertheless, in view of the diversity of implicit memory phenomena, the activation, processing, and multiple-memory system views need not be mutually exclusive. Each may account well for certain aspects of the data, and may be useful in generating different questions and problems for future research.

The generality of implicit/explicit dissociations: a theoretical challenge

Recent research has revealed that implicit/explicit dissociations are not restricted to situations involving memory for recent events. These studies have produced dissociations that are remarkably similar to some of those discussed here in one crucial respect: subjects demonstrate that they possess a particular kind of knowledge by their performance on a task, yet they are not consciously aware that they possess the knowledge and cannot gain access to it explicitly. In cognitive psychology, evidence of this kind, although somewhat controversial, has been provided by previously mentioned studies on perception without awareness (e.g., Cheesman and Merikle, 1986; Marcel, 1983).

Neuropsychological research has demonstrated that patients with various lesions and deficits show implicit knowledge of stimuli that they cannot explicitly perceive, identify, or process semantically. First, patients with lesions to primary visual projection areas, who do not have conscious perceptual experiences within their hemianopic field, nevertheless perform at above-chance levels when given forced-choice discrimination tests concerning location, orientation, and other dimensions of a visual stimulus (e.g., Weiskrantz, 1986; see Campion *et al.*, 1983, for a critique). This phemonenon of 'blind-sight' occurs in patients who claim that they are guessing the location and identity of the visual stimulus but do not 'see' anything at all. A second, similar dissociation has been reported in patients with lesions of the right parieto-occipital cortex who have deficits orienting and attending to stimuli which are presented in their left visual fields. Such patients can make accurate same–different judgments regarding stimuli that are presented simultaneously in the left and right visual fields, despite the fact that they cannot state the identity of the stimulus in the left visual field and often deny the presence of any left-field stimulus (Volpe *et al.*, 1979). Third, patients with facial recognition deficits (prosopagnosia) show stronger galvanic skin responses to familiar than to unfamiliar faces, even though patients do not explicitly recognize any faces as familiar (Bauer, 1984; Tranel and Damasio, 1985). Fourth, alexic patients, who have serious problems reading common words, perform at above chance levels when required to make lexical decisions and semantic categorizations regarding words that they cannot explicitly or consciously identify (Coslett, 1986; Shallice and Saffran, 1986), or to point to objects corresponding to words that they deny seeing (Landis *et al.*, 1980). Fifth, aphasic patients with severe comprehension deficits show semantic priming effects for related word pairs without conscious understanding of the semantic relation that links the words (Blumstein *et al.*, 1982; Milberg and Blumstein, 1981).

The foregoing phenomena differ from one another, and from the implicit memory phenomena discussed earlier, insofar as the performance of each type of patient reflects somewhat different residual or preserved capacities (for more detailed review, see Schacter *et al.*, 1988). The striking similarity, however, is that in all cases knowledge is expressed implicitly and does not give rise to a conscious experience of knowing, perceiving, or remembering. This observation suggests that conscious or explicit experiences of knowing, perceiving, or remembering are all in some way dependent upon the functioning of a common mechanism, a mechanism whose functioning is disrupted in various brain-damaged patients. Elsewhere, I have outlined a model that delineates some properties of this mechanism, describes how it is related to various memory structures, and suggests that it can be isolated or disconnected from specific memory and processing systems in different neuropsychological syndromes (Schacter, 1987). For the present purposes, the observation of implicit–explicit dissociations in multiple domains has several implications: it provides a possibly important clue for development of theories of implicit memory, it suggests that the study of implicit memory should be pursued in close conjunction with the study of related phenomena in normal and brain-damaged populations, and it highlights again the generality and pervasiveness of dissociations between implicit expressions of memory and knowledge.

References

Adams, J. K. (1957). Laboratory studies of behavior without awareness. *Psychological Bulletin*, *54*, 383–405.

Bargh, J. A., Bond, R. N., Lombardi, W. J., and Tota, M. E. (1986). The additive nature of chronic and temporary sources of construct accessibility. *Journal of Personality and Social Psychology*, *50*, 869–878.

Bargh, J. A., and Pietromonaco, P. (1982). Automatic information processing and social perception: The influence of trait information presented outside of conscious awareness on impression formation. *Journal of Personality and Social Psychology*, *43*, 437–449.

Barkworth, T. (1891). Some recent experiments in automatic writing. *Proceedings of the Society of Psychical Research*, *7*, 23–29.

Bauer, R. M. (1984). Autonomic recognition of names and faces in prosopagnosia: A neuropsychological application of the guilty knowledge test. *Neuropsychologia*, *22*, 457–469.

Bergson, H. (1911). *Matter and memory.* New York: Macmillan.

Binet, A. (1890). *On double consciousness.* Chicago: Open Court.

Blumstein, S. E., Milberg, W., and Shrier, R. (1982). Semantic processing in aphasia: Evidence from an auditory lexical decision task. *Brain and Language*, *17*, 301–315.

Bowers, K. S. (1984). On being unconsciously influenced and informed. In K. S. Bowers and D. Meichenbaum (Eds.), *The unconscious reconsidered* (pp. 227–272). New York: Wiley.

Brewer, W. F. (1974). There is no convincing evidence for operant or classical conditioning in adult humans. In W. B. Weimer and D. S. Palermo (Eds.), *Cognition and the symbolic processes* (pp. 1–42). Hillsdale, NJ: Erlbaum.

Brooks, D. N., and Baddeley, A. D. (1976). What can amnesic patients learn? *Neuropsychologia*, *14*, 111–122.

Brooks, L. (1978). Nonanalytic concept formation and memory for instances. In E. Rosch and B. B. Lloyd (Eds.), *Cognition and categorization* (pp. 169–211). Hillsdale, NJ: Erlbaum.

Bruce, V., and Valentine, T. (1985). Identity priming in the recognition of familiar faces. *British Journal of Psychology*, *76*, 373–383.

Butters, N. (1987). *Procedural learning in dementia: A double dissociation between Alzheimer and Huntington's disease patients on verbal priming and motor skill learning.* Paper presented at the meeting of the International Neuropsychological Society, Washington, DC.

Campion, J., Latto, R., and Smith, Y. M. (1983). Is blindsight an effect of scattered light, spared cortex, and near-threshold vision? *Behavioral and Brain Sciences*, *6*, 423–486.

Carpenter, W. B. (1874). *Principles of mental physiology.* London: John Churchill.

Cermak, L. S., Talbot, N., Chandler, K., and Wolbarst, L. R. (1985). The perceptual priming phenomenon in amnesia. *Neuropsychologia*, *23*, 615–622.

Cheesman, J., and Merikle, P. M. (1986). Word recognition and consciousness. In D. Besner, T. G. Waller, and G. E. Mackinnon (Eds.), *Reading research: Advances in theory and practice* (Vol. 5, pp. 311–352). New York: Academic Press.

Claparède, E. (1951). Recognition and 'me-ness.' In D. Rapaport (Ed.), *Organization and pathology of thought* (pp. 58–75). New York: Columbia University Press. (Reprinted from Archives de Psychologie, 1911, *11*, 79–90).

Clarke, R. G. B., and Morton, J. (1983). Cross modality facilitation in tachistoscopic word recognition. *Quarterly Journal of Experimental Psychology*, *35A*, 79–96.

Cofer, C. C. (1967). Conditions for the use of verbal associations. *Psychological Bulletin*, *68*, 1–12.

Cohen, N. J. (1984). Preserved learning capacity in amnesia: Evidence for multiple memory systems. In L. R. Squire and N. Butters (Eds.), *Neuropsychology of memory* (pp. 83–103). New York: Guilford Press.

Cohen, N. J., and Squire, L. R. (1980). Preserved learning and retention of pattern-analyzing skill in amnesia: Dissociation of 'knowing how' and 'knowing that.' *Science, 210,* 207–209.

Coslett, H. B. (1986). *Preservation of lexical access in alexia without agraphia.* Paper presented at the 9th European Conference of the International Neuropsychological Society, Veldhoven, The Netherlands.

Craik, F. I. M. (1983). On the transfer of information from temporary to permanent memory. *Philosophical Transactions of the Royal Society of London, 302,* 341–359.

Craik, F. I. M., and Tulving, E. (1975). Depth of processing and the retention of words in episodic memory. *Journal of Experimental Psychology: General, 104,* 268–294.

Crovitz, H. F., Harvey, M. T., and McClanahan, S. (1979). Hidden memory: A rapid method for the study of amnesia using perceptual learning. *Cortex, 17,* 273–278.

Darwin, E. (1794). *Zoonomia; or the laws of organic life.* (Vol. 1) London: J. Johnson.

Diamond, R., and Rozin, P. (1984). Activation of existing memories in the amnesic syndrome. *Journal of Abnormal Psychology, 93,* 98–105.

Dixon, N. F. (1971). *Subliminal perception: The nature of a controversy.* London: McGraw-Hill.

Dixon, N. F. (1981). *Preconscious processing.* New York: Wiley.

Dulany, D. E., Carlson, R. A., and Dewey, G. I. (1984). A case of syntactical learning and judgment: How conscious and how abstract? *Journal of Experimental Psychology: General, 113,* 541–555.

Dulany, D. E., Carlson, R. A., and Dewey, G. I. (1985). On consciousness in syntactic learning and judgment: A reply to Reber, Allen, and Regan. *Journal of Experimental Psychology: General, 114,* 25–32.

Dunn, R. (1845). Case of suspension of the mental faculties. *Lancet, 2,* 588–590.

Ebbinghaus, H. (1885). *Über das Gedächtnis* [Memory]. Leipzig: Duncker and Humblot.

Eich, E. (1984). Memory for unattended events: Remembering with and without awareness. *Memory & Cognition, 12,* 105–111.

Ellenberger, H. F. (1970). *The discovery of the unconscious.* New York: Basic Books.

Erdelyi, M. H. (1970). Recovery of unavailable perceptual input. *Cognitive Psychology, 1,* 99–113.

Eriksen, C. W. (1960). Discrimination and learning without awareness: A methodological survey and evaluation. *Psychological Review, 67,* 279–300.

Eslinger, P. J., and Damasio, A. R. (1986). Preserved motor learning in Alzheimer's disease: Implications for anatomy and behavior. *Journal of Neuroscience, 6,* 3006–3009.

Feustel, T. C., Shiffrin, R. M., and Salasoo, A. (1983). Episodic and lexical contributions to the repetition effect in word identification. *Journal of Experimental Psychology: General, 112,* 309–346.

Forbach, G. B., Stanners, R. F., and Hochhaus, L. (1974). Repetition and practice effects in a lexical decision task. *Memory & Cognition, 2,* 337–339.

Forster, K. I., and Davis, C. (1984). Repetition priming and frequency attenuation in lexical access. *Journal of Experimental Psychology: Learning, Memory, and Cognition, 10,* 680–698.

Fowler, C., Wolford, G., Slade, R., and Tassinary, L. (1981). Lexical access with and without awareness. *Journal of Experimental Psychology: General, 110,* 341–362.

Freud, S., and Breuer, J. (1966). *Studies on hysteria.* (J. Strachey, Trans.). New York: Avon Books.

Gardner, H., Boller, F., Moreines, J., and Butters, N. (1973). Retrieving information from Korsakoff patients: Effects of categorical cues and reference to the task. *Cortex, 9*, 165–175.

Giddan, N. S. (1967). Recovery through images of briefly flashed stimuli. *Journal of Personality, 35*, 1–19.

Giddan, N. S., and Eriksen, C. W. (1959). Generalization of response biases acquired with and without verbal awareness. *Journal of Personality, 27*, 104–115.

Glisky, E. L., Schacter, D. L. and Tulving, E. (1986). Computer learning by memory-impaired patients: Acquisition and retention of complex knowledge. *Neuropsychologia, 24*, 313–328.

Gordon, P. C., and Holyoak, K. J. (1983). Implicit learning and generalization of the 'mere exposure' effect. *Journal of Personality and Social Psychology, 45*, 492–500.

Graf, P., and Mandler, G. (1984). Activation makes words accessible, but not necessarily more retrievable. *Journal of Verbal Learning and Verbal Behavior, 23*, 553–568.

Graf, P., Mandler, G., and Haden, P. (1982). Simulating amnesic symptoms in normal subjects. *Science, 218*, 1243–1244.

Graf, P., and Schacter, D. L. (1985). Implicit and explicit memory for new associations in normal and amnesic subjects. *Journal of Experimental Psychology: Learning, Memory, and Cognition, 11*, 501–518.

Graf, P., and Schacter, D. L. (1987). Selective effects of interference on implicit and explicit memory for new associations. *Journal of Experimental Psychology: Learning, Memory, and Cognition, 13*, 45–53.

Graf, P., Shimamura, A. P., and Squire, L. R. (1985). Priming across modalities and priming across category levels: Extending the domain of preserved function in amnesia. *Journal of Experimental Psychology: Learning, Memory, and Cognition, 11*, 385–395.

Graf, P., Squire, L. R., and Mandler, G. (1984). The information that amnesic patients do not forget. *Journal of Experimental Psychology: Learning, Memory, and Cognition, 10*, 164–178.

Greenspoon, J. (1955). The reinforcing effect of two spoken sounds on the frequency of two responses. *American Journal of Psychology, 68*, 409–416.

Haber, R. N., and Erdelyi, M. H. (1967). Emergence and recovery of initially unavailable perceptual material. *Journal of Verbal Learning and Verbal Behavior, 6*, 618–628.

Haldane, E. S., and Ross, G. R. T. (Eds.). (1967). *The philosophical works of Descartes.* Cambridge: Cambridge University Press.

Hashtroudi, S., Parker, E. S., DeLisi, L. E., Wyatt, R. J., and Mutter, S. A. (1984). Intact retention in acute alcohol amnesia. *Journal of Experimental Psychology: Learning, Memory, and Cognition, 10*, 156–163.

Herbart, J. F. (1896). *A text-book in psychology.* New York: D. Appleton.

Hering, E. (1920). Memory as a universal function of organized matter. In S. Butler (Ed.), *Unconscious memory* (pp. 63–86). London: Jonathan Cape.

Holender, D. (1986). Semantic activation without conscious identification in dichotic listening, parafoveal vision, and visual masking: A survey and appraisal. *Behavioral and Brain Sciences, 9*, 1–66.

Hull, C. L. (1933). *Hypnosis and suggestibility.* New York: Appleton Century.

Irwin, F. W., Kauffman, K., Prior, G., and Weaver, H. B. (1934). On 'learning without awareness of what is being learned.' *Journal of Experimental Psychology, 17*, 823–827.

Jacobs, W. J., and Nadel, L. (1985). Stress-induced recovery of fears and phobias. *Psychological Review, 92*, 512–531.

Jacoby, L. L. (1983a). Perceptual enhancement: Persistent effects of an experience. *Journal of Experimental Psychology: Learning, Memory, and Cognition, 9*, 21–38.

Jacoby, L. L. (1983b). Remembering the data: Analyzing interactive processes in reading. *Journal of Verbal Learning and Verbal Behavior, 22*, 485–508.

Jacoby, L. L. (1984). Incidental versus intentional retrieval: Remembering and awareness as separate issues. In L. R. Squire and N. Butters (Eds.), *Neuropsychology of memory* (pp. 145–156). New York: Guilford Press.

Jacoby, L. L., and Dallas, M. (1981). On the relationship between autobiographical memory and perceptual learning. *Journal of Experimental Psychology: General, 110*, 306–340.

Jacoby, L. L., and Witherspoon, D. (1982). Remembering without awareness. *Canadian Journal of Psychology, 36*, 300–324.

Janet, P. (1893). L'amnésie continue [Continuous amnesia]. *Révue Générale des Sciences, 4*, 167–179.

Janet, P. (1904). L'amnésie et la dissociation des souvenirs par l'émotion [Amnesia and the dissociation of memories by emotion]. *Journal de Psychologie Normale et Pathologique, 1*, 417–453.

Johnson, M. (1983). A multiple-entry, modular memory system. In G. H. Bower (Ed.), *The psychology of learning and motivation* (Vol. 17, pp. 81–123). New York: Academic Press.

Johnson, M. K., Kim, J. K., and Risse, G. (1985). Do alcoholic Korsakoff's syndrome patients acquire affective reactions? *Journal of Experimental Psychology: Learning, Memory, and Cognition, 11*, 27–36.

Johnston, W. A., Dark, V. J., and Jacoby, L. L. (1985). Perceptual fluency and recognition judgments. *Journal of Experimental Psychology: Learning, Memory, and Cognition, 11*, 3–11.

Kihlstrom, J. F. (1980). Posthypnotic amnesia for recently learned materials: Interactions with 'episodic' and 'semantic' memory. *Cognitive Psychology, 12*, 227–251.

Kihlstrom, J. F. (1984). Conscious, subconscious, unconscious: A cognitive perspective. In K. S. Bowers and D. Meichenbaum (Eds.), *The unconscious reconsidered* (pp. 149–211). New York: Wiley.

Kinsbourne, M., and Wood, F. (1975). Short term memory and the amnesic syndrome. In D. D. Deutsch and J. A. Deutsch (Eds.), *Short-term memory* (pp. 258–291). New York: Academic Press.

Kirsner, K., Milech, D., and Standen, P. (1983). Common and modality-specific processes in the mental lexicon. *Memory and Cognition, 11*, 621–630.

Kirsner, K., and Smith, M. C. (1974). Modality effects in word identification. *Memory and Cognition, 2*, 637–640.

Kolers, P. A. (1975). Memorial consequences of automatized encoding. *Journal of Experimental Psychology: Human Learning and Memory, 1*, 689–701.

Kolers, P. A. (1976). Reading a year later. *Journal of Experimental Psychology: Human Learning and Memory, 2*, 554–565.

Komatsu, S.-I., and Ohta, N. (1984). Priming effects in word-fragment completion for short- and long-term retention intervals. *Japanese Psychological Research, 26*, 194–200.

Korsakoff, S. S. (1889). Etude médico-psychologique sur une forme des maladies de la mémoire [Medical-psychological study of a form of diseases of memory]. *Révue Philosophique, 28*, 501–530.

Krieckhaus, E. E., and Eriksen, C. W. (1960). A study of awareness and its effects on learning and generalization. *Journal of Personality, 28,* 503–517.

Kunst-Wilson, W. R. and Zajonc, R. B. (1980). Affective discrimination of stimuli that cannot be recognized. *Science, 207,* 557–558.

Lacey, J. L., and Smith, R. L. (1954). Conditioning and generalization of unconscious anxiety. *Science, 120,* 1045–1052.

Landis, T., Regard, M., and Serrant, A. (1980). Iconic reading in a case of alexia without agraphia caused by a brain tumor: A tachistoscopic study. *Brain and Language, 11,* 45–53.

Lazarus, R. S., and McCleary, R. (1951). Autonomic discrimination without awareness: A study of subception. *Psychological Review, 58,* 113–122.

Leibniz, G. W. (1916). *New essays concerning human understanding.* Chicago: Open Court.

Lewicki, P. (1985). Nonconscious biasing effects of single instances on subsequent judgments. *Journal of Personality and Social Psychology, 48,* 563–574.

Lewicki, P. (1986). Processing information about covariations that cannot be articulated. *Journal of Experimental Psychology: Learning, Memory, and Cognition, 12,* 135–146.

Light, L. L., Singh, A., and Capps, J. L. (1986). Dissociation of memory and awareness in young and older adults. *Journal of Clinical and Experimental Neuropsychology, 8,* 62–74.

Luria, A. R. (1976). *The neuropsychology of memory.* Washington, DC: V. H. Winston.

Maine de Biran. (1929). *The influence of habit on the faculty of thinking.* Baltimore: Williams and Wilkins.

Mandler, G. (1980). Recognizing: The judgment of previous occurrence. *Psychological Review, 87,* 252–271.

Mandler, G. (1989). Memory: Conscious and unconscious. In P. R. Solomon, G. R. Goethals, C. M. Kelley, and B. R. Stephens (Eds.). *Memory – Interdisciplinary approaches.* New York: Springer Verlag.

Mandler, G., Nakamura, Y., Van Zandt, B. J. S. (1987). Nonspecific effects of exposure on stimuli that cannot be recognized. *Journal of Experimental Psychology: Learning, Memory, and Cognition, 13,* 646–648.

Marcel, A. J. (1983) Conscious and unconscious perception: Experiments on visual masking and word recognition. *Cognitive Psychology, 15,* 197–237.

Markus, H., and Kunda, Z. (1986). Stability and malleability of the self-concept. *Journal of Personality and Social Psychology, 51,* 858–866.

Masson, M. E. J. (1984). Memory for the surface structure of sentences: Remembering with and without awareness. *Journal of Verbal Learning and Verbal Behavior, 23,* 579–592.

McAndrews, M. P., Glisky, E. L., and Schacter, D. L. (1987). When priming persists: Long-lasting implicit memory for a single episode in amnesic patients. *Neuropsychologia, 25,* 497–506.

McAndrews, M. P., and Moscovitch, M. (1985). Rule-based and exemplar-based classification in artificial grammar learning. *Memory and Cognition, 13,* 469–475.

McDougall, W. (1924). *Outline of psychology.* New York: Charles Scribner's Sons.

McKoon, G., and Ratcliff, R. (1979). Priming in episodic and semantic memory. *Journal of Verbal Learning and Verbal Behavior, 18,* 463–480.

McKoon, G., and Ratcliff, R. (1986). Automatic activation of episodic information in a semantic memory task. *Journal of Experimental Psychology: Learning, Memory, and Cognition, 12,* 108–115.

McKoon, G., Ratcliff, R., and Dell, G. (1986). A critical evaluation of the semantic–episodic distinction. *Journal of Experimental Psychology: Learning, Memory, and Cognition, 12*, 295–306.

Metcalfe, J., and Fisher, R. P. (1986). The relation between recognition memory and classification learning. *Memory and Cognition, 14*, 164–173.

Milberg, W., and Blumstein, S. E. (1981). Lexical decision and aphasia: Evidence for semantic processing. *Brain and Language, 14*, 371–385.

Milner, B. (1962). Les troubles de la mémoire accompagnant des lésions hippocampiques bilatérales [Disorders of memory accompanying bilateral hippocampal lesions]. In *Physiologie de l'hippocampe.* Paris: Centre National de la Recherche Scientifique.

Milner, B., Corkin, S., and Teuber, H. L. (1968). Further analysis of the hippocampal amnesic syndrome: 14 year follow-up study of H. M. *Neuropsychologia, 6*, 215–234.

Miss X. (1889). Recent experiments in crystal visions. *Proceedings of the Society of Psychical Research, 5*, 486–521.

Morton, J. (1979). Facilitation in word recognition: Experiments causing change in the logogen models. In P. A. Kolers, M. E. Wrolstad, and H. Bouma (Eds.), *Processing of visible language* (Vol. 1, pp. 259–268). New York: Plenum.

Moscovitch, M. (1982). Multiple dissociations of function in amnesia. In L. S. Cermak (Ed.), *Human memory and amnesia* (pp. 337–370). Hillsdale, NJ: Erlbaum.

Moscovitch, M., Winocur, G., and McLachlan, D. (1986). Memory as assessed by recognition and reading time in normal and memory-impaired people with Alzheimer's disease and other neurological disorders. *Journal of Experimental Psychology: General, 115*, 331–347.

Murrell, G. A., and Morton, J. (1974). Word recognition and morphemic structure. *Journal of Experimental Psychology, 102*, 963–968.

Neisser, U. (1954). An experimental distinction between perceptual processes and verbal response. *Journal of Experimental Psychology, 47*, 399–402.

Nelson, T. O. (1978). Detecting small amounts of information in memory: Savings for nonrecognized items. *Journal of Experimental Psychology: Human Learning and Memory, 4*, 453–468.

Nisbett, R. E., and Wilson, T. D. (1977). Telling more than we can know: Verbal reports on mental processes. *Psychological Review, 84*, 231–259.

Nissen, M. J., and Bullemer, P. (1987). Attentional requirements of learning: Evidence from performance measures. *Cognitive Psychology, 19*, 1–32.

Nissen, M. J., Knopman, D. S. and Schacter, D. L. (1987). Neurochemical dissociation of memory systems. *Neurology, 37*, 789–794.

Nissen, M. J., Ross, J. L., Willingham, D. B., Mackenzie, T. B., and Schacter, D. L. (1988). Memory and awareness in a patient with multiple personality disorder. *Brain and Cognition, 8*, 117–134.

O'Keefe, J., and Nadel, L. (1978). *The hippocampus as a cognitive map.* Oxford: Clarendon Press.

Osgood, C. E., and Hoosain, R. (1974). Salience of the word as a unit in the perception of language. *Perception and Psychophysics, 15*, 168–192.

Parkin, A. (1982). Residual learning capability in organic amnesia. *Cortex, 18*, 417–440.

Perry, C., and Laurence, J. R. (1984). Mental processing outside of awareness: The contributions of Freud and Janet. In K. S. Bowers and D. Meichenbaum (Eds.), *The unconscious reconsidered* (pp. 9–48). New York: Wiley.

Pine, F. (1960). Incidental stimulation: A study of preconscious transformations. *Journal of Abnormal and Social Psychology, 60,* 68–75.

Poetzl, O. (1960). The relationship between experimentally induced dream images and indirect vision. Monograph No. 7. *Psychological Issues, 2,* 41–120.

Prince, M. (1914). *The unconscious.* New York: Macmillan.

Reber, A. S. (1976). Implicit learning of synthetic languages: The role of instructional set. *Journal of Experimental Psychology: Human Learning and Memory, 2,* 88–94.

Reber, A. S., Allen, A., and Regan, S. (1985). Syntactical learning and judgment, still unconscious and still abstract: Comment on Dulany, Carlson, and Dewey. *Journal of Experimental Psychology: General, 114,* 17–24.

Roediger, H. L. III, and Blaxton, T. A. (1987). Retrieval modes produce dissociations in memory for surface information. In D. S. Gorfein and R. R. Hoffman (Eds.), *Memory and cognitive processes: The Ebbinghaus centennial conference* (pp. 349–379). Hillsdale, NJ: Erlbaum.

Roediger, H. L. III, and Weldon, M. S. (1987). Reversing the picture superiority effect. In M. A. McDaniel and M. Pressley (Eds.), *Imagery and related mnemonic processes; theories, individual differences, and applications* (pp. 151–174). New York: Springer-Verlag.

Rosenfeld, H. M., and Baer, D. M. (1969). Unnoticed verbal conditioning of an aware experimenter by a more aware subject: The double-agent effect. *Psychological Review, 76,* 425–432.

Ross, B. H. (1984). Remindings and their effects in learning a cognitive skill. *Cognitive Psychology, 16,* 371–416.

Rozin, P. (1976). The psychobiological approach to human memory. In M. R. Rosenzweig and E. L. Bennett (Eds.), *Neural mechanisms of learning and memory.* Cambridge, MA: MIT Press.

Salasoo, A., Shiffrin, R. M., and Feustel, T. (1985). Building permanent memory codes: Codification and repetition effects in word identification. *Journal of Experimental Psychology: General, 114,* 50–77.

Scarborough, D. L., Cortese, C., and Scarborough, H. S. (1977). Frequency and repetition effects in lexical memory. *Journal of Experimental Psychology: Human Perception and Performance, 3,* 1–17.

Scarborough, D. L., Gerard, L., and Cortese, C. (1979). Accessing lexical memory: The transfer of word repetition effects across task and modality. *Memory and Cognition, 7,* 3–12.

Schacter, D. L. (1982). *Stranger behind the engram: Theories of memory and the psychology of science.* Hillsdale, NJ: Erlbaum.

Schacter, D. L. (1983). Amnesia observed: Remembering and forgetting in a natural environment. *Journal of Abnormal Psychology, 92,* 236–242.

Schacter, D. L. (1985). Priming of old and new knowledge in amnesic patients and normal subjects. *Annals of the New York Academy of Sciences, 444,* 41–53.

Schacter, D. L. (1987). *On the relation between memory and consciousness: Dissociable interactions and conscious experience.* Paper presented at the Conference on Memory and Memory Dysfunction, Toronto, Ontario, Canada.

Schacter, D. L., and Graf, P. (1986a). Effects of elaborative processing on implicit and explicit memory for new associations. *Journal of Experimental Psychology: Learning, Memory, and Cognition, 12,* 432–444.

Schacter, D. L., and Graf, P. (1986b). Preserved learning in amnesic patients: Perspectives from research on direct priming. *Journal of Clinical and Experimental Neuropsychology, 8,* 727–743.

Schacter, D. L., Harbluk, J. L., and McLachlan, D. R. (1984). Retrieval without recollection: An experimental analysis of source amnesia. *Journal of Verbal Learning and Verbal Behavior*, *23*, 593–611.

Schacter, D. L., McAndrews, M. P., and Moscovitch, M. (1988). Access to consciousness: Dissociations between implicit and explicit knowledge in neuropsychological syndromes. In L. Weiskrantz (Ed.), *Thought without language*. London: Oxford University Press.

Schacter, D. L., and McGlynn, S. M. (1989). Implicit memory: Effects of elaboration depend on unitization. *American Journal of Psychology*, *102*, 151–181.

Schacter, D. L., and Moscovitch, M. (1984). Infants, amnesics, and dissociable memory systems. In M. Moscovitch (Ed.), *Infant memory* (pp. 173–216). New York: Plenum.

Schacter, D. L., and Tulving, E. (1982). Memory, amnesia, and the episodic/semantic distinction. In R. L. Isaacson and N. E. Spear (Eds.), *The expression of knowledge* (pp. 33–65). New York: Plenum.

Schneider, K. (1912). Über einige klinisch-pathologische Untersuchungsmethoden und ihre Ergebnisse. Zugleich ein Beitrag zur Psychopathologie der Korsakowschen Psychose [On certain clinical-pathological methods of research and their results. Together with a contribution to the psychopathology of Korsakoff's psychosis]. *Zeitschrift für Neurologie und Psychiatrie*, *8*, 553–616.

Seamon, J. G., Brody, N., and Kauff, D. M. (1983). Affective discrimination of stimuli that are not recognized: Effects of shadowing, masking, and cerebral laterality. *Journal of Experimental Psychology: Learning, Memory, and Cognition*, *9*, 544–555.

Shallice, T., and Saffran, E. (1986). Lexical processing in the absence of explicit word identification: Evidence from a letter-by-letter reader. *Cognitive Neuropsychology*, *3*, 429–458.

Sherry, D. F., and Schacter, D. L. (1987). The evolution of multiple memory systems. *Psychological Review*, *94*, 439–454.

Shevrin, H., and Fritzler, D. E. (1968). Visual evoked response correlates of unconscious mental processes. *Science*, *161*, 295–298.

Shimamura, A. P. (1986). Priming effects in amnesia: Evidence for a dissociable memory function. *Quarterly Journal of Experimental Psychology*, *38A*, 619–644.

Shimamura, A. P., and Squire, L. R. (1984). Paired-associate learning and priming effects in amnesia: A neuropsychological study. *Journal of Experimental Psychology: General*, *113*, 556–570.

Shimamura, A. P., and Squire, L. R. (1987). A neuropsychological study of fact learning and source amnesia. *Journal of Experimental Psychology: Learning, Memory, and Cognition*, *13*, 464–474.

Slamecka, N. J. (1985a). Ebbinghaus: Some associations. *Journal of Experimental Psychology: Learning, Memory, and Cognition*, *11*, 414–435.

Slamecka, N. J. (1985b). Ebbinghaus: Some rejoinders. *Journal of Experimental Psychology: Learning, Memory, and Cognition*, *11*, 496–500.

Sloman, S. A., Hayman, C. A. G., Ohta, N., Law, J., and Tulving, E. (1988). Forgetting in primed fragment completion. *Journal of Experimental Psychology: Learning, Memory, and Cognition*, *14*, 223–239.

Squire, L. R. (1986). Mechanisms of memory. *Science*, *232*, 1612–1619.

Squire, L. R., and Cohen, N. J. (1984). Human memory and amnesia. In J. McGaugh, G. Lynch, and N. Weinberger (Eds.), *Proceedings of the conference on the neurobiology of learning and memory* (pp. 3–64). New York: Guilford Press.

Squire, L. R., Shimamura, A. P., and Graf, P. (1985). Independence of recognition memory and priming effects: A neuropsychological analysis. *Journal of Experimental Psychology: Learning, Memory, and Cognition, 11*, 37–44.

Squire, L. R., Shimamura, A. P., and Graf, P. (1987). Strength and duration of priming effects in normal subjects and amnesic patients. *Neuropsychologia, 25*, 195–210.

Squire, L., Wetzel, C. D., and Slater, P. C. (1978). Anterograde amnesia following ECT: An analysis of beneficial effects of partial information. *Neuropsychologia, 16*, 339–348.

Starr, A., and Phillips, L. (1970). Verbal and motor memory in the amnesic syndrome. *Neuropsychologia, 8*, 75–88.

Storms, L. H. (1958). Apparent backward associations: A situational effect. *Journal of Experimental Psychology, 55*, 390–395.

Thorndike, E. L., and Rock, R. T., Jr. (1934). Learning without awareness of what is being learned or intent to learn it. *Journal of Experimental Psychology, 17*, 1–19.

Tranel, D., and Damasio, A. R. (1985). Knowledge without awareness: An autonomic index of facial recognition by prosopagnosics. *Science, 228*, 1453–1454.

Tulving, E. (1972). Episodic and semantic memory. In E. Tulving and W. Donaldson (Eds.), *Organization of memory* (pp. 381–403). New York: Academic Press.

Tulving, E. (1983). *Elements of episodic memory.* Oxford: The Clarendon Press.

Tulving, E. (1985a). On the classification problem in learning and memory. In L.-G. Nilsson and T. Archer (Eds.), *Perspectives on learning and memory* (pp. 67–94). Hillsdale, NJ: Erlbaum.

Tulving, E. (1985b). Ebbinghaus's memory: What did he learn and remember? *Journal of Experimental Psychology: Learning, Memory, and Cognition, 11*, 485–490.

Tulving, E. (1985c). Memory and consciousness. *Canadian Psychology, 25*, 1–12.

Tulving, E. (1986). What kind of a hypothesis is the distinction between episodic and semantic memory? *Journal of Experimental Psychology: Learning, Memory, and Cognition, 12*, 307–311.

Tulving, E., Schacter, D. L., and Stark, H. A. (1982). Priming effects in word-fragment completion are independent of recognition memory. *Journal of Experimental Psychology: Learning, Memory, and Cognition, 8*, 336–342.

Volpe, B. T., LeDoux, J. E., and Gazzaniga, M. S. (1979). Information processing of visual stimuli in an 'extinguished' field. *Nature, 282*, 722–724.

Warrington, E. K., and Weiskrantz, L. (1968). New method of testing long-term retention with special reference to amnesic patients. *Nature, 217*, 972–974.

Warrington, E. K., and Weiskrantz, L. (1970). Amnesia: Consolidation or retrieval? *Nature, 228*, 628–630.

Warrington, E. K., and Weiskrantz, L. (1974). The effect of prior learning on subsequent retention in amnesic patients. *Neuropsychologia, 12*, 419–428.

Warrington, E. K., and Weiskrantz, L. (1978). Further analysis of the prior learning effect in amnesic patients. *Neuropsychologia, 16*, 169–176.

Warrington, E. K. and Weiskrantz, L. (1982). Amnesia: A disconnection syndrome? *Neuropsychologia, 20*, 233–248.

Weiskrantz, L. (1985). On issues and theories of the human amnesic syndrome. In N. M. Weinberger, J. L. McGaugh, and G. Lynch (Eds.). *Memory systems of the brain* (pp. 380–415). New York: Guilford Press.

Weiskrantz, L. (1986). *Blindsight.* New York: Oxford University Press.

Weiskrantz, L., and Warrington, E. K. (1979). Conditioning in amnesic patients. *Neuropsychologia, 17*, 187–194.

Williamsen, J. A., Johnson, H. J., and Eriksen, C. W. (1965). Some characteristics of posthypnotic amnesia. *Journal of Abnormal Psychology, 70*, 123–131.

Wilson, W. R. (1979). Feeling more than we can know: Exposure effects without learning. *Journal of Personality and Social Psychology, 37,* 811–821.

Winnick, W. A., and Daniel, S. A. (1970). Two kinds of response priming in tachistoscopic recognition. *Journal of Experimental Psychology, 84,* 74–81.

Witherspoon, D., and Moscovitch, M. (1989) Stochastic independence between two implicit memory tasks. *Journal of Experimental Psychology: Learning, Memory, and Cognition, 15,* 22–30.

Young, A. W., McWeeny, K. H., Hay, D. C., and Ellis, A. W. (1986). Access to identity-specific semantic codes from familiar faces. *Quarterly Journal of Experimental Psychology, 38A,* 271–295.

SECTION EIGHT
INDIVIDUAL DIFFERENCES

Editor's introduction

People differ enormously in their memory abilities, and the study of individual differences has provided many important insights into the functioning of the memory system. One of the most intriguing claims about individual variations is that, as with other skills, they are attributable to practice. **Ericsson** (Chapter 13) describes the case for this view, including the startling evidence that digit span can be greatly increased by practice. He also presents a theoretical framework for understanding skilled memory performance.

Plainly, the most obvious way in which people's memories differ is in terms of their recollections about events in their own lives. The study of so-called *autobiographical* memory has become popular in the last few years. The interested reader should consult Conway (1990). Another important topic of research concerns changes in memory performance during the lifespan. Kail (1990) provides a thorough discussion of the changes seen in memory performance during child development, while Craik and Jennings (1992) review the effects of ageing on memory. For a review of evidence on the relationship between memory and factors such as arousal, stress, emotion, motivation, and intelligence, see Searleman and Herrmann (1994).

References

Conway, M. A. (1990). *Autobiographical memory: an introduction.* Open University Press, Milton Keynes.

Craik, F. I. M., and Jennings, J. M. (1992). Human memory. In *The handbook of aging and cognition* (Eds. F. I. M. Craik and T. A. Salthouse), pp. 51–110. Erlbaum, Hillsdale, NJ.

Kail, R. (1990). *The development of memory in children* (3rd edn). W. H. Freeman, New York.

Searleman, A., and Herrmann, D. (1994). *Memory from a broader perspective.* McGraw-Hill, New York.

13 K. Anders Ericsson
'Memory Skill'

Reprinted in full from: *Canadian Journal of Psychology* **39**, 188–231 (1985)

There are many kinds of individual differences with regard to memory. Some people around us are able to remember facts, episodes, and names much better than we can. These people seem able to retain their memories for longer periods of time. Occasionally, we meet people who have extensive portions of books, songs, or music accurately memorized. There are reports in the literature about people who have memorized entire books (cf. Neisser, 1982) or the weekdays of dates for several hundred or even thousands of years back (Barlow, 1952) or the complete multiplication table for all numbers between 1 and 100 (Smith, 1983). These memory feats are very interesting, but little information is available on how these memories developed or were acquired through practice.

Recent studies have indicated that systematic research might significantly change our understanding of some of these alleged skills. By recording people's consecutive recall of the same story or text with a tape recorder, it is now clear that strict verbatim recall is rare and that these narrative recalls often contain a considerable amount of generation and reconstruction (Hunter, 1984). In this article, we will discuss the acquisition and structure of such extensive memories only as they pertain to storing new information.

Furthermore, we will restrict our review to research, where the entire process of memorization occurs under experimental control. This restriction does not seriously limit the kind of memorization we can discuss because a wide range of materials can be memorized within a single session. To be able to use observations on memory performances, it is necessary that the experimenter has selected materials and can decide on the mode and duration of presentation. Recall or retention can be studied by systematically varying the order of recall and type of memory test. As soon as the subject leaves the test situation, however, the experimental control ceases, and we don't know if the subject rehearses or takes notes on the information presented during the session. Tests of retention weeks and years later might be completely unrepresentative as the subject might be able to anticipate and prepare for such recalls. In this paper, we will limit our review to studies using controlled study time and recording of recall within the same session.

Within these constraints this paper reviews the empirical evidence on large individual differences and the possible mechanisms underlying such differences. In particular, we explore the source of these observed memory differences. A few people emerge with such superior memory ability that they are considered exceptional and are assumed to have an organization of memory which is structurally different from that of normal people. Any serious discussion of the nature of such an individual or of structural differences requires a theory of the organization of normal memory. Given such a theory one can then argue whether differences in different types of memory systems are genetically endowed or a result of acquired cognitive processes and structures. We propose that memory ability is a complex skill acquired through extensive practice. We call this the *memory skill hypothesis*. In this paper we will argue that most or all variability in memory ability can be accounted for by differences in acquired memory skill.

The view that sensory impressions are stored without mediation, and hence that memory ability is determined directly by basic innate processes, lies at another extreme.

These theoretical ideas are important in themselves, and they have also determined indirectly many of the experimental paradigms for studying normal and exceptional memory. First, we will trace some important ideas and models of normal memory. After some discussion and criticism of these models, we will propose the skilled memory theory (Chase and Ericsson, 1982) as the framework for accounting for individual differences in memory ability. The first elements of this theory were originally derived from a detailed analysis of a single subject's improvement of his digit span with extensive practice (Ericsson *et al.*, 1980). Analyses of more subjects' memory skills allowed Bill Chase and me to identify some general elements underlying memory skills and skilled memory (Chase and Ericsson, 1981, 1982). This paper shows the power of these ideas by using them to organize the available data on exceptional memory and memory skills. In the first section we will test the assertions of the skilled memory theory against the data from many analyses of exceptional memory feats which had not been available to us earlier (Chase and Ericsson, 1982). Then, we will review the effects of practice in memorization and memory training on normal subjects in terms of the skilled memory theory. In the two final sections the relation between memory skill shown by experts and memory for meaningful information by normal subjects, and the relation of memory skills to other skills, will be discussed.

Brief theoretical background

Philosophers and early investigators of psychology realized that familiar and meaningful material was committed to memory using pre-existing knowledge and associations. In the same way that elementary sensations were seen as the proper starting point for studying perception, material lacking pre-existing associations was seen as the beginning point for experimental research on memory.

Much of the early work was influenced by the structuralist view that all mental elements (including memory) were images in some sensory modality. Hence, a lot of research was directed toward identifying the sensory type of memory. A subject with visual memory was assumed to encode the information as a visual image and have access to the information as immediately as if it were perceptually available in visual form, albeit not as clearly. Subjects with auditory memory were restricted to sequential access of information, limited just as they would be by the sequential structure of auditory presentation.

In an attempt to study the basic and direct processes of forming new associations in memory, meaningless materials like digits and nonsense syllables were used, because such materials would not have prior associations attached to them. Since Ebbinghaus (1885/1964), and particularly during the behaviorist era, these types of materials were used almost exclusively in learning and memory experiments. There was little or no discussion of different types of memory stores and mediating encodings, in keeping with behaviouristic theorizing and the assumption that no pre-existing associations were used in the memorization of such materials.

Given the assumption that basic and direct memory formation was being studied with these materials, it was also necessary to assume that individual differences in speed of memorization reflected differences in these basic processes. Without any mediating steps in memorization, an account in terms of acquired memory skill is theoretically impossible. Hence, it has been claimed that people who can rapidly memorize meaningless information (e.g., digits or names) have exceptional memory (cf. Luria, 1968).

A radically different view of human cognition was proposed in the emerging human information processing models (Bower, 1975; Newell and Simon, 1972). These models postulate that information can be retained in several different kinds of memory stores and that cognitive processes mediate different storage and recall from memory. For our current purposes, we will consider only short-term memory, long-term memory, and various cognitive processes that operate on the information in these two types of stores.

Short-term memory is assumed to contain recently perceived and attended information. Miller (1956) showed that normal people's memory spans are fairly stable over many types of material and fall in a very narrow range (around seven items). Many cognitive psychologists have taken this invariant memory span as an estimate of the capacity of short-term memory (STM). It is appropriate to view STM as an intermediate and temporary step before storage in long-term memory (LTM). There are a couple of pieces of evidence suggesting that LTM is not involved in immediate recall during memory span testing. After a sequence of memory span tests, subjects can recall hardly anything from the presented sequences of items (Ericsson and Karat, 1981). Some studies have reported better recall when the same digit sequences are presented again later in the test series (Bower and Winzenz, 1969; Hebb, 1961; Melton, 1963); but the improvement is very small (generally less than 5%) and appears to disappear completely when the digit sequence is segmented into different groupings at the later presentation. Furthermore, subjects' digit span is virtually unaffected by large changes in speed of presentation (Murdock, 1974).

By associating presented items in STM with each other, or with other patterns or elements retrieved from LTM, a permanent memory trace is formed in LTM. The rate at which normal subjects are estimated to memorize meaningless materials for long-term retention, like digits and nonsense syllables, is so slow (Simon, 1974) that little or no information can be stored in

LTM with the rapid presentation rates used in memory span experiments. In order for an item stored in LTM to be recalled, it needs to be accessed by retrieval cues held in STM (Anderson, 1980; Raaijmakers and Shiffrin, 1981). Hence, storage in LTM is not by itself sufficient for recall of the corresponding information.

The distinction between the limited STM with directly accessible information and the vast LTM with indirectly accessible information has been enormously useful to account for constraints on people's ability to process information and solve problems (Atwood and Polson, 1976; Newell and Simon, 1972), comprehend text (Kintsch and van Dijk, 1978), make decisions (Payne, 1976), and perform other cognitive tasks.

The STM-LTM model of memory has been extended to account for memory performance using material varying in degree of familiarity and meaningfulness. According to Miller's (1956) model, meaningful materials consist of chunks which organize several presented elements into a single unit. For example, the letters *c-a-t* are encoded as the word *cat*. Memory span is extended for meaningful material because a much larger number of presented items can be combined into the same number of chunks. Given a constant rate of committing chunks to LTM, the storage time per presented item will be much less for familiar information (Simon, 1974).

There are several lines of research suggesting that this attractively simple STM-LTM model needs to be extended and changed. We will focus on the psychometric analyses of memory ability and analyses of immediate memory by experts for briefly presented familiar information.

Individual differences in memory ability

In its most direct form, the STM-LTM model states that each individual's memory could be described in terms of the capacity of STM in number of chunks and the rate of transfer from STM to LTM. The capacity of STM is measured by memory span tests. Several studies have shown high correlations between individuals' memory span for unrelated sequences of items for a variety of different kinds of materials, such as words, digits, and consonants (Brener, 1940; Crannell and Parrish, 1957). The high correlations do not extend to memory spans for related sequences of items, like words in meaningful sequences or sentence span (Ericsson and Karat, 1981). Most interestingly, the memory spans for unrelated sequences are almost unrelated to many measures of long-term retention, such as free recall, cued recall of paired associates, and recognition. The remarkably low correlations cause us to reject any hypotheses about a general memory factor (Anastasi, 1931; Kelley, 1964; Thurstone, 1941; Underwood *et al.*, 1978).

Within Baddeley's (1981) concept of STM as working memory, one can easily account for the only major evidence of systematic individual differences – the relations between memory span for unrelated material. Baddeley has argued convincingly that STM is not a single structure but consists of different systems for temporary storage. One of these systems is the articulatory loop where verbal items are kept through continuous rehearsal. The time required to rehearse or articulate some type of information appears to be a strong predictor of the corresponding memory span for unrelated materials (Baddeley, 1981). Another system is called the visuo-spatial scratch pad and is used to keep the information in complex visual images temporarily available. These systems provide only temporary storage, and without further attention the information decays rapidly.

Experts' immediate memory for familiar information

The chunking model of STM was used by Chase and Simon (1973a, 1973b) to account for the dramatic differences in memory for briefly presented chessboard configurations between chess masters and novices (de Groot, 1966, 1978). It is clear that a chessboard configuration would be more meaningful to a chess master who has played for over 10 years than to a novice chess player. Chase and Simon argued that both the chess master and the novice held the information regarding the chessboard in chunks (patterns of chess pieces) in STM. The better recall of the chess master was due to the availability of more complex chunks, which held more pieces per chunk. With chess pieces arranged randomly on the chessboard, the chess master and the novices performed equally poorly and could not remember more than the memory span for unrelated information would predict.

   The superior memory of experts for briefly presented information in their domain of expertise has been demonstrated many times – in chess (Charness, 1976; Frey and Adesman, 1976; Lane and Robertson, 1979), in bridge (Charness, 1979; Engle and Bukstel, 1978), and for diagrams of electronic circuits (Egan and Schwartz, 1979). Further investigations have shown that memory for the briefly presented chessboard configurations is not stored only in STM. Charness (1976) found no decrement in recall after interpolating other tasks assumed to fully occupy STM, although he did find a longer latency to initiate recall with interpolated tasks, which is consistent with storage of memory for the chessboard configuration in LTM. Interpolating memorization and recall of another chessboard had only a minor effect on recall of the originally presented board (Frey and Adesman, 1976). Chess masters need not actively memorize a chessboard configuration, but memory in LTM is formed incidentally from observing it in a meaningful way. Lane and Robertson (1979) found that good chess players selecting the best move for a chess position (meaningful encoding) remembered as much about the chess configuration in a surprise recall (incidental condition) as when they had been told about the recall in advance (intentional condition). When the task was changed to finding the number of chess pieces on light and dark squares, a large difference in memory was found between intentional and incidental memory conditions. Lane and Robertson viewed their study as extending the evidence on levels of processing (Craik and Lockhart, 1972) from verbal learning to chess.

   There appear to be clear parallels between the chess expert's memory for chess and the normal subject's memory for meaningful materials, such as texts and pictures. When a text is read, long-term memory for the text's meaning is formed rapidly and extensively and without an intentional effort to memorize (Kintsch, 1974). Pictures appear to be committed to long-term memory very rapidly – in less than a second (Potter and Levy, 1969).

To summarize, there is compelling evidence that, at least for meaningful and familiar information, storage in LTM can be quite rapid.

Quite early in the development of information-processing models of human cognition and memory, Hunt (1971) proposed an intermediate-term memory (ITM) to hold information about the context of a given task as well as to augment STM in holding relevant information available for successful performance of the task. In tasks like comprehension of text (van Dijk and Kintsch, 1983) and design of computer programs (Jeffries *et al.*, 1981), it has been forcefully argued that all relevant information cannot be contained in STM, but that STM must be supplemented by some additional storage with possibly slower access times (cf. Hunt, 1971). Shiffrin's (1976) discussion of how the current context can serve as an efficient retrieval cue for information stored in LTM suggests that episodic information stored in LTM may be sufficiently accessible for use in many tasks.

Chase and Ericsson (1982) proposed a theory of skilled memory to account for how LTM could be used to store and maintain information with direct access and storage characteristics similar to STM. Based on studies of acquisition of memory skills and analyses of existing memory skills, three general principles of skilled memory were postulated. First, information, either externally presented or internally generated, is encoded in terms of knowledge structures in semantic memory through meaningful associations (*meaningful encoding*). Second, during encoding or storage, retrieval cues are explicitly associated with the memory encoding, where the retrieval cues are sufficient to retrieve the memory encoding at some later time from LTM (*retrieval structure*). Lastly, encoding and retrieval operations can be dramatically sped up by practice, so that memory encoding and retrieval have storage and access characteristics of STM and can be performed within a few seconds (*speed-up*).

Most of the original evidence for the theory of skilled memory came from a series of detailed studies of improvement in digit span with extensive practice. These studies identified the cognitive structures and processes that allowed improvement from initially normal levels of memory performance to exceptional levels of performance. A review of this research allows us to specify how the three principles of skilled memory account for emerging memory skill.

Acquisition of exceptional memory skill

In our characterization of the acquisition of skill in digit span we will describe the original performance first, then the emergence of encoding processes and the retrieval structure, and finally some characteristics of the acquired skill. The focus of the account will be on our first subject (SF), who discovered the means to improve his memory performance by himself.

SF was selected to be a representative and average college student with respect to intelligence and memory ability. His original digit span was about seven digits. During his first session with the digit-span task, he relied almost exclusively on rehearsal of all presented digits to remember them. In the second session he started trying to commit the first three digits of a series to memory and to rehearse the remaining digits of the presented series. Once the rehearsed digits had been committed to memory, he would retrieve the first three digits and initiate recall. The primary mode of encoding was repetition of digits and different numerical relations.

During Session 5, SF suddenly realized that a three-digit sequence could be interpreted as a running time for a mile. For example, 418 could be a 4-minute, 18-second mile time. His average digit span for this session jumped four standard deviations from the previous session. SF was a long-distance runner with extensive knowledge of both specific and general categories of running times for a large number of different races. During the following sessions, SF retrieved a set of races (1/4-mile, 1/2-mile, 3/4-mile, mile, 2-mile) that would cover the range of most three-digit numbers from 100 to 959. However, no three-digit numbers with a middle digit of 6, 7, 8, or 9 (e.g., 483, 873) can be interpreted as meaningful running times. In one experiment we presented digit sequences made up of only such uncodable three-digit sequences to SF, and his memory span was reduced almost to the level prior to practice. An improvement relative to his then current digit span (27%) was obtained by presenting SF with stimuli exclusively made up of three-digit sequences encodable as running times. When SF started to encode four-digit sequences they were encoded as 2942 (29 minutes, 42 seconds [10 km time]) or as 4246 (4 minutes, 24.6 seconds [miletime]). Later, SF realized that three-digit and four-digit sequences uninterpretable as times could be encoded as ages (for example, 592 is 59.2 years old and 4976 is 49 and 76 years old). For an encoding to be effective at presentation rates of one digit per second, rapid access to knowledge in semantic memory to form meaningful encodings was essential for SF's ability to store digit groups in memory.

In parallel with the emergence of new and more effective encodings of three- and four-digit groups, SF started to store up to four different groups in memory, in addition to the four to five digits in the rehearsal buffer. In order to recall these digit groups in their correct order, SF encoded the order of presentation of each digit group as first, middle, and last. At the time of recall, SF could use this as the main cue to retrieve the encoded digit groups in the presented order. The encoding of these additional cues integrated with memory traces for the purpose of subsequent retrieval we call retrieval-structures. In order to be able to store more groups in memory, SF introduced a new level of organization and used two super groups to organize encoded digits as either four-digit groups or three-digit groups. This hierarchical organization is illustrated in Figure 13.1 and is evidenced in SF's retrospective verbal reports on how he encoded the digit sequence as well as in the pauses and intonation patterns of his recall of the digit sequence.

In one experiment we presented SF with digit sequences well below his current memory span, which he encoded as illustrated in Figure 13.1. After successful recall of the sequence, we showed him different subsequences of

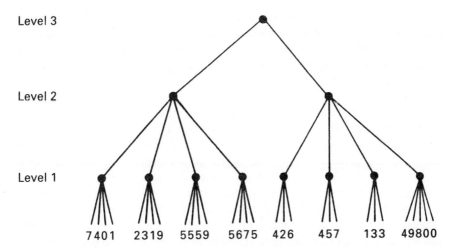

Level 3

Level 2

Level 1

7401 2319 5559 5675 426 457 133 49800

Figure 13.1 Proposed hierarchical organization of SF's memory encoding of 30 presented digits. The first level contains mnemonic encodings of digit groups, and the second level consists of super groups where the relative locations of several digit groups are encoded.

digits (probes) selected from the memorized sequence and asked him to name adjacent digits. In any one session, only one type of probe was used. SF was very rapid in naming the last digit of groups, when the first two or three digits of that group were presented. Using the digit sequence in Figure 13.1 as an example, the visual probe 231 would elicit 9 as a response. Thus, retrieval within the lowest level of the hierarchy (encoded digit groups) is quite fast (1.8 sec). We also presented SF with one of the digit groups (e.g., 426) and asked him to generate the preceding or following digit group, which would be 5675 and 457 respectively in this case (see Figure 13.1). There was a remarkable difference in retrieval time depending on whether or not the retrieved digit group was part of the same super group as the probe. When both groups belonged to the same super group (when retrieval was within the second level of organization), the average retrieval time was 4.4 seconds. When the two groups belonged to different super groups (retrieval with the third level of organization), the average retrieval time was much longer: 10.1 seconds. We asked SF to point out where a presented digit group was located in a schematic drawing similar to Figure 13.1. Also, we would point to a location and ask for recall of the corresponding digit group. SF was much faster giving the location of a probe (1.2 sec) than giving the digit group at a specified location (7.5 sec). As SF's memory span increased the complexity of the retrieval structure increased, and further levels of organization were introduced.

So far, we haven't given any direct evidence showing that improved digit span reflected storage in LTM rather than STM, which digit span supposedly measured. After the sessions, SF was able to recall about 90% of the 200–300 digits presented during the session. Interestingly enough, he did not recall entire or even partially presented digit sequences, but rather individual three-digit and four-digit groups organized around associated mnemonic associations like mile times, 10-km times, and ages. Although he had accurate memory for the location of a digit group within the retrieval structure, he was unable to remember which digit groups belonged to the same digit sequence.

In several experiments we explored how important storage in STM was for SF's ability to recall a presented digit sequence. The experimental procedures forced SF to suppress auditory or visual rehearsal of the digits for 20 seconds, just after the presentation of the digits but before recall. Suppression of rehearsal of visual images had no effect, whereas suppressing auditory rehearsal led to the reduction of digit span by about four digits, which corresponds to the hypothesized content of the rehearsal buffer.

When our work with SF ended, he had developed a large retrieval structure and a large number of mnemonic encodings to allow his final digit span to be 84 digits. We also found that SF's speed of encoding digit groups had been increased. Rather than using the fixed presentation rate used in digit span, we allowed him to pace the presentation of individual digits himself using a cathode ray tube. During the 2-year period, his study times for 10-, 25-, and 50-digit sequences were reduced by 50–80%. In the early stages of practice, his digit span could be reduced to its original value (seven digits) by increasing the presentation rate, which showed that his encoding of digits required sufficient time. Toward the end of practice, his digit span was 11 even when digits were read at a rate of three digits per second. This presentation rate is three times faster than the standard presentation rate and strongly suggests that digits could be encoded much faster with more practice.

A second subject (RE) reached an average memory span of 18 digits by encoding digits as dates, times, and patterns. She capitalized on patterns in the digit sequences and had no fixed grouping of digits, and she was not able to develop a retrieval structure. Instead, she built higher-level groupings of digit groups (e.g., 93 65 342 = September 3, 1965 at 3: 42 p.m.), and only four such higher-level groups could be retrieved on a given trial. After some 40 sessions without further improvement, she decided to terminate the experiment. About 1 year later, without any interim practice, she was able to attain her old digit span within a couple of hours. In order to replicate SF's performance, another long-distance runner (DD) was trained to use SF's methods. After an initial period of faster improvement, DD followed SF's rate of improvement and has now surpassed SF's record digit span with a current memory span of 101 digits. A detailed analysis (Chase and Ericsson, 1982) shows similarities between DD and SF in all important respects regarding the structure of their memory skill.

In this paper, we will use Chase and Ericsson's (1982) three principles of skilled memory (meaningful encoding, retrieval structure, and speed-up) as hypotheses to organize our examination of three areas of research related to memory skill. First, and most importantly, we will review studies of people with exceptional existing memory skills. Next, we will examine the extent and structure of improvements through moderate amounts of practice and/or instruction in group studies. Finally, we will discuss evidence for parallels to skilled memory in normal subjects for highly practised skills, like language comprehension.

Studies of subjects with existing memory skills

There has always been a fascination with people with superior and exceptional memory. The literature is full of anecdotal reports of exceptional memory feats (Barlow, 1952; Mitchell, 1907; Scripture, 1891). However, many of these reports are so poorly documented that their scientific value is unclear and highly disputable. Binet (1894) conducted the first systematic memory study of two mental calculators (Inaudi and Diamondi) and a mnemonist (Arnould). The most extensive and in-depth study was conducted on a mathematics professor (Rueckle), by G. E. Mueller (1911, 1913, 1917). The Japanese mnemonist (Isihara) was studied in laboratory settings (Chiba and Susukita, 1934; Susukita, 1933, 1934; Susukita and Heindl, 1935). Several investigators made minor studies of a Polish mental calculator, Dr. Finkelstein (Bousfield and Barry, 1933; Sandor, 1932; Weinland, 1948). Luria (1968) reported on his extensive study of a mnemonist (Shereshevskii). More recently, Hunt and Love (1972) and Gordon *et al.* (1984) studied mnemonists with experimental procedures used in modern laboratory research on memory.

Experimental analyses of memory performances have also been made of mental calculators, Dr. Aitken (Hunter, 1962, 1977), Griffith (Bryan *et al.*, 1941), expert abacus operators (Hatano and Osawa, 1983) and a restaurant waiter (Ericsson and Polson, 1988a, 1988b). Interesting analyses of other memory performances have been performed by Gummerman and Gray (1971) for a subject with exceptionally good memory for pictures, and by Coltheart and Glick (1974) for a subject with exceptional iconic memory.

These studies examined different aspects of memory skill or ability. Several were concerned with the generality of the superior memory performance for memorization of different types of materials. Others focused on detailing the elements or components of the memory skill.

First, we will discuss generality of performance and level of performance. Then we will discuss research uncovering the structure of a small number of memory skills in detail.

Performance

It is remarkable that the majority of memory experts are most exceptional when the material to be memorized is numbers, nonsense syllables, and other meaningless types of information. Luria's (1968) subject Shereshevskii (S) claimed to memorize numbers directly without using any mnemonic associations, which he reported using for other types of meaningless information.

Unfortunately, there is relatively little consistency between studies in how memory for digits has been measured. Many of the studies have used auditory presentation of individual digits (digit span) and simultaneous visual presentation of matrices of numbers as well as digit sequences of different lengths.

We will limit our review to one test of STM (auditory digit span) and two tests of LTM. The first test of LTM measures the time taken to memorize a matrix of 25 digits. The second test concerns memorization of long sequences of digits presented visually in full view.

Digit span

In Table 13.1 are shown all available estimates of auditory digit span for the memory experts discussed earlier. Data from subjects who received practice on digit span are included, as well as some data on digit spans from testing of large populations of normal subjects. Unfortunately, the procedures used in assessing the reported digit span were different, but we have tried to estimate the digit spans which would have been attained with an auditory presentation rate of 1 digit per second.

All of the reported digit spans are quite high and above the normal range of 4 to 10 digits. Several investigators have argued that the range of digit spans is much wider and that normal educated people can have digit spans up to 14–15 digits (Binet, 1894; Oberly, 1928). In Table 13.1 we have also compiled reported evidence regarding mediation in memory span, or grouping of digits and associations with pre-existing knowledge and meaning of similar numbers. The similarity across studies in reported types of mediation is particularly impressive given the investigators' lack of knowledge of one another's results (as judged by the absence of references to previous work). Several studies show that such encoding processes mediate the higher digit-span performance

Table 13.1 Digit spans for different types of memory experts and information on explicit evidence on grouping and meaningful encoding of the presented digits

Subject	Digit span	Preferred grouping of digits	Meaningful encoding of digits	Source
Mental calculators				
Aitken	13	5	?	Hunter (1977)
Rueckle	18	6(3–3)	Yes	Mueller (1911)
	60	6(3–3)	Yes	Mueller (1913)
Griffith	17	3	Yes	Bryan et al. (1941)
Inaudi	12	3	?	Binet (1894)
Mental abacus operators				
AH	15	?	?	Hatano & Osawa (1983)
HT	16	?	?	Hatano & Osawa (1983)
YH	16	?	?	Hatano & Osawa (1983)
Practiced normal subjects				
SF	82	3 or 4	Yes	Chase & Ericsson (1982)
DD	101	3 or 4	Yes	Staszewski (1984)
RE	21	Variable	Yes	Chase & Ericsson (1981)
Mnemonists				
VP	17	3–5	Yes	Hunt & Love (1972)
TE	15	3	Yes	Gordon et al. (1984)

by demonstrating normal digit spans for these experts at presentation rates which are too fast to allow the encoding processes to operate.

With a presentation rate corresponding to about 2 seconds per digit, Inaudi could report back 36 digits (Binet, 1894, p. 48). However, Inaudi's digit span at 0.5 seconds per digit was seven digits, which is just average! His digit span could be improved to 12 at that relatively fast presentation rate by reading the digits rhythmically and in groups of two digits each (Binet, 1894, p. 46).

Mueller (1911) showed that Rueckle (R) needed either a slower presentation rate to recall 25 digits correctly or to have them read as five-digit numbers with the normal rate (1 second per digit). At the normal rate he could recall 18 digits, a performance he could maintain even at twice the presentation rate (almost 2 digits per second). When R was tested after 5 years and many memory experiments, he could recall 60 digits presented at the normal rate (Mueller, 1913).

The digit span of Griffith (Bryan *et al.*, 1941) was measured for presentation rates of 4 digits, 2 digits, 1 digit, 0.5 digits per second and slower. Griffith's memory span was quite normal at faster presentation rates: 9 and 8 digits for rates of 4 and 2 digits per second, respectively.

How fast encoding processes can become with extensive practice, and hence what presentation rates are required to eliminate meaningful encoding, is unclear. However, we know that even at a rate of 3 digits per second, which was believed earlier to eliminate possibilities of meaningful encoding, several memory experts are able to generate encodings and exhibit exceptionally high digit spans (Chase and Ericsson, 1982; Gordon *et al.*, 1984; Hunter, 1977; Mueller, 1911).

The digit-span results in Table 13.1 are also consistent with the notion that encoding digit groups into a retrieval structure takes additional time. All the memory experts (except R and the two trained subjects, SF and DD) can recall the equivalent of only four to six groups of digits. As this corresponds to the span for unrelated words, no additional retrieval structure is necessary. Using a slower presentation rate of 10 seconds per digit, Griffith (Bryan *et al.*, 1941) was able to create a hierarchically organized memory representation and encode 9 digit numbers (three 3-digit groups) and recall three such numbers, or 27 digits. As we noted earlier, Inaudi (Binet, 1894) was able to improve his span dramatically at slower presentation rates. Smith (1983) reports that Hans Eberstark, a mental calculator, was able to recall 40 digits if they were presented at just below 2 seconds per digit.

Memorization of digit matrices

The 5 × 5 digit matrix originally used by Binet (1894) is shown in Figure 13.2. Once subjects had memorized the matrix, they were instructed to recall the digits in the matrix according to certain predetermined orders (shown in Figure 13.2). The time to complete a given recall was recorded. Binet's reason for using many different orders of recall was to discriminate auditory and visual encoding in memory. With auditory encoding the digits would be memorized as a single list, and they could be recalled only in a single

4	7	1	0	2
3	0	4	3	6
2	1	1	4	8
8	7	4	2	9
1	5	2	7	9

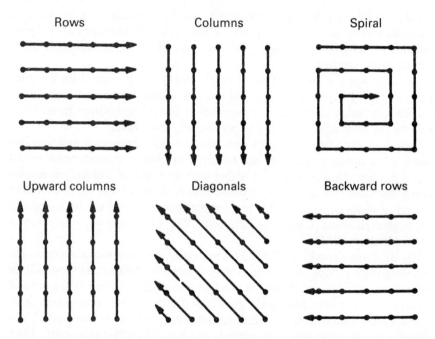

Figure 13.2 At the top is a 25-digit matrix of the type used by Binet to test his memory experts. He asked subjects to repeat the whole matrix in the various orders shown, or to repeat an individual row as a 5-digit number.

sequential way (cf. rigid sequential access of the *Pledge of Allegiance*). A visual memory encoding would allow flexible access similar to that used in the immediate report of a visually available digit matrix, albeit somewhat slower. The available study and recall times for different subjects on Binet's matrix are given in Table 13.2.

The study times in Table 13.2 show the expected superiority of the memory experts over the untrained normal subjects. When we examine the recall times, it is clear that the pattern of, or relation between, recall times for different orders of recall is remarkably similar. Ericsson and Chase (1982) showed the correlation coefficients between the recall times of normal subjects and the corresponding recall times for each of the different memory

Table 13.2 Time (in seconds) needed to study and retrieve Binet's matrix

	Binet[a] himself	Inaudi[a]	Diamondi[a]	Rueckle[b]	Rueckle[b] (more than 1 year later)	SF[c]	Normal subjects[d]	Number of retrievals
Study time	—	45	180	20.2	12.7	26.8	229.6	—
Retrieval time								
Rows	14	19	9	7.2	8.7	41.8	24.0	5
Individual row as 5-digit no.	15	7	9	7.8	8.3	28.7	31.2	5
Backward rows	—	—	—	9.0	7.0	22.9	33.9	5
Columns	55	60	35	23.9	19.1	64.0	71.6	25
Upward columns	60	96	36	24.6	18.5	58.5	—	25
Spiral	—	80	36	29.7	8.5	43.3	73.8	11
Diagonals	112	168	53	58.7	18.4	92.6	124.0	25

[a] Binet, 1894
[b] Mueller, 1917
[c] Ericsson and Chase, 1982
[d] An average based on the times of eight subjects reported by Mueller (1917)

experts to be .90 and above, which suggests a similar retrieval process and memory representation for all subjects.

Hence, Binet's (1894) argument that Inaudi's slower retrieval times were based on auditory list-like encoding and Diamondi's faster retrieval times were based on visual encoding seems incorrect. A more refined analysis shows the predominant similarity of the pattern of recall times.

We will now seek an encoding of the digit matrix in memory that gives an account for the systematic differences in retrieval times for different recall instructions. The fact that both normal and expert subjects can efficiently recall the digits according to these different spatial orders indicates mediation by similar organizing cues, or what we call retrieval structures. For several subjects (SF: Ericsson and Chase, 1982; R: Mueller, 1911; Arnauld and Binet himself: Binet, 1894), we know that the five digits in each row were encoded using mnemonic and meaningful associations; that is, the matrix was encoded as five memory units, each corresponding to one of the rows. Binet (1894) himself encoded three of the rows using the embedded dates 1415, 1893, and 1789 with a leading or succeeding digit. Based on verbal reports from SF, Ericsson and Chase (1982) proposed that the recall of a memory unit (corresponding to a row of digits) from LTM takes considerable time, whereas extracting more digits from an already recalled row takes very little time in comparison. As a first order of approximation, our model will consider only the time required for retrieval of different digit groups.

According to this model, recall by rows would require only five retrievals of different memory units and would take the same time whether done in a forward or backward direction (see Figure 13.2). Recall by columns (starting at the top and proceeding downwards or starting at the bottom and going upwards) would require retrieval of a new row-unit for each recalled digit (a total of 25 retrievals) and would take longer than recall by rows. These predictions are borne out (see Table 13.2). A regression model using the number of required retrievals predicts the observed time for a given recall order remarkably well (Ericsson and Chase, 1982).

The retrieval times for a given matrix appear to be influenced surprisingly little by recalling the same matrix many times. Binet (1894) recalled the matrix several times with each recall order. Retrieval became faster on subsequent recalls, but the increase in speed was roughly proportional for the different recall orders. The correlation between the initial recall (see Table 13.2) and the last recall with each order of recall was 0.997 ($N = 5$).

It may be that the most intriguing finding about recall is that subjects (normals as well as experts) are about as rapid in recalling the digits in forward as in backward order for this 25-digit matrix. There is evidence that memory experts encode linear sequences of digits in a very similar manner, as shown by our discussion of digit span. In addition, several of the mental calculators (Hatano and Osawa, 1983; Hunter, 1977; Weinland, 1948) and memory experts (Mueller, 1911) could recall briefly presented digit sequences in forward as well as backward order.

A very similar pattern of results emerged from Ericsson and Chase's (1982) analysis of the study and recall times from memorization of 50 digits arranged in a matrix with four columns. This digit matrix was originally used by Luria (1968) with his subject S, but has since been used with several memory experts as well as normal subjects (Chase and Ericsson, 1982; Gordon *et al.*, 1984; Hunt and Love, 1972). The pattern of times for different recall instructions was remarkably similar for both memory experts and normal subjects.

Improvement of memory experts with further practice

Only a few memory experts have been given the same memory tests several times at intervals of several years. The study times on the later occasion were dramatically shorter (see R in Table 13.2) and the digit span much longer (see R in Table 13.1). Here we will examine the memory testing of R by Mueller in 1906 (Mueller, 1911) and in 1911 (Mueller, 1913), and also the memory tests performed on Finkelstein by several different laboratories.

In Figure 13.3 we have compiled the study times required for memorization of digit sequences with lengths varying from 12 to 200 digits. On the left side of Figure 13.3, we can see the normal subjects with the slowest study times. On the right side of Figure 13.3, we can see the rapid study time for R. Particularly notable are R's extremely rapid study times (far right) recorded during the second test occasion. One should note the uniform improvement in R's performance: study times for both 102 and 204 digits were improved by around 50%. It is possible to compare these study times for simultaneous visual presentation with total duration of the sequential presentation of digits in auditory digit span. For sequences close to 100 digits in length, the trained subjects DD and SF are actually memorizing the digits faster with sequential auditory presentation than did any of the memory experts with simultaneous visual presentation. Chase and Ericsson (1982) noted that, when their digit span had increased, SF and DD were able to memorize digit sequences (shorter in length than their maximum span) at rates much faster than 1 digit per second. In order to explore the generality of memory improvement during 6 years of memory testing, Mueller (1913) also retested R on material other than digits. In contrast to his remarkably improved performance for digits, R did not improve his performance on colour names and became worse on consonants and nonsense syllables. The effects of R's extensive memorization of digits during the intervening 5 years between tests had selectively improved his memory for digits, which is consistent with the specificity of practice effects observed for other skills.

Susukita (1933) noted a remarkable training effect on Isihara's ability to memorize lists with over 2000 digits. On the first test occasion, Isihara required around 6 hours for memorization and about 2.5 hours for recall with 245 incorrectly recalled digits (9.8%). When he memorized a new list on a second occasion, 12 sessions later, he required a little over 6 hours and recalled all digits with only seven errors (0.3%) within a 2-hour interval.

A lot of information is available about Finkelstein's improvement, both from studies within the same laboratory and from improvements inferred from comparing results on the same memory task from different laboratories.

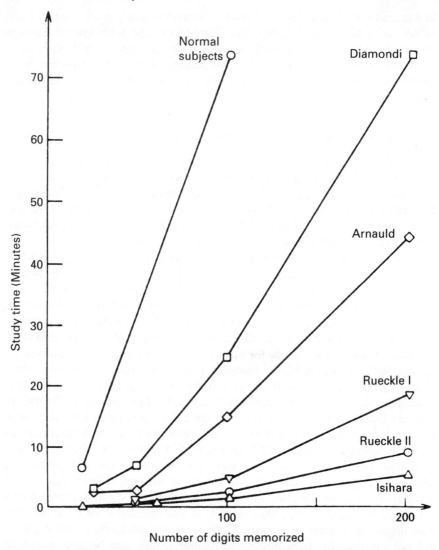

Figure 13.3 The amount of study time required for memorization of a given number of digits for normal subjects (average study time for a group of subjects, Lyon, 1917), for the mental calculator Diamondi and the mnemonist Arnauld (the reported times by Binet, 1894, include time to recall the digits), for R in 1906 (I) and in 1911 (II), (Mueller, 1913), and for Isihara (Susukita, 1933).

However, the scientific rigour and detail of these reports is often meagre. Nonetheless, the first reported study time of Finkelstein for Binet's 25-digit matrix was 26 seconds and was recorded while he was still in Poland (Weinland, 1948). Soon after Finkelstein's arrival in the United States, Wein-land measured his study time on the same type of matrix and found it to be 17.9 seconds (average based on three correct memorizations reported in Weinland, 1948). During his subsequent stay at Ohio State University, his initial performance of 17.5 seconds was improved until he was able to memorize such matrices in less than 9 seconds, a phenomenally short time (Barlow, 1952). Thus, he reduced his study time by more than 65% over a 5-year period.

In sum, existing memory experts can also increase their speed of memorization with the type of material they practise.

Types of memory representation

Many of the early researchers of memory had strong theoretical biases toward viewing the basic memory representation as sensory in nature; that is, as visual or auditory images. This bias was often confirmed by the subjects' introspective reports. Luria's (1968) S reported that he committed the digit matrix to memory as a visual image and at the time of recall he simply read off the information from the image. He reported using mediating associations for all other types of memory materials, such as nonsense syllables or verbatim information in a foreign language. Finkelstein (Bousfield and Barry, 1933) reported using a wide range of associations to aid his memorization of numbers. Once the numbers had been committed to memory he reported accessing them on an imagery basis. Finkelstein was remarkably detailed in his account of imagery. He perceived the numbers, even after auditory presentation, as written in 'chalk on a freshly washed chalkboard' in 'Finkelstein's own handwriting' (Bousfield and Barry, 1933, p. 335). Mueller's (1911, p. 197) R also reported perceiving a visual image of digits in a 'Komplex' of six numbers which, during recall, allowed him to report the digits backward almost as fast as forward. When coloured sequences of digits were memorized, the memory image also contained the colour of the digits.

The notion that a visual image is stored directly (cf. photographic memory) lacks empirical support from performance. In fact, the available data are inconsistent with such an idea. R required additional time to memorize the colour of the coloured digit sequences, corresponding roughly to the time needed to memorize only the colours (Mueller, 1917). The pattern of recall times for the two matrices was remarkably similar across all experts as well as control subjects. In addition, Hunt and Love (1972) compared VP's memorization of a normal digit matrix to a staggered digit matrix of the same size, in which the blanks had been inserted randomly so the columns no longer were aligned. They found a similar pattern of times to recall rows, columns, and individual digits using the two types of matrices, a pattern which was quite different from the corresponding retrieval times for the same information with a perceptually available staggered matrix. Gordon *et al.* (1984) replicated these results with TE.

The most obvious refutation of visual or photographic memory comes from the fact that different kinds of materials are memorized at different rates. Several of these memory experts had superior memory for only one type of material. Mental calculators who showed exceptional memory for digits have had extensive experience with numbers. Generally, previous extensive practice with a certain material appears to be necessary to obtain exceptional memory with that material. Finkelstein (Sandor, 1932) memorized letters at only an average rate and was even worse than average in his memory for shapes and forms. The memory spans of Hatano and Osawa's (1983) mental abacus masters were no different from normal spans for letters and fruit names. Inaudi (Binet, 1894) had average to below-average memory span for consonants and memory for prose. The digit-span expert (SF) showed no improvement in his normal memory span for consonants (Ericsson *et al.*, 1980). Griffith (Bryan *et al.*, 1941) had normal memory span for letters, as well as for series of alternating letters and digits. In a review of mental calculators, Smith (1983) showed that improved memory is almost invariably limited to numbers and digits. The Japanese mnemonist Isihara was shown to have no better than normal recognition memory for colour stimuli (Susukita and Heindl, 1935).

Subjects with superior memory for a wide range of material have always shown that superiority in the rate at which they could memorize materials relative to normal subjects. It is important to note that these faster study rates would not be sufficiently fast to be usable for memory span, where items are presented at 1 item per second. Isihara's memory was superior for nonsense syllables and personal names (Chiba and Susukita, 1934; Susukita, 1934). Mueller (1911) found that R was much better than normal subjects when memorizing sequences of colour names, consonants, nonsense syllables, and geometric figures. Both R and Isihara required 2.5 and 5.0 seconds per item for those other types of material. In a subsequent section we will discuss generalizable aspects of memory skills, which would allow some transfer to materials other than the practised material.

Hunt and Love (1972) administered a variety of psychometric tests to VP and also recorded his performance on several memory tests (e.g., memory for prose and lists of words). VP's performance was usually much higher than average, but was never decisively outside the range of college students.

Up to this point, we have described general characteristics of memory experts' performance in terms of the three principles of skilled memory. To understand the mechanisms underlying these memory skills in detail, it is necessary to obtain more explicit empirical evidence. The experimental tests will be tailored to the description of a specific memory expert's skill. These detailed analyses are important for at least two reasons. First, it is important to demonstrate that expert-level memory skills can be described at the same level of detail as given for our digit-span experts (Chase and Ericsson, 1981, 1982). Second, these detailed analyses contain the best evidence for encoding processes and retrieval structures. Below we give three detailed analyses of different memory experts.

The structure of Professor Rueckle's memory skill

Mueller (1911) argued that Professor Rueckle's (R) memory for a visually presented string of numbers was based on memory encodings of groups of six digits (Komplexe). Each 6-digit group consists of two 3-digit numbers (Teil-Komplexe), where the 3-digit numbers constituted units. At age 12, R had allegedly already memorized how all numbers between 0 and 1000 could be represented as products of prime numbers or as genuine prime numbers, (e.g., 543 = 3*181). The 6-digit group was encoded as a memory unit by generating associations between the two 3-digit numbers. For example: 451697 → 451 = 11 × 41, 697 = 17 × 41; 893047 → 893 = 19 × 47, 047 = 47; 286219 → 219 = 3 × 73, log (73) = 1.86 → 286. In order to account for how long sequences of digits were stored in memory, Mueller proposed associations between these Komplexe to form a higher-level unit, Komplexverbande. This unitization could be achieved either by sequential associations between Komplexe or by place-associations within this higher-level unit. Mueller argued that a 48-digit sequence would be represented as shown in Figure 13.4.

According to Mueller (1911) the 6-digit Komplex is simultaneously attended to during study (encoding) as well as during recall. In a series of small studies, Mueller (1911) gave strong evidence for his proposed structure as well as strong evidence against the view that R stored raw sensory images of the visually presented digit sequence. Mueller (1917) showed that R needed much more time to memorize digits in different coloured inks when both the digit and its colour had to be recalled. R reported memorizing the digits and colours separately and Mueller (1917) could confirm that the study time for memorizing both colours and digits was roughly the same as the sum of the study time for memorizing digits and colours separately. By presenting the digits as Roman numerals instead of as Arabic numerals, R's required study time was more than doubled (Mueller, 1911). Interestingly enough, R encoded Roman numerals in terms of 3-digit Komplexe rather than the normal 6-digit

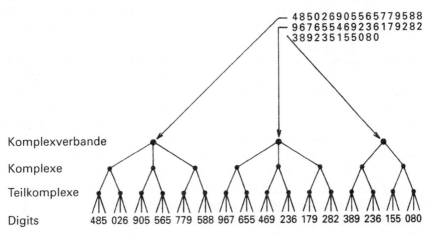

Figure 13.4 The memory representation of 48 digits presented visually in three rows of 18, 18, and 12 digits, respectively (see upper portion of the figure). The hierarchical memory encoding of the digits in each row is shown in the lower portion. The main units of encoding are Komplexe, which consist of two encoded 3-digit groups (Teilkomplexe). Associations between Komplexe form the next level of the hierarchy (Komplexverbande).

Komplexe, which is consistent with a slowing down of encoding processes by the additional step of decoding the Roman numerals into numbers.

Some of the best evidence for the psychological reality of the 6-digit Komplexe comes from experimental variation of the study and recall conditions. When R was forced to encode a 48-digit string into Komplexe of 8 and 4 digits, more study time was required than normal. In another series of studies the speed of R's recall sequences was systematically studied. R was able to recall the digit sequences with remarkable speed. Sequences of 72 digits were recalled in the forward order in 16 seconds (average rate of about 4 digits per second) and in the backward order in 37 seconds. In another recall condition, R was asked to start to recall the last Komplex, then the next to last Komplex, etc., but the digits within a Komplex were recalled in forward order. His recall speed in that condition was about 3 digits per second (23.5 seconds total), which is remarkably similar to the forward recall. The most striking evidence comes from asking R to recall the digit sequence as multi-digit numbers (e.g., 54 691 = fifty-four thousand, six hundred ninety-one) rather than as single digits (R's preferred mode of recall). Recall in 6-digit numbers is structurally consistent with the 6-digit Komplexe and was much faster than recall by 5-digit numbers, which is inconsistent with the memory encoding.

The higher-level organization of Komplexe (Komplexverbande) was evidenced by longer pauses between certain Komplexe during recall (Mueller, 1911). The importance of place cues for retrieval of Komplexe was demonstrated by Mueller (1917) in two different experiments. Digit sequences ranging in length from 42 to 204 digits were memorized by R in matrix format. For example, 204 digits were presented as six rows of 30 digits (five Komplexe of 6 digits each) and the seventh row as 24 digits (four Komplexe of 6 digits). R was presented with either a place description (e.g., third Komplex on the fifth row) or a 6-digit string corresponding to a Komplex, and was asked to rapidly recall the 6-digit Komplex following the referenced Komplex. For short digit sequences (42 digits) both forms of probes led to rapid retrieval: 2.4 seconds for place description and 2.1 seconds for Komplex probes. With sequences of 204 digits, both probes were responded to more slowly: 4.9 seconds (place description) and 5.6 seconds (probe). Many of the errors for the 204-digit sequence were the recall of a Komplex from an adjacent row but with the correct placement within the row (correct Komplex number but wrong row). This experiment demonstrates clearly that spatial cues are directly associated with the Komplexe. However, Mueller noted that the recall latencies are too long to account for the recall of the digit sequence during normal recall.

Subsequently, Mueller (1917) instructed R to recall either the Komplex referred to in the place description or the following Komplex (as in the experiment above). For digit sequences of 60 and 102 digits, the recall latencies for the directly indicated Komplex were 2.9 and 4.8 seconds, respectively. Recall latencies for the following Komplexe were 3.0 and 5.3 seconds, respectively. The differences between these latencies correspond roughly to the time necessary to access the next Komplex once the preceding

Komplex has been retrieved, and are consistent with access times observed during normal recall.

The structure of TE's memory skill

Gordon *et al.* (1984) studied a subject (TE), who had practised mnemonic methods for about 20 years. TE began his memory training at age 15 when he read a book describing mnemonic methods. He studied these techniques more in depth during his time at the university.

TE's basic method for encoding digits involved recoding digits into words. The mnemonists Arnauld (Binet, 1894) and Isihara (Susukita, 1933) used a variant of the same method. Ericsson and Chase (1982) also studied a student, AB, who had used the same mnemonic method for a couple of years. As shown in Table 13.3, each digit corresponds to one or several distinct consonant sounds (Gordon *et al.*, 1984).

When a subject is presented with a digit sequence, such as 43, they would first retrieve that 4 corresponds to an *r*-sound and 3 to an *m*-sound (see Table 13.3). Then a word would be retrieved that contains the consonant sounds *r* and *m* in the correct order, like a*rm*, *room*, *rum*, *rim*, *ram*, or *rhyme*, because the vowels and *w*, *h*, and *y* do not have a digit correspondence and are disregarded. With a few additional rules regarding silent letters and double letters, for example, a given remembered word can be uniquely decoded into the corresponding presented digits.

TE's memory performance replicated VP's (Hunt and Love, 1972) on the memory tasks given to VP. From TE's retrospective reports after the completion of a memory test, Gordon *et al.* (1984) got a remarkably detailed account of his encoding processes during the test.

One of the memory tasks Gordon *et al.* (1984) used with TE was Atkinson and Shiffrin's continuous paired-associate task. This task consists of only four nonsense syllables (e.g., ROQ, JAQ) which are paired with different 2-digit numbers (e.g., ROQ-52). Interspersed in the list of presented paired-associates were test trials where only the stimulus was presented, and the subject was to report the number most recently paired with that stimulus. TE encoded the presented number as words and formed interactive images with physical locations suggested by a meaningful associate to the nonsense syllable; for example, ROQ → Rock → → Rockery in the garden → his garden. When a new 2-digit number was to be associated with a location, TE relied on

Table 13.3 A list of digit to consonants-sound mappings (adapted from Gordon *et al.*, 1984)

1	2	3	4	5	6	7	8	9	0
T	N	M	R	L	J	K	F	P	Z
D	Ng				G (soft)	G (hard)	V	B	S
Th					Ch	Q			C (soft)
					Sh	C (hard)			

Note: Any one of the consonant-sounds in each column can be used to represent the corresponding digit.

chaining together the new image with the earlier. For example, TE visualized a ruler lying on the earth for ROQ-52, where 52 is *line*. When he encountered ROQ-08 (08 is *sieve*) he visualized the sifting of rulers in a garden sieve. During test trials TE would recode the nonsense syllable into a location which would be the retrieval cue for the image, which gave the word and its corresponding digits. Except for a very small number of errors, he responded correctly to all test probes regardless of the number of intervening study trials with other stimulus terms. His latency to report the correct number on test trials was fast, usually around 4 seconds, and in most cases he reported being directly able to find the last image of his generated chain of images associated with a given location or nonsense syllable. After the end of this experiment TE was able to recall virtually the entire sequence of presented paired-associates. Unfortunately, no information is given about TE's study times in this self-paced version of the continuous paired-associates memory task.

In memorizing Luria's (1968) 50-digit matrix, TE encoded each row of 4 digits into one or two words. The words corresponding to the digits of the row were converted into a visual image also containing the scene or object which was part of a previously learned list of words (pegs), where the first word (e.g., *eat*) corresponded to the first row, the second (e.g., *inn*) corresponded to the second row, etc. Using a previously learned list of words as a retrieval structure is called the *peg-word method*. At the time of recall, the first scene of the prelearned list was recalled, then the associate image with the words which was decoded into the presented numbers, and so on. Given all those required cognitive processes, TE's study times and recall times are very fast and also remarkably similar to those recorded for Luria's S and Hunt and Love's VP as well as the student AB using the same method (Ericsson and Chase, 1982).

TE's digit span was found to be around 15 digits, which is comparable to those of other mnemonists and mental calculators (see Table 13.1). Gordon *et al.* (1984) argued that TE converted 3 digits into two-syllable words and that his span corresponded to four or five such words. This limit was not caused by too little time for encoding digits into words, because TE's digit span was virtually unaffected by an increase of the rate of presentation from 1 to 3 digits per second. We argued earlier that the real limit is the number of recoded units which can be reliably retrieved in sequence without an acquired retrieval structure.

There doesn't appear to exist any clear upper bound on the amount and speed of memorization with methods similar to TE's. The professional mnemonist Isihara, who used such methods, had the fastest study times of sequences of digits and also memorized the most digits in a single session. Isihara relied on phonemic recoding of 2 to 4 digits into a word, for example 0605→*omuretsu* (English *omelette*) (Susukita, 1933). Susukita found Isihara took between 1.0 to 1.5 seconds to recode digits into a word and form a clear visual image. Instead of using the pegs in the peg-word method, Isihara used a fixed sequence of physical locations (loci), like a brook close to his house and a friend's house. He had over 400 such locations readily accessible in a given order. Susukita found that Isihara could visualize these different locations at a rate of about 2 every second. By storing up to three images of recoded words in each location Isihara was able to memorize 2400 digits in about 6 hours. Beyond this information based on verbal reports, Susukita also gives evidence on errors to validate that Isihara used the methods described above.

A memory skill for dinner orders

A waiter who could memorize up to 20 complete dinner orders in a normal restaurant setting was studied for a 2-year period by Ericsson and Polson (1988a, 1988b). A laboratory analog was generated, where each person at a table was represented by a card with a picture of a face and each order was a random combination of one of eight meat entrées, one of five meat temperatures (rare to well-done), one of five salad dressings, and one of three starches (baked potato, rice, or french fries), forming a pool of 600 possible orders. The presentation procedure was self-paced and the subject indicated when the next order should be read. Subjects were allowed to request any information to be presented again. Tables with three, five, and eight customers were used throughout these studies.

After a session to familiarize college students with this memory task, their study times and recall performances were recorded. These subjects stored the orders as a list and recalled the orders in the order presented.

The waiter (JC) required dramatically less study time in this task than did the college students, and he made fewer errors (i.e., virtually none). Rather than recalling all the information from an order together, JC recalled all information in a category together: first, all salad dressings, then, all entrées, etc. For each category, JC encoded the items with a different mnemonic strategy. Salad dressings were encoded as a group of the initial letters of their names (e.g., Bleu cheese, Oil-and-vinegar, Oil-and-vinegar, Thousand island = BOOT or *boot*). With only three different starches, repetitions were frequent, and JC encoded starches in patterns (e.g., baked potato, rice, rice, baked potato = *abba*). Temperatures of the meat were all ordered by the degree to which they were cooked (rare to well-done), and JC would encode these relations spatially; that is, Rare, Medium-rare, Medium-well, Rare, would be a linear increase from rare to medium-well (jumping over medium) down to rare again, expressed by the numbers 1241. The entrées were encoded primarily by association to the position of the person ordering.

It is important to note that these encodings are configural; that is, that all or at least most of the items need to be attended to simultaneously to access the mnemonic pattern. JC encoded up to five items in a single encoding, which is sufficient for tables of three and five people. For tables of eight people, he grouped the items for the first four and last four people together, two encodings for four items each.

During our early studies of JC, he was asked to think aloud during study and recall of the dinner orders, as well as give retrospective verbal reports after each memory task. His concurrent verbalization of his thoughts during the memorization showed that he reliably retrieved earlier presented items of each category to encode them with the corresponding item from the just-presented dinner order. For tables of eight people he did not retrieve the items from the first four people while studying the last four. Hence, no retrieval of earlier items was required when studying the fifth order. This was confirmed by analyzing the time spent studying each dinner order for tables of eight people. The study time increased from Order 1 to Order 4, but the study time for Order 5 was much lower than that for Order 4, and was similarly increased for Orders 6 through 8. Thinking aloud protocols demonstrated that only items within the same group of dinner orders were encoded together.

The experimental evidence for the cognitive processes and structures described above come from three lines of experiments. First, Ericsson and Polson (1988a, 1988b) changed the order of presentation (the information) about dinner orders. In one experiment, JC was presented with lists of items of categories (all salad dressings together, etc), as well as the traditional presentation of complete dinner orders. Although JC had no previous experience with this compatible form of presentation, his performance was indistinguishable from that with the standard presentation format described earlier. This experiment also demonstrated that the required study times for different categories of information were reliably different, thus providing support for different mnemonic encoding processes for the four types of materials. In a second experiment, JC was given dinner orders for randomly selected people around the table, along with the regular presentation of orders from people in a clockwise order around the table. In both conditions of the experiment, JC recalled by category and in the same clockwise order, based on the placement of individuals. Hence, JC must encode the information in terms of the placement of the individual giving the order. Somewhat surprisingly, no reliable differences between conditions were found for tables of three and five people, but a large difference was found for tables of eight. For tables of three and five, items might be put into a single group. If information is stored with a location cue, a random order of presentation would have no effect. However, for tables of eight people, JC would need to keep two groups of information simultaneously. Thinking-aloud protocols and detailed *post hoc* analyses gave additional support to this interpretation.

In two experiments, Ericsson and Polson (1988a, 1988b) examined whether JC's memory skill would transfer to informaton other than dinner orders. The first experiment used materials with categories which had been selected to have the same structural properties as the matching category for the dinner orders. For example, the ordered category of meat temperatures ranging from rare to well-done was matched up with the category of time intervals ranging from second to week. After two to three sessions JC showed close to the same performance on the new category items as he did for dinner orders in the first experiment. Several analyses of individual study times, order of recall, and thinking-aloud protocols have provided evidence that the same mnemonic encoding processes and memory organization were used for this new type of information. In the second experiment on transfer, JC was presented with items from categories in formats designed to hinder JC from using his mnemonic encoding processes and his category-based storage. In sum, his performance was dramatically impaired and, in at least one condition, his recall was no longer based on category but was based on the order in which the information was presented. However, even with these types of materials, his performance was superior to that of the naïve college students, which constitutes evidence for generalizable aspects of acquired memory skill. In a later session we will discuss cognitive structures and mechanisms which could mediate such transfer.

Finally, Ericsson and Polson (1988b) examined JC's post-session recall of up to 12 memorized lists or tables. JC showed extremely good recall for the last instance of dinner orders from a table with a certain number of people. For earlier memorized instances of tables with the same number of people, he showed almost no recall of the corresponding dinner orders. When cued with the faces corresponding to the studied list, his recall performance improved and his recall for the last instance of a given number of dinner orders was virtually perfect. Recall of earlier instances was better with face cues than without, but clearly inferior to the last instances. His recall was organized by category, and occasionally a whole list of items would intrude from another table with the same number of people.

These three detailed descriptions of the cognitive processes and structures involved in memory skill show the important role of mediation in exceptional memory. For many of the other exceptional subjects, evidence for similar mechanisms is much more spotty and incomplete.

Summary of analyses of memory experts and trained subjects

The great consistency in the basic findings is even more remarkable, since most investigators did not seem to be aware of each other's work. The evidence for mediation by pre-existing knowledge (cf. principle of meaningful encoding) is clear, and, even in the rare cases where affirmative evidence is lacking, no counter evidence is available. Verbal reports concerning consistent grouping of digits in threes and fours, and concerning recognized patterns, associations to knowledge, or mnemonic recodings are the most common evidence. Evidence from post-session recall according to mnemonic categories and from experimental manipulation of mnemonic encodability is stronger. The specificity of all memory skills to certain materials (really only a single type of material) at fast presentation rates and the sensitivity to small changes in presentation rates provide the strongest evidence for some form of mediation.

Strong evidence for retrieval structures is obtained from a small number of detailed case studies. A large number of subjects give predictable recall times for different orders of recall on the two types of digit matrices, which gives strong indirect support. Several memory experts have also shown remarkable speed in recalling memorized digit sequences forwards or backwards.

The speed-up principle originally emerged from the analysis of the studies of practice in digit span (Chase and Ericsson, 1981, 1982). Given the traditional short-term studies of memory experts, no relevant information could possibly be obtained. Results from retests were available for two memory experts, and clear evidence for speed-up was found.

The improved and superior memory can thus be attributed to acquired knowledge, retrieval structures, and rapid encoding and retrieval processes. One of the real advantages of the skill view is that it suggests a continuum of memory skill (or memory performance) where memory experts occupy one extreme end and novices the other. The data from the memorization of digit matrices showed that normal subjects required considerably more study time. Once the information was committed to LTM, a remarkable similarity in the pattern of retrieval times was observed, suggesting a similar structure of the memorized information between novices and memory experts. In two later sections we will examine data on novices' memorization in more detail.

Memory skill versus memory ability in normal subjects

According to the memory skill hypothesis, there are not only large differences in memory performance (memory experts vs normal people), but there are also memory differences in normal subjects. It will be hard to prove that all systematic differences in memory performance are due to acquired memory skill, but we will look at some evidence consistent with it and also consider evidence inconsistent with an innate account of memory ability. In the following, we will review an extensive body of primarily older research reporting improvement in memory as an incidental result of a large number of sessions of memory testing. Recent studies of memory usually test subjects' memory for a single session only. Some of the older studies with many sessions have tried to describe the cognitive processes used by the subjects to memorize information and the changes in the cognitive processes mediating improved speed of memorization. In a separate section, we will review attempts to instruct and train subjects to use efficient methods for memorization. The elements of these efficient methods will be discussed in terms of the three principles of skilled memory. As the final piece of evidence, we will compare normal subjects' memory performance in their areas of highly developed skill with the experts' performance described earlier.

Practice effects in regular laboratory studies

The fact that subjects improve with practice in a specific memory task is well established. Here we will be concerned only with studies giving more practice than is given in the traditional 1- to 3-hour memory experiment. Speed and efficiency of memorization is dramatically improved after 5 to 15 training sessions. After 15 sessions, the study times for a list of 12 nonsense syllables were reduced by over 50% on the average and by over 85% for some individuals (Reed, 1917). For 10 nonsense syllable lists, Harcum and Coppage (1965) observed over 75% reduction of the number of errors prior to memorization during a 12-session period. Greater reduction was observed for two subjects given 30–40 practice sessions. Similar dramatic improvements have been observed for lists of nonsense syllables (Ebert and Meumann, 1904;

Lepley, 1934; Meyer and Miles, 1953; Ward, 1937), lists of coloured geometric forms (Jensen and Roden, 1963), and for learning of paired-associates (Greenberg and Underwood, 1950; Keppel *et al.*, 1968; Warr, 1964, Exp. 1).

Verbatim memorization of prose appears to be improved by practice (Dearborn, 1910; James, 1890; Peterson, 1912), but a small number of subjects and a lack of counterbalancing of texts make numerical estimates of the size of improvement inexact. Cofer (1940) achieved such counterbalancing for memorization of 12 short texts and found 62% reduction of trials required for complete verbatim memorization of these texts as a result of practice. Interestingly enough, Cofer did not find any improvements when only the content and meaning of these stories were memorized.

In addition to the studies described earlier by Chase and Ericsson (1981, 1982), several investigators have observed improvements on memory span and recall of briefly presented digit lists and matrices. Two subjects were given over 50 sessions of practice on digit span by Martin and Fernberger (1929). They increased their span up to 15–16 digits from their rather high original spans of 8.9 and 10.9 digits respectively. The reported method underlying their improvement was to form groups of digits and increase the number of digits in each group. Towards the end of the study they were able to form groups of 5 digits. No further details are given about the structure and mechanisms underlying the improvement. Another remarkable case study (Barlow, 1952) concerns the study time necessary to memorize a sequence of 21 digits with simultaneous visual presentation. After 75 hours of practice a college student at Ohio State University was able to memorize 21 digits in just 4.37 sec, which was even faster than the memory expert Finkelstein. Group experiments have also demonstrated similar improvements of memory span and immediate recall. After 78 days of practice, Gates and Taylor (1925) showed that kindergarten children had improved their digit span by about 50% (4.3 to 6.4 digits). Pollack *et al.* (1959) studied how many of the last consecutive series of digits subjects could recall from a super-span length list (running memory span) read at different presentation rates. After over 100 hours of practice, subjects improved their spans (1 digit per second presentation rate) from about 4.5 to 9.5 digits for digit sequences of unknown length and from about 7.0 to 11.6 when the length of the presented digit sequence was known. Fracker (1908) found an increase of over 20% for immediate memory of sequences of four tones after about 10 daily training sessions. Junior high school students were tested daily on their recall of a digit matrix which was presented for 2 minutes (Murphey *et al.*, unpublished MS). Throughout the 54 daily tests, the subjects increased the number of correctly recalled digits close to threefold, from 15.3 digits to 41.3 digits. During the final sessions two subjects were able to memorize the 64-digit matrix perfectly during the allotted 2-minute interval. These results are even more remarkable when one realizes that Luria's S and all other mnemonists required more time (around 3 minutes) to memorize fewer digits (50-digit matrix).

In summary, normal motivated subjects display remarkable (up to fivefold) improvements in memorization and immediate memory after rather moderate amounts of practice. Unfortunately, much less is known about the structure and mechanisms of these improvements.

In accord with the studies of memory discussed earlier, skill improvements in memory through practice reflect storage in LTM. The improvements in learning rate are greater for the first half of the list (primacy effects) than for the second half of the list (recency effects) (Harcum and Coppage, 1965; Jensen and Roden, 1963; Lepley, 1934; Ward, 1937). Waugh (1960) found that the improved performance of well-practised subjects occurred in the primacy portion of the serial position curve and that the recency portion was unaltered. A similar result was obtained in comparing subjects with high and low memory spans (Jensen and Roden, 1963).

More information about mechanisms comes from those studies above which evaluated transfer of the observed practice effect to other memorization tasks. Pollack *et al.* (1959) found perfect transfer of the increased running memory spans to visual presentation of digits when auditory presentation was used during practice. Ebert and Meumann (1904) demonstrated remarkable improvements on a wide range of memory tasks from their practice with nonsense syllables. Subsequent research (Dearborn, 1909; Reed, 1917) has shown that Ebert and Meumann's improvements were not due to a generalized improvement of memory caused by the practice series. The initial memory testing prior to the memory practice turned out to be crucial to the generalized improvement on the memory tests observed after practice. A control group receiving only the initial and final testing showed improvement similar to that of the experimental group receiving practice.

When these retest effects are subtracted, the improvements are much smaller and, in general, not statistically reliable. Complete reviews of transfer of memory improvement are given by Orata (1928) and Woodworth (1938). A study by Fracker (1908) is particularly interesting: he isolated an abstract spatial encoding of groups of four different tones in the practice series (discussed below). We will briefly review his transfer study, which included a small control group not given practice. His subjects showed considerable transfer (beyond the improvement of the control group) to immediate memory tasks involving four shades of gray and four other tones, and some transfer to memory tasks involving nine different shades of gray and nine different tones. Introspective reports support the hypothesis that the abstract spatial encoding was mediating the transfer. Essentially no transfer was seen to memorization of poetry, or memory for arm movements, numbers, or geometric figures.

The performance data discussed above show clear speed-up of memorization with practice, and the above results on transfer are at least consistent with an interpretation in terms of memory skill. In order to establish the mapping of these results from normal subjects onto the skilled memory theory, we need to demonstrate that memorization is mediated by encoding processes and use of retrieval structures; ideally, we should relate the observed improvement to changes in those components.

Encoding processes used for memorization of nonsense syllables and unrelated words have been studied extensively using verbal report techniques. Reed (1918a, 1918b) found that the paired-associate *kimono-stencil* was recalled much better if encoded as 'picture of a design stenciled on kimono' than if no particular encoding technique was used (Reed, 1918b, p. 265). Many investigators have gone as far as to suggest that all forms of memorization involve mediation (cf. Prytulak, 1971; Woodworth, 1938). Reed (1918a) disproved the old saying, 'Quickly learned, quickly forgotten,' by showing that the most rapidly learned material was best retained at a subsequent recall test. This finding can be accounted for best in terms of availability of good mediators, as shown by much subsequent research. The ease of forming meaningful associations to a nonsense syllable (its M-value) is a powerful predictor of ease of learning (cf. Montague, 1972). The greater the number of steps or differences between the nonsense syllables and its mediator, the less likely is correct subsequent recall (Prytulak, 1971). Research showing the validity of verbally reported mediators is reviewed in Montague (1972) and Ericsson and Simon (1984).

With the importance of retrieved mediators for rapid learning demonstrated, the question remains as to how the speed of memorization can be improved with practice. We believe that the main cause of speed-up in memorization is speed-up of access of good mediators. Many subjects do not intentionally try to recall mediators, as demonstrated by improvements observed in experiments where subjects are simply told to try and use them (Montague, 1972). In the next section we will discuss studies where subjects are instructed and trained in the use of specific mediational memory methods. Some of the best evidence that improvement in memorization is related to better availability of mediators, at least during the early stages of practice, comes from Postman's (1969) systematic experimental analysis of warm-up effects.

In at least two of the studies discussed above, encoding processes were identified as having emerged with practice. Pollack *et al.* (1959) gave their trained subjects digit sequences grouped by 1, 2, 3, 4, 5, and 6 digits. When digit sequences of unknown length were presented, subjects' performance with 4-digit groups was reliably better than all other groupings except 3-digit groups, which gave intermediate performance. Performance with 4-digit groups was indistinguishable from performance on sequences of known length, where subjects could adopt their own optimal grouping. This interpretation is supported by the result that digit sequences of known length were unaffected by the group size of the presentation. Fracker (1908) found that reports given after the training session showed that subjects recoded the four tones with different levels of pitch into locations on abstract spatial scales and remembered groups of four tones in terms of the corresponding spatial pattern. Very similar recoding methods have been observed in the waiter's (JC) encoding of temperatures of meat (Ericsson and Polson, 1988b) and also in subjects representing information in the three-term series task (Egan and Grimes, 1979).

The best evidence that normal subjects use retrieval structures comes from the analysis of different recall orders, when digits from a memorized 25-digit matrix were discussed earlier. Several other studies (cf. Woodworth, 1938) have shown that information about the location of an item in the series can be memorized prior to the sequential associations between items.

In sum, normal subjects show speed-up and great improvements of memory performance as a function of practice. The available evidence suggests that practice leads to faster storage in LTM rather than extending STM. Memorization of unrelated and nonsense materials involves extensive use of meaningful encodings, and the cognitive processes, which provide better accessibility to such encodings, appear to account for much of the improvement during the early stages of practice.

Instruction and training of normal subjects

There have been several efforts to validate hypothetical mechanisms (often verbalized in retrospective reports) underlying improved memory performance by experimental techniques. In these studies, randomly selected subjects are instructed to use some specific method of memorization and are compared with naïve subjects on the same memory task. For our purposes the most interesting studies regard instructions to use mnemonics and, in particular, interactive visual imagery. Other relevant studies, which we will not discuss here, have demonstrated improvements through instruction in general methods for improved memory (cf. Woodrow, 1927), methods of study (e.g., rote memorization vs reciting: Gates, 1917), and learning by whole or by parts (Hovland, 1951).

The research on mnemonics has been excellently reviewed elsewhere (Bellezza, 1981; Bower, 1972; Hoffman and Senter, 1978), and we will focus primarily on research relevant to the mechanisms underlying memory skill we discussed earlier.

There is a wide range of different mnemonic techniques, but underlying all of them is the effort to utilize pre-existing knowledge structures. Following our earlier format, we will discuss encoding processes and retrieval structures separately. To encode two or more items (e.g., words or digits), it is necessary to provide a context in which meaningful relations can be established. For example, two unrelated words (*cow-ball*) can be effectively associated to each other by visualizing a scene where the two objects interact (a cow kicking a ball). Similarly effective encodings can be attained by generating a sentence linking the noun pairs (Bower, 1972). However, these associative processes do not work well or at all with abstract words, numbers, names, and nonsense syllables. For such types of material, it is necessary to find associative links to meaningful and, ideally, concrete words. Earlier, we have discussed digit-to-sound conversions and nonsense-syllable-to-word mappings. Similar associative relationships can be used for names and abstract words. In most of these cases, there is not a one-to-one mapping between the associate and the presented stimulus; hence, information about the stimulus beyond the associate must be stored for successful retrieval. Ericsson and Simon (1984) discussed several studies showing better recall for the mnemonic or the associate than for the actual stimulus. Even when a presented word pair is encoded as an interactive image, it is necessary to remember the words corresponding to the elements of the image. Bower showed that if a list of paired-associates contained synonyms (e.g., *boat-ship*), subjects using imagery showed a much higher proportion of such confusion than a control group rehearsing the pair auditorily.

When subjects must remember a long list of items, they need a retrieval structure which is provided by the method of loci and the peg-word method. Bower and Reitman (1972) have shown the two methods to give indistinguishable performance. In the peg-word method, the subject initially learns a list of concrete nouns or pegs, such as one-bun, two-shoe, etc. The first item is stored by forming an interactive visual image with the first word (peg) of the list (bun), the second item is encoded with the second word of the list (shoe), and so on. At the time of recall, the subject simply recalls the first peg of the list and uses it to recall the interactive image and the first-presented word and so on until the entire list of presented words is recalled.

After a minimal amount of training, subjects perform much better with mnemonic-encoding than do control subjects, especially if the list of presented words is significantly longer than the subjects' memory span (Bellezza, 1981). For mnemonic encoding methods to be successful, the subject needs a reasonably slow presentation rate and sufficient time for recall. Few studies have used a self-paced procedure for mnemonic encoding with the peg-word method. Bugelski (1968) found that an average study time of about 8 seconds produced 85% correct recall. Other studies using fixed presentation rates showed no improvement with 2 seconds per item, and increasing improvement for rates slower than 4–5 seconds per item (Bugelski *et al.*, 1968; Wood, 1967).

Maybe the most intriguing finding is that the same list of peg-words can effectively be used repeatedly, even within the same session. Performance appears to be unaffected by earlier memorization of word lists with the same peg-words (Bugelski *et al.*, 1968; Bower and Reitman, 1972), even when the same words are memorized in different orders (Morris and Reid, 1970). Hence, the peg-word lists appear to have the characteristics of a retrieval structure. Analyses of postsession recall show that subjects recall less from lists memorized earlier during the session, although their level of recall is higher than that of subjects in a control group. This decrement in recall of early-presented items can be avoided by instructing subjects to include earlier memorized items in the encoding of a new item (chaining) (Bjork, 1978; Bower and Reitman, 1972).

Crovitz (1971) studied how many items can be associated with the same peg without losing the correct order of presentation in a given list. He found that one and two items per peg preserved exact order information equally well, four items per peg was intermediate, and more items per peg produced performance no better than that of the control group, who memorized the 32-word list without pegs. The professional mnemonist Isihara was reluctant to store more than three objects in each physical location (Susukita, 1933). Hence, the limit of three to four elements within each encoding unit is evidenced also under these conditions.

The speed of retrieval for information stored in loci (cf. pegs) has been examined in an interesting study by Lea (1975). He had subjects memorize an ordered list of 12 locations on the university campus. Then, they stored one word in each location. Once the list was memorized, Lea measured the time taken from naming a location to the subject's responding with the word stored at a location n locations away, where n was 0, 1, 2, or 3 (varied in blocks). He also measured the latency of naming the location which was n locations away from the probe. The retrieval time of a word was a linear function of the number of mediating locations plus a constant. The word at the named location was accessed in 1.4 seconds, and the word in the adjacent location was retrieved in 2.1 seconds. In two subsequent experiments, Lea used a drawing of 12 objects arranged in a circle as loci or pegs and replicated his earlier results with somewhat slower latencies. The word associated with the named object was retrieved in about 1.6 seconds, and the word associated with the adjacent object was accessed in 2.6 seconds. Lea (Exp. 2 and 3) found evidence that retrieving an object using physical location as a cue was not direct, and that it possibly involved searching through subgroups of objects. Because of large individual differences between subjects, the organization was not analyzed further.

Few studies have studied long-term practice effects on memorization using mnemonic associations. Wallace, Turner, and Perkins (cf. Wood, 1967) had subjects memorize 700 paired-associates using visual images. Cued recall for the first 500 pairs was essentially perfect (99%). When all 700 pairs were tested, cued recall dropped to about 95%. The study time for each pair was shortened dramatically, from an initial 20 seconds per pair to 3–5 seconds per pair. In a study by Slak (1970) two subjects received practice encoding each 3-digit group into a unique phonemic sequence consisting of a consonant-vowel-consonant triplet; they also practised decoding these phonemic sequences into the corresponding digits. After about 30 hours of practice, the subjects could encode 3-digit groups at a rate equivalent to 1 digit per second. Using visual presentation of 3-digits at a time, the subjects' memory span was found to be 12–15 digits (cf. the mental calculators' digit span and their 3-digit groups). Slak found that serial learning and free recall of numbers were similarly improved with such phonemic recoding. In his classic paper, Miller (1956) reported on a study by Sidney Smith, who was able to improve his digit span for binary numbers by recoding binary digits into numbers. After an unspecified amount of practice, Smith attained a memory span of over 40 binary digits. In a group experiment, Pollack and Johnson (1965) extended Sidney Smith's finding and demonstrated that even after 28 days of uninstructed practice in remembering binary symbols, further improvement was attained by training subjects to recode 4 binary digits into a decimal number. By systematically varying presentation rates (0.7 to 2.8 binary digits/sec) and grouping of binary digits (segmentation in groups of 4 binary digits vs no segmentation), Pollack and Johnson showed that both segmenting the binary digits into groups of four and encoding groups of 4 binary digits into decimal numbers requires sufficient time. With brief tachistoscopic exposures of binary patterns, no benefit of recoding into decimal numbers has been observed (Klemmer, 1964; Pollack and Johnson, 1965).

It is possible to observe sizable improvements in digit span within a single session. Hunt and Love (1972) found that, given instructions to form digit groups and generate mnemonic associations, a group of college students improved their average digit span from about 9 to about 11 digits.

Memory skill in normal subjects versus expert memory

We have argued that differences in memory ability both within and between subjects can be understood in terms of acquired cognitive processes and structures, or memory skill. Up to this point, we have primarily examined memory performance for materials which are unfamiliar, lacking in meaning, and hard to memorize for normal subjects. The observed dramatic differences in memory ability are not surprising or unexpected from the perspective of memory skill, given the huge differences in practice and familiarity with the type of material. Many of the memory experts have dedicated a major portion of their lives to improving their skill with particular materials, like numbers. For example, Isihara was a professional mnemonist (Susukita, 1933), and Finkelstein performed mental calculations (primarily additions) as a major aspect of his job for over 10 years (Weinland and Schlauch, 1937).

If we allow for dramatic effects of extensive practice, it may not be necessary to attribute exceptional performance to differences in basic memory characteristics. Coltheart and Glick (1974) attributed a woman's ability to spell words and sentences in reverse order (backward-talking) to an unusually durable memory for visual images.

Subsequently, Cowan and his associates (Cowan and Leavitt, 1982; Cowan *et al.*, 1982) reported several people who displayed very similar patterns of memory performance. These subjects all reported having extensively practised backwards spelling during childhood and adolescence. Their achievement of the same skill casts doubt on the need for unusual basic memory characteristics as prerequisites.

Several investigators have pointed out the general relation between mental calculators' superior memory for numbers and regular speakers' superior memory for information given in their own language.

> Dealing constantly with figures, the mental calculator learns to assimilate them readily. A 20-figure number, which for the most of us is a meaningless string of figures devoid of interest, for him 'makes sense,' and so is easy to learn, just as a page of French is more easily learned by a Frenchman than by a foreigner who knows little or nothing of the language. (Mitchell, 1907, p. 116)

Within the realm of interpreting artificial symbols, it is clear that language comprehension and production are the skills that normal subjects develop to the highest level. In the following we will compare memory skills associated with language with the memory skills of the memory experts and mental calculators.

For normal subjects as well as for mental calculators, memory or memorization is not the direct focus, but is, rather, a necessary prerequisite for comprehension or mental calculation. When we examine memory for language or digits we are using tasks that the respective subjects have not practised directly. The three memory tests we will discuss concern memory after brief exposures (attention span), memory span, and memorization of longer lists. The detailed results of digit experts have been discussed earlier and will be used only for reference.

From the early research on tachistoscopic presentation of letters and words it is clear that words are perceived directly (Woodworth, 1938). Only four to five unrelated letters can be perceived with very brief exposures, and longer exposures give only an additional two letters. When the letters form familiar words, up to 20 letters can be correctly reported under the same presentation conditions. Hoffman (1927) conducted a study tracing the emergence of the recognition of words in schoolchildren. Students in the first grade did not show any advantage in reporting letters in familiar words over unrelated letters. The number of letters reported from words increased smoothly as a function of grade level, and eighth graders showed a performance comparable to adults.

Weinland (1948) demonstrated that Finkelstein could reliably extract only seven digits at very brief tachistoscopic exposures. At somewhat longer presentation times (less than a second), Finkelstein could report 12 digits, which he could later do in half a second with practice (Sandor, 1932). During later testing by Weinland (1948), Finkelstein could report over 20 digits after a 1-second exposure. Unfortunately, the procedure and apparatus used for this last feat of Finkelstein was poorly documented (Smith, 1983), and it is likely that a dark postexposure field may have increased the time of availability for the stimulus (Sperling, 1963). The later measurement of Finkelstein's time to memorize 21 digits at Ohio State suggests a study time four times longer (Barlow, 1952).

Mueller (1913) showed that R was not superior in reporting very briefly presented digits, but when presentation times were increased to 0.3 second, his superiority emerged. The evidence for tachistoscopic recognition of digit groups is weak at very brief exposures; however, at only slightly longer presentation times, such recognition appears to occur. The difference between the letters in words and the digits could at least in part be due to the redundancy of letters in real words, because all combinations of digits were admissible. Hoffmann's (1927) results on attention spans for groups of unrelated syllables and unfamiliar words support this interpretation. Attention spans for unrelated syllables and unfamiliar words were hardly different from the attention span for consonants. The only clearly greater attention span was obtained for familiar words.

Memory span for unrelated words is around 6 words, but memory span for words in sentences is several times larger, ranging from about 15 words (Marks and Jack, 1952) to about 25 words (Magne, 1952). The exact mechanism underlying the superior span for words in sentences is still unclear. The most important factor is the meaningfulness of the sentence; syntactical correctness without meaning gives only a minor improvement over unrelated words (Epstein, 1961, 1962; Marks and Jack, 1952). When subjects make errors in recalling the exact words of sentences, the errors almost invariably preserve the meaning of the sentence and concern switches of articles, prepositions, tense, etc. Ericsson and Karat (1981) proposed that in memory span for sentences, subjects actively associated the verbatim form of the sentence to the automatically extracted meaning. We found evidence for storage of the verbatim information in LTM from a surprise cued-recall of all sentences and of unrelated word sequences during the session. Memory for sentences was very good, whereas memory for word sequences was almost nonexistent. Hence, the higher memory spans for words in sentences are mediated by storage in LTM in a manner similar to the extended digit spans for memory experts. There is good evidence that the efficiency of encoding and storage in LTM of the exact wording of the sentence is influenced by the linguistic characteristics of the sentence and by the linguistic knowledge of the subject. The frequency of words in sentences and the perceived natural-ness of sentences have major effects on average span (Nichols, 1965). There are considerable individual differences in memory span for words, which can be well predicted by psychometric tests of verbal ability and language use (correlations .60–.70, Ericsson and Karat, 1981). An influential study by Daneman and Carpenter (1980) has also shown a strong relation between performance in verbal skills tasks (reading comprehension) and the size of working memory during reading (reading span test). Daneman and Carpen-ter's (1980, 1983) interpretation differs from the skilled memory account, in that they assume the individual differences are due to differences in the size of working memory rather than the efficiency of storage in LTM. Some recent studies of Masson and his colleagues (Masson and Goldsmith, 1984; Masson and Miller, 1983) have given strong evidence that memory performance on reading span tests (used by Daneman and Carpenter to assess the size of working memory) primarily reflects encoding and storage in LTM. Assuming that reading span test performance reflects the efficiency of storage in LTM, the results of Daneman and Carpenter, and Masson and his colleagues, are consistent with skilled memory theory.

Let us briefly compare memory span for words in normal subjects to digit span for memory experts. Even under optimal circumstances memory span for words in sentences cannot match the memory span for digits observed for the digit-span experts, who were able to associate the encoded digit groups with the cues in the retrieval structure. These three experts (SF and DD, Chase and Ericsson, 1982; R, Mueller, 1913) have attained digit spans of 60–110 digits. The studies providing extensive practice on the digit-span task show mono-tonic improvement with practice without any signs that a fixed upper bound for digit span exists.

To summarize the results for memory span, there are some interesting parallels between memory experts and normal subjects. It is intriguing to note that mental calculators have digit spans of around 15 digits, which is also the modal span for words in sentences of normal subjects. However, there is reason to believe that the mental calculator remembers digits in a way similar to the way in which normal subjects remember letters which make up words. Digits seem to be handled primarily in groups of three, and for many calculators it is clear that these groups constitute separate psychological units which have been committed to memory, often at an early age. Hence, 15–18 digits can be kept in STM as five to six units, and this compares remarkably well to normal subjects' memory span for sequences of unrelated words. It is possible to extend the analogy above and argue that the three digit-span experts remember digits in a way similar to that in which normal subjects remember the letters in a sentence (Bourne *et al.*, 1986). With an average of four or five letters to a word, a memory span for sentences of 15 to 20 words would correspond to between 60 and 100 letters, which they note is remarkably similar to the performance of the digit-span experts.

The speed of LTM-storage for longer lists of items can be compared by analyzing rates of verbatim memorization of meaningful prose passages and rates for memorization of long sequences of digits. Verbatim memorization of text is no longer very common, but many studies investigated such memorization just after the turn of the century. Lyon (1917) reported that he required 70 hours of study to memorize 10 000 words (corresponding to about 30 pages of text), whereas he memorized 100 and 200 words in 9 and 24 minutes respectively. Although Lyon was relatively experienced, one cannot view his times as even close to an upper bound on memorization. The study times discussed earlier for long lists of digits are remarkably comparable to Lyon's, and both Isihara and R memorized 100 and 200 digits much faster than Lyon memorized the corresponding number of words. Most remarkable is the fact that Isihara memorized lists of over 1000 digits and lists of over 2000 digits faster than Lyon memorized the corresponding number of words (Susukita, 1933).

In summary, variation in memorization performance can be described best in terms of varying degrees of skill. Memory for meaningful materials, like language, can be viewed as one extreme on the skill dimension. The same level of skill can, however, be obtained in other domains, such as digits, when years of practice are dedicated to achieving excellence.

Memory skills and other skills

In this concluding section we will briefly review some evidence showing that memory skills share important characteristics with other types of skills. Finally, we will discuss the relation between acquired skill on memory tasks (pure memory skills) and the improved memory of experts in the domain of their expertise.

We have analyzed memory skills in terms of the three principles of skilled memory. The semantic encoding processes and the use of retrieval structures postulated by the first two principles are directly consistent with cognitive structures and processes proposed for other acquired cognitive skills. The speed-up of list memorization with practice corresponds directly to the practice effects found in a wide range of perceptual-motor and cognitive skills. Newell and Rosenbloom (1981) review and discuss the underlying learning mechanisms for the speed-up of cognitive processes as a direct function of practice.

A general characteristic of skills is their permanence in spite of long periods of disuse. Many perceptual-motor skills, such as typing, ball-tossing, letter cancellation, and inverted writing, show rather little deterioration with absence of practice. Even after 4 years of no practice (see McGeoch and Melton, 1929, for a review), only limited practice was necessary to achieve the previous performance level. More recent studies have extended these findings of permanence of skilled performance with disuse as well as demonstrated small reliable decrements in performance (Kolers, 1976; Salthouse and Somberg, 1982).

We are aware of few studies of mental skills that have found similar retention characteristics. In a study by Gray (1918) subjects received over 10 training sessions in transcribing text into an unfamiliar letter code, where each letter corresponded to a unique symbol. The subjects attained a high level of proficiency during the training and showed only a 60–75% retention of their transcription rate over a 2-week period without practice. Brooks (1924) found that mental multiplication training over 2 weeks led to 60% retention of the original improvement when subjects were tested 2.5 months later. There seems to be no information available on the effects of extensive practice on memory skills. However, one of the subjects (RE) in our memory span experiment terminated her participation in the experiment after about 100 hours of practice. When she was retested 3 and 6 months later, her memory span after a couple of hours of warm-up was not significantly different from her memory span in her last block of training. In sum, the acquired cognitive structures and processes mediating memory skill are not different in kind from those mediating other skills, and they appear to be acquired by similar learning processes.

If memory skills are not structurally different from other skills, how are memory skills different from skills with improved memory for task-relevant information? Pure memory skills are acquired skills on different memory tests, like memory span and recall of memorized lists. In these cases, the degree of skill is defined in terms of performance on literal recall of the presented information. For other skills, like mental calculation and chess, improved memory is a byproduct of acquired expertise in the corresponding skill. Both types of skills were demonstrated earlier to use LTM even for storage of briefly presented information. A similar use of LTM at rapid presentation rates is found for normal subjects reading texts.

In all these instances the capacity of memory for immediately presented information is large and possibly without a measurable upper bound. The crucial issue with information stored in LTM is how to access it and, especially, how to access it efficiently when it is relevant. Chase and Ericsson (1982) proposed that associating selected retrieval cues with the information at encoding would provide known access cues. From research on cued recall in paired-associate learning, we know that normal subjects can retrieve the associate within a couple of seconds, even after a considerable delay from the time of learning (Anderson, 1980; Reed, 1918a; cf. Woodworth, 1938). Hence, such retrieval would be sufficiently rapid if the subject could reliably generate the cue (cf. the stimulus of the paired-associate).

Returning to the comparison between pure memory skills and skills with memory improvement, we propose that the two types of skill differ with respect to the type of retrieval cues which are used to retrieve the information from LTM. In most skills, the relevant information in LTM needs to be accessed on the basis of the content of the stored information. For example, in reading a novel or writing a large computer program we need rapid access to relevant information encountered earlier, ideally through effortless reminding. Pure memory skills, on the other hand, rely on structural retrieval cues, cues that allow the subject to retrieve the stored information without knowing the contents of it. For example, if asked whether a digit matrix contained a row with an 8 followed by 3, it is likely that the subject would have to retrieve and scan each row before being able to answer that question. If the digit pair had been 88, the subject might be able to answer directly because he or she stored a pair of eights as part of the memory encoding for the digits in that row. Chase and Ericsson (1982) found that the digit-span experts SF and DD reported automatically retrieving digit groups memorized earlier in the session that had the first 2 or 3 digits in common (in the same mnemonic category) with the digit group currently being encoded. When measured experimentally, this retrieval was achieved within about 1 second. Such automatic retrieval based on meaning would provide a sufficiently powerful mechanism to account for skilled memory in chess players, bridge players, computer programmers, normal subjects comprehending text, and any other skills that require planning, integration, and design. We are still far away from specifying the processes of encoding and the cognitive processes used to elicit this information when it is relevant. If or when such a description is achieved, our understanding of memory will be integrated with our understanding of human skills in general.

Concluding remarks

The principles of skilled memory were originally proposed to account for the impressive memory skill of a single subject acquired through extensive practice. The same principles provide a remarkably good account of performances reported in all available case studies of memory experts. Several of the discussed memory experts (Finkelstein, Isihara, and R) display memory performances that widely surpass several more well-known subjects with exceptional memory and approach, or even match, the performance characteristics of normal subjects' memory for meaningful material. Whether adult subjects' memory for meaningful material can be viewed successfully as a memory skill acquired after extensive practice is, at this point, only a conjecture. The above analyses of performance characteristics and structure of memory skill have shown that such a conjecture is possible and even plausible. It is likely that our future understanding of meaningful memory will be based on laboratory studies of individuals with acquired skills.

References

Anastasi, A. (1931). A group factor in immediate memory. *Archives of Psychology*, **18** (120), 5–61.

Anderson, J. R. (1980). *Cognitive psychology and its implications.* San Francisco: W. H. Freeman.

Atwood, M. E., and Polson, P. G. (1976). A process for water jar problems. *Cognitive Psychology*, **8**, 191–216.

Baddeley, A. (1981). The concept of working memory: A view of its current state and probable future development. *Cognition*, **10**, 17–23.

Barlow, F. (1952). *Mental prodigies.* New York: Greenwood Press.

Bellezza, F. S. (1981). Mnemonic devices: Classification, characteristics and criteria. *Review of Educational Research*, **51**, 247–275.

Binet, A. (1894). *Psychologie des grands calculateurs et joueurs d'echecs.* Paris: Libraire Hachette.

Bjork, R. A. (1978). The updating of human memory. In G. H. Bower (Ed.), *The psychology of learning and motivation* (Vol. 12). New York: Academic Press.

Bourne, L. E., Dominowski, R. L., Loftus, E. F., and Healy, A. F. (1986). *Cognitive processes* (2nd ed.). Englewood Cliffs, NJ: Prentice Hall.

Bousfield, W. A. and Barry, H. (1933). The visual imagery of a lightning calculator. *American Journal of Psychology*, **45**, 353–358.

Bower, G. H. (1972). Mental imagery and associative learning. In L. W. Gregg (Ed.), *Cognition in learning and memory.* New York: Wiley.

Bower, G. H. (1975). Cognitive psychology: An introduction. In W. K. Estes (Ed.), *Handbook of learning and cognitive processes* (Vol. 1). Hillsdale, NJ: Erlbaum.

Bower, G. H., and Reitman, J. S. (1972). Mnemonic elaboration in multilist learning. *Journal of Verbal Learning and Verbal Behavior*, **11**, 478–485.

Bower, G. H., and Winzenz, D. (1969). Group structure, coding, and memory for digit series. *Journal of Experimental Psychology Monograph*, **80** (2), 1–17.

Brener, R. (1940). An experimental investigation of memory span. *Journal of Experimental Psychology*, **26**, 467–482.

Brooks, F. D. (1924). Learning in the case of three dissimilar mental functions. *Journal of Experimental Psychology*, **7**, 462–469.

Bryan, W. L., Lindley, E. H., and Harter, N. (1941). *On the psychology of learning a life occupation.* Bloomington, IN: Indiana University Publications.

Bugelski, B. R. (1968). Images as mediators in one-trial paired-associate learning. II: Self-timing in successive lists. *Journal of Experimental Psychology*, **77**, 328–334.

Bugelski, B. R., Kidd, E., and Segman, J. (1968). Image as a mediator in one-trial paired-associate learning. *Journal of Experimental Psychology*, **76**, 69–73.

Charness, N. (1976). Memory for chess positions: Resistance to interference. *Journal of Experimental Psychology: Human Learning and Memory*, **2**, 641–653.

Charness, N. (1979). Components of skill in bridge. *Canadian Journal of Psychology*, **33**, 1–16.

Chase, W. G., and Ericsson, K. A. (1981). Skilled memory. In J. R. Anderson (Ed.), *Cognitive skills and their acquisition.* Hillsdale, NJ: Erlbaum.

Chase, W. G., and Ericsson, K. A. (1982). Skill and working memory. In G. H. Bower (Ed.), *The psychology of learning and motivation* (Vol. 16). New York: Academic Press.

Chase, W. G., and Simon, H. A. (1973a). Perception in chess. *Cognitive Psychology*, **4**, 55–81.

Chase, W. G., and Simon, H. A. (1973b). The mind's eye in chess. In W. G. Chase (Ed.), *Visual information processing.* New York: Academic Press.

Chiba, T., and Susukita, T. (1934). A study of the extraordinary memory. *Japanese Journal of Psychology,* **9**, 44–45. (English abstract).

Cofer, C. N. (1940). *A comparison of logical and verbatim learning of prose passages of different lengths.* Unpublished doctoral dissertation, Brown University.

Coltheart, M., and Glick, M. J. (1974). Visual imagery: A case study. *Quarterly Journal of Experimental Psychology,* **26**, 438–453.

Cowan, N., and Leavitt, L. A. (1982). Talking backward: Exceptional speech play in late childhood. *Journal of Child Language,* **9**, 481–495.

Cowan, N., Leavitt, L. A., Massaro, D. W., and Kent, R. D. (1982). A fluent backward talker. *Journal of Speech and Hearing Research,* **25**, 48–53.

Craik, F. I. M., and Lockhart, R. S. (1972). Levels of processing: A framework for memory research. *Journal of Verbal Learning and Verbal Behavior,* **11**, 671–684.

Crannell, C. W., and Parrish, J. M. (1957). A comparison of immediate memory span for digits, letters, and words. *The Journal of Psychology,* **44**, 319–327.

Crovitz, H. F. (1971). The capacity of memory loci in artificial memory. *Psychonomic Science,* **24**, 187–188.

Daneman, M., and Carpenter, P. A. (1980). Individual differences in working memory and reading. *Journal of Verbal Learning and Verbal Behavior,* **19**, 450–466.

Daneman, M., and Carpenter, P. A. (1983). Individual differences in integrating information between and within sentences. *Journal of Experimental Psychology: Learning, Memory, and Cognition,* **9**, 561–584.

Dearborn, W. F. (1909). The general effect of special practice in memory. *Psychological Bulletin,* **6**, 44–45.

Dearborn, W. F. (1910). Experiments in learning. *Journal of Educational Psychology,* **1**, 373–388.

de Groot, A. (1966). Perception and memory versus thought: Some old ideas and recent findings. In B. Kleinmuntz (Ed.), *Problem solving* (pp. 19–50). New York: Wiley.

de Groot, A. (1978). *Thought and choice in chess.* The Hague: Mouton.

Ebbinghaus, H. (1964). *Memory: A contribution to experimental psychology* (H. A. Ruger and C. E. Bussenius, Trans.). New York: Dover Publications, Inc. (Originally published, 1885).

Ebert, E., and Meumann, E. (1904). Ueber einige Grundfragen der Psychologie der Uebungsphaenomene im Bereiche des Gedaechtnisses. *Archiv fuer die gesamte Psychologie,* **4**, 1–232.

Egan, D. E., and Grimes, D. D. (1979, November). *Differences in mental representations spontaneously adopted for reasoning.* Paper presented at Annual Meeting, Psychonomic Society, Phoenix, Arizona.

Egan, D. E., and Schwartz, B. J. (1979). Chunking in recall of symbolic drawings. *Memory and Cognition,* **7**, 149–158.

Engle, R. W., and Bukstel, L. H. (1978). Memory processes among bridge players of differing expertise. *American Journal of Psychology,* **91**, 673–689.

Epstein, W. (1961). The influence of syntactic structure on learning. *American Journal of Psychology,* **74**, 80–85.

Epstein, W. (1962). A further study of the influence of syntactic structure on learning. *American Journal of Psychology,* **75**, 121–126.

Ericsson, K. A., and Chase, W. G. (1982). Exceptional memory. *American Scientist,* **70**, 607–615.

Ericsson, K. A., Chase, W. G., and Faloon, S. (1980). Acquisition of a memory skill. *Science*, **208**, 1181–1182.

Ericsson, K. A., and Karat, J. (1981). *Memory for words in sequences.* Paper presented at the 22nd Annual Meeting of the Psychonomic Society, Philadelphia, Pennsylvania.

Ericsson, K. A., and Polson, P. G. (1988a). An experimental analysis of the mechanisms of a memory skill. *Journal of Experimental Psychology: Learning, Memory, and Cognition*, **14**, 305–316.

Ericsson, K. A., and Polson, P. G. (1988b). A cognitive analysis of exceptional memory for restaurant orders. In M. T. H. Chi, R. Glaser, and M. J. Farr (Eds.), *The nature of expertise.* Hillsdale, NJ: Erlabum.

Ericsson, K. A., and Simon, H. A. (1984). *Protocol analysis.* Cambridge, MA: MIT Press/Bradford.

Fracker, G. C. (1908). On the transference of training in memory. *Psychological Review Monograph Supplement*, **9**, 56–102.

Frey, P. W., and Adesman, P. (1976). Recall memory for visually presented chess positions. *Memory and Cognition*, **4**, 541–547.

Gates, A. I. (1917). Recitation as a factor in memorizing. *Archives of Psychology*, **7** (Whole No. 40), 1–104.

Gates, A. I. and Taylor, G. A. (1925). An experimental study of the nature of the improvement resulting from practice in a mental function. *Journal of Educational Psychology*, **16**, 583–592.

Gordon, P., Valentine, E., and Wilding, J. (1984). One man's memory: A study of a mnemonist. *British Journal of Psychology*, **75**, 1–14.

Gray, C. T. (1918). A comparison of two types of learning by means of a substitution test. *Journal of Educational Psychology*, **9**, 143–158.

Greenberg, R., and Underwood, B. J. (1950). Retention as a function of stage of practice. *Journal of Experimental Psychology*, **40**, 452–457.

Gummerman, K., and Gray, C. R. (1971). Recall of visually presented material: An unwonted case and bibliography for eidetic imagery. *Psychonomic Monograph Supplements*, **4**, 189–195.

Harcum., E. R. and Coppage, E. W. (1965). Serial-position curve of verbal learning after prolonged practice. *Psychological Reports*, **17**, 475–488.

Hatano, G., and Osawa, K. (1983). Digit memory of grand experts in abacus-derived mental calculation. *Cognition*, **15**, 95–110.

Hebb, D. O. (1961). Distinctive features of learning in the higher animal. In J. F. Delafresnoye (Ed.), *Brain mechanisms and learning* (pp. 37–46). Oxford: Blackwell.

Hoffmann, J. (1927). Experimentell-psychologische Untersuchungen ueber Leseleistungen von Schulkindern. *Archiv fuer die gesamte Psychologie*, **58**, 325–388.

Hoffman, R. R., and Senter, R. J. (1978). Recent history of psychology: Mnemonic techniques and the psycholinguistic revolution. *The Psychological Record*, **28**, 3–15.

Hovland, C. I. (1951). Human learning and retention. In S. S. Stevens (Ed.), *Handbook of experimental psychology* (pp. 613–689). New York: John Wiley & Sons.

Hunt, E. B. (1971). What kind of computer is man? *Cognitive Psychology*, **2**, 57–98.

Hunt, E., and Love, T. (1972). How good can memory be? In A. W. Melton and E. Martin (Eds.), *Coding processes in human memory.* New York: Holt.

Hunter, I. M. L. (1962). An exceptional talent for calculative thinking. *British Journal of Psychology*, **53**, 243–258.

Hunter, I. M. L. (1977). An exceptional memory. *British Journal of Psychology*, **68**, 155–164.

Hunter, I. M. L. (1984). Lengthy verbatim recall (LVR) and the mythical gift of tape-recorder memory. In K. M. J. Lagerspetz, and P. Niemi (Eds.), *Psychology in the 1990s*. Amsterdam: North Holland.

James, W. (1890). *The principles of psychology* (Vol. 1). New York: Holt.

Jeffries, R., Turner, A. A., Polson, P. G., and Atwood, M. E. (1981). The processes involved in designing software. In J. R. Anderson (Ed.), *Cognitive skills and their acquisition*. Hillsdale, NJ: Erlbaum.

Jensen, A. R., and Roden, A. (1963). Memory span and the skewness of the serial-position curve. *British Journal of Psychology*, **54**, 337–349.

Kelley, H. P. (1964). Memory abilities: A factor analysis. *Psychometric Society Monographs*, No. **11**, 1–53.

Keppel, G., Postman, L., and Zavortnik, B. (1968). Studies of learning to learn: VIII. The influence of massive amounts of training upon the learning and retention of paired-associate lists. *Journal of Verbal Learning and Verbal Behavior*, **7**, 790–796.

Kintsch, W. (1974). *The representation of meaning in memory*. Hillsdale, NJ: Erlbaum.

Kintsch, W., and van Dijk, T. A. (1978). Toward a model of text comprehension and production. *Psychological Review*, **85**, 363–394.

Klemmer, E. T. (1964). Does recoding from binary to octal improve the perception of binary patterns? *Journal of Experimental Psychology*, **67**, 19–21.

Kolers, P. A. (1976). Reading a year later. *Journal of Experimental Psychology: Human Learning and Memory*, **2**, 554–565.

Lane, D. M., and Robertson, L. (1979). The generality of levels of processing hypothesis: An application to memory for chess positions. *Memory and Cognition*, **7**, 253–256.

Lea, G. (1975). Chronometric analysis of the method of loci. *Journal of Experimental Psychology: Human Perception and Performance*, **1**, 95–104.

Lepley, W. M. (1934). Serial reactions considered as conditioned reactions. *Psychological Monographs*, **46** (1, Whole No. 205).

Luria, A. R. (1968). *The mind of a mnemonist*. New York: Avon.

Lyon, D. O. (1917). *Memory and the learning process*. Baltimore: Warwick & York, Inc.

Magne, O. (1952). *Perception and learning*. Uppsala, Sweden: Appelbergs Boktryckeri AB.

Marks, M. R., and Jack, O. (1952). Verbal context and memory span for meaningful material. *American Journal of Psychology*, **65**, 298–300.

Martin, P. R., and Fernberger, S. W. (1929). Improvement in memory span. *American Journal of Psychology*, **41**, 91–94.

Masson, M. E. J., and Goldsmith, S. M. (1984). *Individual differences in memory skills and reading comprehension*. Unpublished manuscript, Department of Psychology, University of Victoria, Canada.

Masson, M. E. J., and Miller, J. A. (1983). Working memory and individual differences in comprehension and memory of text. *Journal of Educational Psychology*, **75**, 314–318.

McGeoch, J. A., and Melton, A. W. (1929). The comparative retention values of maze habits and of nonsense syllables. *Journal of Experimental Psychology*, **12**, 392–414.

Melton, A. W. (1963). Implications of short-term memory for a general theory of memory. *Journal of Verbal Learning and Verbal Behavior*, **2**, 1–21.

Meyer, D. R., and Miles, R. C. (1953). Intralist-interlist relations in verbal learning. *Journal of Experimental Psychology*, **45**, 109–115.

Miller, G. A. (1956). The magical number seven, plus or minus two. *Psychological Review*, **63**, 81–97.

Mitchell, F. D. (1907). Mathematical prodigies. *American Journal of Psychology*, **18**, 61–143.

Montague, W. E. (1972). Elaborate strategies in verbal learning and memory. In G. H. Bower (Ed.), *The psychology of learning and motivation* (Vol. 6). New York: Academic Press.

Morris, P. E., and Reid, R. L. (1970). The repeated use of mnemonic imagery. *Psychonomic Science*, **20**, 337–338.

Mueller, G. E. (1911). Zur Analyse der Gedächtnistätigkeit und des Vorstellungsverlaufes: Teil I. *Zeitschrift für Psychologie, Ergänzungsband*, **5**, 1–403.

Mueller, G. E. (1913). Neue Versuche mit Rueckle. *Zeitschrift fuer Psychologie und Physiologie der Sinnesorgane*, **67**, 193–213.

Mueller, G. E. (1917). Zur Analyse der Gedächtnistätigkeit und des Vorstellungsverlaufes: Teil II. *Zeitschrift für Psychologie, Ergänzungsband*, **9**, 1–682.

Murdock, B. B. (1974). *Human memory: Theory and data*. Potomac, MD: Lawrence Erlbaum.

Murphey, M., Quave, J., and Ericsson, K. A. (unpublished ms). *Large memory improvement as a result of extended practice*.

Neisser, U. (1982). *Memory observed: Remembering in natural contexts*. San Francisco: W. H. Freeman and Co.

Newell, A., and Rosenbloom, P. S. (1981). Mechanisms of skill acquisition and the law of practice. In J. R. Anderson, (Ed.), *Cognitive skills and their acquisition*. Hillsdale, NJ: Erlbaum.

Newell, A., and Simon, H. A. (1972). *Human problem solving*. Englewood Cliffs, NJ: Prentice-Hall.

Nichols, A. C. (1965). Effects of three aspects of sentence structure on immediate recall. *Speech Monographs*, **32**, 164–168.

Oberly, H. S. (1928). A comparison of the spans of 'attention' and memory. *American Journal of Psychology*, **40**, 295–302.

Orata, P. T. (1928). *The theory of identical elements*. Columbus, Ohio: The Ohio State University Press.

Payne, J. W. (1976). Task complexity and contingent processing in decision making: An information search and protocol analysis. *Organizational Behavior and Human Performance*, **16**, 366–387.

Peterson, H. A. (1912). Note on a retrial of Professor James' experiment on memory. *Psychological Review*, **19**, 491–492.

Pollack, I., and Johnson, L. B. (1965). Memory-span with efficient coding procedures. *American Journal of Psychology*, **78**, 609–614.

Pollack, I., Johnson, L. B., and Knaff, P. R. (1959). Running memory span. *Journal of Experimental Psychology*, **57**, 137–146.

Postman, L. (1969). Experimental analysis of learning to learn. In G. H. Bower and J. T. Spence (Eds.), *The psychology of learning and motivation* (Vol. 3). New York: Academic Press.

Potter, M. C., and Levy, E. I. (1969). Recognition memory for a rapid sequence of pictures. *Journal of Experimental Psychology*, **81**, 10–15.

Prytulak, L. S. (1971). Natural language mediation. *Cognitive Psychology*, **2**, 1–56.

Raaijmakers, J. G. W., and Shiffrin, R. M. (1981). Search of associative memory. *Psychological Review*, **88**, 93–134.

Reed, H. B. (1917). A repetition of Ebert and Meumann's practice experiment on memory. *Journal of Experimental Psychology*, **2**, 315–346.

Reed, H. B. (1918a). Associative aids: I. Their relation to learning, retention, and other associations. *Psychological Review*, **25**, 128–155.

Reed, H. B. (1918b). Associative aids: II. Their relation to practice and the transfer of training. *Psychological Review*, **25**, 257–285.

Salthouse, T. A., and Somberg, B. L. (1982). Skilled performance: Effects of adult age and experience on elementary processes. *Journal of Experimental Psychology: General*, **111**, 176–207.

Sandor, B. (1932). The functioning of memory and the methods of mathematical prodigies. *Character and Personality*, **1**, 70–74.

Scripture, E. W. (1891). Arithmetical prodigies. *Journal of Psychology*, **4**, 1–59.

Shiffrin, R. M. (1976). Capacity limitations in information processing, attention and memory. In W. K. Estes (Ed.), *Handbook of learning and cognitive processes* (Vol. 4). Hillsdale, NJ: Erlbaum.

Simon, H. A. (1974). How big is a chunk? *Science*, **183**, 482–488.

Slak, S. (1970). Phonemic recoding of digital information. *Journal of Experimental Psychology*, **86**, 398–406.

Smith, S. B. (1983). *The great mental calculators.* New York: Columbia University Press.

Sperling, G. (1963). A model for visual memory tasks. *Human Factors*, **5**, 19–36.

Staszewski, J. J. (1984). Personal communication.

Susukita, T. (1933). Untersuchung eines ausserordentlichen Gedaechtnisses in Japan (I). *Tohoku Psychologica Folia*, **1**, 111–154.

Susukita, T. (1934). Untersuchung eines ausserordentlichen Gedaechtnisses in Japan (II). *Tohoku Psychologica Folia*, **2**, 14–43.

Susukita, T., and Heindl, R. (1935). Der Gedaechtniskuenstler als Zeuge. *Archiv fuer Kriminologie*, **97**, 93–99.

Thurstone, L. L. (1941). *Factorial studies of intelligence.* Chicago: University of Chicago Press.

Underwood, B. J., Boruch, R. F., and Malmi, R. A. (1978). Composition of episodic memory. *Journal of Experimental Psychology: General*, **107**, 393–419.

van Dijk, T. A., and Kintsch, W. (1983). *Strategies of discourse comprehension.* New York: Academic Press.

Ward, L. B. (1937). Reminiscence and rote learning. *Psychological Monographs*, **49** (Whole No. 220).

Warr, P. B. (1964). The relative importance of proactive inhibition and degree of learning in retention of paired-associate items. *British Journal of Psychology*, **55**, 19–30.

Waugh, N. C. (1960). Serial position and the memory-span. *American Journal of Psychology*, **73**, 68–79.

Weinland, J. D. (1948). The memory of Salo Finkelstein. *Journal of General Psychology*, **39**, 243–257.

Weinland, J. D., and Schlauch, W. S. (1937). An examination of the computing ability of Mr. Salo Finkelstein. *Journal of Experimental Psychology*, **21**, 382–402.

Wood, G. (1967). Mnemonic systems in recalls. *Journal of Educational Psychology*, **58**, 1–27.

Woodrow, H. (1927). The effect of the type of training upon transference. *Journal of Educational Psychology*, **18**, 159–172.

Woodworth, R. S. (1938). *Experimental psychology.* New York: Holt.

INDEX